D1207204

Readings in

THE SOCIAL PSYCHOLOGY OF EDUCATION

READINGS IN

Edited by

With a

Allyn and Bacon, Inc. Boston 196

THE SOCIAL PSYCHOLOGY OF EDUCATION

W. W. CHARTERS, Jr. and *N. L. GAGE*
Washington University — *Stanford University*

reword by *GOODWIN WATSON*
Teachers College, Columbia University

Project of the Society for the Psychological Study of Social Issues

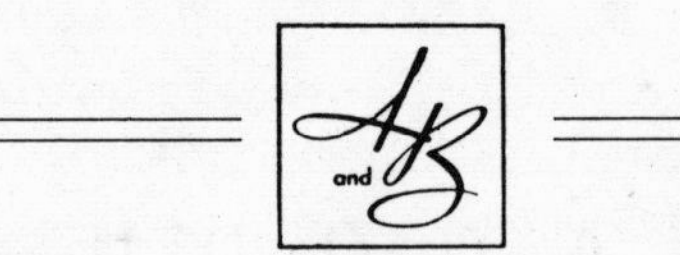

Library of Congress Catalog Card Number: 63-10589

Printed in The United States of America

FOREWORD

A persistent problem for any civilization which tries to make extensive use of scientific research is the gap between the scientist and the practitioner. They differ in their concerns, their procedures, and their language. They work in closely related areas and they are aware of a need to communicate but they seldom understand each other clearly.

The scientist often looks down on the practitioner, grubbing away at the business of production, as if to say, "I am a physicist; let a tradesman repair the TV." "I am interested in psychological theory; let someone else induce scatterbrained adolescents to do their homework."

In a parallel way, the practitioner often becomes impatient with the scientist's qualified, tangential answers and his speculative preoccupation. "Ask him a practical question and all you get is a proposal to do a five-year research project on one small part of the problem!" "I'd like to see one of these university psychology professors try to handle Mrs. Green when she comes in fighting mad!"

The root of the difficulty is that, while the scientist is seeking answers to questions about what is true, the practitioner is trying to cope with a life-situation. Scientific research tests hypotheses; management operates to get things done. When the research report is presented, the operator says, "Very interesting, but so what? How does this help me?" When the practical man asks for help on his complicated problems, the scientific adviser screens out all but the one facet on which he has some data or which fits into his theory. He assumes that if more and more research were done on more and more of these theoretical facets of the complex practical issue, wisdom would emerge. The harried operator doubts that this piecemeal attack on specific questions will ever produce an integrated procedure. In any case he knows he can't wait for generations of research; he must act next week.

The engineering profession has developed to help close the gap between the physical science laboratories and the construction tasks. Mechanical, chemical, and electrical engineers are middle-men who take the confirmed hypotheses and established relationships from the pure scientist and develop the handbooks of formulas, tables, and techniques needed for putting scientific knowledge to practical use. We have learned not to ask the theoretical physicist, the mathematician, or the metallurgist how to build our bridges. Yet, without the basic research, the applied engineering tasks could never be done.

Educators come to the study of social psychology bearing the pressing concerns of practitioners. They want to learn how to improve their way of handling individuals, committees, boards, classes, schools, and public opinion. The editors of this volume have performed a valuable service in selecting pertinent research, but a communication problem still remains. The answers yielded by the studies about social class or school desegregation or other areas do not correspond precisely with the problems faced by administrators and teachers. Educators want to know, for example, how to design a good curriculum for children living in a slum neighborhood. Research studies can answer certain questions about class differences, but their results do not add up to any formula for curriculum design. Scientists can test some theories about pupils and their social backgrounds but cannot prescribe any best method of dealing with the problems arising from the differences in pupils' backgrounds.

Some of the dissatisfaction that the educators have felt with their courses in psychology arises from their adopting an approach based on the wrong expectations. A necessary transition step from such courses to on-the-job problem solving has often been omitted. The "case method" has become popular in the study of law and business because it helps to supply the missing step. Discussion of the case leads to formulation of some assumptions underlying the problem and the proposed lines of action. These assumptions can then be related to factual investigations. Between the practical problem and the findings of scientific laboratories lies the task of asking pertinent questions which research can answer.

The teacher or school administrator will find the study of these readings helpful to the extent that he can derive from them a critique of the assumptions on which he bases his plan of operations. If he can first ask himself, for example, what his proposed procedures assume to be true about adolescents in slum or middle-class or upper-class areas, then he may well find the studies included here will confirm or challenge his postulates. The available research will not tell him what to do or what not to do, but it will help him build his program upon sound conceptual foundations.

The Society for the Psychological Study of Social Issues has tried, from its inception, to improve two-way communication between research workers and practitioners. This volume of readings is intended to acquaint educators with some of the facts and truths which they can use in thinking about their professional responsibilities. But what about communication in the other direction, from the man on the job to the scientist? Research in social psychology could probably speak more directly to the problems of educators if educators were asking more of the questions to be investigated. Educators can become producers as well as consumers of research. One reason why many of the studies in this book are described in some detail is that their methods are fully as important as their findings. The methods, with minor changes, could quite possibly be used to answer somewhat different questions. The student using this collection of readings may be inspired and challenged to try out similar investigations in his own classroom or community. Important as the answers to questions already explored are, they constitute only a tiny portion of those which need checking. The contribution of social psychology to education may lie less in the truths already established than in development of methods applicable to new questions.

The student of this volume is likely to find each reading useful in two ways: (1) as a set of findings and (2) as an exposition of methods.

1. To understand the findings clearly, it is important first to determine what questions the writer was trying to answer. The title of the study gives some clue; the opening paragraphs may state the problems; often a summary at the end makes the general

purpose and findings much clearer. The reader may find it useful to turn to the conclusion before he begins to study the data. Once the question being investigated is understood, the methods can be grasped fairly quickly. The table headings—if there are tables—show the kind of facts being presented to answer the question. The next step is to consider the meaning of the results for education. As emphasized earlier, the findings will not bear directly on "how to do it" but are likely to relate to the assumptions which underlie familiar procedures.

2. In focusing on the research methods, the reader must know how the investigator proceeded. Only then may the reader become able to design other experiments of the same sort to test more precisely the questions that interest him. As the student reads each piece of research, he might well ask himself whether a similar method could be applied in answering questions other than that asked in the study reported.

These two ways of studying the volume—looking at findings and looking at methods—have implications for tests of learning. The most useful tests would go beyond the kind of question which asks what a certain research worker found. To be valuable for educators, these readings must bear on thinking about education and on educational research. Hence, one good kind of test question would ask what assumptions underlying practical operations are confirmed or challenged by the reported research. Another kind of test question would reveal the ability of the student to design a similar study to check a somewhat different hypothesis.

No one likes to devote his intelligence and effort to work of little benefit to others. The social psychologists who wrote the papers assembled here hoped to make a contribution to science and society. Whether they succeed or not depends largely on the reader. If this book is simply read as any other nonfiction book might be, the chances are slim that the reader will gain significant ideas. Viewed as a recipe book, the readings are sure to be disappointing. But the serious reader will achieve two kinds of learning. One kind will correct erroneous assumptions which may have been implicit in his professional activity. The other will yield ways of discovering new truth.

The editors and contributors, in offering herewith the result of scores of man-years of work by able social scientists, require that the reader make an active response to the challenge which each study presents. Here is a book which invites not passive absorption but vigorous response. If readers are able to relate these investigations to ideas behind educational procedures, an important step will have been taken toward reducing the persistent gap between research and practice. Our society takes pride in scientific advance, but the gap between what is known and what is applied continues to be disturbingly great. The methods of study recommended for this volume can help to reduce "social lag" and to make science functional in practice as well as in theory.

Goodwin Watson
Teachers College
Columbia University

CONTENTS

INTRODUCTION xv

part ONE
Extra-classroom Influences on Students

SECTION I. SOCIAL CLASS AND FAMILY INFLUENCES

W. B. BROOKOVER and DAVID GOTTLIEB
Social Class and Education 3

W. W. CHARTERS, JR.
Social Class and Intelligence Tests 12

ELIZABETH DOUVAN AND JOSEPH ADELSON
The Psychodynamics of Social Mobility in Adolescent Boys 21

ELIZABETH MONROE DREWS and JOHN E. TEAHAN
Parental Attitudes and Academic Achievement 35

SECTION II SCHOOL DESEGREGATION

STUART W. COOK
Desegregation: A Psychological Analysis 40

ERNEST Q. CAMPBELL and THOMAS F. PETTIGREW
Racial and Moral Crisis: The Role of Little Rock Ministers 51

MELVIN M. TUMIN
Readiness and Resistance to Desegregation: A Social Portrait of the Hard Core 57

SECTION III SCHOOL AND CAMPUS AS LEARNING ENVIRONMENTS

PAUL HEIST, T. R. McCONNELL, FRANK MATSLER, and PHOEBE WILLIAMS

Personality and Scholarship 65

C. ROBERT PACE

Differences in Campus Atmosphere 73

CLAIRE SELLTIZ, ANNA LEE HOPSON, and STUART W. COOK

The Effects of Situational Factors on Personal Interaction between Foreign Students and Americans 80

JAMES S. COLEMAN

The Adolescent Subculture and Academic Achievement 87

part TWO

The Classroom Setting

SECTION IV STUDENT RELATIONSHIPS IN THE CLASSROOM

NORMAN E. GRONLUND

Typical Sociometric Patterns 97

DORWIN CARTWRIGHT

Achieving Change in People: Some Applications of Group Dynamics Theory 107

ALVIN ZANDER and ELMER VAN EGMOND

Relationship of Intelligence and Social Power to Interpersonal Behavior of Children 114

EUGENIA HANFMANN

Social Structure of a Group of Kindergarten Children 123

MUZAFER SHERIF

Experiments on Group Conflict and Cooperation 126

E. PAUL TORRANCE and KEVSER ARSAN

Experimental Studies of Homogeneous and Heterogeneous Groups for Creative Scientific Tasks 133

SECTION V TEACHER-STUDENT INTERACTION

RONALD LIPPITT and RALPH K. WHITE

An Experimental Study of Leadership and Group Life 141

RICHARD C. ANDERSON

Learning in Discussions: A Résumé of the Authoritarian-Democratic Studies 153

NED A. FLANDERS and SULO HAVUMAKI

Group Compliance to Dominative Teacher Influence 162

N. L. GAGE, PHILIP J. RUNKEL, and B. B. CHATTERJEE

Changing Teacher Behavior through Feedback from Pupils: An Application of Equilibrium Theory 173

ARTHUR J. HOEHN

A Study of Social Status Differentiation in the Classroom Behavior of Nineteen Third-Grade Teachers 181

SECTION VI STUDENT MOTIVATION AND TEACHER CONTROL

JACOB S. KOUNIN, PAUL V. GUMP, and JAMES J. RYAN, III

Explorations in Classroom Management 190

MURRAY HORWITZ

Hostility and Its Management in Classroom Groups 196

W. J. McKEACHIE, DONALD POLLIE, and JOSEPH SPEISMAN

Relieving Anxiety in Classroom Examinations 212

ELLIS BATTEN PAGE

Teacher Comments and Student Performance 219

SECTION VII SHAPING ATTITUDES THROUGH SCHOOLS

A. W. FOSHAY and KENNETH D. WANN

Considerateness and Aggression 226

CARL I. HOVLAND

Yale Studies of Communication and Persuasion 239

JULES HENRY

Attitude Organization in Elementary School Classrooms 254

ALBERTA ENGVALL SIEGEL and SIDNEY SIEGEL

Reference Groups, Membership Groups, and Attitude Change 264

part THREE

Adults in the Educational Setting

SECTION VIII THE AMERICAN TEACHER

EGON G. GUBA, PHILIP W. JACKSON, and CHARLES E. BIDWELL

Occupational Choice and the Teaching Career 271

WARD S. MASON, ROBERT J. DRESSEL, and ROBERT K. BAIN

Sex Role and the Career Orientations of Beginning Teachers 278

PATRICK D. ROCCHIO and NOLAN C. KEARNEY

Teacher-Pupil Attitudes as Related to Nonpromotion of Secondary School Pupils 287

PAUL F. LAZARSFELD and WAGNER THIELENS, JR.

Social Scientists and Recent Threats to Academic Freedom 291

SECTION IX ADULTS IN THE SCHOOL AND COMMUNITY

JACOB W. GETZELS

Conflict and Role Behavior in the Educational Setting 309

JOHN K. HEMPHILL

Leadership Behavior with the Administrative Reputation of College Departments 319

WAYNE E. THOMPSON and JOHN E. HORTON

Political Alienation as a Force in Political Action 327

GLOSSARY 334

INDEX OF NAMES IN INTRODUCTION 339

INDEX OF NAMES IN READINGS 340

SUBJECT INDEX 343

INTRODUCTION

Social psychology is the study of interaction among persons and of the psychological and collective phenomena which cause and result from such interaction. The social psychology of education studies interaction and its social products in the context of educational settings and issues.

Education in this country has always been beset with social issues. Since World War II it has been the scene of increasing controversy and national soul-searching. Education is a massive public institution, exceeded in size only by the military establishment, and today, as never before, it is recognized as a major instrument of national and, indeed, human welfare. Since 1957, the achievements of Soviet technology and training have sharpened American concern with educational problems. Bitter controversies over the curriculum and teaching methods, the hard choice between higher local taxes and federal aid to education, difficulties in maintaining academic freedom in a period of heightened tension between the political right and left, school desegregation, and the place of religious or moral training in the schools—these are some of the social issues that have erupted in the field of education. They are not new problems. But their present intensity is unexampled in American history.

The prototypical educational setting for social interaction is, of course, the classroom. Here assembles the one kind of group that most surely can be found in extended interaction on any weekday in every American community. Such groups are at least as intriguing for scientific study as others that have been studied, and they are certainly not the least important to the healthy functioning of our civilization. But the classroom is not the only setting of interaction relevant to education. The principal's office, the teachers' committee, the school board meeting, the polling place for a bond issue, the teachers college—all these are loci of significant social psychological phenomena. In the perspective of the development of a mature science, study of these settings has barely begun, but this book presents some samples of what social psychological investigation of them can produce.

Social psychology has for many years concerned itself with social interaction in many areas other than education. Industrial and business organizations, military units, mental hospitals and clinics, and the community at large have all received the attention of social psychologists. Until a decade or two ago, however, educators were wont to lament what seemed to be a lack of concern on the part of social psychologists with educational issues and settings. Social psychologists seemed to turn up everywhere—in distant early-warning stations in the Arctic and submarines under the Atlantic, in executive training programs and jury rooms, in German concentration camps and the Kingdom of Father Divine—everywhere except in the schools. But this neglect seems well on its way to being remedied, as the selections gathered in this volume will, we hope, attest. Indeed, the editors and the sponsoring society hope that the present volume will further the application of social psychological theory and method to pressing educational issues.

Initiation of the volume. The sponsor of this volume, the Society for the Psychological Study of Social Issues (a division of the American Psychological Association), consists of more than a thousand psychologists and allied scientists concerned with the psychological aspects of important societal problems. The Society's members share a conviction that such problems deserve the concentrated attention of social psychologists. Such problems, they believe, can profitably be subjected to the kind of rigorous scrutiny that is so often reserved for physical and biological phenomena and for noncontroversial human affairs.

The Society is governed by Kurt Lewin's dictum that "there is nothing so practical as a good theory." In various ways, the Society seeks to bring theory and practice together on human problems of the group, the community, and the nation, as well as the increasingly important ones that transcend national boundaries. The Society has sponsored volumes on civilian morale, industrial conflict, mass communications, the American college, peace, research methods, and three successive editions of *Readings in Social Psychology*. The wide usefulness of the latter volumes in colleges and universities since 1947 has encouraged the Society to sponsor this book.

At its meeting in February, 1959, the Society's council appointed three editors to plan and prepare "a research-oriented book of readings to include existing empirical studies from preschool to the college level." The book was to avoid polemics, the council directive continued. "In cases such as the controversy over ability grouping, the book would not get into the debate nor would it offer opinion but would attempt to get at the underlying values and look at research which examines those values."

Among the editors appointed by the Council was Professor Goodwin Watson, who over many years has helped to form and sustain the best traditions of the social psychological study of education. The present editors regret that Professor Watson was obliged to terminate his co-editorship under the press of other commitments. Herewith they acknowledge the wise counsel he contributed in the most critical, formative stages of the work.

Uses of the book. Under terms of the Council directive, *Readings in the Social Psychology of Education* is intended to encourage as well as to service the growing interest among educators in social psychological theory and research. It is designed primarily as a set of supplementary readings for undergraduate and graduate students in a variety of education courses, including those on the social foundations of education, educational psychology, measurement and evaluation, supervision, curriculum, school administration, guidance, public relations, and, of course, the social psychology of education. This intent—namely, to offer something for a wide variety of education courses—reflects our conviction and that of the sponsoring society that social psychological phenomena pervade educational problems. How well this claim can be supported only the reader of this volume can tell.

Editorial responsibility. Following the precedent set for *Readings in Social Psychology,* the editors established an Advisory Board which included representatives of other associations interested in the social psychology of education. Appointed by their respective organizations were representatives from the American Association of School Administrators, the American Educational Research Association, the American Sociological Association, and the Association for Supervision and Curriculum Development. Their names are listed on the title page of this volume. Also named to the Advisory Board were individuals who represented no organization, but whose interest was unmistakable and from whom good suggestions could be expected. These persons, too, are listed on the title page. As potential members of the Advisory Board were identified, we found the list unexpectedly long; our selection of a smaller number, for the sake of operational efficiency, was highly arbitrary. We also included as working members of the Advisory Committee the officers and council members of the sponsoring society in 1959-60.

The principal function of Advisory Board members was to submit lists of suggestions for readings which might appropriately appear in the volume, and thus to extend the editors' awareness of the scattered literature in the field. A grant from the publisher, Allyn and Bacon, Inc., enabled the editors to undertake their own systematic canvass of the literature. From these two sources, a pool of well over 500 potential selections was assembled. The editors assumed the responsibility for choosing, from this volume of scholarly production, those items which would best represent the quality and diversity of social psychological research in education, and which could be published in a volume of reasonable size.

The publisher's grant also enabled the editors to employ the editorial assistance of Carl E. Pitts, an experienced editorial worker as well as a student of social psychology and education. Mr. Pitts carried a major share of the burden, from abstracting the literature to the preparation of final copy, and stayed on the job long after funds to compensate him were gone.

The division of labor between the editors was uneven. Charters did the larger part: the first large-scale search for papers, the initial winnowing, the preparation of the manuscript, and most administrative details; he also wrote the "Cursory Account" which concludes this Introduction. Gage read the approximately 150 papers surviving the first selection and joined in making the final selection.

Scope of the social psychology of education. Before selecting any of the materials, we had to meet the formidable problem of delineating the social psychology of education. Boundaries had to be set to guide our own search of the literature and the Advisory Board's suggestions. The problem was not eased by our conviction that social psychological theory bears on all manners of educational affairs.

The book was not intended to be a general reader in social psychology for educators. It was to be a book in the social psychology of education. A moment's thought will make this basic distinction clear. The former orientation, social psychology for educators, would open the door to a much wider variety of matter—anything in social psychology that had explicit *or implicit* significance for education. Many topics relate implicity to educational process; many of them have been the focus of social psychological research. Thus, family fertility patterns, processes of decision-making in state legislatures, and labor-management strife in the community all have a distinct bearing upon the operation of the schools. But we did not want to go so far afield. To have done so would have been easier, but it would have made our book less convincing and less useful.

The latter orientation, the social psychology of education, requires that the selections have explicit and direct connections with education. Schools, teachers, pupils, school board members, school achievement, and so on had to be involved directly in the research, not by analogy or by extrapolation.

Our initial approach to the problem was in the form of a definition by denotation, which we gave the Advisory Board to aid them in making their suggestions. It entailed, on the one hand, a 19-item list of major topics and concepts of social psychology and, on the other hand, an 8-item list of educational settings. The intersections of these two dimensions provisionally defined the scope of the volume and gave Advisory Board members an appropriate orientation to their search for ideas. Although the final product does not embrace all of the categories, the two dimensions are offered here to show the breadth of conception with which the project began.

SOCIAL PSYCHOLOGICAL TOPICS

1. Social aspects of perception, including interpersonal perception.
2. Social aspects of cognitive processes, including problem solving, intelligence, memory.
3. Social aspects of motivation (excluding attitudes).
4. Personality development, self, and self concept.
5. Language and stereotypes.
6. Mass communication and public opinion.
7. Modes of face-to-face communication.
8. Modes of interpersonal influence.
9. Attitude formation and change.
10. Multiple-group membership, reference group.
11. Role, role conflict, role set.
12. Ideology, value systems, national character.
13. Socialization—child and adult, professionalization.
14. Social stratification.
15. Division af labor, occupations, social psychology of work.
16. Small group structure.
17. Small group process.
18. Leadership.
19. Group conflict, segregation, discrimination, prejudice.

EDUCATIONAL SETTINGS

1. Teacher-pupil relationship (including parent-child).
2. Classroom group.
3. Peer group, gangs.
4. Student society of the school.
5. Social organization of adults in the school.
6. Community in relation to education and the school.
7. Profession of education.
8. Society and the institution of education.

A more delimited conception of the field, or, more properly, of the scope of the volume, evolved as we began to review the mass of material which came within our provisional formulation. It became obvious that we would have to eliminate topics which belonged traditionally in the provinces of general and educational psychology, child growth and development, and pedagogical method. Similarly, we eliminated selections essentially sociological or anthropological in character, even though they involved the educational institution. We hence rejected studies of relationships between sociological variables which did not centrally involve individuals or interaction between individuals. For example, we rejected studies of ecological processes in the school community, the function of the educational institution in maintaining the societal stratification system, and the effect of educational training on the manpower resources of the nation.

In short, we tried to admit only contributions of a uniquely social psychological character, contributions which embodied an immediate and intimate conception of the interaction of persons with their social environments.

Further, as already noted, we chose to restrict the selections to those with specific and explicit relevance to the educational institution and to persons functioning within it. This criterion meant, for the most part, limiting them to the *formal* educational institution as found in industrial societies. Excluded was work that might involve children or their parents solely within the family and without regard to their roles as pupils in school or as patrons of the school. In this way, parent-child relationships, the gang, and the peer group outside of school were struck from the list of educational settings. To be included, the research had to deal with these matters in some way that embraced people in their roles as pupils, teachers, school administrators, or parents of pupils.

Criteria for selection. Within the boundaries of the social psychology of education as circumscribed, we tried to use the following criteria in making the selections. Although we recognized quickly how difficult it was to apply them, these criteria were satisfied to a major extent.

1. Empirical Grounding. Reports of investigations in which data were generated or collected, variables were measured and interrelated, factors were manipulated and their effects observed—or summary reviews and critical analyses of such investigations—were consistently given preference over programmatic statements, descriptive surveys, insightful commentaries, and the like. In so doing, the editors intended the volume to adhere to the orientation of the society, which maintains that social psychology is an empirical social science and that social issues can best be resolved in the light of the findings of empirical research.

2. Methodological Soundness. In any young field of scientific endeavor, many studies have their prime significance in opening an area to investigation rather than in producing trustworthy knowledge. Nevertheless, one purpose of our volume is to encourage students to apply empirical methods to the investigation of educational issues, and above all, to place their faith in the power of accurate, objective knowledge. Hence, we wanted to display social psychology at its methodological best. In many cases, the choices were hard. Practicing researchers are the first to recognize that any study, no matter how impeccable its design, is open to criticism, reinterpretation, and refutation in the light of new knowledge or new perspectives. Unlike propositions of mathematics and systems of logic, propositions of the empirical sciences are never proven, only supported. Scientific theories are "true" only to the extent that they are capable of organizing the known facts and predicting the still unknown facts within their domain; alternative propositions may account for the same facts equally well and, thereby, become equally "true." And, of course, the research scientist is ever hopeful of discovering a new set of propositions which more thoroughly or more parsimoniously organizes the empirical world. Seen in this way, methodological soundness is largely a function of the knowledge available at a given time. Irrelevant factors which could account for the findings, such as acquiescence set in questionnaire responses, may not have been as fully appreciated at the time a study was conducted as they are now.

Nevertheless, we applied the standards of 1962 to the best of our knowledge and judgment. The criterion of methodological soundness was applied primarily to eliminate those investigations in which the errors were obvious, important, and not open to serious debate.

Accurate, objective knowledge may be achieved in many ways, of course, and one of our objectives in presenting our selections is to display a variety of methodologies and approaches. Accordingly, some of our selections are based upon relatively unstructured observations of complex patterns of human experience, as in Henry's report on teacher-pupil interaction in elementary schools. At the other end of a continuum of rigor, we have studies in which formal experiments were designed, variables were manipulated, highly reliable measurements were taken, and complex statistical analyses were performed, as in the Page investigation of teacher comments on examination papers. Similarly, the data-gathering procedures in our selections include observing, interviewing, questionnairing, testing with self-report devices, and testing with "objective" instruments and carefully constructed scales; commonly, several of these procedures are used in combination. The subjects studied are often found in natural settings, are chosen sometimes so as to constitute probability samples of a population, and sometimes to reflect unusual circumstances or characteristics. Occasionally the subjects are the targets of experimentation in the field; in other studies they are brought into an artificially contrived world in the social psychology laboratory. The ways to the understanding of social issues are manifold, and we have endeavored to slight as few of them as possible.

3. Theoretical Significance. Another criterion, which could not be enforced consistently, was that the research be couched in terms of constructs that went beyond the immediate operational definitions of the variables involved. In some studies, data were reported as if they were sufficient unto themselves, without regard to their connection with general social psychological concepts, such as role, norm, attitude, reference group, cognitive dissonance, or whatever. Such studies had to meet the other criteria to an exceptionally high degree before their excessive specificity to a single circumstance was overlooked.

4. Readability. Not the least of the criteria was the readability of the research report. Profusion of jargon, turgidity of style, obscurity in the development of argument, excessive resort to technicalities of statistics and method—all served to repel us from selections that might otherwise have met the requirements. On the positive side, decided preference was given to reports whose penetrating anecdotes and concrete descriptions enlivened their methodology and statistics. Too often, it seems, social psychological reports fail to give any impression that one is reading about human beings. Readability, however, is a two-sided affair. The reader must be willing and able to meet the author half way. Recognizing our fallibility in estimating the level of understanding of potential readers, we nevertheless have tried to minimize the difficulties in communication and, particularly, those imposed by poor writing.

5. Length. Obvious limitations were imposed by the length of the original research reports. Some were too brief. A report which simply describes findings and discusses their implications, without reference to measuring techniques, data-taking operations, experimental design, or analysis procedures, omits the information necessary to judge the soundness of the findings and to permit replication and refinement of the research. But brevity was a less common problem than excessive length. When an important study had appeared in monograph or book-length form, we sought a brief but comprehensive summary of it in the periodical literature. In some cases, we selected representative sections from such publications. Some lengthy journal articles were abridged by us or the authors. As a result, the length of the selections in the volume conforms generally to that of papers published in major journals devoted to social psychological research.

6. Representativeness. Related to the problem of length was that of representing the variety of studies which had appeared with respect to a single topic or line of investigation. It would have been impossible, of course, to include all of the important research studies even if they met the foregoing criteria. We used several strategies to resolve the problem. Preference was given, normally, to the most recent of the line of studies, especially if the most recent report carried an adequate review of the preceding research. Thus, the volume contains relatively few "classics," i.e., studies that have stimulated much subsequent investigation along the same lines. A second strategy was to search the periodical literature for a careful, well-documented review of work in the area. When this search failed, a third strategy was introduced, that of inviting one of the leading investigators in a field to prepare a summary especially for this volume. For example, Professors Wilbur Brookover and David Gottlieb summarized the extensive literature on social class and education; Professor Murray Horwitz reported several experiments on the conditions for hostility and its relief in classrooms; and Professor Jacob W. Getzels brought together a series of role studies conducted by himself and others. One of the co-editors examined the research on social class "bias" in intelligence tests. Also, the editors are privileged to present a rounded summary of research from the Yale Communication and Attitude Change Program prepared by Carl I. Hovland a few months before his death.

The preceding list does not exhaust the special contributions to the volume. Apart from the selections whose authors generously adapted them to a form suitable for publication in this volume, several research reports were solicited directly by the editors and appear here for the first time.

Organization of the volume. No single, internally consistent, articulated theoretical system underlies the organization of this volume. This is a fact for which the editors do not apologize. Social issues are singularly resistant to attempts to shape them according to the conceptual schemes of social psychologists. Rather, they cut across such arrangements with utter abandon. The editors believe that the concrete problems of education must be viewed from diverse perspectives if they are to be resolved. In any event, this volume brings together a set of empirical studies, chosen according to the criteria outlined above, irrespective of their conceptual unity. Consequently, our section headings and the arrangement of selections are in large part matters of editorial convenience. Our rationale for the organization of the content, as outlined below, is considered to have only modest theoretical utility.

To what extent should the editors of a book of readings such as this inject their own commentary into the text? Differences in practice and in point of view on the question are wide. One common procedure is to introduce each selection with editorial notes and even a synopsis of its content. Other editors abide by the dictum that the best editing is the least obtrusive, that each selection should speak for itself. An interesting case of diversity in judgment regarding the editor's task is found in the reviews of three successive editions of *Readings in Social Psychology,* whose editors consistently refrained from intruding upon the body of the text. In reviewing the first edition, M. Brewster Smith observed approvingly that:

> The volume is presented as an illustrative selection of empirical studies and of approaches to problems which may supplement systematic presentations and conceptual formulations. The editors do not attempt, therefore, to provide a general theoretical framework for social psychology and wisely refrain from embedding the selections in commentary.[1]

On the other hand, Howard Brand, in reviewing the second edition, stated that:

> In conclusion, the reviewer feels disappointed with the 1952 edition of the *Readings*. He had hoped that the new topical arrangement was the beginning of a social psychological theory. It would have been an outstanding contribution to reinterpret systematically the sixty odd papers into a theoretical framework.[2]

Our view, however, is that books of readings are not the places for systematic theoretical formulations. The editors of a book like this one are at the mercy of what is in the literature. And, at any given moment, the literature has gaps; in any growing science there are bound to be lacunae where no research has been done or the findings are still tentative. If a social psychologist wants to develop a systematic theoretical framework and impose it on his field, he should write a book, not edit one.

In his review of the third edition, R. R. Blake asked for an "orientational context," something half-way between no commentary and a systematic theory:

> It is customary, and perhaps right, too, to think that things make sense when they fit together to form a whole. Koffka said so, and Lewin said so, and Helson, and Sherif, and others too. Things make sense in a framework. Anything from a thread to a theme to a thesis to a theory should do. When so few articles are presented in any area, . . . an editorial orientation, spelling out the importance of each problem area, is clearly indicated.[3]

The present editors choose this middle course—that of offering "anything from a thread . . . to a theory." We are convinced that editorial comment frequently adds only banalities and distracts from the readings themselves, except, of course, in volumes intended to develop a unitary theoretical scheme. So we have chosen to absent ourselves from the body of the text. But, recognizing our responsibility to furnish at least a loose rationale for the topical organization and assignment of selections, we offer the following cursory account and commentary.

A cursory account. The readings in this book are arranged by sections which are grouped in three major parts. Part One, Extra-classroom Influences on Students, deals with forces which act upon persons in the role of student but which arise outside the classroom. Part Two, The Classroom Setting, examines the forces acting upon students, and occasionally upon teachers, which arise inside the classroom. In Part Three, Adults in the Educational Setting, attention shifts from forces acting upon students to those acting upon the adult participants in the educational institution.

Section 1. *Social Class and Family Influences.* The family's position in the social class structure of the community undoubtedly has been studied more extensively than any other extra-classroom variable affecting the student's performance in the school. This research movement was stimulated in large measure by the sociologists whose contribu-

[1]*Journal of Abnormal and Social Psychology,* 1948, *43,* p. 240.
[2]*Journal of Abnormal and Social Psychology,* 1953, *48,* p. 457.
[3]*Contemporary Psychology,* 1959, *4,* p. 278.

tions Brookover and Gottlieb review in the opening selection. The influence of social class extends, as psychologists have long known, even to the performance of pupils on intelligence tests. But the charge of "bias" in the tests, made in the late 1940's by a group of sociologists and anthropologists, stirred up a flurry of controversy and research which only recently has run its course. Charters' article recounts the events and issues of this era of intellectual endeavor.

Once the relationship between social class and pupil performance in the educational setting had been established, attention turned to the nature of psychological and social forces which mediate between the social class structure and behavior in the school institution. The paper by Douvan and Adelson concentrates upon the psychological factors, attempting to show fundamental personality differences among high school boys who vary in their strivings for mobility within the class structure. In the latter part of their article, Brookover and Gottlieb point to the mediating, indeed the leveling, influence of the peer group in the school, while other investigators[4] have focused upon the interplay between parental influences and educational aspirations. At this more intimate level of inquiry, social psychological interest goes into questions quite apart from that of the social class system, viz., family influences on academic talent. Thus, Drews and Teahan examine the contributions of parental attitudes to under- and over-achievement among public school pupils.

Section 2. *School Desegregation.* The Supreme Court decisions in the middle 1950's set in motion in the school's environment a profoundly significant chain of events. While little research has yet been conducted to show the effects of desegregation on pupils, the process of school desegregation in the community at large has come under social psychological scrutiny, and we have separated it as an issue worthy of especial attention. Cook's article, which appeared in 1957, brings to bear social psychological knowledge on the desegregation process and poses questions which subsequent research can help to illuminate. Campbell and Pettigrew describe the rending conflict in which clergymen of Little Rock, Arkansas, found themselves during the 1957 crisis. By casting their discussion in the framework of social role, the authors raise the descriptive account to a level sufficiently general to touch upon the lives and circumstances of a wide diversity of people. Tumin used an interview survey procedure among whites in Guilford County, North Carolina, to emphasize the fact that attitudes toward racial integration are not all of one piece in the South. The present article, reporting one part of his research, takes a close look at those whose attitudes toward integration are comparatively intransigent, suggesting among other things that these persons most often are found in the least favorable position in the social status system of the white community.

Section 3. *School and Campus as Learning Environments.* Systematic analysis of the influences which impinge upon the student from the small society of the school has recently captured the interest of social psychologists. More casual research on the matter dates back at least to the work of Waller in the early 1930's.[5] The selections we have chosen represent discrete but, in some instances, convergent lines of contemporary research. One of these lines followed the discovery, reported by Knapp and Goodrich in 1952, that a small number of American colleges produces an overwhelming proportion of the nation's scholars and scientists.[6] The significance of this finding has been traced in studies showing how colleges vary in the academic capabilities of their student bodies and, as in the study by Heist and his co-workers, in the personality attributes of the students they attract. Other studies in this line[7] have looked to academic climates of colleges for an explanation of their differences in productivity of scholars and scientists. These latter studies drew upon a methodological contribution which emerged from an independent line of research —the systematic measurement of environmental *press*. Pace describes one investigation in this line in which measures of college *press* were obtained from well over half a hundred institutions of higher education across the country.

In a related vein, Selltiz and her colleagues center their attention upon the person-to-person interaction between foreign exchange students and their sometimes indifferent hosts in American universities. This study is one of a series, sponsored by the Social Science Research Council's Committee on

[4]See J. A. Kahl, "Educational and Occupational Aspirations of 'Common Man' Boys," *Harvard Educational Review*, 1953, *23*, pp. 186-208; and Anne Roe, *The Making of a Scientist* (New York: Dodd, Mead, & Co., 1952).

[5]Willard Waller, *The Sociology of Teaching* (New York: John Wiley & Sons, Inc., 1932).

[6]R. H. Knapp and H. B. Goodrich, *Origins of American Scientists* (Chicago: University of Chicago Press, 1952).

[7]D. L. Thistlethwaite, "The College Environments and the Development of Talent," *Science*, 1959, *130*, pp. 71-76; and the same author's "College Press and Student Achievement," *Journal of Educational Psychology*, 1959, *50*, 183-191.

Cross-Cultural Education,[8] which looked into the adjustment of exchange students to their American sojourn and their readjustment upon return to their homelands.

While contemporary research on the educational environment has dealt most often with higher education, the social environment of the high school has by no means been ignored. Coleman's investigation of the forces emanating from the adolescent peer culture of the high school is a case in point. He argues, as the reader will see, that the pressures from the peer group often work at cross purposes with the avowed intent of instruction in the educational institution. His investigation into the source of these non-intellectual norms of the high school society leads him to propose positive steps which the school might take to reform them.

Section 4. *Student Relationships in the Classroom.* With this section we turn our attention from the society of students in the school at large to the smaller system of student relationships within the classroom. Unquestionably, the significance of these relationships was most fully impressed upon educators and social psychologists by the development of sociometric measurement by Moreno[9] and his students in the 1930's. In subsequent years such a large research literature on sociometry has arisen that a representative selection seemed hard to choose. The happy solution we reached was to take from Gronlund's book[10] a passage which assembles a composite view of the results of sociometric testing. Concern for the group context of the pupil (or of anyone toward whom change efforts are addressed) arose later in the group dynamics movement, whose theoretical position is synopsized in the article by Cartwright. While Cartwright's general treatment does not concentrate specifically on the classroom, research has indeed extended there. In particular, Zander and Van Egmond examine the interplay between intelligence and social power as these affect the group problem solving processes of elementary school children. Interestingly, Hanfmann's report in 1935 of her observations of kindergarten children, expressing the same interest as that of these other investigators, antedates the group dynamics research and even the sociometric movement by a number of years.

[8]M. Brewster Smith and J. Casagrande, "The Cross-Cultural Education Projects: A Progress Report," Social Science Research Council *Items,* 1953, 7, No. 3.

[9] J. L. Moreno, *Who Shall Survive?* (New York: Beacon House, 1953).

[10]N. E. Gronlund, *Sociometry in the Classroom* (New York: Harper & Row, Publishers, 1959).

Sherif's paper describes a series of studies in which intergroup conflict and then harmony were experimentally produced in a summer camp. His success in manipulating conflict and harmony experimentally suggests that his knowledge touched upon central causal agents in the processes. It affords, too, a productive means for expanding our knowledge of these processes, as Sherif indicates.

A recurrent theme in recent research by social and educational psychologists, reflected in several of our selections, is the study of creativity and its nurturance in the classroom. The Torrance-Arsan research shows how an institutional decision to group pupils "heterogeneously" or "homogeneously" may affect the nurturance of creative responses in children and, particularly, the amount of disruptive social stress in pupil-pupil relationships.

Section 5. *Teacher-Student Interaction.* It is difficult, as the reader may anticipate, to maintain a clear distinction between the previous section on student relationships and the present one on student-teacher relationships. In the public school classroom, the teacher is highly influential in shaping the forms of interaction among pupils. If any doubt ever existed about this, it has long since been dispelled by the classic investigations in the late 1930's by Kurt Lewin and his students on varying styles of leadership. A full-length report of these studies has appeared recently,[11] but we have included here a shorter version by Lippitt and White. The influence of the studies has been widely felt throughout education. Anderson, in his review of research on "autocratic" and "democratic" styles of classroom instruction, cautions against endowing the styles with greater significance than they merit. Indeed, much of the leadership research in social psychology in the years since the Lewin, Lippitt, and White studies appeared has been directed toward analyzing the autocratic-democratic typology into its multifarious dimensions. This effort is reflected here in the investigation by Flanders and Havumaki, in which patterns of teacher influence were allowed to vary solely in the extent to which the teacher directed his remarks to specified members of the pupil group or to the group as a whole.

The study by Gage, Runkel, and Chatterjee, regarding changes induced in teachers by furnishing them with information concerning their pupils' conceptions of them, draws upon one of the most

[11]R. K. White and R. Lippitt, *Autocracy and Democracy: An Experimental Inquiry* (New York: Harper & Row, Publishers, 1960).

recent theoretical developments in social psychology—the equilibrium theories of Heider, Newcomb, Festinger, and Osgood and Tannenbaum. These theories, differing substantially in their details, share the common position that psychological and/or social processes consist of elements tending toward a state of equilibrium and that disruption in the "balance" or "symmetry" among the elements can be restored by a number of alternative strategies. Under some conditions, for example, commitment to an unpleasant course of action will lead, not to a change of behavior, but to a change of evaluation in the "unpleasantness" of the behavior. These theories have wide implications for the social psychology of education.

Hoehn's selection carries into the classroom setting an interest expressed in the first section of the *Readings*. He puts to test the proposition drawn from the social class literature that middle-class teachers behave differently toward middle- and lower-class pupils.

Section 6. *Student Motivation and Teacher Control.* As the preceding section indicated, the student-teacher relationship can be subjected to the same kind of analysis as any social relationship. Social psychologists have adopted this point of view in examining classroom "discipline," or, phrased differently, the problem of inducing in the student the motivation and behavior needed to profit from instruction. Kounin, Gump, and Ryan attack the problem directly by investigating the consequences of various kinds of "desist" techniques used by the teacher—consequences, however, not for the pupils who were the targets of teacher control but for pupils who were more or less innocent bystanders. Horwitz's experiments start from the premise that frustration and its attendant hostility are inescapable ingredients of life in the classroom (or any social group). He shows that frustrating conditions arouse hostile feelings on the part of students in proportion to the degree to which the students' influence is illegitimately reduced. Horwitz also experimented with teacher-controlled procedures which enable the student to relieve the teacher-student relationship of the socially disruptive hostility.

The selections by Page and by McKeachie, Pollie, and Speisman point to the achievement-enhancing character of two simple but manifestly different teaching acts. The latter authors showed that an increase in examination scores among college students resulted from merely inviting the students to comment freely in spaces provided them in their examination papers. Curiously, it was a matter of indifference whether or not the students accepted the invitation to comment. The balance of the article reports a series of investigations attempting to determine the effectiveness of various components of the procedure. In Page's study, the experimental variable was whether instructors wrote motivational comments (freely, or according to plan, or not at all) on students' test papers. The high school students who received instructor comments performed better on a subsequent examination. The study is an excellent specimen of research that is rigorously controlled without upsetting realistic classroom conditions.

Section 7. *Shaping Attitudes through Schools.* Instruction is more than the transmission of skills and knowledge from teacher to student; it also entails, intentionally or unwittingly, the transmission of attitudes and basic values. That the character-forming aspect of teaching proceeds more often through unspoken and subtle social processes than through didactic instruction need hardly be said. The chapter from the book by Foshay and Wann describes a conscious and deliberate effort on the part of school personnel to understand and to use social processes to shape the character of students and illustrates the sophisticated understanding occasionally yielded by "action research" in education. In a markedly different spirit from the foregoing selection, Hovland's summary of the Yale program reflects a patient, systematic, investigation of the conditions under which modes of communication have varying effects upon attitude formation and change.

Not all school-induced influences on student attitudes are matters of deliberate design. Henry's observations on interaction in the elementary school classroom, suggesting the attitude-crystallizing functions of the interplay between teacher and pupil, may encourage teachers to reflect not alone on their lesson plans but on their patterns of behavior in accomplishing even the most "innocuous" tasks. On the college campus, too, student living arrangements carry unexpected consequences for attitude change.[12] Siegel and Siegel use this circumstance to demonstrate the power of the theoretical distinction between membership and reference groups, showing different changes in authoritarian attitudes among girls who aspire to and belong to sororities, who

[12]See also T. M. Newcomb, *Personality and Social Change* (New York: Dryden, 1943) and the same author's *The Acquaintance Process* (New York: Holt, Rinehart, and Winston, Inc., 1961).

aspire to but do not belong, and who neither aspire to nor belong.

Section 8. *The American Teacher.* In the final part of the book, we are concerned no longer with influences acting upon the student but rather with those acting upon teachers, administrators, voters, and other adults. Issues in this area have enormous social significance, and social psychological concepts and methods have especial utility for the analysis of these issues. Yet the literature here is far less abundant than that which focuses upon the student.

One mode of social psychological interest has centered upon the nature of the classroom teacher's career. Guba and his colleagues report studies which trace the pattern of personality attributes among teachers through a series of stages, from the teacher-training institution to the status of veteran teacher in the public school. Mason and his co-workers in the U.S. Office of Education describe their findings from a nation-wide sample survey of teachers, in this case devoted directly to occupational plans and values as they interact with the teacher's sex.

The Minnesota Teacher Attitude Inventory, which has stimulated many investigations, is represented in the present volume by Rocchio and Kearney's novel demonstration of the relationship between teachers' attitudes toward pupils and their inclination to pass or fail high school students. Lazarsfeld and Thielens' summary of their longer work[13] is of a different order. Focusing on the college teacher in the social sciences, it probes the impact upon him of the forces arising in and beyond the institution to constrain his freedom of academic inquiry.

[13]P. F. Lazarsfeld and W. Thielens, Jr., *The Academic Mind* (Glencoe, Ill.: Free Press, 1958).

Section 9. *Adults in the School and Community.* Other categories of adults besides teachers have been the subject of social psychological investigation in the educational setting. In his summary of his own and others' research on social roles in education, Getzels ranges widely over school board members, principals, superintendents, consultants in the state department of education, and teachers to report the underlying regularities in their relationships as suggested by role analysis. Hemphill's study, on the other hand, concentrates upon the leadership role of the department chairman in the university, using the Leader Behavior Description Questionnaire to discern differences in role performance associated with the department's local reputation for being "well administered." The interest of Thompson and Horton lies with the voter in the school community and especially with the voter who harbors a sense of political and social insignificance. Contrary to a common view, these authors suggest that the alienated citizen does not necessarily withdraw apathetically from the voting arena. Indeed, he may enter it vigorously and unpredictably with his feelings of futility, his sense of powerlessness, his distrust of the world, and all the products of his deprived position in the social structure wrapped up in a personal protest vote of "NO!"

The scattered nature of the selections in this final part of the *Readings* should lend credence to our earlier observation that, despite the social significance of the issues, social psychological research has not taken advantage of opportunities in the adult world of education. We hope that future research will yield more studies in the social psychology of teaching and teachers, of school organization and administration, and of school-community relations.

W. W. C.
N. L. G.

Social Class and Family Influences

School Desegregation

School and Campus as Learning Environments

part ONE

Extra-Classroom Influences on Students

I

SOCIAL CLASS AND FAMILY INFLUENCES

*SOCIAL CLASS AND EDUCATION**

By W. B. Brookover and David Gottlieb

There are few sociological reports or texts which do not deal with the question of social class in American society. The impact of this term is such that it has now become part of our everyday language. Through mass media we are told how the middle class lives, what they drive, what they wear, and what they eat. We are reminded that if we want to be identified as an "influential" we should read such and such a book or magazine.

Entertainers are cautioned by their agents to maintain a certain kind of "image" or risk the possibility of alienating a certain social class. Concern with how class background affects the consumer's habits has led to the pre-testing of popular music, movies, food items, etc.

In each case, whether he be a social scientist or an advertising executive, whether his data be based on a few random interviews or a systematic sample, there is agreement that if we are to understand the dynamics of the family, voting behavior, socialization processes, and countless other behavioral phenomena, we cannot go far without considering social class as a crucial variable.

While social scientists do not always agree on the precise meaning of "social class" and how it is best measured, there is general consensus that differences in social class will account for some of the variation in human behavior.[1] Precisely how important social class differences may be in different social situations is, of course, most difficult to answer.

In this paper the goals are two-fold: First, to examine some of the research which has dealt with relationships between social class and various aspects of American education; second, to derive some *schema* which will enable us, at least in part, to answer the question of just how important is social class as a factor affecting education.

---

[1] J. F. Cuber and W. F. Kenkel, *Social Stratification in the United States* (New York: Appleton-Century-Crofts, Inc., 1954); M. M. Gordon, *Social Class* (Durham: Duke University Press, 1958); J. A. Kahl, *The American Class Structure* (New York: Holt, Rinehart & Winston, Inc., 1957).

*Prepared especially for this volume, and to appear in W. B. Brookover and D. Gottlieb, *A Sociology of Education* (2nd. ed.; New York: American Book Company, forthcoming).

REVIEW OF COMMUNITY STUDIES

A brief review of three sociological classics each dealing with social stratification and education will provide a foundation for later analysis.

Middletown. During the years 1924-1925 the Lynds, using the techniques of the cultural anthropologist, carried on a detailed investigation of Middletown, a Midwestern industrial city of about 38,000 population.[2] The Middletown study focused on, among other areas, a social analysis of "training the young."

The Lynds point out that the people of Middletown are very much concerned that the young have an education. They note that "no less than 45% of all money expended by the city in 1925 was devoted to its schools."[3] The authors point out that this concern with education is not limited to elementary and secondary schools but manifests itself in parents' desire to see to it that their children go on to college. This desire for education in Middletown is of such a magnitude that the authors concern themselves primarily with the school drop-outs. They report that potent among the determining factors in matter of continuance in school is the economic status of a child's family. This is indicated by the comments of several Middletown working-class mothers:

> A number of mothers who said that a child had left school because "he didn't like it" finally explained with great reluctance, "We couldn't dress him like we'd ought to and he felt out of it," or, "The two boys and the oldest girl all quit because they hated Central High School. They all loved the Junior High School down here, but up there they're so snobbish. If you don't dress right you haven't any friends." [4]

While little systematic evidence of the two social class groups' variations in attitudes towards education exists, the Lynds describe differences as follows:

> If education is oftentimes taken for granted by the business class, it is no exaggeration to say that it evokes the fervor of a religion, a means of salvation, among a large section of the working class.[5]

The authors go on to discuss how the school system, a product of middle-class values, operates to suppress the educational aspirations of lower social class children.

Two major conclusions are drawn from Middletown. The first is that most Middletown parents, whether from the lower or higher social class levels, recognize the value of an education for their children. It is implied, however, that lower class parents are less likely than middle class parents to instill in their children a desire for a formal education. Secondly, lower class children are penalized within the school system since they do not possess the symbols, attitudes, and behavior characteristics valued by the dominant class group.

Who shall be educated? The extensive research on social prestige conducted by W. L. Warner and those who were later to become identified with Warner began in the early 1930's. The first study of "Yankee City"[6] in New England was followed by *Deep South*[7] and a Midwestern study, *Democracy in Jonesville*.[8] From these studies Warner, Havighurst, and Loeb wrote *Who Shall Be Educated?*[9] to present their conclusions that American schools have a social class screening device which, in actuality, keeps at a minimum the flow of upward mobility:

> This book describes how our schools, functioning in a society with basic inequalities, facilitate the rise of a few from lower to higher levels but continue to serve the social system by keeping down many people who try for higher places. The teacher, the school administrator, the school board, as well as the students, themselves, play their roles to hold people in their places in our structure.[10]

The authors note that education is one of several potential elevators in moving people from one

[2] R. S. Lynd and H. M. Lynd, *Middletown: A Study in American Culture* (New York: Harcourt, Brace & World, Inc., 1929).

[3] *Ibid.*, p. 182.

[4] *Ibid.*, pp. 185-186.

[5] *Ibid.*, p. 187.

[6] W. L. Warner and P. S. Lunt, *The Social Life of a Modern Community* (New Haven: Yale University Press, 1941); W. L. Warner and P. S. Lunt, *The Status System of a Modern Community* (New Haven: Yale University Press, 1942); W. L. Warner and L. Srole, *The Social Systems of American Ethnic Groups* (New Haven: Yale University Press, 1945); W. L. Warner and J. O. Low, *The Social System of a Modern Factory* (New Haven: Yale University Press, 1947).

[7] A. Davis, B. B. Gardner, and M. R. Gardner, *Deep South* (Chicago: University of Chicago Press, 1941).

[8] W. L. Warner and W. C. Bailey, *Democracy in Jonesville* (New York: Harper & Row, Publishers, 1949).

[9] W. L. Warner, R. J. Havighurst, and M. B. Loeb, *Who Shall Be Educated?* (New York: Harper & Row, Publishers, 1944).

[10] *Ibid.*, p. xi.

status position to another, but they add that the elevator does not travel upward for all people. The school curriculum, administrators, and teachers—all, according to the authors, products of middle class values—are viewed as playing an instrumental role in keeping lower class students at the same status position held by their parents.

The authors describe the educational institutions' function to be that of sorting students, rejecting some and re-routing others:

> One large group is almost immediately brushed off into a bin labeled "non-readers," "first-grade repeaters," or "opportunity class" where they stay for eight or ten years and are then released through a chute to the outside world to become 'hewers of wood and drawers of water.' [11]

The intricate conveyor belt is seen to continue through high school and college, at each grade level a bit more selective and certainly less democratic in rejecting and accepting.

> The young people are inspected not only for brains and learning ability, but also for skin color, pronunciation, cut of clothes, table manners, parental bank account.[12]

Evidence to support the conveyor-belt hypothesis comes in the form of two tables which show that the greater the student's parental income the greater the likelihood that he will go to college. In each case it is noted that IQ is not the vital factor in explaining variations in educational attainment. The authors are quick to note, however, that it should not be assumed from these figures that members of the lower class are not interested in higher education for their children. On the contrary, they state that lack of money is a reason frequently given by poorer people for the removal of their children from school. Some evidence which indicates this reason to be true was that with the establishment of the National Youth Administration student aid program of 1935 there was a sharp increase in high school and college enrollment.

It is in their discussion of the school curriculum that Warner and his colleagues are perhaps most emphatic in their statements about the non-democratic aspects of American public schools.

> The evidence is clear that the social class system of Yankee City definitely exercises a control over the pupils' choice of curricula. . . . The children of the two upper and the upper-middle classes, in overwhelming percentages, were learning and being taught a way of life which would fit them into higher statuses. On the other hand, the lower-middle and the lower-class children, in their studies in the high school, were learning a way of life which would help adjust them to the rank in which they were born.[13]

Nor is the teacher spared:

> Teachers represent middle-class attitudes and enforce middle-class values and manners. In playing this role, teachers do two things. They train or seek to train children in middle-class manners and skills. And they select those children from the middle and lower classes who appear to be the best candidates for promotion to the social hierarchy.[14]

We can summarize the material presented in *Who Shall Be Educated?* as follows:

1. Upper class people ordinarily send their children to private schools, especially at the high school level;
2. for others in the community, the school may act as a means of social mobility by teaching skills essential for occupational advancement and the middle class values and attitudes;
3. in high schools there is a relationship between the student's socio-economic status and the curriculum in which he is enrolled and, when intelligence is held constant, the proportion of high school graduates that go on to college decreases with socio-economic status;
4. the type of school curriculum determines, in part, the quality of education, for teachers and administrators give less prestige to vocational training programs than they do to the college-oriented courses;
5. children from the lower socio-economic groups are penalized in the social life of the school because they do not conform to the school's middle class standards.

Elmtown's youth. Hollingshead[15] focused on the relationship of adolescents to the social structure in a Midwestern community which is also analyzed in *Democracy in Jonesville*.

The analysis involved 390 high school students, 345 who had withdrawn from the school, and the 535 families of these adolescents.

[11] *Ibid.*, p. 49.
[12] *Ibid.*, p. 50.

[13] *Ibid.*, p. 62.
[14] *Ibid.*, p. 107.
[15] A. Hollingshead, *Elmtown's Youth* (New York: John Wiley & Sons, Inc., 1949).

The relationship of class level to patterns of school attendance, attrition, dating, school activity, employment, career expectations, and peer association was the focus of attention. Significant differences in social class for each of the variables noted above were presented. These data supplemented by case histories provided the foundations for the conclusion that opportunities for the attainment of desirable rewards and values (those held by members of the middle class) vary positively with the individual's position on the social class ladder.

Hollingshead proposes two explanations for the failure of the lower class adolescent to rise above his present status position. The first is the socialization process in the lower class which Hollingshead believes does not properly fit the working class adolescent for satisfactory educational and occupational adjustment. The second is that middle class adults in the school enforce their class values by "putting down" the lower class adolescents. Finally, Hollingshead presents evidence to support his initial hypothesis that youngsters reflect within the social structure of the school the attitudes, values, and behavior patterns pursued by their parents in the larger society.

The preceding pages have been devoted to a brief overview of three works dealing with social stratification and education. Selection of these for particular attention was deliberate because each has had and continues to have a great impact on educators' views of our schools.

Much of the criticism of these studies is that the relatively small communities analyzed are inadequate samples from which to make generalizations about all of American society. Furthermore, the data do not fully support the hypothesis that variations in school drop-out, curriculum selection, friendship choices, extra-curricular participation, and other variables relevant to education are determined by social class position or by unjust school policies. It is difficult to pinpoint just what causal relationships exist. Generally the authors fail to consider other factors, once a relationship is found to exist between social class and some dependent variable.

Hollingshead's discussion of social class and patterns of friendship among Elmtown's high school youth illustrates the limitations of this analysis. He shows that most students maintain clique associations within their own social class group but also finds that freshmen are more likely to maintain friendship ties with other freshmen, sophomores with sophomores, juniors with juniors, and seniors with seniors. Thus, both social class and school class are related to clique associations. Since drop-out increases with years in school and is highest for the lower classes it should not be surprising to find that social class is related to friendship patterns. We cannot, however, be certain whether the observed differences result from social class discrimination or from the fact that over time there are fewer and fewer lower class students around to choose as friends. A better analysis would have examined the correlation between social class and clique relationships with year in school (freshman, sophomore, etc.) controlled. We would speculate that, in time, social class differences become less important in determining friendship choices than post-high school plans, school activity involvement, and academic interests, or other reference group variables.

These studies also fail to make clear just what there is in the student's socio-economic status that would lead to variations in attitudes, norms, and behavior. Is it, for example, a question of finances alone? Will capable lower class students who are given financial assistance express as strong an interest in college as students from the more affluent families? Is it a question of the values which are stressed by parents from the different class groups? To what extent do members of lower classes use the middle class as a reference group for educational matters and, hence, hold educational values and attitudes like the middle class? Could difference in educational success be due simply to differences in educational sophistication among individuals from the various social strata? Because of their own college experiences and community positions, middle class parents may have a better understanding of how schools operate, where to get information, with whom to speak in the academic bureaucracy, how to fill out applications, and so on.

Probably each of these factors is at play in the total operation of social class and education. The problem is to determine the saliency of each and to measure its impact as the student moves through the various stages of the educational program.

Finally, and here the authors of the works cited above cannot be held accountable, there have been many changes in our schools and communities during the past three decades. Given these changes as well as the recent innovations in methods and techniques of social research, it is necessary to review the more current research in this field.

SCHOOL CONTROL OF EDUCATION AND THE SOCIAL CLASS MATRIX

Investigations of the class composition of school boards have indicated that these boards are heavily populated with the more affluent members of the community. Our purpose is to examine the proposition that middle class control of school boards and administrative bodies will lead to the encouragement and support of policies which reflect the values of the dominant group.

Charters, in discussing control of public education, noted that much of our knowledge about the impact of social class differential on school policy is based on a series of untested assumptions.[16] He indicated that teachers and, in some instances, school administrators are not residents of the community in which they are employed. Involvement with the community is limited to a highly formalized work week and infrequent contact with parents. School administrators, while more active in community life, do not, typically, remain long enough in any one town to become a part of it.

Charters questions the assumption that all individuals internalize, to the same degree, the values of their specific social class group. Adult socialization research demonstrates that numerous influences and pressures act to shape the values, attitudes, and behavior of the individual. The impact of social class may be very much altered by contact with members of other class groups, shifts in institutional identification, and preference for membership in some other group. Implicit in this notion is the belief that personality is a growing, changing, plastic structure that is subject to modification throughout life by social influences that surround the individual at given stages.

While recognizing that attitudes towards education are associated with socio-economic status, Charters questions whether this association should be generalized to maintain that our schools favor a dominant social class group. He also takes exception with the one factor, analytical method which concentrates on the impact of a single variable, in this case, social class. There is reason to doubt that the behavior of school personnel is primarily governed by the values they bring into the school from their positions in the community social structure. If class position were the only factor, there would be little variation among school administrators and teachers who are largely of the same class group. But, important differences are to be found when we look at school personnel at different grade levels, in different schools, in different communities, and with different students.

Charters has called attention in his study to factors which may account for some of the variation in educational attitudes and behavior among members of the same social class group. The operation of non-class factors within the community-school matrix was indicated in the recent work of Gross who also noted that many factors aside from social class help to determine how school board members and superintendents respond to school related questions.[17] Community size, religion of the individual, the issues being considered, the superintendent's self-image, the school board members' images of the school superintendent—all play some part in how these people react even though they have a relatively homogeneous socio-economic status.

He finds that there are significant differences in outlook between school superintendents and their boards and among board members on such subjects as elementary-secondary teacher salary differentials, use of materials in teaching supplied by labor unions, concentration on subject matter, federal aid to education, and international cooperation. These examples indicate that knowledge of an individual's socio-economic status is not enough if we are to understand the values and attitudes of individuals or to understand decision making in education. The social class identification of school board, school staff, and other relevant persons provides some understanding of the forces affecting the school. But the socialization of children and adolescents occurring in the school may be quite dif-

[16] W. W. Charters, Jr., "Social Class Analysis and Control of Public Education," *Harvard Educational Review,* 1953, *23,* pp. 268-282.

[17] N. Gross, *Who Runs Our Schools?* (New York: John Wiley & Sons, Inc., 1958).

ferent than that implied by the social class identification of the dominant adults.

SOCIAL CLASS AND THE SCHOOL SOCIAL SYSTEM

The work of Warner, Hollingshead, and the Lynds show how a student's social class position affects his role within the social system of the school. These authors leave little doubt as to the importance of social class in their discussion of school achievement, school activities, cliques and teacher-pupil relationships. More recent analyses of the social system and norms of behavior which characterize schools throw additional light on the effect of social class on education.

Coleman conducted a study of the "climate of values" among students in nine public high schools.[18] His data suggest that (a) adolescents do not always reflect the values and attitudes of their parents; (b) social class alone will not predict the types of attitudinal orientations held by individuals; (c) educational institutions differ in respect to "social climates" and these differences will alter the impact of social class in respect to values, attitudes, and behavior.

Other investigators have shown that variation in "social climates" is not limited to high schools but also can be found in American universities.[19] Clark and Trow have identified several types of college student sub-cultures. The orientations in these are characterized as academic, collegiate, vocational and non-conformist.[20]

Clark and Trow reported that contemporary trends and forces tend to strengthen the vocational orientations in higher education. The increasing numbers of lower status students in college is probably a major force in this process. Such students view college education as an instrument for obtaining higher status occupations. Gottlieb, in a study dealing with graduate student socialization, found that the "academic climate" of the graduate department, rather than social class origin, played a significant role in the changes in career orientation among graduate students.[21] Among graduate students in the traditional arts and sciences, academic standing, professional orientation of the faculty, contact with the faculty are more significantly related to career orientation than is the student's socio-economic background.

Several other studies dealing with aspects of adolescent behavior support the position that there are norms of school culture which cut across the social class categories. Form and Stone [22] found that adult attitudes and sensitivity to clothing varied sharply by social class identification. Then Vener[23] investigated differences in attitude toward clothing, sensitivity to clothes and other aspects of clothing behavior among secondary-school youth in the Lansing, Michigan, school system according to the social class backgrounds of their families. Guttman-type scales measuring awareness of clothing and feeling of clothing deprivation were developed for these adolescent groups. Except for a feeling of deprivation with regard to clothing, Vener found no significant differences among the boys or girls from the various social strata in any of their age groups. These findings indicate that in spite of differences in family background these adolescents have acquired a relatively common set of attitudes about the importance of clothing. The slightly greater feelings of deprivation among the lower-class students reinforce the other findings; they apparently are less able than higher-status students to acquire the type of wardrobe which they have learned to value.

[18] J. S. Coleman, "Academic Achievement and the Structure of Competition," *Harvard Educational Review*, 1959, *29*, pp. 330-351; also see Coleman's "The Adolescent Subculture and Academic Achievement," reprinted on pp. 87-94 of this volume, and *Social Climates in High Schools* (Washington, D.C.: U.S. Dept. of Health, Education, and Welfare, Office of Education, Cooperative Research Monograph No. 4, 1961).

[19] See C. R. Pace, "Differences in Campus Atmosphere," reprinted on pp. 73-79 of this volume.

[20] B. Clark and M. Trow, "Determinants of College Student Sub-Cultures," in T. M. Newcomb and E. Wilson (Eds.), *The Study of College Peer Groups*, forthcoming.

[21] D. Gottlieb, "Processes of Socialization in the American Graduate School," Unpublished doctoral dissertation, University of Chicago, 1960.

[22] G. Stone and W. Form, *Clothing Inventories and Preference among Rural and Urban Families* (Michigan State University, Agricultural Experiment Station Bulletin, No. 246, 1955); and their *The Social Significance of Clothing in Occupational Life* (Michigan State University, Agricultural Experiment Station Bulletin, No. 247, 1955).

[23] A. Vener, "Adolescent Orientation to Clothing: A Social Psychological Interpretation," Unpublished doctoral dissertation, Michigan State University, 1957; A. Vener and C. Hoffer, *Adolescent Orientation to Clothing* (Michigan State University, Agricultural Experiment Station Bulletin, No. 270, 1959).

In a similar study of seventh-grade girls in the city of Lansing, Michigan, Roach [24] found no differences in clothing behavior by social class. Through interviews with the girls and their mothers she obtained a wide range of data on style, appropriateness, judgment of quality, basis for selecting several sample items of clothing, and related behavior. The only social class difference obtained was from the mothers. Higher-stratum mothers more often reported that they purchased their daughters' clothes at specialty shops while lower class mothers more often shopped at the chain department stores. Apparently, in this community the socialization process for junior and senior high school youth has not closely followed social class lines.

Houser's [25] study of ninth-grade students' attitudes toward minorities suggests that adolescent attitudes vary according to sociometrically identified reference groups rather than according to the social class of the families. This analysis was stimulated by the findings of an earlier investigation in a southern Michigan county showing that although the attitudes of *adults* toward minority groups differed according to their occupational classification, the attitudes of sixth, ninth, and twelfth grade *students* did not vary according to their parents' occupation.[26] Houser hypothesized that the family was not necessarily the relevant reference group for adolescents' attitudes toward minority groups—at least not for all adolescents. Using sociometric choice data, she identified "pure" groups of ninth graders whose families were in a given occupational category and who chose and were chosen by only students from the same category. Attitudes of students composing these "pure" groups were found to vary according to parental occupation in essentially the same way as those of the adults in the community varied. A student who chose and was chosen by only students from a different occupational background than his own, however, expressed attitudes like those in this sociometric reference group different from those in his occupational group. The attitudes of students who chose into another group but were not chosen by members of that group on the sociometric test fell between those of the two relevant "pure" groups.

This analysis indicates that within the adolescent school society there are relevant patterns of interaction which cut across the socio-economic categories characterizing the youths' families. Perhaps a similar analysis of the clothing, dating, school activities, career aspirations, and other behavior of high school students would reveal that such reference group interaction is at least as important as the family's social class in molding the behavior of adolescents and young adults.

Certainly the comprehensive school which draws students from all social strata provides an opportunity for cross-class socialization to occur. The possibility that such interaction produces a relatively different set of behavioral norms in the school than exists in the various adult strata has not been fully explored.

THE SCHOOLS AND SOCIAL MOBILITY

Implicit in some early studies is the assumption that the schools tend to reinforce the social class structure. As Parsons [27] indicated, the schools serve an allocating function in American society. The future status of the child in the adult social structure is determined in significant degree by decisions made in school. Although level of education achieved and curriculum are related to family social class, we are also aware that the school provides an opportunity for many lower class children to rise above the status of their parents.

An examination of the college attendance of students from River City [28] reveals that about four-fifths of youth in the upper and upper-middle class enter college, while only about one-fifth of youth from upper-lower and only a few from lower-lower class families enter college. Since lower class fam-

[24] M. E. Roach, "The Influence of Social Class on Clothing Practices and Orientation at Early Adolescence," Unpublished doctoral dissertation, Michigan State University, 1960.

[25] L. Houser, "A Socio-metric Test of Reference Group Theory in a Study of Prejudice among Youth," Unpublished doctoral dissertation, Michigan State University, 1956.

[26] J. Holland, "Attitude Toward Minority Groups in Relation to Rural Social Structure," Unpublished doctoral dissertation, Michigan State University, 1950.

[27] T. Parsons, "The School Class as a Social System," *Harvard Education Review*, 1959, *29*, pp. 297-318.

[28] R. J. Havighurst, "Social-Class Influences on American Education," in N. B. Henry (Ed.), *Social Forces Influencing American Education*, Sixtieth Yearbook of the National Society for the Study of Education, Part II (Chicago: University of Chicago Press, 1961), p. 123.

ilies, however, constitute a far larger proportion of the River City population than upper-middle class families, the gross number of students from lower class homes who reach college is slightly greater than the number from upper strata homes. National estimates suggest that not only is the total college population composed of students from all strata but that increasingly larger proportions are coming from lower strata.

A study of graduate students in a sample of United States universities revealed that approximately two-thirds of the graduate students in natural science, social science, and the humanities came from lower-middle and lower class backgrounds.[29] This is further evidence that high levels of education are achieved by some youth of lower status. This evidence of mobility through education suggests that the schools' status-allocating function tends to select across as well as within social strata.

The processes by which the status allocation occurs in the school have not been extensively explored. The socialization that occurs in the relatively homogeneous school culture is probably a significant factor. It is generally assumed that teachers play a significant role in this process, but there is little precise knowledge about it.

An analysis of the changes in educational and occupational expectations of sixth-grade students in Flint, Michigan, indicates that the family's status as measured by occupational prestige is not related to pupil changes which occur during the school year.[30] A sizeable proportion of children from both higher and lower strata change their educational and occupational expectations during the sixth grade, but the hypothesis that low stratum children would lower their expectations more than high stratum children during this school year was not generally supported. Tentative findings from a small sample of this sixth-grade group indicate that the child's relationship with the teacher is an intervening factor affecting changes in expectations. Teachers seemed to encourage the mobility aspirations of certain low-stratum students selected on the basis of their perceptions of the child's behavior and how it fits the teacher's stereotype of social class. The teachers involved in the study were all identified with essentially the same middle class stratum, but there is no reason to believe that teachers from different strata would behave differently in their selection of students for mobility.

SOCIAL CLASS AND SCHOOL ACHIEVEMENT

The cold war and the need for highly trained manpower in our industrial society have focused attention on school achievement and excellence in job performance. Much of this attention has been directed to the discovery of talent at an early age on the assumption that the factors producing high achievement and success are relatively stable. The validity of this assumption is limited by evidence that measured abilities, aptitudes, attitudes, motivation, and other aspects of behavior change over time—either these factors are less stable than is commonly believed or our methods for measuring them are unreliable.

It is generally accepted that there is some correlation, though limited, between ability as measured by intelligence tests and school achievement, on the one hand, and adult accomplishment on the other. The variation in both IQ and school grade from time to time and the other factors associated with adult achievement make early talent identification extremely difficult. Social class and other family-background differences in emphasizing the factors associated with achievement are among the basic considerations in this area.

A number of investigators have noted that eventual expression of talent may be a product of differences in child-rearing practices. These investigators point out that need for achievement is strongly affected by parental attitudes and values. Exactly what there is in the family structure which might account for these differences in achievement need is not clearly established. Rosen discusses an "achievement syndrome" which he finds to be more prevalent in middle class families than in lower class families.[31]

In this case Rosen attributes variations in achievement need and intensity to differences in the values held by parents in both social class groups. Middle

[29] Gottlieb, *op. cit.*

[30] A study in process of completion by M. Smith.

[31] B. Rosen, "The Achievement Syndrome," *American Sociological Review,* 1956, *21,* pp. 203-211.

class parents are seen to place the greater emphasis on mobility and success; hence their children are more likely to embrace achievement-oriented behavior. Strodtbeck concludes from his study of differences in achievement and incentive between boys of Italian and Jewish extraction that the higher motivation of the Jewish youth can be explained by family power structure, cultural traditions, and parental attitudes.[32] These and other studies suggest that ethnic or religious values may cut across social class lines and reduce the importance of socio-economic background.

What then can be said about the importance of socio-economic background as a factor related to achievement? At this point, it would seem, not much. McClelland makes the following observation about socio-economic status, IQ, and achievement:

> Since probably no other single assumption is so widely held among both scientists and laymen as that intelligence, as such, regardless of background, is linearly associated with success both in school and in life, the importance of clarifying the whole issue is crucial. It should be accorded high priority in any set of research projects undertaken to improve the predictive efficiency of test scores.[33]

Numerous studies indicate a limited relationship between family social status and both intelligence test scores and school grades.[34] In recognition of this, the fact that these correlations are relatively low is sometimes overlooked. A current Michigan State University study of school achievement among 778 seventh-grade high and low achieving students in a Midwestern city showed the typical relationships with students' social class backgrounds. Yet it is significant that among the lower social class students included in the two achievement groups above and below the middle range 35 per cent were high achievers. The comparable proportions of high and middle class students were 75 and 53 per cent. In spite of the limited educational achievement and occupational status of their parents, a sizeable proportion of the youth from lower-class families are excelling in school. Certainly factors other than those identified as social class are operating in determining school grades.

SUMMARY

This review of investigations of the relation of social class and education may be summarized as follows.

Earlier studies have led to an over-emphasis on social class as a single factor which accounts for variation in attitudes, achievement, and other behavior relevant to the school system.

American schools, particularly comprehensive public schools, provide an arena for the common or cross-class socialization of children and youth. This is evidenced by common social norms and patterns of school behavior that are widely distributed across social class lines.

Variation in reference group, motivation, self perception, school "social climates," teachers' and other adults' expectations of the school, and other factors may account for some differences in educational achievement and other school behavior which have been attributed to social class. Much more examination of such intervening variables is needed.

The large number of lower class youth who enter and complete extended programs of higher education demonstrates that education provides a relatively clear opportunity for social mobility in American society. Although class differences exist, increasingly large proportions of undergraduate and graduate student bodies are drawn from lower strata of the society.

The commonly held assumption that social classes differ in the value they attach to education is questioned. In contrast, the demand for equal educational opportunities indicates that lower socio-economic groups place a high premium on education. Differences in consumption of higher education may be due to the fact that lower strata persons are less sophisticated in knowing how to operate in the educational bureaucracy and in relating specific educational programs to their aspirations.

[32] F. L. Strodtbeck, "Family Interaction, Values and Achievement," in D. C. McClelland *et al.* (Eds.), *Talent and Society* (New York: D. Van Nostrand Co., Inc., 1958).

[33] D. C. McClelland *et al.* (Eds.), *Talent and Society* (New York: D. Van Nostrand Co., Inc., 1958), p. 14.

[34] *Cf.*, W. W. Charters, Jr., "Social Class and Intelligence Tests," pp. 12-21 of this volume.

*SOCIAL CLASS AND INTELLIGENCE TESTS**

By W. W. Charters, Jr.

Few thoughtful people today believe that the Intelligence Quotient reflects a purely innate, hereditary ability of humans. Half a century of intelligence testing and research has made it clear that a person's environmental experiences help to determine the IQ score he achieves.

In the 1920's and 1930's studies were made of the intelligence of orphanage children before and after they had been placed in foster homes, of Negro children from the Deep South attending public schools in Northern cities to which their families had migrated, and of identical twins separated at an early age and reared under differing environmental conditions.[1] These and other studies showed important differences in IQ scores which could not be attributed solely to hereditary or constitutional differences among the subjects.

While demonstrations of the contribution of environmental experiences to measured intelligence have been impressive, they have not led psychologists to assume that biological factors play no part. The question of whether it is heredity *or* environment which makes for differences in intelligence was abandoned many years ago as fruitless. Obviously, both are necessary to produce an intelligently functioning human being. Moreover, psychologists today tend to agree that biological and environmental factors interact with one another in intricate and complex ways to produce intelligent behavior. No longer is it fruitful to ask how much is contributed by heredity and how much by environment, as though their contributions to intelligence were entirely independent of one another. Psychologists still disagree, however, in their conceptions of the particular way the various factors interact to determine differences in intelligence and, to a certain extent, in the relative emphasis they attribute to the biological and environmental determinants.[2]

SOCIAL CLASS DIFFERENCES IN IQ

Shortly after World War II a group of scientists at the University of Chicago began an intensive examination of the impact of family social class position on IQ scores of children. It had long been known that intelligence test scores of children from the lower classes averaged below those of children from the higher social classes. Indeed, Alfred Binet was acutely aware of the influence of social status on children's responses to test items at the time he was developing his pioneer intelligence measure in the early 1900's.[3] A number of studies had accumulated in the intervening years to show that the correlation between socio-economic status and intelligence test scores was in the neighborhood of .35 and that scores for children of professional families typically ran from 15 to 25 points higher on the average than for children of unskilled laborers.[4] But the Chicago group, composed predominantly of sociologists and anthropologists, introduced a new perspective regarding the nature of the environmental influence.

Psychologists of the day explained the relation-

[1] F. N. Freeman, K. J. Holzinger, and B. C. Mitchell, "The Influence of Environment on the Intelligence, School Achievement and Conduct of Foster Children," *Twenty-seventh Yearbook of the National Society for the Study of Education,* Part I, 1928, pp. 103-217; H. H. Newman, F. N. Freeman, and K. J. Holzinger, *Twins: A Study of Heredity and Environment* (Chicago: University of Chicago Press, 1937); O. Klineberg, *Negro Intelligence and Selective Migration* (New York: Columbia University Press, 1935).

* Prepared especially for this volume.

[2] The development of the "heredity-environment controversy" with respect to intelligence testing can be traced conveniently through various Yearbooks of the National Society for the Study of Education. See G. M. Whipple (Ed.), *Intelligence: Its Nature and Nurture,* Thirty-ninth Yearbook, National Society for the Study of Education (Bloomington, Ill.: Public School Publishing Company, 1940), Parts I and II.

[3] A. Davis, "How Does Cultural Bias in Intelligence Tests Arise?" in K. Eells, A. Davis, R. J. Havighurst, V. E. Herrick, and R. W. Tyler, *Intelligence and Cultural Differences* (Chicago: University of Chicago Press, 1951), Ch. 5.

[4] V. E. Herrick, "What is Already Known About the Relation of the I. Q. to Cultural Background?" in Eells *et al., Intelligence and Cultural Differences, ibid.,* p. 12.

ship between social class and intelligence in one of two ways. Some took the position that it was primarily the result of a process of social selection. Those persons with higher levels of intelligence were capable of climbing into and remaining in the upper reaches of the social class structure, leaving behind in the lower ranks the less intelligent members of the society. Other psychologists attributed to the environment a more direct role in shaping the intellectual capacity of individuals. They believed that social environments could be ranked on a continuum of "mental stimulation value"—the extent to which the environment provided experiences necessary for intellectual development. In this view, the important environmental difference between foster homes and orphanages, for example, or between urban schools in the North and the Southern segregated schools, was in the amount of mental stimulation they offered. With respect to social class, the more intellectually nurturant experiences were afforded the child by higher- than by lower-status homes so that the lower-class child was usually deprived of the environmental support vital to the full fruition of his intelligence.

A CULTURAL POINT OF VIEW

The University of Chicago scientists, too, attributed to the environment an active, direct role in shaping individual intelligence, but they disagreed with the prevailing view that environments differed simply in the amount of mental stimulation they provided. Environmental influences, the Chicago scientists argued, differed not only in degree but in *kind* with the consequence that different kinds of intellectual skills were fostered in various environments. The proper explanation for the relationship between intelligence and social class lay in the *cultural* differences existing among the social classes.

It is not surprising that this cultural point of view arose when and where it did. About 1945, major studies of social class in American communities, under the leadership of W. Lloyd Warner, were underway or had recently been completed.[5] Warner and his colleagues had applied to contemporary society the perspectives and methods of cultural anthropology, theretofore reserved largely for the study of primitive societies. Prominent in the anthropological perspective was the concept of *culture.* This concept referred to the observation that groups of people living in relative isolation from others develop standard, more or less distinctive, ways of doing and thinking about things, of expressing themselves, of raising their children, of deciding what is valuable in life, and so on. As these students investigated the cultural patterns in the various social classes of the American community, they found them to be surprisingly diverse. The social classes, of course, were not entirely isolated from one another; they shared in important cultural patterns and institutions of the general American society. But the community studies indicated that the isolation was sufficient to allow the various classes to develop significant variations on the general theme of American society. The variations were sufficiently divergent to warrant regarding them as *sub-cultures* within the society. And, according to the Chicago research workers, children from the lower classes performed poorly on intelligence tests because the tasks required of them by the tests were either unimportant in or alien to their particular sub-cultures.

THE ARGUMENT FOR CULTURAL BIAS IN STANDARD INTELLIGENCE TESTS

Implications of the cultural point of view for intelligence testing were extensively developed by Allison Davis, who had been a prominent participant in the early social class studies.[6] These implications were presented at length in his 1948 Inglis Lecture[7] and more compactly in the contributions of Davis and his colleagues to Part I of their subsequent research monograph.[8] Davis's basic argument was that the social class differentials in IQ scores resulted from cultural biases in intelligence test construction and not from differences in the reason-

[5] See W. B. Brookover and D. Gottlieb, "Social Class and Education," published in this volume, pp. 3-11.

[6] A. Davis, B. B. Gardner, and M. R. Gardner, *Deep South* (Chicago: University of Chicago Press, 1941).

[7] A. Davis, *Social-Class Influences upon Learning* (Cambridge, Mass.: Harvard University Press, 1948).

[8] Eells, *et al., op. cit.*

ing ability of children. In short, intelligence tests were unfair to children of the lower-class culture.

Problem-solving abilities. Davis elaborated the argument in several ways. Most fundamental was his position that intelligence tests were designed to measure only one of several kinds of problem-solving ability—the kind associated with scholastic achievement in what he regarded as the typically middle-class educational program of the schools. From the earliest days, intelligence tests had been validated against the scholastic success of pupils. Those test items which could discriminate between "good" and "poor" students were retained in the tests while those which could not were rejected. Consequently, the tests measured only those forms of mental ability which were adaptive for superior achievement in educational institutions. They stressed verbal facility and ability to deal with abstract problems.

> In nearly all general intelligence tests, the authors have depended chiefly upon two types of verbal questions to furnish the most difficult problems in their tests, and to screen the "mediocre" and "average" pupils from the "superior" pupils. These two types of questions are based upon (1) verbal relationship and complex academic phrasing (such as verbal "analogies" and "opposites," and "syllogisms"); and (2) rare words (used in vocabulary tests and "definitions").[9]

But mental ability—including such things according to Davis as inventiveness, the analysis and organization of observed experiences, and the drawing of inferences—is considerably more than facility with language, and intelligence tests failed to measure these other aspects of problem-solving capacity.

The intensive studies of social class had indicated that it was precisely with respect to an emphasis upon verbal skills and "bookish" abstractions that the cultures of the middle and lower classes departed. Davis illustrated this point in a passage on reading skill.

> These low socio-economic groups fail because their parents themselves have not been trained to read; nor do they regard reading or school curriculums as important. Moreover, neither the parent nor the child's social group urges the child to practice reading or school exercises or sets him an example for attainment in this field. The parents and friends of the average child in the high socio-economic groups, on the other hand, do offer him a powerful example of their skill in reading and in the school type of culture. Furthermore, the latter group of parents consciously and unconsciously reveals an interest in the child's learning this behavior; they likewise afford him practice in such problem-solving.[10]

Middle and lower class cultures differed, too, in the extent of their congruency with the educational institution in which verbal intelligence of the kind measured by intelligence tests is nurtured.

> School is an extension of home to the average middle-class child. It rewards and punishes him for the same things that the home does. It is familiar ground. On the contrary, school is often a strange place to the lower-class child, with strange expectations. It often contradicts the home in its rewards and punishments.
>
> From school experience are drawn many of the items of current intelligence tests. Hence the child who spends the greatest amount of time in school, and who is most receptive to the school's teaching, prepares himself best for intelligence tests. Middle-class children tend to stay longer in school than lower-class children. In many cities the best-equipped schools and the best-prepared teachers are in the higher-status areas of the community, while the lower-class pupils go to run-down schools with less able teachers. Consequently, the experiences of the lower-class children is less conducive to good performance on intelligence tests. There is also more retardation of lower-class pupils, which means that they are exposed to less advanced school work, with a consequent decreased experience with the materials from which the more difficult test items are drawn.
>
> There is a tendency to place and to keep middle-class children in the most academic or "bookish" curriculums in school. Test items which are drawn from these curriculums will probably favor middle-class children. For example, a test item requiring the pupil to know that geometry, algebra, and trigonometry all belong together, but that botany does not belong closely with them, would more probably be known by a pupil in the college preparatory than in the vocational or general curriculum.
>
> The sectioning of children by "ability" tends to place the middle-class children in "high" sections and the lower-class children in "low" sections. . . . The higher groups get more verbal and abstract learning experience, which gives them an advantage with intelligence tests of a verbal or abstract character.[11]

Intelligence tests, then, were designed to measure those aspects of mental ability in which middle-class children, by virtue of their culture and by virtue

[9] A. Davis, *Social-Class Influences . . . , op. cit.*, pp. 78-79.

[10] A. Davis, "What are Some of the Basic Issues in the Relation of Intelligence Tests to Cultural Background?" in K. Eells *et al., op. cit.*, p. 27.

[11] R. J. Havighurst, "What are the Cultural Differences which May Affect Performance on Intelligence Tests?" in K. Eells *et al., op. cit.*, p. 20.

of the orientation of educational methods of the school, were bound to excel and to ignore those other aspects of mental ability in which the lower-class culture would lead its children to perform favorably.

Language forms. Following from his cultural perspective of the social classes, Davis added another facet to his argument. Not only the emphasis upon linguistic skills but the very language itself differs from one class to the next. Intelligence test instructions and items frequently contain words and refer to situations which are common-place for the middle-class child but foreign to the lower-class child. An oft-quoted example of this is the test item the correct answer to which depends upon the pupil's familiarity with the word *sonata*—"a word which will clearly be heard more often in a home in the higher socio-economic brackets than in a family from the low socio-economic group."[12] Another illustration is the following analogies question:

A symphony is to a composer as book is to what?
( ) paper
( ) sculptor
( ) author
( ) musician
( ) man

In this version, 81 per cent of higher- as opposed to 51 per cent of lower-class children marked the answer correctly in a trial administration. Not only were the key words culturally loaded but the linguistic form of the question was highly abstract; the form ". . . is to . . ." was hardly a linguistic structure to which lower-class children would be exposed in the normal course of their lives. A second, less "biased" version was drawn up as follows:

A baker goes with bread, like a carpenter goes with what?
( ) a saw
( ) a house
( ) a spoon
( ) a nail
( ) a man

In this version an equal proportion of children in the lower and higher classes responded correctly.[13]

One of the major research investigations conducted by the University of Chicago group was designed to illuminate the preceding criticisms of intelligence tests. By means of an exhaustive, item-by-item analysis of social class differences in responses of school pupils to standard tests of intelligence, Eells[14] sought to discover what particular kinds of test items favor high-status as compared with low-status children. Ten widely-used group intelligence tests were administered to 9- and 10-year-old and 13- and 14-year-old school children in Rockford, Illinois, in such a way that each age group responded to five tests on five succeeding days. The 5,000 children tested constituted most of the white pupils at these age levels in the city. When the total IQ scores were compared for children in the various social classes, the typical correlations were found—ranging from .20 to .43, depending upon the particular test.

Detailed examination of 650 individual items in the tests showed that social class differences in correct responses appeared on nearly two-thirds of the items among the younger children and on nine out of ten items among the older age group. Eells had hoped to discover the nature of the "bias" in test items by comparing the items which discriminated between the social classes with other items on which social class differences did not appear. But most of the items which showed no social class differences were at the extremes of the difficulty range and were either passed or failed by virtually all children, regardless of their social class. Excluding these, only a small number of items remained on which the lower-status children performed as well as their higher-status peers and which could be used for the purpose of comparison. Hence, Eells could draw no definitive conclusions, but his inferences about these few items followed closely the general arguments advanced by Davis.

> It is shown that, when the test item is expressed in terms of strange, academic, or bookish words, the status differences are much greater than when the item is expressed in simple everyday words. Differential opportunity for familiarity with certain objects is also stressed for a number of items. In other items, status differences are related to formal school learning, or to an assumed greater ability of high-status pupils to handle abstract as opposed to concrete terms.
>
> Practically all the items which show unusually small

[12] A. Davis, *Social-Class Influences . . . , op. cit.*, p. 45.

[13] A. Davis, "Socio-economic Influences upon Children's Learning," *Understanding the Child,* 1951, *20,* pp. 10-16.

[14] K. Eells, in K. Eells *et al., op. cit.,* Parts II and III.

differences either are nonverbal in symbolism or are expressed in relatively simple everyday vocabulary and deal with objects or concepts which are probably equally familiar, or equally unfamiliar, to pupils at both status levels.[15]

But the investigator goes on to warn his readers that on many items there were large status differences for which he could offer no plausible explanation.

It was possible to analyze the items in another way. Besides comparing the few items showing no class differences with those showing large differences, the investigator could inspect the items as they varied in the *amount* of advantage they gave the higher-status children. From this standpoint, Eells first classified items according to the kind of symbolism they employed and then compared the average status differences in correct responses. He found that the greatest status differences occurred for the verbal items and the least for items employing pictures, geometric designs, and stylized drawings. When the items were classified according to the kinds of intellectual operations they required of children (analogies, opposites, and so on), no consistent or meaningful variations in the amount of status difference could be discovered.

Eells was extremely cautious in drawing conclusions from his study. It was clear that status differences in responses to the test items persisted on virtually all items, regardless of their form. Nevertheless, the analysis yielded certain clues as to how items could be written so as to minimize if not to eliminate social class differences.

Motivation and work habits. A third feature of Davis' argument came close to setting a condition which would have made it impossible to *disprove* his argument. He asserted that test-taking itself is alien to the lower-class culture, and that, even if intelligence tests were constructed to measure the IQs of lower-class children fairly, the children still would not have the work habits or motivation in the testing situation sufficient to compete with their middle-class peers. Davis set forth the issue in this passage:

> It is possible that the middle class will also prove superior on all, or nearly all, types of possible test problems, because they have a cultural advantage in habits of work and in test motivation. That is, since *training* is an essential part of all problem-solving, it may be that the superiority of middle-class culture in establishing habits of school work will generalize to all kinds of mental problems, including also those in which the cultural content and symbols are common to all social classes.[16]

If this were true, no empirical evidence could establish the truth or falsity of Davis's overall position. His analysis, however, led to an investigation of the effects of training and motivation on intelligence test scores. The analysis also encouraged Davis and his colleagues, in connection with the intelligence test they eventually developed, to attempt to "relax" the testing situation under which it was administered (by reading test questions to groups of children rather than requiring them to read them for themselves, by encouraging laughter, by fashioning test items to look like comic-strip cartoons) so that the class differences in work habits and test motivation would operate less to the advantage of middle-class children.

In sum, Davis argued that the general intelligence tests in common use were culturally loaded against the lower class. They tested only those mental abilities favoring the cultural experiences of the middle class; they were couched in language and linguistic forms unfamiliar to the lower class; and they called for kinds of work habits and motivation which were not valued or taught in the lower-class culture. The trouble was, Davis believed, that intelligence tests were products of the middle class and incorporated the bias of the middle-class culture.

> [Test-makers and educators] continually make the error of regarding middle-class culture, and even more narrowly, middle-class school culture, as the "true" culture, or the "best" culture. More than 95 per cent of our teachers and professors are middle-class in their socio-economic status. Like all other cultural groups, teachers and professors regard that particular version of culture (those mores, emotional patterns, and social values) which they have learned from their own families, friends, and teachers, as the "best" and only "true" culture. This attitude is powerfully reflected in school curriculums, in intelligence tests, and in teachers' judgments of their pupils.[17]

If Davis' points were true, then social class differences in IQ would disappear when children

[15] *Ibid.*, p. 357.

[16] A. Davis, "What are Some of the Basic Issues . . .?" *op. cit.*, p. 28.

[17] *Ibid.*, p. 26.

were tested on culturally-fair intelligence measures in a testing situation equally motivating to those of higher and lower status.

The Haggard experiment. As mentioned above, another major empirical investigation in the Chicago research program was designed to examine the effects of motivation, training, and certain other conditions on intelligence test scores. Specifically, Haggard[18] predicted that lower-class children would show substantial improvement in their test scores under the following conditions: a) when they were tested on an intelligence test form in which the content was more in keeping with the language and experiences of lower-class children, b) when test items were read aloud to them instead of depending upon them to read the items to themselves, c) when they were given practice in answering questions similar to those which appear on intelligence tests, and d) when either their practice or their test taking was motivated by the promise of a free pass to a movie for a good performance. Haggard evaluated these predictions by measuring the intelligence of nearly 700 high- and low-status children on a conventional test and then separating them into a variety of experimental groups of 40 to 50 children each. These groups, then, were subjected to different combinations of the experimental conditions. All were retested five days later, some with the conventional test and others with a revised form of the test, some under motivating conditions and some not, some with practice during the intervening days and some without such practice, and so on. Haggard's fundamental question was, Would lower-class children *improve more* in their scores than higher-class children under the predicted circumstances?

As one might imagine, the number of comparisons reported from this study was large, and they cannot be itemized in detail here. Generally speaking, the results were mixed and inconsistent. Thus, it was the high-status and not the low-status children who benefitted from the practice sessions, particularly when they were retested on the conventional test. In some experimental conditions the investigator's attempts to motivate the children *decreased* the retest scores of high- and low-status children alike, in other conditions the motivation attempts made no difference, and in still others motivation improved the retest scores of low-status children but not high-status children in accordance with Haggard's prediction. The lower status children showed substantial gains when they were retested on the form of the test deliberately revised to make it more suitable for them, but these gains were overshadowed by the fact that higher-status children also showed remarkable gains on the revised form.

In sum, while Haggard's study was unable to demonstrate that social-class differences in intelligence were fully accounted for by such matters as motivation, practice, test forms, and the like, it did show that test scores of children, whether of low or high status, could be influenced by these factors. Test performance, the investigator concluded, depends upon the experience children bring with them and upon psychological factors in the testing situation itself. The mere revision of current intelligence tests to remove their middle-class bias would not be sufficient to measure mental ability adequately.

AN UNBIASED TEST: CRITICISMS AND DISAPPOINTMENTS

The Chicago scientists culminated their five years and more of intensive work by producing a measure of general intelligence which they believed would not unduly favor children of the upper status levels. In 1953 a series of group tests for elementary-school age levels was commercially published as the Davis-Eells Games.[19] Their anthropological perspective had led the authors to point up limitations in the conventional intelligence tests insofar as these incorporated "biases" which penalized children from the sub-culture of the lower class. Their investigations, in turn, suggested ways in which they might avoid in a new test the shortcomings of their predecessors. Thus, the authors wrote items which required reasoning about everyday events rather than about abstractions, and they avoided language which was academic or bookish in form and content.

---

[18] E. A. Haggard, "Social-Status and Intelligence: An Experimental Study of Certain Cultural Determinants of Measured Intelligence," *Genetic Psychology Monographs,* 1954, *49,* pp. 141-186.

[19] A. Davis and K. Eells, *Davis-Eells Tests of General Intelligence or Problem-Solving Ability* (Yonkers, N.Y.: World Book Company, 1953).

As the word *Games* in the title implies, the test was to be administered in a relaxed atmosphere. Even the test format, giving it an appearance not unlike a comic strip, attempted to remove the impression that the testing session was an examination. This format, too, was designed to engage motivations more universal than that of simply performing well on a school test. But publication of their own test also provided the opportunity to put their whole approach on trial, and scholars across the country were quick to do so.

Criticisms of the approach to test construction. Prior to the appearance of the Davis-Eells Games, however, the academic community had been receiving abridged reports of the work at Chicago. A number of sophisticated criticisms were made concerning the approach and the assumptions on which it was based. Thus, Anastasi wrote:

> Perhaps the principal weakness in the approach of these investigators is their inadequate recognition of the extent to which the cultural differences in information, motivation, and work habits manifested in test performance also influence the individual's overall intellectual development. Removing culturally-biased items from a test does not eliminate cultural differences in behavior. The criteria against which the tests are validated are themselves culturally loaded, and "intelligence tests" are operationally meaningless unless defined in terms of such criteria. To be sure, it is important to investigate behavior differences between cultural groups. But such differences cannot be studied by eliminating culturally loaded items. They can be explored only by constructing tests which sample the behavior functions fostered by each culture.[20]

Some critics questioned the assumption running through the work of Davis and his colleagues that, since the social classes do not differ fundamentally in problem-solving capacity, any test which shows such differences must be biased. With this assumption Davis took a firm "environmentalist" stand, discounting the possibility that members of the social classes may differ in biological constitution as well as in cultural circumstances. The heredity-environment issue was still capable of evoking well-entrenched sentiments which served to add heat to the criticisms.

One of the more balanced of the early criticisms was that of Lorge.[21] He noted that differences in measured intelligence have been well-established between groups classified by education, occupation of father, geographic origin, personality structure, and so on. As a result, psychologists have become "increasingly aware of the multiplicity and intricacies of factors related to test performance of individuals and of groups."[22] Psychologists and test-makers have taken pains to provide "normative data for a variety of groups because they know differences in test performance are related to sex, age, grade-placement, and socio-economic status," and those who use the tests have been cautioned time and again to interpret test scores in the light of the variety of factors, such as the child's motivations and health, which are known to affect them.

> Inevitably some users of tests neglected to profit from the tutelage. They wilfully treated test scores as absolute determinations about individuals, or, even, groups. Others, of course, failed to appreciate fully the range and interaction of circumstances that affect test performance. To overcome such perversity and such ignorance, some psychometricians tried to be quit of the *bias* of the test-user by attempting to eliminate the *differences* from the tests. One procedure long in use is to add items of a certain kind which favor an otherwise unfavored group. In this way, the composite IQ score is adjusted until it is "fair" to each group.
>
> For instance, it is well-known that boys and girls (and men and women) perform differently on tests of verbal, and of numerical, content and process. . . . All of us are fully aware that to overcome the obtained verbal superiority of women, the test-maker adds a sufficiency of numerical reasoning items to make the average total score of men equal that of women. *No difference, ergo, no bias.* Fortunately, there still are differences between the sexes.

Lorge pointed out, however, that the description of a person's intelligence by means of a single, composite score is a practice of convenience and compromise, not an ideal to emulate. Current knowledge has made it plain that intelligence is not a single, unitary capacity, and that to express it in a single-index score is to cover up important differences in the mental organization of different individuals and groups. Better that intelligence

[20] A. Anastasi, "Individual Differences," in C. P. Stone and D. W. Taylor (Eds.), *Annual Review of Psychology* (Stanford, Calif.: Annual Reviews, Inc., 1953), vol. 4, p. 151.

[21] I. Lorge, "Difference or Bias in Tests of Intelligence," in *Proceedings of the 1952 Invitational Conference on Testing Problems* (Princeton, N.J.: Educational Testing Service, 1953), pp. 76-83.

[22] This and subsequent quotations in the following paragraphs have been taken from Lorge, *ibid., passim.*

scores be broken down into their component parts and reported as such, as differential aptitude tests have done in another realm of psychometrics, than to adjust a composite score until it is "fair" to everyone.

Lorge also disagreed with the test-making strategy of Eells and Davis. To select test items principally on the grounds that they do *not* discriminate between groups is to use an extremely restrictive, if not a reversed, approach to the construction of a measure of intelligence. "Some criterion about intellectual functioning, other than the one that the items make for no diversity, seems, at least, a psychological prerequisite." Lorge had no doubt that the Eells method could produce a test, but he, along with other critics of the day, had serious question as to what such a test would measure. Conventional intelligence tests had been eminently successful in predicting behavior with respect to the wide variety of tasks in our society which call for verbal and linguistic skills. If a test were constructed which minimized verbal processes and favored those requiring the manipulation of numbers, geometric designs, and pictures, what meaningful behavior would it predict? The Eells and Davis approach included no clear provision for behavioral criteria against which the test could be validated.

Throughout Lorge's commentary was the fundamental objection that the removal of systematic group differences from intelligence measures reduces the amount of decision-relevant information yielded by the tests, information useful in guiding children to appropriate educational experiences and vital to the further understanding of intellectual processes in both individuals and groups.

> There can be little doubt that among some kinds of groups differences do exist. As a matter of fact, the wide range of general and specific tests of intelligence has made it possible to establish much of the available knowledge of differential psychology. Not only has the awareness of such differences led to the emergence of a more adequate understanding of the relative advantages and limitations of intelligence tests but it also has increased our appreciation of the significance of difference in the understanding of children as individuals, and in groups. In a democracy, such as ours, respect for difference as difference is necessary. There is no virtue in developing instruments so blunted that they decrease the amount of information. Perhaps the best method for reducing bias in tests of intelligence is to use them with the full knowledge that endowment interacting with opportunity produces a wide range of differences. Appraisal of the variation of different kinds of intellectual functioning requires many kinds of tests so that the differences can be utilized for the benefit of the individual and for the good of society. Intellectual functioning certainly does involve the ability to learn to adjust to the environment or to adapt the environment to individual needs and capacities by the process of solving problems either directly or incidentally. Such a concept recognizes a variety of different aptitudes for success with different kinds of problems. The full appreciation of the variety of aptitudes and the development of adequate methods for appraising them, should in the long run, ultimately lead to the production of enough information to eliminate bias.

With this, Lorge returned to the theme with which he started: the *bias* in intelligence tests resides not in the tests themselves—they only show *differences* —but in those who interpret the tests as though the IQ scores were an "absolute determination" of the inherent mental capacity of the individual.

Empirical assessments of the new test. Once the Davis-Eells test was published, the theoretical discussion of the Chicago group's approach gave way to empirical evaluation of the product. The research findings accumulated rapidly, and by 1956 they indicated unequivocally that the test had fallen short of its goal. In view of the amount of time required for its administration, the test had relatively low reliability. But even more to the point, it had not eliminated the social class differences in IQ. In five of six grade-levels of children studied in a Southwestern city, for example, high status-children still averaged 5 points higher than low-status children on the Davis-Eells test.[23] Another investigator found the advantage of the high-status pupils to range from 12 to 17 points in three Tennessee cities, and, moreover, the mean scores from the Davis-Eells test looked no different from mean IQs derived from a conventional intelligence test given at the same time.[24] The Davis-Eells scores still showed a correlation of about .35 with social class among a number of 10-year-olds in the Detroit

[23] H. Angelino and C. L. Shedd, "An Initial Report of a Validation Study of the Davis-Eells Test of General Intelligence or Problem Solving Ability," *Journal of Psychology,* 1955, *40,* pp. 35-38.

[24] W. Coleman and A. W. Ward, "A Comparison of Davis-Eells and Kuhlmann-Finch Scores of Children from High and Low Socio-economic Status," *Journal of Educational Psychology,* 1955, *46,* pp. 465-469.

area—not much different from the correlations obtained with two conventional tests.[25] More recently one investigator found the kind of results initially promised by the test: Among children in a Midwestern suburb the correlations between father's occupation and score on the Davis-Eells Games were close to zero while IQs from a standard test showed the usual correlations with social class.[26] But taken as a whole, these and other studies[27] made it clear that the "culture-fair" test produced by the Chicago workers could not be counted on to equalize the IQs between the classes.

THE RESIDUE

It may have been unfortunate, in one sense, that Davis and his colleagues attempted to produce an intelligence test. The test's publication and the subsequent efforts to assess its promise seemed to divert scholarly attention away from the fundamental issues posed by Davis in his cultural analysis of environment and intelligence. In some quarters of psychology, at least, the failure of the Davis-Eells test to live up to its promise simply closed the chapter on the Chicago group's excursion into the theory of intelligence; the underlying arguments, it seemed, no longer needed to be met.

Other psychologists viewed the work at Chicago in broad perspective, seeing it as one among many attempts to refine the meaning of intelligence and its relation to experience. Lorge took such a view. He opened his critique of the Eells book with the following paragraphs.

> From time to time, scientists need to reappraise the concepts of their science, their methods of measurement, and the application of their knowledges for the general good. Psychologists, during the nature-nurture controversy, have had to reevaluate not only the concept of intelligence but also that of environment. For more than fifty years, they have been revising the *meaning* of intelligence, the various tests and procedures for its estimation, and, more especially, the implication of the evidence from tests for the understanding of children and their achievements. . . .
>
> Psychologists, as well as educators in the fullness of time may feel obligated to the authors for "Intelligence and Cultural Differences." For again, they have asked them to reconsider the meaning of test intelligence. As contemplated, the book has motivated anew serious reexamination of intelligence and of intelligence-tests.[28]

The implication is plain, from this perspective, that the concerns of which Davis wrote represented general movements of thought and work which already existed in the field. For example, there had been a number of efforts, which preceded Davis by many years, to create "culture-free" measures of intelligence and to de-emphasize the verbal and linguistic components of tests. Similarly, the part of Davis' argument suggesting that there were different *kinds* of problem-solving capacity resembled a prominent current of thought among American psychologists, strongly reinforced by the work of Thurstone in the 1930's and epitomized by Guilford's theory of the structure of intelligence.[29] Psychologists of Lorge's perspective, then, found little that was new in the work of the Chicago group and assimilated the underlying arguments largely to ongoing theoretical developments in psychology.

The one relatively novel contribution of Davis and his co-workers—the use of a detailed anthropological-sociological analysis of cultural differences to highlight different kinds of intellectual development—failed to find a foothold in the psychological domain. The main currents of thought among the psychometricians contained little to which it could be assimilated.

In recent years, the research of social psychologists and others has continued to illuminate the bearing of cultural influences upon intellectual functioning and closely allied psychological processes, although quite apart from the rationale and program of Davis and his colleagues. Thus, studies of creativity, studies of the development of talented youth, studies of achievement motivation—all have pointed to the significance of social and cultural factors underly-

[25] W. L. Fowler, "A Comparative Analysis of Pupil Performance on Conventional and Culture-controlled Mental Tests," *Yearbook of the National Council on Measurements Used in Education*, 1957, *14*, pp. 8-19.

[26] V. H. Noll, "Relation of Scores on Davis-Eells Games to Socio-economic Status, Intelligence Test Results, and School Achievement," *Educational and Psychological Measurement*, 1960, *20*, pp. 119-130.

[27] W. G. Warrington and J. L. Saupe, "Development and Applications of Tests of General Mental Ability," *Review of Educational Research*, 1959, *29*, p. 19. These authors review several additional studies, but for a more complete bibliography, see O. K. Buros (Ed.), *Fifth Mental Measurements Yearbook* (Highland Park, N. J.: The Gryphon Press, 1959), pp. 459-462.

[28] Lorge, *op. cit.*, p. 76.

[29] J. P. Guilford, *Personality* (New York: McGraw-Hill Book Co., Inc., 1959).

ing the psychological attributes.[30] But they have shown, too, that the significant factors are not organized simply and uniquely according to social class variations. Indeed, some scholars believe that the particular cultural differences among the social classes of which Davis spoke a decade or more ago are becoming less distinct.[31]

In any event, many school people found something of a revelation in the work of the Chicago group. Davis, Warner, Havighurst, and others often addressed themselves to the education audience, already sensitized to their research on social class patterns in the school. This was an audience, also, rarely reached by the academic psychometricians. The fallibilities of the Intelligence Quotient, of which the test-makers and the psychologists were so fully aware, were not recognized by all schoolmen. Numbered among the educators were some who, in Lorge's words, regarded IQs as "absolute determinations" about their pupils. Despite courses in educational psychology, not a few of the nation's teachers believed the IQ to mark the innate mental capacity of the child, or at least, to indicate a trait so firmly a part of the child that little help could be held out for the dull.

Such faith in the intelligence test was badly shaken by the charges of "bias" which emanated from Chicago and by the dramatic illustrations of "biased" test items. The possibility that low test scores could be a product of cultural experiences and motivational patterns which were different from those stressed by the school gave pause to many educators. It reinforced the pleas from certain leaders for teachers to review their teaching methods and their curriculums in order to fit the school to children from all walks of life. Quite apart from the technical issues, the work of Davis and his colleagues at the University of Chicago helped to remove the bias, if not from tests, at least from the test-users in the education profession.

[30] See D. C. McClelland *et al., Talent and Society* (Princeton, N. J.: Van Nostrand, 1958); E. P. Torrance (Ed.), *Talent and Education* (Minneapolis: University of Minnesota Press, 1960); A. Roe, *The Making of a Scientist* (Dodd, Mead & Co., 1952).

[31] See U. Bronfenbrenner, "Socialization and Social Class through Time and Space," in E. E. Maccoby, T. M. Newcomb, and E. L. Hartley (Eds.), *Readings in Social Psychology* (3rd ed., New York: Holt, Rinehart & Winston, Inc., 1958), pp. 400-424; W. B. Brookover and D. Gottlieb, "Social Class and Education," in this volume, pp. 3-11.

THE PSYCHODYNAMICS OF SOCIAL MOBILITY IN ADOLESCENT BOYS*

By Elizabeth Douvan and Joseph Adelson

There is a large and growing body of literature on social mobility, and the significance of the topic is generally acknowledged; so it is surprising to find that only limited attention has been given to studying the motivational sources of mobility. What we do find is a general disposition to treat *upward* mobility in a vaguely invidious fashion. It would seem that, in this country, the Horatio Alger tradition and the "dream of success" motif[1] have been pervasive and distasteful enough to have alienated, among others, a good many social scientists. The upwardly aspiring individual has apparently become associated with the pathetic seeker after success or with the ruthless tycoon. This image of success is, much of it, implicit—assumption and attitude, and not quite conviction—but it seems to have dominated the thinking of our intellectual community.

Or so it has been until recently. Newer empirical findings have encouraged a more differentiated view of mobility. We begin to get some sense that

[1] K. S. Lynn, *The Dream of Success* (Boston: Little, Brown, & Co., 1955).

* From the *Journal of Abnormal and Social Psychology*, 1958, *56*, pp. 31-44. Used by permission of the authors and publisher.

varying motivations may underlie social striving; we become aware that the direction, the rapidity, and the absolute extent of mobility may reflect differing psychodynamic sources and thus require separate analytic treatment.

In this paper, a first effort is made to explore and clarify one problem in this complex area—to analyze some of the psychic accompaniments of upward and downward mobility strivings among adolescent boys. In the following section, a theory of the personality determinants of mobility is presented; the paper as a whole is devoted to testing some of these formulations.

THEORETICAL CONSIDERATIONS

Upward mobility. We can distinguish at least three separate patterns of motivation which are implicit in discussions of upward social mobility: fear of failure, ambivalence toward success, and hope of success.

The first pattern—perhaps the most common image of the mobile individual—is of the desperately scrambling Philistine, exhausted in his pursuit of status. He has defined his identity and personal worth exclusively by the criteria of success. Perhaps a typical genetic source of this pattern has been described by Ackerman and Jahoda.[2] Competitiveness is taught by the family: "Most of the mothers of our cases . . . apparently did not tell their children 'be happy' but rather 'make money'. . . ." "Success is measured by comparison with others rather than by actual achievement. . . . There are always some who have done better, who have more money and more social prestige; and there is always the danger of being pushed down the social ladder by a competitor."[3]

In the second pattern—ambivalence toward success—the dynamics are more complex. The individual aspiring upward is here seen as responding to the dominance and prestige of the more privileged stratum through a defensive identification with this group and by denying and decrying his own background and status. The genetic sources of this choice of mechanism may be sought in the aspirer's early encounters with authority and status in the original family setting. We discover in the family scene a harsh and forbidding parent, one who allows the child no hostility; we find a child who has accommodated to parental strength through identification. In this formulation, we see the mobile individual showing many of the characteristics of the "authoritarian personality": a conscious over-idealization of the parent and of authority together with unconscious rebellion and hostility, rigidity, conformity, and anti-intraception. As regards mobility, we find the following dynamics: the motive for upward aspiration arises out of the need to emulate the parents; at the same time mobility arouses conflict since it implies a struggle with this powerful authority figure.[4]

Without question, both of these mobility types occur (perhaps frequently) in our society. Yet the recent literature on mobility has suggested that the most common pattern is the one we have called "hope of success."[5] Here we find interest in success directed by a rational ego: the individual who can mobilize his energies effectively, whose aspirations are realistic. The mobility goals are moderate or, in those cases where aspiration is toward a substantial status move, they are nevertheless realistic in view of the individual's talents.

We find a family milieu which encourages autonomy, is not obsessed by status, yet accepts and transmits without ambivalence the culturally central value of achievement. Moreover, the shifts in identity required do not implicate the child in conflict: the family has provided or permitted the child a model for identity consistent with the goal of mobility.

In a society which holds upward mobility to be a central value, which provides opportunity for it, and in which it is, apparently, a very common occurrence, we can expect that the dominant motivational pattern informing upward aspiration is not a defensive one—does not necessitate a personally damaging flight from one's past; rather, we would expect it to accompany effective ego functioning and successful socialization by a family

[2] N. W. Ackerman and M. Jahoda, *Anti-Semitism and Emotional Disorder* (New York: Harper & Row, Publishers, 1950).
[3] *Ibid.*, pp. 88-89.
[4] T. W. Adorno *et al.*, *The Authoritarian Personality* (New York: Harper & Row, Publishers, 1949).
[5] D. C. McClelland *et al.*, *The Achievement Motive* (New York: Appleton-Century-Crofts, Inc., 1953).

which is transmitting a cultural value of which it approves.[6]

Downward mobility. What about the adolescent boy whose aspirations are downward in direction? Here we have someone whose goals are atypical; indeed, they contradict directly a strongly held cultural value. To be sure, the same novelistic tradition which associates upward mobility with Babbittry has sometimes offered us a sentimental image of the downward mobile type, presenting him as an unfettered, romantically sullen child of nature. Our own view is considerably darker.

We see downward aspiration as representing, in many areas, the psychodynamic opposite of upward mobility. If we are correct, these adolescents are demoralized, alienated, anomic. An ambivalent relationship to the parents produces an impoverished ego, vulnerability to conflict, a failure to internalize general cultural values. Ambivalence is, of course, an almost universal outcome of the socialization process; but we conjecture that it is especially acute among the downward mobile. We expect to find a relationship to the parents which is infantile, that is, dependent and hostile. Dependency and aggression accompany, reinforce, and conceal each other. The child who is captured in an infantile tie to his parents has too much of his energy committed in ambivalence; ego functions remain immature and conflict-ridden; the ego is unable to cope adequately with impulses, internalized morality, and the more complex aspects of reality. At its best, the ego enforces a harmony among the psychic institutions and the outside world. But the downward mobile boy, if our formulation is correct, is at the mercy of his impulses, which continually threaten to overwhelm brittle controls. The superego drives are equally primitive and frightening; parental prohibitions are not sufficiently internalized, in part because of their very intensity; superego functioning is consequently immature, in that there is an inadequate fusion of ego and superego processes; the superego stands at some distance from the ego, so that questions of morality are not so much matters of right and wrong as of escape and pursuit. As regards the ego's operations vis-a-vis the outer world, we do not hypothesize that the downward mobile show any gross pathology of reality testing. And yet we feel that the more complex and articulated ego processes—judgment, rapport, control, time-binding—are poorly or unevenly developed.

Hypotheses. In the research reported here, a study of the mobility aspirations of adolescent boys, we test a number of hypotheses based on these conceptions of the sources of mobility strivings. Specifically, the following predictions were made about upward- and downward-aspiring boys.[7]

1. ENERGY LEVEL. The upward-mobile boys possess a high degree of available energy for use in social and work activities. Downward-mobile boys, on the other hand, show a diminished vitality.

2. ACHIEVEMENT MODE. The boys aspiring to higher status show a pervasive achievement orientation and a secure sense of their own effectiveness in reaching goals. The downward mobile are less oriented toward achievement and dominated by a concern with security.

3. ORIENTATION TOWARD THE FUTURE. The time perspective of the upward mobile tends to be extended, while the downward mobile tend to have a constricted orientation in time.

4. PERSONAL STANDARDS. The upward mobile boys manifest well internalized moral values and standards of personal behavior. Internalization is relatively incomplete among the downward mobile.

5. AUTONOMY. The upward aspiring display a precocious independence from the family, and a strong sense of autonomy in choosing values and goals. Downward mobile boys, on the other hand, are tied in a dependent relationship to the family.

[6] One may speculate about those social situations in our culture where upward aspiration necessitates a good deal of emotional stress or induces personal conflict. Generally, we would say, these are situations where a change in status requires a decisive modification of behavior or necessitates a sharp shift in identity models. A number of such situations come to mind: (a) where the status change involves a concomitant ethnic (including religious) shift; (b) where it involves a gross movement up the status ladder; (c) where there has been a limited opportunity to learn the status behavior of the higher status group; (d) at certain points in the status continuum, where the defining criteria of the higher status group are realistically difficult to achieve; e.g., in the movement from lower-upper to upper-upper status, in those cases where a defining criterion is ancestry; (e) where the group-of-origin is ambivalent or hostile to the mobility of its members, necessitating a decisive abandonment of the past as a condition of mobility. Under these conditions, mobility upward will require an unusually high degree of personal motivation.

[7] In this paper we will use the terms "upward aspiring" and "upward mobile" interchangeably. It should be clear that we do not assume that upward aspiration will necessarily lead to successful social mobility.

6. ORIENTATION TOWARD THE SELF. Upward-mobile boys are realistic in assessing themselves, and show a high degree of self-confidence. The downward aspiring reveal ambivalence toward the self and a lack of poise in social situations.

7. FAMILY MILIEU. In this area, our predictions were firmer and more specific about the downward mobile group. Previous research[8] led us to expect a pattern of ambivalent dependency in the downward mobile boys' relations with their families. Rebellion and rejection of parental values combined with a strong dependency stem from inconsistent and punitive treatment at the parent's hand: in short, we anticipated an authoritarian family setting.

In addition to these specific predictions, we were interested in inquiring whether the relationship to the family, in upward mobile boys, is characterized by an ambivalent rejection of family values or by a conflict-free differentiation of the self from the family.

METHOD

Subjects. The data for our analysis derive from a national sample survey of adolescent boys conducted by the Survey Research Center.[9] The sample for the total study consisted of a thousand boys in the 14- to 16-year age range selected by probability sampling methods. Each boy was given a personal interview at school by a member of the research center's field staff. Open-ended questions and projective questions were used, and interviews lasted from one to three hours.

In the present analysis, we have used as the base sample the interviews taken with urban nonfarm youth whose fathers' occupations fell in any of the following categories: small business owners, self-employed artisans, white collar, sales, and clerical workers; skilled and semi-skilled manual workers. The reason for excluding the sons of men occupying positions at the two extremes of the skill hierarchy becomes apparent when the mobility measure is discussed.

Mobility aspiration. Each of our youthful respondents was asked the following questions:

a. What kind of work would you like to do as an adult?

b. Are you pretty sure about this or do you think that you're just as likely to go into something else?

Each boy's aspiration was classed on the occupational scale and compared to his father's position to determine whether it was equivalent to or higher or lower than the father's job in the hierarchy of skills and status.

The distribution of aspiration types by father's occupation is presented in Table 1 for all urban youth in the original sample. An obvious fact is illustrated in this table. Boys whose fathers currently occupy jobs in the top category are by definition limited to equivalent or lower status aspirations, just as those whose fathers are unskilled workers are barred from downward aspiration.

TABLE 1-1

DISTRIBUTION OF ASPIRATION TYPES BY FATHER'S OCCUPATION

	Father's Occupation			
	1	*2*	*3*	*4*
Aspiration	*Profes-sional, Manage-rial (N = 136)* %	*White Collar*[a] *(N = 183)* %	*Manual Skilled*[b] *(N = 335)* %	*Manual Un-skilled (N = 70)* %
Upward		46	58	84
Stable	67	29	34	16
Downward	33	25	08	

Note.—Ten per cent of the total urban sample of boys was lost in the process of rating the boy's aspiration in relation to father's occupation. These were *Ss* who had not decided what they wanted to be, who gave vague answers, or who wished to be farmers.

[a] This category includes small business owners in addition to sales and clerical workers.

[b] This category includes both skilled and semi-skilled workers.

[8] H. Gough, personal communication, 1955.

[9] The survey was sponsored by the Boy Scouts of America. The complete questionnaire used in the study has been deposited with the American Documentation Institute. Order Document No. 5422 from ADI Auxiliary Publications Project, Photoduplication Service, Library of Congress, Washington 25, D.C., remitting in advance $1.75 for 35 mm. microfilm or $2.50 for 6 by 8 in. photocopies. Make checks payable to Chief, Photoduplication Service, Library of Congress.

Because of this limitation on the relative freedom of direction in the aspirations of boys from families in Groups 1 and 4, and because we were interested ultimately in both upward and downward mobility, the sample was restricted to those boys from the two middle categories. The aspiration behavior of boys from the extreme groups may reflect in part a statistical artifact. That is, assuming that by chance a certain proportion of boys will aspire to a status-skill level different from the parent's, the direction of deviation is automatically determined for boys in Groups 1 and 4. In the middle groups, on the other hand, deviation is possible in either direction, and the selection of one or the other type should reflect certain specific motivational factors. One might maintain that the fact of aspiring to a level other than the father's in itself reflects unique psychological characteristics, but since the direction of deviation is a focus of our present concern, opportunity for choice in both directions was controlled.[10]

RESULTS

In the following pages we show contrasts among upward, downward, and stable groups. In most cases, we find linear relationships between status aspiration and other variables: the upward mobile are particularly high or low on a variable, the downward mobile are at the opposite extreme, and the stable group falls somewhere in between. Occasionally we find that either the upward or downward aspiring group clearly distinguishes itself from the other two groups. And in a few relationships, the stables stand out, the linear relationship gives way to a curvilinear one.

Since our predictions all concern the mobility categories and there was uncertainty about the exact position of the stable group, chi square was used to test the significance of variation among the three groups.

Energy level. We see here a sharp contrast between upward and downward subjects (*Ss*): while the upward mobile boy is unusually lively and energetic, the downward aspirer is inactive and apathetic. On all of our measures, the upward group reveals a high commitment of energy to social and recreational pursuits, and yet not at the expense of work involvement; they also seem to show a spirited and enthusiastic love of activity. The downward mobile boy, in contrast, shows an impoverished vitality: he does not participate energetically or enthusiastically in recreational activities.

Looking first at boys' memberships in organizations (Table 1-2, Item 1), we find that three quarters of the upward mobile *Ss* belong to some organized group; while slightly less than half of the downward aspiring boys report membership. The upward mobile also have a relatively high proportion of multiple memberships, compared to the other two groups. A similar relationship appears in the area of general leisure activities: almost half the upward mobile report having tried twenty of more separate activities while only about one quarter of the downward mobile fall in this category; the stable group is approximately midway between the other two (Table 1-2, Item 2). There is a small difference in dating, the upwards being slightly more likely, and the downwards least likely to date (Table 1-2, Item 3).

Although they more commonly engage in leisure pursuits, the aspiring boys are not significantly different from others in having job commitments. One might expect that the reason the downward-aspiring boys play less is that they work more. But this does not seem to be the case (Table 1-2, Item 4), the three groups being approximately equal in the percentage who hold jobs. The more active social life of the upward mobile boy represents an increment in total activity rather than a substitute for work activity. The upward mobile boy is more likely to report leisure reading. He has a more diversified reading pattern, and his reading includes more demanding material. The downward aspiring boy much less often reads novels and mysteries, travel and adventure stories, and technical, scientific literature. Stable boys fall between the other two groups on all specific categories of read-

[10] The group used for analysis consisted of 335 boys from working-class background and 183 from white-collar families. Since the upward mobile group contained a disproportionate number of boys from blue-collar backgrounds, we ran all mobility analyses separately for the two broad occupational groups (Categories 2 and 3 in Table 1-1). Relationships were of approximately the same order within each of these groups. Analysis is presented for the combined group in order to avoid complicating tables unnecessarily, but in all cases relationships reported also held within each of the two background groups.

TABLE 1-2
RELATIONSHIPS BETWEEN MOBILITY ASPIRATION AND INDICES OF LEVEL OF ENERGY

Item	*Mobility* *Up-ward* (N = 277) %	*Stable* (N = 168) %	*Down-ward* (N = 73) %	χ^{2*}	*p Level*
1. Number of group memberships [a]					
a. none	25	33	52	26.91	.01
b. one	32	38	22		
c. two	23	20	17		
d. three or more	20	09	09		
2. Number of leisure activities					
a. fewer than 20	52	65	67	11.65	.01
b. 20 or more	48	35	33		
3. Dating					
a. do date	66	59	52	5.67	.10-.05
b. do not date	34	41	48		
4. Employment					
a. have jobs	49	47	51	.44	.90
b. do not have jobs	51	53	49		
5. Leisure reading					
a. do not read	17	27	25	7.93	.05
b. fiction–novels mysteries	32	23	11	12.31	.01
c. travel and adventure	31	20	18	10.52	.01
d. technical, scientific	09	04	01	11.13	.01
e. sports and hobby books	10	09	04	2.44	.30-.20
f. history, biography	08	07	05	.27	.90-.80
g. animal stories	05	04	05	.73	.70-.50
h. comics, joke books	21	26	27	1.95	.50-.30
i. newspapers, magazines	19	16	19	.96	.70-.50
6. Proportion of activities enjoyed					
a. fewer than half	45	41	59	6.09	.05
b. one half or more	55	59	41		
7. Additional activities desired					
a. suggest activity	63	31	10	87.67	.01
b. do not suggest activity	37	69	90		

ing, but are like the downward mobile in the proportion of nonreaders. The single case in which the trend favors the downward mobile boy is in the category "comics, joke books" (Table 1-2, Item 5).

Upward mobile boys are not only more active currently but also seem to be more enthusiastic about their activities and more receptive to new experiences. After our *Ss* had checked the leisure pursuits they had experienced within the last year, they were asked to check the ones they had especially enjoyed. In general, the two indices bear a low negative relation to each other—that is, boys who do more things are more selective in naming those they "particularly enjoy." Despite this tendency for a negative association, we find that the upward aspiring boys (who take part in more leisure activities) are nevertheless enthusiastic about the things they do. They are like the stables in the proportion of their leisure pursuits that they designate as particularly enjoyable; while the downward mobile, who have tried relatively few leisure activities, are much less enthusiastic about these few (Table 1-2, Item 6). When asked if there are other activities they would like to try, aside from those appearing on the list, almost two-thirds of the upward group name something else they would enjoy. This responsiveness contrasts sharply to the other groups: a third of the stable group, and only one tenth of the downward group suggest any additional unlisted activities that appear to them (Table 1-2, Item 7).

Achievement mode. We expected that the degree of striving reflected in a boy's job aspiration would be part of a general achievement orientation, that upward occupational aspiration would be associated with the pattern of behavior which McClelland *et al.*[11] have termed the "achievement syndrome," and that the upward mobile boy would show concern with achievement as against security and would be interested in meeting self-imposed standards of excellence. The downward aspiring boy, on the other hand, should show the same lack of vigor, the same constriction in setting other goals that we have seen in his choice of a future occupation.

* Unless noted, the chi square was derived from a 3 x 2 table with two degrees of freedom.

[a] In this case, the chi square was derived from a 3 x 4 table with six degrees of freedom.

[11] McClelland *et al., op. cit.*

The most direct evidence on these points is found in response to other questions in the occupation area. The *Ss* were asked to choose among criteria for judging the attractiveness of a job, to choose the two most and the two least important dimensions. Compared to the stable and downward groups, upward mobile boys stress interesting work and have a less dominating concern about security. They are highest of all three groups in desire for status achievement. The downward mobile also strongly wish for status, but their status drive is not bound to a demand for interest in the content of the job; rather, they would most like to have status combined with security. The answers of our stable group are interesting on this item; relatively unattracted by status and fame, they stress security and interesting work (Table 1-3, Item 1).

TABLE 1-3

RELATIONSHIPS BETWEEN MOBILITY ASPIRATION AND INDICES OF ACHIEVEMENT MODE

Item	*Mobility* Upward (N = 277) %	Stable (N = 168) %	Downward (N = 73) %	χ^{2*}	*P* Level
1. Job criteria selected [a]					
a. interesting work	56	51	33	15.74	.01
b. status achievement	44	28	36	22.15	.01
c. security	50	59	65	5.84	.10
2. Reasons for job choice [a]					
a. status	20	09	03	11.65	.01
b. ease of job or ease of obtaining job	04	12	32	15.27	.01
c. interest of work	70	78	58	5.99	.05
3. Preference: success or security					
a. success	52	35	33	12.00	.01
b. security	48	65	67		
4. Savings					
a. do save	30	21	18	6.16	.05
b. do not save	70	79	82		
5. Education plans					
a. beyond high school	69	42	12	140.06	.01
b. not beyond high school	31	58	88		

When we ask boys to rationalize their own job choices, the upward aspiring *S* emphasizes interest in the work itself, while the downward mobile more often adduces the ease of the work, or the ease of obtaining employment in the field (Table 1-3, Item 2).

It would seem, then, that the upward mobile *Ss* are more willing to yield security for the sake of achievement. In answer to a forced-choice question: "Which would you rather have—a job where you're sure you won't be laid off or one you can't be so sure of but where you have a chance to be a big success?" the striving boys choose the challenging, less secure job significantly more often than boys in either of the other groups (Table 1-3, Item 3).

Achievement orientation is often inferred from the willingness to forego immediate gratification for long-term goals. One indication of this appears in answer to the question, "What do you spend your own money for?" The boys who aspire high are more likely to say they save their resources for education or other long term goals (Table 1-3, Item 4). As we would expect, boys aspiring to higher occupations also reveal more extensive educational plans than do other boys (Table 1-3, Item 5).

Orientation toward the future. The upward mobile boys have an extended time perspective and a marked interest in attaining adult status; while the downward group shows constriction in time, as in other aspects of the life space. We asked our *Ss* what decisions they would have to make in the next few years; the answers were rated for the breadth of time perspective. The upward aspiring boys are more likely to mention decisions in the more distant future, such as adult roles and goals. The downward mobile more often name immediate decisions, those within the high school period (Table 1-4, Item 1).

In answer to the question "What things that you do—at home, in school, or with your friends—make you feel important and useful?" the upward striving boy more often states instances in which he has assumed adult roles. He is less likely than the downward mobile *S* to mention peer acceptance as a source of self-esteem. An interesting finding here

* Unless noted, the chi square was derived from a 3 x 2 table with two degrees of freedom.

[a] Categories here are not exhaustive. Tests are run on the presence or absence of particular answers.

TABLE 1-4

RELATIONSHIPS BETWEEN MOBILITY ASPIRATION AND INDICES OF ORIENTATION TOWARD THE FUTURE

Item	*Mobility* Up-ward (N= 277) %	Stable (N= 168) %	Down-ward (N= 73) %	χ^{2*}	*p Level*
1. Time perspective on decisions [b]					
a. within high school	17	18	29	5.21	.10
b. beyond high school	78	73	77	1.75	.50
c. distant future	53	51	26	16.51	.01
2. Sources of self-esteem [b]					
a. assuming adult role	31	23	16	6.91	.05
b. belonging, being part of a group	46	56	32	11.34	.01
c. being accepted by peers	03	07	14	10.90	.01
d. nothing	04	08	11	6.39	.05
3. Preference for coed or all-boy club [a]					
a. all boy	39	48	59	10.60	.05
b. neutral	23	16	14		
c. coed	38	36	27		

* Unless noted, the chi square was derived from a 3 x 2 table with two degrees of freedom.

[a] In this case, the chi square was derived from a 3 x 3 table with four degrees of freedom.

[b] Categories here are not exhaustive of responses given to open questions, and more than one response was often given. Tests are run on the presence or absence of particular answers.

is that the stable group is highest of all three in choosing "belonging, being part of a group," one of the few occasions where this group does not fall somewhere between the other two. We suggest, though very tentatively, that this may reflect a concern with maintaining stable interpersonal ties.

We may also point to the apparently greater social maturity of the upward mobiles. As we have seen, they are somewhat more likely to date. They are also more eager for heterosexual social activities; when asked to choose between an all-boy or a coed social club, the upward aspiring less often prefer the former (Table 1-4, Item 3).

The internalization of personal standards. Another point of difference between the groups concerns the interiorization of standards. Upward mobile boys consistently show a more complete internalization of personal controls. Downward mobile boys show a tendency to externalize standards and to rebel against them.

A set of projective pictures showed an adolescent boy in conflict between a promise made to his parents (to be home at a certain time) and peer pressure (to stay out later). Our *Ss* were asked what the boy would do and how he would feel about it.

In all of our groups, approximately two thirds of the respondents say that the boy will go home. However, the motives attributed to the boy differ sharply. The upward mobile boys more often have the boy go home because "he promised" or because "his parents trust him," whereas the downwards say he will go because of a fear that the parents will find out and punish the transgression (Table 1-5, Item 1).

Regardless of their responses to these questions, all *Ss* were asked: "If the boy decided to say with his friends awhile, do you think he'd tell his parents about it later?" The upward aspiring group answer "yes" more frequently than other boys (Table 1-5, Item 2).

Another series of questions concerned boys' conceptions of and general reactions to rules. Here, again, the upward mobile group reveals a greater degree of internalization. When asked why a boy might break a rule, they focus on uncontrollable emergency situations and those in which a boy is old enough (i.e., responsible enough) to guide his own behavior. On the other hand, the downwards more frequently give responses fitting the categories of "rebellion against the parent," "irresistible impulse," and "when parental authority is not present" (Table 1-5, Item 3). When asked what kind of a rule they would never break, upward mobile *Ss* more often mention those which involve responsibility to others; they less frequently say that there is no rule, or no rule that comes to mind, which they wouldn't break (Table 1-5, Item 4).

Autonomy. We saw earlier that the striving boys are interested in assuming adult-like roles, those, that is, in which they themselves are responsible for their behavior and for a job. We see here a seemingly greater drive towards independence and

TABLE 1-5

RELATIONSHIPS BETWEEN MOBILITY ASPIRATION AND INDICES OF INTERNALIZATION OF PERSONAL STANDARDS

Item	*Mobility* *Up-ward* (*N* = *277*) %	*Stable* (*N* = *168*) %	*Down-ward* (*N* = *73*) %	χ^{2*}	*p Level*
1. Reaction to parent–peer conflict[a]					
a. adheres to promise because of sense of trust	37	19	16	24.03	.01
b. Adheres to promise because of fear of punishment	04	06	14	6.38	.05
2. Honesty with parents					
a. would tell parents	55	42	44	9.15	.05
3. Conditions for breaking a rule[a]					
a. emergency	18	10	10	6.56	.05
b. boy mature enough	11	07	01	6.49	.05
c. rebellion	10	14	22	10.11	.01
d. impulse	05	11	16	11.41	.01
e. parental authority absent	05	10	27	31.50	.01
4. Unbreakable rule					
a. no unbreakable rule	03	17	21	10.85	.01

* Unless noted, the chi square was derived from a 3 x 2 table with two degrees of freedom.

[a] Categories here are not exhaustive of responses given to open questions, and more than one response was often given. Tests are run on the presence or absence of particular answers.

responsibility. In contrast, the downward mobile, though they show signs of rebellion against the parents, are also more dependent on them.

In one series of items, our *Ss* were asked whose advice they would prefer to take on particular problems—their parents' or friends'. The issues ran from such central ones as what time to be in at night to matters of taste, such as personal grooming. While there were no very striking differences in the proportions who would heed their parents on any of these topics, one interesting difference appears in the proportion of boys who inject a note of independence while discussing these issues. Thirty per cent of the striving group spontaneously assert that they would follow their own ideas on at least one of the six issues, and only three per cent of the downwards give such a response (Table 1-6, Item 2).

We find another indication of independence from the family in response to the question, "Can a friend ever be as close as a family member?" The upward mobile *Ss* most often agree to this idea (Table 1-6, Item 3).

TABLE 1-6

RELATIONSHIPS BETWEEN MOBILITY ASPIRATION AND INDICES OF AUTONOMY

Item	*Mobility* *Up-ward* (*N* = *277*) %	*Stable* (*N* = *168*) %	*Down-ward* (*N* = *73*) %	χ^{2*}	*p Level*
1. Independence in allocating funds					
a. no independence	01	01	19	59.27	.01
2. Advice on decisions					
a. interjects own opinions	30	21	03	24.69	.01
3. Intimacy of friendship					
a. can be as close as family relationship	59	54	34	9.92	.01
4. Role of adult leader[a]					
a. helper	58	51	38	9.71	.01
b. decision maker	40	43	51	3.67	.20
5. Authority reliance					
a. high	38	47	54	6.06	.05
b. moderate	62	53	47		
6. Adult ideal[a]					
a. family member	41	50	55	5.99	.05
b. unrelated adult acquaintance and composite	31	24	18	6.74	.05

* Unless noted, the chi square was derived from a 3 x 2 table with two degrees of freedom.

[a] Categories here are not exhaustive of responses given to open questions, and more than one response was often given. Tests are run on the presence or absence of particular answers.

When our *S*s are asked what the role of a club leader ought to be, we again find that the aspiring boys desire independent direction of their behavior. They limit the leader's function to that of a helper (Table 1-6, Item 4). A coder rating based on this question and on one which asked the *S* to describe an adult leader he had liked, revealed that the downward mobile *S* is more authority reliant than other boys (Table 1-6, Item 5).

Finally, a crucial index of independence from the family is yielded when *S*s are asked to choose an adult ideal. As we would expect, the stable group, which includes all boys who choose the same occupation as the father's, also has the largest proportion of boys who choose the father as an ideal. The upwards more often choose a model outside the family, or describe a composite of characteristics from several people. More often than other boys, downward mobiles say there is no adult they wish to be like. And despite the fact that they choose the father less often than stable boys, they give the largest proportion of within-family models of any group, particularly choosing grandfathers and uncles. Here again we can observe the ambivalence of the downward mobile boys; though they are covertly rebellious toward family authority, they cling to within-family models. Another way of viewing this finding is to see in it a reflection of the downward mobile boys' narrowed and immature life space. Havighurst[12] has found that the tendency to choose within-family models characterizes the earlier years of adolescence. Our downward mobile boys retain the more infantile, more restricted image of the adult world.

The upward mobile boys, on the other hand, tend to a certain precocity in the loosening of family ties. Yet we have seen in the previous section on internalization that this is not associated with rebellion from or rejection of the family. Further evidence along these lines appears in the discussion of family milieu.

Until now evidence has been presented bearing on the *sense* of autonomy. Some other data suggest that these differences are related to the objective degree of autonomy permitted upward and downward boys by their parents. We asked: "What are your parents' ideas about the way you spend your money?" One fifth of the downward mobile respondents replied that they do not have funds of their own but ask their parents for money as they need or want some special thing. In the upward mobile group, fewer than one per cent gave this answer (Table 1-6, Item 1). Since there is no difference between the groups with respect to actual spending of money, we may infer that the difference resides in the *control* of spending.

Orientation toward the self. Upward mobile boys show a high degree of self-acceptance, and a confidence in social situations. The downward mobile is more ambivalent toward himself and more unsure and conflicted in social interaction.

Interviewers rated boys on a number of variables, among which were self-confidence, humor, and the clarity with which they organized and presented their opinions and attitudes. We may interpret these ratings, with caution, as reflecting the boy's social skill and ability to handle himself in social interaction with an adult. On each of the ratings, the upward mobile are high; they are more self-assured, show humor more often, and are better organized in the interview. The downward mobile are relatively unconfident, humorless, and disorganized (Table 1-7, Items 1, 2, and 3).

We find signs of self-rejection and demoralization in the downward mobile boys' answers to the question, "What would you like to change about yourself if you could—about your looks or your life or your personality?" They more often desire changes so gross or so central as to indicate alienation from the self; and they more often wish for changes that are unlikely to occur. The upward mobile boy more often refers to changes he has the power to effect himself. He is more realistically critical of himself, and less self-rejecting (Table 1-7, Item 4).

Family milieu. The reader may recall that we felt far more confident of our predictions about the downward than the upward mobile in this area. We believed that the downward group would show a pattern of ambivalence towards the parent, a mingling of dependency and hostility; and we further held that this pattern would arise out of inconsistent, overly harsh methods of discipline. We did not, however, feel we could make any specific statement about the upward mobile: here we were

[12] R. J. Havighurst *et al.*, "The Development of the Ideal Self in Childhood and Adolescence," in J. Seidman (Ed.), *Readings in Adolescence* (New York: Dryden Press, 1953).

TABLE 1-7

RELATIONSHIPS BETWEEN MOBILITY ASPIRATION AND INDICES OF ORIENTATION TOWARD THE SELF

Item	Mobility: Up-ward (N= 277) %	Stable (N= 168) %	Down-ward (N= 73) %	χ^{2*}	p Level
1. Self-confidence [a]					
a. high	30	23	18	7.93	.10
b. average	52	57	57		
c. low	18	20	25		
2. Humor					
a. present	74	67	58	7.14	.05
b. absent	26	33	42		
3. Organization of ideas [a]					
a. high	60	53	50	7.31	.10
b. average	22	27	20		
c. low	18	20	30		
4. Desired changes [b]					
a. self rejecting, major	04	10	15	6.36	.05
b. changes that are impossible	06	07	23	11.33	.01
c. changes within boy's own power	37	29	05	14.10	.01

* Unless noted, the chi square was derived from a 3 x 2 table with two degrees of freedom.

[a] In these cases, the chi square was derived from a 3 x 3 table with four degrees of freedom.

[b] Categories here are not exhaustive of responses given to an open question, and more than one response was often given. Tests are run on the presence or absence of particular answers.

TABLE 1-8

RELATIONSHIPS BETWEEN MOBILITY ASPIRATION AND INDICES OF FAMILY MILIEU

Item	Mobility: Up-ward (N= 277) %	Stable (N= 168) %	Down-ward (N= 73) %	χ^{2*}	p Level
1. Punishment [a]					
a. physical	02	08	15	19.12	.01
b. deprivational	66	69	65		
c. psychological	32	23	20		
2. Portrayal of parental figures					
a. harsh	27	35	48	11.59	.01
b. non-harsh	73	65	52		
3. Disagreements with parents					
a. have disagreements	66	56	49	6.39	.05
b. do not have disagreements	34	44	51		
4. Parents' attitudes toward way boy spends money					
a. disapproval	19	16	05	8.58	.05
b. no disapproval	81	84	95		
5. Leisure activities with parents [a]					
a. share many	19	11	09	17.23	.01
b. share some	73	74	68		
c. share none	08	15	23		

* Unless noted, the chi square was derived from a 3 x 2 table with two degrees of freedom.

[a] In these cases the chi square was derived from a 3 x 3 table with four degrees of freedom.

interested in discovering what we could about the family milieu, in particular whether upward aspiration is associated with a rejection of family values, or a defensive identification with a forbidding parental authority, or by that relatively amiable relationship to the parent which permits the growth of autonomy.

To begin with, we find that deprivation seems to be the dominant method of discipline for all groups; differences here are not significant. Striking differences appear, however, in the relative frequency of "psychological" and "corporal" methods of punishment. Only one in fifty of the upwards say that their parents use physical punishment; approximately one in ten of the stables and one in seven of the downwards report this method. In contrast, the use of "psychological" techniques (such as "given a good talking to") occurs in more than one quarter of the upward mobile responses, about one in five of the stables, and only one in eighteen of the downwards (Table 1-8, Item 1). We find that the parents of the upward aspirers avoid the harshest method of punishment; the "psychological" methods, which we suspect encourage the child's internal controls, are infrequently used by the parents of downward mobile boys.

Are our mobile *Ss* presenting an over-idealized picture of their families? We looked for the pattern of repressed hostility and surface idealization which has been shown to characterize defensive identifiers.[13] But our data reveal that the opposite is true: in the projective materials—where the *S*s are not discussing their own parents and where they have an opportunity to discharge repressed hostility without danger—the upward aspiring portray parents as less harsh than do the other groups (Table 1-8, Item 2). And as we shall see, they are more aware of differences between themselves and their parents. They more commonly report that their parents have some "old-fashioned ideas, or ideas they disagree with," (Table 1-8, Item 5), and that their parents in some respect disapprove of the way in which they spend their own money (Table 1-8, Item 6). We saw previously (Table 1-6, Item 3) that they are not likely to feel that family relationships are necessarily more intimate than friendships; and they less often choose an ideal adult from within the family group (Table 1-6, Item 6). The upward mobile boys are, then, more sensible of differences with parents.

Do the aspiring boys have a detached rather than congenial relationship to their parents? The single bit of evidence on this question suggests that this is not the case: they more often report engaging in leisure activities with their parents (Table 1-8, Item 5).

The downward mobile boy's family relationship is, as we expected, marked by ambivalence: the pattern is one of conscious idealization accompanied by unconscious suspicion and hostility.

We have already seen that the parents of this group are more often severe in their punishment. And in this group we find evidence of repressed hostility: in the projective stories, the downward mobile boys picture parental figures as both harsh and suspicious (Items 3 and 4, Table 1-8). Yet consciously they are more likely to deny differences with their parents. Some of our findings on autonomy have shown this; and in addition we find that these boys most often say they have no disagreements with their parents (Table 1-8, Item 5), and they least often say their parents disapprove of their handling of funds (Table 1-8, Item 6). The downward mobile boy shares leisure activities with his parents somewhat less than do boys in the other two groups (Table 1-8, Item 7).

Alternative hypotheses. Before we discuss the possible meanings of these findings, we must consider briefly alternative hypotheses which might account for them. These are: (*a*) An age differential among the three groups; thus, the upward aspiring *S*s might have given "little boy" job hopes, while the nonmobile group presented more mature aspirations; (*b*) a difference among the groups in frame of reference, so that the upward aspirers may have understood the interviewer to be asking for "fantasy" aspirations while other boys took the question to mean "realistic expectations"; (*c*) objective differences in the social status of the groups: perhaps the upward mobile boys' families are at the upper end of their group in income or education, and so provide their sons with an objectively greater opportunity for mobility; (*d*) a difference in intelligence among the groups.

First, on the question of realism. There were in our total sample fewer than one per cent of the boys who gave as their job choices distinctly "little boy" or "glamour" occupations. Among boys in the mobility analysis subsample, there were no aspirations listed which were obviously or totally based on ideas of glamour. When the boys are asked how sure they feel about the job they've chosen, we find that very few of them say they're not at all sure; more important, the variation that does occur is not related to the type of aspiration they express. Boys in the three groups show approximately equal certainty that they will *get* the jobs for which they are aiming (Table 1-9, Item 1).

Furthermore, we find a difference in educational plans, one which is appropriate for the difference in job aspirations; this indicates at least a minimal degree of realism in our *S*s' understanding of work preparation (Table 1-3, Item 5).

The groups differ neither in age (Table 1-9, Item 2) nor in present socio-economic status. The upward mobile boys are not from homes which are higher economically or in educational background (Table 1-9, Items 3, 4).

The two rough measures of intelligence available both show the striving group to be somewhat superior. The upward aspiring boy is more likely to report leisure reading (Table 1-2, Item 5), and the

[13] T. W. Adorno *et al., op. cit.;* M. L. Hoffman, "Some Psychodynamic Factors in Compulsive Conformity," *Journal of Abnormal and Social Psychology,* 1953, *48,* pp. 383-393; I. Sarnoff, "Identification with the Aggressor: Some Personality Correlates of Anti-Semitism among Jews," *Journal of Personality,* 1952, *20,* pp. 199-218.

TABLE 1-9

RELATIONSHIP OF MOBILITY ASPIRATION TO AGE, CERTAINTY ABOUT ASPIRATION, FAMILY INCOME, FATHER'S EDUCATION, AND INTELLIGENCE

Item	Mobility: Upward (N = 277) %	Stable (N = 168) %	Downward (N = 73)	χ^{2*}	p Level
1. Certainty about aspiration					
a. high	57	58	54	3.22	.70
b. moderate	34	33	33		
c. low	09	09	13		
2. Age					
a. fourteen	33	29	31	1.94	.80
b. fifteen	30	36	33		
c. sixteen	37	35	36		
3. Family economic status [a]					
a. high average	32	35	31	2.76	.70
b. average	53	49	52		
c. low	15	16	17		
5. Father's education					
a. grade school	32	27	25	3.07	.70
b. high school	50	58	55		
c. college	18	15	20		
5. Verbal ability					
a. high	25	11	03	33.92	.01
b. average	69	75	74		
c. low	06	14	25		

* Unless noted, the chi square was derived from a 3 x 3 table with four degrees of freedom.

[a] The measure used for economic status was the Remmers House and Home Scale.

is rated by coders as more facile verbally (Table 1-9, Item 5). The downward mobile are rated low on verbal skills, but their reading pattern does not differ significantly from that of the stable group ($\chi^2 = .10$; $p > .90$ with 1 *df*). We will defer a consideration of this until the discussion.

DISCUSSION

We may interpret our data on the upward aspiring boy in relation to ego structure and functioning. We did not, of course, make a direct investigation of intrapsychic processes; furthermore, our understanding of "normal" ego functioning is, at present, limited and tentative. Nevertheless, it may be of some interest to attempt a formulation of our results in the current vocabulary of ego psychology.

Among upward aspiring boys we find a high level of diversified activity, suggesting that energy is available to the ego for focused use in work and play. We may infer that the antecedent condition for this accessibility is in the ego's having at its disposal a relatively high degree of neutralized energy. If we assume that both groups, mobile and non-mobile, do not differ in primary energy resources, we may conjecture that the aspiring *Ss* have less energy tied to the resolution of conflict, and consequently gain in neutralized, disposable energy.[14]

Another sign of the comparative effectiveness of ego functioning among aspiring boys is seen in the greater degree of cohesion among the three major systems within the personality. On the one hand, ego processes in the mobile boy are less likely to be imperiled by the break-through of impulses (When would a boy break a rule?); on the other hand, he is less likely to show evidence of an excessively punitive super-ego. The greater degree of internalization of moral values among aspiring boys suggests a more harmonious articulation between the ego and super-ego systems. Our data show that this integration is not purchased at the expense of an unusual quantity of guilt.

A consideration of the intelligence factor is relevant here. Although we had no direct measure of intelligence, we saw that the upward mobile boys read more and read more difficult things; and they are judged on the basis of the interview to be more verbally skilled. In all likelihood there *is* an intellectual difference among our groups; one plausible interpretation of many of our findings is that they merely reflect group differences in IQ. We feel, however, that such a formulation assumes an overly simple causal sequence—for one thing it fails to clarify the mechanisms which mediate between IQ and other indices of successful ego functioning. A good deal of recent data points to a high degree of association between intelligence and variables which indicate effective ego functioning. The direction of

[14] Cf. D. Rappaport, *Organization and Pathology of Thought* (New York: Columbia University Press, 1953), p. 353. "In other words, the amount of energy which the person can dispose by investing it in objects, by becoming interested in activities, even when essential drive-aims and drive-objects are in abeyance, is an indicator of ego-autonomy and ego strength."

causality and connection among these variables is by no means understood. Furthermore, to explain our data as a function of intelligence alone would not allow us to generate predictions in the area of family relations. If we assume, however, that our data are best understood by positing differences in intrapsychic organization—and particularly in ego structure and functioning—we may then posit specific expectations about family milieu.

We would expect—on the basis of the higher energy level and the more refined control of impulsivity among upward mobile *Ss*—that they have relatively good relationships within the family and have successfully resolved infantile object ties. We mean by this that there is a relative absence both of covert hostility toward the parents, and of overt dependence upon them, together with a relatively high degree of objectivity about family relations.

We have seen that this is, in fact, the case. The mobile boy asserts (and probably has been encouraged toward) greater independence of judgment and behavior. It will be recalled that he expresses a desire for equalitarian rather than dependent relationships with adults. He frequently uses his own convictions as authority in making decisions.

The aspiring boy more often admits differences between himself and his family. He seems able to assert the legitimacy of an autonomous self-definition—to the extent, at least, of selecting an ego ideal outside the family setting.

The independence we have observed has not occurred through rebellion from or rejection of the family. Despite their ability to differentiate themselves from their parents, the upward aspirers give evidence of a congenial relationship with them. They share their leisure activities; in response to a projective measure they reveal relatively little covert hostility toward parental figures.

Their parents are, in fact, comparatively lenient; they are more likely to employ mild and essentially verbal discipline and use physical punishment infrequently.

We have seen, then, that the upward aspiring boy is characterized by a high energy level, the presence of autonomy, and a relatively advanced social maturity. These attributes may be viewed as derivatives of a generally effective ego organization, one which has developed out of the successful resolution of infantile object-ties and conflicts. We would expect, on theoretical grounds, that this development would be most likely to occur in a family setting where the parents allow the child a non-ambivalent connection with them, where autonomy can emerge without conflict. As we have seen, the data we have suggest that this is the case.

We have already presented, in the introductory section, our view of the internal psychic processes which characterize downward mobile boys. From the specific perspective of ego functioning, we see an apparent blocking or impoverishment of energy which should, ideally, be available to the ego. We may infer that neutralization is not being successfully accomplished. There is a relatively poor articulation among the psychic systems: impulses threaten the ego's integrity; the superego seems overly severe and yet incompletely incorporated. These boys seem humorless, gauche, disorganized—relatively so, at least. Perhaps the most telling and poignant datum which the study locates is their response to the possibility of personal change, their tendency to want to change intractable aspects of the self, and the degree of alienation revealed by their desire to modify major and fundamental personal qualities. As we have seen, this pattern is associated with a certain quality of family interaction: the boy gives evidence of an ambivalent tie to the parents, a mixture of overt dependency and covert aggression. One of the determinants of this ambivalence, we may infer on theoretical grounds, is in the parents' relatively punitive style of discipline which fails to establish self-governing controls in the child.

A final point concerning the mechanisms through which the differing aspirations become established: In the case of upward aspiration we assume a direct connection between the socialization process and the aspiration to social mobility. That is, we assume that the parents transmit the value on mobility during socialization, and that the child incorporates this as part of a complex of values which includes autonomy and general achievement. In contrast, we conjecture that the process in downward aspiration may be more indirect: the rebellion engendered by an ambivalent family atmosphere may be directly expressed in a rejection of general social goals; or we may have a diffuse demoralization which causes (and prepares the child for) failure and isolation in social situations. In turn, these failures result in a general narrowing of goals, and a retreat from success; a central expression of this is the lowering of occupational goals.

SUMMARY

We have only recently begun to recognize that prevalent views of the dynamics of mobility, based as they are largely on literary sources and on extreme instances, require refinement and differentiation. The paper begins by distinguishing varieties of mobility behavior. There is presented a model of the psychodynamics of upward and downward aspiration, which is tested with data from a national sample of adolescent boys. The general formulation holds that upward mobility is found among boys with effective, autonomous ego functioning; downward mobility is seen as a symptom of demoralization. Psychoanalytic ego theory provides the framework from which we make specific predictions of differences in the areas of activity level, achievement mode, time perspective, internalization of values, autonomy, self-esteem, and family milieu. The findings reveal sharp differences, in the predicted directions, between upward and downward aspiring groups.

*PARENTAL ATTITUDES AND ACADEMIC ACHIEVEMENT**

By Elizabeth Monroe Drews and John E. Teahan

PROBLEM

There are two contradictory viewpoints regarding the type of familial atmosphere which is most conducive to achievement motivation, namely the free permissive type of environment and the more authoritarian or restrictive type of home setting. Proponents of the former view cite such animal studies as Christie's[1] and Thompson and Melzack's[2] which showed retardation in various psychological traits as a result of early restriction. Psychoanalysts such as Greenacre[3] have argued that the frustrations engendered by parental restraints may impair intellectual efficiency because of an increase in sadomasochism and resulting anxiety in the child. On the other side of the issue stand Pearson[4] and Liss[5] who look upon the acquisition of knowledge and society's symbols as a process of sublimation. They feel that if a child is allowed too much freedom he will remain at the mercy of the pleasure principle.

Perhaps one source of confusion in this issue has been the tendency to use such words as "democratic" to stand for the "good" parent, and "authoritarian" to stand for the "bad" parent, while the actual operational definitions of these words vary from investigator to investigator. It is questionable whether any parent can completely escape the role of an authoritarian during the formative years of a child's life. In this respect Lewin[6] has identified two different kinds of restrictive parental attitudes, one of which sets certain limits upon the child's behavior while at the same time encouraging him to engage in acceptable activities. The other, however, issues "blanket warnings" leaving the child insecure and afraid to engage in any new behavior. The importance of parental intervention is also contained in

[1] J. R. Christie, "The Effects of Frustration on Rigidity in Problem Solution." Unpublished doctoral dissertation, University of California, Berkeley, 1949.

[2] W. R. Thompson and R. Melzack, "Early Environment," *Scientific American,* 1956, *194,* 1, pp. 38-42.

[3] P. Greenacre, "Infant Reactions to Restraint: Problems in the Fate of Infantile Regression," in C. Kluckhohn and H. A. Murray (Eds.), *Personality in Nature, Society and Culture* (New York: Alfred A. Knopf, Inc., 1949), pp. 390-406.

[4] G. H. Pearson, "A Survey of Learning Difficulties in Children," in A. Freud (Ed.), *The Psychoanalytic Study of the Child* (New York: International University, 1952), 7, pp. 322-386.

[5] E. Liss, "Learning Difficulties—Unresolved Anxiety and Resultant Learning Patterns," *American Journal of Orthopsychiatry,* 1941, *11,* pp. 520-523.

[6] K. Lewin, "Time Perspective and Morale," in G. Watson (Ed.), *Civilian Morale* (New York: Houghton Mifflin Company, 1952).

* From the *Journal of Clinical Psychology,* 1957, *13,* pp. 328-332. Used by permission of the authors and publisher.

the book of McClelland[7] and Winterbottom[8] who have emphasized the importance of parental demands upon achievement motivation. Such demands for certain standards of excellence in the child would seem to imply something different than mere passive permissiveness. It is therefore the thesis of this paper that the parents of high academic achievers will actually be less permissive and accepting in the treatment of their children than the parents of low academic achievers.

SUBJECTS

Parents of gifted students. One group consists of the mothers of forty junior high school students of gifted intelligence (IQ of 130 or more on the Stanford-Binet). Twenty of these students (ten girls and ten boys) had maintained a uniform grade point average of "A" over a previous two-year period and they were identified as high achievers. A group of low achievers (ten girls and ten boys) were matched to these students to within five IQ points on the Stanford-Binet, and to within six months in age. These low achieving students had maintained only a "B minus" or lower grade point average throughout the previous two-year period of their school history. An attempt was also made to equate the groups for socio-economic status by matching high and low achievers on the basis of their fathers' occupations using the classification developed by Warner, Meeker, and Eels[9] (Table 1-10). No significant differences were found in the educational levels of the parents of highs and lows although there was a tendency for both the fathers and mothers of high achievers to have had more years of formal schooling.

Parents of average students. Another group was composed of the mothers of twenty-eight students of average or high average intelligence (IQ's from 93 to 120 on the Stanford-Binet). Fourteen of these students (seven girls and seven boys) had maintained an "A" grade point average for the previous two years, and they were identified as high achievers. The low achieving group was composed of seven girls and seven boys who were matched to the high achievers to within five IQ points on the Stanford-Binet and to within six months in age (Table 1-10). These low achievers had maintained only a "C minus or D" grade point average throughout the previous two-year period of their school history. The two groups were also equated with respect to their father's occupational status in order to control for socio-economic level.

MATERIALS

A Parental Attitude Scale was constructed consisting of 30 items taken from the Parent Attitude Survey (PAS) devised by Shoben.[10] The original scale

[7] D. C. McClelland *et al., The Achievement Motive* (New York: Appleton-Century-Crofts, Inc., 1953).

[8] M. R. Winterbottom, "The Relation of Childhood Training in Independence to Achievement Motivation." Unpublished doctoral dissertation, University of Michigan, 1953.

[9] W. L. Warner *et al., Social Class in America* (Chicago: Science Research Associates, 1949).

[10] E. J. Shoben, Jr., "The Assessment of Parental Attitudes in Relation to Child Adjustment," *Genetic Psychology Monographs,* 1949, *39,* pp. 103-149.

TABLE 1-10

COMPARISON OF THE PARENTS OF GIFTED AND AVERAGE HIGH AND LOW ACHIEVERS ON IQ OF CHILDREN, OCCUPATION OF FATHER AND PARENTS' EDUCATION

	Gifted Intelligence			*Average Intelligence*		
Factors	*High Achiever Means*	*Low Achiever Means*	*t Ratios**	*High Achiever Means*	*Low Achiever Means*	*t Ratios**
Binet IQ of Children	137.60	138.20	.37	110.71	110.07	.32
Occupation of Father	3.25	3.55	.36	3.72	4.55	1.02
Education of Father	13.65	11.75	1.76	11.91	10.83	1.03
Education of Mother	13.70	12.25	1.51	12.76	11.31	1.61

* All t ratios reported here fail to reach a level of statistical significance.

contained 85 items, 75 of which were arranged into three subscales, the Dominating (D) Scale, the Possessive (P) Scale, and the Ignoring (I) Scale. A parent scoring high on the "D" Scale would agree with such items as "It is wicked for a child to disobey his parents" or "A child should always believe what his parents tell him"; a possessive parent would agree with an item like "Babies are more fun for their parents than older children," while a sample "ignoring" item is "Children should not interrupt adult conversation."

The 30 items of the abridged scale used in this study contained an equal number of each of these types of statements (ten of each). The mother was asked to rate each item on a five-point scale from "strongly agree" to "strongly disagree." Care was also taken to insure that the dominating, possessive, and ignoring statements taken from the Shoben scale were worded in such a way that an individual receiving a high score on any subtest would have to agree with half of the items and disagree with the other half. This was to protect against the possibility of obtaining persons with high scores who had simply agreed, or disagreed, with all statements. A copy of the abridged attitude scale is presented in Figure I-1.

Figure I-1. PARENTAL ATTITUDE SCALE. Please read each of the statements as to whether you strongly agree, mildly agree, mildly disagree, or strongly disagree. If you cannot decide whether you agree or disagree with the statement, then rate it as uncertain. There are no right or wrong answers, so answer according to your own convictions. Draw a circle around the pair of letters that best express your feeling.

Strongly Agree —SA   Strongly Disagree —SD
Mildly Agree —MA   Mildly Disagree —MD
Uncertain —UN

*Code**		Statement	*Scores***				
			5	4	3	1	2
(P)	1.	Independent and mature children are less lovable than those children who obviously want and need their parents.	SA	MA	UN	SD	MD
			5	2	1	3	4
(P)	2.	Parents should sacrifice everything for their children.	SA	MD	SD	UN	MA
			3	1	2	5	4
(D)	3.	A child should have strict discipline in order to develop a fine, strong character.	UN	SD	MD	SA	MA
			5	3	2	4	1
(D)	4.	Children should not be punished for doing anything they have seen their parents do.	SD	UN	MA	MD	SA
			2	5	4	3	1
(I)	5.	A child should be seen and not heard.	MD	SA	MA	UN	SD
			5	3	2	1	4
(I)	6.	The most important consideration in planning the activities of the home should be the needs and interests of the child.	SD	UN	MA	SA	MD
			3	2	5	4	1
(P)	7.	The weaning of the child from its emotional ties to the parents begins at birth.	UN	MA	SA	MD	SA
			2	5	4	3	1
(P)	8.	Babies are more fun for parents than are older children.	MD	SA	MA	UN	SD
			1	3	4	5	2
(D)	9.	Children should be allowed to make only minor decisions for themselves.	SD	UN	MA	SA	MD
			3	1	2	4	5
(D)	10.	Strict discipline weakens a child's personality.	UN	SA	MA	MD	SD
			4	5	3	2	1
(P)	11.	Children should be allowed to play with any youngsters they like.	MD	SD	UN	MA	SA
			4	3	1	2	5
(I)	12.	Parents are generally too busy to answer all of a child's questions.	MA	UN	SD	MD	SA
			5	3	2	1	4
(I)	13.	When they can't have their own way, children usually try to bargain or reason with their parents.	SD	UN	MA	SA	MD

*Code**			*Scores***				
(I)	14.	Quiet children are much nicer than little chatter-boxes.	5 SA	4 MA	3 UN	1 SD	2 MD
(P)	15.	A child should be allowed to enter any occupation he or she wishes.	3 UN	4 MD	1 SA	2 MA	5 SD
(P)	16.	In the long run it is better, after all, for a child to be kept fairly close to his mother's apron strings.	1 SD	3 UN	4 MA	5 SA	2 MD
(D)	17.	A child should always believe what his parents tell him.	5 SA	4 MA	3 UN	1 SD	2 MD
(D)	18.	It is sometimes necessary for the parent to break the child's will.	2 MD	5 SA	4 MA	3 UN	1 SD
(I)	19.	Children should not annoy their parents with their unimportant problems.	3 UN	1 SD	2 MD	5 SA	4 MA
(D)	20.	It is wicked for a child to disobey its parents.	1 SD	3 UN	4 MA	2 MD	5 SA
(I)	21.	Children should not interrupt adult conversation.	2 MD	5 SA	4 MA	1 SD	3 UN
(I)	22.	Children should have as much freedom as their parents themselves.	1 SA	2 MA	5 SD	3 UN	4 MD
(D)	23.	Children should not be required to take orders from their parents.	3 UN	4 MD	1 SA	2 MA	5 SD
(D)	24.	Children should be allowed to choose their own religious beliefs.	2 MA	5 SD	4 MD	1 SA	3 UN
(P)	25.	Parents are not entitled to the love of their children unless they earn it.	5 SD	3 UN	2 MA	4 MD	1 SD
(P)	26.	The best child is the one who shows lots of affection for his mother.	2 MD	5 SA	1 SD	4 MA	3 UN
(D)	27.	Children should be allowed to choose their own friends without restrictions.	5 SD	2 MA	4 MD	3 UN	1 SA
(I)	28.	Children should be allowed to manage their affairs with little supervision from adults.	3 UN	4 MD	1 SA	2 MA	5 SD
(I)	29.	Children should have the opportunity to express their opinions to their parents.	1 SA	2 MA	3 UN	5 SD	4 MD
(P)	30.	A child should stand on his own two feet as soon as possible.	5 SD	3 UN	2 MA	4 MD	1 SA

*Code
P = possessive
D = dominating
I = ignoring

**Scores
The scores given to the various responses on each item, and the code letters designating the category of the item were not included in the test administered to the subjects. They are shown here only for the benefit of the reader.

TABLE 1-11

Comparison of Gifted and Average Mothers on the Parental Attitude Scale

	Gifted Mothers (N = 40)			*Average Mothers (N = 28)*		
Scales	*Highs*	*Lows*	*t Ratios*	*Highs*	*Lows*	*t Ratios*
D Scale	31.45	26.45	2.87**	35.07	33.21	.93
I Scale	26.80	22.35	3.71**	27.72	24.93	2.15*
P Scale	21.65	21.35	.19	25.07	25.14	.08

** significant at the one per cent level.
* significant at the five per cent level.

RESULTS

The results in Table 1-11 reveal that the mothers of high achieving students had higher scores on both the Dominating (D) Scale and the Ignoring (I) Scale of the test. In the former case this was significant at the one per cent level of confidence only among mothers of the gifted sample, while in the latter case (I Scale) the results were statistically significant at the one per cent level among the gifted and at the five per cent level among the mothers of students of average intelligence. No differences were noted between high and low achievers on the Possessive (P) Scale.

DISCUSSION

Mothers of high achievers of both gifted and average intelligence were found to receive significantly higher scores on the Ignoring (I) Scale of the test. An examination of the items which make up this subtest seems to indicate that it refers to the limits which have been set up for the child within the home. Examples of a few "I" Scale items are, "Children should not interrupt adult conversation," "Children should not annoy their parents with their unimportant problems," and "A child should be seen and not heard." Thus it would appear that the high achiever is a child who has a rigidly defined place within the home which he is expected to keep with docile acceptance. This was especially true of the gifted sample where the mothers of high achievers also received significantly greater scores on the "D" Scale. Items in this subtest seem to refer to punitive attitudes towards disobedience which would appear to indicate that these mothers are quite authoritarian in their treatment of their children.

If these results reflect the typical attitudes which characterize the parents of high achievers then it is not surprising that Gough[11] discovered his successful high school students to be conforming, orderly, docile and conventional. High achievers appear to come from a family atmosphere in which the adult knows what is best for the child, and where these adult standards are not often questioned. These findings are also in agreement with Pearson[12] and Liss[13] who emphasize that parental intervention is necessary for the development of proper ego controls within the child so that he can adjust to the reality demands of the schoolroom. Certainly it is not difficult to see that a student who readily accepts adult dictums might be perceived as a more ideal student in the eyes of his teachers.

SUMMARY

An attempt was made to determine the attitudes of the mothers of high and low academic achievers of both gifted and average intelligence in terms of permissiveness, protectiveness, and domination. It was found that the mothers of high achievers were more authoritarian and restrictive in the treatment of their children than the mothers of low achievers. The parents of high achievers of gifted intelligence also seemed to have more punitive attitudes with respect to child-rearing.

---

[11] H. G. Gough, "What Determines the Academic Achievement of High School Students?", *Journal of Educational Research*, 1953, *46*, pp. 321-331.

[12] G. H. Pearson, *op. cit.*

[13] E. Liss, *op. cit.*

II

SCHOOL DESEGREGATION

*DESEGREGATION: A PSYCHOLOGICAL ANALYSIS**

By Stuart W. Cook

I want to talk with you about a psychologist's view of a major social change which is taking place in this country. I am referring to the series of events in the South which have followed the Supreme Court's decisions against segregation in public schools.

As *citizens* we may consider the Court's rulings wise or unwise, we may applaud or condemn specific actions taken in the South, we may find the ferment and the turmoil and the apparently inconsistent reactions in the South fascinating or confusing, or both. But as *psychologist*s our approach must be to consider, on the one hand, whether our available knowledge can contribute to an understanding of what is going on, and, on the other hand, to seek in the changing situation opportunities for research which will increase our understanding of the process of change in relations between social groups.

I believe that even in the present rather primitive state of social psychology, we do have knowledge which would suggest a different interpretation of events than everyday common sense provides. Take, for instance, the recent vote in Virginia, in which residents of that state, by a two-to-one majority, approved a plan which will make possible the transformation of public schools into what are technically private schools in order to evade the Supreme Court ruling. A correspondent of the *New York Times,* in commenting on the vote, drew the conclusion that much of the South will not accept racially integrated schools and that desegregation there will have to be a slow evolutionary process. I am doubtful that this is the correct interpretation; I will shortly suggest another possibility.

And, on a much larger scale—what are the long-range implications of the fact that schools are being desegregated in many communities, and probably sooner or later throughout the South? Many interpreters have seen in this event the beginning of the end of racial segregation in the South. How realistic an expectation is this?

I don't know, with any certainty, the answers to

* From *The American Psychologist,* 1957, *12,* pp. 1-13, with minor deletions. Used by permission of the author and publisher. This paper was first given at the annual meeting of the New York State Psychological Association, January 28, 1956.

these questions. In fact, my main argument is going to be that the significance of the Supreme Court's decision, from the standpoint of a *science of psychology,* is that it provides a rare opportunity to acquire more of the kind of knowledge we need in order to make better interpretations of such matters than is now possible.

First, however, I want to indicate that I think we already know enough to suggest alternative—though not necessarily correct—interpretations for each of the points I have just mentioned.

Take the Virginia vote. My expectation would be that when school desegregation does take place in Virginia it will be with as little unpleasantness as there has been in places like Washington, Baltimore, and St. Louis, which have already undergone desegregation. I do not mean to say that I doubt that the people of Virginia are opposed to desegregation; on the contrary, I think the vote is a very clear expression of that opposition. But I do not think it provides a basis for predicting what their behavior will be when school desegregation is initiated. I would suggest that, if similar votes had been taken in other communities before desegregation was started, the balloting would have been about the same.

I base my interpretation on a number of studies which suggest that, in the area of race relations, stated opinion is frequently not a reliable basis for prediction of behavior. The classic example, of course, is the study in which LaPiere,[1] after traveling throughout the United States with a Chinese couple, wrote to the hotels and restaurants which they had visited, asking if the establishment would accept Chinese as guests. What he found was that over 90 per cent of the respondents (all of whom actually had served the Chinese couple) said they would not do so. Saenger's[2] interviews with white women in New York City made the same point. Individuals who had been seen buying goods from Negro salesgirls denied that they would do so.

As it happens, we have *direct* evidence that stated opposition to school desegregation in Southern communities does not necessarily lead to hostile *action* once desegregation has been initiated.

For example, Bower and Walker[3] in interviews with a cross section of the population of Washington, D.C., in June, 1954, found that 52 per cent of the white respondents thought the Supreme Court decision was bad, only 24 per cent thought it was good, and another 24 per cent was neutral. In other words, among those who had definite opinions, feeling was two to one against the decision—the same proportion as the Virginia vote. Yet desegregation took place the following fall. According to Bower and Walker, the first gradual change-over worked so well that the school superintendent decided to speed the process a bit and authorized a large-scale transfer: at this point there was a brief strike by junior and senior high school students, which collapsed after a few days when it received little support from the adult community. Except for this brief strike, desegregation proceeded without incident. When the same sample of respondents were reinterviewed toward the end of the school year, even among those who had disapproved of the Supreme Court decision, 39 per cent conceded that desegregation was going "very well" or "fairly well," and only 29 per cent said it was going "not so well" or "badly."

What about the expectation that the end of school segregation will lead to sweeping changes in the pattern of race relations in the South—and specifically, that it will mean the end of all segregation? In expressing some reservations about this I do not mean for one moment to underestimate the importance of the Supreme Court decisions; I share the general judgment that they constitute a major historic event. But I think there is a tendency to overestimate the probable effects of the change in school patterns, both among liberals who *hope* that desegregation of schools will lead to desegregation in all aspects of life, and among many Southerners who *fear* that it will. One of the clearest findings of studies of the relation between intergroup contact and attitude change is that, while individuals rather quickly come to accept and even approve of association with members of another social group in situations of the type where they have experienced such association, this approval is not likely to be generalized to other situations unless the individuals have quite close personal relationships with mem-

[1] R. T. LaPiere, "Attitudes vs. Actions," *Social Forces,* 1934, *13,* pp. 230-237.

[2] G. Saenger and E. Gilbert, "Customer Reactions to the Integration of Negro Sales Personnel," *International Journal of Opinion and Attitude Research,* 4, 1950, pp. 57-76.

[3] R. T. Bower and H. Walker, "Early Impacts of Desegregation in D. C.," mimeographed, Bureau of Social Science Research, The American University, Washington, D. C.

bers of the other group. Thus, for example, Harding and Hogrefe[4] found that white salesgirls in Philadelphia department stores who worked in departments where there were Negro salesgirls were more likely than those in all-white departments to express willingness to work with Negroes, but were no more willing to have Negroes as neighbors or as friends. A particularly dramatic example of the extent to which behavior may be limited to a specific situation is Minard's description[5] of a mining community in West Virginia where white and Negro miners work amicably together in mixed teams, sometimes with a Negro supervising white workers, but separate at the mine shaft and lead their aboveground lives in complete segregation—living in separate neighborhoods, eating in separate restaurants, participating jointly in no activities save those in the union hall. And one need only look around any Northern community to see that unsegregated schools do not necessarily lead to unsegregated living.

That this kind of compartmentalization occurs also when schools are newly desegregated is evidenced by the descriptions of a number of border communities, reported in the book edited by Williams and Ryan.[6] In community after community they report that, although relations between white and Negro students within the schools are matter-of-fact and even friendly, the two groups go their separate ways outside of school. Time will tell, of course, whether over a period of years school desegregation will gradually extend to desegregation in other areas of living, but there seems no reason to expect an immediate sweeping change.

THE NEED FOR AN ANALYTICAL SCHEMA

These few examples are more than enough to show how our present understanding of social relations leads us to question the more obvious common sense interpretations which are usually offered. We look for meanings other than those which appear on the face of things and, by taking a more comprehensive view of the determinants of human action, less often assume direct correspondence between stated opinion and other kinds of behavior. Such an approach suggests alternative and probably more accurate interpretations of specific events. But, to be most useful, psychological science must go beyond explanations of specific phenomena, and provide a schema within which a range of events can be organized and understood. Can social psychology provide such a framework for viewing the present scene?

My answer—as you may guess—is "yes" and "no." To elaborate this, I must distinguish between two aspects of the events following on the Supreme Court decision: first, those having to do with the decision of policy makers whether to accept the Court's ruling and desegregate the schools; second, those having to do with what happens once desegregation has been initiated. On questions of the second sort—the process and the effects of desegregation—we have a considerable body of relevant information, and, I think, the beginnings of an organized analytical approach. Within this schema we have a basis for at least tentative predictions and for identifying with some certainty the kinds of situations in which research could provide answers to crucial questions. On the first aspect—that of the process of deciding whether to desegregate—we have much less to draw upon; I should say we are in a position of having to develop simultaneously both a systematic approach and ways of testing the hypotheses which grow out of this approach.

ATTITUDE CHANGES FOLLOWING INTERGROUP CONTACT

Let me start with the area in which I think our knowledge and our thinking are relatively far along. After the last war, a number of psychologists and sociologists interested in attitude change turned their attention to problems of intergroup relations. They developed a consensus that some of the most important determinants of attitude change toward other social groups were to be found in the experience of face-to-face contact with members those groups. At first, they tended to the optimistic

[4] J. Harding and R. Hogrefe, "Attitudes of White Department Store Employees toward Negro Co-Workers," *Journal of Social Issues, 8,* 1, 1952.

[5] R. D. Minard, "Race Relations in the Pocahontas Coal Field," *Journal of Social Issues, 8,* 1, 1952.

[6] R. M. Williams, Jr., and M. W. Ryan (Eds.), *Schools in Transition: Community Experiences in Desegregation* (Chapel Hill: University of North Carolina Press, 1954).

view that such personal contact with members of another group was sure to be a powerful influence toward *favorable* attitude change.

However, in spite of the considerable number of studies which found such a relationship, some did not. A much earlier study by Horowitz[7]—and one of the most interesting in the present context—had already reported that attitudes towards Negroes of white boys in racially mixed schools in New York City differed little from attitudes of white boys in segregated schools in Tennessee and in Georgia.

Additional research on the relationship between intergroup contact and changes in attitude gave rise to a variation of the old chicken-and-egg question. A number of studies had found contact with members of an ethnic group other than one's own associated with favorable attitudes toward that ethnic group. But which came first—the contact or the favorable attitude? This methodological difficulty led to an interest in situations of so-called involuntary contact—on the job, in public housing, in the armed forces, etc.—that is, in situations where the individual is in a setting where there are members of another social group, but he is there not because of a desire to associate with that group but because of a strong push or pull from some other source.

Also, it proved helpful to distinguish between mere physical presence of members of different ethnic groups in a common situation, on the one hand, and the occurrence of interaction between them, on the other. We are now thinking in terms of the following schema: individuals from two ethnic groups encounter one another involuntarily in some situation. This encounter may or may not lead to interaction, depending on the characteristics of the individuals involved and on the nature of the situation. When it does, the interaction may vary in amount and quality and this variation, in turn, influences the type of attitude change which takes place.

The influence of conditions under which contact occurs. When we raise the question, "What does the nature of the contact situation have to do with the outcome of the experience?" the need to identify the dimensions in terms of which contact situations can be described becomes apparent.

Here are three examples of what I mean. One of the characteristics of a contact situation is the extent to which it offers the opportunity for the participants to get to know one another—labeled, for short, its *acquaintance potential.* There is great variation in the extent to which the characteristics of individuals are revealed during contact. You may encounter an elevator operator, for example, twice a day for years, without communication about anything other than the weather. A contrasting situation—that of living as neighbors—does not impose comparable limitations on the areas over which communication may take place and individuality emerge.

A second characteristic of contact situations has to do with the way in which they define the *relative* status of participants belonging to the two ethnic groups. For example, in a given work situation, Negroes may have only menial jobs while white persons are in skilled or supervisory positions; in another work situation, Negroes and whites may be doing the same kinds of jobs.

My third example of a dimension along which contact situations differ involves the nature of the *social norm* toward contact of one ethnic group with another. In some situations, the general expectation of persons in authority and of most of the participants may be that friendly association between members of the two groups is appropriate; in other situations, even though for some reason members of the two groups are present, the general feeling on the part of at least one of the groups may be that any unnecessary mingling should be avoided.

I will examine the implications of only one of these three concepts for our thinking about the outcomes of desegregation in the public schools of the South—the social norm regarding interaction with the other group. Several studies have pointed to the significance of this variable.

Thus, Minard,[8] in the study I have already mentioned of the behavior of white workers in coal mines where they worked with Negroes on an unsegregated basis, and of the same workers in the segregated communities where the mines were located, estimated that about three-fifths of the men adapted their behavior, without apparent conflict, to the generally accepted practices in the specific situation—even to the extent of sitting next to

[7] E. L. Horowitz, "The Development of Attitudes toward the Negro," *Archives of Psychology,* No. 194 (New York: Columbia University Press, 1936).

[8] R. D. Minard, *op. cit.*

Negroes in the mine bus but sitting in the white section when they transfer to the public bus.

The perceived norm with regard to contact also has wider effects. In a study of relationships within biracial public housing projects,[9] we found that white housewives differed not only in the extent of their association with Negroes in the project but in their views as to whether other white women in the project approved of associating with Negroes. We found that those who believed that the other white women in the project approved of such association showed much more favorable attitudes toward Negroes than did those who believed that the other white women disapproved of such association. With minor exceptions, this influence of the perceived social norm showed up regardless of whether the women lived in integrated or in building-segregated projects, or of whether they had much or little contact with Negroes: those who believed the other white women in the project approved of interracial association were more favorable in their attitudes toward Negroes than were the comparable white housewives who thought such association was not approved.

The cumulative weight of these and other studies highlights the effect of what is generally referred to as the social climate or social atmosphere. What they tell us is that interracial contacts take place in a social context in which the individual is responding not only to persons from another ethnic group but also to what he believes would be judged proper in such relationships by those whose social approval he needs and seeks. This, of course, is a familiar and pervasive characteristic of human behavior. The fact that it operates generally below the level of conscious awareness and is often accompanied by the production of beliefs and feelings which rationalize otherwise incomprehensible behavior gives it a prominent place in the study of social relations.

Nevertheless not enough progress has been made with the task of studying analytically the effect of social climate on the outcomes of intergroup contact. Some effort has been made to identify factors contributing to it. It seems possible to distinguish several components: first, positions taken publicly by individuals or groups who carry an aura of moral authority or of extremely high prestige (for example, the Supreme Court, the President of the United States, church figures); second, the attitudes and behavior of the general population of the community or the region; third, the statements and practices of persons in authority in the particular situation such as the employer or the school superintendent; and fourth, the behavior, expectations, beliefs, etc., of other members of one's own group with whom one is in direct personal association.

It would be of great interest to know, for instance, the relative weight of a position taken by a powerful but distant authority such as the Supreme Court as compared with the norms of the face-to-face group in influencing an individual's reaction to new experiences of interracial contact. And it would be of interest to know what effect a face-to-face group norm that is in conflict with the position taken by the powerful but distant authority has on the interpretation of the latter's action and how this bears on the individual's reaction to novel contact experiences. Do Southerners, for instance, more than others, perceive the anti-segregation decisions as a political—in the low sense of the term—act rather than as a truly juridical one? And do individuals who so perceive the decisions react differently to contact experiences than do those who believe the Supreme Court justices were honestly and faithfully attempting to abide by strictly constitutional considerations?

In cases where the norm of the immediate group differs from that held by the larger population, we need to know which one is more likely to be followed. And, since the other members of one's immediate group in a situation of intergroup contact are themselves subject to the influences of the contact experience, we need to study changes in the face-to-face group norm itself.

The Supreme Court decisions, and the events which have followed them, provide a rare opportunity for studying questions of this sort. We are, in effect, presented with a ready-made laboratory in which, on the one hand, the position of national figures—notably, of course, of the Court itself—has become prominent and is a constant, but where individual communities present a wide range of variation in terms of the position taken by state and city political leaders, local school authorities, and the residents. Studies of border communities in which school desegregation has already taken place, as

[9] D. M. Wilner, R. P. Walkley, S. W. Cook, *Human Relations in Interracial Housing: A Study of the Contact Hypothesis* (Minneapolis: University of Minnesota Press, 1955).

reported by Williams and Ryan,[10] show an enormous range in this respect. In Cairo, Illinois, for instance, desegregation was initiated reluctantly, as the result of threats that the state would withhold financial aid and of legal action by the NAACP; the local school authorities, apparently the entire white population, and much of the Negro population, appeared to be opposed to desegregation. At the other extreme, Carlsbad, New Mexico, operating under a permissive state law, began to desegregate its schools two years before the Supreme Court decision was actually handed down. All important segments of the community seemed to support the move. The superintendent of schools advocated it; the board of education favored the change on the basis of monetary savings; teachers and principals, on the whole, were not opposed; the Ministerial Alliance cooperated; community leaders in general took the position that times were changing, and "we might as well go along with it since we can't stop it"; the white high school students voted for integration at the high school level. There are still other communities—such as Hoxie, Arkansas—where the school authorities favor desegregation on economic grounds but general community opinion is strongly opposed.

This wide variation among communities provides a striking opportunity—one which it is probably not possible to create under laboratory conditions, and which is not likely to be again duplicated on such a scale in our lifetime—for studying the effects on social change of differences in social norms, and the relative influence of different sources of norms.

Were we able to utilize this real-life laboratory, I would find of especial interest the community which desegregates its schools while all the sources of social climate save those at the national level oppose the step and, where possible, act to limit its effect. It is in such communities that I suspect we may see the really dramatic developments. Under the influence of the social norms which prevail at the outset, the schoolroom contact may seem for some time to be without effect. Then at some later period—and I could not guess how much later—there will be a time during which change in the relationships between white and Negro students proceeds at what will seem an unexpectedly rapid pace. Behind this, if I am right, will lurk unrecognized the influence of a changed social norm among the students themselves. It seems to be often the case that the basis for a shift in norms develops well in advance of the shift itself. When, for some reason, the new norm crystallizes in the perceptions of members of a group they may show very suddenly behavior for which in fact they had been individually ready for some time. A factor which may help encourage such a development in school desegregation is the general readiness of adolescents to rebel against adult authority.

The influence of characteristics of individuals who are in contact. So much for this illustration of the need to think of characteristics of the contact situation when analyzing the outcomes of involuntary presence in intergroup contact situations. Let me mention more briefly another class of variables which seem important: namely, characteristics of the individuals who are in contact. They are of interest from two quite different points of view. First, each group constitutes part of the contact situation for the other group. Characteristics which are relevant from this point of view may be thought of as "characteristics of the individual as object" or "characteristics of the object-group." Second, each group may be looked at as potential changers as a result of the contact. Characteristics which are relevant from this point of view I shall refer to as "characteristics of the individual as subject" or "characteristics of the subject-group."

To the extent that learning about the other group takes place in intergroup contact, it follows that the characteristics of the individuals with whom contact takes place may have an effect on the outcome. With specific reference to the interethnic character of the contact, two aspects of the characteristics of object individuals seem likely to be of particular importance: the extent to which the individuals differ from the commonly held stereotypes about the object group; and the extent to which they resemble the subject individuals in terms of background characteristics, interests, etc.

It seems likely that the great variety of patterns which are appearing in the course of the shift to desegregated schools may give rise to situations which differ in this respect. For example, Valien's report on the process of desegregation in Cairo, Illinois,[11] notes that, because of a variety of community pressures, middle- and upper-class Negro children

[10] R. M. Williams, Jr. and M. W. Ryan, *op. cit.*

[11] R. M. Williams, Jr. and M. W. Ryan, *op. cit.*

remained in segregated schools, and only children of the lowest socio-economic group enrolled in the formerly white schools. Many of these children were below average in intellectual ability, had had poor records in the Negro schools, and did not do well in their new schools; according to the report, they tended, because of this selective process, to confirm the white stereotypes that Negroes are stupid and lazy. On the other hand, there will certainly be other communities where the children of the better-educated Negro families will enter mixed schools. While it will admittedly be difficult to identify in advance situations where the Negro children in a mixed school will tend to conform to the derogatory stereotypes and others where they will not, examination of the characteristics of residential neighborhoods should make it possible to identify schools where each of these situations is likely to occur. Comparisons of attitudes and behavior of white children in the two types of schools should throw considerable light on the importance of characteristics of the object individuals in determining attitudes.

When we consider the individuals in the contact situation as *subjects,* we regard them from a somewhat different point of view. Focusing now upon the attitude changes they may undergo, we would like to know why some change more and others less; some in one direction, others in another. Two classes of personal variables may be thought of as likely to influence the individual's reaction to intergroup contact: the nature and intensity of initial attitudes toward the object group, and aspects of personality or character structure which may predispose one to hostile reactions toward members of outgroups.

The few studies which have attempted to take account of initial attitudes have emerged with a striking diversity of conclusions. Two studies in public housing projects[12] found that white housewives who said they were initially unfavorable to Negroes were *more* likely to report favorable attitude changes than were those who reported themselves as being originally favorable. Another study,[13] of white residents of a block into which Negroes had moved, reported exactly the opposite finding: those who were relatively favorable toward Negroes at the time the first Negro family was about to move in became more favorable after the Negroes had been living there a few weeks; those who were initially unfavorable had become still more unfavorable.

All of these studies took into account simply differences in the degree of favorableness or unfavorableness of the attitudes rather than the particular constellation of beliefs and feelings. It may be, however, that there are other differences in attitudes which make them more or less resistant to change. It has sometimes been stated, for example, that there are at least two distinct constellations of attitudes in the South. According to one, Negroes are gentle, fun-loving, jolly, but childlike and irresponsible; this attitude is said to have a warm, affectionate component; one is fond of Negroes, but just doesn't consider them intellectually and socially the same class of human being as oneself. The second, apparently quite different, attitude constellation is dominated by apprehension of the Negro as potentially dangerous, animal-like, and sexually uncontrolled. It is likely, of course, that the two constellations may often exist simultaneously in the same individual.

If these observations of differences in *kinds* of attitude are correct, it is reasonable to ask whether they differ in the extent to which they can be changed by experience with Negroes. For example, if there is really an attitude which is made up of friendly feelings in combination with unrealistic beliefs about Negroes and a caste feeling that they are a different order of being (and from my personal experience, I believe there is), is it possible that experience with Negroes in a situation where at least officially they are defined as equals might correct the beliefs and gradually eradicate the caste feelings, without destroying the friendliness? Or would the disappearance of the caste distinction result in a threat to self-esteem which would generate hostility? To my knowledge, there are no studies on attitude constellations of this sort, and the outcome should be quite instructive.

The research potential in school desegregation. Many of these questions can be studied as well in situations of involuntary contact in the North as in desegregated schools in the South. Why then do I

[12] M. Deutsch and M. E. Collins, *Interracial Housing: A Psychological Evaluation of a Social Experiment* (Minneapolis: University of Minnesota Press, 1951); D. M. Wilner, *et al.*, *op. cit.*

[13] I. Taylor, Personal communication.

emphasize the importance of research in Southern schools? Partly, it is because of the scale on which desegregation is taking place in the South. It is estimated that more than 150,000 Negro children who formerly attended segregated schools are now in mixed classes for the first time. Since in most of the newly mixed schools Negro children are in the minority, it seems safe to estimate that about half a million white children are for the first time having contact with Negroes in school.

From the point of view of research, the significance of change on such a scale is the probability that contact between Negro and white children will occur under a great variety of conditions and that this would make it possible to find contrasts which highlight the variable one is interested in studying. Moreover, the fact that the change is occurring in so many schools and so many communities means that similar combinations of variables will be repeated, thus making it possible to replicate studies and so check the findings.

The situation also presents a second advantage. Because of the gradualness of the increase in the number of situations of involuntary contact in the North, it is difficult to find comparable or contrasting situations in which interracial contact is about to occur for the first time. Almost all studies have been carried out in situations where whites and Negroes were already in contact at the time of the investigation; initial attitudes had to be recalled by the respondents or inferred by the investigators on the basis of indirect evidence. In contrast, the fact that thousands of children in hundreds of southern communities will be attending mixed schools for the first time offers an unprecedented opportunity for research which can get direct evidence of initial attitude and in which the process of attitude change can be traced rather than inferred.

There is still another advantage—namely, the possibility of checking findings which seem fairly well substantiated in Northern studies, in settings where the over-all milieu is quite different. For example, it seems quite well established that, under certain combinations of circumstances—such as those obtaining in interracial public housing projects in the North—actual physical proximity of residence of whites to Negroes is an important determinant of favorableness of attitudes toward them. Would this finding hold in the quite different setting of a mixed school in a Southern town: will the white children who happen to be seated close to Negro children associate with them more, and become more friendly with them, than those who are seated farther away? Here I predict rather confidently that the answer will be yes.

PUBLIC POSITION-TAKING ON CONSEQUENTIAL ISSUES

You will recall that I said earlier that we could think of the events following the Supreme Court's decision partly in terms of the process of desegregation as I have been discussing it and partly in terms of decisions to desegregate or not to desegregate the schools in a given locality. Let me turn now to this latter aspect.

First we should note that we are involved here in an area of decision-making which is in many respects quite different from those that have been studied by social psychologists up to now. Most of the available studies have dealt with the effect of the conditions under which decisions are made on the subsequent behaviors of the people who decide. Considerable interest has focused on the process of decision-making in situations where the decisions do not have wider reverberations than the small groups in which they are made. Another focus has been upon decisions where the final act is completely private, as in voting behavior. In the present context, by contrast, we are concerned with the act of arriving at a public decision on consequential issues which inevitably involve large-scale public interest.

In relation to desegregation, it is developments in connection with these public decisions which make the headlines, although in my own opinion the real drama is played out in the schools and PTAs once desegregation gets under way. The daily papers bring us reports of reactions which run the gamut from decisions to desegregate immediately to statements that desegregation will never be accepted. For example, within twelve months after the Supreme Court's *first* ruling—that is, even before the Court had issued any directives as to how and when desegregation was to be initiated—scattered communities in eight states, plus the District of Columbia, had undertaken to desegregate their schools. On the other hand, seven states—Virginia, North and South Carolina, Georgia, Alabama, Mississippi, and Louisiana—after the Court's second ruling, passed legislation designed to preserve segregation. Within Virginia, where the citizens were voting two to one against integration in the public schools, the Catholic schools desegregated. While "white citizens' councils" to "defend states' rights and preserve racial purity" were being formed, such groups as the Southern Methodist Conference were passing resolutions favoring desegregation.

What are we to make of this bewildering variety of reactions? Do we have in psychology an approach to such events which would help us to see some order underlying the apparent confusion?

Before I try to suggest the direction which such an approach might take, let me outline tentatively some trends which I think can be observed in recent events in the South. It appears that, other things being equal, desegregation tends to proceed faster in cities than in rural areas, in border regions than in the deep South, in areas where the proportion of Negroes is small, and in areas where there has been a sizable influx of people from outside the South. Persons opposing desegregation seem to be older and less well-educated. Persons who support desegregation do so primarily on the basis of moral and religious allegiance, on the one hand, and on law-abiding grounds on the other. Desegregation seems to be accepted relatively easily within organizations, such as the Army and the Catholic Church, which have strong and enforceable sanctions. Segregation is abandoned more easily when it conflicts with some other need than where there is no such opposing force; for example, a white person who, in a relatively empty train, will not sit next to a Negro may do so when the only vacant seat happens to be next to a Negro. And individuals' views about segregation or integration tend to be brought into line with the position of important reference groups.

While these trends, if they are correctly observed, suggest some orderliness in the apparent confusion of events, they do not in themselves give us a basis for a psychological organization of our thinking in relation to an individual instance of decision making—such as, for example, might be represented by the vote of a member of the School Board of Knox County, Tennessee, on a proposal to desegregate the public schools of the county.

I think that most, if not all, of the complex phenomena that have been observed can be comprehended within the framework of two groups of concepts: one having to do with variables which may be related to the direction the decision takes, the other dealing with factors influencing the extent to which any given one of these possible variables becomes a weighty determinant of the position taken.

Some developments in the town of Hoxie, Arkansas, will illustrate what I mean. At the time of the Supreme Court's decision, the Hoxie School Board was in debt and discouraged about the possibility of improving the financial situation. One of the heavier drains on the school district's budget was the cost of transporting a number of Negro students of high school age to a Negro high school in a nearby community and paying that community for their tuition. The Hoxie School Board interpreted the first Supreme Court decision as invalidating the Arkansas law requiring racial segregation. They saw the possibility of solving their financial crisis by enrolling the Negro high school students in their own high school, and decided to do this. To the outside observer this decision might well appear to be based upon a favorable reaction to racially mixed public schools, and it *was* widely interpreted in this way. Actually, it probably had no such implication whatsoever. Although the Board's public statement of reasons included reference to religious and constitutional values, I understand from observers on the scene that the major factor in their decision was the financial one, that they took the step with great reluctance, and that their personal attitudes, like those of most of the other white residents of the community, favored separation of the races.

This example points to two variables which are potential determinants of the desegregation decision: one, individual attitudes toward Negroes and toward segregation; the other, the incentive represented by financial benefits to be gained by desegregating. The school board made its decision in terms of the latter consideration; the community reacted in terms of its attitude toward segregation. What made the financial consideration the determining one for the school board, who were in other respects not different from other members of the community? It seems clear that what is reflected here is the influence of role requirements. As members of the board of education, they were responsible for the school budget; it was this role requirement which made the economy of integrated schools the dominant consideration for them.

Some determinants of the direction of position-taking. A parallel to what we have found in Hoxie will be found in other situations. Some of the potential determinants of the decision, such as racial attitudes, are of the sort which recur regardless of the specific situation; that is, they have an inherent psychological relation to the desegregation issue. Others, like the financial incentive, are not so related but are made relevant through the operation of some other factor.

Let me mention first some of the first type of variables—those which are inherently relevant to the desegregation decision. I have already referred, in the Hoxie example, to the variables of attitudes toward Negroes and toward racial separation. These attitudes involve both apprehensions and values directly relevant to the segregation issue. You will remember that one of the trends I thought I had noted is that less well-educated persons are likely to be more opposed to desegregation. A possible inference from this might be that underlying one's decision to support or oppose desegregation is a need for social status. For the less well-educated, being white and therefore upper caste, may be the only way in which this need is satisfied. If this is true, apprehension of a possible loss of status if Negro children attend schools on a basis of equality with white children might be expected to run higher for this segment of the population. Another apprehension relating directly to the possible effects of desegregation may be the fear of loss of political and economic power, particularly where Negroes are in the majority.

On the *values* side, the one most directly related to beliefs about the desirability of desegregation would seem to be the political or philosophical creed of the basic equality of individuals. In considering this value as a factor entering into the decision whether or not to desegregate, one would need to know not only its strength for a given individual but the extent to which it is compartmentalized and out of contact with segregation practices.

Factors influencing the relevance and strength of various determinants. I shall not attempt to list the variables which are not inherently related to the question of desegregation but which may become relevant through the operation of other factors; potentially they cover the whole range of human motivation. Rather, I should like to consider some of the major factors which can operate, first, to bring these otherwise irrelevant variables into connection with the desegregation issue and second, to influence the strength of any given variable—whether or not it is inherently related to desegregation—in the decision.

One of these factors has been illustrated in the Hoxie example—that of the requirements of the role which the individual occupies. In that instance, the role requirements brought into prominence the financial incentive to desegregation. In other instances, role requirements may make community opinion the decisive variable. A local political leader, for example, is likely to be especially sensitive to community attitudes, since his continued occupation of his position is dependent on community approval.

Another factor which may bring seemingly unrelated variables into the segregation decision and which may also influence the relative strength of variables is the position taken by reference groups which are important to the individual. Let us say, for example, that an individual places great stress on respect for law. Before the Court's decision, this value exerted no force toward desegregation; in fact, in the South, the value of law-abidingness would operate in support of segregation. But the Court's ruling may bring the value of law-abidingness into play as a force toward desegregation, regardless of the individual's attitudes toward racial mingling. Thus, statements by officials in the border states have frequently had the following tone, "However we as individuals feel about desegregation, as loyal citizens we will of course respect the authority of the nation's highest judicial body."

One can see a similar process with respect to face-to-face reference groups. Consider, for example, the fact that soon after the Court's decision school boards in a number of communities set up plans for studying means of desegregating, with every indication that they were inclined toward a decision to desegregate. As time went on there was a shift. In some cases little more was heard of the plan; in others the plan was explicitly postponed or abandoned. Or take such communities as Milford, Delaware, where the decision to desegregate was officially made, but reconsidered as a result of strong community protests. In such situations, one may suppose that there was to begin with only one effective reference group—namely, the Supreme Court. But as community opinion was mobilized, a new force entered into the situation—the position taken by a reference group which was closer not only physically but probably also psychologically. This force brought into the complex of variables influencing the desegregation decision the desire for approval by persons who are important to the individual. This desire for social approval can be assumed to have existed in the board members all along, but it did not become an important variable in the desegregation decision until the expression of community opinion made it clear that a decision for desegregation would lead to disapproval.

A third factor which may connect otherwise irrelevant variables with the desegregation decision is that of the ability of individuals or groups which have some authority over the individual to invoke sanctions which have objective consequences for him. Even if a group is not a reference group for a given individual, it may objectively have power over him which it can exert in order to bring him into line with its position. Thus, for a school board member who faces the possibility of prosecution for contempt of court, the desire to avoid the unpleasantness of legal proceedings and a possible fine becomes relevant to the question of whether the community's schools are to be desegregated, and may outweigh his own attitudes and beliefs about segregation. The possibility of such sanctions is not limited to persons whose roles carry responsibility for the decision. For the man who faces loss of his job if he signs a petition urging desegregation, or the lawyer threatened with disbarment if he represents a plaintiff in a desegregation suit, the need to earn a living becomes linked with his position on the desegregation issue. The weight which the variable thus invoked has in the decision is likely to bear a direct relation to the seriousness of the objective consequences for the individual's life. It is important to note that not everybody is equally vulnerable to such sanctions. Some individuals may be relatively immune, perhaps because of support from a subgroup, or because of some unique aspects of their position, such as having an independent income.

I want to mention one last factor which may influence the weight of a given variable in the decision; this is an over-all change in the average strength of the variable wherever its influence is felt. We sometimes think of variables in the sense that they have different strengths for different individuals at a given time, but many of the variables which are likely to enter into the desegregation decision are of interest also in the sense that their average strength may be expected to change over time.

To illustrate, a variable whose strength may be expected to change has to do with one aspect of the social norm toward desegregation. Recently a Columbia, South Carolina, newspaper complained in an editorial of the fact that some of the previously segregated states had gone ahead with plans for desegregation. The writer indicated that this would make it harder for other states to hold out for segregation. As desegregation spreads, the social norms regarding segregation to which the decision-makers of the remaining states respond will become increasingly heterogeneous—some favoring and some opposing a change. One can guess that the effect of this will be to greatly weaken the social support for opposing the Court's decision, which is now one of the major factors at work in the still segregated states.

The last considerations I shall mention in relation to the desegregation decision—and on occasion they may be the most important—are those we traditionally encompass under the heading of personality. Perhaps this is only a crude way of saying that when we have taken into account all of the factors that I have discussed up to now, there will remain striking variations in individual behavior still unaccounted for. When, for example, you consider the actions of a man like Governor Folsom of Alabama, situational determinants of behavior seem suddenly insignificant. Imagine a man—a politician we might say under other circumstances—situated in the very heart of the deep South, refusing to sign the legislature's pro-segregation bills and warning the Alabama Education Association against "the excessive noise being made by those who are guided by blind prejudice and bigotry."[14] Some such quality as that which Ries-

[14] *Southern School News,* September, 1955, Nashville, Tennessee: Southern Education Reporting Service.

man has called inner-directedness—the extent of one's independence from social approval—must be invoked to make sense of the decisions of such a person.

Let me make it clear, finally, that in identifying these various determinants of desegregation decisions and suggesting some ways in which they may operate, I am not implying that such considerations put us in a position to predict and anticipate the decisions about desegregation which are yet to be made. The most I would claim for them is that they organize the available experience sufficiently to tell us where to look for some of the more crucial determinants of such decisions.

*RACIAL AND MORAL CRISIS: THE ROLE OF LITTLE ROCK MINISTERS**

By Ernest Q. Campbell and Thomas F. Pettigrew

This paper analyzes the conduct of the ministers in established denominations in Little Rock, Arkansas, during the crisis over the admission of Negro students to the Central High School in the fall of 1957. How do ministers behave in racial crisis, caught between integrationist and segregationist forces?

One might expect that Little Rock's clergymen would favor school integration. All the major national Protestant bodies have adopted forceful declarations commending the Supreme Court's desegregation decision of 1954 and urging their members to comply with it. And southern pastors have voted in favor of these statements at their church conferences—and sometimes have even issued similar pronouncements to their own congregations.[1] But the southern man of God faces serious congregational opposition if he attempts to express his integrationist beliefs publicly in the local community. The vast majority of southern whites—even those living in the Middle South—are definitely against racial desegregation.[2]

The purpose of this study is to determine how the ministers of established denominations in Little Rock behaved in the conflict. In analyzing their behavior, we treat self-expectations as an independent variable. This is contrary to the usual course, in which the actor is important analytically only because he is caught between contradictory *external* expectations. The standard model of role conflict treats ego as forced to decide between the incompatible norms of groups that can impose sanctions for non-conformity. This model—which is essentially what Lazarsfeld means by cross-pressures—skirts the issue of whether ego imposes expectations on itself and punishes deviations. Pressure and sanction are external to the actor. Hence the typical model tends to be ahistorical in the sense that a finite number of cross-pressuring groups are used to predict the actor's behavior. It is assumed that the actor cannot have developed from periods of prior socialization any normative expectations for his behavior which would have an independent

[1] For example, local ministerial groups issued such statements in New Orleans, Louisiana; Richmond, Virginia; Dallas and Houston, Texas; and Atlanta, Macon, and Columbus, Georgia. For a review of national church statements see "Protestantism Speaks on Justice and Integration," *Christian Century*, February 5, 1958, *75*, pp. 164-166.

[2] A 1956 National Opinion Research Center poll indicated that only one in every seven white southerners approves school integration. H. H. Hyman and P. B. Sheatsley, "Attitudes toward Desegregation," *Scientific American*, December, 1956, *195*, pp. 35-39. A 1956 survey by the American Institute of Public Opinion showed that in the Middle South — including Arkansas — only one in five whites approved of school integration. M. M. Tumin, *Segregation and Desegregation* (New York: Anti-Defamation League of B'nai B'rith, 1957), p. 109.

*Reprinted from *The American Journal of Sociology*, 1959, *64*, pp. 509-516, by permission of the authors and The University of Chicago Press. Copyright 1959 by the University of Chicago. This study was supported by a grant from the Laboratory of Social Relations, Harvard University. The authors wish to express their gratitude to Professor Samuel A. Stouffer for his suggestions. Two brief popular accounts of aspects of this study have appeared previously: "Men of God in Racial Crisis," *Christian Century*, June 4, 1958, *75*, pp. 663-665, and "Vignettes from Little Rock," *Christianity and Crisis*, September 29, 1958, *18*, pp. 128-136.

existence.[3] This additional variable—the actor's expectations of himself—is especially meaningful in the analysis.

Though it is a city of approximately 125,000, Little Rock has much of the atmosphere and easy communication of a small town. It is located in almost the geometric center of the state, and physically and culturally it borders on both the Deep South-like delta country to the east and south and the Mountain South-like hill country to the west and north. Thus Little Rock is not a city of the Deep South. Its public transportation had been successfully integrated in 1956, and its voters, as late as March, 1957, had elected two men to the school board who supported the board's plan for token integration of Central High School. And yet Little Rock is a southern city, with southern traditions of race relations. These patterns became of world-wide interest after Governor Faubus called out the National Guard to prevent desegregation and thereby set off the most publicized and the most critical chain of events in the integration process to date.

Only two ministers devoted their sermons to the impending change on the Sunday before the fateful opening of school in September, 1957. Both warmly approved of the step and hoped for its success. Other ministers alluded to it in prayer or comment. It was commonly believed that a majority of the leading denominations' clergy favored the school board's "gradual" plan. This impression seemed confirmed when immediately after Governor Faubus had surrounded Central High with troops fifteen of the city's most prominent ministers issued a protest in, according to the local *Arkansas Gazette,* "the strongest language permissible to men of God."

When Negro students appeared at the high school for the first time, they were escorted by four white Protestant ministers and a number of prominent Negro leaders. Two of the four whites are local clergymen, one being the president of the biracial ministerial association, the other, president of the local Human Relations Council. Many of the more influential ministers of the city had been asked the night before to join this escort. Some demurred; others said they would try to come. Only two appeared.

On September 23, the day of the rioting near Central High School, several leaders of the ministerial association personally urged immediate counteraction on the mayor and the chief of police. Later, support was solicited from selected ministers in the state to issue a declaration of Christian principle, but dissension over the statement prevented its publication. Indeed, *no* systematic attempts were made by the clergy to appeal to the conscience of the community. Such statements as individual ministers did express were usually—though not always—appeals for "law and order" rather than a Christian defense of the principle of desegregation.

Several weeks after the rioting, plans for a community-wide prayer service began to develop. Care was taken to present this service in as neutral terms as possible. Compromise and reconciliation were stressed: never was it described as organized prayers for integration. And indorsements came from both sides of the controversy—from President Eisenhower and from Governor Faubus. As one of the sponsors put it: "Good Christians can honestly disagree on the question of segregation or integration. But we can all join together in prayers for guidance, that peace may return to our city." The services in the co-operating churches were held on Columbus Day, October 12. All the leading churches participated, with only the working-class sects conspicuously missing. The services varied widely from informal prayers to elaborate programs, and attendances varied widely, too, and totaled perhaps six thousand.

These "prayers for peace" may best be viewed as a ritualistic termination of any attempts by the clergy to direct the course of events in the racial crisis. The prayers had met the national demand for ministerial action and the ministers' own need to act; and they had completed the whole unpleasant business. Despite sporadic efforts by a small number to undertake more effective steps, the ministers lapsed into a general silence that continued throughout the school year.

[3] By showing that the actor may have a predisposition toward either a particularistic or a universalistic "solution" to role conflicts in instances where the particularistic-universalistic dimension is relevant, Stouffer and Toby link the study of personality to that of role obligations in a way rarely done. Samuel A. Stouffer and Jackson Toby, "Role Conflict and Personality," *American Journal of Sociology*, 1951, *61*, pp. 395-406. This study, however, treats the personal predisposition as a determinant of conflict resolution rather than a factor in conflict development. Much the same is true of Gross's analysis. Neal Gross, Ward S. Mason, and A. McEachern, *Explorations in Role Analysis: Studies of the School Superintendency Role* (New York: John Wiley & Sons, Inc., 1958), esp. chaps. 15, 16, and 17.

THE DESIGN

We began our work in Little Rock in the week after the peace prayers. Following a series of background interviews and a careful analysis of ministerial action as recorded in the press, twenty-nine detailed interviews with ministers were held.[4] Twenty-seven of them are Protestants and two are Jewish; the Roman Catholics did not co-operate.

This sample was not selected randomly; the so-called "snowball technique" was used in order to include the most influential church leaders. This involves asking each interviewee to name the members of the Little Rock clergy that he considers to be "the most influential." The first interview was made with an announced leader of the peace prayers, and interviewing was continued with all the men mentioned as influential until no new names were suggested. We added a number of ministers who were not named but who had taken strongly liberal positions during the crisis. Thus our sample is most heavily weighted with the pastors of the larger churches with the greatest prestige and the pastors of smaller churches who had assumed active roles in the conflict. These two groups, we anticipated, would have to contend with the greatest amount of incompatibility in role.

Most of the interviews were held in the church offices. Rapport, which was generally excellent, was partly secured by the authors' identification with southern educational institutions. A detailed summary, as nearly as possible a verbatim account, was placed on Audiograph recording equipment shortly after the completion of each interview. Information in three broad areas was sought, and to this end a series of open-ended questions was developed. A series of questions was aimed at determining whether the respondent was a segregationist or an integrationist. A segregationist here is defined as one who prefers racial barriers as presently constituted; an integrationist is one to whom the removal of legal and artificial barriers to racial contact is morally preferable to the present system.[5]

Each interviewee was asked to give a complete account of what he had done and said in both his parish and in the community at large regarding the racial crisis. If he had not been active or vocal, we probed him for the reason and to learn if he had felt guilty over his failure to state the moral imperatives.

A final set of questions dealt with the pastor's perception of his congregation's reaction to whatever stand he had taken. If pressure had been applied on him by his parishioners, we probed him to learn exactly what pressure had been used and how.

The segregationist. Only five of the twenty-nine clergymen we interviewed were segregationists by our definition. None was avidly so, and, unlike segregationist ministers of the sects, none depended on "chapter-and-verse Scripture" to defend his stand. All men in their late fifties or sixties, they did not think that the crisis was a religious matter. One of them was a supervising administrator in a denominational hierarchy. Although all five were affiliated with prominent denominations, they were not among the leaders of the local ministerial body.

These five men have not been publicly active in defending segregation.[6] Each was opposed to violence, and none showed evidence of internal discomfort or conflict. All five co-operated with the neutrally toned prayers for peace. As one of them commented, "You certainly can't go wrong by praying. Praying can't hurt you on anything."

The inactive integrationist. Inactive integrationists had done enough—or believed they had done enough—to acquaint their congregations with their sympathy with racial tolerance and integration, but during the crucial weeks of the crisis they were generally silent. These, representing as they do all major denominations, varied considerably as to age and size of church served. Included among them were virtually all the ministers of high prestige, many of whom had signed the protest against Governor Faubus at the start of the crisis and later were advocates of the peace prayer services. Some had

[4] Thirteen additional interviews were held with the sect leaders of an openly pro-segregation prayer service. None of these were members of the ministerial association or were in personal contact with any ministers of the established denominations. A detailed report on them will be published.

[5] Using the interview, three judges, the two authors and a graduate assistant, independently rated each respondent as either a segregationist or an integrationist. Agreement between the three raters was complete for twenty-seven of the twenty-nine cases.

[6] Again, this is in contrast to the sect segregationists. One sect minister is president and another is the chaplain of the local Citizen's Council.

spoken out in favor of "law and order" and in criticism of violence. They had not, however, defended the continued attendance of the Negro students in the high school, and they had not challenged their members to defend educational desegregation as a Christian obligation. They were publicly viewed as integrationists only because they had supported "law and order" and had not defended segregation.

Altogether, the inactive integrationists comprise sixteen out of the twenty-nine of our sample. Because it was not a random sample, we cannot draw inferences regarding the division of the total ministerial community or of ministers of established denominations into integrationist and segregationist camps. However, since the sample underrepresents the uninfluential minister who had not been in the public eye during the crisis, we may conclude that a large majority of Little Rock's men of God did not encourage their members to define the issue as religious, nor did they initiate actions or participate in programs aimed at integration.

The active integrationist. Eight of our respondents can be designated as active integrationists because they continued to defend integration in principle and to insist that support of racial integration is nothing less than a Christian imperative. They were, on the whole, young men who have headed their small churches for only a few years. Most were disturbed that the churches of the city were segregated; some have urged their churches to admit Negroes.

Most of the active integrationists had serious difficulty with their members because of their activities, evidence of which was lowered Sunday-morning attendance, requests for transfer, diminished giving, personal snubs and insults, and rumors of sentiment for their dismissal. One had concluded that his usefulness to his congregation had ended and accordingly had requested to be transferred. By the end of 1958, several others had been removed from their pulpits.

One thing all twenty-nine of the sample had in common was a segregationist congregation.[7] Without exception, they believed that the majority of their members were strong opponents of racial integration. The highest estimate given by any integrationist of the proportion of his congregation which supported his views was 40 per cent; the median estimate for segregation was 75 per cent. Only three interviewees thought that a majority of their members would "accept" a strong public defense of integration by their minister.

Personal integrity, alone, would lead the liberal Little Rock minister to defend integration and condemn those who support segregation. However, the minister is obligated to consider the expectations of his church membership, especially inasmuch as the members' reactions bear upon his own effectiveness.

When an individual is responsible to a public, we distinguish three systems as relevant to his behavior: the self-reference system (SRS), the professional reference system (PRS), and the membership reference system (MRS). The SRS consists of the actor's demands, expectations, and images regarding himself. It may be thought of as what the actor would do in the absence of sanctions from external sources. We have already seen that typically the SRS would support racial integration.[8] The PRS consists of several sources mutually related to his occupational role yet independent of his congregation: national and regional church bodies, the local ecclesiastical hierarchy, if any, the local ministerial association, personal contacts and friendships with fellow ministers, and, probably, an image of "my church." Finally, the MRS consists simply of the minister's congregation. We have already seen that it favored segregation or at least ministerial neutrality.

The net effect of three reference systems seems to favor the cause of integration. Were they equal in strength, and were there no contrary forces internal to any of them, this conclusion is obvious. The minister would then feel committed to support the official national policy of his denomination; his knowledge that fellow ministers were similarly committed would support him, and the local hierarchy would encourage him to make this decision and reassure him should his congregation

[7] Our study of a modest sample of church members bore out the ministers' estimates of predominantly pro-segregationist sentiment in their congregations.

[8] Although groups make demands, impose sanctions, and significantly affect the actors' self-expectations and self-sanctions, nevertheless, we treat the self-reference system as an independent variable in role conflict. This system seems especially significant where personal action is contrary to the pressure of known and significant groups.

threaten disaffection. These external influences would reinforce his own values, resulting in forthright action in stating and urging the Christian imperatives. However, internal inconsistencies in the PRS and the SRS restrain what on first examination appears to be an influence toward the defense of integration.

The professional reference system. Two overriding characteristics of the PRS minimize its liberalizing influence. First, most of its components cannot or do not impose sanctions for non-conformity to their expectations. Second, those parts of the PRS that can impose sanctions also impose other demands on the minister, inconsistent with the defense of racial integration before members who, in large part, believe in racial separation and whose beliefs are profoundly emotional.

The inability to impose sanctions. The national and regional associations that serve as the official "voice of the church" are not organized to confer effective rewards or punishments on individual ministers. Especially is this true in the case of failure to espouse national racial policy or to act decisively in the presence of racial tension. This is even more true of the local ministerial association; it does not presume to censure or praise its members. Conversely, the local church hierarchy is an immediate source of sanctions. It has the responsibility of recommending or assigning parishes, and of assisting the pastor in expanding the program of his church.

The probability and the nature of sanctions from fellow ministers among whom one has personal contacts and friends are somewhat more difficult to specify. However, it does not appear likely that he is subject to sanctions if he does not conform to their expectations by liberal behavior on racial matters. Should he indorse and actively support segregationist and violent elements, this would be another matter. If he is silent or guarded, however, it is not likely to subject him to sanction. The active integrationists in Little Rock expressed disappointment at the inaction of their associates while at the same time suggesting possible mitigating circumstances. There is no evidence that personal or professional ties had been damaged.

Among the various components of the PRS, then, only the local ecclesiastica, which does not exist for some, and, to a considerably lesser extent, fellow ministers, are conceivable sources influencing the minister's decision to be silent, restrained, or forthright.

Conflicting expectations and mitigated pressures. The role of the minister as community reformer is not as institutionalized (i.e., it does not have as significant a built-in system of rewards and punishments) as are certain other roles associated with the ministry. The minister is responsible for the over-all conduct of the affairs of the church and is judged successful or unsuccessful according to how they prosper. He must encourage co-operative endeavor, reconciling differences, and bring people together. Vigor and high morale of the membership are reflected in increased financial support and a growing membership, and his fellow ministers and his church superiors are keenly sensitive to these evidences of his effectiveness. His goal, elusive though it may be, is maximum support from all members of an ever growing congregation.

The church hierarchy keeps records. It hears reports and rumors. It does not like to see divided congregations, alienated ministers, reduced membership, or decreased contributions. Responsible as it is for the destiny of the denomination in a given territory, it compares its changing fortunes with those of rival churches. In assigning ministers to parishes, it rewards some with prominent pulpits and punishes others with posts of low prestige or little promise. However exalted the moral virtue the minister expounds, the hierarchy does not wish him to damn his listeners to hell—unless somehow he gets them back in time to attend service next Sunday. Promotions for him are determined far less by the number of times he defends unpopular causes, however virtuous their merit, than by the state of the physical plant and the state of the coffer.

Now it is especially commendable if the minister can defend the cause and state the imperative with such tact or imprint that cleavages are not opened or loyalties alienated. If, however, the moral imperative and church cohesion are mutually incompatible, there is little doubt that the church superiors favor the latter. One administrator told two of his ministers, "It's o.k. to be liberal, boys; just don't stick your neck out." Indeed, ecclesiastical officials advised younger ministers, systematically, to "go slow," reminding them of the possibility of permanent damage to the church through rash action.

Under these circumstances pressure from the national church to take an advanced position on racial matters loses much of its force. The minister is rewarded *only* if his efforts do not endanger the membership of the church: "Don't lose your congregation." Similarly, the prospect of an unfavorable response from his congregation protects him from the (possibly liberal) church hierarchy; he need only point to what happened to Pastor X, who did not heed the rumblings in his congregation. The higher officials, themselves keenly aware of local values and customs, will understand. And his fellow ministers, too, are, after all, in the same boat. They give him sympathy, not censure, if he says, "My hands are tied." An informal rationale develops that reassures the pastor: "These things take time," "You can't change people overnight," "You can't talk to people when they won't listen." There is strong sympathy for the forthright pastor who is in real trouble, but he is looked on as an object lesson. Thus the ministers reinforce each other in inaction, despite their common antipathy to segregation.

The self-reference system. We still must reckon with the demands the minister imposes upon himself. It is obvious that the actor has the power of self-sanction, through guilt. A threatening sense of unworthiness, of inadequacy in God's sight, cannot be taken lightly. Similarly, to grant one's self the biblical commendation "Well done" is a significant reward. We have said that the self is an influence favoring action in support of desegregation. Can the inactive integrationist, then, either avoid or control the sense of guilt?

Our data are not entirely appropriate to the question. Nevertheless, four circumstances—all of which permit of generalization to other cases—appear at least partially to prevent the sense of guilt. These include major characteristics of the ministerial role, several ministerial values and "working propositions," certain techniques for communicating without explicit commitment, and the gratifying reactions of extreme opposition forces.

The role structure. The church, as an institutional structure, sets criteria by which the minister may assess his management of the religious enterprise; it does *not* offer criteria by which to evaluate his stand on controversial issues.[9] This encourages, even compels, the minister to base his self-image, hence his sense of worth or unworth, on his success in managing his church. Thus, if church members do not share his goals, three types of institutionalized responsibilities restrain him in reform.

In the first place, the minister is required to be a cohesive force, to "maintain a fellowship in peace, harmony, and Christian love," rather than to promote dissension. Thus some ministers prayed during the Columbus Day services that members "carry no opinion to the point of disrupting the Christian fellowship."

Second, he is expected to show a progressive increase in the membership of his church. Pro-integration activity, lacking mass support, is likely to drive members to other churches.

Finally, his task is to encourage maximum annual giving and to plan for the improvement and expansion of the plant. It is hardly surprising that several inactive integrationists who were engaged in vital fund-raising campaigns shrank from action that might endanger their success.

Working propositions. The minister makes certain assumptions about his work that reduce the likelihood of guilt when he does not defend moral convictions that his members reject. He is, first, a devotee of education, by which he means the gradual growth and development of spiritual assets—in contrast to his counterpart of an earlier period, who was more likely to believe in sudden change through conversion. He also believes that communication with the sinner must be preserved at all costs ("You can't teach those you can't reach") and for long enough to effect gradual change in attitude and behavior. A crisis, when feelings run high, is not the time to risk alienating those one wishes to change. For example, Pastor X acted decisively but, in so doing, damaged or lost his pastorate: "Look at him; he can't do any good now."

Communication techniques. The minister may avoid committing himself unequivocally.[10] Some use

---

[9] Blizzard does not find a "community reformer" or "social critic" role in the ministry. See Samuel W. Blizzard, "The Minister's Dilemma," *Christian Century,* April 25, 1956, *73,* pp. 508-510.

[10] For a full description and illustration of such techniques as used in Little Rock, see our *Christians in Racial Crisis: A Study of Little Rock's Ministers* (Washington, D.C.: Public Affairs Press, 1959).

"every man a priest" technique, for example, the stating of his own opinion while expressing tolerance for contradictory ones and reminding his listeners that their access to God's truth is equal with his. Others use the "deeper issues" approach; generalities such as the brotherhood of man, brotherly love, humility, and universal justice are discussed without specific reference to the race issue, in the hope that the listener may make the association himself. Still another course is to remind listeners that "God is watching," that the question of race has religious significance and therefore they should "act like Christians." There is also the method of deriding the avowed segregationists without supporting their opposites. The "exaggerated southerner" technique, which may be supplementary to any of the others, involves a heavy southern drawl and, where possible, reference to an aristocratic line of planter descent.

These techniques do not demand belief in integration as a Christian imperative. Further, except for the "every man a priest" technique, they do not commit the speaker to integrationist goals as religious values; the listener may make applications as he chooses. The speaker, on the other hand, can assure himself that the connections are there to be made; he supplies, as it were, a do-it-yourself moral kit.

Reaction of the opposition. The ministerial body in Little Rock, except for pastors to dissident fundamentalist sects, is defined by agitated segregationists as a bunch of "race-mixers" and "nigger-lovers." For example, the charge was made that the peace prayers were intended to "further integration under a hypocritical veneer of prayer" and that the sect pastors sponsored prayers for segregation "to show that not all of the city's ministers believe in mixing the races." Indeed, ministers of major denominations were charged with having "race on the mind" so that they were straying from, even rejecting, the biblical standard to further their un-Christian goals.

The effect of opposition by segregation extremists was to convince certain inactive integrationists that indeed they *had* been courageous and forthright. The minister, having actually appropriated the opposition's evaluation of his behavior, reversing its affective tone found the reassurance he needed that his personal convictions had been adequately and forcefully expressed.

Were the force of the membership reference system not what it is, the professional reference system and the self-reference system would supply support to integration that was not limited to "law and order" appeals and the denunciation of violence. However, since "Don't lose your congregation" is itself a strong professional and personal demand, the force of the PRS is neutralized, and the pressure from the SRS becomes confused and conflicting. Inaction is a typical response to conflicting pressures within both the internal and the external system.

It is not surprising, then, that most Little Rock ministers have been far less active and vocal in the racial crisis than the policies of their national church bodies and their sense of identification with them, as well as their own value systems, would lead one to expect. Rather, what is surprising is that a small number continued to express vigorously the moral imperative as they saw it, in the face of congregational disaffection, threatened reprisal, and the lukewarm support or quiet discouragement of their superiors and peers.

*READINESS AND RESISTANCE TO DESEGREGATION: A SOCIAL PORTRAIT OF THE HARD CORE**

By Melvin M. Tumin

It is a popular notion that the South is a homogeneous unit so far as its attitudes towards desegregation are concerned. But this is wrong on the state level where there are strategic and crucial differences between the so-called seven hard-core states and the other ten states most frequently included in the

*From *Social Forces,* 1958, *36,* pp. 256-263. Used by permission of the author and publisher.

southern region. And it is also wrong *within* any one of these states, hard or soft core, for here, too, there are unmistakable differences in the degree of readiness for or resistance to the social changes implied in the term desegregation. To blur these differences is to make a serious mistake. In doing so, one will lose sight of the available points of vantage and leverage, at which the exertion of the proper forces can either harden or soften, spread or diminish the existing resistances.

What is true between and within southern states also applies to southern individuals. For it seems equally unmistakable that—as Myrdal so elegantly asserted—there are rank orders of resistance, such that any single white may offer no resistance or objection at all to working side by side with a Negro, yet may furiously oppose any attempt to make it customary for a Negro to sit on the same seat on the bus.

There is a continuum, then, of resistance, a social and a personal continuum. More properly this should be put in the plural. Each individual, and each social unit, taken as a collective set of attitudes, can be described as a profile defined by different scores or points on a number of scales, his location on any one of these varying with the situation in which it is proposed that the Negro be treated as an equal.[1]

These general assertions are borne out by our findings in a study recently made in Guilford County, North Carolina. The explicit aim was to discover the qualities and quantities of readiness and resistance to desegregation among a group of some 300 white, male, adult (18 years old) members of the work force in Guilford County. Adequate resources made it possible to draw a random, stratified area-probability sample of the white, male, adult work force of the county, in which the rural and urban populations are proportionately represented.

From the data collected in this study we are able to put together a composite social portrait of type-persons, distinguished from each other by their relative resistance to desegregation, as this is revealed in their answers to a set of questions concerning the desegregation of the public schools. One group of these—the hard core—is called by that name here because it rejects desegregation unequivocally and without apparent reservation, but, more importantly, indicated, at variance with its neighbors, that it is willing to use force if necessary to prevent desegregation. Our report here will shortly focus upon this group, examining in what aspects it resembles and how it differs from other, less intransigent and committed southerners.

Material was secured from these persons by a set of questions, put to them in face-to-face interviews, by a group of graduate students enrolled in the Woodrow Wilson School of Princeton University. Generous support by that school, operating on a grant from the Carnegie Corporation, had made it possible to inventory the literature, work over the leading suggestions and hypotheses in the literature during numerous seminars, conduct preliminary field explorations, and engage in pilot and pretesting of our instruments, both in Princeton and in North Carolina. Similarly generous cooperation from the Institute for Research in Social Science at the University of North Carolina and other persons connected with the University, had made it possible for the students to become quickly and efficiently oriented to the local mores and the strategies of interviewing, so that many of the expectable gaffs were avoided. It is our estimate that rapport was generally high and responses correspondingly frank and informative. Loss through refusal was gratifyingly low.[2]

The interview questions were designed explicitly to test current hypotheses concerning the relationship between readiness for desegregation and a host of sociological background variables such as age, education, income, and residence; and between the former, and a set of other variables, such as educational and occupational mobility, contact with Negroes, and exposure to the mass media.

As measures of readiness for desegregation, we

[1] For an excellent review of the range of factors connected with ethnic attitudes, see J. Harding, B. Kutner, H. Proshansky, and I. Chein, "Prejudice and Ethnic Relations," in G. Lindzey (Ed.), *Handbook of Social Psychology* (Cambridge: Addison-Wesley Publishing Co., Inc., 1954), II, chap. 27.

[2] Specific mention must be made of the invaluable assistance of Professors George E. Simpson, Jr. and John Monroe of the University of North Carolina. At Princeton, Professor Stephen K. Bailey, Director of the Graduate program of the Woodrow Wilson School provided indispensable support, intellectual and material, at every phase of the project. Appreciation is due to Mr. Robert Cutler and Mrs. Leila Mattson for their help. Finally, my colleague, Professor Warren Eason, and my co-workers, the graduate students in the Woodrow Wilson School, have worked closely with me throughout.

constructed five sets of questions, all of which later proved to constitute scales of the Guttman type.

The first set probed for the respondent's image of the Negro, as an inferior, superior, or equal creature with the white, in regard to intelligence, ambition, morality, and responsibility.

The second questioned the ideological fancies of the respondent, in terms of how, *in general* he would, if he could, arrange the relations among Negroes and whites in a set of eight situations (the scale was ultimately reduced to six of these eight), including: neighborhood co-residence, co-dining on a private basis, co-dining in restaurants, school attendance, church attendance, having Negroes for supervisors over whites, riding on buses, and working side by side on an equal status basis.

The third scale asked about the same situations but put the question in terms of how the respondent would *feel* if he found himself in such a situation.

The fourth scale then asked what the respondent *would do* if and when he found himself faced with these facts.

The fifth scale focused specifically on the schools and asked the respondent to approve or disapprove of a series of four proposals offered as ways in which to prevent the desegregation of the schools.

In this study, we will focus primarily on the reponses given to this last set of questions. As put to the respondents, they read:

a) Some people have suggested that the Supreme Court Decision ordering desegregation was wrong and that the States ought to be permitted to decide for themselves on this question. The proposal is to go through the process of getting an amendment to the United States Constitution to take power away from the Supreme Court. How do you feel about this kind of proposal to try to amend the U.S. Constitution?

1. strongly approve
2. approve
3. undecided
4. disapprove
5. strongly disapprove

b) In Texas, the Governor has threatened to withhold State school funds from any school district which desegregates the schools, i.e., which permits Negro children to attend the same schools as white children. How do you feel about withholding State money from school districts here in North Carolina—if and when any of these districts start letting Negro children go to school together with white children?

1. strongly approve
2. approve
3. undecided
4. disapprove
5. strongly disapprove

c) Some people have suggested that if need be, the public schools ought to be closed altogether rather than have Negro and white children go to school together. How do you feel about this?

1. strongly approve
2. approve
3. undecided
4. disapprove
5. strongly disapprove

d) Once in a while you hear it said, too, that if need be, people ought to get together and resist with force any attempts to mix Negro and white children in the same schools. How do you feel about this?

1. strongly approve
2. approve
3. undecided
4. disapprove
5. strongly disapprove

Strong approval, approval, and undecided were classed as the segregationist type of response; disapproval or strong disapproval were classed as desegregationist. On this basis, the percentage segregationist response to these questions is shown in Table 2-1. Scale analysis yielded a coefficient of reproducibility of 95.7. The scale consists of five points ranging from extreme segregationist, defined by the score of IV, to extreme desegregationist, who receives a score of 0. The distribution of the respondents through these scale score types is shown in Table 2-2.

We may now examine the extent to which the different scale score groups are distributed on a number of other characteristics, such as age, education, income, and similar sociological characteristics. For purposes of convenience the scale score IV group, that which approves of all alternatives, will be referred to, variously, as the hard core and the resisters, while the 0 group, those who approve of none of the measures, will be referred to as the desegregators and the ready-ones.

AGE

Table 2-3 shows the age makeup of the different scale score groups. Testing reveals no significant difference in mean ages between any of the groups. The hard core group is the youngest, with a mean

TABLE 2-1

RESPONSES TO QUESTIONS ON SCHOOL DESEGREGATION

Question	*Per cent Giving Prosegregationist Answer*
Amend the Constitution	77.3
Withhold state funds	55.6
Close the public schools	43.5
Use force if necessary	24.8

TABLE 2-2

DISTRIBUTION OF SCALE SCORES, QUESTIONS ON SCHOOLS

Scale Score	*Number*	*Per Cent*
0	50	17.5
I	58	20.3
II	53	18.6
III	71	24.8
IV	54	18.9
Total	286	100.0

TABLE 2-3

AGE, RELIGIOSITY, AND RESIDENCE

Scale Score Group	*Mean Age*	*Frequency of Church Attendance**	*Per Cent Stable Residence*	*Per Cent Rural Residence*
0	41.4	2.9	80.0	22.0
I	41.4	3.0	86.4	33.9
II	42.2	3.1	83.0	41.5
III	43.7	2.9	80.3	32.4
IV	39.8	2.8	83.3	51.9

*For calculating mean attendance, never = 1, less than once a month = 2, less than once a week = 3, once a week or more = 4, daily = 5.

age of almost 40 years, and its adjacent scale score group, the III group, is the oldest, with a mean age of almost 44 years. But even this difference failed to reach the .05 level of significance.

RELIGIOUS AFFILIATION

The total sample, according to religious affiliation, is distributed as shown in Table 2-4.

When we compare our scale score groups for the percentage of various denominations present in each, we find that religious affiliation is thoroughly non-discriminating. None of the groups differs significantly from any other in its percentages of Baptists or of Methodists (the two most numerous). The N's in the other categories are too small to warrant testing of differences.

TABLE 2-4

RELIGIOUS AFFILIATION

Religious Denomination	*Number*	*Per Cent*
Catholic	3	1.0
Jewish	1	.4
Other	3	1.0
None	23	8.0
Baptist	103	35.9
Methodist	79	27.5
Episcopalian	10	3.5
Quaker	3	1.0
Presbyterian	20	7.0
Other Protestant Denom.	39	13.6
No information	3	1.0
Total	287	100.0

RELIGIOSITY

Our data also permitted us to divide our sample according to the frequency of their church attendance. We distinguished between (1) those who never attend, (2) those who attend less than once a month, (3) attend less than once a week, (4) once a week or more, and (5) those who attend daily. We assigned the numbers 1-5 to each of these groups in that order, and calculated mean religiosity rates in that way. The results are seen in Col. 3 of Table 2-3. From these data one sees that the most ready and the most resistant groups are the least religious, averaging less than once-a-week attendance. But the other groups are only slightly more religious, and analysis of differences shows no significant differences between the means of religiosity of any of the groups. Not one of the groups averages as much as once-a-week attendance.

RESIDENCE

Does residence matter? Our sample was divided into four groups: (1) those who have resided in a rural area in the country more than five years, or stable-rurals; (2) those in rural area less than five years, or recent-rurals; (3) those in urban area more than five years, or stable-urbans; and (4) those in urban area less than five years, or recent-urbans.[3]

The results of testing here are not regularly patterned. The groups do not differ at all on their percentages of stable residents, whether urban or rural. And, when we focus on the rural-urban difference alone, we find that the IV group, differs from the 0, I and III groups, but not from the II group, on the per cent rural, with the higher percentages in the hard core group. (See Table 2-3.) The only other difference which is significant is between the 0 group and the II group, with the higher per cent rurals in favor of the latter group. The major drift of these differences is generally in favor of a significantly higher percentage of rural residents in the hard core group.

INCOME

The distribution of income reveals a patterned and regular relationship between income and attitudes toward school desegregation. The higher the income, the more ready for desegregation, without exception. Mean annual incomes for the five scale score groups, starting with the least segregationist and going down to the hard core, are shown in Col. 2 of Table 2-5.

TABLE 2-5
INCOME, OCCUPATION, AND EDUCATION

Scale Score Group	*Mean Annual Income (dollars)*	*Per Cent White Collar*	*Per Cent Professional*	*Years of School Completed*
0	$6,194	71.4	22.4	10.1
I	5,915	64.4	10.2	9.7
II	4,940	64.2	9.4	9.3
III	4,592	58.6	5.7	9.5
IV	3,500	35.8	1.8	8.0

[3] Some of these tests are reported in other articles. See M. M. Tumin, "Exposure to the Mass Media and Readiness for Desegregation," *Public Opinion Quarterly*, 1957, *21*, No. 2; M. M. Tumin and R. Rotberg, "Leaders, the Led and the Law: A Case Study in Social Change," *Public Opinion Quarterly*, 1957, *21*, No. 3; and M. M. Tumin, P. Barton and B. Burrus, "Education, Prejudice and Discrimination: A Study in Readiness for Desegregation," *American Sociological Review*, 1958, *23*, 41-49.

Testing for significance of differences between these means shows that the IV, or hard core, group differs significantly from each of the others; and that the 0, or ready, group differs from the II and III as well as from the IV group. The intervening groups do not differ significantly from each other. It is as though there were a polarization of incomes as well as of attitudes toward desegregation.

OCCUPATION

If we raise the ordinary expectation that occupational distributions will closely correspond to income spreads, we will not be disappointed. We tested for this in two ways. First, we examined the per cent white collar workers in each of the scale score groups. Their distributions are seen in Table 2-5. The significant differences here are again between the IV, or hard core, group and each of the others. None of the other differences reaches significance.

If we narrow the focus somewhat and examine the per cent professionals in each of the groups, the results are also indicated in Table 2-5. It is the most ready group which is set off from all the others here. For it is only between this group and each of the others that the differences in per cent of professionals reach significance, with none of the other differences between the other groups getting to this point.

EDUCATION

As one would expect there is a close correspondence between the educational differences and the differences in income. The mean number of years of school completed for the five groups are shown in Table 2-5. Testing for significance of differences here reveals that the IV group differs significantly again from each of the other groups, and that none of the other differences reaches statistical significance. Here, as in previous findings, the hard-core group is set off from all the others. The same finding is repeated when we test differences between the groups on their percentages of respondents who have nine or more years of school.

FATHER-SON EDUCATIONAL MOBILITY

Another comparison of interest takes mobility of son from father's educational achievements as a possible factor, and compares the variously resistant groups on their percentages of those where the father has *less* than nine years of school and the respondent *nine or more years*. Here we find that the groups do not differ at all. Mobility, then, as measured by difference between fathers and sons on formal education does not seem to be related to differences in attitudes toward segregation. Table 2-6 shows the per cent of each scale score group of respondents who had nine or more years of school but whose fathers had only eight or less.

TABLE 2-6

EDUCATIONAL AND OCCUPATIONAL MOBILITY

Scale Score Groups	*Per Cent Respondents with 9 or More Years of School Whose Fathers Had 8 or Less*	*Per Cent White Collar Respondents Whose Fathers Were Blue Collar Workers*
0	44.0	26.0
I	33.9	23.7
II	39.6	32.1
III	46.5	23.9
IV	35.2	20.4

FATHER-SON OCCUPATIONAL MOBILITY

If we define mobility by differences between the respondents and their fathers on white vs. blue collar work, we find that there are no significant differences between any pair of the groups on their percentages of respondents with white collar jobs whose fathers were manual or blue-collar workers. Table 2-6 shows the percentages on this item.

WHITE-COLLAR WORKERS

As we have seen, a difference appears in the per cent of respondents in each group who themselves work at white collar jobs. This difference occurs between the hard core and the other groups, with the former having a significantly lower percentage of white-collar workers than any of the other groups. (Table 2-5.) It appears, in short, that status more than mobility makes a difference, and serves to set off, as did formal education, the hard core from all the other groups.

EXPOSURE TO THE MASS MEDIA

The groups present an interesting pattern of differences in their respective degrees of exposure to the mass media. Again, the hard core has a significantly lower mean exposure rate than all the other groups. But there is further differentiation, such that the III group differs from the 0 group. All these differences are in the expected direction, namely, the more ready for desegregation, the more exposed to the mass media. Table 2-7 shows the distribution of the groups through the various degrees of exposure to the mass media.

TABLE 2-7

EXPOSURE TO THE MASS MEDIA

Scale Score Groups	*Mean Exposure Rate**
0	2.8
I	2.5
II	2.7
III	2.3
IV	2.1

* Maximum exposure = 4

SUMMARY AND EVALUATION

Here, then, are some fundamental similarities and differences among our various attitude types. If we may ignore certain minor reversals and irregularities, in the interest of drawing together a collective portrait of the hard-core group, as it compares with the other four groups, that summary sketch would read as follows:

The hard core is slightly younger than its neighbors.

It belongs to the same churches in about the same proportions.

It attends church about as frequently.

It is as stable in its residence patterns, but is somewhat more concentrated in the rural areas.

Its earning power is significantly lower than all of its neighbors.

There are many fewer white collar workers in the group, and many fewer professionals, proportionately speaking.

All the other groups have significantly higher averages of number of years of school completed, though the actual differences are not very large.

Similarly, the hard core has a significantly smaller percentage of members who have achieved nine or more years of schooling. In this regard, it stands differentiated from all the other groups.

The hard core is not different from the other groups in the percentage of its members who have gone on in school beyond the grammar school level achieved by their fathers.

In the same vein, members of the hard-core group have moved as frequently as members of the other groups out of the manual-work situations of their fathers into white-collar work of their own.

The mass society, through the agencies of the mass media, does not impinge upon the hard core to nearly the same extent as upon the other groups.

Can we distill any over-all patterns? Several suggest themselves in varying degrees of clarity. The most forceful impression is that of a significant difference between the hard core, those who would use force, from all others, on the basic equipment for improving life chances in this society: education, income, and occupation. In these regards, they seem to be at the bottom of the southern heap. It may very well be this relatively low position in the southern status hierarchy which urges them to such intransigent resistance to any improvement of the status of the Negro. For, clearly, in a moving and changing status system, it is they, the low men on the totem pole, who are most threatened by the surge upward of the Negroes.

Where this polarization of hard core vs. all others is not present, the most frequent other pattern is a graduation of scores, almost always, except for the status-contacts, in the directions which the literature of race relations has taught us to expect. That is, the more of the good things in life, the more in contact with the larger world, the more exposed to the urban metropolis and its impulses toward change, the more ready for desegregation does the southern sample here studied appear to be.

The least well indicated, yet the most suggestive pattern, is that of a split between the most ready group and all the other groups. For instance, those who disapprove of all measures proposed as ways to prevent desegregation seem to be recruited from a qualitatively different level of education, occupation, income, alertness to the news, and the larger world. It is as though there is a cut-off point which must be reached, defined by the averages on the various items characteristic of the ready group, before that kind of readiness, indicated by an unwillingness to go against the law of the larger land, becomes a reality.

If we put these three patterns together, one gets the strong impression of a group of people who are graded into each other in many important social characteristics, and who therefore must be considered the *same* kinds of people, with the important reservation that their positions on the graded continua often are correlated with distinct differences in their attitudes. There is no evidence in our study to indicate that the hard core is a sick and malicious group, nor that the ready ones are substantially free of pathologies which affect the other groups. Rather, the hard core seems to be sufficiently far along toward the lower end of the continua to form a distinct and distinguishable entity. So, too, but not quite so forcibly, the ready ones seem to be sufficiently far along toward the more advantageous ends of the continua to emerge as an entity distinguishable from the rest of the population.

We may think of the ways in which these two extreme groups are set off from the others in terms of different sets of norms and responsibility-reward systems into which they are integrated. The hard core seems to view the emergent and changing social system as one which does not contain enough by way of promised satisfaction in return for adherence to the new norms, and so seems to reject the emergent system in preference for the more traditional form of social organization. The ready group, by contrast, has good reason to see the emergent system as containing promises of even more of the relatively advantaged positions which they have come to enjoy, and hence they seem to welcome, or at least, to refuse to impede, the development of the new system.

We are suggesting, in short, that it is not a difference between mental health and mental sickness; or between integration and anomie. Rather, since there is some degree of option between a traditional and a new system and since the balance of responsibility and reward strikes each group as different, one seeks to retain the old, and the other seeks to institute the new.

Yet the metaphor in which we have put this difference carries in its vocabulary too much of the actors' subjective definitions of the situations. For it seems clear, from the materials on self-perception and self-image, relative to various others, that ordinary measures of subjective definitions do not indicate as much difference in the self-images as one would expect from the sharp differences in attitudes toward the new ideas. By contrast, the *objective* indices of difference in such things as income, occupation, education, and the like, do correspond far more closely with the differences in attitudes.

Could it be, then, that the actors here are responding to the pressures of the system upon them in ways unknown to them consciously and unverbalizable by them, and hence not as easily discoverable from a codification of their views of life as from a straightforward analysis of their positions in the social order?

Could it also be, then, that, if the inequalities in position and life chances between the hard core and the others were to be reduced over time, the differences between their attitudes toward the Negroes and desegregation would be correspondingly reduced, again in ways unknown to and unperceived by them, and perhaps in spite of their verbalizations to the contrary? Some such destratification and equalization seem to be strongly indicated by our findings.

III

SCHOOL AND CAMPUS AS LEARNING ENVIRONMENTS

*PERSONALITY AND SCHOLARSHIP**

By Paul Heist, T. R. McConnell, Frank Matsler and Phoebe Williams

Objective studies of the product of the educational process in America's colleges and universities are relatively few. The report by Learned and Wood of a study of the "academic growth of the baccalaureate mind" is still the most comprehensive assessment of the output of higher education that has been published.[1] Two decades ago they demonstrated amazing differences in achievement among the students attending the various colleges in a single state.

More recent landmarks are the studies by Knapp *et al.*, which showed that a relatively small number of higher institutions in the United States were much more productive of scientists and scholars than the great majority of colleges and universities. The index of institutional productivity devised by Knapp and Greenbaum was the number of students per thousand graduates from 1946 to 1951 who later received either (1) Ph.D. degrees, (2) university fellowships, (3) government fellowships, or (4) private foundation fellowships exceeding $400 per year. Fifty institutions with the highest indices for male graduates and 13 with the highest indices for female graduates were designated as institutions of high productivity.

Knapp and Greenbaum suggested some reasons for the striking differences in educational productivity they discovered. Although they did not disregard the quality of the students attracted to the most productive colleges in attempting to explain the institution's records, they nevertheless put the greater emphasis on the institutions—the faculty, the objectives, and the intellectual atmosphere. In referring specifically to the exceptional productivity of a few small liberal arts colleges, they spoke of their "singular hospitality to intellectual values in

[1] W. S. Learned and B. D. Wood, *The Student and His Knowledge* (Carnegie Foundation for the Advancement of Teaching, New York, 1938).

*From *Science,* 1961, *133,* pp. 362-367. Used by permission of the authors and publisher. The collection and analysis of data discussed in this study were part of a larger project made possible through a grant from the Carnegie Foundation. Drs. John Darley, Elwin Farwell, Harold Webster, and Mr. George Yonge served as consultants for the project and the study.

general" and declared that "the climate of values sustained by the institutions elevated the scholar and intellectual to the position of 'culture hero.' "[2]

While serving as a member of a planning committee for research on diversification of American higher education at the Center for the Study of Higher Education of the University of California, Berkeley, Darley[3] shifted the explanation for differential productivity from the institution to the student when he said: "Without cynicism, one might state that the merit of certain institutions lies less in what they do to students than it does in the students to whom they do it."

Subsequently, a study by Holland[4] lent support to this hypothesis. After comparing certain characteristics of National Merit Scholarship winners and near-winners who attended colleges having "high" and "low" indices of productivity, he concluded that differential institutional productivity is a function of the concentration in certain institutions of exceptionally able students with high scholastic motivation. Holland, in another study, also found that the parents of National Merit Scholarship students who attended colleges which ranked high in productivity placed a high value on "learning how to enjoy life, and developing mind and intellectual abilities," while those whose children went to colleges which ranked lower placed less emphasis on intellectual goals.[5]

In several research projects the Center for the Study of Higher Education has explored the hypothesis that particular colleges and groups or types of institutions are differentially selective, not only with respect to scholastic aptitude but also with respect to attitudes, values, and intellectual dispositions. The study reported here was devised to test the general hypothesis that highly productive institutions, by the criteria of Knapp and Greenbaum, are more attractive than less productive ones to National Merit Scholarship students with high scores on certain personality tests designed to measure attributes closely related to intellectual orientation and intellectual functioning.

[2] R. H. Knapp and J. J. Greenbaum, *The Younger American Scholar* (Chicago: University of Chicago Press, 1953), p. 97.

[3] J. G. Darley, "Diversification in American Higher Education," *Proceedings*, Anniversary Conference National Association of Student Personnel Administrators, 38th Conference, Lawrence, Kansas, 1956, pp. 45-66.

[4] J. L. Holland, "Undergraduate Origins of American Scientists," *Science*, 1957, *126*, pp. 433-437.

[5] J. L. Holland, "Determinants of College Choice," *College and University*, 1959, *35*, No. 1, pp. 11-28.

THE SAMPLE

The population of students of high ability from which the sample for the study was drawn consisted of all the winners and a 10-per cent sample of those who received certificates of merit (the near-winners) from the National Merit Scholarship Corporation in the spring of 1956. The longitudinal investigation of the 1956 sample has been conducted with the cooperation of the staff at the National Merit Scholarship Corporation, and the students in this sample were a part of the larger group used by J. L. Holland.[6] In the latter part of the summer of 1956 the students, 956 in number, were invited to participate in one of the Center's investigations of the development of exceptional students during their college careers. Those who acquiesced were mailed packets containing tests and questionnaires on two occasions, the first immediately prior to college entrance and the second just before completion of the first year in college. Almost 90 per cent (843 of the students who were invited to participate) returned their tests and questionnaires on both occasions.

The students who entered the Massachusetts Institute of Technology and the California Institute of Technology were omitted in the study under consideration. Of the remaining students, 216 males and 52 females enrolled in the highly productive institutions. The distribution of students among those institutions is shown in Table 3-1. The institutions are listed in the order of the Knapp and Greenbaum indices of productivity. It may be noted that about 70 per cent of the 216 male students attended the ten most productive institutions. This enrollment represents about 25 per cent of the more than 600 males in the total group of National Merit Scholarship students under study.

The total sample of 268 men and women entered only 31 institutions. This represents a high concentration of students of exceptional ability in a small number of colleges and universities, a finding which corresponds to the distribution of National Merit Scholarship students reported by Holland.[7]

[6] J. L. Holland, *Science, op. cit.*

[7] J. L. Holland, *Science, op. cit.*

TABLE 3-1

DISTRIBUTION OF MALE AND FEMALE NATIONAL MERIT SCHOLARSHIP STUDENTS AMONG INSTITUTIONS RANKED HIGH IN THE PRODUCTION OF SCIENTISTS AND SCHOLARS

School	NMS students	
	No.	No. per 1000 students
Males		
Swarthmore	10	7
Harvard	64	5
Haverford	5	4
Oberlin	11	4
Reed	4	4
University of Chicago	8	3
Carleton	3	2
Princeton	21	2
Yale	23	2
Wesleyan	4	2
Knox	3	2
Cornell	22	2
Pomona	2	2
Grinnell	2	1
DePauw	3	1
Amherst	4	1
Williams	4	1
Johns Hopkins	4	*
University of the South	1	*
Columbia	4	*
Augustana (Ill.)	1	*
Brooklyn	1	*
Brown	4	*
University of Pennsylvania	3	*
Dartmouth	5	*
Total	216	
Females		
Swarthmore	7	6
Radcliffe	14	5
University of Chicago	5	3
Cornell	7	2
Bryn Mawr	2	1
Vassar	3	*
University of Pennsylvania	1	*
Mt. Holyoke	4	*
Smith	6	*
Grinnell	1	*
Barnard	2	*
Total	52	

*More than 0 but less than 1.

Because the sample comprised both scholarship winners and near-winners, it is important to note the proportions falling into the two subgroups. Of the 268 students, 36.4 per cent of the men and 38.6 per cent of the women had been awarded Certificates of Merit. Of greater concern is the matter of equivalence in ability of the winners and near-winners. Differences in scholastic aptitude between the two groups could invalidate a comparison of the differential characteristics of students in high and low institutions, since 71.8 per cent of the male winners attended the high-productivity institutions in comparison with only 28.2 per cent of the near-winners; for the males in the low-productivity institutions, the corresponding percentages are 38.6 per cent and 61.4 per cent, respectively. The higher percentages of winners in the high-productivity sample may be due in large part to the fact that the scholarships had permitted them a greater choice in the selection of schools.

Since measured aptitude was a criterion in selecting the scholarship winners, the combined mean scores (verbal plus mathematical) of both men and women on the Scholastic Aptitude Test were significantly higher in the case of the winners. However, with the exception of one personality scale—Complexity of Outlook—upon which female winners scored higher than near-winners, the difference in scholastic aptitude was the only significant one. The differences in aptitude between winners and near-winners and the differences in the percentages of winners (or near-winners) attending the high- and the low-productivity institutions produced different mean aptitude scores for the students attending schools in the two groups. Because of this, samples of males and females in the two productivity categories were matched on total Scholastic Aptitude Test scores (verbal and mathematical combined) by drawing students at random from the low-productivity institutions and pairing them with students from the high-productivity institutions. The mean aptitude scores of the four groups are presented in Table 3-2.

TABLE 3-2

MEANS AND STANDARD DEVIATIONS (SD) ON THE TOTAL SCORE (VERBAL AND MATHEMATICAL COMBINED) OF THE SCHOLASTIC APTITUDE TEST FOR MATCHED GROUPS OF MALE AND FEMALE STUDENTS ATTENDING INSTITUTIONS RANKED HIGH AND LOW IN PRODUCTION OF SCIENTISTS AND SCHOLARS

Rank of institution	Males (N = 50)		Females (N = 41)	
	Mean	SD	Mean	SD
High	138.78	5.8	139.2	8.6
Low	138.84	5.7	139.6	8.0

The matching resulted in groups whose mean scores were approximately halfway between the mean aptitude test scores of the total groups of males and females (N = 216 and 52) attending the high-productivity institutions and the total groups in the low-productivity institutions. A greater attenuation of the aptitude scores of male students in the higher ranking institutions suggests that this high-ability group (N = 216) is probably underrepresented in the matched sample, and indeed, proportionally more of the less capable students from the original high-productivity group do fall into this matched subgroup of 50 students.

There were, of course, other variables upon which students could have been matched for greater comparability of the groups. However, matching on more than one variable at a time would have resulted in groups too small for satisfactory comparisons.

AVAILABLE DATA

Included in the first packet of material sent to the students, in the late summer of 1956, were a questionnaire covering biographical, socio–economic and attitudinal items, the Strong Vocational Interest Blank (SVIB), and an Omnibus Personality Inventory (OPI).[8] The latter instrument was assembled particularly for this project and for other studies of students of superior ability. At the end of the spring term of their freshman year, the students were asked to respond to another questionnaire, composed chiefly of attitudinal items, and the Allport-Vernon-Lindzey Study of Values (AVL).[9] Additional biographical data, Scholastic Aptitude Test scores, and some pertinent information from the students' high school records were obtained through the cooperation of the National Merit Scholarship Corporation. The analyses for this report were limited to scores on three objective inventories: the Strong Vocational Interest Blank, the Omnibus Personality Inventory, and the Allport-Vernon-Lindzey Study of Values.

[8] P. Heist and P. A. Williams, unpublished manuscript.

HYPOTHESES

The specific hypotheses concerning differences in characteristics between students in the high- and low-productivity institutions are given in Table 3-3. The content and "direction" of these hypotheses were derived from conclusions and implications in the studies by Knapp *et al.*,[10] some general knowl-

[9] G. W. Allport, P. E. Vernon, and G. Lindzey, *Study of Values: A Scale for Measuring the Dominant Interests in Personality, Manual of Directions* (Rev. ed.; Boston: Houghton Mifflin, 1951).

[10] R. H. Knapp and J. J. Greenbaum, *op. cit.;* R. H. Knapp and H. B. Goodrich, *Origins of American Scientists* (Chicago: University of Chicago Press, 1952).

TABLE 3-3

OMNIBUS PERSONALITY INVENTORY MEANS AND STANDARD DEVIATIONS (IN PARENTHESES) FOR NATIONAL MERIT SCHOLARSHIP MALES AND FEMALES ATTENDING INSTITUTIONS OF HIGH PRODUCTIVITY (HP) AND LOW PRODUCTIVITY (LP)

OPI scale	*Males (N = 50)*			*Females (N = 41)*		
	HP	*LP*	*t*	*HP*	*LP*	*t*
Schizophrenia*	12.14(7.6)	11.66(5.8)		9.73(5.4)	11.59(6.5)	
Hypomania*	16.80(4.8)	17.14(3.7)		14.68(3.2)	16.15(4.3)	
Social Introversion	22.92(8.3)	25.94(9.7)	2.29**	24.85(7.9)	26.93(8.5)	
Thinking Introversion	47.44(7.2)	46.06(7.8)		49.71(5.7)	46.27(8.8)	2.23**
Responsibility	41.64(6.4)	41.62(3.7)		43.71(3.0)	44.40(5.2)	
Complexity of Outlook	15.64(4.1)	13.96(3.3)	2.79***	16.71(3.6)	14.90(3.5)	2.87***
Originality	25.86(4.1)	24.16(4.4)	3.20***	26.20(3.3)	25.68(3.7)	
Authoritarianism (F)	7.24(3.9)	9.02(3.7)	2.12**	5.28(2.7)	7.95(3.7)	3.35***
Ego Strength	22.46(2.7)	21.92(2.8)		23.30(2.6)	21.76(2.6)	2.68***
Authoritarianism (F4)	17.86(4.3)	18.96(7.1)		15.48(3.6)	17.51(4.1)	2.16**
Impulse Expression	19.88(8.2)	18.10(7.4)		17.25(6.0)	18.83(6.7)	

* Scales not corrected by K value. ** $p < .05$. *** $p < .01$.

edge of the institutions in the high-productivity group, and some evidence on the academic adjustment and attainment of the more liberal, free-thinking, and nonauthoritarian student.[11]

1. The students in the high-productivity institutions should have significantly higher scores than those in the low-productivity institutions on the following personality variables, all included as scales in the Omnibus Personality Inventory: Schizophrenia, Hypomania, Thinking Introversion, Originality, Complexity of Outlook, Ego Strength, and Impulse Expression.
2. The students in the high-productivity institutions should have significantly lower mean scores than those in the low-productivity schools on the following Omnibus Personality Inventory scales: Social Introversion, Responsibility, and Authoritarianism (both F and F4).
3. The students in the high-productivity schools should have significantly higher mean scores than those in the low-productivity colleges on the Theoretical and Aesthetic scales of the Allport-Vernon-Lindzey Study of Values and a significantly lower mean score on the Religious scale.
4. There should be significant differences between students in the high- and low-productivity schools in the prevalence of theoretical and applied patterns of responses on the Strong Vocational Interest Blank.[12]

RESULTS

Tables 3-3 and 3-4 present the means on the Omnibus Personality Inventory and AVL Study of Values scales, in addition to values for all scales yielding differences significant at or beyond the .05 level. On the OPI, the male groups in the high- and the low-productivity institutions differed significantly on four scales, and on the AVL there were significant differences for two of the three traits tested. The males in the high-productivity group scored higher on the OPI scales of Complexity of Outlook and of Originality and lower on Social Introversion and Authoritarianism (F). On the AVL, the males in the high-productivity group scored higher on the Theoretical and Aesthetic scales and lower on the Religious scale.

The results for the females on these inventories were in general agreement with those for the males. The females in the high-productivity group also scored higher on the Aesthetic and lower on the Religious scales of the AVL (the difference on the Theoretical scale approached the .05 level). On the personality inventory the differences on the Complexity of Outlook and Authoritarianism (F) scales are again significant, and in the same direction as the results for the men. On a second scale, measuring authoritarianism (F4),[13] the women in the high-productivity group had significantly lower scores than those in the other group. In addition, they scored higher on two other scales—Thinking Introversion and Ego Strength.

In the case of the male groups, the scale variances were homogeneous in all instances. In the case of the females, however, the variances on both the Authoritarianism (F) and the Thinking Introversion scales were significantly different at the .10 level. For the reader unacquainted with personality measurement it should also be added that the differences obtained must be interpreted with a concern both for the amount of the difference and the amount of the overlap of scores in the two distributions. However, where the differences are significant, a majority in one group receive scores quite unlike those of a majority in the second group.

One may conclude that the first two hypotheses are supported by the data for *both* sexes on only the Complexity of Outlook and the Authoritarianism (F) scales. For the males, the hypotheses are supported on the Originality and the Social Introversion scales. For the females, the differences on Thinking Introversion, Ego Strength, and Authoritarianism (F4) are in line with expectations. Except for the Theoretical scale, the third hypothesis is supported for both sexes. In a previous analysis of comparable data for *all* students (that is, before matching on Scholastic Aptitude Test scores), significant differences after matching, with the exception of the differences on Social Introversion.

Weissman's method of analyzing Vocational Inter-

[11] G. G. Stern and A. H. Cope, paper read before the American Psychological Association, Chicago, Sept., 1956; H. E. Titus and E. P. Hollander, "The California F Scale in Psychological Research: 1950-1955," *Psychological Bulletin*, 1957, *54*, pp. 47-64.

[12] M. P. Weissman, unpublished thesis, University of California, 1958.

[13] H. Webster, N. Sanford, and M. Freedman, "A New Instrument for Studying Authoritarianism in Personality," *Journal of Psychology*, 1955, *40*, pp. 73-84.

TABLE 3-4

Allport-Vernon-Lindzey Study of Values Means and Standard Deviations (in Parentheses) for National Merit Scholarship Males and Females Attending Institutions of High Productivity (HP) and Low Productivity (LP)

AVL scale	*Males (N = 50)*			*Females (N = 41)*		
	HP	*LP*	*t*	*HP*	*LP*	*t*
Theoretical	48.66(9.7)	46.12(7.7)	1.71*	45.37(7.4)	43.00(8.4)	
Aesthetic	43.50(11.6)	36.20(9.3)	4.15**	49.98(8.7)	45.85(9.9)	2.50**
Religious	39.74(11.6)	46.14(10.3)	2.22*	42.51(8.5)	48.15(11.14)	2.23*

* $p < .05$. ** $p < .01$.

est Blank scores on a theoretical-applied dimension was validated only for the men's form on a male sample.[14] Nevertheless, in line with the theory that the form for men can be used in counseling females of superior ability who have a strong career orientation,[15] Weissman's technique of profile analysis was also used with the women in this study.[16]

The Vocational Interest Blank profiles of the 100 males and 82 females were subjected to a "blind" analysis—that is, they were read, interpreted, and classified before the respective groupings by high- and low-productivity institutions were known. The assignment to categories in this method of profile analysis, in the great majority of cases, is readily determined by relatively objective criteria; interpretive judgment is infrequently involved. The assignments were made independently by two judges, and the two or three discrepancies resulting from the independent work were resolved through later discussions and agreement between the judges.

The frequencies for males and females in the various categories are presented in Table 3-5. Chi square analysis was employed to test the hypothesis that the obtained distributions of the frequencies in the major categories differed from the distribution to be expected on the basis of chance. The chi square values are 10.04 ($p < .01$) and 8.60 ($p < .02$) for the males and females, respectively. Thus, for both sexes, the number of individuals in the major categories is significantly different from the number expected on the basis of chance, a much larger number of students in the high-productivity groups falling in the A category. For both sexes the distinctive differences are in the A0 and A2 subcategories. For the males, the frequencies in the C category differ considerably, with five times as many individuals in the low- as in the high-productivity group. For the females, the second major difference is

[14] G. G. Stern, *op. cit.;* M. P. Weissman, *op. cit.*

[15] J. G. Darley and T. Hagenah, *Vocational Interest Measurement: Theory and Practice* (Minneapolis: University of Minnesota Press, 1955).

[16] M. P. Weissman, *op. cit.* Weissman devised a method of classification of responses on the Strong Vocational Interest Blank on a theoretical-applied continuum representing intellectual disposition or orientation scores. There are three major categories of disposition, with a number of subcategories under the first two. Included under category A are the profiles representing a theoretical and abstract orientation. The other two categories represent a less theoretical and more applied orientation, B being distinguished from C chiefly on the basis of "more applied dispositions at professional rather than technical levels of responsibility." The system makes it possible to assign each profile of scores to a single category. The names of the categories and brief characterizations are as follows:

A: *Theoretical.* A0, abstract: intellectual curiosity centers on the world of ideas, concepts, and theory, often without tangible subject focus. A2, scientific: intellectual activity involves speculative and creative thought, the spirit of inquiry, and the scientific "method"; intellectualism centers on science and especially scientific research. A3, social: intellectual interests center on social institutions, customs, and behaviors.

B: *Applied-professional.* B1, biological: orientation is to the application of principles in a broad area of independent responsibility; focus is on medical, biological, and natural sciences. B2, technical: orientation is to application and independent responsibility in technical fields. B3, welfare: orientation is to application and independent responsibility in work with people. B4, business: orientation is to application and independent responsibility in business. B5, verbal: orientation is to application and independent responsibility in "verbal" activities, often of a political or economic nature.

C: *Applied-technical.* Orientation is to application but with limited aspirations for responsibility. Interests are in active, outdoor, technical, or mechanical affairs.

found in the B category, which contains almost twice as many individuals of the low- as of the high-productivity group. It is of interest to note the frequencies found in the subcategories under the general A and B classifications; they appear to shed some light on the meaning of these distributions. For example, the combined totals in the A0 and A2 categories for males and females in the high-productivity groups (20 in each case) as compared to similar totals in the low-productivity groups (7 in each case) are striking, especially since no such differences are found in the A3 category for either sex. The seemingly consistent direction of the small differences in the B4 and B5 categories for both sexes should also be noted. Certain other differences appear to be peculiar to one sex or the other and are probably related to differences in the orientation of men and women toward future occupations.

TABLE 3-5

Numbers of National Merit Scholarship Males and Females, Categorized by Profile Analysis of Strong Vocational Interest Blank, Attending Institutions of High Productivity (HP) and Low Productivity (LP)

Category	*Males (N = 50)*		*Females (N = 41)*	
	HP	*LP*	*HP*	*LP*
A: Theoretical				
A0 (abstract)	6	0	11	3
A2 (scientific)	14	7	9	4
A3 (social)	3	3	10	11
Total	23	10	30	18
B: Applied — professional				
B1 (biological science)	5	1	0	4
B2 (technical)	3	12	2	2
B3 (welfare)	8	7	5	9
B4 (business)	4	8	0	5
B5 (verbal)	4	1	4	0
Total	24	29	11	20
C: Applied — technical	2	11	0	0
Reject	1	0	0	3

DISCUSSION

That higher institutions are differentially selective with respect to general scholastic aptitude is well established, but relatively few studies have been made of the distribution of such student attributes as values, attitudes, and personality characteristics among particular institutions or groups of institutions. Holland, as noted above, showed that highly productive colleges drew National Merit Scholarship students with higher average Scholastic Aptitude Test scores than the less productive institutions. Holland has also reported the relationship of scores on the California Psychological Inventory and the choice of an institution of high rank on the Knapp-Goodrich and Knapp-Greenbaum indices of productivity. He concluded that "the choice of a high ranking institution is positively associated with a sense of well-being, psychological-mindedness (sensitivity to others), flexibility, good impression, non-stereotypy, and is negatively associated with socialization (propriety)." [17] However, he reported that most of the relationships were not found in more than one sample and that the correlations were in all cases small—the two highest were .28 for non-stereotypy and .21 for psychological-mindedness. In view of the fact that the students in schools of high and low productivity were matched on Scholastic Aptitude Test scores, this study supplies rather striking evidence of differential selectivity or attraction with respect to a number of personality characteristics. The pattern of differences in these characteristics is summarized below.

In previous research, scores on an instrument such as the Minnesota Multiphasic Personality Inventory (MMPI) have resulted in minimal or no differences among institutional groups. The general picture of mental health and emotional stability appears to be very similar for student bodies in different colleges, and incidentally, quite normal. The results of these multi-institutional high- and low-productivity groups on the MMPI Schizophrenia and Hypomania scales are in line with these previous findings, and the lack of differences on the Impulse Expression scale—a measure of the general readiness to express impulses—may be considered supportive of the same finding. The scores on two other scales—Social Introversion and Ego Strength—both composed of items from the MMPI, also support the picture of mental health in the student bodies of schools of both groups. Though the differences on the Social Introversion scale is significant only for

[17] Holland, *Science, op. cit.*

the males and the Ego Strength scale only for the females, the direction of the differences on both scales is the same for both sexes. It can be inferred from content analysis and validity studies of these scales that there is more innerdirectedness and social independence in individuals from the high-productivity institutions. This seems to be in line with what might be predicted from differences in other characteristics between students in the two kinds of institutions.

The other differences discovered can be viewed as reflecting an orientation favorable to learning and intellectual activity among those selecting high-productivity institutions. For example, whatever the "true" meaning of the Authoritarianism (F) scale —whether it indicates rigidity, conventionality, and so on, or whether (at the other extreme) it largely reflects educational and cultural sophistication or "response set"—the differences obtained, in conjunction with those obtained on the AVL Study of Values Religious scale, which assesses a degree of fundamentalism and dogmatism, make it possible to draw a fairly simple conclusion. The scores of students in the high-productivity institutions indicate more freedom and receptivity to learning, more objectivity, and less conservatism and authoritarianism.

The major components of the pattern of differences referred to as a positive orientation toward learning are further supported by the distributions across the Vocational Interest Blank categories presented in Table 3-5. The high-productivity colleges have a greater number of both males and females in the A, or theoretical, category, and particularly in the subcategories, A0 and A2 (abstract and scientific). These people may be described as possessing intellectual curiosity and a spirit of inquiry, as being concerned with ideas and theory, and as being disposed toward speculative and creative thought. In addition, interesting differences are found in the biological science (B1) category for the males and in the verbal (B5) category for the males and the females, but the number involved and the size of the differences are not sufficient to warrant supportive interpretations of the differences in intellectuality between the two groups.

In contrast, the frequencies in the low-productivity schools are concentrated more in the major applied-technical area (C) and in the technical (B2) and business (B4) subcategories for the males; for the females, almost twice as many individuals from the low- as from the high-productivity group are found in the broad applied-professional (B) category, in which the major differences are in the biological science (B1) and business (B4) subcategories. Thus, there is a greater concentration of students with theoretical and non-technical Vocational Interest Blank patterns in the high-productivity institutions and of students with patterns in the applied, and especially in the technical, areas in the low-productivity schools.

The differences on the Aesthetic scale of the AVL Study of Values are consistent with the differences in the Vocational Interest Blank findings. Work at the Center for the Study of Higher Education has indicated that the Aesthetic scale is more closely related to serious intellectual and scholarly interests than is the Theoretical scale, although a high score on *both* scales is especially indicative of intrinsic intellectual interests, and possibly of a creative disposition.[18] In the study under discussion, more than twice as many individuals of both sexes in the high-productivity institutions as in the low-productivity group are at least one standard deviation above the college-student mean on both of these scales.

Both male and female students in the high-productivity schools had significantly higher scores on the Complexity of Outlook scale. The established correlates of this scale indicate that high scorers may be described as independent, critical, liberal, somewhat unconventional, interested in artistic things, tolerant of ambiguity, receptive to the new and the different, and potentially original and creative. The results on two additional scales supplement this picture. The males in the high-productivity schools score higher on the scale measuring a disposition toward originality, and the females in these schools score higher on the Thinking Introversion scale, which assesses the degree of preference for reflective thought, particularly of an abstract nature. The data round out the picture of intellectuality and potential creativity of the students in the highly productive institutions.

The colleges which are noted for the production of future scientists and scholars start with students

[18] D. W. MacKinnon in "Selection and Educational Differentiation," *Proceedings,* Conference Selection and Educational Differentiation, Berkeley, California, 1960.

who apparently have a considerably greater inclination for the intellectual life. The "output" of these colleges must therefore be seen in relation to the "input." This does not necessarily mean that the merit of such a college is in its students rather than in what it does to them, any more than it implies that the character of the institution is of no consequence. As a matter of fact, Thistlethwaite[19] has shown that the productive colleges have rather special cultural characteristics, and that the climate of the institutions which are especially known for turning out future natural scientists differs in certain ways from that of the ones which are noted for the production of social scientists and humanists. The most likely hypothesis is that the productivity of these schools is the outcome of a fortunate combination of faculty and student expectations, interest, and values. This is one major hypothesis which the Center for the Study of Higher Education is testing in its investigation of student development in some eight institutions, including small liberal arts colleges, a large state college, and a complex state university.

[19] D. L. Thistlethwaite, *Science,* 1959, *130,* 71.

SUMMARY

Two groups of National Merit Scholarship students were selected on the basis of attendance at educational institutions ranked high or low in the production of future scholars and scientists. Four hypotheses pertaining to expected personality differences between matched groups from both sources were explored by means of the following instruments: the Omnibus Personality Inventory, the Strong Vocational Interest Blank, and the Allport-Vernon-Lindzey Study of Values. In general, the hypotheses were firmly supported, and it was concluded that students of high ability attending highly productive institutions have a pattern of traits, values, and attitudes which is more closely related to serious intellectual pursuits than have students of high ability attending less productive institutions.

*DIFFERENCES IN CAMPUS ATMOSPHERE**

By C. Robert Pace

What are the experiences and conditions for student learning and living which a college provides? Whatever they may be, they define the environment, the college culture, the campus atmosphere. To some extent, of course, the character of a college is determined by the character of the students it admits. Other information about a college however is much more commonly available. How large is it, is it coeducational or not, where is it located, when was it founded, what degrees does it offer, is it public or private, religious or non-sectarian, what does it cost? Having learned the answer to all these questions, one knows little that is important about a college. Suppose one asked the same kind of questions about a prospective college student. What is his height and weight, sex, residence, age, vocational goal, religious affiliation, and family income? Knowing all these things, one is still left in ignorance about what kind of a person the prospective student really is. The important knowledge concerns his aptitudes and interests, his motivations, and emotional and social maturity. In short, the crucial knowledge concerns his personality. So too with the college. The crucial knowledge concerns its overall atmosphere or characteristics, the kinds of things that are rewarded, encouraged, emphasized, the style of life which is valued in the community and is most visibly expressed and felt.

The concept of environmental press was described in 1938 by the psychologist, Henry Murray.[1]

[1] H. A. Murray, *Explorations in Personality* (New York: Oxford University Press, 1938).

*Adapted by the author from a paper given at a symposium on "Personality Factors on the College Campus," Nov. 2-4, 1960, sponsored by the Hogg Foundation for Mental Health, University of Texas, Austin, Texas.

Individuals were seen as having characteristic needs, and the strength and relationships of these needs was what characterized the personality. In corollary fashion, the environment was seen as having potentials for satisfying or frustrating these needs. The model for studying behavior was thus the interaction between personality needs and environmental press. In 1956, Stern, Stein, and Bloom[2] elaborated this need-press concept by applying it to assessment studies and showing that the prediction of performance was improved as one defined the psychological demands of the situation in which the performance was to occur. The psychological demands of the situation are the environmental press. In 1957 Pace and Stern[3] constructed the first version of a test, called the College Characteristics Index (CCI), applying the concept of environmental press to the study of college atmospheres. The instrument was constructed as a parallel to the Activities Index (AI),[4] which is an inventory of personality needs that had been previously constructed by Stern. Thus, a pattern of personality needs scales was paralleled by a corresponding pattern of environmental press scales. For example, a personality need for Order would be suggested by liking such activities as: "keeping an accurate record of the money I spend," "arranging my clothes neatly before going to bed," etc. An environmental press for Order would be suggested by such features of the college as: "professors usually take attendance in class," "in many classes students have an assigned seat," etc.

Each instrument, the AI and the CCI, consists of 30 scales of 10 items, or a total of 300 items. In answering the CCI, students act as reporters, saying what they believe is generally true or not true of their college. The items refer to a wide range of topics—rules and regulations, facilities, student-faculty relationships, classroom methods, extra-curricular activities, etc. The argument is that all these characteristics and events and practices, added together, constitute an educational press upon the students. The aggregate awareness of students about their college environment constitutes a press in the sense of exerting a directive influence on their behavior. Preliminary results were reported by Pace and Stern[5] in 1958.

Over the past four years, groups of students in approximately 100 different colleges have filled out the CCI.[6] In the Spring of 1959 a norm group of 32 colleges, representing a wide assortment of sizes and locations and shapes, was selected to develop standard scores for the scales. Much is now known about college environments from this testing activity and from various studies that have been made of the data. Some of the major results are described below.

Some things are true about all colleges. Students everywhere agree that certain things are true about their college. By agree is meant that at least 4 out of 5 students across the total norm group of 32 colleges, and at least 3 out of 4 in each sub-category of the norm group (private liberal arts, denominational liberal arts, universities, education, engineering, and business) describe press identically.

Thus, it is generally reported as true everywhere that—

There are many opportunities for students to get together in extra-curricular activities.

There is a lot of excitement and restlessness just before holidays.

Student papers and reports must be neat.

Classrooms are kept clean and tidy.

Most courses are very well organized and progress systematically from week to week.

Most of the professors are dedicated scholars in their fields.

Similarly, it is generally reported as false everywhere that—

If a student wants help he usually has to answer a lot of embarrassing questions.

Students don't argue with the professors; they just admit that they are wrong.

When students dislike a faculty member they make it evident to him.

[2] G. G. Stern, M. I. Stein, and B. S. Bloom, *Methods in Personality Assessment* (Glencoe, Ill.: The Free Press, 1956).

[3] C. R. Pace, and G. G. Stern, *College Characteristics Index, Form 457* (Syracuse, N. Y.: Syracuse University, Psychological Research Center, 1957).

[4] G. G. Stern, *Activities Index, Form 156* (Syracuse, N. Y.: Syracuse University, Psychological Research Center, 1956).

[5] C. R. Pace, and G. G. Stern, "An Approach to the Measurement of Psychological Characteristics of College Environments," *Journal of Educational Psychology*, 1958, *49*, pp. 269-277.

[6] Support for parts of this research program has come from the College Entrance Examination Board, the Carnegie Corporation, the Social Science Research Council, and the Cooperative Research Branch of the U.S. Office of Education.

Students pay little attention to rules and regulations.
The student leaders here have lots of special privileges.
There are practically no student organizations actively involved in campus or community reforms.
Spontaneous student rallies and demonstrations occur frequently.
The campus and buildings always look a little unkempt.
"Alma mater" seems to be more important than "subject matter" at this school.
Students who work hard for high grades are likely to be regarded as odd.

In short, one might say that college campuses and classrooms are generally well manicured, the students are not especially belligerent or demonstrative but neither are they uninterested in reforms, faculty members are scholarly, and there is no stigma attached to hard work and honest inquiry.

Beyond these few common characteristics, however, colleges are vastly different from one another. By comparing the rank order of mean scores on the 30 scales one gets a general index of the degree of similarity between one environment and another. For the 32 institutions these rank order correlations ranged from +.93 to −.87.[7] Among some colleges the relative environmental pressures are nearly identical; among others the relative pressures are almost totally opposite. Between Swarthmore and Hamline, for example, there were 70 items characteristic of both schools, with characteristic being defined as agreement by 3 out of 4 students, or more. Sixteen items, however, were answered in exactly the opposite ways at the two schools, meaning that more than 3 out of 4 students at one school said "yes" and more than 3 out of 4 students at the other school said "no." Here are some of these opposite characteristics:

Most courses require a lot of library work.
The professors really push the students' capacities to the limit.
Concerts and art exhibits always draw big crowds of students.
Students address faculty members as professor or doctor.
Professors usually take attendance in class.
There is a recognized group of student leaders.
Pep rallies, parades, dances, carnivals, or demonstrations occur very rarely.
Education here tends to make students more realistic and practical.

Moreover, the familiar structural classifications of schools—as liberal arts or professional, college or university, non-sectarian or denominational—are not very good indicators of environmental press similarity. Among schools in any one of these structural categories the rank order correlation of the press scales range from high to zero and sometimes negative.

The differences between college environments, across a wide assortment of schools, fall into several fairly clear patterns. There are certain kinds of pressures or characteristics which tend to go together in college environments generally. Five such clusters were recently described.[8] The first two are both strongly intellectual, with one more strongly oriented toward humanism, sentience, and reflectiveness, and the other more strongly oriented toward scientism, uncertainty, and competition. The third cluster emphasizes the practical and applied rather than the abstract or theoretical, and is heavily concerned with establishing status in relation to peers and accepting status in relation to authority. The fourth cluster exhibits a strong press toward group welfare, human relations, and social responsibility. And the fifth cluster suggests a rebellion against the well managed, group welfare oriented community.

These clusters form a pattern of interrelationships. The humanistic and scientific clusters are positively related, owing to their common intellectual component, and both are negatively related to the practical, status-oriented cluster. The humanistic cluster, however, is unrelated to either the social welfare or the rebellion clusters. The scientific cluster, on the other hand, is negatively related to social welfare and positively related to rebellion. The practical, status-oriented cluster has a positive but low relationship to social welfare, and a somewhat higher positive relationship to rebellion.

This same pattern which is true nationally is also true within the environments of individual colleges.

[7] C. R. Pace, "Five College Environments," *College Board Review*, 1960, *41*, pp. 24-28.

[8] *Ibid.*

The profiles of Vassar and Antioch illustrate this point. (See Figure 3-1.) These profiles show the complete range of standard score means for all of the scales included in each cluster. In both colleges the intellectual-humanistic-scientific clusters emerge as the strongest emphasis in the environment, with the practical, status-oriented cluster being correspondingly low. At Vassar the rebellion emphasis is about average. At Antioch the social welfare emphasis is about average. Rebellion is somewhat higher at Antioch and social welfare is somewhat lower at Vassar. Comparing the two schools, one finds Antioch having the stronger scientific press, and also being higher in rebellion and in social welfare.

Syracuse, as its profile shows, emerges as a high practical, status-oriented environment, with correspondingly lower press toward humanism and scientism. It is average in its emphasis on social welfare, and high on the rebellion cluster. Some schools have a relatively flat profile, as seen in the example of San Jose State College. Its strongest press is in the practical, status-oriented direction, but it is neither very high nor very low on any of the press clusters.

For the most part, as the examples indicate, the variables fall into distinctive patterns within individual colleges. There is a dominant character which emerges.

Distinctive patterns of college environments have predictable and demonstrable consequences. A number of validity studies have been made which lend support to this statement. For many of the colleges that have been studied, a variety of additional data from educational directories and other sources has been correlated with the environmental press data. For example, the intellectuality of the college environments, as measured, should have a positive relationship with intellectually motivated behavior of students and with other features of a college commonly supposed to contribute to the intellectuality of the college. The per cent of students who go on to graduate school would be an example of intellectually motivated behavior; the adequacy of li-

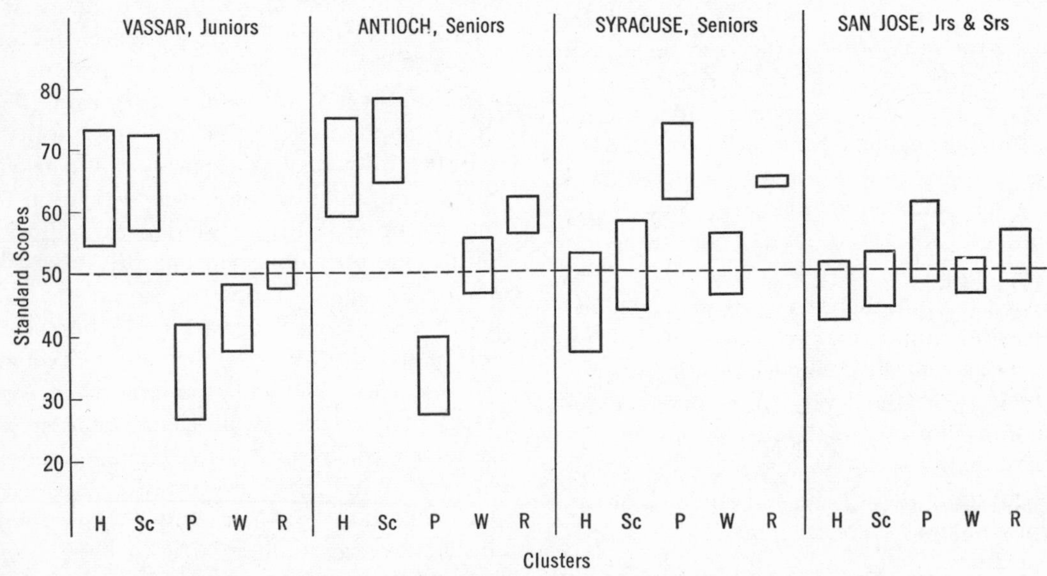

H = Humanistic (Humanism, Reflectiveness, Sentience, Understanding, Achievement, Energy, Objectivity)
Sc = Scientific (Scientism, Change, Fantasied Achievement, Low Supervision, Low Order)
P = Practical (Practicality, Abasement, Dominance, Play, Sex)
W = Welfare (Affiliation, Nurturance, Succorance, Conjunctivity)
R = Rebellion (Aggression, Impulsion)

The standard score scale has a mean of 50, and a sigma of 20. The bars in the chart show the range of mean standard scores for the variables included in each cluster.

Figure 3-1. Four college profiles on the CCI

TABLE 3-6

Correlations between CCI Data and Other Information about Colleges

Number of Colleges	Other Information or Variables	CCI clusters: Intellectual-Humanistic	CCI clusters: Intellectual-Scientific
10	Per cent men who go to graduate school	.80	.79
10	Per cent women who go to graduate school	.84	.93
33	Productivity index AHSS (See note below)	.47	
33	Productivity index NS (See note below)		.25
17	Attainment index (See note below)	.48	*
11	SAT verbal score of applicants	.89	
12	SAT math score of applicants		.50
36	National Merit Scholarship Corporation test score of students	.55	.49
41	Ratio library volumes to enrollment	.61	.66
41	Ratio library periodicals to enrollment	.51	.51
41	Ratio money spent on library to enrollment	.51	.59
15	Per cent Ph.D.s on total faculty	.53	.59
38	Per cent Ph.D.s on full time faculty	.33	*
17	Honors program	*	.45
17	Per cent seniors in Liberal Arts	.62	*
36	Per cent majoring in "intellectual" subjects	.31	.38
		Practical-Status	
17	Per cent seniors in applied fields	.36	
8	Per cent students from same state	.63	
17	Having fraternities or sororities	C† .52	
50	State supported	C .40	
		Group Welfare	
17	Index of student involvement (See note below)	.48	
17	Per cent full-time students	*	
39	Per cent full-time faculty	*	
16	Per cent faculty in American Association of University Professors	.73	
13	Per cent alumni contributing to alumni fund	*	
50	Church-related	C .39	
		Specific CCI scales	
50	Church-related	Abastement	*
50	Church-related	Closeness of Supervision	C .33
50	Church-related	Deference	C .32
50	Church-related	Order	C .31
50	Church-related	Nuturance	C .55
50	Church-related	Succorance	C .40

* Not significant.

† *C* designates contingency coefficient.

Note: Productivity index "Arts, Humanities, and Social Sciences" and "Natural Sciences." For a description of these, see D. L. Thistlethwaite, "College Environments and the Development of Talent," *Science*, 1959, *130*, pp. 71-76.

Attainment index and Index of Student Involvement. For a description of these see Natalie Rogoff, *College Board Members: A Comparative Analysis* (New York: Bureau of Applied Social Research, Columbia University, 1957).

brary resources would be an example of a condition or feature which presumably contributes to intellectuality. Similar logical or expected relationships with other patterns or clusters of environmental press were also studied. The results of these correlational studies are shown in Table 3-6.[9] The correlations are Pearson r's except when labeled otherwise. For the CCI clusters, the mean of the scales comprising the cluster was used to characterize the college.

The table shows 28 correlations with the intellectual-humanistic and the intellectual-scientific press of the environment. Twenty-four of these are significant in the expected direction. Four other correlations are with the practical-status press of the environment. All are significant. Six relationships are reported with the group welfare press. Three of the six are significant. Six relationships are shown between specific CCI scales and the religious orientation of the college. Five of the six are significant. In other words, many features or conditions or types of behavior which one would expect to find associated with different patterns of environmental press are, in fact, associated with them.

The best evidence that different environments have a differential influence on the behavior of students comes from studies made by Thistlethwaite[10] at the National Merit Scholarship Corporation. In a 1959 study, he reported as follows:

> One type of college environment is associated with achievement in the natural sciences, while a different kind of environment is related to accomplishment in the arts, humanities, and social sciences. Productivity in the humanities is positively related to Humanism, Reflectiveness, Sentience, Harm-avoidance, and Understanding. It is negatively related to Pragmatism, Deference, and Abasement. Productivity in the natural sciences is positively related to Scientism, Aggression, and Impulsion, and negatively related to Order, Deference, and Sentience.

He went on to point out that there was some ambiguity in these results owing to the fact that most of the CCI scales contained items which referred to students as well as to faculty or other non-student aspects of the environment. He proceeded, therefore, to revise the scales into two categories, one referring only to the student press, and the other referring only to the faculty press. With these revised scales he found that

> . . . student cultures characterized by Humanism, Breadth of Interest, and Reflectiveness are associated with scholarly productivity (humanistic), whereas cultures characterized by Participation and Aggression are negatively related. . . . Motivation to seek the Ph.D. in the natural sciences, on the other hand, seems to be stimulated by student cultures which are high in Scientism and Aggression and inhibited by those which stress Social Conformity.

Then, considering only the faculty press scales, he found that ". . . colleges outstandingly successful in encouraging undergraduates to get the doctorate in humanistic fields are characterized by excellent social science faculty and resources, a flexible, or somewhat unstructured curriculum, energy and controversiality of instruction, and informality and warmth of student-faculty contacts . . ."

Colleges high in natural science productivity are characterized, also, by informality and warmth of student-faculty contacts, but, beyond this, they are characterized by relatively non-directive or non-predictable teaching methods and the lack of close supervision. In a study in 1960[11] he predicted that motivation to seek graduate education would be associated with certain characteristics of faculty and student press in the undergraduate college environment. He found that all his predictions about faculty press were confirmed, but that there was no evidence that student press influenced the aspirations of the National Merit students he studied. It seems quite clear from these studies that different college environments do have demonstrable consequences on student behavior, over and above the student culture which is part of the total college culture.

To the question, "Do students make the college?," the answer is both yes and no. There are results from the AI and CCI, administered to students in 43 colleges, which show clearly that students with strong needs in certain directions tend to be found at colleges which exert a strong press in those same directions. The public image which a college has makes it especially attractive to students who sense

[9] The correlation data were assembled by Sheila Best as part of a masters thesis at Syracuse University.

[10] D. L. Thistlethwaite, "College Press and Student Achievement," *Journal of Educational Psychology*, 1959, *50*, pp. 183-191.

[11] D. L. Thistlethwaite, "College Press and Changes in Study Plans of Talented Students," *Journal of Educational Psychology*, 1960, *51*, pp. 222-234.

that they would find such an environment congenial to them.

A correlation matrix was developed, based on the mean AI scores, and the mean CCI scores, for this group of 43 schools.[12] This shows the extent to which students with certain kinds of needs are found in institutions with corresponding kinds of press. For three selected and most important scales in the humanistic press cluster—humanism, reflectiveness, and sentience—the median correlation with the three corresponding personality needs scales is .55. For the three most important scales in the science cluster—scientism, change, and negative order—the correlation with the corresponding three personality needs scales is .54. For the three most diagnostic scales in the practical-status cluster—practicality, dominance, and play—the correlation with the three corresponding personality needs scales is .23. For the four scales in the social welfare cluster, the correlation with the parallel personality scales is .60. And for the two scales in the rebellion cluster, the correlation with the parallel personality scales is .54. The median correlation between all thirty parallel need-press scales is .35. For the special scales noted above, it appears that the similarity between student bodies and college environments is indicated by a correlation of about .55. Translating this relationship into other statistical language, and projecting its meaning onto a broader plane, one might suggest that about 30 per cent of the distinctive environment of a school is accounted for by the distinctive character of the students it admits. This leaves much of the potential impact of a college squarely up to the decisions of its faculty, administration, and trustees. Environmental press is clearly more than the student culture alone.

Summarizing, and turning to implications, one can say that it now seems possible and certainly fruitful to think about the college environment as a whole. Many apparently disparate pieces of the environment fit together in a pattern of relationships, and these pieces cut across the familiar parts into which environments have usually been divided. Across the national scene the patterns of college culture illustrate the diversity of higher education. With variations in emphasis, the same patterns are revealed in the environments of individual colleges and illustrate the uniqueness of certain institutions. There are predictable and demonstrable consequences which follow from different major patterns of emphasis in college environments. These consequences cannot be fully explained by the selective distribution of students to environments which are already congruent with their needs. Nor can they be explained fully by the influence of student characteristics or student life within the total culture of the college.

The most important implication for evaluation studies lies in the new awareness of relationship between many different parts of the college environment. Whether a college class is taught by lectures or by discussions, whether the class size is large or small, whether the professor is permissive or strict, whether counseling is directive or non-directive, whether teaching machines or audio-visual aids are used liberally or not at all, whether general education courses are required or are selected from alternative offerings, all these, and many others, are relatively small phenomena in the total college culture. They are separately important, of course. But their real significance, and the clue to their influence, lies in the relationships between them. Do they "add up" to some dominant direction? Or is their possible influence dissipated through isolation and lack of reinforcement from the rest of the college environment? To the extent that a college environment is an unrelated assortment of policies and practices and events and features, its influence upon the student is probably small. To the extent that a college environment is a culture, in the anthropologist's sense of that word, its influence on the student is probably large.

[12] This matrix was prepared by George Stern, as part of an Office of Education sponsored research project, directed jointly by Pace and Stern.

THE EFFECTS OF SITUATIONAL FACTORS ON PERSONAL INTERACTION BETWEEN FOREIGN STUDENTS AND AMERICANS*

By Claire Selltiz, Anna Lee Hopson and Stuart W. Cook

The research being described here is part of a larger study concerned with the influence of personal interaction between foreign students and Americans on the foreign students' attitudes toward various aspects of the United States and its people.[1] This larger study fits into the general context of research on the relation between intergroup contact and attitude change. Within the last two or three decades there have been a number of studies of the effects of association between individuals from different ethnic groups. In spite of considerable diversity of results, a few findings do seem to be emerging as fairly well substantiated. It appears that, when members of different ethnic groups find themselves together in situations which offer opportunity to get to know each other as individuals, where they have equal status, where the individuals of the two groups have common interests and are similar in characteristics such as age or occupation, where the social norms are favorable to association between the two groups, and where the circumstances of the situation favor cooperation or at least do not introduce competition or conflict—given these conditions, it appears that personal association with members of an ethnic group other than one's own leads to favorable changes in attitudes toward that group.

But these findings stem primarily from studies within the United States, in which the individuals in contact were natives, or at any rate permanent residents, of the country. The question presents itself: Would association between citizens of different countries, under similar conditions, also lead to favorable attitude change? There are evident similarities between contact between members of different ethnic groups within a single country and contact between individuals from different countries. There are, however, important differences which must be taken into account in considering to what extent the findings from the one type of personal association may hold for the other.

INTERGROUP RELATIONS AND CROSS-CULTURAL CONTACT

One difference between the two types of situation is likely to be the extent to which individuals have well-structured preconceptions of the group with whose members they are entering into contact. In situations of intergroup contact which have been studied within the United States, members of at least one of the groups generally enter the situation with fairly well structured negative stereotypes about the other group. Typically, these stereotypes are not accurate representations of the group; thus individuals of that group in the contact situation do not conform to them. Further, individuals of the two groups, being products of the same culture, are alike in many ways. They speak a common language; they are likely to have similar values and similar ways of looking at things. Once they enter into communication, it is usually not difficult for them to understand each other. This combination of circumstances leads to a state of affairs in which contact provides an opportunity for observation of individual behavior which does not conform to previously-held negative stereotypes and which may lead to the perception that these individuals are more similar to oneself than one had supposed.

This combination of variables may also occur in cross-cultural contact, but it may not. It may happen that neither party comes with any clear initial stereotypes, or they may come with favorable preconceptions. They may not be sufficiently fluent in a common language to be able to handle all the kinds of topics about which they might want to communicate. Even if language itself does not pre-

[1] With the assistance of Ruby Weinberg and Agnes Niyekawa.

*From *Journal of Social Issues*, 1956, *12*, No. 1, pp. 33-34. Slightly abridged. Used by permission of the authors and publisher.

sent a barrier, differences in frames of reference and in values may mean that one does not really understand what the other is trying to communicate. An individual may be more struck by the differences in behavior and points of view than by similarities. Association under such circumstances might favor the building up of negative stereotypes—just the reverse of what is found to take place in the course of intergroup contact within the United States.

Another important difference between cross-cultural contact and intergroup contact within a country has to do with the influence of the broader context of which the personal interaction is only one element. Within the United States, investigators of the effects of intergroup contact have been able to concentrate on a limited situation—for example, one in which Negroes and whites work together, or live together as neighbors—with relatively little attention to the other contemporaneous experiences of members of either group. The general cultural setting can be assumed to be well known to both groups, and roughly constant for all individuals in the situation; the only major new experience which is a likely determinant of change in ethnic attitudes is the specific experience of personal association. But this is typically not the case for at least one party to cross-cultural contact—the individual who is in a strange country. For him, personal associations are but one part of a total new experience. He is eating new food, reading unfamiliar newspapers, speaking a more or less strange language, observing different ways of doing things, having innumerable casual encounters with storekeepers, taxi drivers, policemen. These other aspects of his experience may influence his attitudes at least as much as do his more intimate personal associations.

There are differences, too, in the range of relevant objects of attitudes. Within the United States, most studies have been concerned with attitudes toward Negroes. Typically, the items which are used to measure attitudes refer to beliefs about characteristics of Negroes as individuals ("Negroes are lazy," etc.), feelings about Negroes, opinions as to whether or not they should be segregated. Even when these beliefs, feelings, etc., refer to Negroes as a group, the reference is essentially to a collection of individuals. Within the United States, there is no distinctive "Negro culture," or "Negro political institutions," nor any official actions of "Negrodom." But in the case of cross-cultural and cross-national contact, the objects of attitudes may range from individuals to foreign policy. Thus the question of the extent of generalization of favorable attitudes developed in the course of interpersonal association becomes even more salient.

These differences between intergroup contact within a country and cross-cultural contact present a challenging opportunity to investigate the dynamics by which personal association leads to attitude change. By making possible investigation of the effects of personal association under conditions different from those in which they have usually been studied, they present the possibility of sharpening statements about the effects of varying conditions on the attitudinal outcomes of personal contact. And, of course, the more that is known about the effects of different conditions, the more possible it is to make inferences about the process of attitude change.

But in studying the relationship between personal interaction and attitude change, one must contend with a familiar problem of interpretation. Suppose we find an association between some aspect of interaction and some aspect of attitude change; which is cause and which effect? To disentangle the causal factors, it is necessary to demonstrate both that the interaction precedes the attitude change in time and that differences in interaction are not due to differences in individual inclination. This requirement, which offers little trouble in the laboratory, is quite difficult to satisfy in a study done under field conditions.

DESIGN OF THE STUDY

The first part of the study—that reported here—was designed to get evidence on these points. Since it was impossible to take a group of students and assign them randomly to situations which would encourage or discourage interaction, we chose settings which we believed might differ in the opportunities they offered foreign students for association with Americans, and compared students in those different settings in terms of the amount and kind of interaction they had with Americans. We made the assumption—subject, of course, to checking within the study—that the reasons for which a student finds himself in one or another of these environments do not include expectations of or predispositions toward association with Americans. We predicted certain differences in extent and nature of interaction solely on the basis of an analysis of the characteristics of the settings. Verification of these predictions may be taken as support for the conclusion that such differences in interaction are not contingent upon attitudinal differences—provided, of course, that our assumption that students are not in these different environments by reason of different attitudinal predispositions is supported. Under these conditions, we may argue that the difference in interaction is environmentally determined, and precedes rather than follows such attitude change as may occur among our subjects.

Although this first part of the study is necessary to meet the logical requirements for testing hypotheses about the relationship between personal interaction and attitude change, it has considerable interest in its own right, as an investigation of the influences that lead to greater or less interpersonal association between members of one social group and those of another.

As the settings for the study, we chose three types of educational institution: small colleges in small towns, large universities in large cities, and large universities in small towns. Foreign students come from a wide variety of cultures—some with customs quite similar to those of the United States, some very different. Some students speak English fluently, others can barely understand and make themselves understood. Some arrive with more favorable feelings toward the United States than others. Some are assured and gregarious, others are hesitant or put a high value on privacy and self-sufficiency. Given all these differences among the students themselves, are the differences among college communities within the United States sufficiently great to lead to systematic differences in the extent and nature of foreign students' associations with Americans?

Suppose a foreign student attends a small college in a small town. Typically, in this setting there will be few other foreigners—whether students, faculty members, or residents of the town. The foreign student is likely to be quartered with American students; he may from time to time be invited into the homes of townspeople. In other words, we would expect that a foreign student in a small college in a small town would, through no choice of his own, find himself often in the company of Americans. We would expect further that in these contact situations a considerable amount of interaction with Americans would develop and that this might go beyond impersonal and superficial interchange to interaction of a more intimate quality.

By contrast, the foreign student attending a large university in a city of several million people is likely to be exposed to quite different influences. Typically, there will be many other foreign students. The university dormitories—if there are any—will usually accommodate only a small fraction of the student body. He may live in an international house where the majority of residents are foreign students, or in a neighborhood where there are many people from his home country. Under such circumstances we might expect the student in the metropolitan university to be drawn much less frequently into contact situations and hence to be likely to experience less interaction with Americans, particularly interaction of a more personal nature.

The large university in a small town presents an intermediate case. Such a setting shares some of the characteristics of the small-college-small-town setting and some of those of the large-university-large-city setting.

Let us put all this in somewhat more theoretical terms.

Take the case of a hypothetical student from India. During the course of a day, he is likely to find himself in a number of situations where there are Americans with whom he may interact. He may, for example, stop at the corner store to buy a newspaper; he is likely to be in classes where there are many Americans; he may eat dinner with three or four Americans. We shall refer to these as *contact situations.* The examples of contact situations which we have given obviously differ in the extent to which they encourage interaction; buying a newspaper does not typically involve extended personal interaction, while eating together usually does. We shall refer to this characteristic of contact situations as their *interaction-potential.*

We need, of course, to distinguish between the fact of being in a contact situation with a given interaction-potential, and the actual occurrence of *interaction.* In any given situation, interaction may or may not take place; in class, for instance, the Indian student may talk to the American next to him, or he may not. The *amount or frequency* of such interaction will vary, of course, from student to student. Also, its *quality* will vary along several dimensions, such as that of intimacy; the Indian student may talk with Americans about something impersonal like his studies or he may discuss with them intimate features of his personal life. There will be variation along other qualitative dimensions—the friendliness or hostility in the interaction, its cooperative or competitive nature, etc.

We must also consider variables which describe the student himself. It is clear that what happens to him will depend, in part, upon what he is like when he comes to this country. His initial feelings about Americans, for example, may be one of the determinants of his relationships with them while here.

Finally, we must also remember the characteristics of the *objects* of the attitudes in which we are interested, namely, Americans and various American practices. While we shall not be dealing with variables of this type in this report, they are obviously of great importance.

We predicted that foreign students in small colleges in small towns would be most likely to find themselves in contact situations with high interaction-potential, and that those in metropolitan universities would be least likely to be in such situations. In turn, we predicted that students in situations with higher interaction-potential would engage in more frequent and more intimate interaction with Americans. Verification of these predictions would be taken as evidence that interaction is influenced by situational factors and is not dependent upon attitudinal or volitional sets on the part of foreign students. Again, of course, such a conclusion would depend on demonstration that a student's being in a situation with high or low interaction potential was not a function of a favorable or unfavorable predisposition toward Americans.

We took several steps designed to insure approximate comparability among the students interviewed at the three types of educational institution. We limited the study to men who had never been in the United States before June 1, 1954. (Our first wave of interviews was conducted in October 1954.) We tried—with reasonable, though not complete, success—to secure similar nationality distributions in the three types of setting. We also examined our groups for comparability in factors such as age, field of study, marital status. Although we found some differences, they do not seem of sufficient importance to affect our findings. We shall report here only one central point—namely, whether students who are predisposed to seek out social contact with Americans choose to attend colleges or universities in small towns rather than large cities. Our data indicate no such bias.

Experienced interviewers, carefully trained for this purpose at our Research Center for Human Relations, interviewed our 348 subjects at the 35 colleges and universities which they were attending, first in October and again in late April. The October interview covered numerous background variables, and an inquiry into the student's beliefs and feelings about various aspects of the United States and its inhabitants. The April interview repeated the latter inquiry so as to make possible the study of attitude change, and in addition, made a comprehensive survey of the student's experiences during the year, including his living arrangement, his interactions with Americans, his satisfactions and dissatisfactions with his year in the United States, and so on.

INTERACTION-POTENTIAL IN THREE TYPES OF INSTITUTIONAL SETTINGS

The first question we asked of the data was: Do foreign students who attend the three different types of colleges find themselves in contact situations which differ in interaction-potential—that is, which offer different degrees of opportunity for interaction with Americans? We constructed two indices expressing the degree of opportunity for interaction. The first of these deals with living arrangements and runs from a high position of living in a fraternity or having an American roommate to a low position represented by living, without an American roommate, in an apartment house or a hotel or in a rented room. The second index of interaction-potential is based upon a variety of activities—classes, job, extracurricular activities, etc.—and reflects the frequency with which the respondent is in situations where Americans whom he knows are present. These two indices of interaction-potential showed a low positive correlation—a phi coefficient of .35.

Since the study considered students in the situations in which we found them (as contrasted with an ideal experimental procedure in which students would have been randomly assigned to situations with varying degrees of interaction-potential), we must consider whether being in a situation with a given interaction-potential might have been the result of choice by the student and thus might have reflected his predisposition toward Americans. In the case of living arrangements, we ascertained whether the student had chosen his quarters or had been assigned to them. Although more than half of the students had had some choice in their living arrangements, analysis of responses to attitude questions on the first interview makes it reasonable to believe that the choice of living arrangements was not a function or favorableness or unfavorableness of predisposition toward Americans.[2]

In the case of the index of interaction-potential based on situations other than residence, it was not possible to determine to what extent a student's presence in situations with high interaction-potential was a matter of his own choice. Undoubtedly there is a volitional element. Nevertheless, it seems to us that there are environmental pressures which make it more likely, for instance, that students in small colleges will engage in extracurricular activities where there are Americans, that they will more often meet, in the buildings where they live and around the campus, Americans whom they know well enough to speak to, etc.

We had predicted that the small colleges would offer the greatest opportunity for interaction, followed by the non-metropolitan universities, with the metropolitan universities lowest. Both indices support our prediction; the differences between the types of college are significant[3] and in the predicted direction. As an example of the differences between types of college: two-thirds of the students in small colleges, as compared to one-fourth of metropolitan university students, have American roommates or live in fraternities.

Are there other factors which are related to the interaction-potential of the situations in which the foreign student finds himself? We have examined two possible ones: nationality[4] and academic status. Both proved to be significantly related to opportunity for interaction, as measured by both indices. For example, proportionately more Europeans than non-Europeans live in fraternities, and fewer Europeans than non-Europeans live in apartments or rented rooms. Similarly, more undergraduates than graduate students live in fraternities, and fewer undergraduates live in apartments or rented rooms.

When nationality and academic status are held constant, however, we still find significant differences in interaction-potential among the three types of college. Among either Europeans or non-Europeans taken separately, among graduate students or undergraduates separately, students in small colleges are highest on both our indices of interaction-potential, and those in metropolitan universities are lowest.

INTERACTION-POTENTIAL AS A DETERMINANT OF INTERACTION

Now that we know that attendance at small colleges leads the foreign student into contact situations with greater interaction-potential than does attendance at large universities, we are prepared to ask of our data the next question: Does being in contact situations which differ in *interaction-potential* lead to differences in the amount and nature of *interaction?* In the April interview we asked a number of questions about how the student spent his time, the kinds of activities in which he engaged, the nationality of the people with whom he associated, etc. From these we derived six measures of interaction.

There were two reasons for this multiplicity of indices. The first was, quite simply, that, since "interaction" is a complex concept, we did not know what single measure would be its best indicator. Secondly, by using different measures of interaction, we hoped to gain some understanding of the dynamics by which interaction leads to attitude change. Some of our measures reflected primarily opportunities to get information about Americans by meeting a variety of people in a variety of situations; another reflected subjective feelings of having made friends; others reflected differences in the kinds of activities engaged in with Americans. If these different measures of interaction showed different relationships to attitude change, we hoped

[2] The data on which this statement is based are too complicated for presentation in the space available here.

[3] All relationships reported are significant at the .01 level or better, except where otherwise noted.

[4] For this part of the analysis, two overall nationality groupings were used: students from Europe or countries where English is the native language, and students from countries other than those — Latin America, the Near East, and Asia.

to be able to draw inferences about the relative influence of increased information, of pleasant emotional experiences, and similar factors, in bringing about attitude change.

Our six measures (all based, of course, upon the students' reports) were:

1. proportion of free time spent with Americans,
2. variety of roles in which Americans had been seen (whether the student had met farmers, businessmen, etc., whether he had visited American homes, dated American girls, etc.),
3. whether the student felt that he had at least one close American friend,
4. the frequency with which he engaged in certain activities with Americans (eating meals, going to the movies, talking about his life at home, etc.),
5. the variety of such activities with Americans, regardless of frequency,
6. his score on a selected number of these items which scale according to Guttman's criteria, along a dimension which we have called, for lack of a better term, "intimacy" (ranging from an impersonal extreme of discussing courses to a personal extreme which was described as "talking about the sort of things you would talk about only with your best friends at home").

The indices of variety of interaction, frequency of interaction, and intimacy, represented different ways of scoring answers to the same set of questions. Naturally, they show positive intercorrelations with each other—phi coefficients of .39, .55, and .68. The other indices were based on separate items; phi coefficients of interrelations among these three indices, and between these three and the three above, are all also positive but lower—ranging from .16 to .34. The lowest correlations are between the students' reports of having or not having a close American friend and the other (more objective) measures of interaction.

Each of the six *interaction* indices was examined in relation to the two indices of interaction-*potential*. Of the twelve relationships examined, all but one are significant at the .01 level or better; in fact, seven are significant at the .001 level or better. The only relationship below the .01 level of significance is that between interaction-potential of living arrangements and the feeling of having a close American friend; this relationship, however, is still significant at the .05 level. In short, the relations between these measures answer our question affirmatively: being in contact situations with greater interaction-potential does lead to more varied, more frequent, and more intimate interaction with Americans. With regard to living arrangements, this holds true regardless of whether one has *chosen* to live in quarters with high interaction-potential or has been *assigned* to them.

OTHER FACTORS INFLUENCING INTERACTION

What about other factors which may be either enhancing or obscuring this relationship? We know that the three types of college differ in the degree of opportunity for interaction which they offer, and that students of different nationalities and of different academic levels find themselves in situations which differ in interaction-*potential*. It should follow that the *interaction* indices show differences among the three types of college, between nationality groups, and between academic levels. We examined types of college and nationality in relation to all six of the interaction indices, and academic status in relation to two of them—proportion of free time spent with Americans, and intimacy of interaction.

On four of the measures, students in the different types of college differ in the expected direction. Students in small colleges spend a greater proportion of their free time with Americans, and engage in more frequent, more varied, and more intimate interactions with them; students in metropolitan universities are lowest, and those in non-metropolitan universities intermediate, on these measures. There is no significant difference between students in different types of college in the variety of roles in which they have seen Americans nor in feeling that they have made close friends.

Nationality is related to five of the measures of interaction at the .001 level. Europeans spend a greater proportion of their free time with Americans than do non-Europeans; they have seen Americans in a greater variety of roles; and they have more varied, more frequent, and more intimate interactions with Americans. They are also somewhat more likely than non-Europeans to report that they have made a close American friend; however the difference between the two nationality groups on this measure is not statistically significant.

There is no systematic relation between academic status and either intimacy of interaction or proportion of free time spent with Americans; the trends differ in the different types of college.

The relationship of initial attitudes to the indices of *interaction-potential* and to the measures of *interaction* were also examined. They proved to be too complex to report within the space available. However, they do not seem to be such as to negate any of the other relationships reported here.

INTERRELATIONSHIPS AMONG FACTORS INFLUENCING INTERACTION

To summarize: Four variables—type of college, nationality, interaction-potential of living arrangements, and interaction-potential of other situations—were found to be related to most, or all, of the interaction indices. What about interrelationships among these four factors in their influence on interaction?

First, *type of college.* Holding nationality constant, type of college still makes a significant difference on each of the four interaction measures which it was earlier found to influence. Among both Europeans and non-Europeans, students in small colleges are highest, and those in metropolitan universities lowest, in proportion of free time spent with Americans, and in frequency, variety, and intimacy of interaction with Americans.

However, when interaction-potential—either of living arrangements or of other situations—is held constant, almost all the differences in interaction between types of college disappear. It is possible, in relation to each interaction index, to consider separately students rating "high," "medium," or "low" on each of the indices of interaction-potential; this makes a total of 36 sub-relationships examined. When interaction-potential is held constant in this way, in only 4 of the 36 relationships do differences between colleges remain important in influencing interaction. Although these differences are not highly significant (3 of the 4 are at the .05 level), they are all in the expected direction. For example, among students who are in situations—both residential and other—which rate low in interaction-potential, those in small colleges have more frequent interaction with Americans than do those in either metropolitan or non-metropolitan universities. It appears, then, that most of the differences between colleges in extent and nature of interaction between foreign students and Americans can be accounted for by differences in the living arrangements they provide and in the extent to which they encourage participation in various activities where Americans are present.

Nationality, however, continues to appear as an important factor even when the others are controlled. With minor exceptions, in each of the three types of college, Europeans score significantly higher than non-Europeans on all of the interaction indices except that of having a close American friend. The combined effects of nationality and interaction-potential were examined in relation to only two of the measures of interaction: intimacy, and proportion of time spent with Americans. Holding constant the level of interaction-potential as described above, Europeans are higher than non-Europeans on both intimacy of interaction with Americans and proportion of free time spent with them. There is, however, one exception to this finding: among students whose living arrangements are low in interaction-potential, the difference between Europeans and non-Europeans on these two measures of interaction is not significant.

In order to see more clearly the effect of *opportunities for association with Americans,* both of the interaction-*potential* indices were examined in combination with type of college in relation to all six of the *interaction* indices. The index of interaction-potential for situations other than residence showed significant relations to all interaction indices within both metropolitan and non-metropolitan universities, and to four of the six indices within small colleges. Within metropolitan and non-metropolitan universities, the rating of interaction-potential of living arrangements showed significant relationships to all the interaction measures except the feeling of having a close American friend. Within the small colleges, the rating of interaction-potential of living arrangements did not relate significantly to the measures of interaction. However, there was a tendency for those living in situations with high interaction-potential to be high on the interaction indices; the failure to show significant relationships seems to be largely a function of the small number of students in small colleges whose living arrangements were rated "low" in interaction-potential.

In addition, both measures of interaction-potential were examined in combination with nationality and with academic status in relation to intimacy and to proportion of free time spent with Americans. Both among Europeans and among non-Europeans, among graduate students and among undergraduates, students in situations with higher interaction-potential spent more of their free time with Americans and entered into more intimate interaction with them.

To sum up this part of the study: We found that there are differences among college communities in the United States which are sufficiently great to lead to systematic differences in the extent and nature of foreign students' associations with Americans, despite the great diversity among the students themselves. These differences between college settings consist largely in the extent to which they provide contact situations with high potential for association with Americans. In turn, being in situations with high interaction-potential does, as predicted, lead to more varied, more frequent, and more intimate association with Americans; it does not as clearly lead to the feeling of having made close American friends.

At least one difference among students, however, is as weighty a determinant of association with Americans as is the interaction potential of contact situations: this is national origin. Nationality and interaction-potential reinforce each other. Europeans are more likely to be in contact situations with high interaction-potential than are non-Europeans; and, in situations at any given level of interaction-potential, Europeans are likely to have more, and more intimate, association with Americans.

*THE ADOLESCENT SUBCULTURE AND ACADEMIC ACHIEVEMENT**

By James S. Coleman

Industrial society has spawned a peculiar phenomenon, most evident in America but emerging also in other Western societies: adolescent subcultures, with values and activities quite distinct from those of the adult society—subcultures whose members have most of their important associations within and few with adult society. Industrialization, and the rapidity of change itself, has taken out of the hands of the parent the task of training his child, made the parent's skills obsolescent, and put him out of touch with the times—unable to understand, much less inculcate, the standards of a social order which has changed since he was young.

By extending the period of training necessary for a child and by encompassing nearly the whole population, industrial society has made of high school a social system of adolescents. It includes, in the United States, almost all adolescents and more and more of the activities of the adolescent himself. A typical example is provided by an excerpt from a high-school newspaper in an upper-middle-class suburban school:

> SOPHOMORE DANCING
> FEATURES CHA CHA
>
> SOPHOMORES, this is your chance to learn how to dance! The first day of sophomore dancing is Nov. 14 and it will begin at 8:30 A.M. in the Boys' Gym. . . .
>
> NO ONE IS required to take dancing but it is highly recommended for both boys and girls. . . .
>
> If you don't attend at this time except in case of absence from school, you may not attend at any other time. Absence excuses should be shown to Miss ——— or Mr. ———.

In effect, then, what our society has done is to set apart, in an institution of their own, adolescents for whom home is little more than a dormitory and

*Reprinted from *The American Journal of Sociology,* 1960, *65,* pp. 337-347, by permission of the author and The University of Chicago Press. Copyright 1960 by the University of Chicago. The research discussed in this paper was carried out under a grant from the United States Office of Education; a full report is contained in "Social Climates and Social Structures in High Schools," a report to the Office of Education. The paper was presented at the Fourth World Congress of Sociology, Milan, Italy, September, 1959.

whose world is made up of activities peculiar to their fellows. They have been given as well many of the instruments which can make them a functioning community: cars, freedom in dating, continual contact with the opposite sex, money, and entertainment, like popular music and movies, designed especially for them. The international spread of "rock-and-roll" and of so-called American patterns of adolescent behavior is a consequence, I would suggest, of these economic changes which have set adolescents off in a world of their own.

Yet the fact that such a subsystem has sprung up in society has not been systematically recognized in the organization of secondary education. The theory and practice of education remains focused on *individuals;* teachers exhort individuals to concentrate their energies in scholarly directions, while the community of adolescents diverts these energies into other channels. The premise of the present research is that, if educational goals are to be realized in modern society, a fundamentally different approach to secondary education is necessary. Adults are in control of the institutions they have established for secondary education; traditionally, these institutions have been used to mold children as individuals toward ends which adults dictate. The fundamental change which must occur is to shift the focus: to mold social communities as communities, so that the norms of the communities themselves reinforce educational goals rather than inhibit them, as is at present the case.

The research being reported is an attempt to examine the status systems of the adolescent communities in ten high schools and to see the effects of these status systems upon the individuals within them. The ten high schools are all in the Midwest. They include five schools in small towns (labeled *0-4* in the figures which follow), one in a working-class suburb (*6*), one in a well-to-do suburb (*9*), and three schools in cities of varying sizes (*5, 7,* and *8*). All but No. *5,* a Catholic boys' school, are coeducational, and all but it are public schools.

The intention was to study schools which had quite different status systems, but the similarities were far more striking than the differences. In a questionnaire all boys were asked: "How would you most like to be remembered in school: as an athletic star, a brilliant student, or most popular? The results of the responses for each school are shown in Figure 3-2,[1] where the left corner of the triangle represents 100 per cent saying "star athlete"; the top corner represents 100 per cent saying "brilliant student"; and the right corner represents 100 per cent saying "most popular." Each school is represented by a point whose location relative to the three corners shows the proportion giving each response.

The schools are remarkably grouped somewhat off-center, showing a greater tendency to say "star athlete" than either of the other choices. From each school's point is a broken arrow connecting the school as a whole with its members who were named by their fellows as being "members of the leading crowd." In almost every case, the leading crowd tends in the direction of the athlete—in all cases *away* from the ideal of the brilliant student. Again, for the leading crowds as well as for the students as a whole, the uniformity is remarkably great; not so great in the absolute positions of the leading crowds but in the direction they deviate from the student bodies.

This trend toward the ideal of the athletic star on the part of the leading crowds is due in part to the fact that the leading crowds include a great number of athletes. Boys were asked in a questionnaire to name the best athlete in their grade, the best student, and the boy most popular with girls. In every school, without exception, the boys named as best athletes were named more often—on the average over twice as often—as members of the leading crowd than were those named as best students. Similarly, the boy most popular with girls was named as belonging to the leading crowd more often than the best student, though in all schools but the well-to-do suburb and the smallest rural town schools *9* and *0* on Figure 3-2) less often than the best athlete.

These and other data indicate the importance of athletic achievement as an avenue for gaining status in the schools. Indeed, in the predominantly middle-class schools, it is by far the most effective achievement for gaining a working-class boy entrée into the leading crowd.

Similarly, each girl was asked how she would like to be remembered: as a brilliant student, a leader in extracurricular activities, or most popular. The various schools are located on Figure 3-3, together

[1] I am grateful to James A. Davis and Jacob Feldman, of the University of Chicago, for suggesting such graphs for presenting responses to trichotomous items in a population.

with arrows connecting them to their leading crowd. The girls tend slightly less, on the average, than the boys to want to be remembered as brilliant students. Although the alternatives are different, and thus cannot be directly compared, a great deal of other evidence indicates that the girls—although better students in every school—do not want to be considered "brilliant students." They have good reason not to, for the girl in each grade in each of the schools who was most often named as best student has fewer friends and is less often in the leading crowd than is the boy most often named as best student.

There is, however, diversity among the schools in the attractiveness of the images of "activities leader" and "popular girl" (Figure 3-3). In five (*9, 0, 3, 8,* and *1*), the leader in activities is more often chosen as an ideal than is the popular girl; in four (*7, 6, 2,* and *4*) the most popular girl is the more attractive of the two. These differences correspond somewhat to class background differences among the schools: *2, 4, 6,* and *7,* where the activities leader is least attractive, have the highest proportion of students with working-class backgrounds. School *9* is by far the most upper-middle-class one and by far the most activities-oriented.

The differences among the schools correspond as well to differences among the leading crowds: in schools *2, 4,* and *6,* where the girls as a whole are most oriented to being popular, the leading crowds are even more so; in the school where the girls are most oriented to the ideal of the activities leader, No. *9,* the leading crowd goes even further in that direction.[2] In other words, it is as if a pull is exerted by the leading crowd, bringing the rest of the students toward one or the other of the polar extremes. In all cases, the leading crowd pulls away from the brilliant-student ideal.

Although these schools vary far less than one might wish when examining the effects of status systems, there are differences. All students were asked in a questionnaire: "What does it take to get into the leading crowd?" On the basis of the answers, the relative importance of various activities can be determined. Consider only a single activity, academic achievement. Its importance for status among the adolescents in each school can be measured simply by the proportion of responses which specify "good grades," or "brains" as adolescents often put it, as a means of entrée into the leading crowd. In all the schools, academic achievement was of less importance than other matters, such as being an athletic star among the boys, being a cheerleader or being good-looking among the girls, or other attributes. Other measures which were obtained of the importance of academic achievement in the adolescent status system correlate highly with this one.[3]

If, then, it is true that the status system of adolescents *does* affect educational goals, those schools which differ in the importance of academic achievement in the adolescent status system should differ in numerous other ways which are directly related to educational goals. Only one of those, which illustrates well the differing pressures upon students in the various schools, will be reported here.

In every social context certain activities are highly rewarded, while others are not. Those activities which are rewarded are the activities for which there is strong competition—activities in which everyone with some ability will compete. In such activities the persons who achieve most should be those with most potential ability. In contrast, in unrewarded activities, those who have most ability may not be motivated to compete; consequently, the persons who achieve most will be persons of lesser ability. Thus in a high school where basketball is important, nearly every boy who might be a good basketball player will go out for the sport, and, as a result, basketball stars are likely to be the boys with the most ability. If in the same school volleyball does not bring the same status, few boys will go out for it, and those who end up as members of the team will not be the boys with most potential ability.

Similarly, with academic achievement: in a school where such achievement brings few social rewards, those who "go out" for scholarly achievement will be few. The high performers, those who receive

[2] This result could logically be a statistical artifact because the leaders were included among students as a whole and thus would boost the result in the direction they tend. However, it is not a statistical artifact, for the leading crowds are a small part of the total student body. When they are taken out for computing the position of the rest of the girls in each school, schools *2, 4, 6,* and *7* are still the most popularity-oriented, and school *9* the most activities-oriented.

[3] Parenthetically, it might be noted that these measures correlate only imperfectly with the proportion of boys or girls who want to be remembered as brilliant students. These responses depend on the relative attractiveness of other ideals, which varies from school to school, and upon other factors unrelated to the status system.

good grades, will not be the boys whose ability is greatest but a more mediocre few. Thus the "intellectuals" of such a society, those defined by themselves and others as the best students, will not in fact be those with most intellectual ability. The latter, knowing where the social rewards lie, will be off cultivating other fields which bring social rewards.

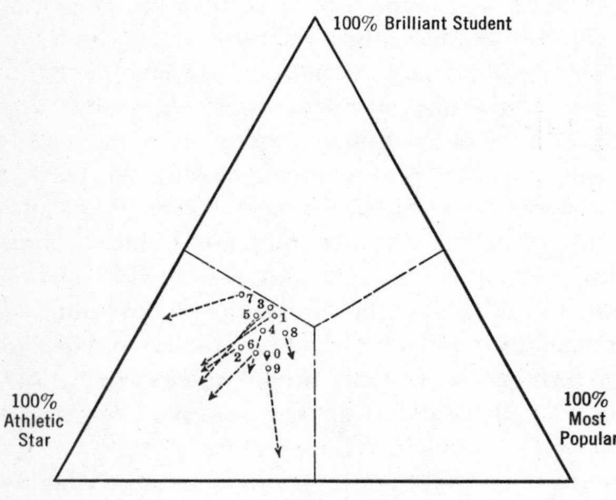

Figure 3-2. Positions of schools and leading crowds in boys' relative choice of brilliant student, athletic star and most popular

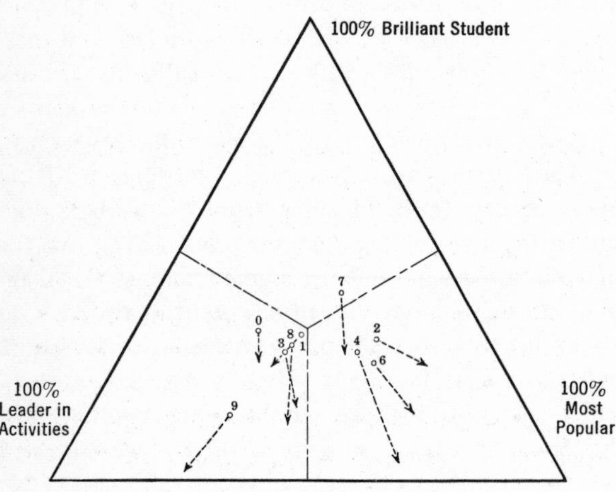

Figure 3-3. Positions of schools and leading crowds in girls' relative choice of brilliant student, activities leader, and most popular

To examine the effect of varying social pressures in the schools, academic achievement, as measured by grades in school, was related to IQ. Since the IQ tests differ from school to school, and since each school had its own mean IQ and its own variation around it, the ability of high performers (boys who made *A* or *A*— average)[4] was measured by the number of standard deviations of their average IQ's above the mean. In this way, it is possible to see where the high performers' ability lay, relative to the distribution of abilities in their school.[5]

The variations were great: in a small-town school, No. *1*, the boys who made an *A* or *A*— average had IQ's 1.53 standard deviations above the school average; in another small-town school, No. *0*, their IQ's were only about a third this distance above the mean, .59. Given this variation, the question can be asked: Do these variations in ability of the high performers correspond to variations in the social rewards for, or constraints against, being a good student?

Figure 3-4 shows the relation for the boys between the social rewards for academic excellence (i.e., the frequency with which "good grades" was mentioned as a means for getting into the leading crowd) and the ability of the high performers, measured by the number of standard deviations their average IQ's exceed that of the rest of the boys in the school. The relation is extremely strong. Only one school, a pa-

[4] In each school but *3* and *8*, those making A and A— constituted from 6 to 8 per cent of the student body. In order to provide a correct test of the hypothesis, it is necessary to have the same fraction of the student body in each case (since IQ's of this group are being measured in terms of number of standard deviations above the student body). To adjust these groups, enough *6's* were added (each being assigned the average IQ of the total group of *6's*) to bring the proportion up to 6 per cent (from 3 per cent in school *3*, from 4 per cent in school *8*).

[5] The IQ tests used in the different schools were: (0) California Mental Maturity (taken seventh, eighth, or ninth grade); (1) California Mental Maturity (taken eighth grade); (2) SRA Primary Mental Abilities (taken tenth grade); (3) California Mental Maturity (taken ninth grade; seniors took SRA PMA, which was tabulated as a percentile, and they have been omitted from analysis reported above); (4) Otis (ninth and tenth grades; taken eighth grade); Kuhlman Finch (eleventh and twelfth grades, taken eighth grade); (5) Otis (taken ninth grade); (6) California Mental Maturity (taken eighth grade); (7) California Mental Maturity (taken eighth grade); (8) Otis (taken ninth or tenth grade); and (9) Otis (taken eighth grade).

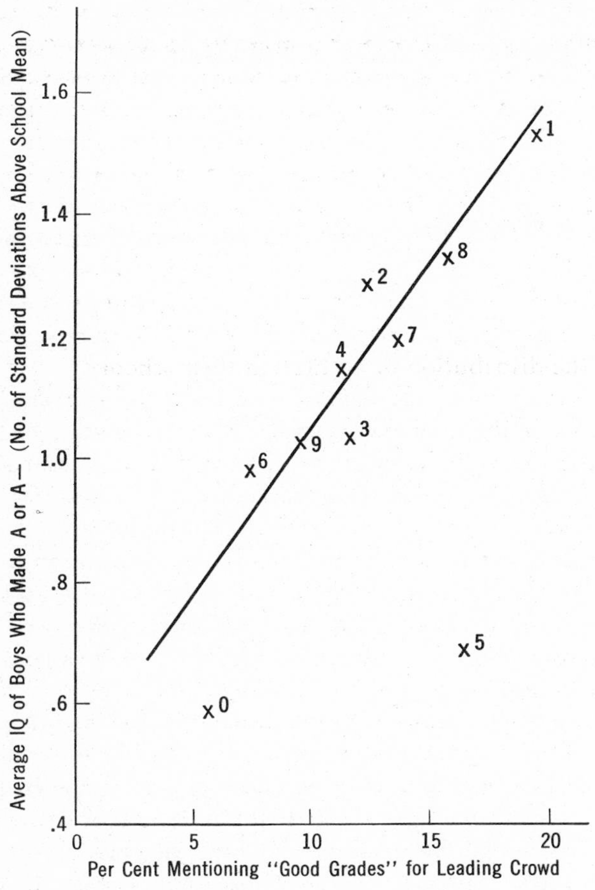

Figure 3-4. IQ's of high achieving boys by importance of good grades among other boys

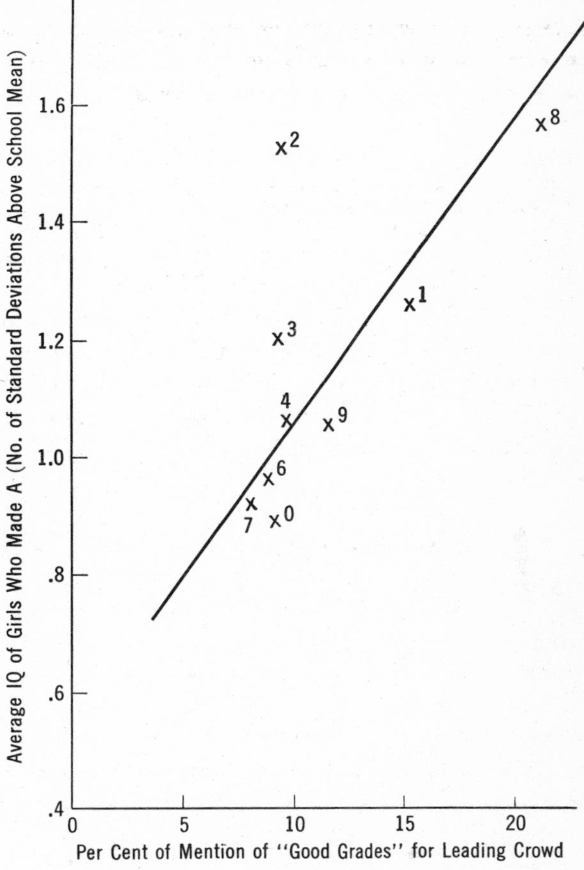

Figure 3-5. IQ's of high achieving girls by importance of good grades among other girls

rochial boys' school in the city's slums, deviates. This is a school in which many boys had their most important associations outside the school rather than in it, so that its student body constituted far less of a social system, less able to dispense social rewards and punishments, than was true of the other schools.

Similarly, Figure 3-5 shows for the girls the IQ's of the high performers.[6] Unfortunately, most of the schools are closely bunched in the degree to which good grades are important among the girls, so that there is too little variation among them to examine this effect as fully as would be desirable. School *2* is the one school whose girls deviate from the general relationship.

The effect of these value systems on the freedom for academic ability to express itself in high achievement is evident among the girls as it is among the boys. This is not merely due to the school facilities, social composition of the school, or other variables:

[6] For the girls, only girls with a straight-A average were included. Since girls get better grades than boys, this device is necessary in order to make the sizes of the "high-performer" group roughly comparable for boys and for girls. Schools differed somewhat in the proportion of A's, constituting about 6 per cent of the students in the small schools, only about 3 per cent in schools *6* and *7*, 1 per cent in *8*, and 2 per cent in *9*. In *8* and *9*, enough girls were added and assigned the average grade of the 7 (A–) group to bring the proportion to 3 per cent, comparable with the other large schools. The difference, however, between the large and small schools was left.

the two schools highest in the importance of scholastic achievement for both boys and girls are *1* and *3,* the first a small-town school of 350 students and the second a city school of 2,000 students. In both there are fewer students with white-collar backgrounds than in schools *9* or *3,* which are somewhere in the middle as to value placed on academic achievement, but are more white-collar than in schools *7* or *4,* which are also somewhere in the middle. The highest expenditure per student was $695 per year in school *9,* and the lowest was little more than half that, in school *4.* These schools are close together on the graphs of Figures 3-4 and 3-5.

It should be mentioned in passing that an extensive unpublished study throughout Connecticut, using standard tests of achievement and ability, yielded consistent results. The study found no correlation between per pupil expenditure in a school and the achievement of its students relative to their ability. The effects shown in Figures 3-4 and 3-5 suggest why: that students with ability are led to achieve only when there are social rewards, primarily from their peers, for doing so—and these social rewards seem little correlated with per pupil expenditure.

So much for the effects as shown by the variation among schools. As mentioned earlier, the variation among schools was not nearly so striking in this research as the fact that, in all of them, academic achievement did not count for as much as other activities. In every school the boy named as best athlete and the boy named as most popular with girls was far more often mentioned as a member of the leading crowd and as someone to "be like," than was the boy named as the best student. And the girl named as best dressed, and the one named as most popular with boys, was in every school far more often mentioned as being in the leading crowd and as someone "to be like," than was the girl named as the best student.

The relative unimportance of academic achievement, together with the effect shown earlier, suggests that these adolescent subcultures are generally deterrents to academic achievement. In other words, in these societies of adolescents those who come to be seen as the "intellectuals" and who come to think so of themselves are not really those of highest intelligence but are only the ones who are willing to work hard at a relatively unrewarded activity.

The implications for American society as a whole are clear. Because high schools allow the adolescent subcultures to divert energies into athletics, social activities, and the like, they recruit into adult intellectual activities people with a rather mediocre level of ability. In fact, the high school seems to do more than allow these subcultures to discourage academic achievement; it aids them in doing so. To indicate how it does and to indicate how it might do differently is another story, to be examined below.

Figures 3-2 and 3-3, which show the way boys and girls would like to be remembered in their high school, demonstrate a curious difference between the boys and the girls. Despite great variation in social background, in size of school (from 180 to 2,000), in size of town (from less than a thousand to over a million), and in style of life of their parents, the proportion of boys choosing each of the three images by which he wants to be remembered is very nearly the same in all schools. And in every school the leading crowd "pulls" in similar directions: at least partly toward the ideal of the star athlete. Yet the ideals of the girls in these schools are far more dispersed, and the leading crowds "pull" in varying directions, far less uniformly than among the boys. Why such a diversity in the same schools?

The question can best be answered by indirection. In two schools apart from those in the research, the questionnaire was administered primarily to answer a puzzling question: Why was academic achievement of so little importance among the adolescents in school *9*? Their parents were professionals and business executives, about 80 per cent were going to college (over twice as high a proportion as in any of the other schools), and yet academic excellence counted for little among them. In the two additional schools parental background was largely held constant, for they were private, coeducational day schools whose students had upper-middle-class backgrounds quite similar to those of school *9*. One (No. *10*) was in the city; the other (No. *11*), in a suburban setting almost identical to that of No. *9*. Although the two schools were added to the study to answer the question about school *9,* they will be used to help answer the puzzle set earlier; that of the clustering of schools for the boys and their greater spread for the girls. When we look at the responses of adolescents in these two schools to the question as to how they would like to be remembered, the picture becomes even more puzzling (Figures 3-6 and 3-7). For the boys, they are ex-

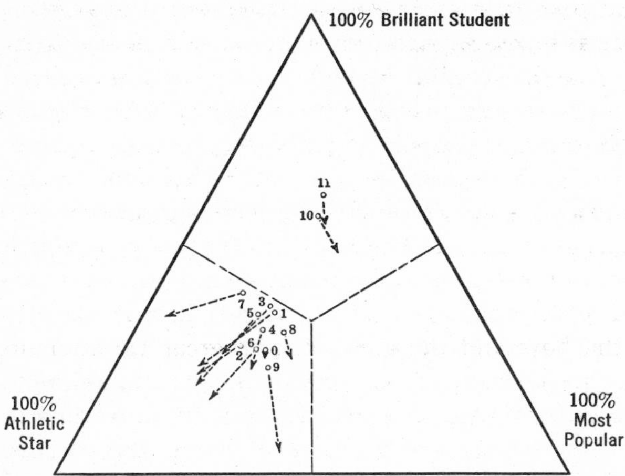

Figure 3-6. Positions of schools and leading crowds in boys' relative choice of brilliant student, athletic star, and most popular (two private schools [*10, 11*] included)

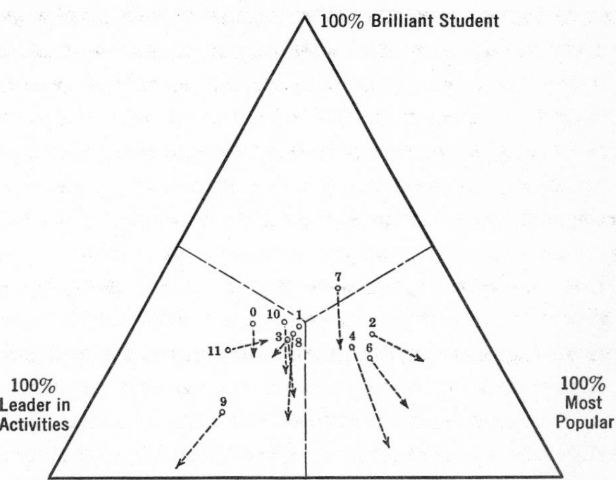

Figure 3-7. Positions of schools and leading crowds in girls' relative choice of brilliant student, activities leader, and most popular (two private schools [*10, 11*] included)

tremely far from the cluster of the other schools; for the girls, they are intermingled with the other schools. Thus, though it was for the boys that the other schools clustered so closely, these two deviate sharply from the cluster; and for the girls, where the schools already varied, these two are not distinguishable. Furthermore, the leading crowds of boys in these schools do not pull the ideal toward the star-athlete ideal as do those in almost all the other schools. To be sure, they pull away from the ideal of the brilliant student, but the pull is primarily toward a social image, the most popular. Among the girls, the leading crowds pull in different directions and are nearly indistinguishable from the other schools.

The answer to both puzzles, that is, first, the great cluster of the boys and now, in these two additional schools, the greater deviation, seems to lie in one fact: the boys' interscholastic athletics. The nine public schools are all engaged in interscholastic leagues which themselves are knit together in state tournaments. The other school of the first ten, the Catholic school, is in a parochial league, where games are just as hotly contested as in the public leagues and is also knit together with them in tournaments.

Schools *10* and *11* are athletically in a world apart from this. Although boys in both schools may go in for sports, and both schools have interscholastic games, the opponents are scattered private schools, constituting a league in name only. They take no part in state or city tournaments and have almost no publicity.

There is nothing for the girls comparable to the boys' interscholastic athletics. There are school activities of one sort or another, in which most girls take part, but no interscholastic games involving them. Their absence and the lack of leagues which knit all schools together in systematic competition means that the status system can "wander" freely, depending on local conditions in the school. In athletics, however, a school, and the community surrounding it, cannot hold its head up if it continues to lose games. It *must* devote roughly the same attention to athletics as do the schools surrounding it, for athletic games are the only games in which it engages other schools and, by representation, other communities. These games are almost the only means a school has of generating internal cohesion and identification, for they constitute the only activity in which the school participates *as* a school. (This is well indicated by the fact that a number of students in school *10*, the private school which engages in no interscholastic games, has been concerned by a "lack of school spirit.") It is as a consequence of this that the athlete gains so much status: he is doing something for the school and the community, not only for himself, in leading his team to victory, for it is a school victory.

The outstanding student, in contrast, has little or no way to bring glory to his school. His victories are always purely personal, often at the expense of his classmates, who are forced to work harder to keep up with him. It is no wonder that his accomplishments gain little reward and are often met by ridiculing remarks, such as "curve-raiser" or "grind," terms of disapprobation which have no analogues in athletics.

These results are particularly intriguing, for they suggest ways in which rather straightforward social theory could be used in organizing the activities of high schools in such a way that their adolescent subcultures would encourage, rather than discourage, the channeling of energies into directions of learning. One might speculate on the possible effects of city-wide or state-wide "scholastic fairs" composed of academic games and tournaments between schools and school exhibits to be judged. It could be that the mere institution of such games would, just as do the state basketball tournaments in the midwestern United States, have a profound effect upon the educational climate in the participating schools. In fact, by an extension of this analysis, one would predict that an international fair of this sort, a "Scholastic Olympics," would generate interscholastic games and tournaments within the participating countries.

Student Relationships in the Classroom

Teacher-Student Interaction

Student Motivation and Teacher Control

Shaping Attitudes through Schools

part TWO

The Classroom Setting

IV

STUDENT RELATIONSHIPS IN THE CLASSROOM

*TYPICAL SOCIOMETRIC PATTERNS**

By Norman E. Gronlund

Sociometric results obtained from different groups will vary according to the sociometric criteria used, the number of choices allotted, the directions used, and the level of socialization achieved by the various groups. ["Sociometric criteria" are the bases on which members of a group are asked to choose other members; for example, if pupils are asked to name classmates next to whom they would like to sit, the criterion would be *seating companion*. "Number of choices" refers to the number of fellow group-members each member is asked or allowed to name on the basis of a given criterion; for example, each pupil might be asked to name *three* classmates on the criterion of seating companion.] Thus, it is not expected that the distribution of sociometric choices or the resulting social structures will be comparable from group to group. Some groups will contain a relatively large number of stars and isolates while others will contain few or none; some groups will have many mutual choices while others will have relatively few; and some groups will reflect a greater cleavage between subgroups than do others. Despite these variations, however, sociometric results from different groups have revealed some common patterns. Certain phenomena have occurred frequently enough in sociometric testing to be considered typical of sociometric findings.

This paper will present some typical sociometric results for various grade levels. The basic data, presented in tabular form, were obtained from several school systems. Sociometric results for grades three through six were obtained from elementary schools in a large city located in the Midwest. The data for grades seven through twelve represent the total population of a junior and senior high school located in a small Midwestern city. The college classes were composed of seniors in a teacher-training curriculum. The sociometric data were gathered in all public school classrooms between six and eight months after the beginning of the school year. The college students had spent seven weeks together at the time of the sociometric testing. This involved class dis-

*From *Sociometry in the Classroom* (New York: Harper & Row, Publishers, 1959), Chap. 4, pp. 93-113. Used by permission of the author and publisher.

cussion in education classes that met daily. Similar directions were used with the sociometric test at all grade levels. In all groups the pupils were instructed to confine their choices to their classmates.

DISTRIBUTION OF SOCIOMETRIC CHOICES

One of the most common phenomena in sociometric testing is the uneven distribution of sociometric choices. A relatively small number of group members receive a large number of sociometric choices, while others receive few or none. When the total distribution of choices is analyzed, it is found to be positively skewed. That is, more group members appear at the lower sociometric status positions than appear at the higher sociometric status positions. This is brought out clearly in Table 4-1.

Table 4-1 presents the percentage of pupils above and below the expected value at various grade levels. Since five sociometric choices were allotted on one criterion, the expected value, or average number of choices received, would be five. With a normal distribution of choices, 50 per cent of the pupils would be above this expected value and 50 per cent would be below. This assumes, of course, that those receiving exactly five choices would be evenly distributed between the above and below average groups. It will be noted in Table 4-1 that between 58 and 68 percent of the pupils received fewer choices than the expected value. In other words, almost two-thirds of the pupils were below average in sociometric status. This, of course, is a result of the undue proportion of choices going to pupils in the above average category. The percentage of pupils above and below the expected value is fairly consistent at all grade levels. Similarly consistent results were found by Bronfenbrenner[1] for pupils enrolled in classes from kindergarten through grade six. He found that approximately 60 per cent of the pupils fell below the expected value in number of sociometric choices received. This tendency for the distribution of sociometric choices to be positively skewed has been designated a *sociodynamic law* by Moreno.[2] He indicates that the uneven distribution of sociometric choices is similar to the uneven distribution of wealth in a society. Thus, few are "sociometrically wealthy" but many are "sociometrically poor."

A more detailed distribution of sociometric choices is presented in Table 4-2. Here the pupils are classified into the five sociometric categories based on Bronfenbrenner's fixed frame of reference.[3] Thus, using five sociometric choices with one sociometric criterion the categories have the following values:

Star	9 or more choices
Above average	5-8 choices
Below average	2-5 choices
Neglectee	1 choice
Isolate	No choices

In calculating the two average groups, those pupils receiving exactly five choices were evenly divided between the above average and below average categories.

It will be noted that the percentage of pupils in each sociometric category remains fairly constant from grade three through grade ten. From grade eleven on, however, there is a consistently smaller percentage of pupils in the star and neglectee cate-

TABLE 4-1

PERCENTAGE OF PUPILS CHOSEN ABOVE AND BELOW EXPECTED VALUE, USING FIVE SOCIOMETRIC CHOICES WITH ONE SOCIOMETRIC CRITERION

Grade Level	Number of Classrooms	Number of Pupils	Percentage of Pupils: Above Expected Value	Percentage of Pupils: Below Expected Value
3	9	270	40	60
4	10	277	41	59
5	10	268	40	60
6	10	284	39	61
7	6	171	38	62
8	6	146	41	59
9	8	173	42	58
10	6	135	38	62
11	6	105	35	65
12	5	105	32	68
College	5	144	38	62

NOTE: Criteria: *Work Companion* (grades 3-6), *Seating Companion* (grades 7-12), and *Teaching Companion* (college).

[1] U. Bronfenbrenner, "The Measurement of Sociometric Status Structure and Development," *Sociometry Monograph* No. 6 (New York: Beacon House, 1945).

[2] J. L. Moreno, *Who Shall Survive?* (New York: Beacon House, 1953).

[3] Bronfenbrenner, *op. cit.*

gories, with an increase in the percentage of pupils in the below average group. This shifting of pupils from the extreme sociometric positions toward the average may be due to the tendency to form more cliques and small subgroups at these grade levels. A larger number of groups at each grade level, however, would be necessary to verify such an assumption.

The extent to which distributions of sociometric choices are positively skewed is readily apparent in Table 4-2. At all grade levels, there are almost twice as many pupils in the below average category as there are in the above average group. The combined percentages in the neglectee and isolate categories also exceed those in the star category, at all grade levels except the fourth. Thus, there is a tendency for groups to contain more pupils with extremely low sociometric status than with high status. An analysis of the percentage of choices received by these extreme groups revealed that the 7 to 17 per cent of the pupils in the star category captured between 17 and 41 per cent of all of the choices given. In contrast, the pupils in the neglectee and isolate categories received less than 3 per cent of the choices although there were between 11 and 22 per cent of the pupils in these groups.

Of special interest in Table 4-2 is the fact that isolates appear at all grade levels. It might be assumed that after attending school for a period of time every pupil would receive at least one choice as a desired associate. Apparently just being a member of a group does not assure acceptance by the group.

Although the percentage of isolates at the secondary school level is similar to that of the elementary school level, it must be taken into account that approximately 90 per cent of the pupils drop out of school between grades nine and twelve. Since Kuhlen and Collister[4] have shown that drop-outs tend to have low social acceptance, fewer isolates would be expected at the secondary school level. Thus, it is possible that the percentage of isolates actually increases during the high school years and that this increase does not appear in Table 4-2 because of the disproportionate number of isolates dropping out of school. Nevertheless, the table does indicate that a certain percentage of pupils at all grade levels need help in improving their social relations. If the neglectees (those receiving only one choice) are included in this category, between 11 and 22 per cent of the pupils could benefit from such help.

Influence of criteria on choice distributions. The uneven distribution of sociometric choices remains fairly consistent over different criteria, as well as

[4] R. G. Kuhlen and F. G. Collister, "Sociometric Status of Sixth- and Ninth-Graders Who Fail to Finish High School," *Educational and Psychological Measurement*, 1952, *12*, pp. 632-637.

TABLE 4-2

PERCENTAGE OF PUPILS IN EACH SOCIOMETRIC CATEGORY AT VARIOUS GRADE LEVELS, USING FIVE SOCIOMETRIC CHOICES WITH ONE SOCIOMETRIC CRITERION

Grade Level	*Number of Classrooms*	*Number of Pupils*	*Percentage in Each Sociometric Category*				
			Star	*Above Average*	*Below Average*	*Neglectee*	*Isolate*
3	9	270	14	26	41	13	6
4	10	277	15	26	45	8	6
5	10	268	15	25	41	14	5
6	10	284	17	22	39	14	8
7	6	171	11	27	49	10	3
8	6	146	11	30	43	15	1
9	8	173	14	28	39	14	5
10	6	135	15	23	46	11	5
11	6	105	8	27	52	7	6
12	5	105	7	25	53	8	7
College	5	144	8	30	51	8	3

NOTE: Criteria: *Work Companion* (grades 3-6). *Seating Companion* (grades 7-12), and *Teaching Companion* (college).

over different age groups. A reanalysis of data[5] obtained from forty sixth-grade classrooms is presented in Table 4-3. It will be noted here that the percentage of pupils appearing in each sociometric category is similar for the criteria of seating companion, work companion, and play companion. The slightly smaller percentage of pupils in the star and neglectee categories on the play companion criterion indicates a more general distribution of choices. However, the positive skewness, discussed earlier, is clearly evident in all three distributions. Approximately 39 per cent of the pupils had higher than average sociometric status with 61 per cent falling somewhere below the average point.

TABLE 4-3

PERCENTAGE OF PUPILS IN EACH SOCIOMETRIC CATEGORY ON THE CRITERIA OF SEATING COMPANION, WORK COMPANION, AND PLAY COMPANION IN FORTY SIXTH-GRADE CLASSROOMS

Criteria (5 Choices Allotted on Each)	*Percentage in Each Sociometric Category*				
	Star	*Above Average*	*Below Average*	*Neglectee*	*Isolate*
Seating	15	24	42	11	8
Work	13	26	41	12	8
Play	11	29	45	8	7

NOTE: There was an average of 16 boys and 16 girls in each classroom.

Since the criteria of seating companion, work companion, and play companion cover the major activities in the pupil's school day, it is discouraging to note the consistency with which a certain percentage of neglectees and isolates appear in all three distributions. The hope that acceptance on the playground will make up for lack of acceptance in classroom activities becomes very unrealistic. To determine the extent to which pupils remained in the same relative position on the three sociometric criteria, their sociometric-status scores were correlated. For the forty classrooms, the mean correlation coefficients ranged from .76 to .89 between the various pairs of criteria.[6] Thus, there was a tendency for pupils to remain in the same sociometric position on all three sociometric questions. Those with high sociometric status as seating companions tended also to have high status as work companions and play companions. Conversely, pupils least accepted as seating companions tended to remain in this position as work companions and play companions. This pervasiveness of the lack of acceptance on the part of some pupils should be of special concern to those interested in improving the social relations of pupils.

Influence of the pupils' sex on choice distributions. Teachers frequently remark that girls are more accepted by their classmates than boys. Although their behavior may be more acceptable to the teacher, sociometric results show no difference in the degree of acceptance they experience among their peers. Table 4-4 presents a comparison of the relative percentage of boys and girls in the extreme sociometric categories. Although the average sociometric categories have been omitted from this table, they follow the same general distribution presented earlier with no distinction between boys and girls.

TABLE 4-4

RELATIVE PERCENTAGE OF BOYS AND GIRLS IN THE STAR, NEGLECTEE, AND ISOLATE CATEGORIES ON THE CRITERIA OF SEATING COMPANION, WORK COMPANION, AND PLAY COMPANION IN FORTY SIXTH-GRADE CLASSROOMS

Criteria (5 Choices Allotted on Each)	*Percentage in Star Category*		*Percentage in Neglectee Category*		*Percentage in Isolate Category*	
	Boys	*Girls*	*Boys*	*Girls*	*Boys*	*Girls*
Seating	13	17	11	11	7	8
Work	12	15	12	11	7	8
Play	12	10	8	9	8	6

NOTE: There was an average of 16 boys and 16 girls in each classroom.

The slightly larger percentage of girls in the star category on the seating companion and work companion criteria and the lower percentage on the play companion criterion can probably be accounted for by random variations in the data. For all practical

[5] N. E. Gronlund, "The Accuracy of Teachers' Judgments Concerning the Sociometric Status of Sixth-Grade Pupils," *Sociometry Monographs,* No. 25 (New York: Beacon House, 1951).

[6] N. E. Gronlund, "Generality of Sociometric Status over Criteria in Measurement of Social Acceptability," *Elementary School Journal,* 1955, *56,* pp. 173-176.

purposes, an equal percentage of boys and girls are socially neglected or isolated among their classmates. The tendency of teachers to view girls as possessing more socially desirable characteristics than boys[7] needs to be overcome, if they are to be most helpful in improving the social relations of both boys and girls.

Influence of the number of choices on choice distributions. It might be assumed that increasing the number of choices allotted to a sociometric criterion would even out the distribution of choices among the pupils. However, it has been found in sociometric testing that when an increased number of choices is made available to a group, the pattern of distribution tends to remain the same. Highly chosen pupils receive an undue proportion of the new choices, and the majority of the isolates remain unchosen. The persistence of this uneven distribution of sociometric choices with varying numbers of choices allotted is illustrated in Table 4-5. This distribution of choices for a sixth-grade class indicates the number of choices each boy and girl received when three, four, and five choices were used with one sociometric criterion. It will be noted that the pupils remained in approximately the same relative position when an increased number of choices was available for distribution. In fact, a rank-order correlation of .92 was obtained between the sociometric status of these pupils based on the use of three choices and their sociometric status based on five choices. Similar correlations for eleven classrooms from the fourth to the sixth grades[8] ranged from .72 to .92. Thus, although nearly twice as many choices are available for distribution when five choices are allotted than when three are used, the distribution follows essentially the same pattern.

It will be noted in Table 4-5, however, that the number of stars increases slightly and the number of neglectees and isolates decreases slightly as the number of choices is increased. This partly accounts for the varying percentages of stars and isolates reported by different investigators.[9] The larger spread of scores with five sociometric choices would seem to favor their use. In fact, Bronfenbrenner's[10] table of critical raw status scores indicates that neglectees cannot be distinguished from isolates on one sociometric criterion unless five choices are allotted.

The persistent tendency for the uneven distribution of choices to remain as the number of sociometric choices is increased has been called *sociodynamic effect* by Moreno.[11] It indicates that the largest number of choices will continue to go to the highly chosen group members, while other group members will be continually ignored in the choosing. Phrasing it in terms of the distribution of wealth, again, "the sociometrically rich get richer" and "the sociometrically poor remain poor."

In summary, the distribution of sociometric choices persistently reveals a larger percentage of pupils with low sociometric status than with high sociometric status. Since this uneven distribution of choices may be found at all age levels, over different sociometric criteria, among both boys and girls, and with varying numbers of choices, it may be con-

TABLE 4-5

RELATIVE NUMBER OF CHOICES RECEIVED BY BOYS AND GIRLS IN A SIXTH-GRADE CLASS, USING THREE, FOUR, AND FIVE SOCIOMETRIC CHOICES ON ONE SOCIOMETRIC CRITERION

Boys	*No. of Choices Received*			*Girls*	*No. of Choices Received*		
	3	*4*	*5*		*3*	*4*	*5*
1	12	12	13	1	11	12	13
2	10	12	12	2	6	7	12
3	4	9	11	3	6	8	11
4	4	6	7	4	5	11	12
5	4	5	5	5	4	6	8
6	2	3	3	6	4	4	6
7	1	1	3	7	3	4	5
8	1	1	2	8	2	3	4
9	0	1	2	9	2	2	2
10	0	0	0	10	1	2	2
11	0	0	0	11	1	1	1
12	0	0	0	12	1	1	1
13	0	0	0	13	0	1	3
				14	0	0	2
				15	0	0	0

NOTE: Criterion: *Work Companion.*

[7] C. M. Tryon, "Evaluations of Adolescent Personality by Adolescents," *Monograph of the Society for Research in Child Development,* No. 4 (Washington, D.C.: National Research Council, 1939).

[8] Gronlund, "The Relative Stability . . ." *op. cit.*

[9] Bronfenbrenner, *op. cit.;* Moreno, *op. cit.*

[10] Bronfenbrenner, *op. cit.*

[11] Moreno, *op. cit.*

sidered typical of sociometric results. Although the relative percentage of pupils in each sociometric category will vary somewhat from one group to another, the positively skewed distribution of choices will remain.

CHOICES BETWEEN BOYS AND GIRLS

It has been noted in sociometric choosing among school children that there is a cleavage between the sexes. That is, boys tend to direct the majority of their choices toward boys, and girls confine the majority of their choices to girls. The extent to which this cleavage exists at various grade levels is shown in Table 4-6. The percentage of choices boys gave to girls varied between 11 and 18 per cent up to the tenth grade where it increased slightly, reaching its peak at the college level. However, even at the college level less than a third of the boys' choices were given to the girls. Somewhat similar results are presented for girls, although no increase in cross-sex choices is apparent at the high school level. Except for the lower percentages at the sixth- and the tenth-grade levels, the percentage of choices girls gave to boys remained consistently between 12 and 17 per cent for grades three through twelve. At the college level the percentage rose to 40 per cent. Thus, it is apparent that a sex cleavage remains even at the college level, although it has lessened considerebly by this time.

TABLE 4-6

PERCENTAGE OF CHOICES BETWEEN BOYS AND GIRLS AT VARIOUS GRADE LEVELS, USING FIVE SOCIOMETRIC CHOICES WITH ONE SOCIOMETRIC CRITERION

Grade Level	Number of Class-rooms	Number of Pupils		Percentage of Choices	
		Boys	*Girls*	*Boys Chose Girls*	*Girls Chose Boys*
3	9	129	141	13	12
4	10	144	133	11	15
5	10	142	126	18	16
6	10	138	146	15	10
7	6	96	75	13	15
8	6	78	68	11	15
9	8	88	85	17	17
10	6	66	69	21	9
11	6	50	55	25	17
12	5	46	59	15	14
College	5	81	63	31	40

NOTE: Criteria: *Work Companion* (grades 3-6), *Seating Companion* (grades 7-12), and *Teaching Companion* (college).

In terms of developmental trends among boys and girls one would expect cross-sex choices to increase considerably during the junior and senior high school period. Although there was a slight trend in this direction among the boys, no such increase was apparent in the girls' choices. This may be due to selective factors in the data analyzed or to the restricted nature of the choosing situation. Since the junior and senior high school classrooms were located in a small community, it is possible that there was less opportunity for boy-girl interaction than would be found in a large city. Limiting the choices to classmates may also partly account for the lack of an increase in cross-sex choices, especially for the girls. They may have had an interest in associating with members of the opposite sex in other classrooms or at other grade levels but were compelled to choose among the members of their own classroom. This restriction on the choosing may have depressed the percentage of cross-sex choices given. Limiting the sociometric test to one criterion may also account for the lack of expected results, as will be noted later. Nevertheless, the tendency for boys and girls to confine the majority of their choices to members of their own sex indicates a sex cleavage that is typical of sociometric results at all grade levels.

Influence of criteria on cross-sex choices. Observation of children's groups indicates the tendency for boys and girls to interact more readily in certain activities than in others. This would lead to the expectation that the degree to which a sex cleavage appeared in sociometric choosing would be partly dependent upon the nature of the sociometric criterion. To test this assumption, the percentage of cross-sex choices was determined for the criteria of seating companion, work companion, and play companion in forty sixth-grade classes.[12] The results are presented in Table 4-7.

It will be noted that the percentage of sociometric

[12] Gronlund, "The Accuracy of Teachers' Judgments . . ." *op. cit.*

TABLE 4-7

PERCENTAGE OF CHOICES BETWEEN BOYS AND GIRLS ON THE CRITERIA OF SEATING COMPANION, WORK COMPANION, AND PLAY COMPANION IN FORTY SIXTH-GRADE CLASSROOMS

Criteria (Five Choices Allotted on Each)	*Percentage of Choices*			
	Boys Chose Girls		*Girls Chose Boys*	
	Total	*Range*	*Total*	*Range*
Seating	11	0-38	9	0-23
Work	8	0-29	6	0-16
Play	4	0-29	5	0-16

NOTE: There was an average of 16 boys and 16 girls in each classroom.

choices boys and girls exchanged with each other shows a steady decline from the choice of seating companions to the choice of play companions. The relatively small percentage of cross-sex choices on the play companion criterion is readily understandable in terms of the distinction between play activities considered suitable for boys and girls in our culture. The terms "sissy" and "tomboy" are well-known labels for the boy and girl who dare venture into the play activities of members of the opposite sex.

The fact that the percentage of cross-sex choices does vary from one sociometric criterion to another limits the interpretations that can be made about boy-girl relations from one sociometric situation. Although a sex cleavage is apparent among school children, the extent of this cleavage cannot be determined except with reference to a particualr activity. A large number of sociometric criteria would be necessary to obtain a true picture of boy-girl relations at various age levels.

Of particular interest in Table 4-7 is the *range* of cross-sex choices among the different classes. In some classrooms none of the boys choose girls, while in others as many as 38 per cent of the choices went to girls. Similar results are indicated for the girls' choices of boys although the range is smaller. This raised an interesting question concerning the degree to which the school influenced the presence or absence of cross-sex choices on the sociometric test. A reanalysis of the data provided at least a partial answer to this question.

Influence of school on cross-sex choices. To determine the extent to which the percentage of cross-sex choices varied among different schools, the forty sixth-grade classrooms, discussed above, were arranged according to the fourteen elementary schools in which they were located. The percentage of cross-sex choices in each school is presented in Table 4-8. Since the percentage of boys choosing girls was so similar to the percentage of girls choosing boys, these were combined to provide one set of percentages indicating cross-sex choices.

TABLE 4-8

PERCENTAGE OF CROSS-SEX CHOICES ON THE CRITERIA OF SEATING COMPANION, WORK COMPANION, AND PLAY COMPANION IN FORTY SIXTH-GRADE CLASSROOMS FROM FOURTEEN DIFFERENT ELEMENTARY SCHOOLS

School	*Number of Classrooms* [a]	*Percentage of Cross-Sex Choices* [b]		
		Seating	*Work*	*Play*
1	3	21	15	7
2	2	17	11	8
3	3	13	12	8
4	2	12	6	5
5	3	11	8	6
6	4	10	9	5
7	3	9	7	5
8	2	9	6	8
9	4	8	7	4
10	3	8	5	4
11	3	8	7	2
12	2	8	3	2
13	3	7	4	2
14	3	6	4	2

a There was an average of 16 boys and 16 girls in each classroom.

b Based on five sociometric choices for each criterion.

A glance at Table 4-8 readily reveals the variation among schools in the percentage of cross-sex choices. Moving from school one down the table to school fourteen, it will be noticed that the percentage of cross-sex choices tends to drop consistently on all three sociometric criteria. This consistency from one criterion to another lends support to the hunch that the nature of the school influences the extent to which pupils express a desire to associate with members of the opposite sex for certain activities. Schools with a relatively small percentage of cross-sex choices, like the last several in the table, in all probability have separate playgrounds for boys and girls, encourage boy-girl competition in the classroom, and in other ways widen the cleavage between the sexes. In contrast, those schools with a relatively large percentage of cross-sex choices probably encourage and arrange for boy-girl interaction in school activities. Although we can only speculate concerning the probable causes of the differences between these schools, the fact that boy-girl relations can be modified is noteworthy.

The decline in the percentage of cross-sex choices, moving across the table, from the seating companion criterion to the play companion criterion is also clearly visible in Table 4-8. The fact that this decline is consistent among the various schools reinforces earlier statements that the percentage of cross-sex choices is influenced by the nature of the sociometric criterion. The relatively small percentage of cross-sex choices on the play companion criterion, in all fourteen schools, also substantiates the belief that the cleavage between boys and girls is greatest in the area of play activities.

Although the percentage of cross-sex choices in sociometric choosing varies with the grade level of the pupils, the nature of the sociometric criterion, and the school in which the test is administered, the fact that a sex cleavage continues to appear under all conditions should not be overlooked. Variations from one situation to another make it difficult to indicate what degree of sex-cleavage is desirable or characteristic for a given age level. However, the preference boys and girls have shown for members of their own sex occurs so persistently in sociometric choosing that a sex cleavage can be considered typical of sociometric results at these age levels.

MUTUAL CHOICES

A mutual choice is indicated when two group members choose each other on the same sociometric criterion. Since mutual choices reflect a common desire to associate together, the number of mutual choices in a group is a general indication of the degree of socialization among the group members. Newly formed groups have relatively few mutual choices, and the number increases as the group members become better acquainted.[13] This variation in the number of mutual choices with the development of the group makes it difficult to indicate the percentage of mutual choices that might typically be expected in classroom groups at a particular time. However, data on mutual choices in groups where the choice process has become stabilized should provide some indication of the extent to which mutual choices might be expected.

Table 4-9 presents the percentage of boys and girls with mutual choices at various grade levels. It will be noted that a relatively large percentage of pupils have mutual choices at all grade levels. This is partly due to the fact that all of the class members, except those in the college group, had been together between six and eight months. Smaller percentages would be expected earlier in the school year. The pupils without mutual choices tend to be those in the low sociometric status categories. This is accounted for primarily by the fact that low status group members tend to choose high status group members and high status group members tend to choose each other.[14] Since low status group members do not choose each other, their choices remain unreciprocated.

Although the percentage of pupils with mutual choices is relatively large at all grade levels, it is interesting to note that the percentage increases at the seventh-grade level and remains above 82 per cent throughout the high school and college levels. This is probably a reflection of the more complex social structures formed during this period.[15] To check on this assumption the percentage of pupils with three or more mutual choices was calculated for each grade level. For grades three through six, between 19 and 31 per cent of the pupils had three or more mutual choices. At grade seven the percentage rose to 45 and remained above 40 per cent throughout the junior and senior high school period. The consistently larger percentage of pupils with three or more mutual choices, at these grade levels, indicates the formation of more complex sociometric patterns characteristic of a higher level of socialization.

Distribution of mutual choices by sex. The sex cleavage between boys and girls in sociometric choosing is strikingly apparent when mutual choices

[13] Bronfenbrenner, *op. cit.;* Moreno, *op. cit.*

[14] M. E. Bonney, "A Study of the Sociometric Process Among Sixth-Grade Children," *Journal of Educational Psychology,* 1946, *37,* pp. 356-372.

[15] Moreno, *op. cit.*

TABLE 4-9

PERCENTAGE OF PUPILS WITH MUTUAL CHOICES AT VARIOUS GRADE LEVELS, USING FIVE SOCIOMETRIC CHOICES WITH ONE SOCIOMETRIC CRITERION

Grade Level	Number of Classrooms	Number of Pupils		Percentage With Mutual Choices	
		Boys	Girls	Boys	Girls
3	9	129	141	78	77
4	10	144	133	74	81
5	10	142	126	81	80
6	10	138	146	67	71
7	6	96	75	87	84
8	6	78	68	82	96
9	8	88	85	86	84
10	6	66	69	88	93
11	6	50	55	84	93
12	5	46	59	83	88
College	5	81	63	90	84

NOTE: Criteria: *Work Companion* (grades 3-6), *Seating Companion* (grades 7-12), and *Teaching Companion* (college).

TABLE 4-10

PERCENTAGE OF MUTUAL CHOICES AT VARIOUS GRADE LEVELS, USING FIVE SOCIOMETRIC CHOICES WITH ONE SOCIOMETRIC CRITERION

Grade Level	Number of Class-rooms	Number of Pupils		Percentage of Mutuals		
				Within Sex		Between Sexes
		Boys	Girls	Boys	Girls	
3	9	129	141	34	38	2
4	10	144	133	36	35	2
5	10	142	126	35	37	3
6	10	138	146	31	35	1
7	6	96	75	40	41	2
8	6	78	68	42	48	2
9	8	88	85	41	49	6
10	6	66	69	38	48	4
11	6	50	55	34	39	7
12	5	46	59	33	38	5
College	5	81	63	33	22	12

NOTE: Criteria: *Work Companion* (grades 3-6), *Seating Companion* (grades 7-12), and *Teaching Companion* (college).

are considered. Although between one-third and one-half of the sociometric choices at various grade levels are mutual choices, a relatively small percentage of these mutual choices occur between members of the opposite sex. This tendency for mutual choices to be directed to members of the same sex is brought out clearly in Table 4-10. The percentage of mutual choices reported, within the same sex group and between the sexes, refers to the percentage based on the total number of choices given at each grade level. It will be noted that the percentage of mutual choices between boys and girls varies between 1 and 3 per cent until the ninth grade. Here it rises to 6 per cent and remains at this slightly higher level throughout the high school period. This increase in mutual choices between the sexes during the adolescent period would be expected in terms of the development of heterosexual interests. However, even a larger increase than that reported might be expected. The fact that the percentage of girls choosing boys did not increase during the high school period, as indicated earlier, probably accounts for the relatively small percentage of mutual choices between the sexes at these grade levels. It can only be surmised that more mutual choices between adolescent boys and girls would have occurred if the sociometric test had not restricted their choices to pupils in their own classroom.

There are a few interesting things to note concerning the percentage of mutual choices boys and girls exchanged with members of their own sex. First, the percentage of choices that were mutual is relatively high at all grade levels. It indicates that approximately two of the five choices given on the sociometric test were reciprocated by a mutual choice from a member of the same sex. In other words, the average boy and girl had approximately two mutual friends among their classmates.

The larger percentage of mutual choices from the seventh to the tenth grades indicates the increased socialization among adolescents, referred to earlier. The slight decline for boys from the eleventh grade on can probably be accounted for by the increased percentage of choices directed toward girls at these grade levels. The more noticeable drop in percentage for girls at the college level is also probably due to the relatively large percentage of cross-sex choices. It will be recalled that 40 per cent of the college girls' choices went to members of the opposite sex.

Except for the fourth grade and the college level, girls had a consistently larger percentage of mutual choices than boys. This greater tendency of girls to form mutual pairs lends support to Moreno's[16] hypothesis that girls tend more toward socialization than boys. Since the largest differences between boys and girls occurred during grades eight to twelve, it appears that this tendency might be greatest during the adolescent period.

As with the other distributions of sociometric choices presented in this chapter, the data on mutual choices have been presented to indicate some typical sociometric results at various grade levels. However, the percentages reported here should not be considered a desirable goal or a set of norms by which to evaluate sociometric results from a specific classroom. So many factors enter into sociometric choosing that a specific set of standards or norms would be inappropriate for sociometric testing. Typically one can expect more mutual choices to appear as the level of socialization of the group members increases. The specific number of mutual choices obtained, however, must be evaluated in terms of the type of sociometric test used and the nature of the group being tested.

SUMMARY

Although sociometric results can be expected to vary from one group to another, certain phenomena occur with such persistence that they may be considered typical sociometric patterns. One of the most common findings in this regard is the positively skewed distribution of sociometric choices. This tendency for a larger percentage of the pupils to appear in the low sociometric status categories than in the high status categories has been shown to occur at all age levels, over different sociometric criteria, among both sexes, and with varying numbers of sociometric choices. The consistency with which this positive skewness has appeared in sociometric results has led to the formulation of Moreno's *sociodynamic law*. This law states that distributions of sociometric choices are positively skewed.

When an increased number of sociometric choices is made available to a group, there is a tendency for the largest number of choices to continue to go to the group members with high sociometric status while those with low sociometric status continue to receive a disproportionately small share of the choices. This tendency has been called *sociodynamic effect* by Moreno. Typical sociometric results, presented in this chapter, have illustrated the operation of the *sociodynamic law* and the *sociodynamic effect* among pupils at various grade levels in the public school.

The persistence with which socially neglected and socially isolated pupils appear in the classroom, at all grade levels, indicates their need for help in improving their social relations. Sociometric results at various grade levels indicated that between 11 and 22 per cent of the pupils were neglected or ignored by their classmates.

Another common phenomenon appearing in sociometric results of children and adolescents is the sex cleavage. Boys and girls both show preference for members of their own sex in sociometric choosing. The extent of this cleavage, however, varies with the grade level of the pupils and the nature of the sociometric criterion. A slightly larger percentage of cross-sex choices has been shown to occur at the high school and college levels. The lowest percentage of cross-sex choices appeared on the play companion criterion, at all grade levels. It was also shown that the percentage of cross-sex choices varied from one school to another.

The extent to which mutual choices occur in sociometric choosing is a general indication of the socialization level of the group. Sociometric results at various grade levels have indicated an increase in mutual choices during the junior and senior high school periods. There was also a general tendency for girls to have more mutual choices than boys, indicating a possible trend toward greater socialization on the part of girls. The percentage of mutual choices between boys and girls was relatively low at all grade levels but showed a slight increase during the adolescent period. Although mutual choices can be typically expected in sociometric choosing, it was pointed out that the percentage of such choices will be influenced by the type of sociometric test used and the nature of the group being tested.

The sociometric results presented in this paper were intended to illustrate some typical sociometric patterns among school children and adolescents. However, the percentages of pupils occurring in various distributions should not be considered as norms or standards for a given grade level. The complexity of factors entering into sociometric choosing makes norms and standards inappropriate for sociometric testing.

[16] *Ibid.*

*ACHIEVING CHANGE IN PEOPLE: SOME APPLICATIONS OF GROUP DYNAMICS THEORY**

By Dorwin Cartwright

We hear all around us today the assertion that the problems of the twentieth century are problems of human relations. The survival of civilization, it is said, will depend upon man's ability to create social inventions capable of harnessing, for society's constructive use, the vast physical energies now at man's disposal. Or, to put the matter more simply, we must learn how to change the way in which people behave toward one another. In broad outline, the specifications for a good society are clear, but a serious technical problem remains: How can we change people so that they neither restrict the freedom nor limit the potentialities for growth of others; so that they accept and respect people of different religion, nationality, color, or political opinion; so that nations can exist in a world without war, and so that the fruits of our technological advances can bring economic well-being and freedom from disease to all the people of the world? Although few people would disagree with these objectives when stated abstractly, when we become more specific, differences of opinion quickly arise. How is change to be produced? Who is to do it? Who is to be changed? These questions permit no ready answers.

Before we consider in detail these questions of social technology, let us clear away some semantic obstacles. The word "change" produces emotional reactions. It is not a neutral word. To many people it is threatening. It conjures up visions of a revolutionary, a dissatisfied idealist, a trouble-maker, a malcontent. Nicer words referring to the process of changing people are education, training, orientation, guidance, indoctrination, therapy. We are more ready to have others "educate" us than to have them "change" us. We, ourselves, feel less guilty in "training" others than in "changing" them. Why this emotional response? What makes the two kinds of words have such different meanings? I believe that a large part of the difference lies in the fact that the safer words (like education or therapy) carry the implicit assurance that the only changes produced will be good ones, acceptable within a currently held value system. The cold, unmodified word "change," on the contrary, promises no respect for values; it might even tamper with values themselves. Perhaps for this very reason it will foster straight thinking if we use the word "change" and thus force ourselves to struggle directly and self-consciously with the problems of value that are involved. Words like education, training, or therapy, by the very fact that they are not so disturbing, may close our eyes to the fact that they too inevitably involve values.

Another advantage of using the word "change" rather than other related words is that it does not restrict our thinking to a limited set of aspects of people that are legitimate targets of change. Anyone familiar with the history of education knows that there has been endless controversy over what it is about people that "education" properly attempts to modify. Some educators have viewed education simply as imparting knowledge, others mainly as providing skills for doing things, still others as producing healthy "attitudes," and some have aspired to instil a way of life. Or if we choose to use a word like "therapy," we can hardly claim that we refer to a more clearly defined realm of change. Furthermore, one can become inextricably entangled in distinctions and vested interests by attempting to distinguish sharply between, let us say, the domain of education and that of therapy. If we are to try to take a broader view and to develop some basic principles that promise to apply to all types of modifications in people, we had better use a word like "change" to keep our thinking general enough.

The proposal that social technology may be employed to solve the problems of society suggests that social science may be applied in ways not different

*From *Human Relations,* 1951, *4,* pp. 381-392. Used by permission of the author and publisher. This paper is based on a lecture delivered at Wayne University, Detroit, in the Leo M. Franklin Lecture Series, 1950-51.

from those used in the physical sciences. Does social science, in fact, have any practically useful knowledge which may be brought to bear significantly on society's most urgent problems? What scientifically based principles are there for guiding programs of social change? In this paper we shall restrict our considerations to certain parts of a relatively new branch of social science known as "group dynamics." We shall examine some of the implications for social action which stem from research in this field of scientific investigation.

What is "group dynamics"? Perhaps it will be most useful to start by looking at the derivation of the word "dynamics." It comes from a Greek word meaning force. In careful usage of the phrase, "group dynamics" refers to the forces operating in groups. The investigation of group dynamics, then, consists of a study of these forces: what gives rise to them, what conditions modify them, what consequences they have, etc. The practical application of group dynamics (or the technology of group dynamics) consists of the utilization of knowledge about these forces for the achievement of some purpose. In keeping with this definition, then, it is clear that group dynamics, as a realm of investigation, is not particularly novel, nor is it the exclusive property of any person or institution. It goes back at least to the outstanding work of men like Simmel, Freud, and Cooley.

Although interest in groups has a long and respectable history, the past fifteen years have witnessed a new flowering of activity in this field. Today, research centers in several countries are carrying out substantial programs of research designed to reveal the nature of groups and of their functioning. The phrase "group dynamics" has come into common usage during this time and intense efforts have been devoted to the development of the field, both as a branch of social science and as a form of social technology.

In this development the name of Kurt Lewin has been outstanding. As a consequence of his work in the field of individual psychology and from his analysis of the nature of the pressing problems of the contemporary world, Lewin became convinced of society's urgent need for a *scientific approach* to the understanding of the dynamics of groups. In 1945 he established the Research Center for Group Dynamics to meet this need. Since that date the Center has been devoting its efforts to improving our scientific understanding of groups through laboratory experimentation, field studies, and the use of techniques of action research. It has also attempted in various ways to help get the findings of social science more widely used by social management. Much of what I have to say in this paper is drawn from the experiences of this Center in its brief existence of a little more than five years.[1]

For various reasons we have found that much of our work has been devoted to an attempt to gain a better understanding of the ways in which people change their behavior or resist efforts by others to have them do so. Whether we set for ourselves the practical goal of improving behavior or whether we take on the intellectual task of understanding why people do what they do, we have to investigate processes of communication, influence, social pressure—in short, problems of change.

In this work we have encountered great frustration. The problems have been most difficult to solve. Looking back over our experience, I have become convinced that no small part of the trouble has resulted from an irresistible tendency to conceive of our problems in terms of the individual. We live in an individualistic culture. We value the individual highly, and rightly so. But I am inclined to believe that our political and social concern for the individual has narrowed our thinking as social scientists so much that we have not been able to state our research problems properly. Perhaps we have taken the individual as the unit of observation and study when some larger unit would have been more appropriate. Let us look at a few examples.

Consider first some matters having to do with the mental health of an individual. We can all agree, I believe, that an important mark of a healthy personality is that the individual's self-esteem has not been undermined. But on what does self-esteem depend? From research on this problem we have discovered that, among other things, repeated experiences of failure or traumatic failures on matters of central importance serve to undermine one's self-esteem. We also know that whether a person experiences success or failure as a result of some undertaking depends upon the level of aspiration which he has set for himself. Now, if we try to dis-

[1] D. Cartwright, *The Research Center for Group Dynamics: A Report of Five Years Activity and a View of Future Needs* (Ann Arbor: Institute for Social Research, 1950).

cover how the level of aspiration gets set, we are immediately involved in the person's relationships to groups. The groups to which he belongs set standards for his behavior which he must accept if he is to remain in the group. If his capacities do not allow him to reach these standards, he experiences failure, he withdraws or is rejected by the group and his self-esteem suffers a shock.

Suppose, then, that we accept a task of therapy, of rebuilding his self-esteem. It would appear plausible from our analysis of the problem that we should attempt to work with variables of the same sort that produced the difficulty, that is to work with him either in the groups to which he now belongs or to introduce him into new groups which are selected for the purpose and to work upon his relationships to groups as such. From the point of view of preventive mental health, we might even attempt to train the groups in our communities—classes in schools, work groups in business, families, unions, religious and cultural groups—to make use of practices better designed to protect the self-esteem of their members.

Consider a second example. A teacher finds that in her class she has a number of trouble-makers, full of aggression. She wants to know why these children are so aggressive and what can be done about it. A foreman in a factory has the same kind of problem with some of his workers. He wants the same kind of help. The solution most tempting to both the teacher and the foreman often is to transfer the worst trouble-makers to someone else, or if facilities are available, to refer them for counselling. But is the problem really of such a nature that it can be solved by removing the trouble-maker from the situation or by working on his individual motivations and emotional life? What leads does research give us? The evidence indicates, of course, that there are many causes of aggressiveness in people, but one aspect of the problem has become increasingly clear in recent years. If we observe carefully the amount of aggressive behavior and the number of trouble-makers to be found in a large collection of groups, we find that these characteristics can vary tremendously from group to group even when the different groups are composed essentially of the same kinds of people. In the now classic experiments of Lewin, Lippitt, and White[2] on the effects of different styles of leadership, it was found that the same group of children displayed markedly different levels of aggressive behavior when under different styles of leadership. Moreover, when individual children were transferred from one group to another, their levels of aggressiveness shifted to conform to the atmosphere of the new group. Efforts to account for one child's aggressiveness under one style of leadership merely in terms of his personality traits could hardly succeed under these conditions. This is not to say that a person's behavior is entirely to be accounted for by the atmosphere and structure of the immediate group, but it is remarkable to what an extent a strong, cohesive group can control aspects of a member's behavior traditionally thought to be expressive of enduring personality traits. Recognition of this fact rephrases the problem of how to change such behavior. It directs us to a study of the sources of the influence of the group on its members.

Let us take an example from a different field. What can we learn from efforts to change people by mass media and mass persuasion? In those rare instances when educators, propagandists, advertisers, and others who want to influence large numbers of people have bothered to make an objective evaluation of the enduring changes produced by their efforts, they have been able to demonstrate only the most negligible effects.[3] The inefficiency of attempts to influence the public by mass media would be scandalous if there were agreement that it was important or even desirable to have such influences strongly exerted. In fact, it is no exaggeration to say that all of the research and experience of generations has not improved the efficiency of lectures or other means of mass influence to any noticeable degree. Something must be wrong with our theories of learning, motivation, and social psychology.

Within very recent years some research data have been accumulating which may give us a clue to the solution of our problem. In one series of experiments directed by Lewin, it was found that a method of group decision, in which the group as a whole made a decision to have its members change their behavior, was from two to ten times as effec-

[2] K. Lewin, R. Lippitt and R. K. White, "Patterns of Aggressive Behavior in Experimentally Created 'Social Climates,'" *Journal of Social Psychology,* 1939, *10,* pp. 271-299.

[3] D. Cartwright, "Some Principles of Mass Persuasion: Selected Findings of Research on the Sale of United States War Bonds," *Human Relations,* 1949, *2,* pp. 253-267.

tive in producing actual change as was a lecture presenting exhortation to change.[4] We have yet to learn precisely what produces these differences of effectiveness, but it is clear that by introducing group forces into the situation a whole new level of influence has been achieved.

The experience has been essentially the same when people have attempted to increase the productivity of individuals in work settings. Traditional conceptions of how to increase the output of workers have stressed the individual: select the right man for the job; simplify the job for him; train him in the skills required; motivate him by economic incentives; make it clear to whom he reports; keep the lines of authority and responsibility simple and straight. But even when all these conditions are fully met we are finding that productivity is far below full potential. There is even good reason to conclude that this individualistic conception of the determinants of productivity actually fosters negative consequences. The individual, now isolated and subjected to the demands of the organization through the commands of his boss, finds that he must create with his fellow employees informal groups, not shown on any table of organization, in order to protect himself from arbitrary control of his life, from the boredom produced by the endless repetition of mechanically sanitary and routine operations, and from the impoverishment of his emotional and social life brought about by the frustration of his basic needs for social interaction, participation, and acceptance in a stable group. Recent experiments have demonstrated clearly that the productivity of work groups can be greatly increased by methods of work organization and supervision which give more responsibility to work groups, which allow for fuller participation in important decisions, and which make stable groups the firm basis for support of the individual's social needs.[5] I am convinced that future research will also demonstrate that people working under such conditions become more mature and creative individuals in their homes, in community life, and as citizens.

As a final example, let us examine the experience of efforts to train people in workshops, institutes, and special training courses. Such efforts are common in various areas of social welfare, intergroup relations, political affairs, industry, and adult education generally. It is an unfortunate fact that objective evaluation of the effects of such training efforts has only rarely been undertaken, but there is evidence for those who will look that the actual change in behavior produced is most disappointing. A workshop not infrequently develops keen interest among the participants, high morale and enthusiasm, and a firm resolve on the part of many to apply all the wonderful insights back home. But what happens back home? The trainee discovers that his colleagues don't share his enthusiasm. He learns that the task of changing others' expectations and ways of doing things is discouragingly difficult. He senses, perhaps not very clearly, that it would make all the difference in the world if only there were a few other people sharing his enthusiasm and insights with whom he could plan activities, evaluate consequences of efforts, and from whom he could gain emotional and motivational support. The approach to training which conceives of its task as being merely that of changing the individual probably produces frustration, demoralization, and disillusionment in as large a measure as it accomplishes more positive results.

A few years ago the Research Center for Group Dynamics undertook to shed light on this problem by investigating the operation of a workshop for training leaders in intercultural relations.[6] In a project, directed by Lippitt, we set out to compare systematically the different effects of the workshop upon trainees who came as isolated individuals in contrast to those who came as teams. Since one of the problems in the field of intercultural relations is that of getting people of good will to be more active in community efforts to improve intergroup relations, one goal of the training workshop was to increase the activity of the trainees in such community affairs. We found that before the workshop there was no difference in the activity level of the people who were to be trained as isolates and of those who were to be trained as teams. Six months after the workshop, however, those who had been trained as isolates were only slightly more active than before the workshop whereas those who had been members of strong training teams were now

[4] K. Lewin, *Field Theory in Social Science* (New York: Harper & Row, Publishers, 1951), pp. 229-236.

[5] L. Coch and J. R. P. French, Jr., "Overcoming Resistance to Change," *Human Relations,* 1948, *1,* pp. 512-532.

[6] R. Lippitt, *Training in Community Relations* (New York: Harper & Row, Publishers, 1951).

much more active. We do not have clear evidence on the point, but we would be quite certain that the maintenance of heightened activity over a long period of time would also be much better for members of teams. For the isolates the effect of the workshop had the characteristic of a "shot in the arm" while for the team member it produced a more enduring change because the team provided continuous support and reinforcement for its members.

What conclusions may we draw from these examples? What principles of achieving change in people can we see emerging? To begin with the most general proposition, we may state that the behavior, attitudes, beliefs, and values of the individual are all firmly grounded in the groups to which he belongs. How aggressive or cooperative a person is, how much self-respect and self-confidence he has, how energetic and productive his work is, what he aspires to, what he believes to be true and good, whom he loves or hates, and what beliefs and prejudices he holds—all these characteristics are highly determined by the individual's group memberships. In a real sense, they are properties of groups and of the relationships between people. Whether they change or resist change will, therefore, be greatly influenced by the nature of these groups. Attempts to change them must be concerned with the dynamics of groups.

In examining more specifically how groups enter into the process of change, we find it useful to view groups in at least three different ways. In the first view, the group is seen as a source of influence over its members. Efforts to change behavior can be supported or blocked by pressures on members stemming from the group. To make constructive use of these pressures the group must be used *as a medium of change*. In the second view, the group itself becomes the *target of change*. To change the behavior of individuals it may be necessary to change the standards of the group, its style of leadership, its emotional atmosphere, or its stratification into cliques and hierarchies. Even though the goal may be to change the behavior of *individuals*, the target of change becomes the group. In the third view, it is recognized that many changes of behavior can be brought about only by the organized efforts of groups *as agents of change*. A committee to combat intolerance, a labor union, an employers association, a citizens group to increase the pay of teachers—any action group will be more or less effective depending upon the way it is organized, the satisfactions it provides to its members, the degree to which its goals are clear, and a host of other properties of the group.

An adequate social technology of change, then, requires at the very least a scientific understanding of groups viewed in each of these ways. We shall consider here only the first two aspects of the problem: the group as a medium of change and as a target of change.

Principle No. 1. If the group is to be used effectively as a medium of change, those people who are to be changed and those who are to exert influence for change must have a strong sense of belonging to the same group.

Kurt Lewin described this principle well: "The normal gap between teacher and student, doctor and patient, social worker and public, can . . . be a real obstacle to acceptance of the advocated conduct." In other words, in spite of whatever status differences there might be between them, the teacher and the student have to feel as members of one group in matters involving their sense of values. The chances for re-education seem to be increased whenever a strong we-feeling is created.[7] Recent experiments by Preston and Heintz have demonstrated greater changes of opinions among members of discussion groups operating with participatory leadership than among those with supervisory leadership.[8] The implications of this principle for classroom teaching are far-reaching. The same may be said of supervision in the factory, army, or hospital.

Principle No. 2. The more attractive the group is to its members the greater is the influence that the group can exert on its members.

This principle has been extensively documented by Festinger and his co-workers.[9] They have been able to show in a variety of settings that in more cohesive groups there is a greater readiness of members to attempt to influence others, a greater

[7] K. Lewin, *Resolving Social Conflict* (New York: Harper & Row, Publishers, 1948), p. 67.

[8] M. G. Preston and R. K. Heintz, "Effects of Participatory vs. Supervisory Leadership on Group Judgment," *Journal of Abnormal and Social Psychology*, 1949, *44*, pp. 345-355.

[9] L. Festinger *et al., op. cit.*

readiness to be influenced by others, and stronger pressures toward conformity when conformity is a relevant matter for the group. Important for the practitioner wanting to make use of this principle is, of course, the question of how to increase the attractiveness of groups. This is a question with many answers. Suffice it to say that a group is more attractive the more it satisfies the needs of its members. We have been able to demonstrate experimentally an increase in group cohesiveness by increasing the liking of members for each other as persons, by increasing the perceived importance of the group goal, and by increasing the prestige of the group among other groups. Experienced group workers could add many other ways to this list.

Principle No. 3. In attempts to change attitudes, values, or behavior, the more relevant they are to the basis of attraction to the group, the greater will be the influence that the group can exert upon them.

I believe this principle gives a clue to some otherwise puzzling phenomena. How does it happen that a group, like a labor union, seems to be able to exert such strong discipline over its members in some matters (let us say in dealings with management), while it seems unable to exert nearly the same influence in other matters (let us say in political action)? If we examine why it is that members are attracted to the group, I believe we will find that a particular reason for belonging seems more related to some of the group's activities than to others. If a man joins a union mainly to keep his job and to improve his working conditions, he may be largely uninfluenced by the union's attempt to modify his attitudes toward national and international affairs. Groups differ tremendously in the range of matters that are relevant to them and hence over which they have influence. Much of the inefficiency of adult education could be reduced if more attention were paid to the need that influence attempts be appropriate to the groups in which they are made.

Principle No. 4. The greater the prestige of a group member in the eyes of the other members, the greater the influence he can exert.

Polansky, Lippitt, and Redl[10] have demonstrated this principle with great care and methodological ingenuity in a series of studies in children's summer camps. From a practical point of view it must be emphasized that the things giving prestige to a member may not be those characteristics most prized by the official management of the group. The most prestige-carrying member of a Sunday School class may not possess the characteristics most similar to the minister of the church. The teacher's pet may be a poor source of influence within a class. This principle is the basis for the common observation that the official leader and the actual leader of a group are often not the same individual.

Principle No. 5. Efforts to change individuals or subparts of a group which, if successful, would have the result of making them deviate from the norms of the group will encounter strong resistance.

During the past few years a great deal of evidence has been accumulated showing the tremendous pressures which groups can exert upon members to conform to the group's norms. The price of deviation in most groups is rejection or even expulsion. If the member really wants to belong and be accepted, he cannot withstand this type of pressure. It is for this reason that efforts to change people by taking them from the group and giving them special training so often have disappointing results. This principle also accounts for the finding that people thus trained sometimes display increased tension, aggressiveness toward the group, or a tendency to form cults or cliques with others who have shared their training.

These five principles concerning the group as a medium of change would appear to have readiest application to groups created for the purpose of producing changes in people. They provide certain specifications for building effective training or therapy groups. They also point, however, to a difficulty in producing change in people in that they show how resistant an individual is to changing in any way contrary to group pressures and expectations. In order to achieve many kinds of changes in people, therefore, it is necessary to deal with the group as a target of change.

Principle No. 6. Strong pressure for changes in the group can be established by creating a shared

---

[10] N. Polansky, R. Lippitt, and F. Redl, "An Investigation of Behavioral Contagion in Groups," *Human Relations*, 1950, *3*, pp. 319-348.

perception by members of the need for change, thus making the source of pressure for change lie within the group.

Marrow and French[11] report a dramatic case-study which illustrates this principle quite well. A manufacturing concern had a policy against hiring women over thirty because it was believed that they were slower, more difficult to train, and more likely to be absent. The staff psychologist was able to present to management evidence that this belief was clearly unwarranted at least within their own company. The psychologist's facts, however, were rejected and ignored as a basis for action because they violated accepted beliefs. It was claimed that they went against the direct experience of the foremen. Then the psychologist hit upon a plan for achieving change which differed drastically from the usual one of argument, persuasion, and pressure. He proposed that management conduct its own analysis of the situation. With his help management collected all the facts which they believed were relevant to the problem. When the results were in they were now their own facts rather than those of some "outside" expert. Policy was immediately changed without further resistance. The important point here is that facts are not enough. The facts must be the accepted property of the group if they are to become an effective basis for change. There seems to be all the difference in the world in changes actually carried out between those cases in which a consulting firm is hired to do a study and present a report and those in which technical experts are asked to collaborate with the group in doing its own study.

Principle No. 7. Information relating to the need for change, plans for change, and consequences of change must be shared by all relevant people in the group.

Another way of stating this principle is to say that change of a group ordinarily requires the opening of communication channels. Newcomb[12] has shown how one of the first consequences of mistrust and hostility is the avoidance of communicating openly and freely about the things producing the tension. If you look closely at a pathological group (that is, one that has trouble making decisions or effecting coordinated efforts of its members), you will certainly find strong restraints in that group against communicating vital information among its members. Until these restraints are removed there can be little hope for any real and lasting changes in the group's functioning. In passing it should be pointed out that the removal of barriers to communication will ordinarily be accompanied by a sudden increase in the communication of hostility. The group may appear to be falling apart, and it will certainly be a painful experience to many of the members. This pain and the fear that things are getting out of hand often stop the process of change once begun.

Principle No. 8. Changes in one part of a group produce strain in other related parts which can be reduced only by eliminating the change or by bringing about readjustments in the related parts.

It is a common practice to undertake improvements in group functioning by providing training programs for certain classes of people in the organization. A training program for foremen, for nurses, for teachers, or for group workers is established. If the content of the training is relevant for organizational change, it must of necessity deal with the relationships these people have with other subgroups. If nurses in a hospital change their behavior significantly, it will affect their relations both with the patients and with the doctors. It is unrealistic to assume that both these groups will remain indifferent to any significant changes in this respect. In hierarchical structures this process is most clear. Lippitt has proposed on the basis of research and experience that in such organizations attempts at change should always involve three levels, one being the major target of change and the other two being the one above and the one below.

These eight principles represent a few of the basic propositions emerging from research in group dynamics. Since research is constantly going on and since it is the very nature of research to revise and reformulate our conceptions, we may be sure that these principles will have to be modified and improved as time goes by. In the meantime they may serve as guides in our endeavors to develop a scientifically based technology of social management.

In social technology, just as in physical tech-

---

[11] A. J. Marrow and J. R. P. French, Jr., "Changing a Stereotype in Industry," *Journal of Social Issues,* 1945, *1,* No. 3, pp. 33-37.

[12] T. M. Newcomb, "Autistic Hostility and Social Reality," *Human Relations,* 1947, *1,* pp. 69-86.

nology, invention plays a crucial role. In both fields progress consists of the creation of new mechanisms for the accomplishment of certain goals. In both fields inventions arise in response to practical needs and are to be evaluated by how effectively they satisfy these needs. The relation of invention to scientific development is indirect but important. Inventions cannot proceed too far ahead of basic scientific development, nor should they be allowed to fall too far behind. They will be more effective the more they make good use of known principles of science, and they often make new developments in science possible. On the other hand, they are in no sense logical derivations from scientific principles.

I have taken this brief excursion into the theory of invention in order to make a final point. To many people "group dynamics" is known only for the social inventions which have developed in recent years in work with groups. Group dynamics is often thought of as certain techniques to be used with groups. Role playing, buzz groups, process observers, post-meeting reaction sheets, and feedback of group observations are devices popularly associated with the phrase "group dynamics." I trust that I have been able to show that group dynamics is more than a collection of gadgets. It certainly aspires to be a science as well as a technology.

This is not to underplay the importance of these inventions nor of the function of inventing. As inventions they are all mechanisms designed to help accomplish important goals. How effective they are will depend upon how skilfully they are used and how appropriate they are to the purposes to which they are put. Careful evaluative research must be the ultimate judge of their usefulness in comparison with alternative inventions. I believe that the principles enumerated in this paper indicate some of the specifications that social inventions in this field must meet.

*RELATIONSHIP OF INTELLIGENCE AND SOCIAL POWER TO THE INTERPERSONAL BEHAVIOR OF CHILDREN**

By Alvin Zander and Elmer Van Egmond

There are contradictory beliefs about the behavior of highly intelligent children in school, and particularly about their participation in problem-solving discussions. These children are described as both influential and impotent, tolerant and impatient, supporting and rejecting, eager and bored. Little information exists which can help us to separate fact from fancy among these assertions, nor do we know much more about the ways in which intelligent persons differ from less intelligent ones in these respects.

There is a reason for this lack of information. Intelligence as a concept is primarily intended to describe an ability to deal with cognitive problems. There are few elements in definitions of intelligence which suggest that variations in intellectual ability are associated with variations in face to face behavior. Hence, intelligence has seldom been used as an independent variable in studies of social behavior.

In a decision-making group, however, a person with high intelligence may perhaps offer wiser observations than one with low intelligence. Because of his greater usefulness, we can anticipate that a brighter child would be more influential than a less intelligent one. Because he is more expert, he should have greater social power, that is, a greater ability to influence others. On the basis of assumptions like these, it is apparent that intelligence can be a cause for particular types of interpersonal behavior. Some children, regardless of their degree of intelligence are able to exercise strong influence on their

*From the *Journal of Educational Psychology*, 1958, *49*, pp. 257-268. Used by permission of the authors and publisher. The research reported herein was performed pursuant to a contract with the United States Office of Education, Department of Health, Education and Welfare.

peers, while others are consistently ignored by classmates.

How then does a person's intelligence affect the way he acts toward others when his group must reach a decision? Does he behave differently when he is used to having his ideas accepted (has high social power) than when he is used to being ignored? These are primary interests in this study.

Boys and girls are expected and required to behave differently in social settings. Boys, for example, are more often pressed than are girls to be concerned with achievement and influence. Because prescriptions for the two sexes differ, it is probable that the meaning and effects of intelligence or social power differ for boys and girls. A secondary purpose of this study is to examine the impact of intelligence and social power on the interpersonal behavior of boys compared to girls.

Toward these purposes, measures were made of the intelligence and social power of all children in a number of classrooms. These persons were then put in standardized, small, problem-solving groups. Their participation was observed in terms of precoded categories to see how those with different degrees of power and intelligence differed in their behavior. Data were also obtained from teachers and classmates concerning characteristics of these children in regular classrooms.

MAJOR ISSUES

In the small discussion groups, we assumed children would behave in the ways they typically do in their classes to try to win acceptance for their ideas.

It was expected that intelligence should make a difference in the actions initiated by them, as already mentioned, because intelligent persons have more resources to offer in a problem-solving discussion than do less intelligent ones. Also, they might have more confidence in their own proposals, stemming from the ready acceptance of them in the past. Highly intelligent pupils, therefore, were expected to make more efforts to influence others, to have their ideas accepted more often than less intelligent pupils, and to behave in ways which could be taken as typical of persons with confidence in themselves.

Children with greater social power were expected to make more efforts to influence others, to be more successful in doing so, and to behave in ways which have been shown in other studies to be typical of persons with greater power.[1]

How do teachers characterize children who have different degrees of intelligence and social power? To determine this, teachers were asked to rate the behavior of *S*s in categories roughly similar to those used in observing the behavior of the children in the small groups. What aspects of the teachers' opinions, based on day-by-day experience with these children, support or contradict the behavior shown in the standardized group situations? Were teachers able to differentiate between the behavior of one type of person and that of another?

Finally, it is useful to know how classmates characterized the children to whom they ascribed high social power as compared to those to whom they attributed little power. The *S*s were rated by their peers concerning their ability in schoolwork, their attractiveness, and their ability to coerce or threaten others. These personal qualities were considered to be separate sources of social power as suggested by French and Raven.[2] It was anticipated that persons with greater social power, in contrast to those with less, would have these qualities ascribed to them more often by classmates. Do highly intelligent persons differ from the less intelligent in these respects?

METHOD

Data used in this research were originally collected by colleagues for a different but related purpose.[3] In the original investigation, measures were

[1] J. R. P. French and B. Raven, "The Basis of Social Power," in D. Cartwright (Ed.), *Studies in Social Power* (Ann Arbor, Mich.: Institute for Social Research, 1959); J. Hurwitz, A. Zander, and B. Hymovitch, "Some Effects of Power on the Relations among Group Members," in D. Cartwright and A. Zander (Eds.), *Group Dynamics Research and Theory* (Evanston, Ill.: Harper & Row, Publishers, 1953); R. Lippitt, N. Polansky, F. Redl, and S. Rosen, "The Dynamics of Power," *Human Relations,* 1952, *5,* pp. 37-64; A. Zander and A. R. Cohen, "Attributed Social Power and Group Acceptance," *Journal of Abnormal and Social Psychology,* 1955, *51,* pp. 490-492; A. Zander, A. R. Cohen, and E. Stotland, *Role Relations in the Mental Health Professions* (Ann Arbor: Institute for Social Research, 1957).

[2] French and Raven, *op. cit.*

[3] The collection of the original data was supported by Grant-in-Aid (M-919) from the National Institute of Mental Health, National Institutes of Health, U. S. Public Health Service. Ronald Lippitt was project director.

obtained concerning all children in 16 second grade and 16 fifth grade classrooms, representing all socioeconomic levels in a medium-sized city. Children were selected in that study for a field experiment concerned with the creation of changes in the social position and behavior of group members. The measures were made in order to establish a baseline, so that the amount of change in a participant's behavior could be determined. The data employed in the present investigation are from these pre-experimental measures.

From the original population of 638 children on whom measurements were available, *S*s were chosen for this study who had degrees of intelligence and power in required combinations. Pupils designated as high in intelligence were those in the upper 33 per cent of their class and those designated as low in intelligence were in the lower 33 per cent. Children designated as high in power were in the upper 50 per cent of their class and those designated as low in power were in the lower 50 per cent of their class on this measure. The sample included 226 boys and 192 girls, 230 second grade children and 188 fifth graders.

The type of data available for each child and the source of each are as follows:

Intelligence. Intelligence scores were obtained from school records. They were based on the results of the Kuhlman-Anderson test, administered in a group form.

Ratings by classmates. Every class member rated every child in his class on four characteristics: social power (who can most often get you to do things for him?), attractiveness, ability in school work, and ability to threaten others. To obtain these ratings, photographs of every child in the classroom were printed on sheets with a four-point rating scale next to each picture.

Observed behavior in groups. The members of a class were divided into four smaller groups on a random basis and each group was sent to a corner of the room where they worked on assigned problems. A trained observer was stationed in each corner who recorded on a precoded observation schedule the quantity and quality of behavior initiated by each child.[4] Four problems were assigned to the groups, each of which required a group decision as a first step in progress toward completion of the task. In one problem, for example, the group built a large tinker-toy and in another arrived at a decision as to how many beans were in a bottle. At the end of each task new groups were formed for the next problem, thus providing maximum opportunity for each child to interact with every other child in the room. No chairmen were designated for these discussions.

The observed behavior was coded into the following categories:

1. Influence attempts—efforts to influence others regardless of the manner employed.
2. Successful influence attempts—efforts in which compliance was obtained from others.
3. Unsuccessful influence attempts—efforts in which compliance was not obtained from others.
4. Demanding influence attempts—comments made in an ordering or directing manner, implying autonomy for the actor.
5. Suggestions—comments indicating weak proposals to, or requests of, others.
6. Valuing of others—behavior indicating recognition of either high or low resourcefulness of another person in an area of knowledge or skill.
7. Positively valuing others' behavior—comments indicating recognition of high value in others' behavior.
8. Negatively valuing others' behavior—comments indicating recognition of low value in others' behavior.
9. Affect-laden behavior—behavior in which overt friendliness or unfriendliness is observed which is not a direct attempt to influence another.
10. Aggressive behavior—acts of aggression which are either inflicted or threatened.
11. Mean weighted directness in style—ratio of frequency of forceful to nonforceful forms of behavior toward others.

Perceptions by teachers. Every child was rated by his teacher on seven characteristics descriptive of the typical social behavior of the person in his schoolroom. The teacher was asked to indicate on a five-point scale the extent to which each child showed the behavior under consideration (from "hardly ever" to "most often"). The qualities rated are shown in Table 4-16.

Teachers did not know how much social power classmates had attributed to the *S*s at the time they made their own ratings. Information concerning the intelligence of these children was available to teachers in school records.

[4] The observers had satisfactory reliability among them. Information concerning reliability of the observations will be available in publications concerning the project from which these data were borrowed.

RESULTS

Characteristics attributed to the *Ss* by their peers, for boys and girls with different degrees of power, are first discussed. Results are then presented for (*a*) the observed behavior of *Ss* in the small groups and (*b*) the perceptions of *Ss*' daily behavior by teachers. Finally, the results are summarized and interpreted.

For the sake of brevity the data in tables are usually limited to statistically significant findings. The omission of results for a specific category of behavior indicates that no significant differences were obtained for it.

At the outset it should be noted that social power is not highly correlated with intelligence. The correlation for boys was .20 and for girls .28. The low relationships between intelligence and power indicate that they may vary quite independently. Since both of these correlations are significant at the .01 level of probability, however, it is also clear that brighter children tend to have more power than less intelligent ones.

Characteristics attributed to subjects by classmates. Both boys and girls who were attributed high social power were more attractive to classmates than those low in power, regardless of their intelligence. These results may be seen in Table 4-11. Girls with greater power were rated as more able in school work than girls low in power irrespective of their intelligence, while boys were described as more able in school work to a significant degree only among those high in power and intelligence. Boys with higher power were described as more threatening. This was not true for girls.

Boys and girls with higher intelligence were seen by classmates as significantly more able in school work than less intelligent persons (*M* 2.24 and 1.76, *p* of diff. = .01). Girls high in intelligence were rated as more attractive than those low in intelligence (*M* 2.40 and 2.01, *p* of diff. = .005). Ability to threaten was not related significantly to intelligence.

Behavior of boys in small groups. We consider the types of behavior boys used in the problem solving discussions.

EFFECTS OF VARIATIONS IN POWER. Among highly intelligent boys, those high in social power were not significantly different in any category of observed behavior from those low in power.

TABLE 4-11

MEANS OF CHARACTERISTICS ATTRIBUTED BY CLASSMATES TO CHILDREN WITH VARIED SOCIAL POWER

	Boys			Girls		
	Social Power			*Social Power*		
	High M	*Low M*	*t*	*High M*	*Low M*	*t*
Children high in intelligence						
Attractive	2.13	1.52	6.42**	2.09	1.50	7.66**
Able in school work	2.19	1.43	6.33**	2.14	1.58	7.18**
Threatening	3.02	2.76	3.29**	2.89	2.86	.39
N	58	38		73	42	
Children low in intelligence						
Attractive	2.21	1.59	6.59**	2.39	1.65	11.69**
Able in school work	2.44	1.73	1.15	2.55	1.76	16.28**
Threatening	2.91	2.78	1.86*	2.98	2.90	.90
N	46	84		26	51	

* $p = .05$.
** $p = .001$.

Among less intelligent boys, those high in power, compared to those low in power, revealed a vigorous, inconsistent, and competitive pattern of behavior. The quantitative results may be seen in Table 4-12.

TABLE 4-12

BEHAVIOR OF LESS INTELLIGENT BOYS VARYING IN SOCIAL POWER

	Social Power		*t*
	High M	*Low M*	
Total influence attempts	24.34	16.00	3.18**
Freq. successful influence attempts	13.87	7.96	3.16**
Freq. unsuccessful influence attempts	10.48	8.04	1.98*
Freq. demanding influence attempts	5.33	3.46	2.10*
Freq. suggestions	18.90	12.30	3.13**
Total valuing of others' behavior	2.48	1.73	2.03*
N	46	84	

* $p = .05$.
** $p = .001$.

Effects of Variations in Intelligence. Among boys with high power, the behavior of the more intelligent was in no way significantly different from that shown by the less intelligent.

Among boys with low power, those with greater intelligence, compared to those with less, were active, effective, and supportive of others. These data are summarized in Table 4-13.

TABLE 4-13

Group Behavior of Boys with Low Social Power Varying in Intelligence

	Intelligence		*t*
	High M	*Low M*	
Total influence attempts	21.63	16.00	2.02*
Freq. successful influence attempts	11.97	7.96	2.06*
Freq. suggestions	16.86	12.30	2.04*
Freq. positively valuing others' behavior	1.37	.89	2.58**
N	38	84	

* $p = .05$.
** $p = .01$.

Behavior of girls in small groups.

Effects of Variations in Power. Among girls with high intelligence, those with high power were not observed to behave differently from those with low power.

Among girls who were less intelligent, those with high social power were only a little different from ones low in power. Those with more power were more often successful in their influence attempts (M 8.81 and 5.61, p of diff. = .01) and were more positive in their remarks about others' behavior (M 1.28 and .58, p of diff. = .01).

Effects of Variations in Intelligence. Regardless of their social power, variations in intelligence were not associated to a significant degree with differences in girls' observed behavior.

Behavior of boys and girls directly compared. A direct comparison of the behavior used by boys and girls, regardless of their power of intelligence indicates the actions most typical of each sex. The following behaviors were observed among boys significantly more often than among girls: attempts to influence, successful influences, unsuccessful influences, aggression, and demands. Girls did not display any type of behavior significantly more often

TABLE 4-14

Behavior of Highly Intelligent Boys Versus Girls Varying in Social Power

	Social Power		*t*	*Social Power*		*t*
	Low Boys M	*Low Girls* M		*High Boys* M	*High Girls* M	
Total influence attempts	21.63	13.57	2.30*	25.55	16.69	3.08***
Freq. successful influence attempts	11.97	7.21	1.80*	15.76	9.79	2.62***
Freq. unsuccessful influence attempts	9.66	6.36	2.39**	9.78	6.90	1.79*
Freq. suggestions	6.87	10.04	3.13***	19.95	13.80	2.75***
Total valuing of others' behavior	2.16	1.67	.97	2.29	2.09	.48
Freq. demanding influence attempts	4.63	3.14	.28	5.17	2.61	2.64***
Freq. aggressive behavior	2.97	1.50	1.89*	2.79	1.54	2.36**
Total affect-laden remarks	1.95	2.02	.15	2.46	1.63	3.92***
M weighted demandingness in behavior	21.15	20.95	.31	22.64	21.25	1.50
N	38	42		58	73	

* $p = .05$.
** $p = .01$.
*** $p = .001$.

than boys. It is evident that boys were considerably more active and demanding in their groups than were girls.

When members of both sexes were high in intelligence but low in power, boys were more active and aggressive than were girls. These data are shown in Table 4-14.

Where members of both sexes were high in both intelligence and power, the patterns of behavior were similar to those just described. In addition, high-high boys were demanding in their comments and used more affect-laden types of behavior than high-high girls (see Table 4-14).

In contrast to the girls, then, highly intelligent boys were likely to be active in their groups regardless of their social power and likely to be aggressively insistent in stating their opinions when high in both power and intelligence.

Among the less intelligent children the boys again appeared to be more involved in their groups than the girls if they were high in power. A comparison of the behavior of boys and girls is presented in Table 4-15. Boys with low intelligence and low power were very little different from girls with low intelligence and power.

Teachers' Perceptions of Boys. We turn to an examination of the qualities teachers attributed to these children.

EFFECTS OF VARIATIONS IN POWER. Among highly intelligent boys, the teachers made clear distinctions on every category between boys who were high in power and those who were low in power. These results are shown in Table 4-16.

Among less intelligent boys, the teachers made similar distinctions in the characteristics they attributed to boys high in power and those low in power. These results are listed in Table 4-16. In the eyes of teachers, boys with greater power are strikingly different in their social behavior from those with less power.

EFFECTS OF VARIATIONS IN INTELLIGENCE. Teachers made no distinctions to a significant degree between boys high in intelligence and those low in intelligence, regardless of their social power.

Teachers' perceptions of girls.

EFFECTS OF VARIATION IN POWER. Among girls high in intelligence, those with high social power were seen to be different from girls low in power as shown in Table 4-17.

Among girls low in intelligence those with high social power were perceived by teachers to be different from those with low social power in only two respects. Girls with higher power were seen as more often successful in influencing others (*M* 4.82 and

TABLE 4-15

BEHAVIOR OF LESS INTELLIGENT BOYS VERSUS GIRLS AS RELATED TO SOCIAL POWER

	Social Power			*Social Power*		
	High Boys M	*High Girls M*	*t*	*Low Boys M*	*Low Girls M*	*t*
Total influence attempts	24.34	15.96	2.44**	16.00	13.49	1.09
Freq. successful influence attempts	13.87	8.81	1.99*	7.96	5.61	1.59
Freq. unsuccessful influence attempts	10.48	7.15	1.90*	8.04	7.88	.12
Freq. suggestions	8.89	13.23	2.07***	12.31	9.75	.84
Freq. positively valuing others' behavior	1.19	.61	2.04*	.89	.58	1.63*
Total valuing others' behavior	2.48	1.54	1.96*	1.76	1.41	.99
M weighted demandingness	21.98	19.70	.30	21.95	20.09	2.86***
Freq. aggressive behavior	3.24	2.00	1.40	3.13	2.20	1.50
N	46	26		84	51	

* $p = .05$.
** $p = .01$.
*** $p = .001$.

TABLE 4-16

CHARACTERISTICS TEACHERS ATTRIBUTE TO BOYS WITH DIFFERENT DEGREES OF SOCIAL POWER

	Boys high in intelligence			*Boys low in intelligence*		
	Social Power		*t*	*Social Power*		*t*
	High M	*Low M*		*High M*	*Low M*	
Freq. influence attempts	4.05	3.70	1.50	4.10	3.52	2.40**
Amt. success as influencer	4.10	3.24	3.69***	4.46	3.50	4.38***
Friendliness	3.95	3.41	2.43**	4.27	3.41	3.63***
Depends on teacher	3.57	4.62	3.84***	3.76	4.32	3.08***
Depends on peers	3.68	4.45	3.00***	3.56	4.04	2.23*
Self-centeredness	3.58	4.26	2.93***	4.03	3.68	1.60
Degree of forcefulness	3.68	4.44	3.00***	3.56	4.04	2.23*
N	58	38		46	84	

* $p = .05$.
** $p = .01$.
*** $p = .001$.

3.77, p of diff. = .005) and more friendly (M 4.30 and 3.46, p of diff. = .005).

EFFECTS OF VARIATIONS IN INTELLIGENCE. Among girls with greater social power, teachers saw girls with high intelligence as being little different in their classrooms from those with low intelligence: the more intelligent girls were viewed as making more attempts to influence classmates (M 4.26 and 3.80, p of diff. = .02) and as more successful in these attempts (M 3.77 and 3.19, p of diff. = .005).

Among girls with little social power, highly intelligent girls compared to less intelligent ones were seen by teachers as making more frequent attempts to exercise influence in the class (M 4.29 and 3.76, p of diff. = .02), as more successful in these efforts (M 4.82 and 3.78, p of diff. = .005), and as more friendly (M 4.29 and 3.62, p of diff. = .005).

Teachers perceptions of boys and girls compared. The perceptions teachers had of boys and girls differed to a significant degree only where the members of both sexes were high in power while low in intelligence. Here, boys were seen as more active in making attempts to influence classmates and more self-centered in doing so than were girls.

Differences due to ages of subjects. The results on all dimensions for second graders were compared with those of fifth graders. There was no acceptable evidence that differences in ratings of *Ss* by peers or teachers, or in their observed behavior in the small groups, were associated with differences in age.

TABLE 4-17

CHARACTERISTICS TEACHERS ATTRIBUTE TO HIGHLY INTELLIGENT GIRLS WITH DIFFERENT DEGREES OF SOCIAL POWER

	Social Power		
	High M	*Low M*	*t*
Amt. success as influencer	3.78	3.19	3.39**
Friendliness	3.62	3.07	2.75**
Depends on teacher	4.00	4.38	1.80*
Self-centeredness	3.93	4.63	3.16**
N	73	42	

* $p = .05$.
** $p = .001$.

SUMMARY AND DISCUSSION OF RESULTS

Charactristics attributed by peers. Boys and girls were smiliar in that those with greater power, compared to those with less, were better liked by their peers. Attractiveness then was an important basis of power for both sexes.

Boys and girls were different in that boys with greater power were seen by classmates as more threatening, and girls with greater power were rated as more expert "in the things you do in school."

These results suggest that among these children the two sexes won social power in part on the basis of different attributes, boys earned it by being threatening and girls earned it by being skilled in the things required of a school child.

Observed behavior in groups. The behavior of boys may be briefly summarized by noting that those who were low in social power and low in intelligence (low-lows) were strikingly different from boys with all other combinations of intelligence and power. The significant differences we have seen in the behaviors of boys stem primarily from the fact that the low-lows were passive persons in their groups, more than boys who were high in either power or intelligence. The low-lows significantly less often tried to influence others, were less successful in doing so, were less demanding in manner, less often evaluating in respect to others' contributions, and less often suggestors of tentative proposals. Boys with various combinations of power and intelligence other than low-low were in no way different from one another to a statistically significant degree in their observed behavior, that is, high-highs were not different from high-lows or from low-highs. It is worth special note that highly intelligent boys whose social power was low behaved in no way different from those whose social power was high.

Because the low-lows were different from boys with more power or intelligence in ways that were quite comparable, and because the high-highs were in no way different from the high-lows or low-highs; it appears that the possession of greater intelligence may be the same as the possession of greater power insofar as the effect upon behavior in these groups is concerned.

This similarity is due, we believe, to the fact that the contributions made by highly intelligent boys in a problem solving discussion represent resources which are valuable to the group. The possession of these resources, we assume, provided power for the owners to influence those who valued them. It is highly probable, although it cannot be demonstrated with the data available here, that boys with high intelligence were treated by group members as though they were persons with high power. As a consequence, boys with high intelligence became aware of the value of their ideas and of the influence they were having on the discussion. Although they had little power accorded to them previously by their classmates, boys with high intelligence apparently behaved in the groups like those who had come to the group with social power already attributed to them by their peers.

It is noteworthy that boys low in intelligence yet high in social power tended to be more inconsistent than low-lows in that they made both demands and weak proposals, and praised as well as criticized others, whereas boys high in intelligence but low in power more consistently proposed ideas and supported others' behavior than did the low-lows. The possibility is suggested by these findings that greater power among boys generated more inconsistent and coercive group behavior while greater intelligence evoked a consistency and readiness to be considerate in relations with others. This conjecture is supported by the findings that peers characterized boys with greater power as threatening but did not so describe boys with greater intelligence.

Girls who were low-lows were less successful in influencing their groups and less often made positive remarks than girls high in power but low in intelligence. This indicates that low-low girls, like the low-low boys, were passive in their groups' discussions. Low-low girls were not different in any respect from girls low in power and high in intelligence, which suggests that high intelligence was not similar to power among girls, as was earlier noted for boys.

In most combinations of intelligence and power, boys were significantly more active in seeking to influence others, more often successful, more often unsuccessful, and more likely to evaluate the comments made by others than were girls. Low-low boys were very much like girls and most like low-low girls, differing from them in only two respects: they were significantly more likely to be demanding and to be positive in commenting upon the contributions made by others.

In sum, the possession of either power or intelligence by boys appeared to stimulate vigorous and successful participation in their groups' work while the possession of low power and low intelligence together generated passivity in boys. The amount of intelligence or power a young person possesses affected a boy's behavior more than it did a girl's behavior in these problem solving discussions.

To explain the consequences of power and intelligence for boys and girls we assume that these two attributes have a differential significance for the sexes in allowing them to conform to the expectations society puts upon them. Barry, Bacon, and Child[5] have reported that boys are expected to be self-reliant and to strive for achievements, while girls are urged to be nurturant, obedient, and responsible in almost all societies, including ours.

We assume that, in their group behavior, the boys and girls were attempting to conform to these prescriptions for their sexes. Boys who were high in either intelligence or social power more clearly fulfilled their sex roles than those lacking in both of these. Boys who were low in both intelligence and power least often showed the behavior required of their sex. The low degree of their intelligence and power apparently made them unable to perform in ways typically expected of them. Thus, either social power or intelligence was necessary for boys if they were to act as boys are expected to act. There is some indication that social power was more important than intelligence in this respect.

Girls who were high in power and intelligence were little different from those who were low in either of these qualities because, we believe, high social power and intelligence were not needed in order to be the nurturant, obedient, or responsible persons required by society. Girls could fulfill these expectations regardless of the amount of power or intelligence they possessed.

Perceptions by teachers. The children who were accorded higher social power by their classmates were viewed by teachers as most influential, since the teachers rated boys and girls with higher power as more successful in influencing others than those low in social power.

On almost every category, teachers distinguished between boys low in power and those high in power, regardless of the boys' intellectual abilities. It is striking in this connection that teachers saw those with greater power as less forceful and more friendly than those with less power, whereas boys with greater power (and low intelligence) were demanding and less friendly than those with less power when observed in the small groups. Clearly teachers did not perceive the boys with greater social power as threatening persons in the way that classmates saw them.

In their considerations of girls, apparently those who were high in either intelligence or power were seen as more effective members of their classes than those low in these respects.

Why did the teachers characterize boys who had greater power (but low intelligence) as more considerate of others than was observed among them in the small groups? The most likely explanation is that their behavior actually was different in their classrooms from what it was in the discussions. In a class the teacher is in charge so that nondemanding, friendly behavior is required and becomes the standard way for interacting with peers during school. It is also probable that teachers approved of achievement oriented and influential efforts when they were used by boys since such behavior is in accord with the demands that teachers, among other adults, place upon young males. Thus, teachers attributed positive characteristics to the boys whom they viewed as most influential in their classrooms.

In the small groups no one was in charge. Hence, the boys with greater power, but less intelligence, were free to insist upon having their opinions accepted and were free to use coercion when necessary in order to be influential.

Teachers did not perceive differences in classroom behavior between boys who were high in intelligence and those who were low in intelligence although differences between these two groups were evident in the problem solving discussions. It appears that variations in intelligence do not generate variations in social behavior in a classroom, of the kind that teachers were asked to report.

We assume that girls were less active in their classes and therefore less visible to the teachers than the boys. Thus, teachers made fewer distinctions in characterizing the behavior among girls with different amounts of power than they did among boys. Girls with higher power were seen by teachers as most friendly to classmates, which suggests that through this friendliness they won influence in the classroom. Girls with higher intelligence were also seen by teachers as being more friendly and as mak-

[5] H. Barry, M. Bacon, and I. Child, "A Cross-Cultural Survey of Some Sex Differences in Socialization," *Journal of Abnormal and Social Psychology*, 1957, *55*, pp. 327-332.

ing more attempts to influence others than girls with low intelligence. It is probable that the girls with high intelligence did use acceptable forms of social influence in their schoolroom relations since they were rated as attractive by their classmates, more so than those with low intelligence. This acceptance by their peers apparently gave them confidence to exercise their influence freely and teachers noted this in characterizing highly intelligent girls.

In summary, teachers perceived the behavior of girls as pretty much alike regardless of their power or intelligence. They made no significant distinctions among boys with different degrees of intelligence, but they saw many distinctions in the behavior of boys who differed in social power. Assuming that the teachers' perceptions are accurate, it is evident that a boy's social power determines his behavior in the classroom more than his intelligence does, whereas differences in the power or intelligence of a girl has little effect upon the behavior she employs in the schoolroom.

*SOCIAL STRUCTURE OF A GROUP OF KINDERGARTEN CHILDREN**

By Eugenia Hanfmann

In order to investigate the interrelationship of dominance within a kindergarten group consisting of ten five-year-old boys, the method of comparison in pairs was introduced: two children at a time were taken to a separate room and allowed to play freely with colored blocks for 15 to 30 minutes, while two observers recorded everything both children did and said. Every child was paired with every other child of the group and was thus observed playing with nine different partners. For control purposes some of the combinations were repeated with changed play material.

After each session an estimate was made by two observers as to which child of the pair was the dominant one. The child who was considered dominant was the one who, in his play, carried through what he himself wanted, and also had the other child do what he—i.e. the first child—wanted, in other words he controlled both his own play and that of his companion. In doubtful cases the decision was reached by determining how frequently during a session each child controlled the other and was himself controlled. Usually the impression of the observers was confirmed by this analysis.

On the basis of these estimates we arrived at a rank order of dominance, measured by the number of partners whom the child dominated. This rank order is shown on the chart. One child is omitted from the chart because he was not paired with all nine children. If the dominance were based upon one factor, varying in degree from child to child, but constant for each child, we would expect to find that, if child X dominated child Y, and latter in his turn dominated child Z, then X would also dominate Z, and we would have a linear rank order. Such relationship is actually found in the lower half of our rank order. However, the interrelationship of the four children ranking highest is more complicated: while A dominates B, and B dominates C and D, each of these: C and D in his turn dominates A. This circular connection suggests that the dominance does not mean the same thing in all cases, and actually we find that these four or five children represent different patterns and different methods of dominance.

We start with child E who occupies the middle position: he is dominated by four children and he himself dominates four. His dominance, however, conforms only to the first part of our criterion: he plays as he wants, but he does not control the play of his partner, except by resisting the latter's wishes. He anxiously protects the blocks that have become his, and consistently opposes the attempts of any other child to bring about joint play. In seven of

*From the *American Journal of Orthopsychiatry*, 1935, *5*, pp. 407-410. Used by permission of the author and publisher.

nine combinations in which E takes part, the play is parallel play throughout, each child building by himself. Thus the dominance is reached by this apprehensive child by way of isolation: it is a negative rather than a positive dominance.

The opposite tactics are employed by the four highest ranking children who actively control the others: every one of them tends to break rather than to strengthen the barrier between himself and his associate, but each does it in a different way and to a different extent.

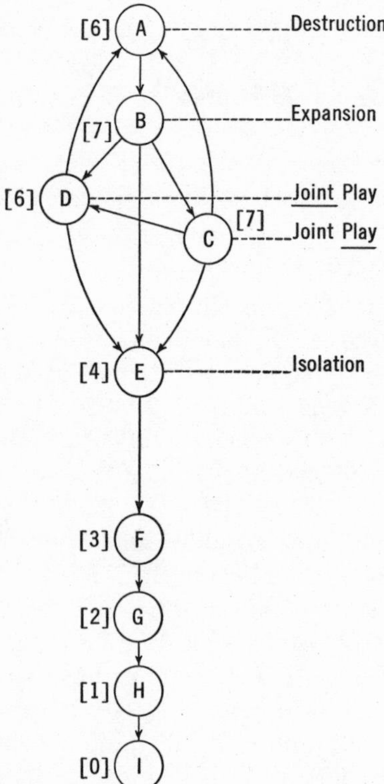

Figure 4-1. Figures in brackets refer to the number of partners dominated by the child.

Child C is himself dominated and dominates the other children by his strong interest in the constructive play, of which he is a great master. He has very definite plans for his play; usually he succeeds in imparting them to the other child and then he will lead and direct the joint activity, mostly giving suggestions, but also frequently taking them. He gets what he needs from his companion—his play material, his assistance—by clearly explaining to the latter his purpose and needs, by earnestly stressing the requirements of the play and insisting on them, but never by violence. If a conflict arises, he tries to solve it by a compromise, e.g., by giving a block in exchange for the one he needs, by making a pact about taking turns, or by combining ingeniously two proposed activities into one. If the conflict cannot be solved by any one of these methods, he will occasionally deliberately dissolve the joint play declaring, for instance: "I'll make a chimney, and you make what you like!" Thus, on the whole, his play with another child results as frequently in parallel as in joint play, the social aspect being subordinated to the requirements of the play activity as such. We could speak of this child as an *objective leader.*

For child D, on the other hand, not play in itself, but play with another child, is the ultimate goal. He tries to induce and to maintain the joint play whenever he can, and actually succeeds with six children out of nine. His methods of controlling the other child are similar to those of C, for he bases his demands upon the requirements of the play, never coercing his playmate and never flatly refusing his requests. But he goes further than that: he actually takes into account the attitude of his companion and displays an astonishing skill and flexibility in trying to remove rather than break his resistance. He introduces mutual play not by taking the other child's blocks but by offering his own; he takes care to announce and to explain his actions in advance, especially when taking the blocks away; while the blocks are in his possession, he keeps telling the other one reassuringly that he will return them soon, and actually does so; if he meets with resistance, he never presses the point, and lets some time pass before repeating his request, usually in a modified form; occasionally he simply ignores a refusal or, by treating it as a joke, makes the other child treat it in the same way. Usually these varied diplomatic methods are successful but, in the case of a serious conflict, he will give way, at least temporarily, to his comrade's plans, rather than give up the joint play. We may speak of this child as a *social leader.*

For child B social play has a totally different function—it is a means of expanding and displaying his own power. Though extremely active, he is less interested in the play itself than in getting all blocks for himself, in being the initiator of all activities, and in having an unrestricted command over the other child. This latter is not allowed any possession or any activity, except in a subordinate role; he is practically thrust out of the play. Yet C does not leave him alone; he keeps requiring the other's services and attention and refers to his own activities as if they were a joint enterprise: "We are making a big train," etc. Thus with this boy social play degenerates into pseudo-social play, with one child having no real part in it. The methods he uses to bring about this situation are as primitive as they are effective; grabbing blocks violently, disregarding protestations, denying the other's requests by saying merely "No, you can't. They are mine. I will do it myself"; suppressing the other's attempts at activity by force, for instance by holding his hands; boasting of own possessions and actions and belittling his partner. In short, the methods used are those of a little *gangster*. They are characterized by great forcefulness and by complete disregard for the rights and wishes of the other child.

It seems that the child using such methods should be invincible. Yet, as the medium for his expansion and dominance is still play activity, he is powerless against the child (A) who deliberately disrupts the situation of orderly play. The method of child A is destruction. He himself does not build, and when the other child starts building, he purposely destroys his work, throwing the blocks to the floor, and meeting protests merely with outbursts of laughter. This procedure is repeated until the other child gives up all attempts at continuing his play. (At this point A usually introduces a new activity, e.g., counting objects in the room—an activity in which he takes the lead, or in which both children continue relatively independent of each other.) As destroyer this child is invincible. Yet, with children C and D he made only half hearted attempts at destruction, and mostly observed with interest their intensive play. Another time he watched for a while spellbound the constructive play of the other child, for a moment tried to imitate him, and then suddenly burst into wild destruction. These variations of his usual behavior suggested, that with play material sufficiently interesting and yet not too difficult for him, the destructive behavior of this child could be checked. This expectation was fully fulfilled. With the new play material the behavior of A changed to a quiet absorption in his play, and he assumed methods of controlling the other child similar in all details to those of C and D. This shows that even though a pattern of dominance can be typical for one child, it is not rigid and unchangeable and depends both upon his partner and upon the activity. That is why we prefer to speak of the patterns of dominance rather than of the types of dominators.

We cannot discuss here what conflicts arise, when the different dominance patterns meet, but we must consider briefly how these different patterns affect the dominated children. Patterns represented by C and D make for a happy and harmonious play, those represented by A and B lead to continuous conflict and dissatisfaction. When the children were asked by their teacher, after the completion of the experiment, with whom they liked best to play, 8 of the 10 named either C or D, thus proving that they preferred the leadership of this type both to the other patterns of dominance and to the absence of any strong leadership.

Summarizing, we find that the pattern of dominance by destruction is the most effective, but also the least stable one, because it disappears as soon as interest in the play is aroused. That is why the "destroyer" may dominate the "gangster," yet be himself dominated by children whose primary interest is play and whose methods are far from violent. The pattern of dominance based upon expansion of personal power is a much stabler one, even though it can also be modified by a strong interest in play as such.

Both of these patterns, however, are unacceptable to the dominated child. Only the child who is mostly interested in play as such or in social play, becomes a real leader, gladly followed by other children. In every instance the social behavior of a child is part of a total structure including the interrelationship of both children involved and the medium in which it takes place, and can be influenced and changed through changes of this structure.

*EXPERIMENTS ON GROUP CONFLICT AND COOPERATION**

By Muzafer Sherif

Conflict between groups—whether between boys' gangs, social classes, "races," or nations—has no simple cause. Its roots often lie in a complex of social, economic, religious, historical, and personal factors. Social scientists have long sought to bring these factors to light by studying the "natural histories" of groups and relations between them. On the basis of their empirical findings it is possible to identify certain general conditions which have crucial influences on the positive or negative nature of the attitudes of members of one group toward another.

Intergroup conflict and cooperation is not a subject that lends itself easily to laboratory experiments. The findings I shall report here are from a program of experimental studies begun in 1948 which combine field and laboratory methods in studying group formation and intergroup relations under controlled yet lifelike conditions.[1]

Various measures have been proposed to reduce intergroup conflicts and hostilities, including spread of information, exchange of persons, social contacts, conferences of leaders, and measures to propagate democratic methods within the groups in question. However, there are few established generalizations concerning the circumstances in which such measures are effective. The experiments to be summarized stem from the conviction that realistic measures to reduce intergroup hostilities can be achieved only by first clarifying the conditions conducive to conflict and cooperation between groups.

What acts can properly be called "intergroup behavior"? If some definitions were not agreed upon, we might be studying acts of transitory congeniality or annoyance. The definitions used were based on empirical findings about group relations which we had surveyed.[2] Obviously, we had to start by defining a group.

A group was defined as a social unit consisting of a number of individuals whose interactions at a given time have the following measurable properties: (1) more or less definite and interdependent status and role relationships among the individuals, and (2) a set of values, standards, or norms which are peculiar to them and regulate their behavior, at least in matters of consequence to the group, such as its existence and perpetuation. "Intergroup relations," therefore, refers to relations between two or more groups, thus defined, and their members. When individuals belonging to one group interact, collectively or individually, with members of another group in terms of their group identifications, we have an instance of intergroup behavior.

Our surveys of sociological and psychological literature on group relations revealed important lessons about intergroup behavior, with implications for practice. In the process of interaction within a group, the group is endowed by its members with positive qualities. Individual members tend to develop these qualities through example, verbal dictums, and correctives. These qualities, which reflect the group's particular brand of ethnocentrism, are products of participation in group activities by its "good" members, who constitute the majority of membership as long as group solidarity and morale are maintained.

Similarly, group members come to attribute certain qualities to other groups and their members. The qualities attributed to other groups may be

[1] Among those working with me were M. B. Sussman, R. Huntington, O. J. Harvey, B. J. White, W. R. Hood, and C. W. Sherif. This report gives a composite of the findings from three experiments conducted in 1949, 1953, and 1954. For full accounts see: M. Sherif and C. W. Sherif, *Groups in Harmony and Tension* (New York: Harper & Row, Publishers, 1953); M. Sherif, B. J. White, and O. J. Harvey, "Status in Experimentally Produced Groups," *American Journal of Sociology*, 1955, *60*, pp. 370-379; and M. Sherif, O. J. Harvey, B. J. White, W. R. Hood, and C. W. Sherif, *Intergroup Conflict and Cooperation, The Robber's Cave Experiment* (Norman, Oklahoma: University Book Exchange, University of Oklahoma, 1961).

[2] Sherif and Sherif, *op. cit.*

*Adapted by the author from his article "Experiments in Group Conflict," *Scientific American*, 1956, *195*, pp. 54-58. Permission granted by the publisher.

favorable or unfavorable, depending upon the positive or negative nature of relations between the groups. A number of field studies show that if the goals of two groups are harmonious or complementary, favorable attitudes are formed in each group toward the other group. But, if the goals of the groups conflict, if one can be gained only at the expense of the other, members within the groups form unfriendly attitudes and unfavorable stereotypes of the other group.

Finally, the major conclusion drawn from surveys of literature on intergroup relations was the effectiveness of *superordinate* goals in reducing intergroup conflict. Superordinate goals are goals which are compelling and highly appealing to members of two or more groups, but which cannot be attained by the resources of any single group separately. In other words, to be attained, superordinate goals require that groups pull together.

In studying intergroup conflict and its reduction, we wanted to "start from scratch" with persons who were not acquainted prior to the experiments. The groups studied would be informal, with group organization and norms evolving during the course of the research, but under controlled conditions which could be specified and reproduced in the future. Therefore, summer camps distant from towns and completely devoted to the research were chosen as sites. This choice led to the selection of subjects who would find camping natural and fascinating, boys between 11 and 12 years old.

The most general hypothesis concerning intergroup behavior was that the nature of relationships between the groups' major goals is the limiting condition determining the way members of one group come to regard and treat members of another. To test this hypothesis, we had to eliminate, as much as possible, any prior bases for friendship or hostility among the subjects. This involved long and careful procedures for selecting subjects. We interviewed each boy's teachers and school officials, studied his school and medical records, observed him in classes and at play with schoolmates, obtained his scores on psychological tests, and interviewed his family. The subjects chosen were similar in background: all were healthy, well-adjusted boys, somewhat above average in intelligence and from stable, white, Protestant, middle-class homes. To insure that experimental results could not be attributed to severe frustrations and neurotic tendencies, we were especially careful that neurotic symptoms or background conditions conducive to them were not present among the subjects.

None of the boys was aware that he was part of an experiment on group relations at the time. They met first on buses that took them to camp, and in their eyes, the time was spent at a normal summer camp. The research staff appeared as a regular camp staff—directors, counselors, caretakers, etc. They did not write down notes or comment on behavior in the boys' presence. This was necessary, for the presence of a person ever-observing, ever-recording what we say necessarily influences our actions, especially when our behavior toward other persons is in question.

To keep the experimental situation as lifelike as possible, all activities were within the framework of normal camp functions and games. The boys' interests were studied both before and during the experiments, in order to control conditions without direct verbal instructions or manipulation by the experimenters. The activities chosen were sufficiently appealing to the subjects that they could hardly help discussing them, initiating plans, and carrying them through. For example, a canoe was placed near their cabin, about a mile from the water. Of course they wanted to use it, so they formed a plan and transported it to the water. Or, when the boys were becoming quite hungry, food was provided in bulk form (uncut meat, unprepared beverage, whole watermelon, etc.). Such situations were compelling as problem situations, and the boys attacked them without suggestions from the experimenters.

Methods used to collect data were disguised or made a natural aspect of the setting. The validity of the findings was cross-checked by using a combination of research methods at every step, for example, observations and ratings by participant "counselors," independent ratings in "test" situations by observers not familiar with the groups, sociometric techniques, and judgment tasks presented as games. Conclusions made here are based on data obtained by two or more techniques.

Starting with unacquainted individuals to study group relations meant that the experiments had to be designed in successive stages, each lasting about a week. Stage 1 was devoted to the formation of two groups, so that relationships between them could be studied. In Stage 2, the two groups were brought into contact in situations such that the attainment of its goal by one group necessarily meant that the other group failed to reach its goal. It was predicted that a series of such encounters would in time produce group conflict and the rudiments of hostile stereotypes and social distance. Finally, Stage 3 of the 1954 experiment was devoted to measures to reduce existing conflict between groups.

The first experiment was conducted in the hills of northern Connecticut. When the boys arrived they were all housed in one large bunkhouse, because we wanted to reduce the importance of sheerly personal attractions in the formation of two groups. This was done in the following way: after the boys had begun to choose buddies or form friendship clusters, we asked each informally who his best friends were. The boys were put in two different cabins, so that about two-thirds of their best friends were in the other cabin. (The pain of separation was assuaged by allowing each cabin to go at once on a hike and camp-out.) Figure 4-2 shows how the friendship choices were reversed after groups had actually formed in Stage 1. We assumed that under the conditions of Stage 1, groups would form even though they were not composed of preferred individuals and that fellow group-members would come to be seen as one's "best friends." This assumption proved to be accurate and was substantiated in the 1953 experiment.

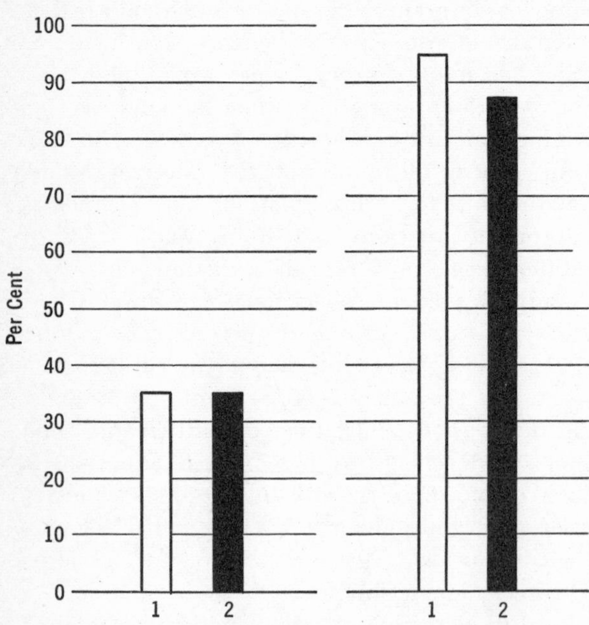

Figure 4-2. Friendship choices of campers for others in their own cabin are shown for Red Devils *(white)* and Bulldogs *(black)*. At first a low percentage of friendships were in the cabin group *(left)*. After five days, most friendship choices were within the group *(right)*.

GROUP FORMATION IN STAGE 1

The boys engaged in many activities in Stage 1, but all were in harmony with experimental specifications for this stage. All required interdependent activities among the boys in a cabin to reach a common goal. Such conditions were specified as conducive to the formation of groups with some kind of organization (status and role relations) and with unwritten rules (norms) for behavior.

As they faced the problem situations, played, and worked together the boys in each unit pooled their efforts, organized duties, and divided up tasks in work and play. Different individuals assumed different responsibilities. One excelled in cooking, another led in athletics. Others, though not outstanding in any particular skill, could be counted on to pitch in and do their best in anything the group attempted. One or two boys seemed to disrupt activities, to start teasing at the wrong moment or offer useless suggestions. A few boys consistently had good suggestions and showed ability to coordinate the efforts of others in carrying them through. Within a few days, one person had proved himself more resourceful in this respect than the others. Thus, rather quickly, a leader and lieutenants emerged. Some boys sifted toward the bottom of the heap, while others jockeyed for higher positions of respect.

This process of group formation may be illustrated during a cook-out in the woods. The staff supplied the boys with unprepared food. When they got hungry, one boy started to build a fire, asking for help in getting wood. Another attacked the raw hamburger to make patties. Others prepared a place to put buns, relishes, and the like. Two mixed soft drinks from flavoring and sugar. One boy who stood around without helping was told by the others to "get to it." Shortly the fire was blazing and the cook had hamburgers sizzling. Two boys distributed them as rapidly as they became edible. Soon it was time for the watermelon. A low-ranking member took a knife and started toward the melon. Some of the others protested. The most highly regarded boy in the group took over the knife, saying, "you guys who yell the loudest get yours last."

The relative positions in the group were rated by observers and independent raters primarily on the basis of effective initiative in the group. These ratings were also checked by informal soundings of the boys' opinions as to who got things started, who got things done, and who could be counted on to support group activities. (See Figure 4-3.) When these measurements checked, we could conclude that a group organization had formed.

In the 1953 experiment, we also measured the status relations in each group through a game requiring each boy to evaluate the performance of his fellow members. Before an important baseball match, a target board was set up on the pretense of making practice in throwing more interesting. There were no marks on the front of the board for the boys to judge objectively how close the ball came to a bull's-eye, but, unknown to them, the board was wired to flashing lights behind so that an observer could see exactly where the ball hit. The result was that the boys consistently overestimated the performances by the most highly regarded members of their group and tended to underestimate the scores of low ranking members. In other words, estimated performance and status in the group, as determined from observation, were significantly correlated.

As the group became an organization, the boys coined nicknames. The big, blond, hardy leader of one group was dubbed "Baby Face" by his admiring followers. A boy with a rather long head became "Lemon Head" to his group. Each group developed its own jargon, special jokes, secrets, special ways of performing tasks, and preferred places. For example, one group, after killing a snake near a place where they had gone swimming, named the place "Moccasin Creek" and thereafter preferred this swimming hole to any other, though there were better ones nearby.

Wayward members who failed to do things "right" or who did not contribute their bit to the common effort found themselves receiving reprimands, ridi-

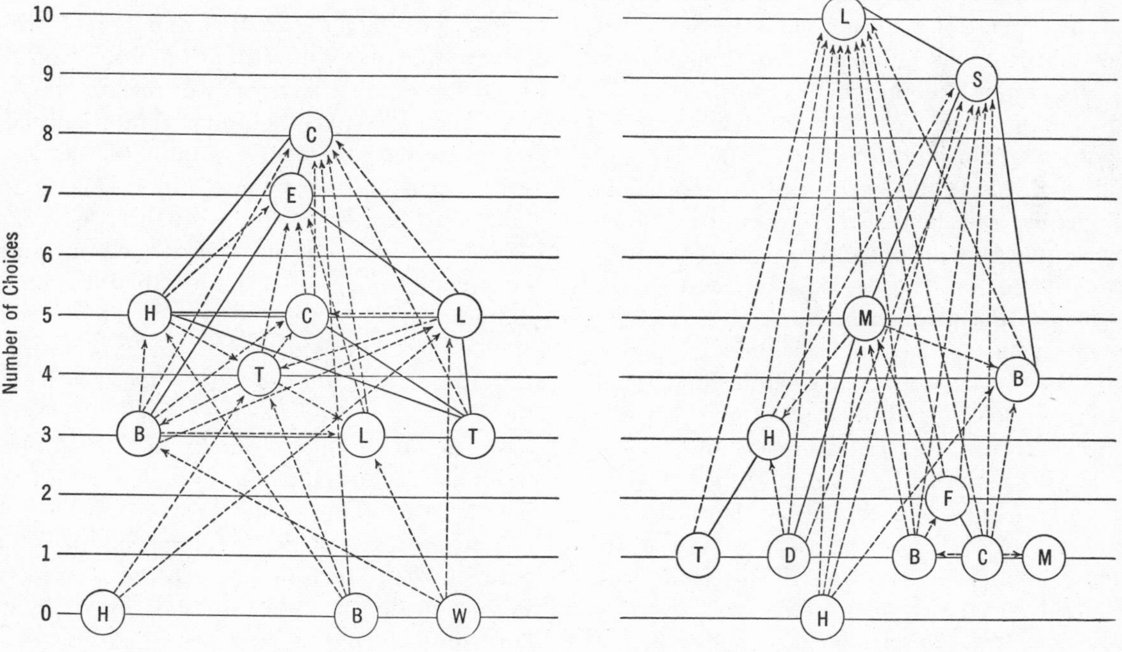

Figure 4-3. Sociograms represent patterns of friendship choices within the fully developed groups. One-way friendships are indicated by broken arrows; reciprocated friendships, by solid lines. Leaders were among those highest in the popularity scale. Bulldogs *(left)* had a close-knit organization with good group spirit. Low-ranking members participated less in the life of the group but were not rejected. Red Devils *(right)* lost the tournament of games between the groups. They had less group unity and were sharply stratified.

cule, "silent treatment," or even threats. Each group selected symbols and a name, and they put these on their caps and T-shirts. The boys in Connecticut called themselves the "Red Devils" and the "Bull Dogs." The 1954 camp was conducted in Oklahoma near a famous hideaway reputed to have been used by Jesse James and Belle Starr and called Robber's Cave. These groups called themselves the "Rattlers" and the "Eagles."

When it was clear that two groups, as defined, had formed, Stage 2 of the experiments began.

INTERGROUP CONFLICT IN STAGE 2

In order that contact between groups could be specified, the groups had no encounters prior to Stage 2. Indeed in the 1954 experiment at Robber's Cave, the two groups came on separate buses and were not even aware of each other's presence until just before Stage 2.

Our hypothesis was that when two groups have conflicting aims such that one can achieve its ends only at the expense of the other, their members will become hostile to each other, even though each group is composed of normal, well-adjusted individuals. Because these were boys to whom competitive sports were an abiding interest, the necessary experimental conditions were easily created. As though acceding to their own requests, the staff arranged a tournament of games; baseball, touch football, tug of war, a treasure hunt, and so on, with prizes to the winning group.

The tournament started in a spirit of good sportsmanship, but as it progressed good feeling began to evaporate. Soon members of each group began to call their rivals "stinkers," "sneaks," and "cheaters." The boys in the 1949 camp turned against buddies whom they had chosen as "best friends" when they first arrived. The rival groups made threatening posters and planned raids, collecting secret hoards of green apples as ammunition.

In the Robber's Cave study, the Eagles, after a defeat in a tournament game, burned a banner left behind by the Rattlers. The next morning the Rattlers seized the Eagles' flag when they arrived on the athletic field. From that time on, name-calling, scuffles, and raids were the rule of the day. A large proportion of the boys in each group gave negative ratings of the character of *all* boys in the other. When the tournament was over, they refused to have anything more to do with members of the other group.

However, the effect of intergroup conflict was to increase solidarity, cooperativeness, and morale *within* each group. It is noteworthy that the heightening of cooperativeness and democratic interaction within each group did not carry over to the group's relations with the other group.

Stage 2 provided the conditions necessary to investigate the reduction of intergroup conflict and the production of cooperativeness between hostile groups.

INTERGROUP COOPERATION IN STAGE 3

How can two groups in conflict be brought into cooperative interaction and friendly intercourse? Various measures could have been tried. The introduction of a common enemy in the form of another group is effective, as we found in the 1949 experiment. But this device implies widening intergroup conflict on a larger scale. Dissemination of favorable *information* about the groups was not seriously considered, because a large body of research has shown the limited effectiveness of information unrelated to the central concerns of a group. *Individual competition* cutting across group lines is sometimes used in classroom and recreation situations but seems to have limited value if one is interested in producing intergroup cooperation rather than breaking up the groups.

The measures used in the 1954 experiment were introduced with the objective of clarifying conditions in which *contact as equals* may be effective in reducing intergroup conflict. As a first phase, a series of situations was introduced involving contact between the groups in activities extremely pleasant to both groups but not involving interdependence between them, such as going to the movies, eating in the same dining room, and shooting off fireworks. Far from reducing conflict, these situations served as opportunities for the rival groups to berate and attack each other. In the dining-hall line, they shoved each other, and the group that lost the contest for the head of the line shouted "Ladies first!" at the winner. They threw paper, food, and vile names at each other. An Eagle bumped by a

Rattler was admonished by his fellow Eagles to brush "the Dirt" off his clothes.

The measure which was effective was suggested by a corollary to our assumptions about intergroup conflict. If conflict develops from mutually incompatible goals, common goals should promote cooperation. But what kind of common goals? In considering group relations in the everyday world, it seemed that the most effective and enduring cooperation between groups occurs when *superordinate goals* exist, that is, goals which have a compelling appeal for members of each group, but which neither group can achieve without the others' participation. To test this hypothesis experimentally, we created a series of urgent and natural situations which challenged individuals in both groups.

One was a breakdown in the water supply. Water came to the camp in pipes from a tank about a mile away. The flow of water was interrupted, and the boys were called together to be informed of the crisis. Both groups promptly volunteered to search the water line for trouble. They explored separately, then came together and jointly located the source of the difficulty. Despite the good spirits aroused, however, the groups fell back to their old recriminations.

A similar opportunity was offered when the boys requested another movie. They were told that the camp could not afford to rent one. The two groups got together, figured out how much each group would have to contribute, chose the film by a common vote, and enjoyed the show together.

One day the two groups went on an outing at a lake some distance away. A large truck was to go for food. But when everyone was hungry and ready to eat, it developed that the truck would not start. (The staff had conveniently taken care of that.) The boys got a rope—the same rope they had used in their acrimonious tug of war—and all pulled together to start the truck.

Joint efforts in situations such as these did not immediately dispel hostility. But gradually the series of activities requiring interdependent actions did reduce conflict and hostility between the groups. The members of the two groups began to feel more friendly. For example, a Rattler whom the Eagles had disliked for his sharp tongue and skill in defeating them became a "good egg." The boys stopped shoving in the meal line. They no longer called each other names and began to sit together at the table. New friendships developed cutting across group lines.

In the end, the groups were actively seeking opportunities to mingle, to entertain and "treat" each other. Procedures which "worked" in one activity were transferred to others. For example, the notion of "taking turns" developed in the dining room and was transferred to a joint campfire, which they decided themselves to hold. They took turns presenting skits and songs, alternating between the groups. Members of both groups requested that they go home together on the same bus, rather than on separate buses. No one paid attention to a few diehards who muttered "Let's not." On the way home, the bus stopped for refreshments. One group still had five dollars won as a prize. They decided to spend this sum on refreshments for both groups, rather than using it solely for themselves and thereby having more to eat. On their own initiative they invited their former rivals to be their guests for malted milks.

Interviews with the boys confirmed the change in their attitudes. From choosing their best friends almost exclusively in their own group, many of them shifted to listing some boys in the other group. (See Fig. 4-4.) They were glad to have a second

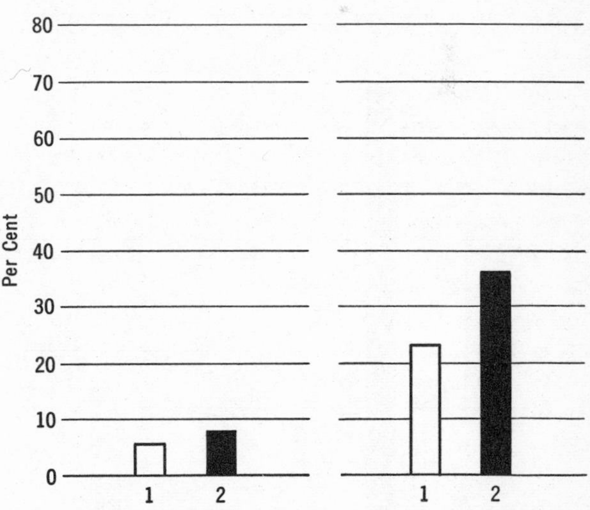

Figure 4-4. During conflict between the two groups in the Robber's Cave experiment there were few friendships between cabins *(left)*. After cooperation toward common goals had restored good feelings, the number of friendships between groups rose significantly *(right)*.

chance to rate the boys in the other group as to personal qualities, some of them remarking that they had changed their minds since the first rating made after the tournament. Indeed they had. The new ratings were largely favorable. (See Fig. 4-5.)

The results of the experiments warrant the following conclusions:

1. Intergroup conflict and its by-products of hostility and negative stereotypes are not *primarily* a result of neurotic tendencies on the part of individuals, but occur under given conditions even when the individuals involved are normal, healthy, and socially well-adjusted.

2. Cooperative and democratic procedures *within* groups are not directly transferable to intergroup relations. On the contrary, cooperativeness and solidarity within groups were at their height when intergroup conflict was most severe.

3. Consequential intergroup relations have an impact on the patterning of relationships and the norms within each group. One group deposed a leader who could not "take it" in contests with the adversary. Another made something of a hero of a big boy who had previously been regarded as a bully. Similarly, the change to intergroup cooperation was accompanied by shifts in the status structure, particularly in one group where some members looked back to former days of rivalry.

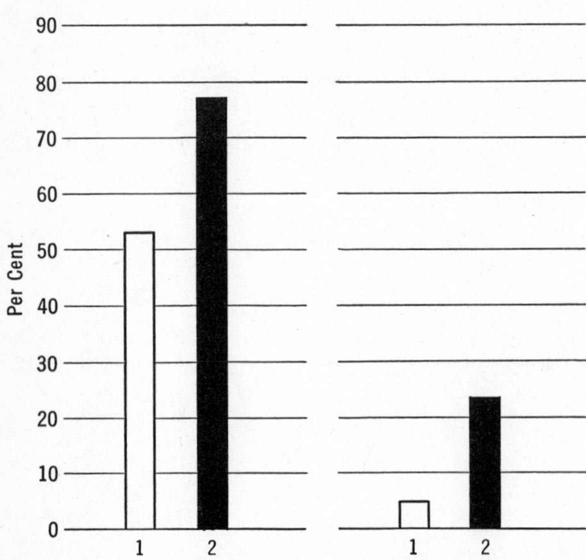

Figure 4-5. Negative ratings of each group by the other were common during the period of conflict *(left)* but decreased when harmony was restored *(right)*. The graphs show per cent who thought that *all* (rather than *some* or *none*) of the other group were cheaters, sneaks, etc.

4. Contact between hostile groups as equals in contiguous and pleasant situations does not, in itself, necessarily reduce conflict between them.

5. Contact between groups involving interdependent action toward superordinate goals is conducive to cooperation between groups, but single episodes of cooperation are not sufficient to reduce established intergroup hostility and negative stereotypes.

6. A series of cooperative situations toward superordinate goals has a cumulative effect in reducing intergroup hostility. This cumulative effect involves the successful development of procedures and their transfer to new situations, such that established modes of intergroup cooperation are recognized.

7. Tools and techniques found useful in problem solving within groups and in intergroup conflict may also serve in intergroup cooperation. But their use in intergroup cooperation requires recognition that the procedures involve not merely so many individuals within a group, but different groups of individuals contributing to the attainment of a common goal.

8. Cooperative endeavor between groups toward superordinate goals alters the significance of other measures designed to reduce existing hostility between them. Intergroup contacts in the course of actions toward superordinate goals were used for developing plans, making decisions, and having pleasant exchanges. Information about the other group became interesting and sought after, rather than something to be ignored or interpreted to fit existing conceptions of the out-group. Exchange of persons for the performance of tasks was not seen as "betrayal" of one's own group. Leaders found that the trend toward intergroup cooperation widened the spheres in which they could take positive steps toward working out procedures for joint endeavors and future contacts. In fact, a leader who tried to hold back from intergroup contacts found that his group was ceasing to listen to him.

In short, the findings suggest that various methods used with limited success in reducing intergroup hostility may become effective when employed within a framework of cooperation among groups toward goals which are genuinely appealing to all and which require equitable participation and contributions from all groups.

*EXPERIMENTAL STUDIES OF HOMOGENEOUS AND HETEROGENEOUS GROUPS FOR CREATIVE SCIENTIFIC TASKS**

By E. Paul Torrance and Kevser Arsan

In assigning creative tasks in elementary-school classes, it is frequently necessary to divide pupils into small groups. If each group is to undertake a different task, the basis for the grouping is usually some kind of similarity of interest. If all groups are assigned the same task as a common educational experience, the problem is different. There are many possibilities. Strevell and Oliver,[1] for example, have identified 24 types of classroom grouping practices. If the task to be assigned requires creative thinking, one logical basic for grouping would be scores on tests of creative thinking. The question then becomes, "Should the groups be homogeneous or heterogeneous?"

In grouping pupils for tasks requiring creative thinking, one must consider a number of special problems. The groupings should help to create conditions which will free each child to think, to express his thoughts, and to have them considered honestly. Disruptive social stress should be reduced as much as possible, and positive, productive interaction should be fostered.

There is a considerable body of literature concerning homogeneous and heterogeneous grouping in reading, mathematics, and other subjects. Using scores on tests of reading achievement as the basis of homogeneity and heterogeneity, research workers have generally given the nod to homogeneous grouping.[2] Some, however, stress flexibility in grouping.[3]

Hardly any attention has been given, however, to the special problems of grouping for tasks requiring creative thinking. One exploratory experiment with young adults as subjects in laboratory tasks requiring group creativity has been reported by Fiedler, Meuwese, and Oonk.[4] Homogeneity and heterogeneity were based on religious and collegiate affiliations. The subjects were students in Calvinist and Catholic colleges in Amsterdam, Holland. The same subjects took part in both homogeneous and heterogeneous groups under both formal and informal organizations. Under both forms of organization, the heterogeneous groups showed much social strain and impeded communication. The homogeneous groups showed little social strain and had few problems of communication.

Some of the findings from Elizabeth Drews' studies of homogeneous and heterogeneous ability groupings in ninth-grade English classes provide clues concerning what we may expect in creative activities.[5] Her results indicate that slow students read more, recited more, were more confident, liked school better, and were more accepted socially and intellectually in the homogeneous groups. Superior students wrote many more compositions, did more research, discussed at a more mature level, used more difficult words, expressed more complex and abstract thoughts, and were more interested in learning in homogeneous than in heterogeneous groups. They were also much more modest in their ratings of self in relationship to others.

The purpose of the study reported herein is to explore the differential effects of homogeneous and

[1] W. H. Strevell and P. Oliver, "Grouping Can be Flexible within the Classroom," *Nations Schools,* 1957, *59,* pp. 89-91.

[2] W. B. Barbe and T. S. Waterhouse, "An Experimental Program in Reading," *Elementary English,* 1956, *33,* pp. 102-104.

[3] N. Bremer, "First Grade Achievement under Different Plans of Grouping," *Elementary English,* 1958, *35,* pp. 324-326.

[4] F. E. Fiedler, W. Meuwese, and S. Oonk, *Performance on Laboratory Tasks Requiring Group Creativity: An Exploratory Study* (Urbana: Center for Research in Social Psychology, University of Illinois, 1960).

[5] E. M. Drews, "Recent Findings about Gifted Adolescents." In E. P. Torrance (Ed.), *New Ideas: Third Minnesota Conference on Gifted Children* (Minneapolis: Center for Continuation Study, University of Minnesota, 1961).

*Adapted by the authors from a paper presented at meetings of Association for Educators of Gifted Children, Statler Hilton Hotel, Detroit, April 8, 1961. Another version of the paper appeared as, "Can Grouping Control Social Stress in Creative Activities?" *Elementary School Journal,* 1961, *62,* pp. 139-145. The research reported herein was supported in part by the Cooperative Research Program of the United States Office of Education.

heterogeneous groups within classes in doing a task requiring creative scientific thinking. Both creative thinking ability and intelligence quotients are explored as bases of the groupings.

PROCEDURES

Subjects. The subjects of the study were fourth-, fifth-, and sixth-graders in three Minneapolis elementary schools. School A is a private school which limits its enrollment to twenty-five per class. Schools B and C are public schools, each having two classes at each grade level.

In 1959, the pupils in each class of School A were divided heterogeneously into groups of five on the basis of *Form A, Test of Imagination* developed by the senior author.[6] In 1960, each class was divided homogeneously on the basis of *Form DX, Test of Imagination,* also developed by the senior author.

In School B, one class in each grade was grouped homogeneously and the other heterogeneously on the basis of creativity scores on Form DX. In all, twenty groups from this school were included in the study.

In School C, one class in each grade was grouped homogeneously and the other heterogeneously on the basis of intelligence quotients as determined by the California Test of Mental Maturity. In this school, twenty-three groups were included in the study.

To summarize, subjects were grouped according to the following design:

School	*Year*	*4th Grade*	*5th Grade*	*6th Grade*	*Basis of Grouping*
A	1959	He	He	He	Form A
	1960	Ho	Ho	Ho	Form DX
B	1960	He	He	He	Form DX
	1960	Ho	Ho	Ho	Form DX
C	1960	He	He	He	Calif. Mental Maturity
	1960	Ho	Ho	Ho	Calif. Mental Maturity

[6] E. P. Torrance and Staff, *Assessing the Creative Thinking Abilities of Children* (Minneapolis: Bureau of Educational Research, University of Minnesota, 1960).

Homogeneous groups were formed by ranking all pupils in a class on the measure (intelligence quotient or creativity score) used as the basis for grouping and placing the first five pupils in one group, the next five in a second, and so on. In forming heterogeneous groups, one of the top-ranking pupils was placed in each group, followed by one of the next highest ranking pupils, and so on. Subjects were not informed of the basis used in forming the groups. Each of the five-person groups was about equally divided insofar as sex is concerned.

Creative thinking tests. As already indicated, two different batteries of creative thinking tasks, Form A and Form DX, were used as the basis for the grouping. Form A consists of six tasks adapted from Guilford's battery.[7] These include, Uses of Common Objects (Tin Cans), Impossibilities, Consequences, Situations, Problems, and Improvements. Form DX consists of the following tasks: Product Improvements (Toy Dog), Unusual Uses of Toy Dog, Unusual Uses of Tin Cans, Circles (sketching objects with circles as main part of design), Asking Questions, Guessing Causes, and Guessing Consequences. Both batteries were scored for fluency of ideas (number of ideas), flexibility (number of different categories of approaches represented by ideas), and originality (uncommonness of ideas). Form DX yielded in addition scores for inventiveness, constructiveness, curiosity, and hypothesis-making. The total raw score was used in making the groupings.

The coefficients of correlation between total scores derived from Forms A and DX, given a year apart, were .55 from fourth to fifth and .58 from fifth to sixth grades. Between Stanford-Binet intelligence quotients and Form A in School A, a mean coefficient of correlation of .22 was obtained by computing coefficients of correlation within grades. Between the IQ based on the California Test of Mental Maturity and total scores on Form DX in School B, a mean coefficient of correlation of .24 resulted. Reliability of scoring has been kept consistently above .90 for both Forms A and DX.[8] Evidence concerning the validity of Forms A and DX

[7] J. P. Guilford *et al., A Factor-Analytic Study of Creative Thinking: I, Hypothesis and Description of Tests* (Los Angeles: University of Southern California, 1951).

[8] E. P. Torrance, *op. cit.*

is encouraging and is described in detail elsewhere.[9]

Experimental Procedures. In each class, all groups were tested simultaneously, each in a different room under a trained experimenter who made detailed observations of the interaction. Tabulations were made for ideas or action initiated, uses discovered, explanations advanced, and reasons suggested during the exploratory period. In addition, the experimenters described how the group got organized and underway with the task, how the members grouped themselves, the general activity level of the exploratory period, the special roles of members, how the demonstrations were planned, special roles in planning and demonstrating, and the like.

To set the creative scientific task, after the homogeneous or heterogeneous groups had been formed, each group was provided with a box of science toys and toy parts obtainable from Science Materials Center, the Library of Science, 59 Fourth Avenue, New York 3, New York. Each toy illustrates at least one basic principle of science. Science Toy Collection Number 2 was used in the 1959 administration in School A. This collection includes a sparkler, a finger trap, a pin trick, a four-ball puzzle, a topsy-turvy top, a blow ball, a flying saucer, and nutty putty. To this collection was added a magnifying glass, a magnet, and a whistle. Science Toy Collection Number 3 was used in all other administrations and includes a bang gun, a string telephone, a siren, a busy bee, a calliope whistle, a cat cry, a Tower of Hanoi puzzle, a tetrahedron puzzle, and other puzzles. A magnet and a magnifying glass were added to this collection.

Before a class was divided into groups, the senior author gave the entire class the following orientation: "Once again, I would like to ask you to help us find out more about the ways people learn how to think of new ideas. During this next hour, we have arranged what is a kind of test of how inventive you can be about science things, and how well you can develop ideas as groups. We will divide you into groups of five and each group will work in a separate place with a different observer. Each group will be given a box of science toys. Your job will be to find out as many things as you can that these toys can do or be used for. Some of you will recognize the scientific principles that these toys were made to illustrate. But we want you to be concerned about any possible uses of these toys, not just the ones they were made for.

"For 25 minutes, you may experiment with these toys and try to find out as many things as you can that you can do with them. Then we will give you another 25 minute period in which to demonstrate what these toys can do and explain the principles behind them.

"The object is to see how many science principles you can demonstrate and explain. We are not interested in individual performance but in how well the group does. One of my helpers will be with each group and will take down your ideas and record some things about the way you do your job. In addition to seeing how you can use and figure out scientific principles, we want to see how you work as a group on problems like this.

"To make this more interesting, we shall award a prize to each member of the group which demonstrates and explains the largest number of science principles."

The membership and places of meeting for each group were then announced. When the five-person groups had assembled, the experimenter gave each person a colored arm band, according to a pre-determined code. He then gave the following instructions for the exploratory phase:

"Here is a box of science toys. All of them were made to illustrate some scientific principle. I am sure that you can think of many other uses than the ones originally intended. Your job is to find out as many things as you can that these toys can do and explain them. Don't give up when you have discovered one use; there are several possible uses for each toy. You can combine them in different ways. You will have 25 minutes to do this."

At the end of this phase, the following instructions were given:

"Now, I would like for you to demonstrate these toys to me just as though I were a class you are trying to teach what these toys can do and why they do it. You will have only 25 minutes to do this. Remember that group performance is what counts. First, demonstrate what the toy can do. Second, explain the principle or reason why it does what it does. All right, go ahead."

At the end of the experiment, each subject was asked to rank each member of his group, including

[9] E. P. Torrance, *Guiding Creative Talent* (New York: Prentice-Hall, Inc., 1962).

himself, according to the value of his contribution to the success of the group. In all the 1960 administrations, subjects were also asked to indicate how well they had enjoyed the activity and how they thought their own group had performed in comparison with the others in the class.

Upon completion of the experiment, the observers prepared their records which consisted of the tabulations and descriptions for the exploratory and planning phases, accounts of the demonstrations and explanations, and other observations of interaction during the ratings and demonstrations. Except for checks on reliability of observers, each group was observed by only one experimenter. The same persons observed both homogeneous and heterogeneous groups on various occasions.

Analysis of data. A score was obtained for each individual on number of ideas initiated, number of ideas demonstrated and explained, reported enjoyment of the activity, self-ranking of performance, and rating of own group. At each of the five ability levels, comparisons were made between the homogeneous and heterogeneous groups separately for each school.

The record of each group was then analyzed for positive and negative signs. This was done by first drawing up lists of words which would be accepted as indicators of social stress and of positive, productive interaction. A high degree of agreement ($r = .95$) was achieved by raters in scoring records according to these lists.

The following terms appearing in the records were classified as indications of disruptive social stress or tension:

Bickering, fighting, squabbling, uncontrolled behavior, disorder, disorganization, dominating, squelching, reprimanding, loss of temper, apathy or passivity, refusal to cooperate, loss of interest, sarcasm, and disruptive talking and joking.

The following terms were classified as signs of positive, productive interaction or tension-reducing behaviors:

Co-operating, helping, working together, organizing, absorption in task, praising one another, respecting others' ideas, listening, considering others' ideas, trying

TABLE 4-18

MEAN NUMBER OF IDEAS INITIATED BY PUPILS OF FIVE ABILITY-LEVELS IN HOMOGENEOUS AND HETEROGENEOUS GROUPS IN THREE ELEMENTARY SCHOOLS AND TESTS OF SIGNIFICANCE

Ability Level	*Homogeneous*		*Heterogeneous*		*F-ratio*	*Level of Signif.*
	Number of Pupils	*Mean*	*Number of Pupils*	*Mean*		
School A						
1 (Most Creative)	14	13.07	15	13.00	0.00	NS
2	14	12.71	13	8.53	4.41	<.05
3	13	7.61	15	5.86	0.96	NS
4	13	8.84	14	5.21	4.30	<.05
5 (Least Creative)	14	13.42	13	4.69	17.47	<.01
School B						
1 (Most Creative)	8	8.00	13	11.30	1.60	NS
2	8	10.30	12	9.50	0.06	NS
3	8	8.90	13	9.20	0.03	NS
4	7	5.40	12	5.50	0.00	NS
5 (Least Creative)	8	7.00	13	3.75	2.11	NS
School C						
1 (Most Intell.)	12	5.60	10	10.00	12.07	<.01
2	12	7.10	10	7.30	0.03	NS
3	13	9.00	10	5.40	4.62	<.05
4	13	12.70	10	5.00	8.92	<.01
5 (Least Intell.)	13	9.13	10	7.90	0.35	NS

out others' ideas, communicating ideas, consulting with one another, congenial, interested, questioning, curious, etc.

A tabulation of both positive and negative signs was made for each group. Homogeneous and heterogeneous groups in each of the three schools were compared by means of chi-square analysis.

RESULTS

Number of ideas initiated. The mean number of ideas initiated by subjects in each of the five ability levels in homogeneous and heterogeneous groups in each of the three schools studied is shown in Table 4-18, together with tests of significance. In School A, it will be noted that in the homogeneous groups, those at the second, fourth, and fifth ability levels initiated significantly more ideas than did their counterparts in the heterogeneous groups. In the heterogeneous groups, it will be noted that there is a tendency toward a linear relationship between ability level and mean number of ideas initiated. This tendency does not prevail under homogeneous conditions; those in the fourth and fifth ability levels diverge from the linear tendency.

In School B, there are no statistically significant differences at any ability level under the two conditions. The trends noted in School B, for subjects at the second and fifth levels of ability to initiate more ideas in homogeneous than in heterogeneous groups, were not statistically significant. Those at the highest ability level, however, tended to initiate more ideas in heterogeneous than in homogeneous groups. Again the linear trend between ability level and mean number of ideas initiated appears in the heterogeneous but not in the homogeneous groups, the second and fifth ability levels diverging most sharply from the linear trend.

In School C, where IQ was the basis for grouping, those in the highest ability level in heterogeneous groups excel their counterparts in the homogeneous groups, while the reverse is true for those at the fourth ability level. Contrary to what was found in Schools A and B, where creativity scores were used as a basis for grouping, there is no linear trend under any condition between IQ level and mean number of ideas initiated. The linear trend in the heterogeneous groups was upset by those in the lowest ability level who excelled their peers at the second, third, and fourth ability levels. In the homogeneous groups, there is almost a linear trend in reverse. The lowest mean was achieved by groups composed of children with the highest IQs, the highest by those at the fourth and fifth levels.

Ideas demonstrated and explained. Table 4-19 shows the mean number of ideas demonstrated and explained by subjects in the five ability levels in homogeneous and heterogeneous groups in each of the three schools, together with tests of significance.

It will be noted that none of the differences is statistically significant in School A. The linear trend between ability level and mean number of ideas demonstrated and explained is spoiled somewhat by

TABLE 4-19

MEAN NUMBER OF IDEAS DEMONSTRATED AND EXPLAINED BY PUPILS OF FIVE ABILITY LEVELS IN HOMOGENEOUS AND HETEROGENEOUS GROUPS IN THREE ELEMENTARY SCHOOLS AND TESTS OF SIGNIFICANCE

Ability Level	*Means*		*F-ratio*	*Level of Signif.*
	Homogeneous	*Heterogeneous*		
School A				
1 (Most Creative)	7.49	12.46	2.04	NS
2	6.92	9.22	1.56	NS
3	4.61	7.26	1.99	NS
4	5.30	4.85	0.10	NS
5 (Least Creative)	8.35	5.61	3.51	NS
School B				
1 (Most Creative)	5.30	6.23	0.35	NS
2	4.80	7.50	1.78	NS
3	2.30	5.30	4.90	<.05
4	2.20	5.33	5.22	<.05
5 (Least Creative)	8.75	4.30	10.34	<.01
School C				
1 (Most Intelligent)	6.90	11.00	2.24	NS
2	10.40	8.10	0.58	NS
3	5.70	4.00	2.13	NS
4	5.60	7.90	1.22	NS
5 (Least Intelligent)	7.26	7.80	0.00	NS

TABLE 4-20

COMPARISON OF REPORTED ENJOYMENT OF SCIENCE-TOY TASK IN HOMOGENEOUS AND HETEROGENEOUS GROUPS IN SCHOOLS B AND C

Degree of Enjoyment Reported	School B		School C		Total	
	Homog.	Heterog.	Homog.	Heterog.	Homog.	Heterog.
	%	%	%	%	%	%
Very much; most fun of anything today	56	58	81	67	72	62
Quite well; would like to do again	38	30	14	24	24	27
All right; wouldn't mind doing again	6	12	5	9	4	11
TOTAL PER CENT	100%	100%	100%	100%	100%	100%
(NUMBER OF CASES)	(39)	(64)	(63)	(49)	(102)	(113)

those in the lowest group. In the homogeneous groups, those at the lowest ability level actually achieved the highest mean of any ability level.

In School B, those at the third and fourth ability levels demonstrated and explained significantly more ideas in heterogeneous groups than in homogeneous groups. The reverse is true, however, for those in the lowest ability level. As in School A, those in the lowest ability level turned in the best performance of any ability level.

In School C, the linear trend in the heterogeneous condition is disturbed by the fourth and fifth ability levels. Again, subjects in the highest ability level turn in a rather mediocre performance under homogeneous conditions.

Enjoyment of task. Complete data concerning enjoyment of task were available only for Schools B and C. As will be seen from Table 4-20, in these two schools there was a consistent tendency for pupils under homogeneous conditions to report greater enjoyment than those under heterogeneous conditions. The difference is statistically significant only at the second ability level, however, and this occurs in both schools. When tabulations are made of the number choosing each category for the entire school, the chi square is significant for School C but not for School B. In School C, 81 per cent of those in the homogeneous groups reported that they enjoyed the activity "very much" compared with 67 per cent in the heterogeneous groups.

Self-rankings. As shown in Table 4-21, there was a general tendency for the more able subjects in both schools to be more modest or self-depreciating and for the less able ones to be less modest or less self-depreciating under homogeneous conditions than under heterogeneous conditions. In School B,

TABLE 4-21

MEAN SELF-RANKING OF PERFORMANCE ON SCIENCE-TOY TASK BY CHILDREN OF FIVE ABILITY LEVELS IN HOMOGENEOUS AND HETEROGENEOUS GROUPS IN TWO ELEMENTARY SCHOOLS AND TESTS OF SIGNIFICANCE

Ability Level	Means: Homogeneous	Means: Heterogeneous	F-ratio	Level of Signif.
School B				
1 (Most Creative)	4.00	2.69	8.19	<.01
2	2.70	2.25	0.99	NS
3	3.00	2.76	0.20	NS
4	2.60	3.25	0.67	NS
5 (Least Creative)	2.50	3.53	1.63	NS
School C				
1 (Most Intelligent)	2.90	2.50	0.33	NS
2	3.60	2.60	2.92	NS
3	3.90	3.10	1.11	NS
4	2.70	3.00	0.33	NS
5 (Least Intelligent)	2.50	3.53	1.63	NS

subjects at the top ability level are extremely self-depreciating in homogeneous groups. Their mean self-ranking is fourth, where the lowest ranking is five. They are significantly more self-depreciating than their counterparts under heterogeneous conditions (.01 level).

Rating of group performance. Only at the top level of ability are there statistically significant differences between subjects in the two conditions in their ratings of their own group's performance. When creative thinking is the basis for the grouping, the top ability subjects rate their group's performance less favorably under homogeneous than under heterogeneous conditions. The reverse is true when IQ is used as the basis for grouping.

Social stress. Comparisons of the homogeneous and heterogeneous groups in each of the three schools on the number of signs of disruptive social stress and positive interaction are presented in Table 4-22. The results are consistent from school to school, and in all cases the differences are significant at better than the .01 level of confidence. There were fewer signs of social stress in the homogeneous than in the heterogeneous groups. This result held when the same classes constitute the homogeneous and heterogeneous groups about a year apart, when one class at each grade-level is divided homogeneously and another in the same school divided heterogeneously, when pupils are grouped according to measures of creativity, and when they are grouped according to intelligence quotient.

DISCUSSION

From the data presented it seems reasonably clear that we may expect greater disruptive social stress when we divide classroom groups heterogeneously than when we divide them homogeneously for creative activities. These results seem to hold both when the groupings are based on IQs and when they are based on measures of creative thinking. In the authors' observations, there did seem to be one major differences between the heterogeneous groups based on IQ and those based on creativity. There seemed to be far less effort to "unseat" the high-IQ member than the highly creative member. The status of the child with the high IQ seemed far more secure than that of the highly creative child.

These results should not be interpreted to mean that teachers should always form homogeneous groups for creative tasks. There are signs that some homogeneous groups tend to be dull and uninteresting and unproductive when new ideas are required. There seem to be times when it is advantageous to increase social stress. On the basis of research[10] on the effects of varying intensity of stress, creative

[10] E. P. Torrance, *Mastery of Stress,* School Counselor Note 4 (Wright-Patterson Air Force Base, Ohio: United States Air Force Orientation Group, 1958).

TABLE 4-22

NUMBER OF POSITIVE AND NEGATIVE INTERACTIONS IN HOMOGENEOUS AND HETEROGENEOUS GROUPS DURING SCIENCE-TOY TASK

School	*Homogeneous*				*Heterogeneous*			
	No. of Groups	*No. of Pupils*	*No. Interactions*		*No. of Groups*	*No. of Pupils*	*No. Interactions*	
			Positive	*Negative*			*Positive*	*Negative*
A	15	70	136	53	15	70	36	77
B	8	39	53	32	12	63	52	73
C	12	63	107	37	11	55	63	53

X^2 (School A) $= 46.3873$; $df = 1$; $p < .001$
X^2 (School B) $= 8.6940$; $df = 1$; $p < .01$
X^2 (School C) $= 11.3360$; $df = 1$; $p < .01$

thinking is likely to be stimulated by increasing social stress to a point, after which thinking is disrupted and productivity diminishes. Thus, it would seem that a classroom teacher may within limits control the degree of social stress in work groups by choosing varying bases of grouping. Of course, still other methods of grouping need to be investigated and effects of groupings other than social stress need to be studied.

Although the findings concerning individual behavior are not nearly as impressive as those relevant to social stress, several rather strong tendencies are worth noting. One of these is the fairly consistent and frequently dramatic "all-out" performance of the low-ability groups under homogeneous conditions. The consistent linear trend in the heterogeneous group provides some rather convincing evidence concerning the validity of the tests of creative thinkings used in forming the groups. Those who produced the most ideas on the written tests administered several months earlier also produced the most ideas in this task. The failure of this linear trend to hold under homogeneous conditions suggests that many of our ability measures, including the IQ, might lose some of their predictive value under conditions of homogeneous grouping, when the performance of one individual is not experimentally independent of that of his fellow group-members.

The findings concerning enjoyment of the activity and self-rankings support those of Drews.[11] They tend to contradict popular beliefs that homogeneous grouping will make children unhappy, especially the low ability ones, and that high ability pupils will become conceited and low ability ones overwhelmed by their feelings of inferiority. In both studies, the very reverse seems to be true.

[11] E. M. Drews, *op. cit.*

V

TEACHER-STUDENT INTERACTION

*AN EXPERIMENTAL STUDY OF LEADERSHIP AND GROUP LIFE**

By Ronald Lippitt and Ralph K. White

The study here reported, conducted in 1939 and 1940, attempted in an exploratory way to discover the extent to which various aspects of leadership behavior and of total group life could be fruitfully studied by experimental procedures of controlled matching and planned variation in conditions. The study had as its objectives:

1. To study the effects on group and individual behavior of three experimental variations in adult leadership in four clubs of eleven-year-old children. These three styles may be roughly labeled as "democratic," "authoritarian," and "laissez-faire."

2. To study the group and individual reactions to shifts from one type of leadership to another within the same group.

3. To seek relationships between the nature and content of other group memberships, particularly the classroom and family, and the reactions to the experimental social climates.

4. To explore the methodological problems of setting up comparative "group test situations," to develop adequate techniques of group process recording, and to discover the degree to which experimental conditions could be controlled and manipulated within the range of acceptance by the group members.

The major experimental controls may be described briefly as follows:

1. *Personal characteristics of group members.* Because a large group of volunteers were available from which to select each of the small clubs, it was possible to arrange for comparability of group members on such characteristics as intelligence, and on such social behaviors (measured by teachers' ratings) as obedience, amount of social participation, leadership, frequency of quarreling, amount of physical energy, etc.

2. *The interrelationship pattern of each club.*

*From *Readings in Social Psychology,* E. E. Maccoby, T. M. Newcomb, and E. L. Hartley (3rd ed.; New York: Holt, Rinehart, and Winston, Inc., 1958), pp. 496-510. Used by permission of the authors and publisher.

In each group, by the use of a sociometric questionnaire in each classroom, it was possible to select groups which were very closely matched in terms of patterns of rejection, friendship, mutuality of relationship, and leadership position.

3. *Physical setting and equipment.* All clubs met in the same clubroom setting, two at a time in adjacent meeting spaces, with a common equipment box.

4. *Activity interests.* It was important to know the extent to which initial interest in the planned activities might be responsible for differences in degree of involvement in activity during the experiment. Therefore it was ascertained in the beginning that all groups of boys were comparably interested in the range of craft and recreational activities in which they would later be engaged.

5. *Activity content.* It is clear that the structure and content of an activity often exerts a powerful influence on the patterns of interdependence, cooperation, competition, etc. in group life. Therefore, it was important that activity content should be equated in these three types of leadership situations. In order to insure this, the clubs under democratic leadership met first in time during the week, and the activities which were selected by those clubs were automatically assigned to the parallel clubs under authoritarian leadership. In the laissez-faire situation, there were a number of potential activities of the same type as that selected by the "democratic clubs."

6. *The same group under different leadership.* The experimental design also made it possible to have a perfect matching of club personnel on the same analysis by comparing the same club with itself under three different leaders.

EXPERIMENTAL VARIATIONS

In the beginning the experimenters had planned for only two major variations in adult leader behavior: an authoritarian pattern and a democratic pattern. Later it was decided that it would be more fruitful to add a third variation of "laissez-faire" adult behavior, although with the four available clubs it would make the experimental design less rigorous. The method of systematic rotation can be noted in the chart below, which refers to the earlier experiment (the same method was followed in the later experiment).

The three types of planned variation were as follows:

1. *The sequence of social climates.* A number of the hypotheses focused upon the effect of a particular type of group history in determining the reactions of a group to a present pattern of leadership. The chart indicates the variety of group history sequences which were selected for exploratory study.

2. *"Leader role" and "leader personality."* There was a question as to the extent to which certain basic personality characteristics of the adult leaders would be important determinants in the individual and group behavior patterns which resulted. To study this variable, four adults with very different personality patterns were selected as leaders and all of

	Period 1 (7 weeks)	*Period 2 (7 weeks)*	*Period 3 (7 weeks)*
Treatment	Autocracy	Autocracy	Democracy
Club	Sherlock Holmes	Sherlock Holmes	Sherlock Holmes
Leader	I	IV	II
Treatment	Autocracy	Democracy	Autocracy
Club	Dick Tracy	Dick Tracy	Dick Tracy
Leader	II	III	I
Treatment	Democracy	Autocracy	Democracy
Club	Secret Agents	Secret Agents	Secret Agents
Leader	III	II	IV
Treatment	Democracy	Democracy	Autocracy
Club	Charlie Chan	Charlie Chan	Charlie Chan
Leader	IV	I	III

them after proper indoctrination took two or three different leadership roles with different groups during the course of the experiment as indicated on the chart. This made it possible to discover whether certain of the leaders induced common reaction patterns which could be traced to their "personality" as contrasted to their "leadership role."

3. *The three planned leadership roles.* The three variations in leader role which were worked through in careful detail by the four club leaders may be summarized as follows:

Plan for authoritarian leadership role. Practically all policies as regards club activities and procedures should be determined by the leader. The techniques and activity steps should be communicated by the authority, one unit at a time, so that future steps are in the dark to a large degree. The adult should take considerable responsibility for assigning the activity tasks and companions of each group member. The dominator should keep his standards of praise and criticism to himself in evaluating individual and group activities. He should also remain fairly aloof from active group participation except in demonstrating.

Plan for the democratic leadership role. Wherever possible, policies should be a matter of group decision and discussion with active encouragement and assistance by the adult leader. The leader should attempt to see that activity perspective emerges during the discussion period with the general steps to the group goal becoming clarified. Wherever technical advice is needed, the leader should try to suggest two or more alternative procedures from which choice can be made by the group members. Everyone should be free to work with whomever he chooses, and the divisions of responsibility should be left up to the group. The leader should attempt to communicate in an objective, fact-minded way the bases for his praise and criticism of individual and group activities. He should try to be a regular group member in spirit but not do much of the work (so that comparisons of group productivity can be made between the groups).

Plan for laissez-faire leadership role. In this situation, the adult should play a rather passive role in social participation and leave complete freedom for group or individual decisions in relation to activity and group procedure. The leader should make clear the various materials which are available and be sure it is understood that he will supply information and help when asked. He should do a minimum of taking the initiative in making suggestions. He should make no attempt to evaluate negatively or positively the behavior or productions of the individuals or the group as a group, although he should be friendly rather than "stand-offish" at all times.

The data below will indicate the extent to which these planned variations were carried out and the pattern of social stimulation which was represented by the leader behavior in each of the clubs.

The three patterns of leader behavior. From the great variety of observations recorded on the behavior of each leader it was possible to compute quantitative profiles of leader performance which could be compared to see the extent to which the three different types of leadership role were different and the degree to which the adults carrying out the same role were comparable in their behavior patterns. Figure 5-1 illustrates some of the major differences in the patterns of behavior of the three leadership roles. Most of the comparisons on the graph meet the test of statistical significance. The "average leader" comparisons are based on four democratic, four authoritarian, and two laissez-faire leader roles. The first three classifications of behavior, "leader orders," "disrupting commands," and "nonconstructive criticism," may be thought of as representing adult behavior which has a limiting

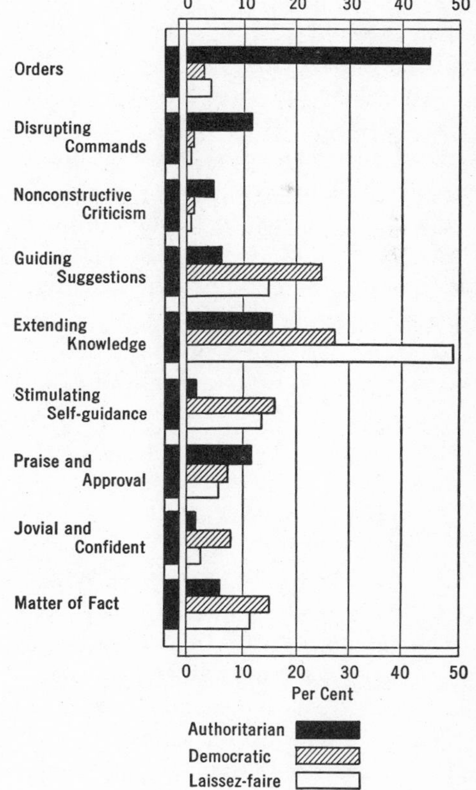

Figure 5-1. Comparison of behavior of average authoritarian, democratic, and laissez-faire leader.

effect upon the scope and spontaneity of child activity. About 60 per cent of all of the behavior of the average authoritarian leader was of these types as compared to 5 per cent for the democratic and laissez-faire leaders. The data show that the authoritarian leader usually initiated individual or group activity with an order, often disrupted ongoing activity by an order which started things off in the new direction not spontaneously chosen, and fairly frequently criticized work in a manner which carried the meaning, "It is a bad job because I say it is a bad job" rather than, "It is a poor job because those nails are bent over instead of driven in."

The next three behavior classifications, "guiding suggestions," "extending knowledge," "stimulating self-guidance," may be thought of as extending individual and group freedom and abilities. We note here some of the major differences between the democratic and the laissez-faire leadership role. Whereas the democratic leader took the initiative (where he felt it was needed in making guiding suggestions) much more frequently than the laissez-faire leader, a major proportion of the latter leadership role was giving out information when it was asked for. It is clear, however, that the democratic leader did not take initiative for action away from the group as indicated by the fact that the average democratic leader showed a greater proportion of "stimulating self-guidance" than even the laissez-faire leader. The category of "stimulating self-guidance" was made up of three main items: "leader's requests for child's opinions on individual and group plans," "use of child judgment as criterion," and "taking consensus of opinion." The data indicate that the democratic leaders stimulated child independence eight times as often as the authoritarian leader and about twice as often as the laissez-faire leader, although the latter two types of adults showed about the same proportion of this behavior in their total pattern of activity.

The classification on the graph entitled, "praise and approval" is made up of such behavior items as "praising," "giving credit," "giving O.K.s," etc. It indicates largely the functioning of the adult as a dispenser of social recognition. The authoritarian adult was significantly more active in this regard than either of the other two types of leaders.

The extent to which the adult discussed personal matters unrelated to the club situation (home, school, etc.) and also joked on a friendly basis with the club members, is indicated by the "jovial and confident" classification. The democratic leader had social interactions of this type with the group members about eight times as often as either the authoritarian or laissez-faire leaders. This is perhaps one of the best indices of the extent to which the democratic leaders were "on the same level" as the club members.

The last classification on Figure 5-1, "matter of fact," indicates one measurement of the extent to which the various social atmospheres were "fact-minded" as compared to "personal-minded" as far as the behavior of the adults was concerned.

The degree to which all the adult leaders, delegated to assume a given leadership role, behaved in a comparable fashion on these major aspects of leadership role is indicated by the fact that, on all comparisons differentiating major characteristics of the three roles, there is no overlapping of the behavior of any representative of one role with any representative of a different role. Thus it is possible to conclude that three clearly different leadership patterns were created with a much smaller range of individual differences in leader behavior within each pattern than between the patterns.

Leadership Role and Personality Style. An examination of the behavior patterns of the different leadership roles by the same individuals reveals that on the items of leader behavior there is no greater similarity between the different performance patterns of the same individual than between those of different individuals. If we turn to the data of the three interviews with each club member in which at each transition stage in their club life they compared their leaders and talked very fully about them, we find again that there is no evidence of any adult personality being rated favorably or unfavorably independently of their particular leadership role (i.e., authoritarian, democratic, laissez-faire). All leaders stood high as well as low for one group or another and all the comments about their "personalities" were concerned with attributes of their leadership roles which had been measured.

The following excerpts from interviews of club members who had just completed six months of club life which included an authoritarian, a laissez-faire, and a democratic leader (in that sequence) indicate rather clearly the aspects of "leadership personality" which were perceived as important.

RW (democratic) was the best leader and DA (laissez-faire) was the poorest. RW has good ideas and goes right to the point of everything . . . and always asked us what to do next time the club met, which was very nice. . . . DA gave us no suggestions like RW did, and didn't help us out at all, though he was very nice to us . . . but let us figure things out too much. I liked RL (authoritarian) pretty well for that kind of work.

RL (authoritarian) was best, and then RW (democratic) and DA (authoritarian). RL was the strictest and I like that a lot. DA and RW let us go ahead and fight, and that isn't good, though RW didn't do it as much as DA did. DA just didn't give us much to do. RW was OK, but he didn't have so many ideas as RL did. RW wanted to do what we did; RL didn't want to go with us lots of times, and he decided what we were to do.

I liked RW (democratic) best, then DA (laissez-faire) and then RL (authoritarian). RW was a good sport, works along with us and helps us a lot; he thinks of things just like we do and was just one of us—he never did try to be the boss, and wasn't strict at all, but always had plenty to do (the golden mean). DA didn't do much, just sat and watched; there wasn't much I didn't like about him, but he didn't help us much . . . not like with RW when we had regular meetings and that was very good. RL was all right mostly; he was sort of dictator like, and we had to do what he said pretty nearly; he helped us work but he was sort of bossy.

I liked RW (democratic) the best and RL (authoritarian) the least. RW was in between DA and RL, I like everything about him. I once said I didn't want to change from DA but I'm glad we changed. We could do what we pleased with DA but he was too easy going, not hard enough nearly, but he's a real nice person. With RL we always had something to do, and we did get a lot of things done, but I didn't like anything about him; he was much too strict. He was not cross, but very direct.

I'd take RW (democratic) for a club leader, and DA (laissez-faire) was the worst. RW was just the right sort of combination; RL (authoritarian) was just about as good as RW, but he was kind of cross once in a while. RW had interesting things to do, he was just about right in everything. DA was too easy; he didn't know anything about the club—didn't know about its ways. He didn't understand us boys at all. . . . I didn't like him as well as RL because he had too few things for us to do.[1]

Another indirect indication that individual personality characteristics were not of any great significance in influencing group life in this study might be inferred from the finding that the total patterns of group reactions of different clubs to the same atmosphere tend to be remarkably homogeneous in spite of differences in adult leadership.

DATA COLLECTION AND ANALYSIS

Before continuing to summarize the individual and group behaviors which resulted from these three variations in leadership role, we will indicate briefly the types of data collection and analysis in the total study.

Eight types of club records were kept on each group, of which the four most important were kept by four different observers as follows:

1. A quantitative running account of the social interactions of the five children and the leader, in terms of symbols for directive, compliant, and objective (fact-minded) approaches and responses, including a category of purposeful refusal to respond to a social approach.
2. A minute-by-minute group structure analysis giving a record of activity subgroupings, the activity goal of each subgroup, whether the goal was initiated by the leader or spontaneously formed by the children, and rating on degree of unity of each subgrouping.
3. An interpretive running account of strikingly significant member actions and changes in the atmosphere of the group as a whole.
4. Continuous stenographic records of all conversation.

These data were synchronized at minute intervals so that placed side by side they furnished quite a complete and integrated picture of the on-going life of the group.

Five other types of data covering the lives of the club members were collected, the three most important being:

1. Interviews with each child by a friendly "non-club" person during each transition period from one kind of group atmosphere and leader to another. These interviews elicited comparisons of the various club leaders with one another, with the teacher and the parents as well as other data about how the club could be run better, who were the best and poorest types of club members, what an ideal club leader would be like, etc.
2. Interviews with the parents, concentrating on kinds of discipline used in the home, status of the child in the family group, personality ratings on the same scales used by the teachers, discussion of the child's attitude toward the club, school and other group activities.

[1] Besides indicating the leadership characteristics perceived as important by the boys, the reader will note that one boy in this club (an army officer's son) preferred his authoritarian leader and that the other four split in that two preferred their authoritarian leader second best and two liked their laissez-faire leader second best.

3. Talks with the teachers concerning the transfer to the schoolroom of behavior patterns acquired in the club and vice versa.

The reliability of the eleven trained observers ranged from .78 to .95 with an average reliability of .84. Another reliability computation on the coding of three thousand units of conversation into twenty-three categories of behavior showed a per cent agreement of 86. The analyses of what constituted a "group life unit" showed reliabilities ranging from .90 to .98. A number of methodological researches carried on since the date of this study seem to suggest that it is possible to get much more meaningful and reliable observation data than has been generally believed if much more time and effort are spent on a careful "calibration" of psychologically well-trained observers.

The experimenters also postulated that a fruitful way to discover some of the major differences between the three types of group atmosphere would be to arrange comparable "test episodes" in each club. So at regular intervals the following situations occurred:

1. Leader arrives late.
2. Leader called away for indeterminate time.
3. Stranger ("janitor" or "electrician") arrives while leader out and carries on critical attack of work of individual group member, then of group as a whole.

The four resultant styles of group life. Some of the major findings, summarized from stenographic records and other case material which are elsewhere reproduced, are as follows: Two distinct types of reaction were shown to the same pattern of authoritarian leadership. All of the data, including the documentary films, indicate that three of the clubs responded with a dependent leaning on the adult leader, relatively low levels of frustration tension, and practically no capacity for initiating group action, while the fourth club demonstrated considerable frustration and some degree of channelized aggression toward the authoritarian leader. (This latter pattern is much more comparable to the behavior of the club under authoritarian leadership in a previous experimental study of two clubs.)

Figure 5-2 indicates the major differences in the relations which developed between the group members and the adult leaders in the four resultant social atmospheres. In both types of authoritarian

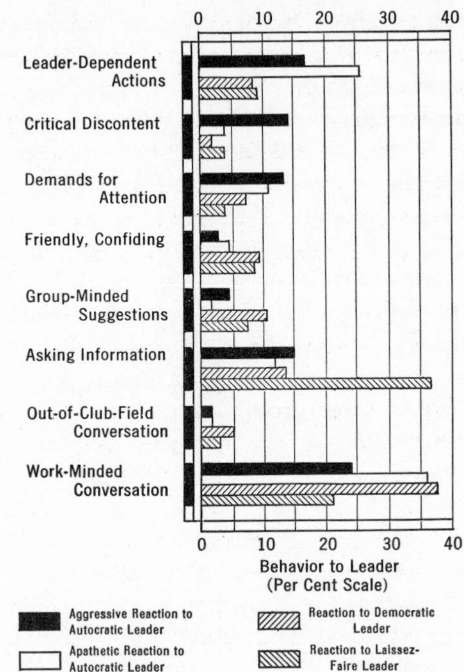

Figure 5-2. Four patterns of group reaction to the three different types of leadership.

atmosphere the members were markedly more dependent upon the leader than in either the democratic or laissez-faire situations, dependence being somewhat greater in the more passive clubs. All other clubs showed a somewhat greater feeling of discontent in their relations with the adult leader than did the members of the democratic clubs, members of the "aggressive autocracy" being outstanding in their expression of rebellious feelings. There is evidence from other sources that the actual "felt discontent" in the "apathetic autocracies" was somewhat higher than indicated by the conversation which was considerably more restricted than was that of the democratic and laissez-faire club members.

In both types of authoritarian situations the demands for attention from the adult were greater than in the other atmospheres. It seemed clear that getting the attention of the adult represented one of the few paths to more satisfactory social status in the authoritarian situation where all of the "central functions" of group life were in the hands of the dominator.

The category "friendly, confiding" indicates that the members of the democratic and laissez-faire clubs initiated more "personal" and friendly approaches to their adult leaders, and the data on "out-of-club-field conversation" further indicate the more spontaneous exchanging of confidences about other parts of one's life experience in the democratic club atmosphere.

The data on "group-minded suggestions" to the leader show that the members in the democratic atmosphere felt much freer and more inclined to make suggestions on matters of group policy than in the other three group atmospheres. It is clear from other data that the lower level of suggestions in the laissez-faire situation is not because of any feeling of restricted freedom but because of a lack of a cooperative working relationship between the adult and the other group members.

The much greater responsibility of the members of the laissez-faire clubs to get their own information is shown by the fact that about 37 per cent of their behavior toward their leader consisted of asking for information, as compared to about 15 per cent in the other three club situations.

The final category in Figure 5-2, "work-minded conversation," indicates that a considerably larger proportion of the initiated approaches of the club members to their leaders were related to on-going club activity in the democratic and in the apathetic authoritarian situations than in the other two types of social climate.

Resultant Relationships of Club Members. The relationships between the club members also developed along quite different lines in the four social climates. Expressions of irritability and aggressiveness toward fellow members occurred more frequently in both the authoritarian atmospheres and the laissez-faire situation than in the democratic social climates. Unlike the relationships of high interpersonal tension and scapegoating which developed in the previous aggression autocracy, the club in this experiment seemed to focus its aggression sufficiently in other channels (toward the leader and toward the out-group) so that in-group tension did not rise to a dangerously high point.

There were more requests for attention and approval from fellow club members to each other in the democratic and laissez-faire situations than in the two authoritarian climates. It seems clear that the child members depended upon each other to a great extent for social recognition and were more ready to give recognition to each other in the democratic and laissez-faire situations.

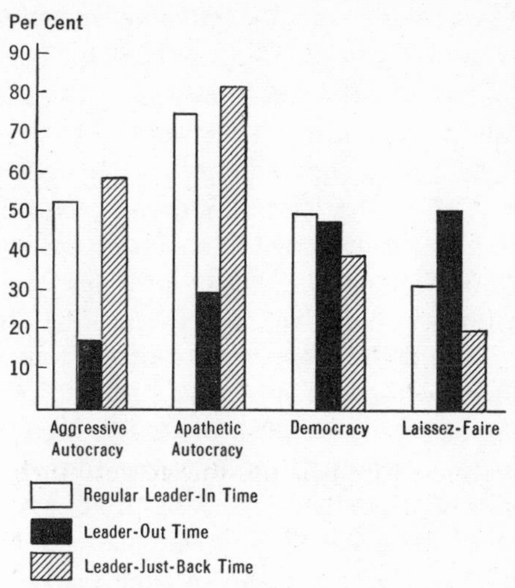

Figure 5-3. Per cent of time spent in high activity involvement.

It is interesting to find nearly as high a level of interpersonal friendliness in the authoritarian situations as in the democratic and laissez-faire atmospheres. The underlying spirit of rebellion toward the leader and cooperation in out-group aggression seem to be the "cohesive forces" in aggressive autocracy, while in apathetic autocracy with its much lower level of felt frustration, the shared submissiveness seemed to do away with all incentive to competition for social status.

Intermember suggestions for group action and group policy were significantly lower in both types of autocracy than in the laissez-faire and democratic atmospheres. The dissatisfactions arising from any lack of feeling of real progress in the laissez-faire situation led to a high frequency of expression of ideas about "something we might do." Contrary to the democratic situation, these suggestions seldom became reality because of the lack of the social techniques necessary for group decision and cooperative planning. The group achievement level, as contrasted to the "wish level," was far lower in laissez-faire than in any of the other three atmospheres.

Other Differences. By having the leaders arrive a few minutes late at regular intervals in each club life, it was possible to discover that in the five authoritarian situations no group initiative to start new work or to continue with work already under way developed, as contrasted with the democratic situations where leaders who arrived late found their groups already active in a productive fashion. The groups under the laissez-faire leaders were active but not productive. Figure 5-3 shows the percentage of total club time in each of the four social atmospheres which was spent in giving major attention to some planned club project. For each atmosphere there is a comparison between the time when the leader was in the room, the time when the leader had been called out for planned experimental periods, and the unit of time just after the leader returned. The data here give striking evidence of the extent to which work motivation was leader-induced in the two types of authoritarian situation. "Working time" dropped to a minimum with the leader out, and most of what was done was in the minutes just after the leader had left the room. We see that in the democratic atmosphere the absence or presence of the leader had practically no effect. The apparent increase in group productive time with the laissez-faire leader out of the room may or may not be a meaningful result. Two or three times it was noted that when the adult left, one of the boys exerted a more powerful leadership and achieved a more coordinated group activity than when the relatively passive adult was present.

The behavior of the groups under authoritarian domination after their transition to a freer social atmosphere provided a very interesting index of

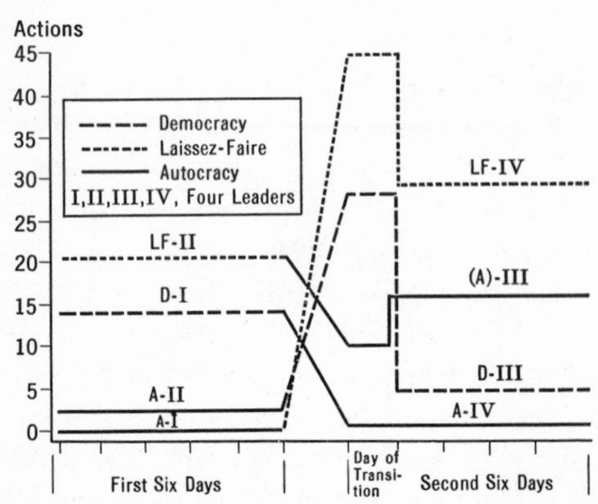

Figure 5-4. Horseplay.

unexpressed group tension. In Figure 5-4 it can be noted that both of these apathetic authoritarian clubs showed great outbursts of horseplay between the members on the first day of their transitions to a laissez-faire and a democratic group situation. This need to "blow off" disappeared with more meetings in the freer atmosphere.

It will be recalled that in certain situations all groups were subject to the same frustration of hostile criticism by a strange adult (e.g., "janitor") while the adult leader was gone. Under the different types of leaders, the groups handled these frustrations differently. Members of the apathetic authoritarian clubs tended to accept individually and to internalize the unjust criticism or, in one or two cases, they "blew off steam" in aggressive advances toward an out-group (the other club meeting in the adjacent clubroom; see Figure 5-5). In the aggressive authoritarian situation, the frustration was typically channeled in aggression toward the out-group, although in several cases there was some direct reaction to the source of frustration, the hostile stranger (see Figure 5-5). In the democratic atmospheres there was evidence of a greater readiness to unite in rejection of the real source of frustration, the stranger, and to resist out-group aggression. Figure 5-5 shows an interesting case of a democratic club which first expressed its aggression directly against the stranger, then showed a slight rise in intermember tension, followed by an aggressive outburst against a sheet of three-ply wood with hammer and chisels accompanied by a striking rise in in-group friendliness and a quick return to cooperative harmony. It was particularly interesting to discover that the clubs under democratic leaders resisted scapegoating as a channel of aggressive release.

The data indicate that the democratic type of adult role resulted in the greatest expression of individual differences, and that some type of uniformity-producing forces brought about a slightly lessened individual variability in the laissez-faire situation, and a much reduced range of individuality in the authoritarian clubs. Figure 5-6 gives an example of this analysis for the same group of individuals under three different leaders.

Individual differences and the group atmospheres. We now come to the question of to what extent it is correct to report the data as though all indi-

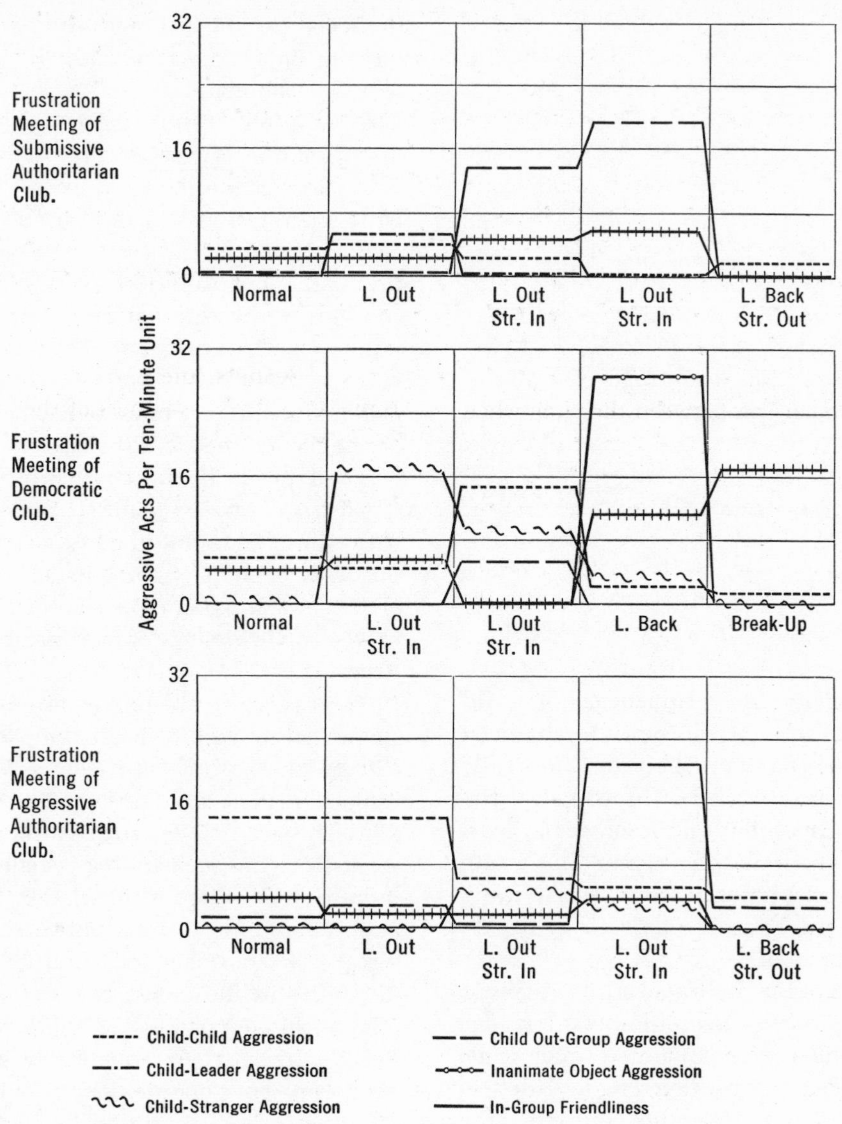

Figure 5-5. Channels of group tension release in clubs of eleven-year-old boys under different types of leadership.

viduals and all groups under the same type of adult leadership role reacted with a high degree of uniformity to the induced social climate. Before turning to the final section of interpretation of individual differences in reaction to the same social climate, it will be interesting to look at the various club lives and see the extent to which the personalities making up each club or the different social atmospheres in which they lived seemed to be the most determining influence in the resulting behavior patterns. Two of the clubs had all three types of leadership. For these two groups it was possible by the techniques of analysis of variance to compare the effects of differences in child personnel and differences in all three experimental treatments. All four clubs were compared in the same way on various items of behavior for the two treatments of autocracy and democracy. It can be reported that in

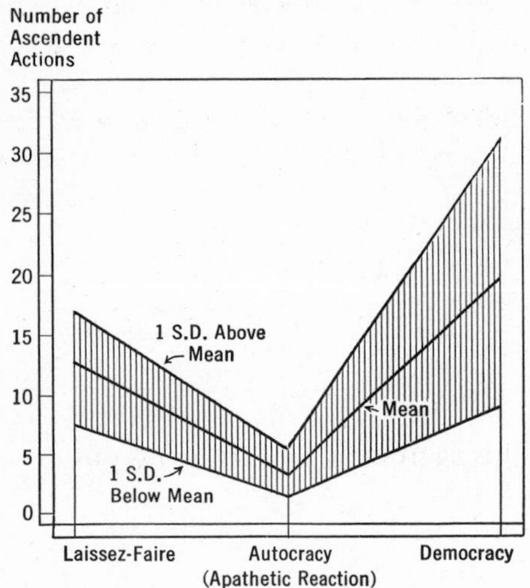

Figure 5-6. The effect of changed atmosphere upon the range of individual differences within the same group.

nearly all cases differences in club behavior could be attributed to differences in the induced social climate rather than to constant characteristics of the club personnel. One club showed a consistent variation from the rest through all atmospheres in level of friendliness between members, and one group showed a consistently lower level of social interaction which was not related wholly to their particular club environment.

Boys in the same club indicated quite different social perceptions of the behavior of the same leader and also made differing comparative judgments about their preferred leaders after having had two or three. Although all but one boy preferred the democratic leader to the other two types, there was quite a split in the population as to whether they preferred as a second choice the laissez-faire or authoritarian type of adult. To get some clews as to the basis for these differences the experimenters made an attempt to study the personality structure of each individual boy as it showed itself in his reactions to the other boys, to his adult leaders, and to his school and home environments. The records taken during the experiments constituted a type of data which is infrequently found in other approaches to personality study. The most commonly used techniques for studying an individual include interviews, questionnaires, Rorschachs, thematic apperception tests, psychoanalytic free association, and the social case history, consisting of interviews with parents and relatives, but not direct observations of social behavior.

It is not felt, of course, that such records are more useful than interviews, social case histories, or other customary techniques, but only that *when combined* with other techniques they are a valuable part of the total picture and are an extremely useful addition to the tool chest of the clinical psychologist, the educator, the vocational counselor, and others who want to understand and to help a particular individual.

To show this concretely, one condensed case study is summarized below. Like our other case studies, it is based primarily upon club behavior data with much less interview material and home study data than would be found in a first class clinical analysis, but with enough of these data to suggest how the club behavior data can be combined with other sorts in the building up of an integrated personality structure.

The case chosen is one of two extremes, not in a single trait only, but in the large structure of intercorrelated traits, which has been found to be more important than any other trait cluster in our data. This cluster includes such variables as not being aggressive, not demanding attention, high work-mindedness, contentment in the strict but orderly atmosphere of autocracy, discontent in the free but disorderly atmosphere of laissez-faire, consistency of discipline in the home, and warmth of emotional relationship to parents. These variables are statistically correlated to a marked degree; that is, the boys who show one of them usually show most of the others also. The reader can form his own judgment as to an appropriate name for the cluster. The boys who stand low in the cluster as a whole would often be called "bad" by the exasperated adults who have to deal with them, while those who stand high in it would be called "good." Goodness, then, or conscientiousness, might be as good a name as any. It should be noticed, though, that the cluster includes some things, such as liking autocracy better than laissez-faire, which are not included in the ordinary connotations of the word "conscientious." It should be noticed too that the boys who stand low in the cluster—boys like Reilly[2] who is described here—are not neces-

[2] Names and other identifying data have been changed here.

sarily "bad" or antagonistic to adult values and requirements; they may be only heedless and relatively indifferent to those values. In groups such as ours which contain only healthy "normal" children, with no actual delinquents, it would do violence to common usage to call any of the boys "bad."[3] For these and other reasons the rather cumbersome term "adult-value-centeredness" seems more accurate than "conscientiousness" as a name for the cluster.

REILLY

Club Personality. Reilly was the most talkative, the most conspicuous, and the most popular member of the Charlie Chan club. He was also one of the most irritating to those of his adult leaders who found themselves unable to cope with him. It was Reilly, for instance, who gleefully shouted, "Let's make war!" at the beginning of the first big water battle with the Secret Agents; it was Reilly whose vociferousness, as much as Fred's and Leonard's more aggressive horseplay, led to the complete disintegration of the group under laissez-faire leadership; and it was Reilly who led the "sitdown strike" against the autocratic leader, which was the one instance in any of the clubs of more or less organized rebellion against authority.

While he was so heedless of adult values and adult wishes, he was at the same time very popular with the other boys. He was the best-liked boy in his schoolroom, as determined by a sociometric questionnaire, and he had been elected president of his class. Yet he asserted his personality as vigorously in competition with other boys as in competition with adults. His personality contrasts sharply with that of Eddie, who was the best-liked boy in the other schoolroom from which our club members were selected. Where Eddie was conscientious, quiet, unassuming, and genuinely friendly with everyone, Reilly was exuberant, self-advertising, constantly bombarding the eyes and ears of others with his demands for attention, and, as the statistics showed, relatively low in both friendly and group-minded conversation. He was not actually a leader in the sense that he showed any planning or organizing ability; he was too impatient and too lacking in time-perspective for that. He was a leader only in the sense that he was liked, and also, perhaps, in the sense that his head-long, self-centered activity was imitated by others in the group.

It is interesting to find that, unlike the other two boys who stood with him at the bottom of the total group in the trait-cluster of "conscientiousness," he was never sullen, hostile, or maliciously mischievous. His scores in aggression were only about average, and his aggression (i.e., criticisms of other boys and playful collective aggression) was never really hostile in character. Even toward adults he was competitive rather than hostile. He ranked highest among the seventeen boys[4] in the proportion of his adult-contacts which had an attention-demanding character. Characteristically, he would loudly interrupt when the adult was talking to some other club member, and vociferously demand that the adult pay attention to him rather than to the other boy. The absolute frequency of this behavior was also very high, as evidenced by the fact that he also ranked highest, out of 17, in the absolute volume of his verbal contacts with the adult leader, in both autocracy and democracy. (The motivation behind these contacts, to be sure, was probably rather different in the two atmospheres. In autocracy it seems to have been almost entirely an expression of competition for power—perhaps in order to win boy-admiration—while in democracy it was also an expression of genuine man-to-man friendliness.) It would seem, then, that his somewhat paradoxical popularity was not due to the kind of warm liking which drew other boys to the quiet and unassuming Eddie. Rather, it seems to have been due to the fact that he was so successful in getting a rather gullible public to accept him at his own valuation, while at the same time the absence of malice in his self-assertion kept it from arousing hostility in others. In spite of his competitiveness and essential self-centeredness, the group accorded him a sort of hero worship, perhaps largely because each of them would have liked to be the sort of vital and self-confident person—completely uncowed by adults—which he unquestionably was.

[3] The Freudian concept of the "super-ego" is relevant here; a "weak super-ego" does not necessarily mean active "badness" or antisocial tendencies. It may be noticed also that the cluster found in our data is similar to one which seems to have been discovered independently by a number of other investigators. It closely resembles Webb's "w" factor, which Thurstone renamed "conscientiousness."

[4] All statistics are based on a population of 17 rather than 20, since there were three boys about whom there was not an adequate amount of home background information.

The statistical club-behavior data and interview data support this impressionistic picture. In addition to the quantitative data already mentioned, we find that he had unusually high scores in volume of conversation (with boys as well as with the adult leader), and in per cent of "out-of-field" conversation, which in his case represented such things as bragging about his father's hardware store, his own chemistry set at home, etc. In the interviews he expressed a preference for his laissez-faire leader as compared with his autocratic leader, indicating, probably, that his need for orderliness was less than his need for free self-assertion. He also showed unusual frankness in his avowed preference for the boy-valued activity of "fighting," as compared with the adult-valued activity of working. In describing his autocratic leader he said, "We didn't have any fun then—we didn't have any fights."

Summarizing his club personality, we can say first that he was not noticeably motivated by any of the adult-sponsored values which were conspicuous in the conscientious boys—obedience, respectfulness, nonaggression, order, self-control, hard work; second, that his primary goal in the club situation was apparently competition, or *superiority* in the eyes of the other boys; and third, that he tended to perceive adults, not as objects of obedience, respect, or hostility, but as equals, with whom he could compete (or be friendly, as he was with his democratic leader) on very much the same basis as with any of the other boys. These more basic characteristics of his present personality-structure, and not the peripheral behavior-traits of talkativeness, attention-demanding, etc., are what must be especially taken into account, whether our interest is the practical interest of the adult group-leader who has to cope with him, or the scientific interest of the clinical investigator who wants to trace the origins of his present personality-structure in his home background and the behavior of his parents.

Home Background. His indifference to adult-sponsored values becomes intelligible when we discover that neither of his parents seems to have given him any incentive—neither fear of punishment nor hope of loving approval—to develop these values. His indulgent father apparently enjoyed his company (in a man-to-man relationship which offers a clew to his warm reaction to his democratic club leader), but his father was extremely busy and apparently accepted little or no responsibility for his training. His mother apparently disliked him, but felt helpless in relation to him; in the constant feud between them, there was neither the warmth which might have made him want to win her love by being "good," nor the firmness which might have made him fear her restrictions when he was "bad." These two attitudes, rejection and a feeling of helplessness, repeatedly came out in the interview with his mother. According to her, he is impudent, he is irresponsible, he is lazy, he is impatient and unable to stay long at one thing, he continually quarrels with his older brother and teases his younger brother. She blurted out these criticisms in a weary but almost defiant way. According to her, "punishment doesn't do him any good. I used to lose my temper and whip him; I was pretty mean, I guess," but he would be just as bad or worse afterward, so that now she doesn't ever punish him. "He sasses me back, and I can't stand a sassy child." Sometimes he argues for hours at a time; "maybe it's because I've given in to him several times," and he knows it's a good way to get things. For a while he had an allowance, but "he'd borrow on the next week's allowance and then expected to get it just the same," so the plan was discontinued. He now gets money for movies at least twice a week; if she tells him he can't go, he often goes to his father and gets the money from him.

Not only his indifference to adult values, but also his desire for superiority and his tendency to perceive adults as equals now seem more intelligible. Since his father does not try to exert much authority, and his mother lets the authority situation become a feud in which he often gets the upper hand, he naturally tends to look upon adults as equals. Since his father's affection is always present and his mother's never is, his life is not geared to the winning of affection; the goal of superiority, first of all in relation to his mother and his brothers, has tended to take its place. And, finally, his exuberant vitality and absence of hostility, which were noted as major reasons for his popularity, now make sense in the light of the fact that his home life contains no major frustrations, and no repressed hostilities. Though his personality-structure may bring him trouble later in life, his existence at the moment is full of affection from his father, triumph over his mother, and exciting, successful competition with other boys.

INTERPRETIVE SUMMARY

The foregoing condensed and highly selective research report has attempted to show some of the interdependencies of leadership role, group composition, group history, and membership personality structure in this study of four experimental clubs of preadolescent boys.

The leader-induced social atmosphere of the group, together with the group history (the preceding club atmospheres), established a hierarchy of channels of expression of response to frustration. Whereas the "aggressive autocracy" club was more ready to express its frustrations in interclub wars, the "apathetic autocracies" were prone to internalize the aggression, and the "democratic" and "laissez-faire" groups to react against the source of frustration.

Passive acceptance by the group of the socially induced frustrations of authoritarian leadership was found in some cases to mean a non-frustrated acceptance of a dependent relationship, and in other cases to mean a frustrated hopelessness in the face of overwhelming power. When a transition to a freer atmosphere occurred these latter cases gave evidence by their "blow-off" behavior of their previous frustrations.

The adult restrictiveness of the benevolent authoritarian role and the environmental unstructuredness of the laissez-faire situation were both found to inhibit greatly genuine "psychological freedom" as contrasted to "objective freedom."

The adult-leader role was found to be a very strong determiner of the pattern of social interaction and emotional development of the group. Four clear-cut types of social atmosphere emerged, in spite of great member differences in social expectation and reaction tendency due to previous adult-leader (parent, teacher) relationships.

It was clear that previous group history (i.e., preceding social climates) had an important effect in determining the social perception of leader behavior and reaction to it by club members. A club which had passively accepted an authoritarian leader in the beginning of its club history, for example, was much more frustrated and resistive to a second authoritarian leader after it had experienced a democratic leader than a club without such a history. There seem to be some suggestive implications here for educational practice.

It was found in this exploratory study that the process of small-group life could be experimentally manipulated in a satisfactory way for scientific study and could be recorded adequately for meaningful quantitative analysis. There emerged a variety of meaningful clusters of correlations between member case history, member social perception of the group situation, member and group behavior, and leader behavior.

*LEARNING IN DISCUSSIONS: A RÉSUMÉ OF THE AUTHORITARIAN-DEMOCRATIC STUDIES**

By Richard C. Anderson

In most teaching methods textbooks you will find reference to two basic teaching styles which can be called teacher-centered and learner-centered. (See, for example, Brandwein, Watson, and Blackwood, 1958; Burnett, 1957; Burton, 1952; Cronbach, 1954; and Grambs, Iverson, and Patterson, 1958.)[1] If you consult a book on industrial management, a book on counseling or psychotherapy, or, indeed, the section on leadership in a textbook on social psychology, you will very likely find a similar statement about leadership. Leadership is universally defined in terms of a hypothetical authoritarian-democratic dimension. Many labels have been applied to this dimension—perhaps it should be called a dichotomy, for such it has been in practice: dominative-integrative, employer-centered—em-

[1] References are listed at the end of the article.

*From *Harvard Educational Review,* 1959, *29,* pp. 201-215. Used by permission of the author and publisher.

ployee-centered, teacher-centered—learner-centered, therapist-centered—client-centered, supervisory—participatory, directive—non-directive; but the idea is basically the same.

As the reader is no doubt well aware, authoritarian-democratic theory and research are the subject of lively controversy in education today. Some educators claim that learner-centered methods are most desirable. For example Mursell concluded:

> Thus the importance of a "democratic" classroom situation is no mere fancy, nor is it based on sentimentalism, or on any far-fetched philosophy. It is a highly significant factor in the realistic organization of learning for the sake of authentic results (1954, p. 146).

Others argue that teacher-centered methods are most satisfactory. Grambs, Iverson, and Patterson (1958, pp. 115-116) have asserted that the average teacher leans toward authoritarian teaching, stating that "the school . . . is by tradition authoritarian. . . . Teachers who seek more democratic ways sometimes find that a number of their colleagues strenuously oppose their new approach." The critical student of educational method and policy will want to be in a position to assess the validity of claims from these opposing points of view.

This paper hopes to shed some light on issues basic to this controversy by returning to primary sources. Forty-nine experimental studies in which authoritarian leadership has been compared with democratic leadership will be reviewed. Two questions will be asked of this research:

1. Is there sufficient evidence that one of these two styles of leadership is more effective?
2. Does the authoritarian-democratic continuum provide an adequate conceptualization of leadership?

Later it will be suggested that failure to define carefully "authoritarian" and "democratic," or whatever synonyms were used, has been a general shortcoming of leadership research. For the present, rough working definitions of these terms will be attempted. Authoritarian leaders generally act in an impersonal manner; punish members who disobey or deviate; decide what the group will do or talk about; decide upon division of labor; determine how work shall be done; judge the soundness of ideas; do more talking than the other members of the group. Democratic leaders generally act in a friendly, personal manner; allow the group as a whole to plan the agenda; allow group members to choose the tasks they will perform; allow group members to talk with one another without permission from the leader; accept suggestions from the group about how the work shall be done; talk only a little more than the average group member. In short, the authoritarian leader makes most decisions for the group whereas the democratic leader shares decision-making with the other members. Just how the democratic leader handles deviation is a moot question. Proponents of democratic leadership argue that deviation rarely occurs in democratically-led groups, maintaining that when it does occur the whole group punishes the offending member. This punishment takes the form of withdrawal of love rather than the aggression and overt hostility which are the rule in autocratically-led groups. Observation suggests that people committed to democratic leadership are placed in severe conflict when the situation seems to require open aggression in order to thwart deviation.

This paper will avoid philosophical issues except insofar as they have influenced the kind and quality of research. Rather, authoritarian and democratic leadership styles will be compared in terms of two criteria of effectiveness which can be experimentally investigated. The first criterion is productivity. The definition of productivity varies according to the institutional setting of the experiment. In industrial research productivity refers to work done or units produced, and also to the quality of the work. In educational experiments productivity means the amount learned. Learning also has qualitative aspects, and these will be considered whenever there are data available. In still another type of study "changes in behavior" will be identified with productivity.

Morale is the second criterion of effectiveness. Morale can be defined as the extent to which group members find the group personally satisfying and the extent to which they believe the group is successfully progressing toward its goals.

There is a problem worth noting in connection with these definitions. The actual definitions of productivity and morale have varied immensely from study to study depending partly upon the kind of institutional setting in which the research was done and partly on the authors' judgments about what was important to observe and measure. In addition, the extensiveness and quality of measures of productivity and morale have varied tremendously. In one case the estimation of morale consisted of the impression of casual observers that "the children seemed to be enjoying themselves a great deal." In another case the measure of productivity was the number of comments showing insight into child psychology (Perkins, 1951). In the latter instance the investigator was faced with a type of discussion in which there necessarily was no tangible product. This kind of problem frequently arises. Whether the solution by any one experimenter is adequate remains to be seen. One thing is evident: the solutions differ. It might well be asked whether these diverse studies are comparable and whether generalization from these studies will have any meaning. One reason the present author is willing to review these studies as though they had some measure of generality is that many synthesizers, specifically the writers of educational textbooks, have assumed that quite unqualified generalization is possible. For instance, after reviewing some of the relevant literature, Burton (1952) stated that,

> Learners *accomplished more* with the help of cooperative, democratic teachers, both in subject matter learning and in the development of personal-social-moral traits. The superiority of settings for learning under the guidance of democratic personalities was overwhelming (p. 297). (Italics in original.)

REVIEW AND CRITIQUE

The classic research—which had a great effect on subsequent investigation—was conducted by Lewin, Lippitt, and White (1953) who studied the effects of authoritarian and democratic leadership on groups of boys whose task was making papier-mâché masks. They found that there were least interpersonal conflict, least aggression, least scapegoating, and highest morale in groups with democratic leaders. The largest number of masks was produced by groups with authoritarian leaders, though democratic groups were capable of more sustained work when the leader was not present than were authoritarian groups. Laissez-faire groups showed both low morale and low productivity.

A multitude of studies investigating authoritarian and democratic leadership followed the research of Lewin, *et al.* However, the results have been disappointing. It is still impossible to demonstrate that either of the two styles is most closely associated with high productivity or high morale. After an extensive review of the literature, Hare (1959) offered the conclusion that democratic leadership is associated with low productivity and high morale whereas authoritarian leadership is associated with high productivity and low morale.

This conclusion demands serious qualifications, however, on the basis of situational factors. The finding that morale is high in democratic groups holds for such groups as fraternities, sororities, boys' clubs, grade school classes, therapy groups, and temporary groups (Adams, 1943-1946; Anderson, 1937, 1939; Bovard, 1951, 1952; Bills, 1952, 1957; Deignan, 1956; Faw, 1949; Flanders, 1951; Hemphill, 1949; Lewin, 1953; McKeachie, 1951, 1954; Perkins, 1951; Rasmussen, 1956; Roseborough, 1953; Sheldon and Landsman, 1950; Thelen and Withall, 1949; White and Lippitt, 1953; Wischmeier, 1955; Zeleny, 1940), but does not always hold in military groups, business groups, and college classes (Berkowitz, 1953; Guetzkow *et al.*, 1954; Hemphill, 1949; Heyns, 1949; Krumboltz, 1955; McCurdy and Lambert, 1952; Wispe, 1951). Some of the discrepancy in research findings may be accounted for as follows: Democratic leadership is associated with high morale when a primary group goal is social, as in the case of the recreational and fraternal groups, or emotional catharsis, as in the case of the therapy groups. Morale is higher under authoritarian leadership, however, in groups which are primarily committed to some task goal rather than a social-emotional goal.

The picture is also somewhat cloudy in regard to productivity. There is wide agreement that authoritarian leadership is most effective when the task is simple and concrete (e.g., Adams, 1954). Some investigators claim that democratic groups are most productive when the task is a complex one requiring insightful behavior, and particularly when it requires cooperation between members. This finding has not been supported by all studies, however. For example, McCurdy and Lambert (1952) compared "miniature dictatorships and democracies" on a switching problem involving cooperation and found no difference in number of correct choices.

Some dramatic evidence often cited to support the contention that democratic leadership results in superior productivity compares democratically led discussions with lectures. These studies, which are summarized by Lewin (1953), generally show that after a democratically led discussion there is more change in behavior than after a lecture. In one representative study conducted during World War II, six groups of Red Cross volunteers were asked to increase their use of beef hearts, sweetbreads, and kidneys. Three groups were given "attractive lectures . . . which linked the problem of nutrition to the war effort" and included recipes for preparing "delicious dishes" from the three meats (pp. 287-288). In each of the other three groups a discussion was started in order to get housewives to use the three meats "without attempting any high pressure salesmanship" (p. 288). After the discussions the women were asked to show, by raising their hands, who was willing to try one of these meats within the next week. Women attending lectures were not asked to make a decision. According to the results of a follow up study, only 3 per cent of the women who heard lectures served one of the meats never served before, while of the women who took part in the group discussion and decision, 32 per cent served one of them.

This difference in behavior could be due to the discussion, the decision, or both. Lewin himself emphasized the importance of the decision, though he felt that people are "more ready . . . to make a decision after a group discussion than after a lecture" (p. 290). Proponents of democratic leadership techniques have tended to overlook the possible significance of the decision. They choose to believe that this study—and other similarly ambiguous studies by followers of Lewin—demonstrates that democratic methods of leadership are superior to lectures and, by implication, to authoritarian leadership in general.

The relative influence of discussion and decision on changes in behavior has been examined by Bennett (1955). This study, which is fully discussed by Festinger (1957), was concerned with getting students to volunteer to serve as subjects in psychological experiments at the University of Michigan. A third of the subjects heard a lecture which tried to persuade them to volunteer, another third (in groups of thirteen) engaged in discussions about the desirability of volunteering, while the final third was simply reminded that requests would be made for volunteers. One-fourth of the subjects from each group was not asked to make any decision about volunteering. The remaining three-fourths were asked to make a decision, some anonymously, some publicly. The subjects of the three groups were matched according to their responses to a questionnaire about their attitudes toward volunteering for psychological experiments. Thus one may regard the subjects in each of the experimental groups as having the same initial willingness to volunteer. Shortly after the "treatment" the experimental subjects were sent letters requesting them to come to a certain place at a certain time if they wished to volunteer. The percentages of subjects from the lecture, discussion, and "simple reminder" groups who showed up at the designated time and place were 22, 21 and 19 respectively. In other words, the lecture, discussion, and simple reminder were equally effective in persuading people to volunteer. The data show, however, that 15 per cent of the "no decision" subjects (N = 135) volunteered, whereas 22 per cent of the subjects (N = 338) who had been asked to make a decision showed up. Bennett (1955) reported that this difference was significant at the .07 level of significance. These data suggest that changes in behavior should be attributed to making a decision rather than engaging in discussion. Perhaps the greater magnitude of change following decision in the Lewin food studies stems from the fact that, unlike the lecture groups, the discussion-decision groups were told that there would be a follow-up study (Lewin, 1953, p. 293).

Research findings from educational investigations are especially contradictory. We cannot state with any certainty that either teacher-centered or learner-centered methods are associated with greater learning. Some researchers claim superior learning for learner-centered groups (Allport, 1950; Bovard, 1952; Brandwein, 1958; Faw, 1949; Flanders, 1951; Neuman, 1957; Perkins, 1951; Peters, 1948; Sheldon and Landsman, 1950; Thompson and Tom, 1957; Zeleny, 1940). In one of the early investigations, Zeleny (1940) conducted a series of five small experiments with college classes in sociology, found a slight advantage for learner-centered groups in each case. Faw (1949) showed that college students in non-directive groups learned more about psychology than did students in directive groups. Similarly, Allport (1950) has reported that students in a college social relations course believed they learned more in permissive than in directive sections.

Thompson and Tom (1957) found that students in learner-centered groups acquire and retain significantly more information about dairy farming than do those in teacher-centered groups. Unfortunately, the observed superiority of learner-centered groups in this study cannot be attributed wholly to the classroom behavior of the teacher since elaborate steps were taken to provide students from learner-centered groups with a chance to carry out dairy projects at home, whereas students from teacher-centered groups were insured of no such opportunity. Perkins (1951) has reported that teachers attending in-service classes in educational psychology with permissive instructors made more comments indicative of psychological insight than those in teacher-centered classes. Flanders (1951) found that pupils taught by a learner-centered teacher showed superiority over the students of an autocratic teacher in the acquisition and retention of four principles of human relations. After observing three science classes under autocratic, laissez faire, and democratic conditions, Brandwein (1955) felt that students in the democratic situation learned more. A study of "non-directive group therapy with students in academic difficulty" (Sheldon and Landsman, 1950) shows marked superiority for the non-directive over the directive method. In the same vein, Neuman (1957) found that students who learned lists of words using their own techniques showed better recall than students directed to use a learning technique developed by a group of psychologists familiar with verbal-learning research.

A number of investigations have found no difference between learner-centered and teacher-centered methods (Bills, 1952; Deignan, 1956; Eglash, 1954; Farquhar, 1955; Haigh and Schmidt, 1956; Landsman, 1950; McKeachie, 1951; Ostlund. 1956; Rasmussen, 1956; Rehage, 1951; Slomowitz, 1955; Smith and Johnson, 1952; Wispe, 1951). In a typical study, Wispe found no over-all difference between groups on the objective part of a final examination in an introductory college course in social relations, but did find that students of low ability did better if taught by teacher-centered methods.

Using content analysis of discussion transcripts to measure learning, Ostlund (1956) found slightly greater learning on the part of learner-centered groups; however, the difference was statistically significant for only one index of learning. It may be wondered whether the Ostlund study and other similarly inconclusive investigations would have showed a significant advantage for learner-centered methods if the treatment had lasted longer. With a few exceptions, the longest experiments have run no more than a semester. Many have been only a few weeks in duration. If we are to believe proponents of democratic teaching, our schools are essentially authoritarian, and it may take considerable exposure before students become acculturated to learner-centered methods. A study by Peters (1948) which lasted two years is suggestive in this respect. Peters found a slight advantage for democratic teachers at the end of the first year, which became a marked superiority by the end of the second year. Directly opposed to Peters' finding is a survey study of sixty-six history teachers and twelve hundred seventy-five students by Brookover (1943), who found a significant negative relationship between student ratings of teachers' permissiveness and mean gains in information on a history test. In Brookover's words, "Apparently the students like the friendly teachers better, but they learn more when taught by the more authoritarian ones" (p. 300).

It is also argued that investigations which use final examinations as a measure of learning and which fail to remove anxiety connected with grades provide an inadequate comparison of teacher-centered and learner-centered methods. It is suggested (McKeachie, 1951) that in a truly democratic situation no external authority would evaluate achievement. Rather, each student would provide his own internal yardstick, evaluating his own progress. Under these conditions, it is argued, learner-centered groups would probably show superiority. A series of experiments at the University of Michigan illustrate this point nicely. In the original experiment Guetzkow, Kelley, and McKeachie (1954) found that students in teacher-centered groups showed slight superiority on a final examination. What is more, morale was higher in teacher-centered groups, and students in these groups expressed more desire to take additional courses in psychology and major in psychology than did students from other groups. Subsequently, McKeachie (1951) conducted an experiment in which an effort was made to reduce grade anxiety. He found no difference on a final examination. In a companion study, Bovard (1952) found that students in the learner-centered groups showed greater insight into psychological processes than students in the teacher-centered groups. Haigh and Schmidt (1956) found that "when students are permitted to choose between a teacher-centered and a group-centered class and when the students in the group-centered class are not required to learn subject matter by the examination-grade system there is no significant difference between these two types of classes at the end of the term" (pp. 301-302). However, reducing the anxiety surrounding grades provides no guarantee that learner-centered groups will do as well or better than teacher-centered. This is evidenced in a study by Asch (1951) in which the instructor-centered group achieved higher grades on both objective and essay portions of a final examination in psychology, despite the fact that the score on the examination was not a basis for grading in the learner-centered group.

One other factor may weigh against discovering possible advantages inherent in the learner-centered method. It may be that the sorts of learning best implemented by teacher-centered methods are measured with relative ease, where as the more intangible learnings of learner-centered groups elude quantification. A study by DiVesta (1954) is enlightening in this respect. He found greater gains on knowledge and attitude tests for students taught by the instructor-centered method, but superior improvement in leadership skills for students taught by the learner-centered method. Rehage (1951) conducted an investigation of teacher-pupil planning in which he found no difference between groups on measures of learning and attitude change, though the experimental group did much more extra work, seemed to have more insight into the process of group planning, and seemed to have more interest in the subject matter than did the control group. Anderson (1956) found that the group taught by a directive teacher recalled much more information than other groups while the non-directive group scored significantly higher on a measure of interest in the subject studied than did the directive group.

In addition to the studies cited above, Burke (1956), Husband (1951), and Ward (1956) all have reported greater learning in teacher-centered groups.

To summarize the educational research reviewed in this article, eleven studies have reported greater learning for learner-centered groups, thirteen have shown no difference, and eight have found teacher-centered methods superior to learner-centered. It should be noted that while some investigations have reported a *statistically* significant difference favoring one method or other, it is doubtful if any of these differences are of *practical* or *social* significance. Some writers, such as Bills (1957), argue that despite—or because of—the failure to find a striking difference in regard to learning, we should prefer the learner-centered method because of its greater association with high morale and psychological well-being.

It is a rather general finding that morale is higher in learner-centered groups (e.g., Thelen and Withall, 1949). The only exceptions to this generalization appear to occur in situations in which there is high anxiety about grades which are awarded on the basis of final examination scores (Guetzkow *et al.,* 1954; Krumboltz, 1955; Wispe, 1951).

There are probably several factors, in addition to the suggestions above, which contribute to the confusing and contradictory pattern of research findings. The first of these is lack of methodological rigor and inadequate research design.[2] Furthermore, many experimenters in this field display a surprising lack of familiarity with other research. This is evidenced by bibliographies which fail to list any experimental studies of authoritarian-democratic leadership styles except, of course, Lewin, Lippitt, and White. Study after study has been conducted with basically the same conception and execution and in apparent isolation from other research. The results of twenty years of investigation remain embarrassingly non-cumulative.

Another serious defect in this research stems from the fact that operational definitions of leadership styles have lacked precision. Herein lies an important reason for contradictory findings. The present author believes that the lack of precise operational definitions of leadership styles is symptomatic of a larger problem; the authoritarian-democratic construct is an inadequate basis for research because, for one thing, it presumes to summarize the complexity of group life into a single

[2] For a critical review of some of the authoritarian-democratic studies which pays some attention to methodological problems, see Roseborough (1953). See also McKeachie (1954), who discusses the teacher-centered—learner-centered controversy in an analysis which stresses methodological shortcomings and weak experimental design.

dimension. There are probably many variables of leadership and group life. Hemphill (1949), after analysis of some five hundred existing groups, arrived at sixteen descriptive variables. Factor analyses of Hemphill's variables (Gekoski, 1952), as well as several factor analyses by Carter (1953), yield three dimensions which the present author likes to interpret as follows:

1. *The Affective area.* Includes degree of interpersonal warmth or coolness, tension or relaxation; degree of antagonism or solidarity. Opposes friendly pleasant exchange to hostility and constraint.

2. *The Procedural area.* Includes statement and control of agenda, control of communication, division of labor. Refers to amount of structure and degree of organization as opposed to degree of disorganization or looseness of structure.

3. *The Task area.* Includes quantity and quality of work done, units produced, ideas presented, solutions considered. Opposes solution reached, problem solved, high performance maintained to no solution, problem unsolved, poor performance. Productivity versus sterility.

No doubt there are other dimensions and subdimensions yet to be conclusively identified. In view of the probable complexity of leadership, the authoritarian-democratic construct appears to be an ill-defined and over-simplified conception of leadership variables. As such this construct cannot be defended on functional grounds. To say that a style of leadership is authoritarian does not adequately describe the behaviors which the leader actually exhibited. Very likely many studies, all of which labeled leadership styles in the same way, actually differed a great deal at the concrete level of what the leaders said and did. These variations in behavior could, of course, lead to variable results. Use of these simplifying labels tends to limit our thinking about leadership. For example, because we have grown used to thinking of the authoritarian leader as impersonal, cool, and sometimes hostile, the possibility of a leader who maintains complete control of the decisions of the group and yet is friendly and personal does not seem very real to us.

Moreover, the words "authoritarian" and "democratic" contain surplus meanings. The proliferation of synonyms for "authoritarian" and "democratic" can be interpreted as an effort to escape the normative overtones of the original terms; in other words, an effort to be "objective." "Authoritarian" and "democratic" have been purposely used in this paper because the present writer believes that behind the façade of objectivity expressed in less-loaded words there lurks an essentially moralistic interpretation of leadership by many researchers and theorists and the bulk of the popularizers.

It serves no practical or scientific objective to prove that unreasonably extreme leadership types are ineffective; yet, there is reason to feel that a number of researchers have been led to this specious demonstration by the moralism inherent in the authoritarian-democratic conceptualizations. The greatest number of studies in which the "bad" leadership type is overdrawn have a democratic bias. Cronbach (1954) has put this point very well, stating that,

> When teacher-control was branded as "autocracy," and contrasted with so-called "democratic" teaching, all the research seemed to be trying to prove that teacher-control cannot possibly work. These studies are usually made by training some leaders to use each particular style of leadership, so that different styles can be compared. Almost without exception, the dominative leaders are taught to be harsh, to use hostile comments in criticizing students, and to discourage student initiative. This means that we lack research on friendly, adaptable teacher control, which is the pattern most teachers are presently trying to use (pp. 455-456).

It is hard to tell how many investigations have been seriously damaged by the biased distortion of one of the leadership styles. A handful of studies is clearly affected, as shown by protocols and incidents reported as well as by descriptions of leadership behavior. This bias has probably operated to a marked degree in a number of other studies, and to some degree in most investigations.

This leads directly to a further and very serious inadequacy in the authoritarian-democratic conceptualization. Even if, as the present writer contends, "authoritarian" and "democratic" conveys a grossly over-simplified picture of leadership behavior, it would still be possible to defend these concepts if there were some good reason for believing that the complex of behavior which "democratic" or "authoritarian" seems to encompass is likely to be associated with high productivity and high morale. Unfortunately no such mediating body of theory and knowledge exists. This statement is probably true of most areas of applied social science, and it is certainly applicable to educational research. There are no adequate notions of how the authoritarian-democratic construct is related to learning. With the exception of a few clinically-derived, *ad hoc* hypotheses emanating largely from the Rogerian school of psychotherapy and *The Authoritarian Personality,* the research on leadership styles seems to flow more from ethical generalization than from scientific hypothesis. Much of the research on teaching methods in the last twenty years seemed bent on discovering whether "The meek shall inherit the earth," or whether, on the other hand, "Nice guys lose."

Whatever the motivation behind it, a principal difficulty of research in teaching methods—and leadership research in general—has been the rather low level of empiricism. Teacher-centered and learner-centered methods have been repetitiously investigated not because there were well conceived ideas as to *how* one would lead to superior learning, but merely to find out *if* one style was superior to the other. We were not fortunate enough to find that one method is consistently better than or even consistently different from the other; thus, we are now forced to explore new avenues. In short, the authoritarian-democratic construct, as far as education is concerned at least, has far outlived its usefulness either as a guide to research or as an interpretation of leadership behavior.

CONCLUSION

The evidence available fails to demonstrate that either authoritarian or democratic leadership is consistently associated with higher productivity. In most situations, however, democratic leadership is associated with higher morale. But even this conclusion must be regarded cautiously, because the authoritarian leader has been unreasonably harsh and austere in a number of investigations reporting superior morale in democratic groups. In the educational setting, morale appears to be higher under learner-centered conditions, at least when anxiety over grades is reduced.

The authoritarian-democratic construct provides an inadequate conceptualization of leadership behavior. When a satisfactory body of knowledge about learning in social situations is available it will then be possible to describe the behaviors which a teacher can exhibit to achieve a given learning outcome. It seems reasonable to suppose that leadership styles or teaching methods emanating from knowledge about learning will have a higher probability of meeting criteria of effectiveness than do *a priori* styles or methods. At least, studies based on two *a priori* styles have not led to consistent or easily interpretable results.

REFERENCES

R. G. Adams, "The Behavior of Pupils in Democratic and Autocratic Social Climates," *Abstracts of Dissertations* (Stanford University, 1943-1946), *91-21,* pp. 83-86.

S. Adams, "Social Climate and Productivity in Small Groups," *American Sociological Review,* 1954, *19,* pp. 421-425.

T. W. Adorno, *et. al., The Authoritarian Personality* (New York, Harper & Row, Publishers, 1950).

G. Allport, "How Shall We Evaluate Teaching the Social Sciences," in Bernice B. Cronkhite (Ed.), *A Handbook for College Teachers* (Cambridge: Harvard University Press, 1950).

H. H. Anderson, "An Experimental Study of Dominative and Integrative Behavior in Children of Pre-School Age," *Journal of Social Psychology,* 1937, *8,* pp. 335-345.

H. H. Anderson, "Domination and Social Integration in the Behavior of Kindergarten Children and Teachers," *Genetic Psychology Monographs,* 1939, *21,* pp. 287-385.

R. C. Anderson, "Teacher Role, Personality and Productivity." Unpublished manuscript, available from the author, 1956.

M. J. Asch, "Non-directive Teaching in Psychology," *Psychology Monograph,* 1951, *65,* p. 4.

E. B. Bennett, "Discussion, Decision, and Consensus in 'Group Decision,'" *Human Relations,* 1955, *8,* pp. 251-273.

L. Berkowitz, "Sharing Leadership in Small, Decision-Making Groups," *Journal of Abnormal and Social Psychology,* 1953, *48,* pp. 231-238.

R. E. Bills, "Personality Changes During Student-Centered Teaching," *Journal of Educational Research,* 1957, *50,* pp. 121-126.

R. E. Bills, "An Investigation of Student-Centered Teaching," *Journal of Educational Research,* 1952, *46,* pp. 313-319.

E. W. Bovard, "The Experimental Production of Interpersonal Affect," *Journal of Abnormal and Social Psychology,* 1951, *46,* pp. 521-528.

E. W. Bovard, "Clinical Insight as a Function of Group Process," *Journal of Abnormal and Social Psychology,* 1952, *47,* pp. 534-539.

P. BRANDWEIN, *The Gifted Student as Future Scientist* (New York: Harcourt, Brace, and World, Inc., 1955).

P. BRANDWEIN, F. WATSON, and P. BLACKWOOD, *Teaching High School Science: A Book of Methods* (New York: Harcourt, Brace, and World, Inc., 1958).

W. B. BROOKOVER, "The Social Roles of Teachers and Pupil Achievement," *American Sociological Review*, 1943, *8*, p. 391.

W. B. BROOKOVER, *A Sociology of Education* (New York: American Book Company, 1955).

H. R. BURKE, "An Experimental Study of Teaching Methods in a College Freshman Orientation Course," *Dissertation Abstracts*, 1956, *16*, pp. 77-78.

R. W. BURNETT, *Teaching Science in the Secondary School* (New York: Holt, Rinehart & Winston, Inc., 1957).

W. H. BURTON, *The Guidance of Learning Activities* (Second Edition, New York: Appleton-Century-Crofts, Inc., 1952).

L. F. CARTER, "Leadership and Small Group Behavior," M. SHERIF and M. WILSON (Eds.), *Group Relations at the Crossroads* (New York: Harper & Row, Publishers, 1953).

L. J. CRONBACH, *Educational Psychology* (New York: Harcourt, Brace & World, Inc., 1954).

F. J. DEIGNAN, "A Comparison of the Effectiveness of Two Group Discussion Methods," *Dissertation Abstracts*, 1956, *16*, pp. 1110-1111.

F. J. DIVESTA, "Instructor-Centered and Student-Centered Approaches in Teaching a Human Relations Course," *Journal of Applied Psychology*, 1954, *38*, pp. 329-335.

A. EGLASH, "A Group Discussion Method of Teaching Psychology," *Journal of Educational Psychology*, 1954, *45*, pp. 257-267.

W. H. FARQUHAR, "An Investigation of the Relationship of Three Teaching Methods to Student Behavior in a How to Study Course," *Dissertation Abstracts*, 1955, *15*, p. 2442.

V. A. FAW, "A Psychotherapeutic Method of Teaching Psychology," *American Psychologist*, 1949, *4*, p. 104.

L. FESTINGER, *A Theory of Cognitive Dissonance* (Evanston, Illinois: Harper & Row, Publishers, 1957).

N. A. FLANDERS, "Personal-Social Anxiety as a Factor in Experimental Learning," *Journal of Educational Research*, 1951, *45*, pp. 100-110.

N. GEKOSKI, "Predicting Group Productivity," *Personnel Psychology*, 1952, *5*, pp. 281-292.

J. D. GRAMBS, W. J. IVERSON, F. K. PATTERSON, *Modern Methods in Secondary Education* (Rev. ed.; New York: The Dryden Press, 1958).

H. GUETZKOW, E. L. KELLEY, and W. J. MCKEACHIE, "An Experimental Comparison of Recitation, Discussion, and Tutorial Methods in College Teaching," *Journal of Educational Psychology*, 1954, *45*, pp. 193-207.

G. V. HAIGH and W. SCHMIDT, "The Learning of Subject Matter in Teacher-Centered and Group-Centered Classes," *Journal of Educational Psychology*, 1956, *47*, pp. 295-301.

A. P. HARE, *Social Interaction: An Analysis of Behavior in Small Groups* (New York: John Wiley & Sons, Inc., 1959).

J. K. HEMPHILL, "Situational Factors in Leadership," *Ohio State University Educational Research Monographs*, No. 32, 1949.

R. W. HEYNS, "The Effects of Variation in Leadership on Participant Behavior in Discussion Groups," *Microfilm Abstracts*, 1949, *9*, Part II, pp. 161-163.

R. W. HUSBAND, "A Statistical Comparison of the Efficacy of Large Lectures Versus Smaller Recitation Sections upon Achievement in General Psychology," *Journal of Psychology*, 1951, *31*, pp. 297-300.

J. D. KRUMBOLTZ, "An Investigation of the Effect of Three Teaching Methods on Motivational Outcomes in a How-To-Study Course," *Dissertation Abstracts*, 1955, *15*, p. 2470.

T. LANDSMAN, An Experimental Study of a Student-Centered Learning Method. Unpublished Doctoral Dissertation, Syracuse University, 1950.

K. LEWIN, "Studies in Group Decision," in D. CARTWRIGHT and A. ZANDER (Eds.), *Group Dynamics: Research and Theory* (Evanston, Ill.: Harper & Row, Publishers, 1953).

H. G. MCCURDY and W. E. LAMBERT, "The Efficiency of Small Human Groups in the Solution of Problems Requiring Genuine Co-operation," *Journal of Personality*, 1952, *20*, pp. 478-494.

W. J. MCKEACHIE, "Anxiety in the College Classroom," *Journal of Educational Research*, 1951, *45*, pp. 153-160.

W. J. MCKEACHIE, "Student-Centered Versus Instructor-Centered Instruction, *Journal of Educational Psychology*, 1954, *45*, pp. 143-150.

O. H. MOWRER, "Authoritarianism Versus Self-Government in the Management of Children's Aggressive Reactions as Preparation for Citizenship in a Democracy," *Journal of Social Psychology*, 1939, *10*, pp. 121-126.

J. MURSELL, *Successful Teaching: Its Psychological Principles* (2nd ed.; New York: McGraw-Hill Book Co., Inc., 1954).

S. E. NEUMAN, "Student Versus Instructor Design of Study Method," *Journal of Educational Psychology*, 1957, *48*, pp. 328-333.

L. A. OSTLUND, "An Experimental Study of Case-Discussion Learning," *Journal of Experimental Education*, 1956, *25*, pp. 81-89.

H. V. PERKINS, "Climate Influences on Group Learning," *Journal of Educational Research*, 1951, *45*, pp. 114-119.

C. C. PETERS, *Teaching High School History and Social Studies for Citizenship* (Coral Gables, Florida: University of Miami Press, 1948).

G. R. RASMUSSEN, "Evaluation of a Student-Centered and Instructor-Centered Method of Conducting a Graduate Course in Education," *Journal of Educational Psychology*, 1956, *47*, pp. 449-461.

K. J. REHAGE, "Pupil-Teacher Planning," *Journal of Educational Research,* 1951, *45,* pp. 111-114.

M. E. ROSEBOROUGH, "Experimental Studies of Small Groups," *Psychological Bulletin,* 1953, *50,* pp. 275-303.

J. L. SINGER and G. D. GOLDMAN, "Experimentally Contrasted Social Atmospheres in Group Psychotherapy with Chronic Schizophrenics," *Journal of Social Psychology,* 1954, *40,* pp. 23-27.

W. D. SHELDON, and T. LANDSMAN, "An Investigation of Non-directive Group Therapy with Students in Academic Difficulty," *Journal of Consulting Psychology,* 1950, *14,* pp. 210-215.

M. SLOMOWITZ, "A Comparison of Personality Changes and Content Achievement Gains Occurring in Two Modes of Instruction," *Dissertation Abstracts,* 1955, *15,* p. 1790.

H. C. SMITH, and D. JOHNSON, "An Experimental Study of Attitudes and Achievement in the Democratic Classroom," 1952 meetings of American Psychological Association.

H. A. THELEN and J. WITHALL, "Three Frames of Reference; The Description of Climate," *Human Relations,* 1949, *2,* pp. 159-176.

O. THOMPSON and F. TOM, "Comparison of the Effectiveness of a Pupil-Centered Versus a Teacher-Centered Pattern for Teaching Vocational Agriculture," *Journal of Educational Research,* 1957, *50,* pp. 667-678.

J. N. WARD, "Group-Study Versus Lecture-Demonstration Method in Physical Science Instruction for General Education College Students," *Journal of Experimental Education,* 1956, *24,* pp. 197-210.

R. WHITE and R. LIPPITT, "Leader Behavior and Member Reaction in Three 'Social Climates,' " D. CARTWRIGHT and A. ZANDER (Eds.), *Group Dynamics: Research and Theory* (Evanston, Ill.: Harper & Row, Publishers, 1953).

R. R. WISCHMEIER, "Group-Centered and Leader-Centered Leadership: An Experimental Study," *Speech Monograph,* 1955, *22,* pp. 43-49.

L. G. WISPE, "Evaluating Section Teaching Methods," *Journal of Educational Research,* 1951, *45,* pp. 161-186.

L. D. ZELENY, "Experimental Appraisal of a Group Learning Plan," *Journal of Educational Research,* 1940, *34,* pp. 37-42.

GROUP COMPLIANCE TO DOMINATIVE TEACHER INFLUENCE*

By Ned A. Flanders and Sulo Havumaki

THE PROBLEM

A teacher sometimes faces a situation in which there is an issue that is a matter of opinion. In its simplest form, the issue may involve two alternatives, say *A* and *B*. Suppose the teacher prefers *A* and nearly all the students prefer *B*. Ideally, the ensuing social interaction tends to reduce the difference of opinion by seeking "the best" solution. But teacher-pupil relationships are essentially superior-subordinate, and the teacher has ultimate authority. Not only does the teacher's opinion carry more weight than students' opinions, but students expects the teacher to be "right." In such a situation, changing opinion from *B* to *A* is an act of compliance requiring the students to give up their preferences. Holding fast to opinion *B* is to resist complying to the teacher's influence.

Given the difference of opinion, a teacher usually exerts logical persuasion, explains the problem as he sees it, outlines certain facts or reasons that support his own point of view, and frequently asks questions designed to stimulate student discussion. Modern practices notwithstanding, a teacher usually will talk much more than all the students combined and will control the communication pattern by responding to each student's statement. Soon all student comments are directed to the teacher, and even though the teacher is pleasant, respects the students, and appears to be fair, the basic superior-subordinate relationship is maintained. These are precisely the conditions that were created in our laboratory study.

Our theoretical analysis of the foregoing situation makes use of two independent variables that affect compliance. The first independent variable is the

*From *Human Relations,* 1960, *13,* pp. 67-82. Used by permission of the authors and publisher. This research was conducted as part of the research program of the Laboratory for Research in Social Relations, University of Minnesota.

"pattern of influence" used by the teacher. Clearly *how* the teacher (*T*)[1] uses his influence will affect student (*S*)[1] compliance. The second independent variable is group contagion or the tendency of a *S* to comply because he thinks others are complying or not to comply if he thinks others are resisting the *T*'s influence.

The pattern of teacher influence is limited, first of all, to logical, friendly argument without threat of punishment or promise of special reward other than *T* commendation. Within this limitation, two patterns are used. In one-half of the experimental groups, the *T* directed his arguments only to individuals while the rest of the group listened. In the individual treatments of our experimental design, the *T* called on only those *S*'s who happened to be seated in the odd-numbered seats, always referred to *S*'s by name, addressed his remarks to individuals, and spoke to the group as infrequently as possible. As one would expect, this behavior caused *Ss* to raise their hands to be called on by the *T* and in this way he was able to restrict communication with ease. In the other one-half of the experimental groups, the *T* directed his arguments to the total group. He spoke only to the group, told the group that anyone should speak right out without raising his hand or waiting to be called on, reacted to ideas expressed as if they belonged to the group, and did not single out individuals by the use of names.

The variable of group contagion was manipulated[2] by the use of special equipment in the laboratory room. All experimental groups were taught to use individual levers hidden from view to indicate their preference for either alternative *A* or alternative *B*. A light panel, hidden from the *T*'s view but in full view of all *Ss*, purported to show the total lever movements for both alternatives. Each *S* could determine the total group opinion by noting the proportion of red and green lights. In one-half of the experimental groups the light panel, which was actually controlled by the *E*, who sat in an observation room, consistently showed throughout the discussion an almost unanimous preference for alternative *B*, the original preference of the *Ss*. In this condition *Ss* perceived others as not complying to the persuasion of the *T*. In the second experimental condition the light panel gradually changed, during the discussion, from a nearly unanimous preference for *B* to a nearly unanimous preference for *A*. In this condition *Ss* gained the perception that the group was shifting its opinion from *B* to *A*. In this manner group perceptions essential to contagion were controlled.

HYPOTHESES AND EXPERIMENTAL DESIGN

The first three hypotheses are concerned with differences in compliance that one might expect when the individual or the group approach is used by the *T*.

Hypothesis 1.0: The individual approach will result in greater compliance than the group approach.

Sub-Hypothesis 1.1: Group cohesiveness will be lower with the individual approach, compared with the group approach.

Sub-Hypothesis 1.2: Dependency on the teacher will be higher during the individual approach, compared with the group approach.

The rationale behind these hypotheses is that the direct influence attempts of the individual approach are divisive. Each contact emphasizes the *T*'s concern with the individual's opinions and disregards relationships between individuals. This laboratory procedure simulates the common classroom practice of dealing with the *Ss* "one at a time." In a situation in which the *T* is trying to persuade *Ss*, it is the divide-and-conquer theory. One would predict, in these circumstances, that a measure of cohesiveness, or the strength of each individual's desire to remain in the group, will be lower in the individual approach.

Superimposed on the divisive aspects of the individual approach is the expectation that dominative teacher influence creates dependency. Dependency differs from compliance in the following way. A direct act of persuasion, if successful, leads to compliance if the *S* shifts his opinion; i.e., compliance

[1] The letter *T* will refer to the teacher; the letters *S* or *Ss* will refer to the singular or plural of student; and the letter *E* will refer to the host experimenter who is in charge except during class discussions.

[2] Manipulation involves professional ethics. The authors feel that these procedures are justified to control experimental conditions only when (a) no individual or group suffers emotionally, and (b) no one leaves the experiment proper with any misconceptions that might adversely affect his social adjustment.

is an act that is in response to an order or to general pressure. An act of dependency is a voluntary act such that a *S* seeks approval or direction from the authority figure. In one sense, it is a voluntary seeking of additional areas in which acts of compliance can be carried out.

Lower group cohesiveness and higher dependency on the teacher will weaken the ability of the group to resist teacher influence; thus, compliance should be higher. The group approach does not restrict or limit the group resources to the same extent. Given hypotheses 1.1 and 1.2, the main hypothesis 1.0 naturally follows.

The second major hypothesis is concerned with the differences in compliance that one might expect when group contagion is manipulated.

Hypothesis 2.0: Compliance increases when students perceive that others are changing their opinion in response to the teacher's persuasion.

This hypothesis is based on well-established principles of conformity to group pressures. In this experiment, however, the forces of group contagion sometimes support and sometimes oppose the persuasive efforts of the *T*. Control of contagion forces by manipulating the light panel combined with the two methods of *T* influence provide four treatments in our experimental design. These four treatments are:

Treatment	*Teacher Approach*	*Group's Perception*
G-O	Group	Opposition
I-O	Individual	Opposition
G-C	Group	Compliance
I-C	Individual	Compliance

If hypotheses 1.0 and 2.0 are to be supported by the data, compliance should be greatest in the I-C treatment and smallest in the G-O treatment. The rank-order of treatment I-O and G-C, according to compliance, will depend on the relative magnitude of the force toward compliance created by the contrasting approaches of the teacher versus the relative magnitude of the contagion manipulation. If the forces associated with contagion are greater, the rank-order as listed above should occur.

THE PROCEDURE

1. Each experimental group of exactly ten members was brought by bus from a local high school to the University laboratory rooms, where they were welcomed by the *E*. The *S*s were told they had been chosen by chance to form a school team for a city-wide high-school competition that would operate like a "Quiz Kid Show." Five members of the team would be called "participators" and five would be called "helpers." The participators would do the talking during the quiz show. The helpers would also be present in the studio, seated right behind the participators, and could coach or help the participators in case the latter did not know the answer. The *S*s were told that the main reason for designating participants and helpers was that, if the twenty boys and girls from both teams were all permitted to talk, there would be too much confusion. The whole introduction, the rules for the contest, and general build-up were carefully planned to convince even the most skeptical *S* that the competition was real and serious. It was explained that each team could choose to compete on either radio or television. Several statements were made about TV shows being lots of fun and that most *S*s would prefer TV. At the time, TV was quite new in Minnesota and very attractive to *S*s.

2. Ballots, inconspicuously coded, were used to collect the prediscussion preferences for TV or for radio. The private ballots were collected and the *S*s informed that the results would be revealed to them in a few minutes.

3. The levers and the light panel were then explained and the *S*s practised using them. The demonstration was designed to convince the *S*s that *their* lever movements controlled the proportion of red (TV) and green (radio) lights. Through discussion with the *E*, the *S*s were persuaded that the levers could be used by them in a discussion that was about to follow to indicate their preferences continuously and automatically. The equipment would permit them to know just how the entire group felt about the two alternatives as the discussion progressed, and this would result in a more adequate group decision because everyone's opinion could be expressed at all times.

4. The *S*s were then told that each team in the contest was guided by a teacher-trainer, and that the teacher-trainer (*T*) assigned to their team would now meet with them to lead their group's discussion. During the discussion they would reach a final decision about radio or TV. The *S*s were again reminded of the light panel. You can use the light

panel to see if your own opinion is the same or different from the rest of the group. The results of the earlier secret ballot were then announced. Regardless of how the group actually voted, the results for each group were: "According to your vote, most of the members of this group prefer TV. Therefore, when the light panel is turned on most of the lights will be red." At the beginning of each group discussion 12 red lights and 2 green lights appeared.

5. The *T* was then introduced to the group by the *E*. The *T* began the discussion by asking what they thought about TV versus radio as media for their group. Depending on the treatment, either an individual or a group approach was used by the *T* throughout the discussion, the light panel either remained red or gradually shifted to green except for continuous minor fluctuations that coincided with real *S* lever movements. Each discussion lasted between 12 and 14 minutes. During each discussion the *T* brought out four reasons for preferring radio: (1) radio has greater coverage in our state and would reach a larger audience; (2) more *S*s could participate because radio time costs less and there would be more contests; (3) radio shows will take fewer rehearsals and impose on their free time less; and (4) a participant will get nervous on TV with thousands watching every move; on radio their team could give a better performance.

6. After the discussion a paper-and-pencil "opinionaire" was filled out by the *S*s. This paper-and-pencil instrument permitted *S*s to (a) indicate their preference for radio vs. TV; (b) indicate their awareness of the movement of the light panel; (c) give an indication of their interest in further participation; (d) react to three items to test their cohesiveness; (e) give an indication of their dependency on the teacher; and (f) indicate those members of their group that they thought would do the best job on the program (sociometric). As soon as the students had filled out the post-discussion questionnaire the *T* collected them and left the room as the *E* re-entered.

7. The *E* told the *S*s that the sponsor wanted to make sure that each team had the best possible opportunity to compete. Therefore, if they had any reservations at all about working with this particular *T*, it would be possible to make a change. There were quite a number of *T*s employed for this purpose and this particular one need not necessarily be assigned to their group. In order to find out their reactions they were asked five questions. These items included: (a) whether they would like to continue to work with the same *T*, (b) how well he explained the radio vs. television issue, (c) whether or not he was fair, (d) whether he appeared to be more interested in each individual or mostly interested in the group as a whole, and (e) whether they were aware of the fact that the teacher-trainer preferred either radio or television.

8. The *E* then went through a carefully planned deflation procedure that revealed the deceptions used in the experiment and also notified the *S*s that there would be no competition. The nature of the experiment and the reasons for using deception were explained. During this 'decompression' session each *S* was encouraged to express his feelings about the experiment. Each *S* was requested to cooperate in not revealing the nature of the experiment to others who might become *S*s, and there were usually verbal pledges given for cooperation in this respect. The students were then taken back to their school.

THE ANALYSIS OF THE DATA

The experimental population. The experimental population consisted of 360 students from seven different high schools in Minneapolis and St. Paul, Minnesota. Local high-school principals or counselors selected groups of ten such that (a) within any one group friendships and acquaintanceships would be at a minimum, and (b) among groups academic ability would be randomly distributed. This necessitated contacting large high schools that had ten or more tenth-grade home-rooms in order to form groups that approached the two specifications by selecting one *S* from each home-room. Three of the high schools were in above average socio-economic areas, two were definitely below average, and two were average. The average age of the *S*s was about sixteen years. There are no reasons to suspect that the experimental population differed significantly from a random sample of urban high-school tenth-graders.

Evidence of T consistency between treatments. The design called for an individual approach by the *T* in treatments I-O and I-C, a group approach in treatments G-O and G-C, with other aspects of the *T*'s behavior to be as consistent as possible. Seven trial runs with different *S*s were used to train the *T* to behave consistently in each approach; the same trained *T* was used in each of the 36 discussions to control personality factors. During each discussion the *E* used electrical recording equipment to keep an accurate record of the total time the *T* talked as well as the *S*s. Later analysis of the records showed that no statistically significant variations of the total time the teacher talked occurred between treatments. In addition, the *T*'s verbal statements were classified according to whether they were directed toward individuals or toward the group as a whole. The results showed that the *T*'s approach varied in a manner consistent with the experimental design.

As a further check on the consistency of the *T*'s behavior, all the *S*s rated the *T* immediately after he left the room, using the item, "The teacher-trainer helped explain the advantages and disadvantages of radio and television so that I: (1) understood it very well, (2) understood it fairly well, (3) am not sure that I understand it, (4) am puzzled about a number of points, or (5) do not understand it at all." Assigning values of one through five to the responses, the mean scores for the various treatments were calculated, and no statistically significant differences were found between treatments.

All data concerning the consistency of the *T*'s behavior are not presented here, to conserve space. An analysis of these data is available upon request. The authors conclude that there were no known behavior differences of the *T*, beyond those required by the individual and group approaches, that could reasonably bias the variables under study.

The effectiveness of the experimental manipulations. In an experiment that is complicated by the attempt to create a special social situation complete with particular individual perceptions, it is reasonable that some manipulations would fail to convince some *S*s. A number of *S*s did not respond as planned, and thus they existed in a situation that is not a proper test of the hypotheses of this study.

First, three groups were discarded because: one group was highly suspicious, nervous, and obviously upset—this was later traced to an unfortunate statement made by a counselor just as the *S*s left their high school; a second group, from a low socio-economic district, contained two uncooperative *S*s who refused to follow directions, used profanity, and tried to smoke during the experiment; and a third group was discarded because it showed unmistakable signs of knowing about the deceptions of the experiment prior to participating. The elimination of these 30 *S*s from the study reduced the population to a total of 330 *S*s.

Second, a total of 87 *S*s indicated a preference for radio before the discussions took place. They obviously could not be influenced to shift their preference from TV to radio. The incidence of these *S*s by treatment as shown in Column 2 of Table 5-1.

TABLE 5-1

INCIDENCE OF MISPERCEIVERS BY TREATMENT

Treatment (1)	*Preferred Radio* (2)	*Other Misper-ceptions* (3)	*Potential Shifters* (4)	*Total* (5)
G-O	14	16	50	80
I-O	23	15	52	90
G-C	23	28	29	80
I-C	27	15	38	80
Total	87	74	169	330

$\chi^2 = 18.36$; at 6 d.f., $p < .01$

Third, a total of 74 *S*s failed to respond properly to some other manipulation; 28 failed to see the *T*'s preference for radio; 41 failed to show understanding of the light panel; and 5 failed at both perceptions. The incidence of these misperceivers by treatment is shown in Column 3, Table 5-1.

The net result of the manipulations is shown in Column 4 of Table 5-1, which indicates that 169 *S*s were in the social situation described at the beginning of this article. The analysis of compliance to test our major hypotheses will make use of these 169 cases.

It would be nice if these misperceptions had occurred without any relationship to the experimental treatment. A simple contingency calculation of chi square, testing whether there is any particular relationship among the cells of Table 5-1, yields a chi square of 18.36, which is significant, at six degrees of freedom, beyond the .01 level. The incidence of misperceivers is higher whenever the light panel is used to indicate a shift of group opinion toward radio (Treatments G-C and I-C) and is particularly high in the G-C Treatment. No plans were made to collect data that might reveal why *S*s misperceived the manipulations; therefore the significant differences revealed in Table 5-1 cannot be interpreted systematically. The most obvious explanation is that most *S*s held their preference for TV strongly and were not willing to accept evidence of group opinion shift toward a preference for radio.

Compliance in the different treatments. Compliance was measured as a shift in opinion from TV to radio on the pre- and post-discussion ballots. Hypothesis 1.0, predicting more compliance in the individual treatments I-O and I-C, can be tested by analysing the opinion shift of the 169 *S*s shown in Table 5-2. Hypothesis 2.0, predicting more compliance in the compliance treatments G-C and I-C, can be similarly tested. First, a 2×4 chi square calculation of the entire table rejects the hypotheses that there are no differences among the cells, $p<.001$. A 2×2 chi square test of the greater compliance in the I-O and I-C Treatments rejects the hypotheses of chance differences, $p=.018$, thus supporting hypothesis 1.0 regarding teacher influence. Finally, a 2×2 chi square test of the greater compliance in Treatments G-C and I-C also rejects the hypothesis of chance difference, $p=<.001$, supporting hypothesis 2.0 concerning group contagion.

TABLE 5-2

OPINION SHIFT OF SUBJECTS WHO PERCEIVED MANIPULATIONS, PRE-DISCUSSION PREFERENCE COMPARED TO POST-DISCUSSION

($N = 169$)

	Preferred TV Before Discussion				
				Seat Position	
Treatment	*Potential Shifters (1)*	*Shift to Radio (2)*	*Per Cent Shifting (3)*	*Odd (4)*	*Even (5)*
G-O	50	7	14.0	3	4
I-O	52	10	19.2	3	7
G-C	29	14	48.3	6	8
I-C	38	22	57.9	13	9
Total	169	53		25	28

$\chi^2 = 26.6$; at 3 d.f., $p<.001$

Limiting the test of our major hypotheses to the 169 *S*s in Table 5-2 may be qusetioned by some readers. The data for all 330 *S*s are not shown, in order to conserve space, but the trends and differences for all 330 *S*s are similar to those for 169 *S*s. The per cent shifting opinion, for example, for 330 *S*s are: G-O, 19.7 per cent; I-O, 23.9 per cent; G-C, 29.8 per cent; and I-C, 43.4 per cent. The same chi square tests for the 330 *S*s are: for the entire 2×4 table, $p=.03$; for teacher influence, $p=.15$ (not significant); and for group contagion, $p= .114$. Apparently, when *S*s who either did not understand or refused to accept the experimental manipulations are added to those *S*s who did, the trends remain the same, and only the differences regarding teacher influence become non-significant.

These data on compliance show that when a *T* talks to the *S*s "one at a time" and, at the same time, the individual *S*s believe that the rest of the group is complying to the *T*'s influence, then maximum compliance occurs. When the *T* talks to the group and most members of the group believe that others are not complying to the *T*'s influence, then minimum compliance occurs. Finally, when the force of the *T*'s influence is compared with the forces of group contagion, the latter are more effective in causing compliance.

The effect of the T's behavior on cohesiveness. Hypothesis 1.1 predicts the cohesiveness will be lower in the individual treatments. Two post-discussion questions used to measure cohesiveness reflect the desire of the *S*s to remain in their group. (1) "If the group should decide to broadcast over TV or radio in a way that is the opposite to what you prefer, would you like to remain with this group or transfer to another group from your school?" (2) "Suppose you do not get your choice about being a participant or a helper. In such a case would you like to remain with this group or transfer to another group from your school?" The response form permitted a *S* to indicate his choice.

The results from the two questions on cohesiveness are presented in Table 5-3 and show that 65 *S*s among the 330 indicated a desire to transfer from the group. When Treatments I-O plus I-C (individual approach) are compared with G-O plus G-C (group approach), there are about twice as many respectively who wish to transfer. The difference (43

TABLE 5-3

SUBJECTS WHO DESIRE TO TRANSFER OUT OF GROUP

Treatment	*N*	*Choices to Transfer*			*% Inds. in Each Treatment** *N = 65*
		Odd	*Even*	*Total*	
	(1)	*(2)*	*(3)*	*(4)*	*(5)*
G-O	80	2	3	5	7.7
I-O	90	15	15	30	46.2
G-C	80	10	7	17	26.1
I-C	80	5	8	13	20.0
Total	330	32	33	65	100.0

*The percentage distribution of column (4).

compared to 22) is significant beyond the .01 level of significance and supports hypothesis 1.1. As expected, there are no significant differences when this same comparison is made between Treatments G-O plus I-O vs. G-C plus I-C.

Evidence of dependency on the teacher. Hypothesis 1.2 predicts that the individual approach will create more dependency than the group approach. One aspect of dependency is measured by the post-discussion question. "Would you like the teacher or the group to select the five 'program participants' "? The percentage of *S*s (N=330) requesting that the *T* make this choice in each experimental treatment is: I-O, 40 per cent; I-C, 37.8 per cent; G-O, 32.5 per cent; and G-C, 31.3 per cent. This measure of dependency is higher for the individual treatments, but the difference could have occurred by chance about one out of three times, p=.3. The individual or group approach, apparently, did not significantly influence the responses of the *S*s to this question.

Additional evidence on dependency can be secured, however. One test can be made within the individual treatments, ignoring the group treatments. One can reason that the *T*'s individual contacts with *S*s in the odd-numbered seats should make these *S*s more dependent than *S*s seated in the even-numbered seats. During each contact the *T* would try to praise the individual, yet at the same time turn his ideas into arguments for radio; failing this, the *T* would confront the *S* with counter-arguments in favor of radio. During these contacts the *T*'s attention was centered on the individual. The *S*s in the even-numbered seats were only spectators to these more personal experiences. Data from the same question (see above) are shown in Table 5-4 for all *S*s in the individual treatments. A significantly greater (p<.01) number of *S*s seated on the odd-numbered seats wanted the *T* to select the five program participants, which tends to support hypothesis 1.2.

TABLE 5-4

PREFERENCES FOR APPOINTING PROGRAM PARTICIPANTS, ODD VERSUS EVEN SEATS IN INDIVIDUAL TREATMENTS

Seat	*Choice*		
	Teacher	*Group*	*Total*
Odd	40	42	82
Even	25	62	87
Total	65	104	169*

*One student did not answer. Total *N* should be 170; 90 *S*s in treatment II; 80 *S*s in treatment III.

Finally, it is shown in another paper growing out of this study that those *S*s who sat in the odd-numbered seats and talked with the teacher were chosen significantly (p=.01) more frequently than others in response to the question, "which five *S*s would make good program participants?" Since these are the same *S*s who, in turn, gave evidence of dependency on the *T*, the overall relationship seems to be: the *T* praises and argues with certain *S*s; these same *S*s are more likely to show dependency on the *T*; these same *S*s are chosen by others for positions of responsibility.

Spontaneous lever movements. One can accept the devisive effects of the *T*'s influence on cohesiveness, the development of dependence and compliance, and still wonder about the more private, inner reactions of the *S*s. In particular, we wish to turn to the *S*s who shifted their opinions from TV to radio. Did these opinion shifts occur with private, inner acceptance or with private inner resistance? "Inner acceptance," in this discussion, is defined as not only being satisfied with one's shift of opinion, but, in addition, actively influencing others in the group to shift to radio. "Inner resistance," similarly, means not only being dissatisfied with the shift to radio, but, in addition, actively influencing others in the group to resist this change. The spontaneous lever movements that were recorded when the *Ss* thought they were secretly influencing the group's opinion, provide considerable evidence on this question.

Interviews and post-experimental discussions indicate that none of the *Ss* realized that their lever movements were being recorded. The lever movements could be made secretly and the *Ss* could not trace lever movements, even their own, by observing the light panel. Their "spontaneity" resulted primarily from the *Ss*' perception that they could use the lever to influence the immediate situation.

Before turning to the data, a word about their form. Lever movements were averaged for three-minute periods. Average lever movements were calculated by adding all lever movements for radio and dividing by 10, the number of *Ss* in a group for each three-minute period. TV average lever movements were calculated in an identical manner. The standard errors of the means vary from 0.2 to as high as 2.5 depending on the number of *Ss* involved. For $N=15$ or larger the standard error is usually less than 0.5. An extensive statistical treatment of these averages does not seem justified in terms of the limited inferences to be made. Simple *t*-tests of the significance of differences between means have been used. Whenever the word "significant" is used in reference to the comparison of lever movements, the *t* calculation indicates a p value of .01 or less.

The first question that can be asked is "Are the lever movements valid?" Any question about the validity of lever movements really refers to what lever movements are supposed to express compared with what they do express. According to the directions given to the *Ss*, lever movements should be an expression of personal opinion. One way to check this is to compare the lever movements of *Ss* who voted consistently in favor of radio with those of *Ss* who consistently voted in favor of TV. We would expect to find predominately TV lever movements for pro-TV *Ss* and predominately radio lever movements for pro-radio *Ss*. Average lever movements per three-minute period for *Ss* who voted TV-TV are shown in *Figure 5-7, Graphs 1* and *2*; those for *Ss* who voted radio-radio in *Graphs 3* and *4*. The data are grouped according to the opposition and compliance conditions, because the differences attributed to the *T*'s approach are insignificant.

When *Graph 1* is compared with *Graph 3,* and when *Graph 2* is compared with *Graph 4,* the TV-TV *Ss* have significantly more TV lever movements and the radio-radio *Ss* have significantly more radio lever movements. It is clear from these comparisons that *Ss* used the levers to express their preference for either TV or radio.

Another aspect of validity is the question, "Did the *Ss* attempt to influence others in the group?" Evidence concerning this question can also be obtained from *Graphs 1* through *4*. First, we would predict that *Ss* who preferred TV would express more lever movements in the compliance condition when it appeared that the group was shifting to radio; in the opposition treatments they could tell that the group still preferred TV and would be less inclined to use their levers to influence the group. The fact that there are significnatly more TV lever movements in *Graph 2,* compared with *Graph 1,* suggests that the *Ss* did try to influence the group by using the levers. For those *Ss* who preferred radio, we would expect more radio lever movements during the opposition condition when it appeared that the group was not shifting to radio. There are slightly more radio lever movements in *Graph 3* compared with *Graph 4,* but this difference is not significant. Perhaps the awareness that such efforts were not just resisting the group, but in addition an aid to the *T*'s arguments, may have curtailed the lever movements of pro-radio *Ss*. Nevertheless, we can assume that those *Ss* who prefer TV can and do use their levers in an attempt to influence the group.

The total picture from *Graphs 1* through *4* strongly supports the validity of average lever movements. To these objective comparisons could be added the subjective impressions of the *E* who observed all sessions and whose own light panels, in the observation room, indicated the true lever movement of the *Ss*. To him the spontaneous lever movements seemed both logical and persuasive. *Ss* with strong convictions "rode" their levers in an effort to influence the group. The authors have accepted spontaneous lever movements as valid indications of the secret preference of the *Ss* and their efforts actively to influence others.

Next we turn to the average lever movements of *Ss* who shifted their opinions from TV to radio and thus complied with the influence of the *T*. Their average lever movements are shown in *Graphs 5* and *6*. In both these figures, there is an orderly

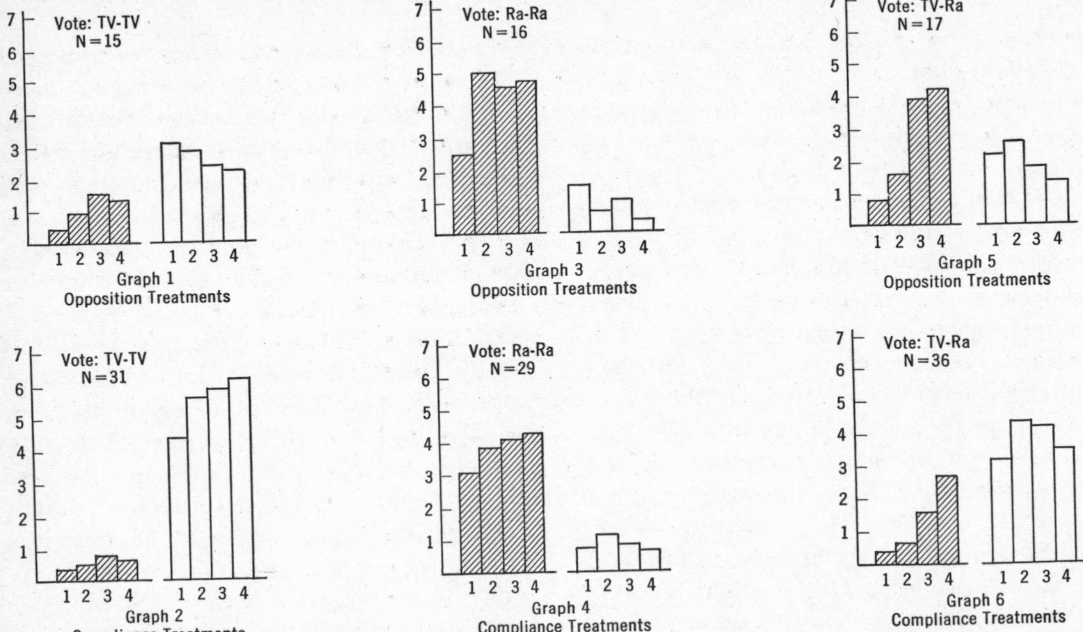

Figure 5-7. Opposition and Compliance Treatments. The four time periods of three minutes each are indicated by the use of a separate bar. The average of radio lever movements during the first period is shown by the first shaded bar on the left, the average of TV lever movements during the same period is shown by the first clear bar on the right. The pre- and post-discussion voting pattern is indicated on each figure; e.g. Graph 2, 31 *Ss* voted for TV before and after the discussion in the compliance treatments; during the second time-period they averaged about one-half lever movement per person for radio and, during the same period, the same *Ss* averaged about 5.6 lever movements for TV.

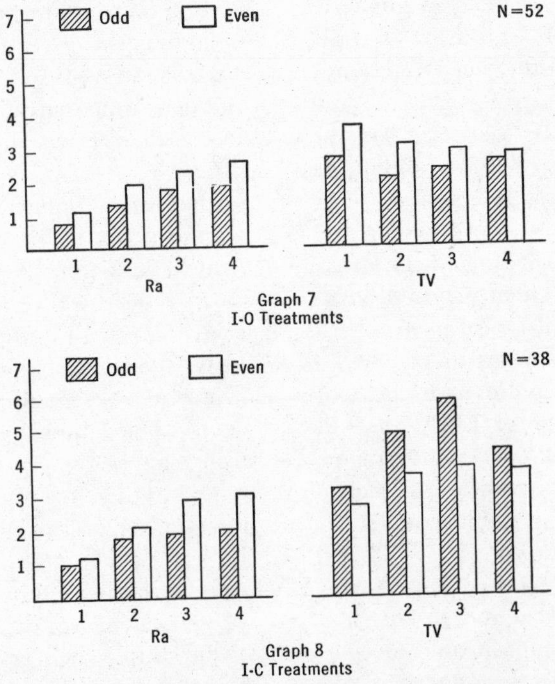

Figure 5-8. I-O and I-C Treatments. The average of lever movements for *Ss* in the odd and even seats are shown separately in these two figures. For each three-minute time-period separate bars show the odd-even averages for radio, on the left, and for TV, on the right.

increase in the number of lever movements in favor of radio as the discussion proceeds. In all treatments the highest number of radio movements occurs in the last three-minute period. This must be due to the logical persuasion of the *T*'s arguments. For the 17 *S*s in the opposition condition, *Graph 5,* their shift of opinion seems to occur with inner acceptance. This inference is made from the fact that the TV lever movements decrease as the radio lever movements increase, so that in the final three minutes of discussion, their radio lever movements occur three times as frequently as their TV lever movements. These *S*s shift their opinions in spite of the apparent opposition of the group and are not conforming to group pressures but are complying to *T* persuasion.

In *Graph 6,* when the group was apparently complying to the *T*'s influence, the proportion of TV and radio average lever movements is significantly different. At all times the average lever movements for TV exceed those for radio. The consistent inference here is that these *S*s wrote down their final vote for radio with considerable inner resistance and perhaps even a secret preference for TV.

Combining the TV average lever movements for the G-C and I-C Treatments in *Graph 6* does hide one significant difference between these two treatments. The TV average lever movement in the I-C Treatment is 4.17, the same average for the G-C Treatment is 3.12. This difference is significant and means that the highest inner resistance of all occurs in the I-C Treatment. In both of these treatments *S*s who shift are conforming to apparent group opinion as well as complying to *T* persuasion.

One final piece of evidence about active resistance can be obtained by making a graph that shows the average lever movements separately for *S*s seated in the odd- and even-numbered seats. This was done by excluding *S*s who voted for radio both before and after the discussion, since their TV lever movements are very infrequent, as is shown in *Graphs 3* and *4*. Next, the graphs for all *S*s participating in the treatments involving the group approach of the *T* are not shown because no significant differences appear or would be expected. There remain 52 *S*s in the I-O Treatment whose radio and TV average lever movements are shown in *Figure 5-8, Graph 7,* and 38 *S*s in the I-C Treatment whose same lever movements are shown in *Graph 8*.

The differences between the odd and even seats are not significant for radio and TV average lever movements in *Graph 7* and also for the radio movements in *Graph 8*. However, the TV lever movements in *Graph 8* averaged over all four discussion periods are 4.71 for *S*s in the odd-numbered seats, which is significantly different from the average of 3.75 for *S*s seated in the even-numbered seats. Inner resistance is not only highest in the I-C Treatment, as reported earlier, but it is also highest for *S*s seated in the odd-numbered seats who participated in the verbal interaction.

To summarize, the lever data shed light on the inner acceptance or rejection of the pressures of group conformity as well as teacher compliance. It is clear that those *S*s whose pre- and post- opinions are consistent, voting either TV-TV or Ra-Ra, expressed stable, inner convictions in their use of the levers. These *S*s, who were in the majority, resisted either the *T* or the group according to their own preferences and the treatment.

Those few *S*s who shifted from TV to radio in the opposition treatments in spite of perceived group resistance, appear to be logically persuaded and are willing to ignore or reject group pressure to follow the teacher. In the case of the compliance treatments, when the group appeared to be shifting, more *S*s also shifted publicly, but inner resistance to their own compliance and conformity is clearly visible. The *S*s seated in the odd-numbered seats, in direct verbal contact with the *T*, show the highest inner resistance of all.

CONCLUSIONS AND INTERPRETATIONS

Conclusions. Hypotheses 1.0 and 2.0, concerning the effects of the *T*'s influence and group contagion on compliance, are strongly supported. Equally clear evidence can be found to support hypothesis 1.1 that the individual approach of the *T* is divisive and reduces group cohesiveness. Fairly strong evidence has been found to support hypothesis 1.2 about the development of dependency as an outcome of restrictive *T* domination.

The logical persuasion of the *T* appears as a constant force toward compliance in all four treatments. With the group approach, this force is reduced somewhat by an implied support of the group caused by the *T*'s group approach. The other major social force affecting opinion shift is perceived group opinion. In the opposition treatments, this force favors resisting compliance; in the compliance treatments this force favors compliance.

Under conditions of this experiment, the more potent of these two forces is the force of group conformity. It is not surprising that *S*s, brought together as a team to represent their school, are more sensitive to their group opinion than they are to the efforts of a strange *T* who presents four logical arguments in the short period of 12 or 13 minutes.

In Treatment G-O, 85 per cent ($N=50$) of the *S*s do not change their preference for TV. The freedom to express ideas spontaneously appears to lend support to the group, in spite of the *T*'s arguments. In this treatment the fewest number of *S*s wish to transfer to another group and dependency on the *T* is lowest. Apparently dependency is less likely to develop in the presence of strong group resistance. The few *S*s who do shift their opinion seem to be logically persuaded with inner conviction.

In Treatment I-O, 80 per cent ($N=52$) of the *S*s keep their preference for TV. Freedom to express ideas is restricted to those in the odd-numbered seats and then only with the permission of the *T*. The *T*'s persuasive efforts center on individuals and ignore the group as a whole while the group appears to oppose shifting to radio. This treatment has the highest incidence of *S*s desiring to leave the group (see Table 5-3). Perhaps this is due to an increasing anxiety, which some *S*s might feel, because the more potent individual approach is being openly resisted by *S*s.

In Treatment G-C, 48 per cent ($N=29$) shift their opinion from TV. The greater impact of group conformity is clear, for those who shifted publicly. But for those who preferred TV initially, including those who shifted, private resistance increases, judging by the higher TV lever movements compared with the first two treatments. For the *S*s who shifted, this can be interpreted as a lack of inner conviction, almost ambivalence. For those who did not shift from TV, this can be interpreted as resistance to group conformity as well as resistance to *T* compliance.

In Treatment I-C, 58 per cent ($N=38$) shift from TV preferences. Here the 'divide and conquer' mechanism seem to operate. The *T*'s restrictive, persuasive methods appear to be supported by a total group shift of opinion, as indicated by the light panel. Increased dependence on the *T* appears as a trend. For those *S*s who did shift, lack of inner conviction is the highest of all treatments. In fact, during the last three-minute period, those who publicly shifted in favor of radio registered more lever movements for TV compared with radio. *Apparently, the situation that produced the highest public compliance also produced the greatest inner resistance for those shifting.*

Implications. This experiment was conducted in the context of teacher-pupil relationships. Our findings contain some implications for classroom situations in which a similar issue is involved.

1. A teacher who sets out to persuade a class to shift its opinion by a "divide and conquer" technique is likely to find that this method is most successful, but, at the same time, very likely to produce inner resistance. It is reasonable to expect that such resistance would be expressed sooner or later if the teacher remained in contact with the class over longer periods of time than obtained in this experiment.

2. In situations where students can judge and discuss the effectiveness of the teacher's persuasive efforts, the success of the persuasion will be influenced by the freedom with which students share their perception of the teacher's efforts. A perception of teacher ineffectiveness is likely to create group pressures strong enough to resist the logical persuasion of the teacher, even in groups that are newly formed. It seems reasonable to expect that these group pressures would be greater in classrooms where the students had the opportunity to develop stronger bonds of friendship and class cohesiveness.

3. By implication, this study clarifies a kind of vicious circle that exists in some classrooms in which teachers assume a dominant, friendly, and successfully persuasive role centered primarily on individuals. In this role the teacher is most likely to achieve temporary success and thus feel rewarded. But when the inner resistance develops and is expressed, the teacher is likely to reassert his authority in the same fashion and this tends to sustain class resistance. On the other hand, when the goals of the teacher and the class are not in conflict and the teacher's efforts are supported by the development of group pressure, then the strongest influence forces are created.

CHANGING TEACHER BEHAVIOR THROUGH FEEDBACK FROM PUPILS: AN APPLICATION OF EQUILIBRIUM THEORY*

By N. L. Gage, Philip J. Runkel, and B. B. Chatterjee

The practice of collecting ratings of teachers from their pupils has had a moderate vogue for about 30 years. Advocates of this practice have claimed many values for such ratings, among them the improvement of teacher behavior. After reviewing the literature on the matter, however, Morsh and Wilder[1] concluded that the research evidence was insufficient to support such a claim. Savage's subsequent experiment, performed in 1956-1957 with student teachers at the junior high school level, did not brighten the picture.[2] She was unable to demonstrate that the student teachers had changed their behavior as a result of learning how their pupils rated them. Studies focusing upon the ability of the teacher to perceive her pupils accurately have also yielded negative results.[3]

Despite the paucity of empirical evidence, it seems reasonable that giving teachers information about the relevant feelings and wishes of their pupils would influence their teaching performance. Under everyday conditions, the teacher gets feedback by glancing at her class and noticing signs of interest or boredom, comprehension or puzzlement, favorable attitudes or resentment. She asks direct questions, gives tests, and talks informally with her pupils. She also gets feedback from other teachers, parents, people in the community, and her principal. Through this feedback, the teacher gauges the learning requirements of her pupils and makes her teaching more appropriate to their needs and desires.

The present experiment, designed and executed in 1956, attempted to examine part of this argument. We asked, To what extent does an increase in the amount of feedback to teachers regarding their pupils' perceptions of them as teachers—an increase over what is normally available to them—affect the teachers' performance and the accuracy with which they are able to estimate their pupils' perceptions of them? In brief, we gave an experimental group of sixth-grade teachers information as to how their pupils described their teaching behavior and how the pupils view the ideal teacher; we withheld this information from a different, randomly equivalent control group of teachers. The information had been obtained during an earlier testing period when pupils in both the experimental and control classrooms had responded to a 12-item form for rating teacher behavior. One to two months after the experimental teachers received a summary of their pupils' responses, the pupils again described their teachers on the rating forms. A comparison of changes in pupil descriptions of their teachers between the two testing periods, then, provided a measure of the amount of change in teacher behavior during the elapsed time. We hypothesized that teachers furnished with feedback concerning their pupils' responses would change more than those who received no such information and, more particularly, that these teachers would then more closely resemble their pupils' conceptions of the ideal teacher.

Data also were obtained from teachers in the two testing periods regarding their own behavior and regarding their estimates of the way pupils perceived them. These data permitted tests of sev-

[1] J. E. Morsh and Eleanor W. Wilder, *Identifying the Effective Instructor: A Review of the Quantitative Studies, 1900-1952* (Lackland AFB, San Antonio, Tex.: Air Force Personnel and Training Research Center, Research Bulletin, TR-54-44), p. 39.

[2] Marjorie L. Savage, "Pupil Ratings Used in Student Teaching," *American Vocational Journal,* 1962, *37,* pp. 19-29.

[3] N. L. Gage, "Explorations in Teachers' Perceptions of Pupils," *Journal of Teacher Education,* 1958, *9,* pp. 97-101.

*Prepared especially for this volume as a condensation of N. L. Gage, P. J. Runkel, and B. B. Chatterjee, *Equilibrium Theory and Behavior Change: An Experiment in Feedback from Pupils to Teachers* (Urbana: Bureau of Educational Research, University of Illinois, 1960). This investigation was supported by a research grant (M-650 R) from the Institute of Mental Health of the National Institutes of Health, Public Health Service.

eral subsidiary hypotheses. We report here on one of these—the hypothesis that information feedback increases the accuracy with which teachers estimate their pupils' expectations of them.

EQUILIBRIUM THEORY

Why do we predict that teachers will change their classroom behavior when they are furnished with information regarding their pupils' expectations of them? Common sense might predict that the "teacher knows best" how to govern her professional conduct in the classroom and that she would ignore discrepant ideas which pupils harbor. The theoretical framework which has often been called "equilibrium theory" and which Zajonc has called "consistency theory" offers a systematic way to consider the alternative courses of action open to a teacher and to understand her choice among them.[4] This theory is represented by the recent contributions of Heider, Newcomb, Osgood and Tannenbaum, and Festinger.[5] It will be sufficient to say a few words about the theories of Heider and Newcomb.

HEIDER. Heider's ideas hinge upon the concepts of unit formation, sentiment, and balanced state.[6] The tendency toward the balanced state can be seen in a triadic system composed of a perceiving person, *p*, an observed other person, *o*, and a third phenomenal object, *x*, these being bound together by the relations of unit formation (e.g., belonging, owning, producing, causing) and sentiment (e.g., liking, respecting, admiring). Heider states the formal conditions of balance as follows: "A triad is balanced when all three of the relations are positive or when two of the relations are negative and one is positive."[7] Further, "If two negative relations are given, balance can be obtained either when the third relation is positive or when it is negative, though there appears to be a preference for the positive alternative."[8]

Suppose the teacher is given evidence that *o* dislikes *x*, for example, that her pupils are critical of her behavior and would like it to change in a certain direction. At the same time she approves of her own behavior (*p* likes *x*) and continues to be attracted to, or to respect, her pupils (*p* likes *o*). We can infer that there will be an influence on the teacher to alter the system; one thing she might do is to change "*p* likes *x*" to "*p* dislikes *x*" (assuming that "*p* likes *o*" will remain true). That is, the teacher can resolve the imbalance by beginning to "dislike" her own behavior and to change in the direction of the pupils' ideal teacher. This will be likely if she has knowledge of the pupils' ideal and if changing in this direction will not send into strong imbalance other co-existing *p-o-x* systems.

NEWCOMB. "Communicative acts" in their simplest form, according to Newcomb, consist of one person (A) transmitting information to another person (B) about something (X).[9] Suppose the teacher (A) has a positive orientation toward her pupils (B). Suppose we inform the teacher as to the pupils' orientations toward the teacher's behaviors (X). Then we set up what Newcomb labeled "strain toward symmetry" (a concept similar to Heider's "imbalance") on the part of the teacher. Such strain tends to make the teacher develop the same orientation toward X which her pupils have. What responses might a teacher make when she finds herself under such a "strain?" From Newcomb's analysis, we can derive the following alternatives:

1. Influencing pupils toward her own orientation to the behaviors;
2. Changing her own orientation toward the behaviors, i.e., adopting the same attitude toward the behaviors as she perceives the pupils to have;
3. Cognitively distorting the pupils' orientation, i.e., reinterpreting her perception of her pupils' orientation so that it becomes more like her own;
4. Modifying her attraction toward the pupils, i.e., liking them less;
5. Modifying her judgment of her own attractiveness to the pupils, i.e., feeling that the pupils like her less;
6. Modifying her own evaluation of herself, i.e., liking herself less;

[4] R. Zajonc, "The Concepts of Balance, Congruity, and Dissonance," *Public Opinion Quarterly*, 1960, *24*, pp. 280-296.

[5] F. Heider, *The Psychology of Interpersonal Relations* (New York: John Wiley & Sons, Inc., 1958); T. M. Newcomb, "Individual Systems of Orientation," in S. Koch (Ed.), *Psychology: A Study of a Science* (New York: McGraw-Hill Book Co., Inc., 1959), Vol. 3, pp. 384-422; C. E. Osgood and P. H. Tannenbaum, "The Principle of Congruity in the Prediction of Attitude Change," *Psychological Review*, 1955, *62*, pp. 42-55; L. Festinger, *A Theory of Cognitive Dissonance* (Evanston, Ill.: Harper & Row, Publishers, 1957).

[6] Heider, *op. cit.*

[7] *Ibid.*, p. 202.

[8] *Ibid.*, p. 206.

[9] Newcomb, *op. cit.*

7. Modifying her judgment of the pupils' evaluation of themselves, i.e., perceiving the pupils to like themselves less;
8. Tolerating the asymmetry without change.

How likely is each of these alternatives under the conditions of classroom life? We interpreted Heider's theory by means of Alternative *2:* The teacher, becoming dissatisfied with her present behaviors after learning of her pupils' views of them, changes her behaviors to conform more closely to the pupils' ideal. It is also possible to interpret this kind of response to feedback from the pupils in terms of Alternative *1:* If the teacher feels that a certain behavior is very much like her own, while she is informed that her pupils do not consider it so but would like it to be so (i.e., they say it would characterize their ideal teacher), the strain toward symmetry will lead her to communicative acts intended to make the pupils also consider the behavior very much like her own. In the classroom, these communicative acts will probably take the form of performing these behaviors more frequently or conspicuously. Alternatives *1* and *2,* or some combination of them, seemed to us the most likely outcome of strain toward symmetry among our experimental teachers. For lack of space we shall not set forth our reasons for considering the other alternatives to be less likely.

Obviously, our hypothesis ignores many other influences upon the teacher and variations among teachers in susceptibility to the kind of influence from pupils which we hypothesize. Our hypothesis implies that influence from pupils will be strong enough, relative to other influences, to make the predicted effects observable. Our experimental design sought to randomize the other influences.

METHOD

Because a number of instruments were used and because some important precautions were taken during data collection, this section will need to be rather lengthy. We chose sixth-grade classes for our experiment. At that grade level the pupils are mature enough to understand printed test materials. Also, since most sixth-grade classes are not departmentalized, the teacher and pupils are together throughout the school day.

Procedure in selecting subjects and collecting data. Our first step was to ask every superintendent of schools in Illinois (outside of Chicago) whose jurisdiction included a sixth grade to send us the name of the first teacher in the alphabetical list of all his sixth-grade teachers; we told him that we would in turn invite this teacher to participate in the research. We tried to retain every possible teacher and her class for use in the final working sample but, since the entire data collection and the treatment were conducted by mail, the beginning list of teachers was inevitably subject to attrition. Some returns came in too late, a few were indecipherable, some losses occurred in the mails, and the like. Of 489 teachers originally receiving our invitation to participate in the research, 208 finally returned usable materials from themselves and their pupils at both pretest and posttest.

Teachers in departmentalized schools or in schools where special circumstances made parts of our questionnaire inappropriate were dropped. We ended, after attrition of various kinds, with 176 sixth-grade teachers in Illinois and approximately 3900 pupils. The teachers were assigned at random to the experimental and control groups at the time the pretest answer sheets of their pupils were received. The distributions of class size among the control and experimental groups were about the same; the median class size was 22 in both groups, and the quartiles of class size were also almost identical. There were 25 males and 65 females among the control teachers, 25 males and 61 females among the experimentals. The final sample was probably biased in having a more than representative proportion of teachers who were interested in what their pupils think of their actions and who were willing to trust information gathered for them by a university research bureau.

Developing the items of teacher behavior. Our experiment called for four kinds of protocol, each obtained near the beginning (pretest) and end (posttest) of the fall semester, 1956-1957:

1. SELF: description by the teacher of *herself*
2. PERCEIVED: the teacher's *perception* of how she would be described by "a pupil who belongs to the majority"
3. ACTUAL: descriptions by the pupils of their *actual* teacher
4. IDEAL: descriptions by the pupils of their *ideal* teacher.

All four of these protocols consisted of responses to the following set of 12 "stimuli," or brief verbal descriptions of teacher behavior:

A. Enjoys a funny remark made by a pupil.
B. Praises what a pupil says in class discussion.
C. Tells pupils about some interesting things to read.
D. Explains arithmetic so pupils can understand it.
E. Suggests to pupils new and helpful ways of studying.
F. Talks with a pupil after school about an idea the pupil has had.
G. Asks a small group of pupils to study something together.
H. Shows a pupil how to look up an answer when the pupil can't find it himself.
I. Asks the pupils what they'd like to study in tomorrow's lesson.
J. Acts disappointed when a pupil gets something wrong.
K. Explains something by using examples from games and sports.
L. Asks the class what they think of something a pupil has said.

These items were intended to be meaningful to sixth-grade pupils; hence they were made brief, with few qualifying phrases. Each item was intended to describe a recognizable and reasonably frequent teacher behavior so that pupils could more easily agree with one another as to whether the behavior occurred. The items were intended to deal with attributes which the teacher could change (more or less) within the time-span of the research and which were determined by teacher-pupil interaction rather than by physical circumstances. (For example, an item asking whether the teacher "shows movies often" might be determined primarily by her having a movie projector and films rather than by motives and attitudes that could be influenced by our feedback.) Finally, to maximize the teachers' acceptance of the procedure, we sought to avoid highly threatening items. From another point of view, however, "threat" should be great enough to exert pressure on the teacher to change. We compromised between these two opposed criteria as well as our judgment permitted. The final items were selected only after a number of trial administrations and analyses.

Instruments. The covering letter and the introductory material in the Teacher's Questionnaire portrayed our project as offering a service to the teacher—that of providing her with information about how her pupils perceived her classroom behavior. (Eventually we did send every teacher a summary of the responses given by her pupils.)

THE QUESTIONNAIRE FOR TEACHERS. The questionnaire booklet was in three colors with sprightly drawings, designed with special care since we depended entirely upon it and a one-page mimeographed follow-up letter to solicit the teacher's participation in the study. The first seven pages described the project and invited the teacher to participate. The care taken with this booklet seemed justified; we got back 360 (or 74 per cent) of the 489 sent out. In view of the time, work, and dislocation of daily routine asked of the teachers, this rate of return seemed gratifyingly high.

Although the Teacher's Questionnaire contained four sections, only two are pertinent to this report. Each section presented the 12 items listed above. Excerpts from the instructions for the pertinent parts of the questionnaire are given below. Section *b* asked the teacher to describe herself and Section *d* asked her to estimate how her pupils would describe her.

Section b: "First, read the sentence which tells what a teacher might do. Then, pick one of the six answers. Like this:

"Enjoys a funny remark made by a pupil.

☐ Very much LIKE me.
☐ Somewhat LIKE me.
☐ A little bit LIKE me.
☐ A little bit UNLIKE me.
☐ Somewhat UNLIKE me.
☐ Very much UNLIKE me."

Section d: "Please answer the items on the next two pages according to your best estimate as to how this pupil who is typical of the majority would answer them if he were asked to: 'Read the sentence which tells what your teacher might do. Then make an 'X' in front of one of the six answers.' "

THE PUPIL OPINION BOOKLET. The Pupil Opinion Booklet contained the same sections as the Teacher's Questionnaire, but, of course, the instructions differed:

Section b: "First read the thing which tells what your teacher might do. Then mark 'X' after one of the six answers."

Section d: "This time, think of the best teacher you can imagine. (Do *not* think any more about the teacher you really have.) Then mark 'X' after the answer which tells how much this thing would be like the best teacher you can imagine."

These instructions were supplemented by mimeographed material for the teacher to read aloud as her pupils prepared to answer the questionnaires. Careful provision was made to assure pupils of the anonymity of their answers. The booklets were provided with separate gummed answer sheets which folded in the middle. The face of the booklet bore this legend:

"Your answers will be sealed up tight when you are finished. Then they will be sent to the University of Illinois. No one in your town—not your teacher, nor your principal, nor anyone else—will ever know how you answered these questions."

The instructions to the teacher on administering the pupils' questionnaires strongly urged her to keep the pupils' answer sheets confidential in every way. One indication of the success of these instructions was that we received no unsealed answer sheet.

The posttest materials were identical with the pretest materials, except that the introductory part of the Teacher's Questionnaire was omitted.

COMMUNICATING FEEDBACK: THE "REPORT ON YOUR PUPILS' OPINIONS." Each teacher in the experimental group received a special booklet filled in with data obtained from her own pupils. This "Report on Your Pupils' Opinions," attractively printed, was designed so that individual information could be entered for each teacher. In each booklet, 12 charts appeared, one for each of the 12 items. The chart for each item had two parts: (a) a histogram concerning the actual teacher, showing how many of her pupils chose "Very much like my teacher," "Somewhat like my teacher," etc., and (b) a histogram concerning the ideal teacher, showing how many of her pupils chose "Very much like a 'best' teacher," "Somewhat like a 'best' teacher," etc. Also, on each histogram, an arrow was fixed to show the position of the median answer. Other explanatory material was also included in the Report booklet.

The experimental design. Our experiment embodied what Campbell has termed *the pretest-posttest control group design,* taking the form shown above in the next column.

	Approximately Mid-October	*Approximately Early November*	*Approximately Mid-December*
Experimental group:	pretest	feedback ("Report on pupils' opinions")	posttest
Control group:	pretest	no feedback (letter explaining delay)	posttest

Our design offers no basis for generalizing to unpretested teachers. In strict logic, our conclusions can apply only to teachers who not only receive feedback but who were also pretested, i.e., prerated by their pupils and by themselves. Since we would have had no information to feed back to the teachers without the prerating by pupils, this limitation is a realistic and necessary one.

We relied on ratings as our measurement devices in this experiment. Ratings like those we obtained are intrinsically significant, quite apart from their relation to other measures of teacher behavior. Yet the generalizability of the present experiment is limited in that no measures other than ratings were used. To overcome this limitation, we should eventually use a variety of ways of describing teacher behavior, "all having in common the theoretically relevant attribute but varying widely in their irrelevant specificities."[10]

RESULTS ON CHANGE OF TEACHER BEHAVIOR

This section will discuss the results obtained from three protocols:

pre-ACTUAL—the pupil's description of his *actual* teacher on the *pre*test

post-ACTUAL—the pupil's description of his *actual* teacher on the *post*test

pre-IDEAL—the pupil's description of his *ideal* teacher on the *pre*test

Adjusted post-ACTUAL. The most important single concern of this study was, would teachers—as described by their pupils—change more if given information about how their pupils described them and their ideal teachers than if not given such information? Specifically, would the experimental and control groups of teachers differ in the posttest descriptions pupils gave of their actual teachers?

[10] D. T. Campbell, "Factors Relevant to the Validity of Experiments in Social Settings," *Psychological Bulletin,* 1957, *54,* p. 310.

A straightforward attack on this question would determine whether the "post-ACTUAL" means on each item were significantly different. This approach would, however, neglect the possibility that the teachers in the two groups may have differed in their initial status—at the time of the pretest ratings. Such differences, even if not statistically significant, would affect the comparisons of post-ACTUAL ratings.

Analysis of covariance was used to control such initial differences. The pretest rating (pre-ACTUAL) on each item served as the control variable, the posttest rating (post-ACTUAL) as the dependent variable, and the feedback as the independent variable. For each of the 86 teachers in the experimental group and the 90 teachers in the control group, the median pretest rating given her by her pupils on each item was determined. Using those median ratings, we performed an analysis of covariance to determine the adjusted post-ACTUAL means of the median ratings. For each item, then, the *adjusted* post-ACTUAL rating of a given teacher is the median posttest rating given by her pupils after the following quantity had been subtracted: the difference between (1) the post-ACTUAL mean predicted from the group's pre-ACTUAL mean and (2) the grand post-ACTUAL mean based on all teachers.

Means for each item of the adjusted post-ACTUAL ratings are shown in Columns 2 and 3 of Table 5-5. As can be seen in the table, the means for the experimental group were closer to 1 (1 being the code for "Very much like my teacher") than were the means for the control group on 10 out of the 12 items; for four of these items, the difference between experimental and control groups was significant beyond the .05 level.

Adjusted post-ACTUAL minus pre-IDEAL. The analysis so far has not considered the direction in which the teacher's pupils might wish her to change. Is the difference between adjusted post-ACTUAL means in the direction of the influence exerted by the feedback? To answer this question, we referred to the means of the pupils' median preratings of their ideal teacher (pre-IDEAL). That is, we hypothesized that the feedback given the teachers in the experimental group concerning their pupils' pre-IDEAL ratings would exert influence on the teachers to change in that direction. The absolute difference between adjusted post-ACTUAL and pre-IDEAL would then be smaller for the experimental group. The results shown in Columns 6 and 7 of Table 5-5 bore out this prediction for 10 of the 12 items. Item A was tied, and the remaining item (J) went against the hypothesis.

Columns 6 and 7 of Table 5-5 make clear that there was ample room for influence among these 12

TABLE 5-5

MEANS OF ADJUSTING POST-ACTUAL AND PRE-IDEAL RATINGS

Item	*Adjusted post-ACTUAL mean*		*pre-IDEAL mean*		*Adjusted post-ACTUAL minus pre-IDEAL*		*Is difference between Columns 6 and 7 in hypothesized direction?*
	Exp.	*Cont.*	*Exp.*	*Cont.*	*Exp.*	*Cont.*	
(1)	*(2)*	*(3)*	*(4)*	*(5)*	*(6)*	*(7)*	*(8)*
A	2.57	2.57	2.20	2.20	.37	.37	No
B	3.46	3.61*	3.21	3.02	.25	.59	Yes
C	2.33	2.42	2.09	1.96	.24	.46	Yes
D	1.15	1.18*	1.13	1.12	.02	.06	Yes
E	2.22	2.30	1.60	1.51	.62	.79	Yes
F	4.07	4.20	3.31	3.14	.76	1.06	Yes
G	3.35	3.46	2.81	2.83	.54	.63	Yes
H	2.19	2.16	1.66	1.57	.53	.59	Yes
I	5.29	5.30	4.06	3.83	1.23	1.47	Yes
J	4.27	4.33	4.54	4.44	−.27	−.11	No
K	3.24	3.44*	2.64	2.66	.60	.78	Yes
L	2.84	2.96*	2.77	2.80	.07	.16	Yes

*Significantly different at the .05 level (one tail) from the value for the experimental group.

items. On no item did the mean adjusted post-ACTUAL rating in either group reach the mean post-IDEAL rating. (This was also true of Item J, since the "desirable" direction for this item was opposite to that of the other items.) The item on which teachers fell farthest from their pupils' ideal was Item I (Asks the pupils what they'd like to study in tomorrow's lesson); the item on which they came closest was Item D (Explains arithmetic so pupils can understand it).

It is invalid to make simple tests of the statistical significance of the combined results here (e.g., by using the binomial theorem or chi square) because each item does not constitute an independent experiment or replication; i.e., the same subjects (teachers and pupils) were involved in all items. The consistency in the direction of the results, however, does suggest that the hypothesized effect of the feedback did occur. We shall have to rely on such a judgment of consistency in this report.

While these results are difficult to assess statistically, the pattern seems clear enough. It seems apparent that the feedback booklet had an effect on the behavior of the teachers. Even so, these results do not seem strong enough to be of great practical importance. That is, the differences between the control group and the experimental group seem small. It should be remembered, however, that this experiment was primarily a test of a hypothesis, not an attempt to demonstrate the most effective strategy for influencing teacher behavior. One small booklet sent by mail constituted the entire influence exerted on the teacher. The booklet contained only twelve simple charts and a few explanatory remarks; it contained no exhortation or suggestion that the teacher do one thing or another; no explicit pressure or prestige was brought to bear. Furthermore, in most of the feedback booklets it was perfectly clear that some pupils felt the ideal teacher would have characteristics opposite to those felt to be ideal by the majority of the pupils. Such a "minority report" must have weakened markedly the influence of the feedback. This study demonstrated that teacher behavior could be changed by a brief package of information about pupils' opinions. The demonstration of such an effect, beyond all other influences acting upon the teachers, seems to us to justify the claim that the effects of pupil expectations on teachers deserve further investigation.

RESULTS ON ACCURACY OF TEACHERS' PERCEPTIONS

So far we have examined differences between our experimental and control groups in the protocols of pupils alone. Now what of the relations between the protocols of pupils and those of teachers? In our experiment, data were available on the accuracy of the teacher's perception or estimation of the typical pupil's response, as measured by its closeness to the pupils' median description of their actual teacher. It seemed reasonable to expect that the experimental group of teachers would become more accurate than the control group; simply remembering or extrapolating from the information in the feedback booklet (the pupils' pretest ratings of their teachers) should have enabled these teachers to estimate their pupils' post-ACTUAL ratings more accurately than could those in the control group.

Adjusted post-ACCURACY. One measure of accuracy can be obtained by computing the difference between the median post-ACTUAL ratings of the pupils (adjusted for pre-ACTUAL medians) and their teacher's posttest perceptions or estimates (post-PERCEPT for short) of her pupils' ratings (adjusted for the teacher's pre-PERCEPT). Taking the difference between these two variables gives us the adjusted post-ACCURACY measures shown in Table 5-6 where we see that our expectation was,

TABLE 5-6

Adjusted Post-ACCURACY: Accuracy of Teachers' Perceptions of Their Pupils' Ratings of Them Based on the Difference between Means in Adjusted Post-ACTUAL and Adjusted Post-PERCEPT

Item	*Adjusted post-ACCURACY*		*Is difference in hypothesized direction?*
	Exp.	*Cont.*	
A	.35	.44	Yes
B	1.03	1.30	Yes
C	.10	.44	Yes
D	−.25	−.42	Yes
E	.16	.18	Yes
F	.23	.69	Yes
G	.25	.22	No
H	.42	.51	Yes
I	.56	.65	Yes
J	.67	.63	No
K	.78	.58	No
L	−.20	.25	Yes

for the most part, borne out. For 9 of the 12 items the mean adjusted post-ACCURACY of the experimental group is better (i.e., shows a lower absolute difference between pupils' adjusted post-ACTUAL and teacher's adjusted post-PERCEPT) than that of the control group.

Accuracy in correlational terms. Accuracy can be measured in one form by the closeness of two averages and in another form by the size of a correlation coefficient. Accuracy of the latter kind reflects how well the relative position of the teachers' PERCEPT followed that of their pupils' ACTUAL (description of their actual teacher) on a given item. Table 5-17 shows changes in the *r*s obtained between PERCEPT and ACTUAL for the two groups on the pretest and posttest. Eight of the items showed changes from pre- to posttest that were more positive or less negative in the experimental group than those of the control group. A Wilcoxon matched-pairs test shows these changes to be significantly different in the two groups, p being less than .025. Measured in correlational terms, accuracy again seems to improve as a result of feedback. This result adds weight to the findings on accuracy in terms of nearness of averages. The findings on accuracy are

TABLE 5-7

CHANGES IN ACCURACY OF TEACHERS' PERCEPTIONS OF THEIR PUPILS' RATINGS OF THEM, BASED ON CORRELATION BETWEEN TEACHERS' PERCEPTION AND PUPILS' ACTUAL RATINGS

Item	*Change in accuracy (posttest correlation minus pretest)*		*Is Exp. minus Cont. difference in hypothesized direction?*
	Exp.	*Cont.*	
A	.21	.27	No
B	.22	−.30	Yes
C	.04	.00	Yes
D	.57	.36	Yes
E	.12	−.10	Yes
F	.09	−.01	Yes
G	−.09	−.02	No
H	−.01	−.21	Yes
I	.12	−.01	Yes
J	.07	.08	No
K	.18	.13	Yes
L	.03	.06	No

consistent with the hypothesis that giving the teacher information about pupils' opinions of her improved the accuracy of her perceptions of those opinions.

SUMMARY AND IMPLICATIONS

Can a teacher's behavior be changed by telling her how her pupils describe her behavior and that of their ideal teacher? In our experiment, some teachers (the experimental group) were given information concerning their pupils' opinions; the remaining teachers (the control group) were not given this information. A month or two later, the pupils again indicated how well the behaviors characterized the teachers. Briefly stated, our major hypothesis was that the experimental group of teachers would change its behaviors (as described by pupils) more than the control group. This hypothesis was derived from an equilibrium theory of social influence.

All in all, our results have the following theoretical and practical implications: Equilibrium theory is given support by the changes in teachers' behaviors, as described by pupils, resulting from the feedback of pupils' opinions. The feedback not only produced change in behavior; it also produced improvement in the accuracy of teachers' perceptions of their pupils' opinions.

For practical purposes, our results suggest that feedback of pupils' ratings can be used to improve teacher behavior. Whether a procedure specifically designed to maximize influence on the teacher would produce changes great enough to have educational significance, whether changes would be found if teachers' behaviors were described and measured by expert observers rather than pupils, whether the changes toward pupils' ideals are also toward educators' ideals—all these are questions for further investigation.

Finally, a couple of notes to researchers are in order. First, our instruments seemed to be highly "reactive"; that is, they focused the attention of teachers on their classroom behaviors and seemed to produce changes even in the control group (without feedback). Only powerful statistical methods enabled us to detect the effect in which we were interested. The reactivity of this kind of measurement should be kept in mind in planning; a "posttest only" group would have aided us in interpreting our results.

Second, the design of this experiment should not be confused with that of some other studies in which attitude change has been attempted through written persuasion. Our "Report on Your Pupils' Opinions" was a message from the teacher's pupils. No arguments attributed to some authority inside or outside the school were presented; in fact, the booklets contained no explicit argument or persuasion whatsoever. In no way did we reveal any opinion about whether the teacher should change her behavior, much less in what direction she should change it. Our intent was to test not the influence of written persuasion on teacher behavior, but rather the influence of opinions of the teacher's own pupils. The outcome of our feedback was left to the working of the processes described by equilibrium theory.

*A STUDY OF SOCIAL STATUS DIFFERENTIATION IN THE CLASSROOM BEHAVIOR OF NINETEEN THIRD GRADE TEACHERS**

By Arthur J. Hoehn

INTRODUCTION

A number of statements have appeared in recent literature to the effect that teachers accord better treatment to pupils of high social status than to pupils of low social status. Thus, in a well-known treatise dealing with the impact of social stratification upon education, Warner, Havighurst, and Loeb[1] say that teachers "exhibit a good deal of unconscious discrimination against lower class children." Similar statements have been made by Warner, Meeker, and Eells,[2] Havighurst,[3] Davis and Dollard,[4] Neugarten,[5] Hughes,[6] and Hollingshead.[7]

While several writers have claimed that teachers deal differently with their high than with their low status pupils, only one major study bearing upon the matter has been made. Clifton[8] selected 25 second grade classrooms from three different socio-

[1] W. L. Warner, R. J. Havighurst, and M. Loeb, *Who Shall Be Educated?* (New York: Harper & Row, Publishers, 1944).

[2] W. L. Warner, M. Meeker, and K. Eells, *Social Class in America* (Chicago: Science Research, 1949).

[3] R. J. Havighurst, "Caste and Class in a Democracy," *Childhood Education,* 1945, *22,* pp. 116-120.

[4] A. Davis and J. Dollard, *Children of Bondage* (Washington, D.C.: American Council on Education, 1940).

[5] M. N. Hughes, "When the Middle Meets the End," *Childhood Education,* 1948, *24,* pp. 226-231.

[6] B. L. Neugarten, "Social Class and Friendship among School Children," *American Journal of Sociology,* 1946, *51,* pp. 305-313.

[7] A. Hollingshead, *Elmtown's Youth* (New York: John Wiley & Sons, Inc., 1949).

[8] D. E. Clifton, *Dominative and Socially Integrative Behavior of Twenty-Five Second Grade Teachers,* Unpublished Doctoral Dissertation, University of Illinois, 1944.

*From *The Journal of Social Psychology,* 1954, *39,* pp. 269-292. Abridged. Used by permission of the author and publisher.

economic areas in Oakland, California. Using an adaptation of the Anderson-Brewer "Dominative-Socially Integrative" observation scheme,[9] she recorded teacher behavior in each classroom. She found that, on the average, teachers of the three socio-economic areas (Waterfront, Central, and Hill) showed close similarity in their classroom contacts with their pupils. However, Hill area teachers, i.e., teachers in the area of highest status level, were found to have slightly fewer conflict contacts and slightly more "highly integrative" contacts with individual pupils than did teachers in the other areas.

Because of the importance of teacher-pupil relationships from the standpoint of pupil adjustment, status discrimination in such relationships, if it exists, is especially invidious. The present study was designed to provide further information as to whether teachers favor their high status children. More specifically, the problem dealt with is whether third-grade teachers tend, either consciously or unconsciously, to have different amounts and kinds of classroom contacts with high than with low status pupils.

DEFINITION OF THE PROBLEM

The hypotheses. The hypotheses considered were as follows:

1. The amount of attention a pupil receives from the teacher varies directly with pupil social status.
2. The proportion of teacher contacts with pupils which are conflict contacts varies inversely with pupil social status.
3. The proportion of teacher contacts in which the teacher shows a high degree of respect for pupil goals varies directly with pupil social status.
4. The "mental hygiene" value of teacher contacts with pupils varies directly with pupil social status.

Each of these hypotheses was tested in a preliminary way on the basis of data from 19 third grade classrooms.

Definitions and assumptions. *Social status* is used here in the sense in which it is employed by Warner and his associates, i.e., it refers to position in the social prestige hierarchy of a community. A social class, by Warner's definition, is a group of people who are all placed by those who know them at about the same level on the social scale.[10] The social classes, so conceived, form a single hierarchy of social status strata. The terms "middle class" and "lower class" refer to the lowest two of the three major status strata in the Warner class system.

In the present study, the social status and class of a child was considered to be that of the family with which he was most closely identified, whether his family was that of his parents, grandparents, or of other persons. A "lower class child" was thus one who was identified with a lower class family or adult, and a "middle class child" one who was identified with a middle class parent or adult.

The concept of "teacher contacts" was taken directly from Anderson and Brewer.[11] In their studies of teachers' classroom personalities, they have defined a "contact" as any behavior of the teacher which is directed toward one or more of her pupils. Anderson and Brewer distinguish between an individual contact, which is a teacher contact with one pupil, and a group contact, which is a teacher contact with two or more pupils. Only individual contacts were studied in the present investigation.

The Anderson-Brewer observation scheme arranges teacher behavior along a scale of domination-integration. "Dominative contacts" are defined as contacts characterized by teacher pressure upon the pupil. In these contacts, the teacher retains partial or complete control over the child's activities. In "integrative" contacts, the teacher is trying to find the interests of the child, or is making suggestions which the child is free to accept or decline, or, in one way or another, is reacting favorably toward the child's expressed interests.

Both dominative (*D*) and integrative (*I*) contacts are subdivided into less inclusive categories. Dominative contacts are subdivided into (1) "domination with evidence of conflict," or *DC* contacts, (2) "domination with no evidence of working together," or *DN* contacts, and (3) "domination with evidence of working together," or *DT* contacts. Integrative contacts are subdivided into (1) "integration with no

[9] H. H. Anderson, J. E. Brewer and M. F. Reed, "Studies of Teachers' Classroom Personalities: III Follow-up Studies of the Effects of Dominative and Integrative Contacts on Children's Behavior," *Applied Psychological Monographs,* 1946, No. 11.

[10] W. L. Warner, M. Meeker, and K. Eells, *op. cit.,* p. 116.

[11] H. H. Anderson, J. E. Brewer, and M. F. Reed, *op. cit.*

evidence of working together," or *IN* contacts, and (2) "integration with evidence of working together," or *IT* contacts.

This classification of teacher behavior is based upon assumptions as to the kinds of contacts which are desirable and the kinds which are undesirable from the standpoint of pupil adjustment. It is assumed that dominative contacts, and particularly those marked by conflict (*DC* contacts) are of low mental hygiene value; and that integrative contacts, especially the IT contacts, are of high hygiene value. High *I/D* and *IT/DC* ratios are assumed to be indicative of teacher behavior contributing to pupil adjustment.[12]

In the present study, each aspect of teacher behavior involved in the hypotheses was equated to one or more of the Anderson-Brewer categories of teacher contacts or to one or more ratios of such contacts. Table 5-8 indicates the teacher behavior variables dealt with in the hypotheses and the Anderson-Brewer contacts or contact ratios with which they were equated.

The first hypothesis has to do with *quantity* of contacts and the index of this was simply contact frequency. The other three hypotheses are concerned with *quality* of contacts. Here the contact indices were proportions or ratios rather than simple frequencies. Proportions or ratios were used instead of raw frequencies because the effect upon pupils of any given number of contacts of a given type is probably relative to the total number of contacts or to the number of contacts of one or more other types.

[12] H. H. Anderson and J. H. Brewer, "Studies of Teachers' Classroom Personalities: II Effect of Teachers' Dominative and Socially Integrative Contacts on Children's Classroom Behavior," *Applied Psychological Monographs,* 1946, No. 8, pp. 31-32.

THE MEASURES

The measure of teachers' classroom behavior. The procedure for observing and recording teacher contacts was essentially the Anderson-Clifton simplification of the Anderson-Brewer scheme. Contacts were recorded only by major category, i.e., only as *DC, DN, DI, IN,* or *IT,* and by the pupil involved. The investigator tabulated five hours of observations in each of the 19 third grade classrooms included in the study. In most classrooms, all of the observations were completed over a period of two school days. Because differences in teacher contacts with pupils of different status levels are likely to be most evident in individual contacts, no group contacts were recorded.

The reliability of the investigators' recording of teacher-pupil contacts was determined by comparing the observational tallies of the investigator with those of a second trained observer. Data on observer consistency were collected in two classrooms. The

TABLE 5-8

For Each Hypothesis, the Teacher Behavior Variable Involved and the Anderson-Brewer Contacts or Contact Ratios Equated to This Variable

Hypothesis	*Teacher behavior variable*	*Anderson-Brewer contact index*
1.	Amount of attention given child	Number of teacher contacts involving child
2.	Tendency to have conflict with pupils	Proportion of contacts which are in the category "Domination with conflict"
3.	Tendency to show high degree of respect for pupil goals	Proportion of contacts which are in the category "Integration with evidence of working together"
4.	"Mental hygiene value" of teacher contacts with pupil	Ratio of "Integrative" to "Dominative" contacts; also, ratio of "Integrative with evidence of working together" to "Dominative with conflict"

indices used were "percentages of agreement."[13] Limitations of space do not permit presentation of all the obtained percentages of agreement, but it can be said that, in general, the observer consistency was much the same as that obtained by other researchers who have used the Anderson-Brewer scheme of tallying teacher behavior. For example, when all contacts were considered to be in agreement which were recorded in the same major category of teacher behavior (*DC, DN,* etc.), the percentages of agreement generally exceeded 90 for each category.

A question related to reliability is that of whether teachers display consistency from one time to another in the way they deal with their pupils. If teachers do show a fairly high degree of consistency, then one may assume that the results obtained for individual teachers are not strongly determined by the choice of some dates of observation rather than others. Data are available which tend to show that teachers are fairly consistent in their contacts with individual pupils. Eleven teachers were taken at random from among the 19 in the present study. For each of the teachers the "dominative with conflict" (*DC*), "dominative" (*D*), "integrative with evidence of working together" (*IT*), "integrative" (*I*), and total (*S*) contacts with each pupil were determined for the first half of the observation period and then for the second half. For each classroom and for each of the five categories, the "first-half contacts" were correlated with the "second-half contacts." The resulting correlations are shown in Table 5-9. Systematic errors in tallying observations would tend to increase these coefficients. On the other hand, variable errors would serve to attenuate them. While the data are not such that one can determine the relative importance of these effects, most of the obtained correlations seem to point to an appreciable degree of consistency in the way teachers deal with individual pupils.[14]

[13] Percentages of agreement are computed by dividing twice the number of tallies in agreement by the sum of the tallies for the two observers. A more complete description as well as an evaluation of the method are found in a paper by R. E. Arrington, "Interrelations in Behavior of Young Children," *Child Development Monographs,* 1932, No. 8.

[14] The reader will note that except for total contacts, the analysis which ensues is concerned with ratios of contacts rather than with raw frequencies. However, evidence of consistency of raw frequencies does provide some evidence of consistency in the ratios as well.

TABLE 5-9

FOR EACH OF ELEVEN CLASSROOMS, CORRELATIONS OF TEACHER CONTACTS DURING THE FIRST 150 MINUTES OF OBSERVATION WITH CONTACTS DURING SECOND 150 MINUTES OF OBSERVATION

		Contact category				
Class-room (1)	*Number of pupils* (2)	*Conflict contacts (DC)* (3)	*Dominative contacts (D)* (4)	*Highly integrative contacts (IT)* (5)	*Integrative contacts (I)* (6)	*All contacts (S)* (7)
1	20	.64	.48	.29	.29	.92
2	22	.69	.55	.43	.49	.71
4	35	.78	.65	.54	.50	.69
7	31	.38	.43	.50	.58	.47
8	34	.42	.32	.37	.26	.35
9	24	.62	.61	.67	.60	.70
10	31	.65	.60	.66	.69	.80
11	32	.56	.32	.28	.38	.54
14	28	.69	.19	.29	.32	.29
16	23	.45	.46	.40	.45	.58
18	23	.37	.29	.66	.59	.60
Median *r*		.62	.46	.43	.49	.60

The measure of pupils' social status. The Index of Status Characteristics, a scale constructed and validated by Warner, Meeker, and Eells,[15] was used in this study to measure pupils' status positions. The scale, as used here, has three items: (*a*) Area Lived In, (*b*) House type, and (*c*) Occupation. Each item consists of a seven-point rating scale. In obtaining an *ISC* for a given individual, one obtains the three ratings, multiplies each rating by its appropriate weight, and sums the weighted ratings. Weights for the items in the scale as used here are 5, 4, and 3, respectively. Scores have a maximum range of 12 to 84. A low *ISC* represents high status; a high *ISC*, low status.

The reliabilities of the House Type and Occupation Items were estimated by comparison of independent ratings of the writer and a second person. The second rater studied the house-typing scale and practiced with the writer over a period of several days. The aim was not simply to reach agreement with each other but also agreement with the intent of Warner and his co-workers. After the period of practice, 85 houses were rated independently by both raters. In 73 (or 85 per cent) of the cases, the ratings assigned were the same; in the other 12 cases, the independent ratings differed by one point on the seven-point scale.

Measures of achievement. In the analysis of the data, consideration was given to the influence of the achievement factor upon the results. To make this possible, achievement measures were obtained for almost all of the pupils. For 17 of the classrooms, these achievement measures are scores on the reading subtest of the Progressive Achievement Test.[16] For the other two classrooms, they are scores on the reading subtest of the Metropolitan Achievement Test.[17]

Reading scores, rather than total achievement scores, were used largely because they were much more readily obtainable than total scores. Also, for the nine classrooms of pupils for whom both total and reading achievement scores on the Progressive Achievement Test were available, high correlations were found between the two scores. These correlations, calculated separately for each classroom, ranged from .77 to .98 and had a median of .89.

COLLECTION OF DATA

The data used in the study were collected in two central Illinois communities having populations of between 50,000 and 75,000.

Selection of these communities was largely incidental to the location of classrooms with teachers and pupils having some specified characteristics. The criteria used in the selection of classrooms were that any classroom included should: (*a*) be a third grade classroom with at least 25 pupils, (*b*) consist entirely or almost entirely of children of the white race and of Old American stock, (*c*) include pupils varying considerably in social status, (*d*) receive all instruction, with the possible exceptions of music and drawing, from the regular teacher, and (*e*) have a female teacher of "middle class" status.

The study was made in classrooms of a single grade level in order to control roughly the pupil age factor. The third grade level, rather than some other, was chosen chiefly for a practical reason, namely that in exploratory observations using the Anderson-Brewer scheme, the writer found that the frequency of teacher contacts in third grade classrooms is quite high, yet not so high as to prevent recording of contacts with acceptable reliability. Teachers' individual contacts in second grade classes seemed more difficult to record with accuracy. At grade levels above the third, individual contacts could be recorded with considerable accuracy, but their frequency was relatively low. The third grade level appeared to be the best for obtaining the highest frequency of tallies consistent with the requirements of observer reliability.

Nineteen classrooms were selected for observation. Hereafter these classrooms will be referred to by numbers ranging from 1 to 19. Classrooms 1 through 13 are in one community; classrooms designated by the numbers 14-19 are in the second community. Each of the 19 teachers is referred to by the same number assigned the classroom in which she is teaching.

All of the teachers whose classroom behavior was studied are women and, in the Warner system, were clearly of middle class status and expressed middle

---

[15] Warner, Meeker, and Eells, *op. cit.*

[16] E. W. Tiegs and W. Clark, *Progressive Achievement Tests —Primary Battery* (Los Angeles: California Test Bureau, 1943).

[17] G. Hildreth, *Metropolitan Achievement Tests, Primary II Battery* (Yonkers, New York: World Book, 1946).

class values. In respect to age, the teachers ranged from 21 to 64 years. The mean age was 37. Fourteen of the teachers had four or nearly four years of college training. None of the teachers had less than one year of teaching experience, and one teacher had taught in the elementary school for over 43 years. For the 19 teachers the average number of years of experience was almost 15 years. Eleven of the teachers were married, eight unmarried.

Order of collection. After the classrooms had been selected by methods described above, the following data were collected in this order: (*a*) observation data; (*b*) sex, age, and achievement test data for the pupils; (*c*) social status of pupils; (*d*) personal data on teachers.

The observation data were collected before pupil status data as a means of preventing bias in the interpretation and tallying of teacher contacts. Otherwise, the order of data collection was largely decided on the basis of convenience.

Collection of observation data. In most classrooms, the five hours of observation were completed in two days, but, in a few cases, the investigator found it necessary to return a third or even a fourth day. Each teacher was given some, but not complete, information regarding the study. Knowledge of the exact nature of the variable under observation was withheld in order to avoid the possibility that it would cause the teacher to alter her usual pattern of classroom behavior. The teacher was told that the observer wished to see the classroom under normal conditions and would not be interested in special demonstrations of teaching methods or special pupil activities. Assurances were given that the data would not be used in any way that might affect the teacher's personal or professional status or which might have an unfavorable effect upon the pupils.

An attempt was made to equate the observation samples from the various classrooms in respect to the times of the school day at which they were obtained. Also, in each classroom the investigator tried to include observations of teacher behavior in each area of subject matter (reading, arithmetic, etc.).

Collection of status data. Occupational data obtained from school records were checked against information given by teachers and principals and against entries in city directories. Each house in which one or more of the pupils were living was located and rated. Finally, "Area Lived In" ratings were secured by methods already described.

ANALYSIS AND RESULTS

Method of testing the four hypotheses under the assumption of the Warner class system. The first step in the analysis of the data was to divide the pupils in each classroom into lower and middle class groups. Then, for each of the four hypotheses, the appropriate teacher contact indices were computed separately for middle and for lower class pupils in each classroom. In testing a given hypothesis, the procedure was as follows: (*a*) For each classroom, the magnitude of the appropriate contact index computed for contacts with middle class pupils was compared with the magnitude of the corresponding index for contacts with lower class pupils. (*b*) Each of the nineteen differences, so obtained, was designated a positive or a negative difference depending upon whether or not it was in the direction expected on the basis of the hypothesis. (*c*) Reference was made to tables of the binomial distribution to determine whether the obtained number of positive differences would occur less than five per cent of the time by chance alone. Where this was the case, the hypothesis being tested was considered to be supported by the data.

The procedure just described may be clarified by illustrating its application in testing Hypothesis 1. This hypothesis is that in third-grade classrooms, the amount of attention a pupil receives from the teacher varies directly with pupil social status. Assuming the Warner status structure, this hypothesis may be translated as follows: Third-grade teachers tend to give more attention to their middle class pupils than to their lower class pupils. In analyzing the data bearing upon this hypothesis, the mean frequency of all contacts involving middle class pupils and the mean frequency of all contacts involving lower class pupils were computed separately for each classroom in which observations were made. It was found that in only 10 classrooms did the mean frequency of contacts involving middle class pupils exceed that for lower class pupils. Tables of the binomial distribution indicate that such a result would occur 50 per cent of the time in samples of 19 cases when the probability of success in any one case is one-half. Thus the data could not be said to support the hypothesis that middle class pupils tend to receive more attention than lower class pupils.

A second test of Hypothesis 1 has been made using *median* frequencies of contacts.

Hypothesis 1 has to do with *quantity* of contacts. Hypotheses 2, 3, and 4, on the other hand, involve consideration of the quality of contacts. The first step in testing these hypotheses was to compute the *DC/S, IT/S, I/D* and *IT/DC* ratios for teachers' contacts with middle and lower class pupils. From this point, the procedure for testing Hypotheses 2, 3, and 4 was the same as that used to test Hypothesis 1.

Hereafter, an analysis wherein teacher contacts involving pupils of a given classroom status group are summed in the computation of contact indices will be referred to as a Type *A* analysis. An analysis by medians will be referred to as a Type *B* analysis. Neither type of analysis determines the degree of teachers' differentiation between pupils of different social class levels. They aim simply to ascertain the direction of differentiation.

Method of testing the four hypotheses under the assumption of continuity of status. To test the hypotheses under the assumption of continuity of status, product-moment correlations between teacher behavior indices and pupil social status are computed separately for each classroom. For each hypothesis, the number of classrooms in which the direction of the correlation is that predicted on the basis of the hypothesis is then determined. The null hypothesis in each case is that there is no tendency for the particular teacher behavior variable to vary with pupil social status. Under the null hypotheses, the chances are even that, for a particular classroom, the obtained direction of correlation will be that expected on the basis of the hypothesis being tested. If, under the null hypothesis, the obtained number of correlations in the predicted direction would occur less than five per cent of the time by chance alone, the null hypothesis is rejected. In this event, the data are said to support the hypothesis being tested.

The analyses assuming continuity of status and involving the computation of product-moment correlation coefficients will hereafter be referred to as analyses of Type *C*.

Statistical results for the four hypotheses. A summary of the principal statistical results bearing upon the four hypotheses is presented in Tables 5-10 and 5-11. These tables show for each teacher con-

TABLE 5-10

FOR EACH TEACHER CONTACT INDEX: (1) THE NUMBER OF CLASSROOMS IN WHICH THE TEACHER WAS FOUND TO FAVOR HIGH STATUS OVER LOW STATUS PUPILS, AND (2) THE SIGNIFICANCE LEVEL OF EACH SUCH RESULT

	Total number of classrooms—19					
Teacher contact index	*Analysis A**		*Analysis B***		*Analysis C****	
	No. of classrooms	*Significance level*	*No. of classrooms*	*Significance level*	*No. of classrooms*	*Significance level*
(1)	*(2)*	*(3)*	*(4)*	*(5)*	*(6)*	*(7)*
Frequencies of contacts	10	50%	11	32%	9	68%
DC/S Ratio	12	18	11	32	12	18
IT/S Ratio	14	3	14	3	13	8
I/D Ratio	16	0.2	14	3	15	1
IT/DC Ratio	15	1	13	8	—	—

*Type *A* analyses are those in which teacher contacts involving pupils of a given classroom status group were summed in the computation of the teacher contact indices. Status is considered to be discontinuous.

**Type *B* analyses are the analyses by medians. This type of analysis involved (*a*) the computation of separate teacher contact indices for each pupil in each classroom, and (*b*) the determination of the medians of these indices for each status group in each classroom. Status is considered to be discontinuous.

***Analyses of Type *C* are based upon correlations of pupil status and the teacher contact indices. Status is here assumed to be continuous.

tact index and for each type of analysis, the number of classrooms in which the teacher was found to "favor" high status pupils over low status pupils. It also shows the significance level of each such result. In addition to results of analyses in which both boys and girls were involved, findings are presented which are based upon analyses made separately for boys and for girls.

The first rows of Tables 5-10 and 5-11 show that none of the results involving frequencies of contacts are significantly different from those expected on the basis of chance. This indicates that regardless of whether or not the sex factor be controlled, the data are consistent with the null hypothesis that there is no relationship between "pupil social status" and "number of contacts received by the pupil."

In the second rows of Tables 5-10 and 5-11 are the statistical results which provide a basis for testing Hypothesis 2. The analyses involving both boys and girls fail to support this hypothesis that teachers tend more strongly toward conflict with low than with high status pupils. However, more weight probably should be given to the results in which the sex factor is controlled than to those in which it is not controlled, since effects of extraneous variables prevent one from generalizing results beyond the specific classrooms studied. When the sex factor is controlled, the findings lend support to Hypothesis 2. Both analyses for only girls yield results which are significant at the 5 per cent level. The Analysis *A* result for boys is statistically significant, while that using median ratios is not. The discrepancy between the two analyses for boys may be due to a tendency for teachers to have a relatively large number of conflict contacts with a few lower class boys, but no unusual number with most boys of this status level.

The evidence for the hypotheses that teachers tend to show respect less often for the goals of lower class than of middle class children appears strong when only the analyses for both boys and girls are considered. Results of these analyses are given in the third rows of Tables 5-10 and 5-11. Both the Type *A* and Type *B* analyses given results which are significant at the 3 per cent level, while the Type *C* (correlational) analysis yields results significant at the 8 per cent level. When the sex factor is controlled, results are less conclusive. Neither of the analyses for boys, and only one of the two analyses for girls, gives significant results.

In Rows 4 and 5 of Tables 5-10 and 5-11 are shown the findings which provide a basis for testing the hypothesis (Hypothesis 4) that the "mental hygiene value" of teacher behavior toward high status pupils is higher than that of teacher behavior

TABLE 5-11

For Each Teacher Contact Index: (1) the Number of Classrooms in which the Teacher Was Found to Favor High Status Boys or Girls Over Low Status Boys or Girls, and (2) the Significance Level of Each Such Result. Total Number of Classrooms: for Boys, 19; for Girls, 18

	Boys				*Girls*			
	*Analysis A**		*Analysis B***		*Analysis A**		*Analysis B***	
Teacher contact index (1)	*No. of Class-rooms* (2)	*Significance level* (3)	*No. of Class-rooms* (4)	*Significance level* (5)	*No. of Class-rooms* (6)	*Significance level* (7)	*No. of Class-rooms* (8)	*Significance level* (9)
Frequencies of contacts	9	68%	10	50%	11	24%	11	24%
DC/S Ratio	14	3	11	32	13	5	13	5
IT/S Ratio	13	8	13	8	12	12	15	0.4
I/D Ratio	12	18	14	3	11	24	12	12
IT/DC Ratio	14	3	14	3	12	12	13	5

*Type *A* analyses are those in which teacher contacts involving pupils of a given classroom status group were summed in the computation of the teacher contact indices. Status is considered to be discontinuous.

** Type *B* analyses are the analyses by medians. This type of analysis involved (*a*) the computation of separate teacher contact indices for each pupil in each classroom, and (*b*) the determination of the medians of these indices for each status group in each classroom. Status is considered to be discontinuous.

toward low status pupils. Actually the hypotheses (2 and 3) tested by means of *DC/S* and *IT/S* ratios have implications with respect to whether the behavior of teachers toward high status pupils is more desirable from the standpoint of mental hygiene than the teacher behavior toward pupils of lower social rating. However, the indices advocated by Anderson and Brewer for determining the "mental hygiene value" of teacher contacts with a pupil or a group of pupils are the *I/D* and *IT/DC* ratios. The *I/D* ratio is the ratio of all integrative contacts to all dominative contacts. The *IT/DC* ratio is the ratio of the most highly integrative contacts to the most highly dominative contacts.

Entries in Rows 4 and 5 of Table 5-10 strongly indicate that, at least in the classrooms studied, the "mental hygiene value" of teachers' contacts is higher for high than for low status pupils. With the sex factor uncontrolled, all three analyses (*A, B,* and *C*) yield statistically significant results when the criterion of mental hygiene value is *I/D* ratio. When the criterion is *IT/DC* ratio, one of the two analyses indicates statistical significance and the other closely approaches it.

When the sex factor is controlled, the results are somewhat different. For *I/D* ratios, only the analysis using medians, Analysis *B,* gives a significant result where boys are concerned; neither analysis gives significant results for girls. However, for *IT/DC* ratios, both results for boys, and one of the two for girls are statistically significant.

Although achievement has not been controlled in the preceding analysis, a study was made to determine how the above results were affected by achievement differences. This was done by partialling out achievement test scores from the correlations between social status studies and contact indices. The results of this analysis suggested these tentative hypotheses:

1. Third grade teachers' behavior is differentiated *quantitatively* on the basis of achievement, low achievers tending to receive more contacts than high achievers.
2. Third grade teachers' behavior toward pupils is *differentiated qualitatively* on the bases of achievement, high achievers being "favored" over low achievers.
3. Failure to find that teachers tend to have more contacts with high than with low status pupils is due to the tendency of the teachers to concentrate their efforts on low achievers rather than on high achievers.
4. The found qualitative differentiation of teachers' behavior on the basis of status is simply incidental to the tendency of the teachers to "favor" pupils of high achievement over pupils of low achievement.

VI

STUDENT MOTIVATION AND TEACHER CONTROL

EXPLORATIONS IN CLASSROOM MANAGEMENT*

By Jacob S. Kounin, Paul V. Gump, and James J. Ryan, III

The origins of the research to be summarized here lay in the authors' feelings of inadequacy in trying to help teachers, especially beginning ones, with problems of importance to them. Discipline is one problem frequently verbalized by teachers. Teachers' questions about "what to do when Johnny disturbs" have been shrugged off with impatience, or have been answered with slogans or "principles." Scientific research about the technology and theory of controlling misbehavior in a classroom is either lacking or inadequate.

Consequently, we turned our attention to a study of the practical problem of classroom management, from the standpoint of technology. We wanted to see whether there is not some lawfulness about discipline in classrooms or, on the other hand, whether the variety of variables involved is so great as to preclude the possibility of predicting pupils' reactions from the qualities of disciplinary techniques employed.

Since the teacher must work with groups or, at least, "aggregates" of pupils, we shifted the focus from the effects of disciplinary measures upon an individual child to that of the audience reactions, or the "ripple effects."

Specifically, how does a teacher's method of handling the misbehavior of one child (henceforth to be referred to as a *desist-technique*) influence *other* children who are audiences to the event but not themselves targets?

The factors to be discussed can be grouped into two major classifications: (1) variables operating at the time of the desist-technique (e.g., the qualities of the desist-technique, the social position of the

*From *The Journal of Teacher Education,* 1961, *12,* pp. 235-246. Abridged. Used by permission of the authors and publisher. The studies discussed in this paper have been supported by Grant M-1066 from the National Institute of Mental Health, United States Public Health Service.

target) and (2) prevailing variables (e.g., the audience-pupils' intensity of motivation to learn and their liking for the teacher).

VARIABLES OPERATING AT THE TIME OF THE DESIST-TECHNIQUE

Threatening vs. supportive desist-techniques. In a fashion characteristic of psychologists, we started with an experiment using college students (these are "captive subjects" that do not require administrative clearances and parental approvals). Four classes of students in a college of education were used as subjects. Two classes were taught by a young instructor of educational methods; two classes were taught by an older professor of psychology.

The experiment was conducted as follows:

1. At the second meeting of the class a researcher, posing as a graduate student, obtained questionnaire data on the attitudes of students regarding their instructors, the degree of seriousness of classroom misbehaviors (including "coming late to class"), and causes of racial prejudice. The student reports were anonymous.
2. The two instructors of each of the four classes began the third class period with a lecture which gave "his own evidence" that the single most important cause of racial prejudice was repressed hostility toward punitive parents that is displaced upon minority groups.
3. A male student, previously informed about the experiment, arrived late to class—toward the end of the instructor's lecture.
4. The instructor directed either a threatening or a supportive desist-technique at the late-comer. Both desist-techniques stated that coming late interfered with the instructor's presentation and should cease. The supportive desist-technique went on to offer the late-comer help in acquiring the lecture material he had missed. The threatening one stated coldly that "this cannot help but affect my evaluation of you and your grade."
5. The "graduate student" readministered his attitude questionnaire.

Two conclusions emerged from this preliminary experiment:

1. Students who are not themselves targets of a desist-technique *are* affected by it.
2. The *two methods* of handling misbehavior in a classroom *produce* statistically significant *different results.* That is, there is a degree of predictability from some dimensions of desist-techniques to some effects upon audience students.

Threatening desist-techniques, for both instructors, resulted in significantly lowered judgments of the instructors' helpfulness, likability, freedom from authoritarianism, and fairness; threatening techniques also raised ratings of the amount of classroom tension.

For the young instructor—but not for the professor—differences between the two desist-techniques produced significant changes in ratings of the instructor's competence in his subject-area and in the freedom of the students to communicate with the instructor.

Students in none of the groups changed their attitudes about the seriousness of the deviancy (coming late), and all groups shifted significantly towards the position of the instructors about the causes of racial prejudice.

It would seem, then, that differences in the effects of certain qualities of desist-techniques are more marked in some areas than in others; that the prestige of the emitter of the desist-technique makes some difference; and that some norms of classroom behavior are so well established in colleges as to be rather resistant to change by an instructor's stand on the issue. Influence attempts of instructors that are directly related to course content are not readily changed in relation to a single example of their desist-technique style.

However, another finding may well serve to limit the generalizability of the above results. Although 97 per cent of the students reported that they did *not* perceive that the event was contrived, the students who witnessed either technique were surprised that a college instructor would take time out to correct a student for coming late, even though they rated coming late as a serious misbehavior. Most of them, especially those who witnessed the threatening desist-technique, felt that the behavior was *not* typical for the instructor. There were frequent comments on a post-incident questionnaire such as: "He must have had an argument with his wife," or "He probably got caught in a traffic jam." This reaction to an unexpected behavior of an instructor,

* Discussion of the prevailing variables is omitted. Ed.

in a sense "excusing it away," may actually function to reduce the changes produced by differences in desist-techniques. From the viewpoint of research methodology and strategy these findings also point to the advisability of using teacher-style variables that are within expectations and that have some ecological prevalence.

Punishing vs. reprimanding vs. ignoring. In an experiment with eighth and ninth graders (for whom teachers' use of desist-orders is not unexpected) Ryan, Gump, and Kounin[1] investigated whether qualities of a desist-technique make any difference in audience-pupils' reactions.[2] Volunteer paid subjects were recruited from three metropolitan junior high schools during the summer months to come to a university campus for the purpose of participating in a research studying different methods of teaching. Volunteers were randomly assigned to groups of about twenty-five each where they were asked to consider themselves as being in a regular classroom.

After each group assembled it experienced the following sequence of events: the experimenter introduced the activities of the day; a female teacher (the same for each group) introduced herself to the class; the subjects filled out a questionnaire containing mostly ratings of their first impression of the teacher; the teacher taught a lesson, using slides, about Turkey; a pretrained pupil (also the same person for all groups) misbehaved (got up and sharpened a pencil while the slides were being shown); the teacher issued a desist-technique; the subjects filled out another questionnaire about the activities, the teacher, and the deviancy-event.

Three desist-techniques were used: (1) punitive and intense (walked toward him, saying "Hey you, who do you think you are?" in a firm, irritated voice, put her arm on his shoulders in a gesture of pushing him into his seat, saying, "Now sit down! If you ever do that again, I'll really make trouble for you."); (2) simple reprimand (saying in a matter-of-fact tone: "Don't do that again. Please sit down in your seat now."); and (3) ignoring (indicated awareness of the behavior, but did nothing).

The "take" of the experimental manipulation was evidenced by the existence of a significant difference between all groups in the predicted direction regarding the subjects' ratings of the teacher's meanness, anger, and degree of determination to stop the misbehavior.

Compared to the others, the punitive technique resulted in the subjects' rating the *deviancy* as "most serious," the degree of *interference* with attention to the task as "greatest," the *teacher* as "making too much of an issue" over the event, the experience "most discomforting," and the *teacher* "best able to maintain order in a class of 'tough kids.' "

The simple reprimand produced the highest ratings for teacher fairness and also resulted in the subjects' reporting their paying more attention to the lesson following the event and to the teacher being judged as best able to maintain order in "most classes."

Subjects witnessing "ignoring" as the desist-technique thought the misbehavior most likely would recur, but rated the teacher highest in her degree of liking her pupils.

There were no differences between the groups in subjects' ratings of how much the teacher knew about the subject or how well she could explain it. When equivalent effects are considered (likability, fairness, felt discomfort) it should be noted that the results of punitiveness in this experiment are quite similar to the results obtained from the threatening desist-technique in the college experiment.

Clarity, firmness, and roughness. In one study by Kounin and Gump[3] fifty observers were trained to record critical incidents in Barker and Wright's[4] specimen-record style. These were incidents in which an audience-child was aware of a teacher directing a desist-technique at another child. Twenty-six kindergarten classes were selected to represent the range of socio-economic and ethnic neighborhoods in a large city. All observations were made during the first four days of beginning kindergarten. The observers were instructed to record: (1)

[1] J. J. Ryan, P. V. Gump, and J. S. Kounin, "An Experiment on the Effect of Motivation to Learn Upon Students' Reactions to Teachers' Desist Techniques." (In preparation.)

[2] This experiment was actually started at a later time in the sequence of explorations in order to study the effects of pupil-motivation. (It will be referred to later as the "high school experiment.") We are referring to it here because it does show that qualities of the desist technique make some predictable differences in audience-pupils' reactions.

[3] J. S. Kounin and P. V. Gump, "The Ripple Effect in Discipline," *Elementary School Journal,* 1958, *62,* pp. 158-162.

[4] R. G. Barker and H. F. Wright, *Midwest and Its Children* (Evanston, Ill.: Harper & Row, Publishers, 1954), p. 532.

what the deviant and the audience-child were doing immediately before the teacher intervened, (2) the full content and manner of the desist-technique and the deviant's immediate reaction, and (3) the behavior of the audience-child during and for two minutes following the desist-technique.

When the resulting 406 incidents were analyzed, it was possible to reliably characterize both the teachers' desist-techniques and the behavior of the audience-children.

The qualities of the desist-technique were rated along dimensions of: (1) clarity (defining the deviancy and stating what to do to stop it); (2) firmness (this included items conveying an "I mean it" quality—walking closer to the deviant, or continuing to look at the deviant until he stopped); and (3) roughness (angry remarks and looks, or punishment).

The reactions of the audience-child were classified as (1) no reaction (no overt behavior which the coder could interpret as related to the desist-technique incident); (2) behavior disruption (overt signs of negative emotionality such as fear, anxiety, and restlessness or a shift away from an originally constructive direction); (3) conformance (stops a deviancy of his own or behaves even better, i.e., sitting more "correctly" himself); (4) nonconformance (engages in a misbehavior of his own); and (5) ambivalence (both conforms and misbehaves).

Statistically significant differences were obtained in the overt behavior of the audience-children as related to the desist-technique used by the teacher. Techniques of increasing "clarity" resulted in increased "conformance," but had no effect upon "behavior disruption." Techniques of increasing "roughness," on the other hand, had no effect on "conformance or nonconformance," but did increase "behavior disruption." The effects of "firmness" differed from both.

Some of the conclusions of this study are as follows:

1. What teachers *do* makes a difference. There is some lawfulness about the effects of techniques. It was not necessary to obtain personality ratings or IQ tests of the teachers as persons; it was only necessary to find out what they do and how they do it. (Whether teachers with personality factor-*x* can or cannot *do* things certain ways is another issue.)

2. There are contextual or prevailing variables that also affect how an audience-child will react to an event. Two such contextual variables stand out from the kindergarten study. One refers to the degree of familiarity the pupil has with the teacher and the situation. (Such familiarity, of course, relates to the amount of time one has spent in a particular experience. For example, there were more "no reactions" on the *last* three days than on the first day.) The other contextual variable is the audience-child's orientation at the time of the incident. Techniques high in "firmness," for example, produced increased "conformance," but *only* for audience-children who were themselves oriented toward, or interested in deviancy at the time of the event.

3. "Roughness" is not an increased degree of "firmness." In terms of their effects, it is evident that these are different dimensions.

Although it does not deal specifically with the ripple effect, we would like to summarize another study on the effects of "punitiveness" since it is closely related to the dimension of "roughness." In a study by Kounin and Gump[5] we attempted to determine the influence of teachers judged to be punitive upon children's attitudes toward misconduct. Three pairs of first-grade teachers, each pair from the same school, were *selected.* One of a pair was rated as "punitive" (anti-child, ready to threaten and inflict harm) by principals, assistant principals, the two investigators, and a supervisor of student teachers; the other member of the pair was rated as "nonpunitive." All teachers were rated as having good organization and as achieving the learning objectives for their grade. Children from these classes were interviewed individually during the third month of attendance at school. The interview consisted of the question: "What is the worst thing a child can do at school?" and, following the reply, "Why is that so bad?" The misconducts talked about were coded for content and for certain qualities. The following was found:

1. Children with teachers judged to be punitive showed more preoccupation with aggression—their misconducts were more serious, their targets suffered more harm; they more frequently cited physical assaults on others as misconduct, and their replies contained more gory—or "blood and guts"—phrases.

[5] J. S. Kounin and P. V. Gump, "The Comparative Influence of Punitive and Non-punitive Teachers upon Children's Concepts of School Misconduct," *Journal of Educational Psychology*, 1961, *52*, pp. 44-49.

2. Children with punitive-rated teachers had more conflicts and were more unsettled about misbehavior in school. They selected misconducts to talk about for which they expressed abhorrence and yet which required premeditation, or "malice aforethought."

3. The children with nonpunitive teachers gave more "reflexive justifications" as explanations for why given misconducts were bad. This was coded when a child gave no consequence for either himself or others in his explanation of why the misconduct was bad—the reason given being "because it's not nice" or "because it's bad." We suggested two interpretations for this finding: (a) that children with nonpunitive teachers have less conflicts about misconduct than have children with punitive teachers—to say "you don't do *x* because it's not nice" reflects a settled issue; and (b) a sort of naive faith and trust in the teacher is reflected by children with nonpunitive teachers—a reflexive justification for a school misconduct is like, say, "*x* is bad because teacher says so."

4. Punitiveness of teachers detracts from childrens' concern with school-unique values and results in less internalized socialization. Children with punitive teachers talked more about physical attacks on peers—misconduct by no means unique to the classroom setting. Children with nonpunitive teachers talked more about learning, achievement losses, and violations of school-unique values and rules.

Task-focus vs. appraisal-focus. Since discipline is centrally related to problems of power and influence and methods of exerting power and influence, another study was undertaken in which Alden[6] dealt with some variables pertaining to these factors. Following French,[7] she hypothesized the following bases for teacher power and influence: the coercive role (the teacher as one who can punish); the "legitimate" role (the teacher as an official leader); reward; pupils' liking for a teacher, and teacher expertness.

The base of a new teacher's power (specifically, "expertness" and "liking") was manipulated by varying the experimenter's introduction of the teacher. All classes were given a lesson in secret writing. A "high expert" was introduced as knowing all about codes and as having a high position in the military intelligence for coding and decoding secret codes; the "low expert" was introduced not as an expert but simply as a teacher who had agreed to teach the lesson. The "high liking" new teacher was introduced as being very fond of children and the "low liking" as not caring about children one way or another.

The desist-techniques used by the teacher were related to these concepts. Some desist-techniques focused upon liking and teacher approval ("I see a boy playing with some paper clips. I just don't like a boy who plays with things when he should be paying attention."). Other desist-techniques related to expertness and focused upon the task ("I see a boy playing with some paper clips. Because secret writing demands concentration, I don't see how he can learn much about it when he plays with things instead of paying attention").

Fifth graders were divided randomly into eight classes in which a new teacher taught a lesson (in a pedantic, "academic" manner) about secret writing. In this manner, both "high" and "low expert" and "high" and "low liking" teachers used both approval-focused and task-focused desist-techniques. In each group three desist-orders were directed at three children who had been trained to act the role of misbehaving pupils. In four of the groups, the desist-technique focused upon teacher liking and approval and in four groups the desist-technique focused upon the task.

One of Alden's most impressive findings was the following: in all cases, desist-techniques focusing upon the task were more effective in eliciting desirable student reactions than desist-techniques focusing upon the teacher's approval. (With the exception of scores on a test of how much was learned from the lesson, measurements of results were all based upon differences between measures given before the lesson and measures given after the lesson.) For some effects, the superiority of the task-focused desist-techniques held, regardless of whether the introduction of the teacher focused upon her expertness or her liking for children. Thus, in all groups, task-focused desist-techniques increased audience-childrens' ratings of the teachers' skill in handling children and increased their rated degree of interest in secret writing.

[6] E. Alden, *The Effects on Non-Target Classmates of the Teacher's Use of Expert Power and Liking Power in Controlling Deviant Behavior*. Unpublished Doctoral Dissertation, Wayne State University, 1959, p. 158.

[7] J. R. P. French, Jr., "A Formal Theory of Social Power," *Psychological Review*, 1956, *63*, pp. 181-195.

For some effects, the use of a task-focused desist-technique combined with the teacher's expertness to effect the pupils' reactions. Thus, when an expert teacher used a task-focused technique it increased the children's judgment of how much she liked pupils and would be inclined to reward pupils; it resulted in the pupils considering the deviancies she corrected as being more serious and feeling less inclined to misbehave themselves; and it led to a greater amount of information recalled by the pupils from the lecture itself. The influence of being introduced as having high liking for children made a significant difference on one measurement: a teacher with high liking for children *and* high expertness using task-focused desist-techniques resulted in pupils feeling more inclined toward discussing personal matters with her.

The deviant's reaction and prestige. An experiment by Gnagey[8] was directed at two questions: (1) What is the effect of the deviant's reaction to a teacher's desist-technique upon audience-pupils? (Specifically, does whether the deviant submits to or defies the teacher's desist-order make any difference on how audience-children react to the event?) (2) Does the prestige of the deviant among his classmates influence audience-pupils' reactions to a desist-order event?

In this study, four intact classes of fifth graders were shown a science film during which a male classmate "misbehaved" (saying aloud, "Hey, is this film about over?"). This deviant boy then became the target of a desist-order exerted by the teacher. This teacher, who was new to the class, directed the deviant to leave the room and report to the principal. The deviants were pre-selected on the basis of sociometric scores. (Of course, their classmates didn't know that the deviancies were part of an act.) Two male deviants had high attributed influence among their classmates and two had low influence. Two (one high-influence and one low-influence) were trained to behave in a *submissive* manner (saying, "Yes ma'am, I'm sorry," on leaving the room) and two were trained to react in a *defiant* manner (saying belligerently, "I'll leave the room, but I won't go to the principal's office. The heck with you!").

Gnagey found that the target's reaction did make a predictable difference in audience-pupils' reactions. Compared to pupils who saw the deviant defy the teacher, pupils who witnessed the deviant submit to the teacher rated the teacher as "more capable of handling kids" and as more expert in showing films; they rated the desist-technique as fairer; and they recalled more facts from the film. The magnitude of the differences between the effects of the two kinds of deviant reactions was greater for boys than for girls and was greater for boys who were audience to a high-influence deviant than boys who were audience to a low-influence deviant.

The Gnagey study also points up one reason for an audience-person to be affected by a desist-order directed at someone else, namely, some sort of linkage with the deviant. In this case it is a sociometric linkage—the linkage of an audience-pupils' motivation to identify with a same-sexed person in a high prestige position. Hence, the finding, for boys only, of a greater effect of a high-influence male's reaction than that of a low-influence male's reaction. Another sort of linkage—to the deviancy event—was illustrated by the previously mentioned kindergarten study. Here, when the audience-child was either deviant himself or was watching the deviancy, he was more likely to react to the desist-technique than if he had no such relationship to the deviancy. In both the Gnagey study and the kindergarten study, then, linkages are shown to be important: linkages to the defiant person, and linkages to the deviancy event.

[8] W. J. Gnagey, "Effects on Classmates of a Deviant Student's Power and Response to a Teacher-Exerted Control Technique," *Journal of Educational Psychology,* 1960, *51,* pp. 1-9.

HOSTILITY AND ITS MANAGEMENT IN CLASSROOM GROUPS*

By Murray Horwitz

Hostility seems hardly avoidable in any extended interaction between persons or groups. It may vary in degree from annoyance to hatred, be fleeting or enduring, be expressed directly or indirectly. Whatever its form, hostility appears among persons in diverse groups—in families, work groups, social clubs, classrooms. It also appears, frequently as a chronic condition, in relationships between groups —gangs, university departments, religious organizations, nations.

While there is no present agreement about whether frustration is a sufficient condition for the arousal of hostility,[1] there is fair agreement that frustration is a necessary condition. From an individual standpoint, frustration may be defined as an interference with a goal-response.[2] From the standpoint of one individual in relation to another, such goal-blocking may imply in addition that something is amiss in their relationship. The present paper proposes a theory about the conditions under which frustrating acts create disturbances in interpersonal relationships. In the series of experiments which is described below, hostility is examined as a function of the degree of such interpersonal disturbance. The experiments, conducted with classroom groups specially formed in the laboratory, deal in turn with (a) arousal, (b) inhibition, and (c) reduction of student hostility.

THE AROUSAL OF HOSTILITY

Interpersonal relationships can be characterized by the amount of *weight* which each person gives the other's desires. If another person frustrates us, we may under conditions which are discussed below, perceive him as giving our desires less weight than we expected. The arousal of hostility is hypothesized to be related to the discrepancy between expected and actual weight, rather than to the frustration *per se*. The theory of interpersonal weight, as illustrated by a teacher-student relationship, may be stated as follows:

1. The strength of desire: A teacher's decision whether to perform an act depends partly on the strength of his desire, D_T. Assume, similarly, that this decision depends partly on the teacher's perception of the strength of the student's desire, D_s.
2. The weight of a desire: Assume that the influence on the decision of a student's desire of given strength, D_s, also depends on the weight, W_s, which the teacher gives this desire, where weight can be assigned values ranging from zero to one. Students may receive close to zero weight from a dominating teacher, a weight of perhaps .5 from an equalitarian teacher, a weight of close to 1.0 from a submissive teacher. The same teacher will ordinarily give less weight to students' desires about his out-of-class activities than to their desires about his in-class activities. Weight thus varies with different interpersonal relationships and with different classes of desire.
3. Weighted desire: It follows from the preceding assumptions that a student's influence on the teacher's decision is a joint function of the strength, D_s, and the weight W_s, of the student's desire. Assume that the combined effect of the two factors equals their product, $W_s D_s$—or weighted desire.
4. Relation between weights: If the teacher and student have conflicting desires, the greater the weight the teacher gives the student's desire, the less the weight he gives his own desire. Assume that the weight the teacher gives his own desires, W_T, equals one minus the weight he gives the student's

[1] N. E. Miller, "The Frustration-Aggression Hypothesis," *Psychological Review*, 1941, *48*, pp. 337-342; F. Heider, "Social Perception and Phenomenal Causality," *Psychological Review*, 1944, *51*, pp. 358-374.

[2] J. Dollard, L. W. Doob, N. E. Miller, O. H. Mowrer, and R. R. Sears, *Frustration and Aggression* (New Haven: Yale University Press, 1940).

* Prepared especially for this volume. The research was supported by grants from the Office of Naval Research and the National Science Foundation. The collaboration of Dr. Morton Goldman and Dr. Francis J. Lee in all phases of the present series of studies is gratefully acknowledged.

desire ($W_T = W_s$). The weight the teacher gives his own desire may thus be close to 1.0 for a dominating teacher, around .5 for an equalitarian teacher, close to zero for a submissive teacher.

5. The teacher's decision: If the teacher and student have conflicting desires, it further follows that the teacher's decision will tend to be determined by whichever is greater from his standpoint, the student's weighted desire (W_sD_s) or his own weighted desire (W_TD_T). The teacher should therefore act in accordance with the student's desire if he perceives that the student's weighted desire exceeds his own weighted desire; the teacher should act in accordance with his own desire if he perceives that his weighted desire exceeds that of the student.

6. Expected weight: Just as weighted desires operate to determine the teacher's action, so they are assumed to determine the student's evaluation of the action. Assume that with regard to the teacher's action, the student weights his and the teacher's desires. Where it is the teacher who makes the decision, the weights he applies in deciding upon the action are called "actual weights"; the weights the student applies in evaluating the action are called "expected weights."

7. Reduction of expected weight: Suppose that the teacher frustrates the student. The occurrence of the frustrating act indicates (a) that the desires of the two parties are in conflict, (b) that the teacher perceives his weighted desire to be greater than that of the student. The student, too, may perceive the teacher's weighted desire to be greater than his own; in this case, the frustrating act implies no discrepancy between the students' expected and actual weights. However, the student may perceive his own weighted desire to be greater than the teacher's. If he believes that neither he nor the teacher has underestimated the other's strength of desire, the frustrating act implies that the teacher has reduced the student's expected weight. It follows from the preceding assumptions that the *degree* of weight reduction implied by a frustrating act is greater, the more the student perceives that his weighted desire exceeds the weighted desire of the frustrating teacher.

A reduction in expected weight has consequences beyond the frustration of a particular desire. With weight reduced, a class of our desires which would otherwise have been strong enough to influence another against performing a frustrating act, now becomes insufficiently strong to forestall the frustration. If we acquiesce in the reduction of our weight, we do not simply accept the immediate frustration, but accept a probable increase in future frustrations as well. We should therefore react strongly against any perceived reduction in expected weight and be activated to restore our actual weight to its expected level.

On this analysis, weight reduction should lead to "hostile" perceptions of the frustrating agent. His weight-reductive act, if performed in the context of an informal interpersonal relationship, should be perceived as "inconsiderate"; if performed in the context of a relationship defined by formalized rules, the weight-reductive act should be perceived as "illegitimate." Weight reduction should also lead to actions to recover the weight "usurped" by the frustrating agent. These may include aggressive actions, i.e., the use of punishments or the withholding of rewards. The following hypothesis is tested in two experiments reported below: With immediate frustration held constant, hostility varies directly with the degree to which a frustrating agent is perceived as reducing one's expected weight.

Procedure. Experiment 1.[3] *S*s were 153 volunteers from the freshman ROTC at the University of Illinois. They were informed that the study had a twofold purpose: (a) to evaluate teaching practices for the Armed Forces; (b) to compare the abilities of students in ROTC units at different universities.

*S*s were divided into 30 groups of four to six persons each, with each group set up as a miniature classroom. After being introduced to a "student teacher," *T*, actually a second experimenter, *S*s indicated their first impressions of him on an adjective check list. On the pretext of enabling *S*s "to get to know something about each other," *E* led the group in a five-minute discussion about whether they believed students should budget their study time.[4]

*S*s were then informed that they would be instructed by *T* in making a number of objects, e.g.,

[3] Additional details of the experimental procedure and results are given in F. J. Lee, *Frustration and Hostility: The Effects of Differential Reduction in Power over Decision Making*. Unpublished doctoral dissertation, Boston University, 1955.

[4] This step was introduced to maintain comparability with the experiment on inhibition of hostility, described below.

a pinwheel, a pyramid, out of paper. Rules were laid down for deciding whether or not *T* should repeat his instructions on any object. These decisions were to be made on each object and were to be determined by a procedure in which weights were assigned to the respective desires of the students, the teacher, and the Armed Forces. *S*s were led to expect a relatively "student-centered" classroom with regard to these decisions: the desires of the students and the Armed Forces' desire were each to be weighted 1, while *T*'s desire was assigned a weight of only ¼.[5]

The experimental variations hinged on the procedure used for making decisions about whether *T* should repeat his instructions. This procedure will therefore be described in greater detail. Midway on each object, each *S* indicated on a nine-point scale how strongly he desired the instructions to be repeated or not repeated. *E* collected *S*s' forms and pretended to compute *S*s' average desire, which in all treatments was announced as varying around 4.5 units in favor of "going back." The announcement was credible since the instructions were given at a rapid pace and *S*s usually did vote to repeat. *T*, on the other hand, announced his desire as varying around 4 units in favor of "going on," which was reduced to 1 unit after being weighted by ¼. The Armed Forces' desire—announced by *E* as based on evaluations of training needs allegedly obtained from the Training Command—varied according to the experimental treatment. Figure 6-1 summarizes the respective weighted desires of the three parties as presented to *S*s in the three treatments.

According to the rules, the decision about repeating was to be determined by algebraically summing the weighted desires of the three parties. In Treatment A, the group's weighted desire to "go back" (4.5) was subtracted from the sum of the teacher's weighted desire to "go on" (1.) and the Armed Forces' weighted desire to "go on" (7.5); thus the resultant in Treatment A was 4 units to *go on*. Correspondingly, the resultants of the weighted desires were 1 unit to *go back* in Treatment B, and 8 units to *go back* in Treatment C. However, in each treatment, irrespective of the legitimate decision, *T* always went *on* in line with his own expressed desire. His frustrating action implied no reduction of *S*s' expected weight in Treatment A, but some reduction in Treatment B, and greater reduction in Treatment C.

Each time *T* completed the instructions on an object, *E* requested that *S*s write notes for delivery to their classmates concerning their feelings about budgeting study time, the topic which *S*s had discussed at the beginning of the session. *S*s were seated in booths which enabled them to see *T*, but not each other. Since conversation was prohibited, the communication by notes was explained to *S*s as an attempt "to have this resemble a real classroom a little more closely." Along with writing the notes, *S*s filled out a series of incomplete sentences, which purportedly enabled *E* to assess their personalities.[6]

*S*s were taught to make five objects. At the midpoint of each object, a "decision" about repeating was made; at the end of each object, a note was exchanged and an incomplete sentence filled out. Shortly after the instructional period, *T* left the room. Measures of *S*s' performance and of their reaction to *T* were obtained. At the conclusion, the experimental deceptions were explained.[7] The total session took approximately two hours. To examine possible effects of *T*'s personal characteristics, two *T*s were employed, each instructing five groups within a given treatment.

Results. *S*s exhibited equally strong desires to "go back" in all three treatments. The strength of individual desires for repetition is given by *S*s' actual ratings during their votes. The mean number of times *S*s voted to "go back" was 3.56, the mean strength of their desire was 3.26 to "go back," with no significant difference among treatments on either measure.[8] The strength of *S*s' acceptance of the group goal for repetition was measured by a post-session question in which *S*s indicated on seven-point scales how much they wanted the group's desire followed. The mean rating was 5.36 in favor of following the group's desire, again with no significant difference among treatments. The frustrations of *S*s' goal responses, thus appears to be equiva-

[5] The weights 1: 1: ¼ used in this procedure correspond to theoretical weights of .44: .44: .12 in terms of the assumptions stated above.

[6] The note-writing and the incomplete sentences, which are described more fully below, were used to maintain comparability with a subsequent experiment, described below.

[7] Twenty-four *S*s, randomly distributed among treatments, stated that they had "caught on" to one or more of the deceptions; these *S*s, are eliminated from the analysis of results.

[8] In these results and those which follow, no differential effects were obtained for the two teachers.

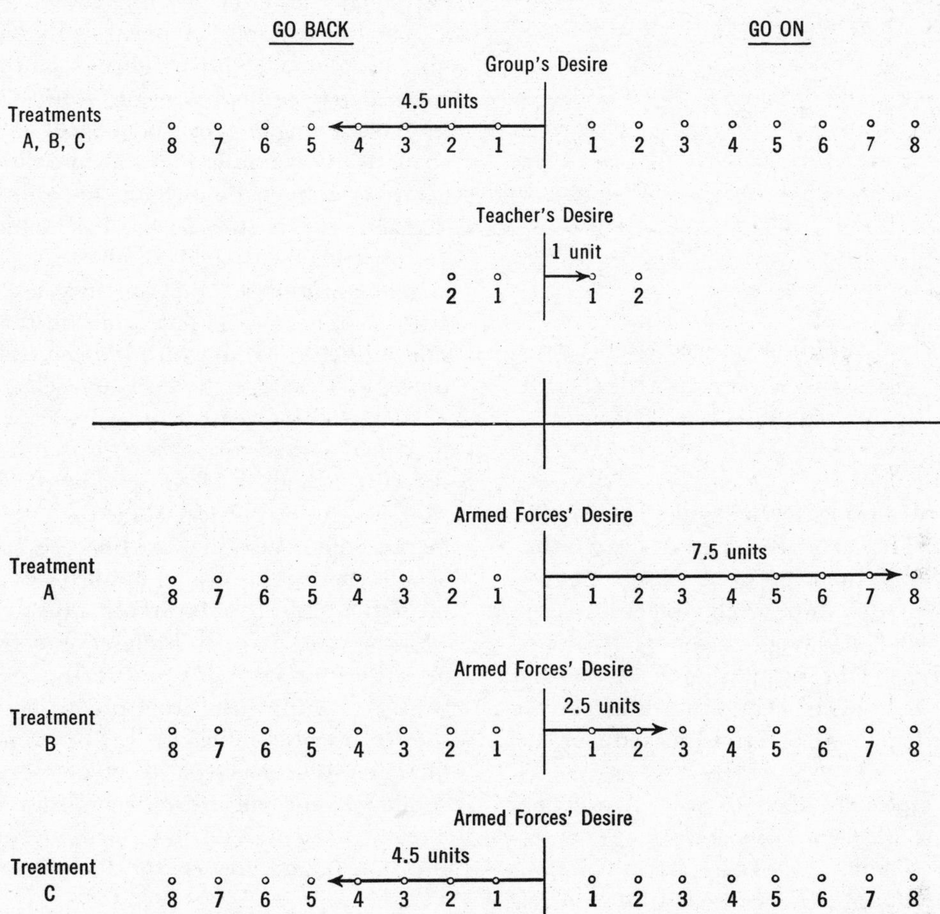

Figure 6-1. Announcements of Average Weighted Desires in Three Treatments (showing the constant averages announced for group and teacher and the varying averages announced for the Armed Forces).

lent across treatments, whether considered from the standpoint of the individual's goal or of his internalization of the group's goal for repetition.

However, *T*'s frustrating acts affected *S*s' weight in different degree among the treatments. In Treatment A, *T* acted in accordance with his assigned weight of .25. But in Treatment B, he acted as if his vote were weighted more than .50, and in Treatment C, he acted as if his vote were weighted more than 2.25. When *S*s were asked, "Considering the way the instructor behaved, how much weight did he act as if his vote had?", their mean responses differed significantly among treatments: .63 in Treatment A, 1.96 in Treatment B, 3.72 in Treatment C (Table 6-1). The data show that *T* was regarded as increasing his weight at others' expense even in Treatment A, perhaps because his rapid-fire instructions were perceived as somewhat illegitimate. In any case, the variations in *S*s' perceptions accord with the variations in *T*'s actual usurpation of weight. *S*s' perceptions, moreover, were reflected in their attributions of personal characteristics to *T*. When *S*s were asked how frequently, if at all, T would tend to build up his authority at others' expense in "real life," their mean response for Treat-

TABLE 6-1

MEAN SCORES ON PERCEIVED WEIGHT REDUCTION

	Treatments		
	A. Zero Reduction (N = 45)	*B. Medium Reduction (N = 45)*	*C. High Reduction (N = 39)*
Students' Judgment of Weight Assumed by *T**	.63	1.96	3.72
T's Misuse of Authority*	2.07	2.88	4.06

*$p < .001$.

ment A was between "never" and "sometimes" (2.07), their mean for Treatment B shifted to near "sometimes" (2.88), and their mean for Treatment C shifted further to a point between "sometimes" and "frequently" (4.06). Although *T* always frustrated *Ss*' desire to repeat the instructions, it is evident that the three treatments were effective in varying degree to which he was perceived as reducing *Ss*' weight.

Hostility is especially likely to occur in response to a frustrating act which is perceived as "intentional"[9] or as "arbitrary."[10] These are attributions about the causality of the act which appear to correspond to the perception that the act is determined by "internal" rather than "external" factors.[11] In Treatment A, *T* behaved as required by the rules; his frustrating acts should therefore be perceived as externally determined. In Treatments B and C, *T*'s acts departed from these external requirements and should more likely be perceived as internally caused. *Ss* were asked to check one of four possible reasons as to why the teacher *voted* as he did, where the item, "wants his own way," is assumed to denote the perception of internal causality. This item was checked by 11.6 per cent of *Ss* in Treatment A, 33.3 per cent in Treatment B, and 50.0 per cent in Treatment C ($p < .01$). The result is particularly noteworthy since *Ss* were informed that *T* had cast his votes at home, without advance information about the weighting procedure; moreover, *T* handed his votes to *E* in full view of *Ss*, before beginning his instructions. Thus *Ss* had no grounds for assuming that *T* had deliberately exaggerated his strength of desire in order to win the decisions. To say that *T* voted as he did because he "wanted his own way" would therefore seem to be a generalization of the causality ascribed to *T*'s frustrating acts. The data indicate that, as a function of the degree to which *T* is perceived as reducing *Ss*' expected weight, his vote itself is increasingly perceived as internally caused.

The hypothesis to be tested is that hostility varies directly with the degree to which *T* augments his own weight or reduces *Ss*' expected weight. Both before and after the teaching session, *Ss* rated *T* on three-point scales applied to a list of 35 favorable and 25 unfavorable adjectives. Each list was scored by taking the differences between the sum of ratings for favorable and for unfavorable adjectives. A drop in score from pre- to post-administration of the lists indicates that *S* has moved in the direction of less favorable ratings. As shown in Table 6-2, the mean drop in ratings was least for Treatment A (−2.72), intermediate for Treatment B (−11.13), and greatest for Treatment C (−14.42).

TABLE 6-2

MEAN SCORES ON REACTIONS TOWARD THE TEACHER

	Treatments		
	A. Zero Reduction (N = 45)	*B. Medium Reduction (N = 45)*	*C. High Reduction (N = 39)*
Pre to Post Shift[a] in Adjective Ratings*	−2.72	−11.13	−14.42
Feelings of Hostility**	2.11	2.63	3.45
Recall of Favorable Minus Unfavorable Examples of *T*'s Behavior **	+2.11	+1.29	−0.59

[a] The higher the (absolute) score, the less favorable the reaction.

*$p < .01$.

**$p < .001$.

[9] Heider, *op. cit.*

[10] N. Pastore, "The Role of Arbitrariness in the Frustration-Aggression Hypothesis," *Journal of Abnormal and Social Psychology*, 1952, *47*, pp. 728-731.

[11] J. W. Thibaut and H. W. Riecken, "Some Determinants and Consequences of the Perception of Social Causality," *Journal of Personality*, 1955, *24*, pp. 113-133.

It is conceivable that a drop in adjective ratings represents a devaluation of *T* rather than feelings of hostility, although many adjectives on the list, e.g., "arrogant," "autocratic," have a distinctly hostile flavor. However, *S*s were also asked to give direct ratings of their feelings of hostility toward *T*. As shown in Table 6-2, the mean responses on this item indicate that as a function of weight-reduction, self-ratings of hostility progressively increase from Treatment A (2.11) to Treatment B (2.63) to Treatment C (3.45).

Finally, *S*s were asked to write down examples of *T*'s behavior during the teaching session which would illustrate any one of a list of six favorable and six unfavorable adjectives. The number of unfavorable examples given by each *S* was subtracted from the number of his favorable examples. Table 6-2 shows that *S*s recalled a greater mean number of favorable than unfavorable examples in Treatment A (+2.11), that this difference was reduced in Treatment B (+1.29), and that it was reversed in Treatment C (—0.59). As a function of the reduction in their expected weight, *S*s not only rated *T* less favorably and rated themselves as more hostile, but they displayed greater selective recall of actions which they interpreted to reflect adversely upon *T*.

There is evidence that hostility toward *T* led to increased attention to his personal characteristics. During the teaching session, *T* enacted six items of behavior which were irrelevant to the content of his instructions, e.g., fumbling his papers, stating his personal preference for one of the objects, etc. Few of these standard behaviors were recalled by *S*s after the instructional period, but the mean number recalled was significantly greater ($p < .01$) in Treatments B and C (1.34, each) than in Treatment A (.83). If hostility thus engendered increased attention to *T*'s personal characteristics, one might suppose it would interfere with *S*s' attention to the task and result in poorer performance. Several measures of performance, described in detail below, were administered to *S*s following the teaching session. To our surprise, we found no difference among treatments with respect to *S*s' learning of the paper objects—nor with respect to their performance on other measures which tapped attention span and rigidity in problem-solving. This finding reappears in subsequent experiments: performance seems unaffected by variations in hostility. However, it will be seen below that performance is markedly affected by the inhibition of hostility.

It is clear from the preceding experiment that *T*'s immediate interference with *S*s' goals cannot alone explain the hostility which he evoked; but there is a possible alternative to the interpretation that hostility varies with the reduction of expected weight. In view of the treatment variations in the strength of the Armed Forces desire (Figure 6-1), *S*s could have perceived the Armed Forces as mainly responsible for the frustrating act in Treatment A, as less responsible in Treatment B, and as not at all responsible in Treatment C. As the Armed Forces are perceived to be less responsible for frustrating *S*s, *T* should be perceived to be more responsible. It can thus be maintained that the equal goal-blocking among the three treatments may have actually produced an equal amount of hostility in each treatment, but that *S*s apportioned increasing amounts of this fund of hostility to *T* as they perceived him to be increasingly responsible for the frustrating acts from Treatments A through C.[12] To decide the issue, a second experiment was run in which *T* again frustrated *S*s, but could not be said to share responsibility with a third party.

Experiment 1A. Forty ROTC cadets were again organized into small classroom groups and instructed by one of the previous teachers in making paper objects. The procedure was modified so that *S*s' desires for repeating instructions were pitted against the desires of *T* alone. Two treatments were employed. In one treatment, *S*s were led to expect a "teacher-centered" classroom in which *T*'s vote was assigned *twice* the weight of the group. The rationale given *S*s was that *T* knew better than they how instruction on any object would contribute to *S*s' ultimate learning. In the second treatment, *S*s were led to expect a "student-centered" classroom in which *T*'s vote was assigned *one-fourth* the weight of the group. The rationale was that *S*s knew better than *T* how well they were learning and how much repetition they therefor needed. In both treatments,

[12] By the same token, hostility toward the Armed Forces should be greatest in Treatment A, intermediate in Treatment B, least in Treatment C. This prediction differs from our own expectation that no treatment differences would appear in feelings about the Armed Forces, but no test could be run since *S*s' feelings about the Armed Forces were not measured.

Ss' desires were always announced as varying around eight units (on a 15-point scale) in favor of "going back" over the instructions and *T*'s desires as varying around eight units in favor of "going on." After multiplying these desires by their assigned weights, the legitimate decision always favored *T*'s desire in one treatment and always favored *Ss*' desire in the other. *T*, however, persisted in going on with his instructions in both treatments. His frustrating action implied no reduction in *Ss*' expected weight in one condition (*Zero Weight Reduction*), but considerable reduction in their expected weight in the second condition (*High Weight Reduction*).

RESULTS. When *Ss* were asked, "How much weight did the teacher act as if his vote had," their mean rating in the Zero Reduction Treatment was 1.33 (where 1 = same as assigned weight), but the mean rating in the Zero Reduction Treatment was 4.48 (where 4 = four times assigned weight). The means differ by a *t*-test beyond the .001 level.[13] When *Ss* were asked how frequently *T* would tend to build up his authority at others' expense, their mean rating in *Zero Reduction* was 1.28 (where 1 = "never"), but 3.36 in *High Reduction* (where 3 = "sometimes"), the difference being significant beyond the .01 level. Finally, when *Ss* were asked to indicate their perceptions of the causality of *T*'s voting behavior, the item, "wants his own way," was checked by 29 per cent of *Ss* in the *Zero Reduction* Treatment, but by 64 per cent of *Ss* in the *High Reduction* Treatment ($p < .05$ by the chi square test). The two treatments not only produced the intended difference in perceptions of weight reduction, but again evoked differential attributions of "internal" causality to *T*.

Hostility toward *T* was again assessed as above by before and after ratings on the adjective check list. The mean drop in favorability of ratings was −3.50 for *Zero Weight Reduction* and −14.27 for *High Weight Reduction;* these values differ beyond the .01 level. In addition, *Ss*' feelings about *T* were more directly tapped by ratings on seven-point scales of how much annoyance, if any, they felt toward the teacher. Significantly less annoyance was expressed in *Zero Weight Reduction* (2.83) than in *High Weight Reduction* (4.55), these means differing beyond the .01 level. When *Ss* were asked to recall examples of *T*'s behavior which would illustrate any of six favorable and six unfavorable adjectives, they recalled an excess of favorable to unfavorable examples in *Zero Weight Reduction* (+2.33), but an excess of unfavorable to favorable items in *High Weight Reduction* (−1.45). This difference in selective recall is significant beyond the .001 level. In the face of these data, it would be difficult to maintain that the same degree of goal-blocking engenders the same degree of hostility. Since *T* had sole responsibility for frustrating *Ss* in the present experiment, the difference in hostility between the two treatments seems to be interpretable as a function of the weight-reduction variable alone.

Measures of learning, attention span, and rigidity in problem-solving were also administered to *Ss*. As in the preceding experiment, no differences appeared between treatments—variations in hostility again appeared to be unrelated to performance.

Discussion. The preceding experiments have examined the impact of frustrating acts upon interpersonal weight. We have shown that if a frustrating act implies a reduction in expected weight, it tends to both be perceived as "internally" caused and to arouse hostility. Heider has suggested that causal attributions to a frustrating agent directly influence the arousal of hostility.[14] He states that a hostile intention on the part of a frustrating agent may be more threatening than the frustrating act, since the hostile intention may imply longer-range consequences than the temporary act. It should be noted, however, that long-range consequences are also implied by an altered relationship due to weight reduction. Weight designates the degree to which one party is responsive to the desires of the other. From this standpoint, the reduction of one's weight decreases the likelihood of reaching any present or future goal whose attainment can be influenced by another's actions. Whether because of effects upon causal attributions or upon the interpersonal relationship, it should be no surprise, therefore, that *Ss* appear to react to a reduction in expected weight as a threatening, hostility-producing event.

The present theory is that interferences with goal responses need not arouse hostility—that a person may indeed choose to be frustrated if he sufficiently

[13] Unless otherwise noted, all comparisons between pairs of treatments are based on two-tailed tests.

[14] Heider, *op. cit.*

"internalizes" the desire of the frustrating agent.[15] The present experiments cannot, however, resolve the issue of whether the occurrence of frustration is sufficient to produce hostility. It could be said that weight-reduced *S*s showed increased hostility because they were subject to a double frustration, the initial interference by *T* and the weight-reduction itself. Dollard, *et al.*, regard the strength of frustration as varying *directly* with the strength of desire of the frustrated individual.[16] If weight reduction is a second form of frustration, then strength of frustration must also be said to vary inversely with the perceived strength of desire of the frustrating agent (Experiment 1) and with his expected weight (Experiment 1A). To understand the arousal of hostility, in any case, one would need to consider interpersonal as well as individual variables.

When a teacher evokes hostility, he may swing to a "soft" approach, which avoids frustrating students, or resign himself to being "hard" if he judges that the frustrations are unavoidable. The present findings suggest a third alternative. The teacher would be well-advised to inquire whether he is perceived as reducing the student's expected weight. He might then be led to the effort to be "fair," i.e., to ensure that students perceive his frustrating acts as legitimate. Supporting this view are the findings of a number of educational studies which show that "fairness" is ranked high among the traits of well-liked teachers.[17]

With respect to achieving legitimacy, there is no clear advantage in "democratic" versus "authoritarian" classroom leadership.[18] Authoritarian leaders are as well esteemed by members who expect low weight as are democratic leaders by members who expect equal weight.[19] An authoritarian teacher runs a greater risk than a democratic teacher of being perceived as weight-reductive and of arousing hostility if students expect more than negligible weight for themselves. On the other hand, the weight-expectations of students can be changed, as we saw in Experiment 1A. If students come to accord great weight to an authoritarian teacher, he can legitimately frustrate a greater range of student desires than can a democratic teacher; the authoritarian teacher would then run lesser risk than the democratic teacher that a given frustration will generate hostility. Moreover, any inconsistency by an authoritarian teacher will tend to be in the direction of increasing the students' weight, and such weight-enhancing inconsistency tends to be favorably evaluated.[20] Inconsistency by a democratic teacher will more often be in the direction of decreasing the student's expected weight, and will evoke hostility. From this standpoint, the burden of consistent leadership rests more heavily upon a democratic than an authoritarian teacher.

A teacher may believe that his frustrating act is legitimate. But it need not be so perceived by students if (a) the teacher underestimates the strength of the student's opposing desire, (b) the students underestimate the strength of the teacher's desire, or (c) either underestimates the weight expected by the other. Frustrations are probably unavoidable in interpersonal relationships; for it is hardly likely that one person's actions will always provide immediate, unobstructed gratification for the other's desires. With so many points at which the occurrence of frustration can disturb a weight relationship, hostility should recur even between persons with irreproachable intentions.

THE INHIBITION OF HOSTILITY

If hostility does arise, how can its potentially destructive effects be controlled? Among the modes of control which have been considered are prohibiting hostile actions but encouraging verbali-

[15] M. Horwitz, "The Recall of Interrupted Group Tasks: An Experimental Study of Individual Motivation in Relation to Group Goals," in D. Cartwright and A. Zander (Eds.), *Group Dynamics: Research and Theory* (Evanston, Ill.: Harper & Row, Publishers, 1953), pp. 361-386.

[16] Dollard, *et al., op. cit.*

[17] A. T. Jersild, "Characteristics of Teachers Who Are 'Liked Best' and 'Disliked Most,'" *Journal of Experimental Education,* 1941, *9,* pp. 139-151.

[18] R. Lippitt, "An Experimental Study of the Effects of Democratic and Authoritarian Group Atmospheres," *University of Iowa Studies in Child Welfare,* 1940, *16,* No. 3, pp. 43-195.

[19] U. G. Foa, "Relation of Worker's Expectation to Satisfaction with Supervisor," *Personnel Psychology,* 1957, *10,* pp. 162-168; M. Horwitz, "Managing Hostility in the Laboratory and the Refinery," *An Action Research Program for Organization Improvement* (Ann Arbor, Mich.: Foundation for Research on Human Behavior, 1960), pp. 49-65.

[20] Horwitz, "Managing Hostility . . . ," *op. cit.*

zation,[21] punishing both action and verbalization,[22] additionally punishing hostile thoughts by inducing guilt.[23] All such methods of discipline are similar in that they block the hostile impulse from activating some psychological function, such as acting, communicating, or thinking. They differ in the range of functions to which the inhibition applies. Barker, *et al.*, have demonstrated that when action toward one goal is inhibited, performance on other activities deteriorates.[24] Their theory implies that deterioration should be greater, the greater the range of inhibition. The experiment which follows was designed to test the hypothesis that, as long as an instigation to hostility persists, performance deteriorates as a direct function of the range of inhibition of hostility.

Procedure.[25] Again recruited from freshmen ROTC classes, 171 *S*s were instructed as in Treatment C of Experiment 1. In this treatment, which aroused a high level of hostility, *T* illegitimately persisted in going on with his instructions in opposition to the desires of both *S*s and the Armed Forces. Four treatments, designated *Action, Catharsis, Suppression,* and *Repression,* respectively, were designed to vary the range of inhibition of *S*s' hostility (Figure 6-2).

In Treatment I, *Action,* the experimental manipulations were intended to facilitate *S*s' acting, communicating, and thinking hostilely with respect to *T*'s illegitimate behavior. In Treatment II, *Catharsis,* forces were induced against acting, but not against communicating or thinking. In Treatment III, *Suppression,* forces were induced against acting and communicating, but no effort was made to influence *S*s' thinking. Finally in Treatment IV, *Repression,* forces were induced against acting, communicating, and thinking. In all treatments, *T* persisted in his illegitimate actions. The successive treatments differed only in that each progressively extended the range of *S*s' inhibition of their hostility.

The manipulations employed in each treatment depended on three devices: (a) a group discussion at the beginning of each session, (b) fictitious classmate notes delivered to *S*s after instructions in making each object, (c) a fictitious personality diagnosis of each S reported to him during the session. Each of these devices was used to build particular social standards about the expression of hostility, with implied rewards for compliance and punishments for deviation.

TREATMENT I. ACTION. a) The group discussion conducted for five minutes before the instructional period, was introduced as a means of helping *S*s to get better acquainted with each other. *E* stated that as the supervisor of the student teacher, he wanted to consider any of *S*s' suggestions about how *T*'s teaching could be improved. *S*s were asked to

[21] Dorothy Baruch, *New Ways in Discipline* (New York: Whittlesey House, 1949).

[22] R. R. Sears, E. E. Maccoby, and H. Levin, *Patterns of Child Rearing* (Evanston, Ill.: Harper & Row, Publishers, 1957).

[23] O. H. Mowrer, "Changing Conceptions of the Unconscious," *Journal of Nervous and Mental Disorders,* 1959, *129,* pp. 222-234.

[24] R. G. Barker, T. Dembo, and K. Lewin, "Frustration and Regression: An Experiment with Young Children," *Studies in Topological and Vector Psychology II, University of Iowa Studies in Child Welfare,* 1941, *18,* No. 1.

[25] Additional details of the experimental procedure and results are given in M. Goldman, *Alternative Classroom Standards Concerning Management of Hostility and Effects on Student Learning.* Unpublished doctoral dissertation, University of Illinois, 1955.

FUNCTIONS INHIBITED

Treatments		*Acting*	*Communicating*	*Thinking*	*Range of Inhibition*
I	Action				0
II	Catharsis	X[a]			1
III	Suppression	X	X		2
IV	Repression	X	X	X	3

[a] "X" denotes the existence of forces to inhibit the particular psychological function.

Figure 6-2. Treatment Variations in Range of Inhibition of Hostility

discuss the topic: "If the student teacher's methods can be improved, should students make suggestions about this to *E*?" Acknowledging that *S*s were starting the discussion "cold," *E* provided each *S* with a different typewritten statement of "fact," which was slanted to show the advantage of students' taking steps to correct deficiencies in teaching. To insure that each *S*'s fact would color his discussion, *S*s were requested to repeat the statements of the facts provided them "in their own words" during the discussion, although *S*s were assured that it was desirable to "make up their own minds." A secret poll was taken at the end of the discussion, and *S*s were informed that the group was very similar in outlook, the majority believing that students "definitely should" take corrective action.

b) Each *S* wrote a note for delivery to one of his classmates after each of the five objects and in turn received notes which he believed came "from a different person each time." The classmate notes contained space for free comments, preceded by a scale on which *S*s indicated how strongly they felt about whether or not to "take steps to have the student teacher improve his teaching methods in the second half of the session." In the present treatment only, *S*s also sent counterparts of their classmate notes to *E*. *S*s were led to believe that during a mid-session recess, *E* would read these notes and solicit suggestions about what might be done to improve *T*'s teaching. The notes which *S*s received from their classmates were fictitious ones and conveyed the impression that all others in the group strongly favored *E*'s correcting the teacher's illegitimate actions; the notes urged *S*s to join in developing a plan of action for influencing *E* during the "break."

c) *S*s also filled out a series of five incomplete sentences along with their classmate notes. The incomplete sentences were described as a personality test of each *S*'s willingness to take action to remedy undesirable situations. After the third sentence, *E* delivered a private communication to each *S* which stated that the test results showed him to be somewhat unwilling to take action and which advised him "to try to improve." As a bit of additional pressure, *S*s were told that the test results would be publicly posted at the end of the experiment, so that each "could compare himself with others."

TREATMENT II. CATHARSIS. The three preceding manipulations were modified in this treatment to inhibit hostile action but not hostile communication or thinking. a) The topic for group discussion was whether a student who disliked an instructor's behavior should talk freely about this to other students or should control his feelings. The "facts" provided *S*s and the group "vote" strongly favored free expression of feelings. b) The classmate notes required *S*s to check a scale on their feelings of liking or disliking the teacher. The fictitious notes —by means of both ratings and free comments— conveyed the impression that all others in the group disliked the teacher. c) The incomplete sentences test was described as measuring *S*s' tendencies "to hold back" and "get tied up with" their feelings. Each *S* was informed that he did not express his feelings freely enough and was advised to improve.

TREATMENT III. SUPPRESSION. Here *S*s were blocked from hostile action and communication, but no effort was made to inhibit hostile thinking. a) The group discussion and "facts" concerned an issue which was irrelevant to *S*s' reactions to *T*. The topic was whether students should budget time "to allow for a balance between studies and extracurricular activities." b) The classmate notes required *S*s to rate their attitudes about budgeting time and allowed for free comments on this question. c) The incomplete sentences purported to measure *S*s' tendencies to "live from day to day" and "avoid long range planning"; *E*'s communication exhorted them to try to improve.

TREATMENT IV. REPRESSION. This treatment was designed to extend the range of inhibition to hostile thinking as well as hostile action and communication. a) As in Treatment II, *Catharsis,* the group discussed the topic of whether students should freely talk to each other about their dislike of a teacher's behavior. However, in *Repression,* the "facts" given to *S*s and the announced group vote strongly favored students "controlling their feelings." b) *S*s again indicated on their classmate notes how much they liked or disliked *T*. The ratings on the fictitious notes which *S*s received, as well as the free comments, were designed to show *S*s that all others in the group *liked* the teacher. As in the Asch manipulation,[26] *S*s received information from

[26] S. E. Asch, "Effects of Group Pressure upon the Modification and Distortion of Judgments," in G. E. Swanson, T. M. Newcomb, and E. L. Hartley (Eds.), *Readings in Social Psychology* (2nd ed.; New York: Holt, Rinehart & Winston, Inc., 1952), pp. 2-11.

the group which belied their own judgments, although the judgments in the present case were not about physical reality but about Ss' own feelings. c) The incomplete sentences test was described as measuring Ss' tendency to have "unpleasant thoughts" about people in authority and to be overly "rebellious." *E* transmitted the diagnosis that each *S* tended to be rebellious, not in sufficient control of his feelings, and advised improvement.

Eight groups of four to six Ss each were run in each of the four treatments. Following the instructional period, measures of the effectiveness of the experimental inductions[27] and of Ss' performance were obtained. At the time of administration of these measures, Ss were not aware the teaching session was completed, but believed they had arrived at the mid-session "break."

Results. In the present experiment, environmental pressures were used in an attempt to vary internal, inhibitory processes. These processes resemble personality defenses which are usually regarded as relatively stable and not easily altered characteristics of the person. We shall therefore consider the effectiveness of the manipulations in some detail.

Table 6-3 presents data concerning the effects of the treatments on Ss' hostile "thinking." The pre-to-post shifts in adjective ratings of *T* differ significantly among treatments ($p < .001$). In particular, the drop in favorability for *Repression* (—5.00) is significantly less by *t*-tests than in any other treatment ($p < .001$). With respect to differences between Ss' recall of favorable and unfavorable examples of *T*'s behavior, the mean differences varied significantly among treatments ($p < .001$), in the same pattern found for the adjectives (Table 6-3). Only in the *Repression* Treatment does recall of favorable examples exceed recall of unfavorable ones (+1.44), differing by *t*-tests beyond the .001 level from all other treatments. We assume that Ss' responses in the post-session questionnaire would be only slightly influenced, if at all, by awareness that the questionnaire might be processed by *E*. On this assumption, the data of Table 6-3 suggest that the *Repression* Treatment succeeded in generating forces which inhibited the emergence of hostile content into Ss' private thoughts.

[27] Twenty-five Ss, randomly distributed among treatments, stated that they had "caught on" to one or more of the experimental deceptions; these Ss are eliminated from the analysis which follows.

TABLE 6-3

MEAN RESPONSES RELATING TO HOSTILE "THINKING"

	Treatments			
	I *Action* ($N = 35$)	*II* *Catharsis* ($N = 35$)	*III* *Suppression* ($N = 37$)	*IV* *Repression* ($N = 39$)
Pre to Post Shift in Adjective Ratings*	—18.31	—32.23	—16.95	—5.00
Recall of Favorable minus Unfavorable Examples of *T*'s Behavior*	—1.20	—3.15	—.37	+1.44

*$p < .001$.

While the level of hostile thinking in *Repression* is similar to the *Zero Weight-Reduction* conditions of Experiments 1 and 1A, above, the levels in *Action* and *Suppression* (Table 6-3) are similar to that in the *High Weight-Reduction* conditions of these earlier experiments. Only in *Catharsis* do Ss exhibit a marked rise in hostile thinking (Table 6-3). By *t*-tests, the drop in favorability of their adjective ratings of *T* is significantly greater ($p < .001$) in *Catharsis* (—32.23) than in any other treatment; the recall of favorable minus unfavorable examples of *T*'s behavior is significantly less ($p < .001$) in *Catharsis* (—3.15) than in any other treatment. Thus *Catharsis* appears to stimulate rather than reduce hostile thinking, a finding which corresponds with the data of Sears, *et al.*[28]

An overall assessment of the effectiveness of the four treatments in inducing differential inhibition of hostility can be obtained from the free comments which Ss wrote in their classmate notes. On this criterion, the *Action Treatment* appears least successful of all. Only 19 of the 35 Ss in this treatment wrote at least one action-oriented note, which suggests the operation of strong built-in restraints against action in our sample of Ss. *Catharsis* was completely successful; none of the 35 Ss wrote an action-oriented comment and all wrote at least two unfavorable free comments. *Suppression* also succeeded; none of the 39 Ss wrote a single action-oriented or unfavorable comment. *Repression* was more successful than anticipated, with 31 of 37 Ss

[28] Sears, Maccoby, and Levin, *op. cit.*

writing at least one *favorable* free comment about the weight-reductive teacher, a type of response which appeared in no other treatment. To summarize: 16 of the 35 Ss in *Action* were over-inhibited, as evidenced by their failure to write an action-oriented note; all Ss in *Catharsis* and *Suppression* evidenced the degree of inhibition appropriate to their treatments; 6 of the 37 Ss in *Repression* were under-inhibited, as evidenced by their failure to write a favorable note about *T*.[29] In considering how inhibition affects performance, we shall distinguish below between those Ss who did or did not give evidence of the degree of inhibition which their particular treatment was designed to induce.

Three different types of performance were measured: retention of learning, attention span, and rigidity in problem solving.

Retention of Learning. During the post session, Ss were asked to remake the paper objects without instruction. Ss in the four treatments showed no difference in ability to make the objects

TABLE 6-4

Performance under Four Conditions of Inhibition[a]

	Treatments			
	I Action	II Catharsis	III Suppression	IV Repression
	(N = 19)	(N = 35)	(N = 39)	(N = 31)
Mean loss in retention*	.235	.308	.421	.485
	(N = 19)	(N = 35)	(N = 39)	(N = 31)
Mean attention span**	33.00	32.08	26.41	25.48
	(N = 13)	(N = 31)	(N = 28)	(N = 26)
Percentage of Ss not breaking set***,[b]	7.7%	9.7%	25.0%	38.5%

*$p < .01$.
**$p < .08$, computed by means of Incomplete Beta Function. See C. J. Burke, *Psychological Bulletin*, 1951, *48*, pp. 392-397.
***$p < .05$.
[a] Excluding Ss who failed to evince the degree of inhibition which their treatment was designed to induce. See text.
[b] Excluding Ss for whom set was not established during training trials. See text.

[29] Two independent raters obtained 97 per cent agreement in classifying the two categories of Ss in *Action* and 89 per cent agreement in classifying the two categories of Ss in *Repression*.

during the instructional period. Table 6-4 shows that half-an-hour later, however, retention of learning differed significantly ($p < .01$) among the four conditions for those Ss who gave evidence of the degree of inhibition intended for their treatments.[30] As measured by the proportion of initially correct folds which were forgotten at the time of testing, the loss in retention was least in *Action* (.235), next in *Catharsis* (.308), next in *Suppression* (.421), and greatest in *Repression* (.485). In agreement with the hypothesis, retention progressively worsens as the range of inhibition increases.

According to this hypothesis, the 16 over-inhibited Ss in *Action* who did not write action-oriented notes should show greater forgetting than the 19 Ss who did. The mean loss in retention was .362 for the more inhibited Ss, as compared with .235 for the less inhibited Ss ($p = .05$, one tail).[31] Similarly, we should expect greater deterioration for the 31 Ss in *Repression* who denied their feelings by writing favorable notes about *T* than for the 6 Ss who did not write favorable notes. As compared with a mean loss in retention of .485 for the more inhibited Ss, the loss was only .161 for the less inhibited ones ($p < .01$, one tail). Both within Treatments I and II and across all four treatments, the evidence is clear that increasing inhibition adversely affects retention of learning.

Attention span. After *T* completed his teaching, but before he was dismissed, *E* asked his assistance in reading aloud a series of numbers, which Ss were to write down in reverse order. The series was constructed so that each successive pair of numbers increased in length by one digit.[32] Each *S* was scored by the number of digits he correctly recalled up to the point at which he missed two numbers of the same length. The means for digit span differ near-significantly among treatments ($p < .08$) and fall in the expected order (Table 6-4).[33] Digit span was greatest in *Action* (33.00), next in *Catharsis* (32.08), next in *Suppression* (26.31), least in *Re-*

[30] The means for the total sample of Ss—which are in the same order—differ at approximately the .05 level.

[31] Forgetting progressively diminished for Ss who wrote 0, 1, 2, or 3 action-oriented notes, respectively (the means being .362, .292, .200, .166).

[32] D. Wechsler, *The Measurement of Adult Intelligence* (2nd ed.; Baltimore: Williams and Wilkins, 1943).

[33] The means for the total sample of Ss are in the same order and differ beyond the .05 level, probably because of the increased N.

pression (25.48). The digit-backwards test requires *Ss* to attend to, maintain immediate memory for, and reorganize increasing amounts of information. As range of inhibition increased, *Ss*' ability to perform a task of this degree of complexity diminished.

PROBLEM-SOLVING RIGIDITY. *Ss* were instructed in a rote method of finding a hidden word embedded in a group of apparently scrambled letters. The rote solution—skipping even-numbered letters and combining odd-numbered ones—was practiced for five trials. On trials 6 through 10, the problem could be solved by directly apprehending a whole word formed in letters 2, 3, 4, and 5. To achieve this direct solution, which moreover was the only one possible on trial 8, *Ss* had to break their set for the rote solution within the time allotted for a trial. Table 6-4 shows the percentages of *Ss* within treatments who did not break the set in any trial from six through ten. Since an *S* cannot be said to break a set if he fails to establish one, the table omits *Ss* who failed to use the rote method (and therefore failed the tasks) on trials four or five. By chi square, the four treatments differ significantly in the relative frequencies of *Ss* who did or did not break the set ($p < .05$). The percentages of *Ss* who did not break the set are in the expected order, being least in *Action* (7.7%), next in *Catharsis* (9.7%), next in *Suppression* (25.0%), and greatest in *Repression* (38.5%).[34]

The tasks presented in Table 6-4 can be regarded as tapping relatively independent[35] aspects of psychological functioning: retention of learned material, "attention span," "rigidity" in problem solving. The four treatments show that increasing the range of inhibition of hostility produces increasingly adverse effects upon each of these aspects of performance. If pairs of treatments are compared, Treatments I and II always differ significantly from Treatments III and IV, although the differences between I and II or between III and IV are not significant.[36] We are inclined to interpret these relationships as signifying that given increments in the range of inhibition have unequal effects upon disruption of performance. As compared with zero inhibition, the inhibition of action alone has a relatively small effect, the inhibition of action and communication has a relatively great effect, which is only slightly increased by adding the inhibition of thinking.

Discussion. The preceding experiment suggests that the hostility which is produced by weight reduction operates as a motivational system. The theory underlying the frustration-regression hypothesis is that if motivational tension remains unreduced, it will tend to lower the level of organization of the person and lead to a decrement in performance.[37] A property of any motivational system is that it activates a variety of psychological functions.[38] The present finding that performance deteriorates as a function of the number of these functions which are inhibited supports the view that hostility operates as a tension system which has not been reduced.

In Experiments 1 and 1A, above, different levels of hostility were aroused, but the pressures to suppress hostility were equal among treatments.[39] It might be thought that with range of inhibition thus held constant, *Ss* should generate a greater degree of inhibition where they suppress high rather than low hostility—yet no differences in performance appeared. By contrast, performance was systematically affected in the present experiment where the instigation to hostility was held constant, but the range of inhibition was varied. Apparently, the range of inhibition contributes more to disruption of performance than does degree of inhibition. It may be that the frustration-regression hypothesis should be modified to state that regression is a function of the range, rather than the degree, of inhibition of a motivational system.

If students are encouraged to act in accordance with their hostility, the coordinated work of the

[34] For the total sample of *Ss*, *Action* is out of the expected order and the difference among treatments is not significant.

[35] Eight correlations were run between pairs of the three tasks within the four treatments—four correlations were infeasible because of small numbers. Of the eight correlations, only one was significant, a biserial r of .55 ($p < .05$) between retention and problem solving in Treatment IV. Three of the seven remaining correlations had negative and four had positive signs; none was as high as .20.

[36] The probability that the predicted order for Treatments I *versus* II *and* for Treatments II *versus* IV would occur by chance on three independent tests is .016.

[37] Barker, Dembo, and Lewin, *op. cit.*

[38] M. Horwitz, "Psychological Needs as a Function of Social Environments," in L. D. White (Ed.), *The State of the Social Sciences* (Chicago: University of Chicago Press, 1956), pp. 162-183.

[39] The inhibitory pressures in these experiments were identical with those in the present Suppression Treatment.

classroom may suffer. Teachers must therefore seek to prevent certain types of hostile actions. From the standpoint of minimizing the effects of such discipline upon students' capacity to learn, the present findings seem to support Baruch's view that discipline should be confined to preventing hostile acts and should be coupled with encouragement to verbalize hostile feelings.[40] It should not be expected, however, that verbal cartharsis will diminish hostile thinking so long as the conditions for hostility arousal persist, as shown in the present data and in the data of Sears, *et al.*[41] But in any event, the findings suggest that if teachers desire to encourage an optimal level of student functioning, they should be less concerned with such evidences of hostility than with evidences of its inhibition.

THE REDUCTION OF HOSTILITY

Given the adverse effects of inhibition, one is led to inquire how hostility can be reduced rather than inhibited. If hostility is aroused by a loss in expected weight, it follows that hostility should be reduced to the degree that weight is restored.

The hypothesis that hostility will be reduced by restoring weight can be tested by comparing the reactions of students who do or do not succeed in correcting a weight-reductive teacher. There is an interesting intermediate situation where the change in the teacher's behavior is mediated by a third party, e.g., a parent or principal. In this case, even though the frustrating teacher is induced to act in accordance with the students' desires, he should be perceived as only partially restoring their weight. For the weight the teacher now accords the students should appear conditional on the influence an outside agent chooses to exert. If this assumption is correct, then the level of hostility in such situations of "mediated change" should remain higher than in situations of "direct change," but be lower than in "no change." These expectations, based on the hypothesis that reduction of hostility varies directly with restoration of expected weight, are tested in the experiment which follows.

[40] Baruch, *op. cit.* The prescription is not as simple as it may sound. Communication of feelings can itself constitute a hostile act which will disrupt classroom activities, e.g., one student's engaging in hostile teasing of another.

[41] Sears, Maccoby, and Levin, *op. cit.*

Method. In Treatment I, *Action,* described above, *S*s addressed a series of five notes to *E* concerning steps "to improve" the teacher, which they expected *E* to read during a later recess. Treatment I corresponds to a situation of "no change" or *Zero Weight-Restoration,* since hostility toward the teacher was measured before the expected recess arrived.

The *Partial Weight-Restoration Treatment* was identical with Treatment I through the first three objects. After the third object, *E* read *S*s' notes, announced that "practically all" *S*s were complaining about *T*'s not repeating his instructions, and advised *T* to change. *T* nodded his assent. On the fourth and fifth objects, *T* indicated that he still desired to go on, but now complied with the vote and repeated the instructions. In this situation of "mediated change," *T*'s illegitimate behavior was changed through *E*'s intervention.

The *Full Weight-Restoration Treatment* was designed to enable *S*s to change *T* directly. In this condition, *S*s sent notes to *T* rather than *E*. *T* read the notes after the third object, announced that "practically all" *S*s were complaining about his not repeating, and acknowledged that he might have been "stubborn." *T* again indicated that he desired to go on during the fourth and fifth objects, but complied with the vote and repeated the instructions. In this situation of "direct change," *T*'s illegitimate behavior was changed in direct response to *S*s' influence.

The *Partial* and *Full Restoration* treatments were run following the administration of Treatment I, using the same teacher and experimenter, and drawing on *S*s from the original pool of volunteers. Although it was necessary that the teacher repeat some of his instructions in the two new treatments, the two-hour experimental period could not be extended. For this reason it was decided to decrease the number of objects on which *T* acted illegitimately. The decision that *T* perform three illegitimate acts was based on an analysis within Treatment I of the ratings of how strongly *S*s favored taking steps to correct the teacher. These ratings rose rapidly from classmate notes one to three, but appeared to level off asymptotically from notes three to five. We interpret these data as indicating that three consecutive weight-reductive acts by *T* give *S*s about as much evidence as five weight-reductive acts that their weight has been reduced. To the degree that this interpretation is correct, the three treatments can be taken to show the respective effects of *Zero, Partial,* and *Full-Weight-Restoration* upon hostility reduction.

Results. Table 6-5 presents data which show that the three treatments were effective in inducing differential perceptions of *T*'s actual weight.

TABLE 6-5

MEAN SCORES ON PERCEPTIONS OF THE TEACHER'S ACTUAL WEIGHT

	Treatments		
	Zero Restoration (N = 35)	*Partial Restoration (N = 11)*	*Full Restoration (N = 14)*
Student's Judgment of Weight Assumed by *T***	3.37	3.20	2.05
T's Misuse of Authority*	4.10	3.18	2.85

* $p < .01$.
** $p < .025$.

After the teaching session, *S*s were asked how much weight *T* acted as if his vote had. *S*s' mean responses were in the expected order and differed significantly ($p < .01$) among treatments. *T* was perceived to give greatest weight to his own vote in *Zero Restoration* (3.37), next in *Partial Restoration* (3.20), least in *Full Restoration* (2.05). Similar results were obtained when *S*s were asked to generalize about *T*'s probable behavior in other situations. In estimating the frequency with which *T* would tend to build up his authority at other's expense "in real life," *S*s' mean responses were again in the expected order and again differed significantly among treatments ($p < .025$). The mean was greatest in *Zero Restoration* (4.10, where 4 = "frequently"), next in *Partial Restoration* (3.18), and least in *Full Restoration* (2.85, where 3 = "sometimes"). We have assumed that the perceived degree of weight reduction approaches an asymptote after *T*'s third weight-reductive act. On this assumption, the treatment variations, which followed *T*'s third act, were successful in varying *S*s' perceptions that their weight had been restored.

Two measures were used to assess *S*s' hostility: the before- and after-shifts in adjective ratings of *T* and self-ratings of annoyance with him (Table 6-6).

TABLE 6-6

MEAN SCORES ON REACTIONS TOWARD THE TEACHER

	Treatments		
	Zero Restoration (N = 35)	*Partial Restoration (N = 11)*	*Full Restoration (N=14)*
Mean shift in pre-post impressions**	−18.31	−5.09	+7.07
Mean annoyance*	4.65	3.50	3.29

* $p < .05$
** $p < .001$

The mean shifts in adjective ratings differ significantly ($p < .001$) among treatments and are in the expected order. The relatively great shift toward unfavorable ratings in *Zero Restoration* (−18.31) was markedly reduced in *Partial Restoration* (−5.09) and was reversed in *Full Restoration* (+7.07).

The treatment means for *S*s' ratings of annoyance with *T* differ beyond the .05 level and are again in the expected order. *S*s rated themselves as most annoyed with *T* in *Zero Restoration* (4.65), as less annoyed in *Partial Restoration* (3.50), and as least annoyed in *Full Restoration* (3.29). Both measures reveal a progressive decrease in hostility as a function of increasing restoration of *S*s' actual weight.

We have cited evidence for the assumption that perceived weight-reduction by *T* is as great after three consecutive weight-reductive acts as after five such acts. If this assumption is incorrect, *Zero Restoration* could not properly be compared with the other two treatments. There is no question, however, about the comparability of *Partial* and *Full Restoration*. Comparing these treatments by two-tailed *t*-tests, *S*s judged *T* to have assumed significantly ($p < .02$) greater weight for his vote in *Partial* than in *Full Restoration* (Table 6-5). The treatment difference is not significant for the less direct question which asked *Ss* to generalize about *T*'s probable misuse of authority in real life, although this difference is in the predicted direction (Table 6-5). With regard to hostility, the adjective ratings of *T* are significantly ($p < .02$) less favorable in *Partial Restoration* than in *Full Restoration* (Table 6-6). Self-ratings of *Ss*' annoyance with *T* do not differ significantly between treatments, although these, too, are in the expected direction (Table 6-6).[42] The differential impact of *Partial* and *Full Restoration* upon *Ss*' judgments of *T*'s actual weight and upon their adjective ratings of *T* is particularly noteworthy in view of the small numbers in these treatments. These data support the hypothesis that weight is more greatly restored and hostility more greatly reduced if a weight-reductive person is changed by direct action rather than by a third party.[43]

Discussion. The foregoing results give further support to the view that hostility operates as a motivational system; if a discrepancy between expected and actual weight generates motivational tension, the correction of this "deficiency" state appears to reduce the tension.[44] In the management of hostility, the process of reducing a hostile impulse should be distinguished from the process of controlling it. As long as the instigation to hostility remains unchanged, such activities as planning action or engaging in verbal catharsis appear to have no hostility-reducing effect, indeed catharsis tends to increase hostile "thinking." Controlling hostility entails some form of intrapersonal inhibition; reducing hostility entails a changed perception of—or an actual change in—one's external environment.

According to the present theory, a significant property of any frustrating act is its effect upon the reduction of expected weight. It is possible that a frustration can be removed without restoring expected weight. In the preceding experiment, frustrations were removed by two different methods, each of which had different value for weight restoration. Although the initial frustrations were equally removed by either method, hostility appeared to persist to the degree that expected weight was not fully restored. It should not be surprising, therefore, that conditions will be found where a teacher conscientiously strives to rectify his frustration of students, yet finds no abatement in their hostility, much less gratitude for his effort.

It also follows from the present theory that weight can be restored and hostility reduced without removing the frustration. Thus, a teacher may be led to frustrate students on the basis of a strong desire which, if known to the students, would legitimize the frustrating act. The students may regard the act as weight-reductive, however, because they perceive it to be based on a relatively weak desire, e.g., a mere whim. If the teacher could correct their misperception, he might restore the students' expected weight, even though he continues his frustrating act. Just as one can vary weight-reduction while holding frustration constant, so can one vary weight-restoration with frustration held constant.

Since restoring weight will usually depend on some change in the external environment, the organizational characteristics of a given classroom may limit the possibilities of reducing hostility. Hostility should be only partially reducible where the classroom is so organized that students are obliged to rely on some outside authority to effect change; it should be more completely reducible where students can effect change directly. Other organizational forms are possible which also have differential value for weight restoration, e.g., students acting through appointed versus elected representatives.[45] To the extent that we learn how to conduct classrooms to facilitate the restoration of weight, hostility could be managed by methods which aim at its reduction rather than its inhibition.

CONCLUSION

There is experimental evidence that a person is motivated not only by his own goals and avoidances, but by the goals and avoidances of others as well.[46]

[42] The annoyance item has a retrospective slant: "Do you feel any annoyance toward the student teacher for anything he has done up to this point?" If this question drew *Ss* attention to how they had felt about *T's* earlier illegitimacy, it could have masked a possible treatment difference in *Ss' present* feelings about *T*.

[43] No differences for digit span appeared among the three treatments nor for retention of learning between *Partial* and *Full Restoration*. Variations in level of hostility again seem to be without effect upon performance.

[44] Horwitz, "Psychological Needs . . . ," *op. cit.*

[45] A. Dispenzieri, *The Role of Institutional Control in the Arousal of Liking and Hostility*. Unpublished doctoral dissertation, New York University, 1961.

[46] Horwitz, "The Recall of Interrupted . . . ," *op. cit.*

In this sense, the person's psychological identity might be said to extend beyond his skin to include other individuals and groups. The construct, "weight," expresses the *degree* to which the person responds to his own or to others' desires, i.e., to his own or to others' goals and avoidances. By means of this construct, one can maintain the distinction between altruism and egoism without abandoning the assumption that behavior is determined by rewards and punishments: In altruistic behavior, the rewards and punishments received by another are given relatively great weight; in egoistic behavior they are given relatively little weight. More generally, the weight construct entails the view that the psychological "person" need not be coterminous with the biological "individual," that there can be varying degrees of interdependence between the two, just as between the person and other individuals.

These assumptions underlie the present view that to understand the nature of a frustrating act it is necessary to examine its interpersonal components. As we balance off our individual desire to avoid a frustrating act and the desire of the frustrating agent to perform the act, our decision need not always oppose, but may sometimes favor the performance of the act. Thus our judgments of the weight and desire of the frustrating agent are essential components in the evaluation of his frustrating acts.

In the first part of this paper, two experiments were reported which support the hypothesis that the arousal of hostility is a function of the impact of a frustrating act upon interpersonal weight. Hostility was found to vary directly with the degree to which the frustrating act is perceived as reducing one's expected weight. The difficulties of avoiding weight reduction give grounds for supposing that social interaction will more or less continually generate conditions which will arouse hostility. In the second part, variations in group conditions were found to produce surprisingly strong effects upon the intrapersonal control of hostility. As the range of inhibition of hostility increased, individual performance progressively worsened. In the last part, we examined the conditions for reducing hostility. Two methods of changing a frustrating agent were found to have different value for weight restoration and for hostility reduction. The present series of experiments indicates that the social environment can be systematically varied to influence the entire course of a hostile impulse—its initial arousal, subsequent inhibition, and final reduction.

*RELIEVING ANXIETY IN CLASSROOM EXAMINATIONS**

By W. J. McKeachie, Donald Pollie, and Joseph Speisman

The concept of anxiety has been one of the most widely used concepts in recent psychological theory. In this paper we will use anxiety to mean the state of an individual in a threatening situation from which he cannot immediately escape. In an earlier paper[1] the senior author suggested some of the ways in which student anxiety may be mobilized by the classroom situation and its possible effects upon his performance. This paper reports a series of investigations concerned with student performance on objective-type classroom achievement examinations. Our basic assumption in these investigations was that such a high degree of anxiety is mobilized by classroom tests that the students' performance is adversely affected.

Basically our theory was this: Most students begin a test with some anxiety as a result of their uncertainty about the outcome of the test and their high degree of motivation for achieving a "good" grade in the course. As they progress through the test they inevitably encounter some questions that are too difficult or ambiguous for them to answer. Each such item adds to the student's anxiety.

[1] W. J. McKeachie, "Anxiety in the College Classroom," *Journal of Educational Research*, 1951, *45*, pp. 153-160.

* From *Journal of Abnormal and Social Psychology*, 1955, *50*, pp. 93-98. Used by permission of the authors and publisher.

As he attacks the succeeding items either the anxiety, or the Zeigarnik effect aroused by the items which he has failed to pass, interferes with his performance, or in Maier's [2] terms, his behavior becomes frustration-instigated, rather than motivated problem-solving behavior.

If the effects of failing items could be diminished in some way, test performance should be improved.

EXPERIMENT I

Our first experiment was based on the theory that if students could "blow off steam" about items that cause them difficulty, performance on succeeding items would be improved. Permitting students to write comments about difficult or ambiguous items might act to discharge feelings or to give the student more closure on the item.

Thus, our hypothesis was: Students who are encouraged to write comments about test items on their answer sheets will make higher test scores than students who have no opportunity to make comments.

Procedure. The tests upon which the experiments were performed were the regular classroom examinations in our general psychology course. They consisted of multiple-choice questions to which students responded by checking the appropriate letter on a separate answer sheet. They were given during the regular class period, and with few exceptions students completed the test in less than the class hour. Those who wished it were given additional time. In this experiment, half of the answer sheets were of the usual form, while the other half contained a blank line beside each place for responding. The instructions for the latter, or experimental group, contained these words: "Feel free to make any comments about the items in the space provided."

Results. The results of the experiment confirmed our hypothesis. Students who used the answer sheets with spaces to comment (even though many made no comments) made significantly higher scores on the test than those who used conventional answer sheets (see Table 6-7). Note that this experiment did not directly test our theory about discharge of anxiety, but merely indicated that an opportunity to comment was beneficial.

TABLE 6-7

EFFECTS OF DIFFERING TYPES OF ANSWER SHEETS UPON TEXT SCORES

Answer Sheet	*N*	*Mean*	*SD*
Usual type	83	29.65	3.9
With space for comments	83	31.09	3.6

NOTE: Difference significant at .01 level.

Discussion. The results of Experiment I were gratifying; yet in view of the many experiments in which different teaching methods failed to produce differences in objective test scores, our results seemed too good to be true. Consequently we asked ourselves a number of questions:

1. Would we get the same results if we repeated the experiment? The obvious way to find out was to repeat the experiment. We did this three times, obtaining results comparable to those of Experiment I.
2. Did the mere appearance of the answer sheet somehow influence scores on the test? To answer this question, Experiment I was repeated with the control group using answer sheets which were identical to those used by the experimental group except that instead of the instructions, "Feel free to comment . . ." their answer sheet contained the instructions, "Do not mark in this space." Again the group with instructions, "Feel free . . ." made significantly higher scores.

EXPERIMENT II

Purpose. If anxiety interferes with test performance, increasing student anxiety should decrease test scores. This was the hypothesis which governed Experiment II.

Procedure. The procedure used in Experiment II was the same as that in Experiment I except that some of the students were told that the test to be given would count as part of the course grade and

[2] N. R. F. Maier, *Frustration* (New York: McGraw-Hill Book Co., Inc., 1949).

some were told that this would be a practice test which would not count on their grades. Both groups had been warned several days in advance of the test that a test would be given, but the information that this was to be only a practice test was given to one group in the examination period. Both types of answer sheets used in Experiment I were used in both groups.

Results. While the effect of the differences between the two types of answer sheets was again significant, our hypothesis (for which we had planned to use a one-tailed test of significance) was not confirmed. The group which thought the test counted toward the course grade did not make lower scores (see Table 6-8).

TABLE 6-8

EFFECT OF DIFFERING SETS TOWARD TEST

Set	*Answer Sheet*	*N*	*Mean*	*SD*
Counts for grade	Space for comments	94	20.1	3.7
	Usual type	131	18.4	4.1
Just for practice	Space for comments	69	19.3	3.4
	Usual type	34	17.5	2.8

Discussion. To attempt to explain negative results is a fascinating but dangerous pastime. One explanation was that the students' experiences with tests had generally been so anxiety ridden that our different sets were not enough to neutralize the effects of the many cues for anxiety present when the student actually took the test. Another was that the announcement that the test was "just for practice" may have so reduced motivation that performance was less. This explanation is congruent with findings that people with high need for achievement do not perform up to capacity in non-achievement situations.[3]

EXPERIMENT III

Purpose. In our early experiments we had been so amazed that the experiment worked that we had not attempted further conceptualization of the way it worked. We thought that allowing students to comment reduced their anxiety, but we had never measured anxiety, and our one attempt to manipulate anxiety had failed to produce differences in behavior. Thus we were eager to learn more of the way in which permitting students to write comments about questions improved their test scores. We had four ideas:

1. When students write a comment about a test item, they must think further about that item. In thus reorganizing their thoughts about the item, they are more likely to be able to select the correct alternative.
2. In commenting about the item the student can explain the reasons for choosing the alternative, and even though this may not make the instructor mark the item right, he will see that the student has some knowledge. Thus the student does not have as great a feeling of failure and may develop a greater sense of closure about the item. This will reduce interference with later items.
3. In commenting on an item, the student can vent his emotions. Since emotions may interfere with problem solving, this release of emotional tension will permit a more rational approach to subsequent items.
4. The fact that the student is allowed to comment changes his perception of the test. He is less likely to feel that the test is intended to be punitive. He is more apt to perceive the instructor as trying to facilitate his success. Thus his anxiety about the test is reduced and whether or not he writes comments, he will be able to perform more rationally.

Our next experiment was designed to test these ideas. Specifically our hypotheses were:

1. Students' performances on a test will be improved if they are permitted to write their feelings about test items, but are not permitted to write explanations, as compared with students who have no opportunity to write comments.
2. Students' performances on a test will be improved if they are permitted to write explanations of their answers, but are not permitted to write their feelings, as compared with students who have no opportunity to write comments.
3. Giving students the opportunity to write comments affects their scores on items succeeding the item which is commented on rather than on the item upon which comments were made.

[3] D. C. McClelland *et al., The Achievement Motive* (New York: Appleton-Century-Crofts, Inc., 1953).

Procedures. Our procedures were much the same as in previous experiments except that we now had two experimental groups. The instructions on their answer sheets read as follows:

Group 1: "In the space provided please state your feelings, only, concerning the question. Do not explain your answer. Your comments may consist of anything whatever you feel about the question —its fairness, clarity, importance, triviality, etc. Your comments will be of aid to us in evaluating your test. Remember you may say whatever you feel."

Group 2: "In the space provided please state your explanations, only, of how you arrived at your particular answer. Do this only in those cases where a solution of the answer entails the application of a principle, fact, or method you have learned about. In other words, explain your answer wherever explanations seem necessary. These will be of aid to us in evaluating the complexity of the questions we have asked you. Use the space for explanations only."

To test Hypothesis 3, the obvious procedure would be to compare scores of the experimental groups with the control group on the items about which most comments were written as well as on the items immediately following. To insure that some items would attract comments and that they would not be too closely bunched together, we inserted six items which had proved very difficult to previous classes in general psychology and spaced these well apart. Unfortunately, even with these insertions no more than 20 per cent of the students wrote comments about any one item, and differences in scores on that or the succeeding item were insignificant. This led us to a different procedure for testing Hypothesis 3. If failing an item creates tension, this tension should increase throughout the test. If having an opportunity to write comments aids in reducing or releasing this tension, the improvement in performance should be more marked on the last half of the test than on the first half. Hence separate scores for each half of the test were computed.

Results. Our attempt to restrict students' comments to feelings (Hypothesis 1) or to explanations (Hypothesis 2) appeared from our results to have dissipated much of the effect of permitting comments. As indicated in Table 6-9, differences between the groups were not significant. However, Hypothesis 3 was verified. The groups that had been given opportunities to write comments were significantly superior to the control group on the last half of the test even though they were not superior on the first half (see Table 6-10).

TABLE 6-9

TEST SCORES FOR GROUPS GIVEN DIFFERENT INSTRUCTIONS

Group	*N*	*Mean*	*SD*
Feelings	66	20.78	2.75
Explanations	75	20.86	2.25
No comments	70	20.07	2.72

TABLE 6-10

SCORES ON FIRST AND LAST HALVES OF TEST FOR GROUPS GIVEN DIFFERENT INSTRUCTIONS

Group	*N*	*First-Half Mean*	*Last-Half Mean*	*Mean of Differences*	*SD of Differences*
Feelings	66	10.79	9.99	.80	1.7
Explanations	73	10.63	10.23	.40	1.8
No comments	70	10.72	9.40	1.32	1.9

NOTE: Difference of differences: Feelings vs. no comments, $p = .11$; explanations vs. no comments, $p < .01$.

In a retest of this hypothesis with other groups, comparable results were obtained with the difference in scores on the last half of the test between "feelings" and "no comments" groups having a probability of .16 and that between "explanations" and "no comments" groups having a probability of .005.

Discussion. This experiment was partly encouraging and partly discouraging. Our prediction was verified. The effects of the opportunity to comment were most pronounced on the last half of the test. Since there were no more comments on the last half of the test than on the first half, this seemed to demonstrate that comments did not affect the scores on the items about which comments were written, but rather succeeding items. This fitted in with our theory that tension is built up throughout the test and that giving opportunity to comment reduces the increasing tension. But we were surprised to find that in general neither the instructions to write explanations nor to write feelings about items seemed to have been as effective as our usual instructions to "Feel free to comment. . . ." We repeated this part of the experiment with the added variation of giving one group answer sheets with the instructions: "In the space provided please state your feelings about a question *and* an explanation of how you arrived at the answer you used. Whenever you come to a question that bothers you, give any feelings you have about its clarity, fairness, triviality, etc., and also an explanation of how you arrived at the answer you used. This will help us to evaluate your test and also help in making out future tests." Surprisingly enough, none of the experimental groups was significantly superior to the group with conventional answer sheets.

The results of this follow-up were disconcerting. It now appeared that the important variable was not whether or not students released emotional feelings or gained closure by explaining their answers. Rather, it now appeared that the over-all set given by the instructions to comment was more important. Obviously, another experiment needed to be done.

EXPERIMENT IV

Purpose. Based on our previous results we now developed the hypothesis that specific instructions to comment actually increase a student's anxiety since they ask him to perform an additional task upon which he may be evaluated. Additional restraint is felt, especially when these instructions specify the kind of comment to be made. Our original instructions to "Feel free to comment" must have worked because they made the situation a permissive one. Our hypothesis for Experiment IV, then, was: Students given answer sheets with the instructions, "If you wish to make any comments about the questions on this exam, do so in the space provided," will make higher test scores than students with instructions to give their feelings and explanations of their answers on difficult items or students who are instructed not to comment.

Procedures. Our procedures were the same as in the preceding experiments. One-third of the students were given answer sheets with the instructions, "If you wish to make any comments about the questions on this exam, do so in the space provided"; one-third of the students received answer sheets with instructions, "In the space provided, please state your feelings about a question *and* an explanation of how you arrived at the answer you used. Whenever you come to a question that bothers you, give any feelings you have about its clarity, fairness, triviality, etc., and also an explanation of how you arrived at the answer you used. This will help us to evaluate your test and also help in making out future tests"; and the remaining third of the students received answer sheets with instructions, "Do not mark in the space to the right of your answers." Except for the instructions all answer sheets were identical.

Results. As indicated in Table 6-11, our hypothesis was confirmed by our results. The students with permissive instructions made significantly higher scores than students receiving the other two types of answer sheets. Since all students in this and the other experiments finished the examination in the allotted time, the results were not due to differences in the time required to write comments.

TABLE 6-11

EFFECT ON PERFORMANCE OF DIFFERING INSTRUCTIONS

Group	*Mean*	*F*	*df*	*p*
Explanations and feelings	32.73	(1 vs. 2) 2.5	1 and 281	NS
Do not comment	33.56	(2 vs. 3) 2.4	1 and 286	NS
Free comment	34.45	(1 vs. 3) 10.5	1 and 267	$<.01$

NOTE: The *F* ratio when all three means were taken together was 4.89, which is just beyond the .01 level of confidence.

[4] R. Teevan and W. McKeachie, "Effects on Performance of Different Instructions in Multiple Choice Examinations," *Michigan Academy of Science, Arts, and Letters*, 1954, *39*, pp. 467-475.

EXPERIMENT V

Purpose. The results of the four experiments conducted up to this point convinced us that test performance is influenced by the stress of the testing situation, and that this stress could be reduced by giving students the opportunity to make comments about the test. At the same time we were interested in personality variables that might make for individual differences in the amount of stress which a student feels in taking a test. To us one of the most interesting possible personality variables was the student's need for achievement. The findings of McClelland *et al.*[5] indicated that their measure of the achievement motive could differentiate students who felt motivated to excel from students who feared failure in achievement situations. We hypothesized that this latter group (low need achievement) would find the test situation more stressful, and that the opportunity to write comments would be of more aid in improving their scores than it would be for students with less anxiety about achievement.

Procedure. Students who took part in the replication of Experiment III were given the measure of achievement motivation. Students were divided at the median on this measure into two groups: (*a*) a high need achievement group, and (*b*) a low need achievement (fear of failure) group. All of these students had been given answer sheets which requested that they write comments about difficult or ambiguous items. The scores of the two groups were compared for the items on the first half of the test and for the items on the last half of the test.

Results. The results were not conclusive but tended to support our hypothesis. On the first half of the test, the high-achievement students scored significantly higher than the fear-of-failure group. On the last half of the examination, there was no significant difference between the scores of the two groups. The probability of the difference in gains was .11 (see Table 6-12). Moreover, the correlation between scores on the last half of the examination and number of comments was .73 for the fear-of-failure group and only .05 for the high-need-achievement group.

[5] McClelland *et al., op. cit.*

TABLE 6-12

ERRORS ON FIRST AND LAST HALVES OF EXAM

Group	*N*	*First Half*		*Second Half*	
		Mean	*SD*	*Mean*	*SD*
Fear-failure	12	6.5	3.6	5.6	2.8
High need achievement	12	2.8	1.9	4.6	1.8

NOTE: Difference of differences, $p = .11$.

DISCUSSION AND GENERAL CONCLUSIONS

What do our experiments add up to? In the sequence of experiments our theory had been building up step by step. We now had ideas about (*a*) the sources of anxiety in the testing situation, (*b*) the effect of anxiety upon performance, and (*c*) methods of reducing the deleterious effects of anxiety upon problem solving.

Sources of anxiety. As we see it, the student's anxiety in the testing situation derives from his helplessness in relation to the instructor's power. The power of the instructor to assign a grade means that the instructor can, by assigning a low grade, bar the student from attaining some of his most important goals, such as admission to graduate professional training, the prestige of college graduation or of Phi Beta Kappa, and the material advantages of good grades in securing a job. While all student-instructor relationships possess some possible threat, the focus of the student's anxiety is course examinations, which are usually the primary basis for grade assignment. The degree of the student's anxiety will be a function of his perception of the instructor's arbitrariness and punitiveness in the use of his power. Our finding that freedom to make comments results in higher test scores could be at least partially explained, we believe, if our instructions to "Feel free to comment . . ." influenced students to perceive the instructor as being a person who was not punitive, not attempting to maintain his superior status, but one who wanted to give students every opportunity to communicate to him.

In addition, the student's anxiety is a function of

uncertainty (as Sinha [6] and Cohen [7] have demonstrated). When we asked for a specific type of comment, e.g., "only feelings" or "only explanations," we did not get the improved performance which we consistently obtained when our instructions were "Feel free to comment. . . ." In retrospect, we suspect that these specific instructions were actually more ambiguous than the free-comment instructions. The student was uncertain as to how much he was expected to comment and how much his comments would influence his instructor's evaluation of him.

Finally, anxiety is a function of individual differences in motivation and security in the situation. Our results indicate that our experimental variation of instructions had little effect upon the person with high need achievement, who in need-achievement theory, is presumed to be stimulated but secure in achievement testing situations. However, students fearing failure were aided by the opportunity to make comments. These results are in harmony with those of Hutt[8], who found that maladjusted children achieved higher IQ's when he followed each failed test item with an easy item. However, such a procedure did not significantly influence scores of normal children.

The effect of anxiety upon performance. While we had no direct measure of anxiety, our findings do appear to support those of Deese and Lazarus,[9] Sarason,[10] and Maier, [11] who have reported decrements in various tasks as a result of anxiety.

How can the decrement in performance due to anxiety be reduced? Obviously, reducing anxiety should reduce the detrimental effects of anxiety, and as we pointed out earlier, this is, we believe, one of the functions of giving students opportunity to comment on test questions. But the fact that scores of students who were allowed to comment improve relatively in the second half of the test suggests that commenting in itself may also be of some value in improving performance. We suspect that when a person is frustrated or anxious, the discharge of the tension through almost any available response will help decrease the effect of the anxiety on later problems. However, we cannot help speculating about the fact that each time we compared instructions to write feelings against instructions to write explanations, the explanations group made slightly, but not significantly, better scores. Can it be that merely "blowing off steam" is not effective, and that catharsis, whether of these superficial feelings or of deeply repressed emotions, should involve verbalizing cognitive as well as affective elements? Or, does the expression of negative feelings arouse fear of incurring the instructor's displeasure? Or is the important thing that the student feels that he is communicating to the person having power over him? Perhaps expression of feelings seems to communicate less than an explanation. Such speculations need to be tested by further research.

SUMMARY

The present experiments attempted to influence student scores on classroom tests by setting up conditions which would permit reduction or dissipation of anxiety.

The results showed that students who were encouraged to write comments about their questions made higher scores than students who had conventional answer sheets. Since students who could write comments did not differ significantly from the control group in their scores on the first half of the test but performed significantly better on the second half of the test, it was concluded that the effect of the comments was not to improve scores on the items about which the comments were written. When students were given specific instructions as to the type of comments to write, their test scores

[6] A. K. P. Sinha, *Experimental Induction of Anxiety By Conditions of Uncertainty.* Unpublished doctoral dissertation, University of Michigan, 1950.

[7] A. R. Cohen, *The Effects of Individual Self-Esteem and Situational Structure on Threat-Oriented Reactions to Power.* Unpublished doctoral dissertation, University of Michigan, 1953.

[8] M. L. Hutt, "A Clinical Study of 'Consecutive and 'Adaptive' Testing with the Revised Stanford-Binet," *Journal of Consulting Psychology,* 1947, *11,* pp. 93-103.

[9] J. Deese and R. S. Lazarus, "The Effects of Psychological Stress upon Perceptual-Motor Performance," *USAF, Human Resources Research Center, Research Bulletin,* 1952, No. 53-19; R. S. Lazarus, J. Deese, and S. Osler, "The Effects of Psychological Stress upon Performance," *Psychological Bulletin,* 1952, *49,* pp. 293-387:

[10] S. B. Sarason and G. Mandler, "Some Correlates of Test Anxiety," *Journal of Abnormal and Social Psychology,* 1952, *47,* pp. 810-817.

[11] N. R. F. Maier, *op. cit.*

were lower than those of students who were told "Feel free to write comments."

On the basis of the McClelland, Atkinson, *et al.* test for achievement motivation, students who feared failure were distinguished from those with positive achievement motivation. When given opportunity to comment, students with fear of failure made lower scores on the first half of the test than students with high need achievement, but did not differ significantly on the last half of the test.

It is suggested that classroom examinations help determine the students' perception of the manner in which the instructor's power to assign grades will be used. Individual anxiety in the situation is partially a function of achievement motivation. Anxiety inhibits performance. Giving students an opportunity to write comments aids not only in reducing the threat but also in channeling the release of anxiety.

*TEACHER COMMENTS AND STUDENT PERFORMANCE: A SEVENTY-FOUR CLASSROOM EXPERIMENT IN SCHOOL MOTIVATION**

By Ellis Batten Page

Each year teachers spend millions of hours marking and writing comments upon papers being returned to students, apparently in the belief that their words will produce some result, in student performance, superior to that obtained without such words. Yet on this point solid experimental evidence, obtained under genuine classroom conditions, has been conspicuously absent. Consequently each teacher is free to do as he likes; one will comment copiously, another not at all. And each believes himself to be right.

The present experiment investigated the questions: 1) Do teacher comments cause a significant improvement in student performance? 2) If comments have an effect, which comments have more than others, and what are the conditions, in students and class, conducive to such effect? The questions are obviously important for secondary education, educational psychology, learning theory, and the pressing concern of how a teacher can most effectively spend his time.

PREVIOUS RELATED WORK

Previous investigations of "praise" and "blame," however fruitful for the general psychologist, have for the educator been encumbered by certain weaknesses: Treatments have been administered by persons who were extraneous to the normal class situation. Tests have been of a contrived nature in order to keep students (unrealistically) ignorant of the true comparative quality of their work. Comments of praise or blame have been administered on a random basis, unlike the classroom where their administration is not at all random. Subjects have often lacked any independent measures of their performance, unlike students in the classroom. Areas of training have often been those considered so fresh that the students would have little previous history of related success or failure, an assumption impossible to make in the classroom. There have furthermore been certain statistical errors; tests of significance have been conducted as if students were totally independent of one another, when in truth they were interacting members of a small number of groups with, very probably, some group effects upon the experimental outcome.

For the educator such experimental deviations from ordinary classroom conditions have some grave implications, explored elsewhere by the present writer.[1] Where the conditions are highly contrived,

[1] E. B. Page, "Educational Research: Replicable *or* Generalizable?" *Phi Delta Kappan*, 1958, *39*, pp. 302-304.

*From the *Journal of Educational Psychology*, 1958, *49*, pp. 173-181. Used by permission of the author and publisher. Portions of this paper were read at the National Research Conference of the American Educational Research Association at San Francisco, March 8, 1958.

no matter how tight the *controls,* efforts to apply the findings to the ordinary teacher-pupil relationship are at best rather tenuous. This study was therefore intended to fill both a psychological and methodological lack by *leaving the total classroom procedures exactly what they would have been without the experiment,* except for the written comments themselves.

METHOD

ASSIGNING THE SUBJECTS. Seventy-four teachers, randomly selected from among the secondary teachers of three districts, followed detailed printed instructions in conducting the experiment. By random procedures each teacher chose one class to be subject from among his available classes.[2] As one might expect, these classes represented about equally all secondary grades from seventh through twelfth, and most of the secondary subject-matter fields. They contained 2,139 individual students.

First the teacher administered whatever objective test would ordinarily come next in his course of study; it might be arithmetic, spelling, civics, or whatever. He collected and marked these tests in his usual way, so that each paper exhibited a numerical score and, on the basis of the score, the appropriate letter grade A, B, C, D, or F, each teacher following his usual policy of grade distribution. Next, the teacher placed the papers in numerical rank order, with the best paper on top. He rolled a specially marked die to assign the top paper to the *No Comment, Free Comment,* or *Specified Comment* group. He rolled again, assigning the second-best paper to one of the two remaining groups. He automatically assigned the third-best paper to the one treatment group remaining. He then repeated the process of rolling and assigning with the next three papers in the class, and so on until all students were assigned.

ADMINISTERING TREATMENTS. The teacher returned *all* test papers with the numerical score and letter grade, as earned. No Comment students received nothing else, Free Comment students received, in addition, whatever comment the teacher might feel it desirable to make. Teachers were instructed: "Write anything that occurs to you in the circumstances. There is not any 'right' or 'wrong' comment for this study. A comment is 'right' for the study if it conforms with your own feelings and practices." Specified Comment students, regardless of teacher or student differences, all received comments designated in advance for each letter grade, as follows:

A: Excellent! Keep it up.
B: Good work. Keep at it.
C: Perhaps try to do still better?
D: Let's bring this up.
F: Let's raise this grade!

Teachers were instructed to administer the comments "rapidly and automatically, trying not even to notice who the students are." This instruction was to prevent any extra attention to the Specified Comment students, in class or out, which might confound the experimental results. After the comments were written on each paper and recorded on the special sheet for the experimenter, the test papers were returned to the students in the teacher's customary way.

It is interesting to note that the student subjects were totally naive. In other psychological experiments, while often not aware of precisely what is being tested, subjects are almost always sure that something unusual is underway. In 69 of the present classes there was no discussion by teacher or student of the comments being returned. In the remaining five the teachers gave ordinary brief instructions to "notice comments" and "profit by them," or similar remarks. In none of the classes were students reported to seem aware or suspicious that they were experimental subjects.

CRITERION. Comment effects were judged by the scores achieved on the very next objective test given in the class, regardless of the nature of that test. Since the 74 testing instruments would naturally differ sharply from each other in subject matter, length, difficulty, and every other testing variable, they obviously presented some rather unusual problems. When the tests were regarded primarily as *ranking* instruments, however, some of the difficulties disappeared.

A class with 30 useful students, for example, formed just 10 levels on the basis of scores from the first test. Each level consisted of three students, with each student receiving a different treatment: No Comment, Free Comment, or Specified Comment. Students then achieved new scores on the second (criterion) test, as might be illustrated in Table 6-13,

[2] Certain classes, like certain teachers, would be ineligible for *a priori* reasons: giving no objective tests, etc.

Part A. On the basis of such scores, they were assigned rankings within levels, as illustrated in Table 6-13, Part B.

TABLE 6-13

ILLUSTRATION OF RANKED DATA

Level	*Part A* (*Raw scores on second test*)			*Part B* (*Ranks-within-levels on second test*)		
	N	*F*	*S*	*N*	*F*	*S*
1	33	31	34	2	1	3
2	30	25	32	2	1	3
3	29	33	23	2	3	1
...	...	...	...	...	...	...
...	...	...	...	...	...	...
...	...	...	...	...	...	...
10	14	25	21	1	3	2
Sum:				19	21	20

NOTE: N is No Comment; F is Free Comment; S is Specified Comment.

If the comments had no effects, the sums of ranks of Part B would not differ except by chance, and the two-way analysis of variance by ranks would be used to determine whether such differences exceeded chance.[3] Then the *sums* of ranks themselves could be ranked. (In Part B the rankings would be 1, 3, and 2 for Groups N, F, and S; the highest score is ranked 3 throughout the study.) And a new test, of the same type, could be made of all such rankings from the 74 experimental classrooms. Such a test was for the present design the better alternative, since it allowed for the likelihood of "Type G errors"[4] in the experimental outcome. Still a third way remained to use these rankings. Summation of each column could be divided by the number of levels in the class, and the result was *a mean rank within treatment within class.* This score proved very useful, since it fulfilled certain requirements for parametric data.

RESULTS

COMMENT VS. NO COMMENT. The over-all significance of the comment effects, as measured by the analysis of variance by ranks, is indicated in Table 6-14. The first row shows results obtained when students were considered as matched independently from one common population. The second row shows results when treatment groups within classes were regarded as intact groups. In either case the conclusions were the same. The Specified Comment group, which received automatic impersonal comments according to the letter grade received, achieved higher scores than the No Comment group. The Free Comment group, which received individualized comments from the teachers, achieved the highest scores of all. Not once in a hundred times would such differences have occurred by chance if scores were drawn from a common population. Therefore it may be held that the comments had a real and beneficial effect upon the students'

TABLE 6-14

THE FRIEDMAN TEST OF THE OVER-ALL TREATMENT EFFECTS

Units considered	*N*	*F*	*S*	*df*	χ_r^2	*p*
Individual Subjects	1363	1488	1427	2	10.9593	$<.01$
Class-group Subjects	129.5	170.0	144.5	2	11.3310	$<.01$

[3] The present study employed a new formula,

$$\chi_r^2 = \frac{6\,\Sigma\,(O - E)^2}{\Sigma\,O}$$

which represents a simplification of Friedman's twenty-year-old notation. (See M. Friedman, "The Use of Ranks to Avoid the Assumption of Normality Implicit in the Analysis of Variance," *Journal of American Statistical Association,* 1937, *32,* pp. 657-701). The new form is the classic chi square,

$$\Sigma \frac{(O - E)^2}{E}$$

multiplied by 6/k where k is simply the number of ranks! This conversion was discovered in connection with the present study by a collaboration of the writer with Alan Waterman and David Wiley. Proof that it is identical with the earlier and more cumbersome variation,

$$\chi_r^2 = \frac{12}{Nk(k+1)}\,\Sigma\,(R_i)^2 - 3N(k+1),$$

will be included in a future statistical article.

[4] Q. McNemar, *Psychological Statistics* (2nd ed., New York: John Wiley & Sons, Inc., 1955).

mastery of subject matter in the various experimental classes.

It was also possible, as indicated earlier, to use the mean ranks within treatments within classes as parametric scores. The resulting distributions, being normally distributed and fulfilling certain other assumptions underlying parametric tests, permitted other important comparisons to be made.[5] Table 6-15 shows the mean-ranks data necessary for such comparisons.

TABLE 6-15

PARAMETRIC DATA BASED UPON MEAN RANKS WITHIN TREATMENTS WITHIN CLASSES

Source	*N*	*F*	*S*	*Total*
Number of Groups	74	74	74	222
Sum of Mean Ranks	140.99	154.42	148.59	444.00
Sum of Squares of Mean Ranks	273.50	327.50	304.01	905.01
Mean of Mean Ranks	1.905	2.087	2.008	2.000
S.D. of Mean Ranks	.259	.265	.276	
S.E. of Mean Ranks	.030	.031	.032	

The various tests are summarized in Tables 6-16 and 6-17. The over-all F test in Table 6-17 duplicated, as one would expect, the result of the Friedman test, with differences between treatment groups still significant beyond the .01 level. Comparisons between different pairs of treatments are shown in Table 6-17. All differences were significant except that between Free Comment and Specified Comment. It was plain that comments, especially the individualized comments, had a marked effect upon student performance.

COMMENTS AND SCHOOLS. One might question whether comment effects would vary from school to school, and even whether the school might not be the more appropriate unit of analysis. Since as it happened the study had 12 junior or senior high schools which had three or more experimental classes, these schools were arranged in a treatments-by-replications design. Results of the analysis are shown in Table 6-18. Schools apparently had little measurable influence over treatment effect.

COMMENTS AND SCHOOL YEARS. It was conceivable that students, with increasing age and grade-replacement, might become increasingly independent of comments and other personal attentions from their teachers. To test such a belief, 66 class-groups, drawn from the experimental classes, were stratified into six school years (Grades 7-12) with 11 class-

TABLE 6-16

ANALYSIS OF VARIANCE OF MAIN TREATMENT EFFECTS
(Based on Mean Ranks)

Source	*Sum of Squares*	*df*	*Mean Square*	*F*	*Probability*
Between Treatments: N, F, S	1.23	2	.615	5.69	<.01
Between Class-groups	0.00	73	.000	. . .	
Interaction T × Class	15.78	146	.108		
Total	17.01	221			

NOTE: Modeled after Lindquist. See *Design and Analysis of Experiments in Psychology and Education* (Boston: Houghton Mifflin Company, 1953.) especially p. 157 *et passim*.

TABLE 6-17

DIFFERENCES BETWEEN MEANS OF THE TREATMENT GROUPS

Comparison	*Difference*	*S. E. of Diff.*	*t*	*Probability*
Between N and F	.182	.052	3.500	<.001
Between N and S	.103	.054	1.907	<.05
Between F and S	.079	.056	1.411	<.10(n.s.)

NOTE: The *t* tests presented are those for matched pairs, consisting of the paired mean ranks of the treatment groups within the different classes. Probabilities quoted assume that one-tailed tests were appropriate.

[5] It may be noted that the analysis of variance based upon such mean ranks will require no calculation of sums of squares between levels or between classes. This is true because the mean for any class will be $(k + 1)/2$, or in the present study just 2.00. An alternative to such scores would be the conversion of all scores to T scores based upon each class-group's distribution; but the mean ranks, while very slightly less sensitive, are much simpler to compute and therefore less subject to error.

TABLE 6-18

THE INFLUENCE OF THE SCHOOL UPON THE TREATMENT EFFECT

Source	Sum of Squares	df	Mean Square	F	Probability
Between Treatments: N, F, S	.172	2	.086	. . .[a]	. . .
Between Schools	.000	11	.000	. . .	. . .
Between Classes Within Schools (pooled)	.000	24	.000	. . .	. . .
Interaction: T × Schools	1.937	22	.088	. . .	. . .
Interaction: T × Cl. W. Sch. (pooled)	4.781	48	.099	. . .	. . .
Total	6.890	107		. . .	. . .

NOTE: Modified for mean-rank data from A. Edwards, *Experimental Design in Psychological Research* (New York: Holt, Rinehart & Winston, Inc., 1950) p. 295 *et passim.*

[a] Absence of an important main treatment effect is probably caused by necessary restriction of sample for school year (N is 36, as compared with Total N of 74), and by some chance biasing.

groups in each school year. Still using mean ranks as data, summations of such scores were as shown in Table 6-19. Rather surprisingly, no uniform trend was apparent. When the data were tested for interaction of school year and comment effect (see Table 6-20), school year did not exhibit a significant influence upon comment effect.

Though Table 6-20 represents a comprehensive test of school-year effect, it was not supported by all available evidence. Certain other, more limited tests did show significant differences in school year, with possibly greater responsiveness in higher grades. The relevant data[6] are too cumbersome for the present report, and must be interpreted with caution. Apparently, however, comments do *not* lose effectiveness as students move through school. Rather they appear fairly important, especially when individualized, at all secondary levels.

One must remember that, between the present class-groupings, there were many differences other than school year alone. Other teachers, other subject-matter fields, other class conditions could conceivably have been correlated beyond chance with school year. Such correlations would in some cases, possibly, tend to modify the *visible* school-year influence, so that illusions would be created. However possible, such a caution, at present, appears rather empty. In absence of contradictory evidence, it would seem reasonable to extrapolate the importance of comment to other years outside the secondary range. One might predict that comments would appear equally important if tested under comparable conditions in the early college years. Such a suggestion, in view of the large lecture halls and detached professors of higher education, would appear one of the more striking experimental results.

[6] E. B. Page, *The Effects Upon Student Achievement of Written Comments Accompanying Letter Grades.* Unpublished doctoral dissertation, University of California, Los Angeles, 1958.

TABLE 6-19

SUMS OF MEAN RANKS FOR DIFFERENT SCHOOL YEARS

School Year	N	F	S
12	21.08	22.92	22.00
11	19.06	23.91	23.03
10	20.08	23.32	22.60
9	22.34	22.06	21.60
8	21.21	22.39	22.40
7	22.04	22.98	20.98

NOTE: Number of groups is 11 in each cell.

TABLE 6-20

THE INFLUENCE OF SCHOOL YEAR UPON TREATMENT EFFECT

Source	Sum of Squares	df	Mean Square	F	Probability
Between Treatments: N, F, S	1.06	2	.530	5.25	<.01
Between School Years	0.00	5	.000		
Between Cl. Within Sch. Yr. (pooled)	0.00	60	.000		
Interaction: T × School Year	1.13	10	.113	1.12	(n.s.)
Interaction: T × Class (pooled)	12.11	120	.101		
Total	14.30	197			

NOTE: Modified for mean-rank data from A. Edwards, *Experimental Design in Psychological Research* (New York: Holt, Rinehart & Winston, Inc., 1950.)

COMMENTS AND LETTER GRADES. In a questionnaire made out before the experiment, each teacher rated each student in his class with a number from 1 to 5, according to the student's *guessed responsiveness* to comments made by that teacher. Top rating, for example, was paired with the description: "Seems to respond quite unusually well to suggestions or comments made by the teacher of this class. Is quite apt to be influenced by praise, correction, etc." Bottom rating, on the other hand, implied: "Seems rather negativistic about suggestions made by the teacher. May be inclined more than most students to do the opposite from what the teacher urges." In daily practice, many teachers comment on some papers and not on others. Since teachers would presumably be more likely to comment on papers of those students they believed would respond positively, such ratings were an important experimental variable.

Whether teachers *were* able to predict responsiveness is a complicated question, not to be reported here. It was thought, however, that teachers might tend to believe their able students, their high achievers, were also their responsive students. A contingency table was therefore made, testing the relationship between *guessed* responsiveness and letter grade achieved on the first test. The results were as predicted. More "A" students were regarded as highly responsive to comments than were other letter grades; more "F" students were regarded as negativistic and unresponsive to comments than were other letter grades; and grades in between followed the same trend. The over-all C coefficient was .36, significant beyond the .001 level.[7] Plainly teachers believed that their *better* students were also their more *responsive* students.

If teachers were correct in their belief, one would expect in the present experiment greater comment effect for the better students than for the poorer ones. In fact, one might not be surprised if, among the "F" students, the No Comment group were even superior to the two comment groups.

The various letter grades achieved mean scores as shown in Table 6-21, and the analysis of variance resulted as shown in Table 6-22. There was considerable interaction between letter grade and treatment effect, but it was caused almost entirely by the remarkable effect which comments appeared to have *on the "F" students*. None of the other differences, including the partial reversal of the "D" students, exceeded chance expectation.

TABLE 6-21

MEAN OF MEAN RANKS FOR DIFFERENT LETTER GRADES

Letter Grade	*N*	*F*	*S*
A	1.93	2.04	2.03
B	1.91	2.11	1.98
C	1.90	2.06	2.04
D	2.05	1.99	1.96
F	1.57	2.55	1.88

NOTE: Each eligible class was assigned one mean rank for each cell of the table.

These data do not, however, represent the total sample previously used, since the analysis could use only those student levels in which all three students received the same letter grade on Test One.[8] Therefore many class-groups were not represented at all in certain letter grades. For example, although over 10 per cent of all letter grades were "F," only 28 class-groups had even one level consisting entirely of "F" grades, and most of these classes had *only* one such level. Such circumstances might cause a somewhat unstable or biased estimate of effect.

Within such limitations, the experiment provided strong evidence against the teacher-myth about responsiveness and letter grades. The experimental teachers appeared plainly mistaken in their faith that their "A" students respond relatively brightly, and their "F" students only sluggishly or negatively to whatever encouragement they administer.

SUMMARY

Seventy-four randomly selected secondary teachers, using 2,139 unknowing students in their daily classes, performed the following experiment: They administered to all students whatever objective test would occur in the usual course of instruction. After

[7] In a 5 x 5 table, a perfect correlation expressed as C would be only about .9 (McNemar, *op. cit.*, p. 205).

[8] When levels consisted of both "A" and "B" students, for example, "A" students would tend to receive the higher scores on the second test, regardless of treatment; thus those Free Comment "A" students drawn from mixed levels would tend to appear (falsely) more responsive than the Free Comment "B" students drawn from mixed levels, etc. Therefore the total sample was considerably reduced for the letter-grade analysis.

TABLE 6-22

THE RELATION BETWEEN LETTER GRADE AND TREATMENT EFFECT

Source	*Sum of Squares*	*df*	*Mean Square*	*F*	*Probability*
Between Treatments: N, F, S	2.77	2	1.385	5.41	<.01
Between Letter Grades	0.00	4	0.000		
Bet. Blocks Within L. Gr. (pooled)	0.00	65	0.000		
Interaction: T × Letter Grades	4.88	8	.610	2.40	.05>p>.01
Residual (error term)	32.99	130	.254		
Total	40.64	209			

NOTE: Modified for mean-rank data from Lindquist (*op. cit.*, p. 269). Because sampling was irregular (see text) all eligible classes were randomly assigned to 14 groupings. This was done arbitrarily to prevent vacant cells.

scoring and grading the test papers in their customary way, and matching the students by performance, they randomly assigned the papers to one of three treatment groups. The No Comment group received no marks beyond those for grading. The Free Comment group received whatever comments the teachers felt were appropriate for the particular students and tests concerned. The Specified Comment group received certain uniform comments designated beforehand by the experimenter for all similar letter grades, and thought to be generally "encouraging." Teachers returned tests to students without any unusual attention. Then teachers reported scores achieved on the next objective test given in the class, and these scores became the criterion of comment effect, with the following results:

1. Free Comment students achieved higher scores than Specified Comment students, and Specified Comments did better than No Comments. All differences were significant except that between Free Comments and Specified Comments.

2. When samplings from 12 different schools were compared, no significant differences of comment effect appeared between schools.

3. When the class-groups from six different school years (grades 7-12) were compared, no *conclusive* differences of comment effect appeared between the years, but if anything senior high was more responsive than junior high. It would appear logical to generalize the experimental results, concerning the effectiveness of comment, at least to the early college years.

4. Although teachers believed that their better students were also much more responsive to teacher comments than their poorer students, there was no experimental support for this belief.

When the average secondary teacher takes the time and trouble to write comments (believed to be "encouraging") on student papers, these apparently have a measurable and potent effect upon student effort, or attention, or attitude, or whatever it is which causes learning to improve, and this effect does not appear dependent on school building, school year, or student ability. Such a finding would seem very important for the studies of classroom learning and teaching method.

VII

SHAPING ATTITUDES THROUGH SCHOOLS

*CONSIDERATENESS AND AGGRESSION**

By A. W. Foshay and Kenneth D. Wann

The romantic notion of childhood, that children enter the world "trailing clouds of glory," that the innocence of children is equivalent to virtue, beguiles many people. Indeed, it is rooted deep in our culture. The idea that sweetness, kindness, or considerateness must be *learned* by children is hard to accept—unless one deals with children constantly! Even then, the idea that children are often inconsiderate, unkind, even cruel to one another is distressing. But it is so.

Some of us in Springfield, having been distressed by inconsiderateness among children and high school youth, sought ways of studying the matter.[1]

WHAT IS CONSIDERATENESS?

Like the other staffs in Springfield, we first defined our "intangible," which we called "considerateness," through observing and recording behavior that seemed to us considerate or inconsiderate. Accordingly, both in the elementary school and in the high school, we gathered examples of these kinds of behavior. Here are some examples of considerate and inconsiderate behavior from the elementary school.

[1] The staff of the York Elementary School (11 teachers, 346 children), and varying groups from the staff of Springfield Senior High School (between 10 and 35 teachers, out of a total staff of approximately 70) were involved in the activities reported in this chapter. The "we" of this chapter refers to members of these staffs, and the three Institute consultants, who worked with the school staffs at different times.
The material that follows was gathered chiefly in the elementary school. We shall report only a small part of the work done in the high school, because circumstances made it impossible for us to bring more than a small portion of our work there to the kind of fruition that would make a report possible.

* From *Children's Social Values,* Chapter 6 (New York: Bureau of Publications, Teachers College, Columbia University, 1954). Abridged. Used by permission of the authors and publisher.

GRADE 1

Considerate

Anna helped erase errors on a note that Freddy was trying to write to his mother. (Freddy's eraser is badly worn and makes dirty marks. Anna has a new eraser.)

Inconsiderate

Jackie put his foot to one side to keep Karen from sitting by him.

GRADE 3

Considerate

Rosalind offered to count change in the classroom for Wanda, who could not make change.

Inconsiderate

Merle knocked Robert's coat off the hook in the cloakroom so that he could hang his own on the hook.

GRADE 5

Considerate

Sue helped a new girl with her lunch order.

Inconsiderate

In front of the other children, Buddy said he wished Jimmie were not on his ball team. He said Jimmy was lazy and made an out every time. This happened on the playground.

GRADE 6

Considerate

Jerry requested that the pitcher slow down the fast ball when it was a timid new boy's turn at the bat.

Inconsiderate

Larry tried to make Frank lose a ball game by fumbling purposely.

In the high school, similar observations were gathered. One reported by an eleventh grade teacher will be given here, because it was thought-provoking:

> I entered the school at eight o'clock in the morning. Albert, a tall sixteen-year-old, ran toward me from the other end of the long school corridor. He must have run seventy-five feet, bearing down on me like a locomotive. He skidded to a stop, a foot from my nose, raised his hand, said, "Hi!" and then vanished before I could say anything. He knew that this was against the school rules; he scared the wits out of me. This was grossly inconsiderate, and I think he meant it to be.

When we talked about Albert's running down the hall, two of us who knew Albert disagreed sharply about the meaning of this incident. The one who had reported the incident was convinced that Albert's behavior was inconsiderate, though in some ways laughable. The other, who also knew Albert quite well, said, "I don't think he meant to be inconsiderate. I don't think he knew that he was frightening you. I think that boy has to be taken at his word. When he says, 'Hi,' that's all he means. I really believe that all he meant to do was to say hello. I suspect that he darted out of the hall when he saw the expression on your face."

We went on talking. Someone else gave this account of Albert: "Albert really seems to me to have a friendly attitude toward everybody. He's a good deal like a setter pup, loose-limbed and gangling, and friendly and clumsy. You have to take him in stride. Just yesterday afternoon, Miss—— and I went to the soda fountain across the street after school. It was filled with students, laughing and talking and taking it easy in general. When we came in, Albert jumped up on a bench, raised his hand, and shouted, 'Silence! There are teachers present!' So help me, I can't get angry at Albert. I think he's trying to find himself, and that he laughs at himself all the time. I think we ought to laugh with him, not at him; and that's what Miss——and I did yesterday. We laughed, had our sodas, and that was the end of the matter."

We agreed that either of these explanations of Albert's behavior could conceivably be true. However, more important than our explanation of his behavior was Albert's own explanation of his behavior. Was there any way for us to find whether Albert saw this thing as we did, or whether, in general, the students in the high school saw inconsiderateness as we did?

Were we and the children talking about the same thing? To examine the possibility that students and teachers interpreted considerateness quite differently, the film "You and Your Friends"[2] was shown to a group of students and a group of faculty members. Each group was asked to indicate the *most* considerate and the *least* considerate act portrayed in the film. Their reactions are shown in Table 7-1.

An examination of these data suggests that, while there are some minor differences in the order of importance assigned to these acts of considerateness and inconsiderateness, students and teachers tended

[2] "You and Your Friends" (7 min. sound film in black and white), produced by Association Films and Look Magazine, Art of Living Series, Association Films, Inc., 347 Madison Ave., New York 17, New York, 1946.

TABLE 7-1

ACTS INTERPRETED AS CONSIDERATE AND INCONSIDERATE BY TEACHERS AND STUDENTS

Acts	*Percentage of Teachers (N = 51)*	*Percentage of Students (N = 31)*
Most Considerate		
Loyalty of girl to boy	49%	29%
Breaking a date in a considerate way	21	48
Dependability	8	0
Acceptance of broken date	8	0
Trying to act pleasant	8	3
Starting a conversation (with a girl who seemed left out)	6	6
Interested in others	0	6
Helping a girl with food	0	6
Least Considerate		
Revealing a secret	65	39
Lack of dependability	12	0
Interrupting a conversation	8	5
Criticizing an absent person	6	10
Breaking a date to make another	6	25
Poor table manners	2	11
Not considering the feelings of others	0	5
Talking too much	0	5

to mention the same things as being considerate and inconsiderate. "Breaking a date in a considerate way" was relatively more important to the students than to the teachers, and loyalty between the girl and the boy seemed somewhat more important to the teachers than to the students. However, both of these behaviors were ranked high by both groups. Insofar as the responses to the motion picture revealed the real judgments of the two groups, they indicated that teachers and students were talking about the same things.

Considerateness and popularity. Continuing our examination of this situation in the high school, we were intrigued by the possibility that what we were calling "considerateness" and "inconsiderateness" were actually reasons for popularity and unpopularity among our high school students. Accordingly, we turned to one portion of a reaction sheet for the film "You and Your Friends," and analyzed responses to that. The question asked in the reaction sheet is: "If you want to be popular in this school, what three things are most important that you be or do?" Students who filled out this form were also asked to name three to five students they considered the most popular in school, and to indicate why they thought they were popular. It was possible, by analyzing the students' responses to the first question and to the "Why?" part of the second question, to draw up a list of sixty-one items mentioned frequently as reasons for popularity. The list could then be made into a check sheet, in which students and teachers could indicate those "reasons for popularity" that in their opinion had most to do with considerateness.

This sixty-one-item form was administered to the seventy-one student members of the student council of the high school and to the sixty-two members of the high school faculty. Those who checked these items were asked to indicate by their response "whether you believe considerate behavior is important to the reason given [for popularity]." There is some reason to suppose that this request was not heeded as the sheet was checked, and that the responses should be read simply as "reasons for popularity." Consequently, we did not base our analysis of the compared responses of students and teachers on the assumption that either group was actually relating these "reasons for popularity" to considerate behavior. However, we thought that it was reasonable to compare the responses of the two groups with respect to their notions of "reasons for popularity."

Before we could make the comparison, however, it was desirable that we test the responses of each of these two groups (students and faculty) for internal consistency. If there was as much or more inconsistency within each group as there was between the groups, we could not consider them as differing. Therefore, each group was divided into chance halves. The two halves of each group were compared with respect to their tendency to rank these items in the same way. The rank-order correlation coefficient for the faculty was .89. The rank-order correlation coefficient for the students was .96. This meant that each group was consistent with itself. Had the groups been internally inconsistent, comparison of the two would have meant little, since to compare groups one must first "pool" the responses of the individuals in a group. "Pooling" means that the responses in a group are similar enough to permit one to treat them as if they were nearly identical. In this case, we found that in each group there was enough similarity (as described by high correlation coefficients) to permit such pooling.

When sixty-two teachers' and seventy-one students' responses were compared, the rank-order correlation coefficient between them was found to be higher than .80. This suggests that the two groups were in substantial agreement concerning the relative importance of the sixty-one "reasons for popularity."

Particularly significant are the items which fell in the first ten ranks of student responses, because the number of responses to the items that fell in these ranks was much larger than the number of responses to the items that ranked lower. The comparison between the student and faculty rank is quite close. The top ten "reasons for popularity" ranked according to student responses are listed below together with the *differences* in ranks between student and faculty responses.

Thinks of others before self	3.5
Courteous	.5
Considerate	11.0
Cooperative	1.0
Friendly with everyone (makes friends)	4.0
Thoughtfulness	.5
Helpful	.5
Kindness	1.0
Good Sport	4.5
Liked by everyone	3.5

The difference between the student and faculty rankings for any one of the items on the check sheet could have been as great as 61. The fact is, however, that the differences in ranking between the two groups were relatively slight all the way down the scale from "thinks of others before self" (rank 1) to "tough" (rank 61). We teachers found this rather reassuring. At least, when we talked about "considerateness" with the students, we tended to talk about the same things. Our agreements certainly outweighed our disagreements. Moreover, the "reasons" considered most important by the students did seem to involve what we were calling "considerateness."

WE STUDY CONSIDERATENESS IN THE ELEMENTARY SCHOOL

We have already given examples of the observations made by the eleven of us who carried on the study of considerateness in the elementary school. These sample observations are our behavioral definition of considerateness. To state the definition in more general terms: By "inconsiderateness" we mean being aggressive and selfish toward one another. By "considerateness" we mean being helpful and generous to one another. However, as our study continued, we found it more helpful to use the examples rather than these general definitions.

Verbal and physical aggression. As we looked at our collection of examples of inconsiderate behavior, it appeared that there was a tendency for such behavior to take the form of overt physical aggression in the early grades and to consist more and more of verbal aggression in the upper grades. We resolved to test this impression of ours by seeing whether the children would reveal such a tendency through their responses to an open-ended question. Accordingly, we asked all of the children in the school to list "Things that make me want to strike back." (The first and second graders responded orally.) In Table 7-2 we offer a summary of the children's responses to this question, categorized according to whether the children named overt physical aggression or verbal aggression. In the category "overt physical aggression" we included such responses as "choke you," "pinch you," "jump on your back." In the category "verbal aggression" we included such responses as "say dirty words," "tattling," "name calling."

TABLE 7-2

NUMBER OF RESPONSES IN EACH CATEGORY, BY ELEMENTARY SCHOOL CHILDREN, TO "THINGS THAT MAKE ME WANT TO STRIKE BACK"*

Grade	*Overt Physical Aggression*	*Verbal Aggression*
1	56	9
2	18	25
3	10	4
4	8	29
6	16	3

* Responses from grade five were not obtained.

What we found when we analyzed the material gathered was that there was no such tendency as the one that had appeared to us when we looked at our observational material. The children in the second grade named what we called "verbal" aggression more frequently than they named "physical" aggression. The children in the sixth grade named physical aggression more frequently than they named verbal aggression. If this was a valid indication of actual aggression, then, verbal aggression appeared prominently by the second grade among these children, and differences in the prominence of verbal aggression among the various grades of our school would have to be accounted for through reasons other than the grade or age of the children.

How I know people don't like me. We wished, however, to discover more about the kinds of things children consider aggressive and thus inconsiderate. We asked another open question of the children in the fourth, fifth, and sixth grades: "How I know people don't like me." A tabulation of the children's answers showed the frequencies for each kind of behavior.

Overt physical aggression (throwing rocks, hitting people, pushing in the lunch line, kicking, jumping on your back)	66
Gossip, teasing, name calling (mocking, call you cheater, profanity, tone of voice)	47
Participation in organized games (refusal to play with one, criticism of failure or mistakes during game play, breaking the rules)	32
Avoidance (refusal to talk, snubbing people, running off to be with someone else)	30
Treatment of others' belongings (tear up my games, "swiping" hat or coat, hiding something, ride your bicycle)	13
Facial expression (refusing to look you in the eye, making faces, sticking tongue out)	13

An analysis of the data above suggested to us a somewhat more detailed version of our original division of "inconsiderateness" into the two categories which we had called physical aggression and verbal aggression. When the upper-grade children responded to our question, "How I know people don't like me," overt physical aggression continued to occupy a prominent place. This was not surprising. After all, communication with a rock or a fist is quite obvious and easy to understand.

What interested us even more, however, was the subtlety of the several varieties of nonphysical aggression that emerged from our analysis of the children's responses. Gossip, bad treatment of others' belongings, refusing to look someone in the eye, and the like are actually quite aggressive behaviors. The sum of the frequencies for these was greater than the frequency for overt physical aggression. All of us remembered from our own childhood experience that gossip, avoidance, and facial expression were very real means of expressing aggression. There are a great many substitutes for a poke in the nose, the children seemed to be saying. These include openly avoiding another person, offering to play with one and then running off to play with someone else, and other such snubbing and cutting.

How much inconsiderateness does a teacher see? When we compared our own observations with the children's responses to these two open questions, it appeared to us that in our elementary school, as in the high school, we and the children were talking about the same thing when we talked about inconsiderateness and considerateness. That is, we were talking about the same thing *insofar as we talked about the behavior we teachers could see.*

Most of our observations in the elementary school would fit into the categories named by the children in the first and second ranks of the children's responses to "How I know people don't like me." Most of what we saw, that is, was either overt physical aggression or overt verbal aggression. The nonverbal inconsiderateness that the children described in the comments we classified as "participation in organized games," "avoidance," "treatment of other's belongings," and "facial expression" appear very rarely in our observations of the children's behavior. Had we been looking for this kind of "inconsiderate" behavior, we might have reported more of it in our observational material. However, the fact that we did not report it means that we did not see it and that we were not in the habit of looking for it.

From this situation, we drew a conclusion of some

importance to us. We concluded that *what we were calling "inconsiderate" amounted to only a fraction of all that the children recognized as "inconsiderate."* Our observations, which fit into the first two ranks of responses to "How I know people don't like me," would account for only 56 per cent of the items of behavior that the children suggested. The other 44 per cent were apparently out of our sight. At least they were sufficiently well out of sight that we did not report them when we were looking for inconsiderateness.

It was useful, therefore, for us to remember that although we and the children agreed about what kinds of behavior were "inconsiderate," we teachers actually observed only about half of the total picture as the children saw it—only the half which includes *overt* behavior.

CONSIDERATENESS AND BELONGINGNESS

Early in our work together, one of us had reported this incident of "considerate" behavior: "Instead of leaving for recess, Sue Ellen stayed in the room and helped Nancy to straighten up her desk." Elsewhere on the sheet of paper used to report this incident, the teacher had written, "Sue Ellen is always going from one friend to another."

This suggested something to us: perhaps Sue Ellen's behavior should be thought of as part of her quest for friends, not just as considerate behavior for its own sake. In fact, Sue Ellen's teacher was strongly persuaded that Sue Ellen was not "fundamentally considerate." Her purpose in recording this incident, in fact, was to raise a question with all of us about the meaning of this kind of behavior and the possibility that we were seriously misinterpreting it.

Perhaps much of the "considerate" behavior we had observed was related to friendship-seeking. We wondered whether we could find any consistent relationship between the acceptance of children in their classes (their group acceptance) and their tendency to behave in a considerate manner. To find out, we outlined our plan of work into a series of steps as follows:

Step 1. Each of us would gather examples of considerate and inconsiderate behavior, making sure that we noted the name of the person initiating the behavior and the name of the person toward whom the behavior was directed—the "initiator" and "receiver," so to speak.

Step 2. Each of us above the third grade would use the Classroom Social Distance Scale to get a measure of group acceptance for each child in our classes. Below the third grade, we would observe children's choices of classmates and friends in an effort to form some judgments about children who were consistently well accepted and children who were consistently lonely in our classes.

Step 3. We would examine our observations of considerate and inconsiderate behavior and our records of group acceptance of each individual to see whether there were any consistent relationships.

Our report of what we found is given in Table 7-3, following. To read this table, note that we are attempting here to state the relationship between the person who initiated the considerate or inconsiderate behavior and the person who received it. There are four possible relationships: 1) the initiator can have higher group acceptance than the receiver; 2) he can have equal group acceptance with the receiver; 3) he can have lower group acceptance than the receiver; 4) one of the two can be new to the class. We have categorized the relationship between the two children involved according to the group acceptance of the person who was on the receiving end of the considerate or inconsiderate behavior.

The comparative group acceptance of initiators and receivers of considerate and inconsiderate behavior is described in the first column ("Group Acceptance") of Table 3. Thus, when Billy snatches

TABLE 7-3

CONSIDERATE AND INCONSIDERATE BEHAVIORS CATEGORIZED ACCORDING TO GROUP ACCEPTANCE OF RECEIVER

Group Acceptance	*Considerate Behavior*	*Inconsiderate Behavior*
Initiator has *higher* group acceptance than receiver.	1	14
Initiator and receiver have *equal* group acceptance.	10	6
Initiator has *lower* group acceptance than receiver.	3	3
Receiver is *new* to the class.	7	0
	21	23

away Jerry's notebook and throws it on a high shelf (and we call this inconsiderate) we look at the *comparative group acceptance* of Billy and Jerry as indicated by our sociometric device. If Billy is higher than Jerry (is mentioned as a friend by more children in his class) we would record the behavior in the first row of the table, under "inconsiderate." If, on the other hand, Billy and Jerry are substantially the *same* (that is, either both relatively high in group acceptance, both in the middle of the class with respect to group acceptance, or both relatively low in group acceptance) we would record the behavior in the second row of the table, in the "inconsiderate" column. And so on. We did not think, in the case of children new to the class, that their "low" group acceptance as measured by the Classroom Social Distance Scale should be taken at its face value. Children who are new to the room, we said to ourselves, have to find their way into the social structure of the classroom. Until they have been in the classroom for a month or so, it is not possible for the teacher to find out what level of group acceptance they will attain. Therefore, we included a separate category for considerate and inconsiderate behavior directed at new children.

What we found. Now let us interpret the table. The figure that stands out is in the first row—the 14 inconsiderate acts, more than half of all we recorded, initiated by a child who had greater group acceptance than the child toward whom the inconsiderate behavior was directed. This observation seemed to indicate that *inconsiderate behavior tended to be directed downward in the scale of group acceptance.*

The other portion of this table that interested us was in the second row, in which the initiator and the receiver have equal group acceptance. While the difference in numbers of behaviors is not very striking (10 considerate acts and 6 inconsiderate acts), nevertheless the fact that nearly half of all the *considerate* behavior we saw took place between children who had approximately equal group acceptance, seemed to us to be significant. Moreover, these 10 considerate acts greatly outnumbered the considerate acts we saw taking place between children who were unequal in group acceptance. The fact that 7 of the 21 observations of considerateness were directed at children new to the room, that only 3 were directed "upward," so to speak (that is, toward a child of greater group acceptance), led us to conclude that, for our children, *considerateness tended to be directed toward social equals,* and to be withheld from social inferiors.

There are some additional interpretations of this material which are not supported strongly enough for us to report them as conclusions. However, we think that they are sufficiently interesting to be reported as questions: Is considerate behavior directed at new children as a means of winning their friendship? Is there any pronounced tendency for children who have generally high group acceptance to commit more considerate acts than inconsiderate acts? Does considerate behavior tend to take place among people of equal and relatively low group acceptance? In a number of cases (but our records are not complete on this point) the considerate behavior directed at children new to the room was initiated by children who had low group acceptance. One example of this was found in the anecdote that led us to study this matter in the first place—the one in which the child who went from one friend to another helped another child during the recess period. The child helped was new to the class. What did this mean?

The classroom "peck order." In our discussion of this material we came back again and again to this: most of the inconsiderate behavior we saw was initiated by people who had higher group acceptance than did the people on whom it was inflicted. What we thought we saw here was a sort of "peck order" in the classroom. In the barnyard, some chickens can peck other chickens without reprisal, and they get the preferred place at the feed box. In the classroom, some children can be inconsiderate to other children without apparent reprisal.

The additional fact, that almost all of the considerate behavior we saw took place between equals, or was directed toward new children, tended to support this "peck order" conclusion.

The more we thought about this, the more we tended to reinterpret what we were calling "considerate" and "inconsiderate" behavior. Possibly "inconsiderate" behavior was actually an expression of differing group acceptance. Perhaps the child's "code" demanded of him that he maintain his status in class, at least in part, by being inconsiderate to certain people. (If we had found many examples of considerate behavior directed from children of low group acceptance to children of high group acceptance, we would have worried still more. Such behavior would have been "toadying.")

On the other hand, we thought that a good many of the youngsters who had low group acceptance were thought by the others to be actually obnoxious much of the time, and that they brought the "inconsiderate" behavior upon themselves. The fact that a child of high group acceptance had initiated some inconsiderate behavior against the youngster of lower group acceptance did not necessarily mean that the inconsiderate behavior was unprovoked.

But the nagging fact remained that most of the inconsiderate behavior we recognized was directed downward in the order of group acceptance. Whatever lay behind it, we certainly were faced with the probability that our interpretation of the meaning of "inconsiderate" behavior had to be re-examined. We concluded by agreeing that *"considerateness" and "inconsiderateness" are so closely related to group acceptance as probably to be an expression of it.*

Building group acceptance. Acting on this conclusion, we resolved to examine the means through which children could achieve group acceptance. If considerate and inconsiderate behavior were considered as expressions of group acceptance, then if we could do things that would make children in the group more acceptable to one another, we might hope that they would be more considerate of one another. (We did not think that we had established a cause-and-effect relationship through our observations as reported in Table 7-3. However, the relationships seemed so close that we thought a cause-and-effect relationship was at least possible. That is why we now turned to a further study of group acceptance.) What were the means through which children could increase their group acceptance? Which could we help them with in school?

Presumably, children like one another because they find one another attractive in some way. If we could discover what made our children attractive to each other, we might help our less attractive children to become more attractive. First, though, we had to know more about what was considered attractive by the children. To gain information from the children about this, we employed another open question: "Things that make me feel important."

What makes children feel important? Our reasoning here was as follows: "Things that make me feel important" in all probability meant to our children the same things that we were calling "factors leading to group acceptance." We thought that there was likely to be a very strong positive relationship between the things that the children would identify as making them feel important and the things which they recognized in others as symbols of high group acceptance (or, in other words, high prestige) in the classroom. We thought that we would attack the matter in this oblique fashion in order to avoid what appeared to us to be the rather superficial findings of studies of factors influencing children's friendships, usually based on direct questions asked of children. Briefly, we thought that those things which children found attractive in themselves would be much more likely to influence their actual choice of friends than would things that they might attempt to identify in someone else as being significantly related to choice of friendships.

In Table 7-4 we have summarized the 185 responses of third, fourth, fifth, and sixth grade children to the "Things that make me feel important" question.

As we examined Table 7-4, we noticed that the first three categories, "academic," "playing games," and "help the teacher," accounted for 67 per cent of all the responses made by the children. The numbers of responses in the other categories were very small.

We had assumed that those things which the children valued in themselves, they would also value in others. Thirty-four per cent of all their responses had to do with academic achievement and the rewards associated with it. Twenty-three per cent of all their responses had to do with the ability to play games well and being chosen to play games. Ten per cent of all of their responses had to do with helping the teacher in one way or another. Could these and other acts that the childen mentioned actually be considered as symbols of the prestige of children in school?

We thought they could. The high frequency of "academic" comments, upon second examination, seemed to us to relate closely to marks of approval by the teacher. What was strongly suggested here was that the teacher's approval, especially as expressed by high grades, actually did contribute

TABLE 7-4

RESPONSES BY 90 CHILDREN IN GRADES 3-6 TO "THINGS THAT MAKE ME FEEL IMPORTANT."

Category and Descriptions of Items	*Frequency*	*Percentage of Total*
Academic (Doing well in school subjects; getting high marks)	63	34
Playing games (Play by the rules; play skillfully; being chosen for a team; people play with me)	42	23
Help the teacher (Run an errand; carry things for the teacher; bring the teacher a gift)	18	10
Class chores (Straighten books; take stamp order or lunch order)	12	6
Help another child (Help with school work; be "big sister" to new child)	8	4
The teacher calls on me (Praises me; displays my work; calls on me in history)	8	4
Gifts (I give and receive gifts and thanks for them)	8	4
Music (Singing; leading the class in singing; play the piano)	6	3
People say kind things to me	6	3
Be nice to (obey) the teacher (Obey the school rules)	5	3
Help the group	3	2
Be chairman	3	2
Have new clothes or shoes	3	2

The following were mentioned once or twice: only 5 more weeks of school; just to come to school; rest, have a party at school; bring something to school; to be trusted; have good ideas; when I went to the dentist; excursion; get in a fight; don't tattle; people come to my house; we have a new baby; eat lunch; buy own clothing; tell the truth.

something to the status of the children with their peers.

We listed the children who had high group acceptance. Did they actually receive these marks of teacher approval? There were two or three striking exceptions; but we found that, by and large, they did. The children who enjoyed high group acceptance were the same ones who tended to receive better-than-average grades. (We wish we had kept better notes at this point. We remember having discussed this matter, and having agreed on this point. However, we cannot find the data that would support it. We are reporting it, nevertheless, because we are convinced of the truth of it, generally speaking, for our children.)

By itself, teacher approval would not account for high group acceptance. However, as we looked at the categories called "teacher calls on me," "be nice to (obey) the teacher," and "help the teacher," the children's responses seemed to imply that the teacher's approval should at least be considered as a major factor in their feelings of personal worth and therefore in their judgment of the worth of others. When we added up the percentages associated with the four categories in which the teacher figured prominently, we found that 51 per cent of all of the responses had to do with these direct indications of teacher approval.

We did not think that teacher approval accounted for 51 per cent of all of the group acceptance of the children. This would have been pushing the significance of the percentages too far. However, the prominence of this type of response made it obvious that overt teacher approval of individual children was, to say the least, a factor of real significance in the self-evaluation of these children and consequently, in all probability, an important factor in their evaluation and acceptance of one another.

What do children like about themselves? Having touched on the crucially important matter of self-evaluation, and having found this evidence that we as teachers were important factors in the children's lives, we resolved to find out more about what children valued about themselves. To do this, we asked these third, fourth, and fifth grade children two more open questions: (1) "What I like about myself" and (2) "What I don't like about myself."

Our purpose here was simply to gather further information about the data the children used in their self-appraisal. We still assumed that those things which they valued in themselves, they also valued in others. The children's responses to these two questions and their responses to the question "Things that make me feel important" should, we thought, be considered as supplementary to one another. From the responses to these three questions we could develop a sort of inventory of the symbols of self-importance that the children were employing. We did not assume that these symbols would amount to a complete list of the factors that actually contribute to a child's feeling of personal worth or to his means of evaluating the worth of others. However, we did think that we could gain through these questions some notion of the factors that the children were able to put into words. Conceivably, if we knew more about what the children could be articulate about, we would be in a better position to help them deepen their own understanding of themselves and thus of others. It was on the basis of this reasoning that we now proceeded to obtain the responses that are summarized below. The responses themselves were of this type: "my hair," "the way I read" (classified as "academic"), "my coat" (classified as "clothing"), "my ways" (classified as "personality").[3] These were the categories for responses to "What I like about myself":

Physical characteristics:
(hair, eyes, figure, face, height, teeth, complexion)
Academic
Clothing
Helping parents
Possessions
Personality

And these were the categories (typical responses are also given) for "What I don't like about myself":

Physical characteristics:
(face, hair, height, figure, complexion, health, color of eyes, eyes, feet, hands, legs, teeth, hearing)
Temper
(my temper, get mad too easily, I lose my temper)
School subjects
(grades, spelling, reading, painting)
"The way I act"
(my ways, habits, the way I do, I absolutely hate myself)
Play skills
(the way I catch, the way I hit, run fast)
Speech
(the way I talk, I say ain't, cussing, bad English)

When we examined the children's responses to the questions "What I like about myself" and "What I don't like about myself," we noticed first that the negative question ("What I don't like about myself") led to more detailed responses than the positive question did. Then, we noticed the striking similarity between the responses to the two questions. In each case, physical characteristics appeared prominently and in considerable detail. In both cases, academic proficiency was mentioned frequently. The categories called "temper" and "the way I act" we thought to be similar in meaning to the category "personality" for "What I like about myself." It was interesting that "play skills" appeared in response to the negative question only and that "clothing" appeared in response to the positive question only. However, we thought that differences of this type between the two tables could not easily be interpreted and that we would do well simply to take all of the categories that appeared in both tables and to interpret them as fairly representative of the things children like and don't like about themselves. We could generalize this, we thought, into a statement that the categories that emerged from the responses to these two questions were legitimately representative of those things the children were articulate about when they evaluated themselves.

The conscious data of prestige. Our conclusions can be put together to explain the conscious elements of classroom prestige, and how they are expressed.

First, we assumed that whatever is consciously used in self-evaluation is also used in evaluating others. We found that in evaluating themselves, our children consciously use the data reported in their responses to "Things that make me feel important," "What I like about myself," and "What I don't like about myself."

Second, we found that the group's acceptance of individuals in it is expressed through considerate and inconsiderate acts and that inconsiderate acts

[3] The categories given here account for all the children's responses. We are neither ranking the categories nor reporting the frequencies, because of a discrepancy in the directions we gave the children. Some of us told the children to state as many things as they pleased. Others restricted the children to one statement. This meant that we could not pool the frequencies from the classes. Therefore, we have reported here the categories we developed and tested. The actual frequencies are high in all the categories.
The reader will be interested in comparing the responses of our children with the responses of children to the same questions, as reported in A. T. Jersild, *In Search of Self* (New York: Bureau of Publications, Teachers College, Columbia University, 1952). The categories we obtained are very similar to those reported by Jersild, to whom we are indebted for the suggestion that we employ these questions.

are catalogued in the children's responses to "Things that make me want to strike back." They are also indicated in the records of our adult observations of considerate and inconsiderate behavior.

The children, having formed judgments about one another partly on the basis of such elements as teacher approval, clothing, play skills, and physical appearance, gave expression to these judgments through such inconsiderate and considerate acts as overt physical aggression, snubbing, name-calling, helping each other, "tempering the wind to the shorn lamb," and complimentary remarks.

We thought we were dealing with two kinds of symbols here. One, the considerate or inconsiderate act, symbolized acceptance or rejection by an individual and ultimately by the class group. Others, the characteristics mentioned in the last three tables above, were the consciously employed symbols of prestige which underlay many of the acts of considerateness and inconsiderateness we saw.

Unmentioned bases for self-evaluation. It was important that we recognize what the children were recognizing. It was equally important, however, that we not assume that these consciously recognized symbols were of themselves a sufficient explanation of the considerate and inconsiderate behavior we had been observing.

One big gap in the children's responses to the questions about their feelings of self-importance and personal worth (possibly a consequence of the questions having been asked in school rather than somewhere else) is the infrequent mention of family. In the three tables having to do with self-evaluation, parents appear in only one category, and that category is not mentioned nearly so frequently as are others that are purely personal or that relate to marks of school approval. It is unlikely that our children's feelings of personal worth and their judgments of the worth of other children are actually influenced as slightly by family membership as their responses suggest.

Another gap is the children's failure to mention physical health. While attitudes toward physical health might be inferred from their responses dealing with play skills and their physical appearance, not a single child ever talked directly about health or illness, fatigue or abundant energy. It is likely, however, that the status of a child's health has considerable influence on his feeling of personal worth and his judgments about the worth and prestige of others.

We were dealing here only with those personal characteristics and behaviors about which the children were specific and articulate. We knew very well that there are other important factors that help to determine the prestige system of the classroom and the feeling of the individual worth of the children in it.

CHILDREN'S INTERPRETATIONS OF STORIES ABOUT CONSIDERATENESS

The observations, responses to open questions, and sociometric material had all been gathered and interpreted by adults. It remained to check these explanations of "considerateness" against the children's own explanations. This behavior had been explained as it appeared to us adults. Possibly what we called inconsiderate was not so thought of by the children. We now attempted to look at it through the children's eyes.

To do this, we changed the names and otherwise disguised some of our anecdotal material, and asked the children to interpret the anecdotes to us. Here, for example, is one of the anecdotes we used:

The "Lunch Pail" Story

Sally was coming to school. She was going up the steps one morning on her way to her room. She was carrying her lunch pail, overshoes, and a box of crayons. She stumbled and fell on the steps and dropped the things she was carrying, and the crayons all rolled out of the box. Now Leonard came along right behind her. What could he say when he came along? [Children give "nice" answer.] Now let's suppose that Leonard did not stop to help Sally. Why didn't Leonard stop?

Five pairs of children in grades three to six were asked to interpret each of these stories to us. The interviews were conducted as follows: the teacher sat with two children in her class and conducted the interview. The entire interview was recorded on tape, and the tape recording was transcribed.

We selected two children in each class, one we thought of as "high" in considerateness, and the other "low." However, when we examined their interpretations of these stories, we could see no particular relationship between the responses of our "high" and "low" children, nor could we find anything consistent that had to do with grade membership of these children. This may arise from the fact that we used such a small number of children. In any case, we shall not discuss the grade membership of the children. We shall, instead, interpret only the social mechanisms that the children seem to imply by their responses.

What quickly appears from the children's responses to these stories is this: there is a kind of back-and-forth to these inconsiderate behaviors. The first thing that the children saw in these stories was a situation involving aggression and counter-aggression. If A did something to B, then B did something to A. In order to understand what happened to Sally, the children turned to Sally's past relations with Leonard, or looked forward to some retaliatory behavior on Sally's part. The children report, we think, an "eye for an eye" kind of social interaction.

Keeping even. In every case in which the story involved what we had called "inconsiderate" behavior, the children's explanation was based on an assumption either that something had happened in the past for which the child was getting even, or that he would have to get even in the future for what had been done to him. If considerate and inconsiderate behavior were expressions of the prestige system in the classroom (and we thought they were), then the children's interpretations of these stories suggested that the prestige of an individual was maintained in part by keeping even in the face of aggression. Now, our comparison of group acceptance and observed inconsiderate behavior suggests that most of the inconsiderate behavior we had observed was directed downward in the prestige system of the classroom. Yet the children implied that it was crucially important to keep even in the face of aggression and counter-aggression. If inconsiderate behavior was usually directed downward, then either some of the children consistently failed to keep even (which might explain their low prestige), or our observations had not revealed the whole situation to us.

The "keeping even" situation suggested by the children's interpretations of these anecdotes was fully as likely to be true as the "peck order" situation which our own observations had implied. If they were both true, then the inconsiderate behavior we had observed was likely to have been part of a back-and-forth series of aggressions in which the child committing the inconsiderate behavior we saw felt that he himself was keeping even. It did not quite add up, however. We still had an impression that a good deal of the inconsiderate behavior we saw was actually initiated by the children we saw doing it. We wondered how the victims of it could keep even. As a matter of fact, they were *not* keeping even, if the results of our sociometric questions were to be trusted, except in the sense that the peck-order *status quo* may not have been disturbed, but actually maintained, by some aggressions.

Our conclusion was that if aggression and counter-aggression are expressions of prestige in the classroom, then the children who were not accepted by the others were actually out of balance with respect to the aggression—counter-aggression pattern. We supposed that the children of low group acceptance either commit too many aggressions (possibly out of our sight) or fail to commit enough counter-aggressions. In either case, the penalty for failing to keep even would be a loss of prestige in class. In a sense, what was exchanged in this "give and take" was prestige.

We thought of it this way. When A hits B, he has taken away some of B's prestige. In order to get it back, B must hit A back. If he does this, they are "even" and the matter comes to an end. If he hits back too hard, then they are out of balance, B having taken away more of A's prestige than was his due. A, then, must hit back again.

Actually this A and B business seemed to us to square with the facts of a great many playground squabbles. When boys start roughhousing, their roughhousing often spirals into a "mad" fight, with thirty other children surrounding them making hysterical noises. We try to prevent such fights on our playground; but they happen on the way to and from school, and sometimes they happen on the playground despite our efforts.

"An eye for an eye" and the teacher. We wondered what our role, as teachers, should be. Here was the situation, as the children reported it—an "eye for an eye" sort of thing.

It was possible that we were sometimes involved

in this spiraling, trading, primitive social mechanism, without knowing it. An incident in the school yard one morning illustrated this situation to us. Here is the teacher's report of what happened:

> During recess two fourth grade boys caught hold of Willa Jean, backed her up against a tree, and kissed her. Cora, who saw this, was outraged. She ran into my room and reported the incident to me. I agreed with her that this kind of thing was intolerable on the playground, called in the two little boys and scolded them for their behavior. After school the two little boys caught Cora and engaged in quite a rough scuffle with her. Cora went home crying. She told the story to her mother, and her mother said, "That's what you get for tattling."

The teacher had been caught squarely in the middle of a spiral of counter-aggressions. The effect of her calling in the two little boys and scolding them had been to get things so "out of balance" that the boys committed aggression against Cora. The series had come to an end only with the mother's rebuff. How might the teacher have avoided being caught?

There was a way to handle this situation that would have dealt with the disciplinary problem on the playground and yet not left Cora "out of balance" with the two little boys. The teacher somehow had to break the spiral of aggression and counter-aggression. The teacher might have broken the spiral by accepting Cora's report of the misdemeanor, but not reacting to it instantly. Rather, the teacher might have waited for an opportunity to put this event with others and discuss the whole matter with the two boys, or in a general way with the whole class, at a later time. Her immediate response to Cora might have been, "Thank you very much, Cora, for reporting this to me. I'll look into it." The teacher's mistake had been made when she immediately went out and called in the two boys for their scolding. In a sense, she simply added velocity to the spiraling aggression and counter-aggression by what she did, and Cora's treatment after school was predictable.

IN SUMMARY

We have reached some conclusions based on the evidence we collected, and think that there are some important implications that grow out of these conclusions.

First, we think that considerate behavior and inconsiderate behavior are thought of in a substantially similar way by our children and by us teachers, insofar as we are talking about the overt behavior we teachers have customarily referred to in these terms. This was true in both the high school and the elementary school. However, the children identify a great deal of covert inconsiderate behavior (in naming "things that make me want to strike back") that we have not usually seen.

Second, we believe that in our elementary school there is a pattern of considerate and inconsiderate behavior which is an expression of the existing social structure of the classroom as revealed through sociometric questions. This leads us to re-examine the significance of such behavior.

Third, the group acceptance of individuals in the classroom depends (among other things) on a number of consciously recognized factors—"things that make me feel important," "things I like about myself," and "things I don't like about myself." These symbols we regard as the currency or data of prestige. We think that these consciously recognized symbols of individual worth should be taken into account by teachers in our school who wish to have a deliberate desirable effect on the children's feelings of personal worth, and consequently on their feelings about the worth of others.

Fourth, we believe our children, who maintain the prestige system in our classroom by means of what we have been calling "considerate" and "inconsiderate" behavior, actually see themselves as keeping a sort of balance with one another when they commit what we call "inconsiderate" behavior. Their interpretations of this behavior strongly imply that, from the child's point of view, most aggression is counter-aggression.

Fifth, the teacher's approval or disapproval is a very important contributing factor in both the personal feeling of worth of our children and the system of aggression and counter-aggression, considerateness and counter-considerateness, that exist in our classrooms. With respect to "inconsiderate" behavior, it is very important that we teachers avoid being caught in a series of aggressions and counter-aggressions of which we are not aware. This bears particularly on what we do about "tattling," and on what we think about the "teacher's pet" situation.

*YALE STUDIES OF COMMUNICATION AND PERSUASION**

By Carl I. Hovland

INTRODUCTION

During the last ten or a dozen years the writer and his colleagues have been pursuing a systematic program of research on how opinions and beliefs are modified by communications. Research of this type, involving psychological experiments in a communication setting, can contribute to our understanding of the processes of memory, thought, motivation, and social influence. The material communicated can be controlled with much the same precision possible in laboratory research, but motivational and emotional factors can be permitted to operate more naturalistically than in the laboratory.

For research purposes it is convenient to define *communication* as the process by which an individual (the communicator) transmits stimuli (usually verbal) to modify the behavior of other individuals. This definition specifies the research task as consisting in the analysis of four factors: *The communicator* who transmits the communication, *the message* transmitted by the communicator, the *predispositions* of the audience, and the *changes* in knowledge and attitudes resulting from the communication. These topics parallel closely the well-known formula of *"who* says *what* to *whom* with *what effect."* Before describing some of our typical studies let me summarize briefly the problems we have investigated in each of these areas.

The communicator. An important factor influencing the effectiveness of a communication is the person or group perceived as originating the communication, and the cues provided as to the trustworthiness, intentions, and affiliations of this source. In some instances, merely perceiving a particular source as advocating the new opinion will be sufficient to induce acceptance. This is generally referred to as "prestige suggestion." The aspects of the problem with which our investigations have been concerned are the effects of variations in the trustworthiness and expertness of the communicator on the recipient's perception and evaluation of the presentation and on his acceptance of the position advocated by the communicator.

Content of the communication. Our research has investigated several aspects of content. The first concerns appeals. This class of stimuli consists of communication contents which arouse emotional states or which are capable of providing strong incentives for acceptance of the new opinion and/or rejection of the original opinions held by the audience.

The second aspect of the content of the communication concerns organization of arguments. The types of arguments employed and their manner of organization will influence what the audience thinks about during exposure to a communication and hence may have a marked effect on their acceptance or rejection. Different types of appeals, orders of presentation, and types of context were studied.

Audience predisposition. The influence exerted by a communicator and by what he says is often dependent upon the individual's adherence to group norms or standards. Thus, one important set of audience predispositions concerns the conformity motives which stem from membership in, or affiliation with, various social groups.

Another aspect of investigation was individual personality factors. Some individuals are likely to be highly responsive to persuasion while others are more resistant. These individual differences in susceptibility to persuasion may arise from differences

* Prepared especially for this volume. Tables and figures are used by permission of the Yale University Press and the American Psychological Association. Figures 7-1 and 7-2 are from the *Journal of Abnormal and Social Psychology*, 1957, *55*, pp. 247, 248. Tables 7-5, 7-6, 7-7, 7-8, and 7-11 and Figures 7-3, 7-4, and 7-5 are from Hovland, Janis, and Kelley. *Communication and Persuasion* (New Haven: Yale University Press, 1953). Table 7-9 is from Hovland *et al.* (Eds.) *Order of Presentation in Persuasion* (New Haven: Yale University Press, 1957), p. 45. Table 7-10 is from Rosenberg *et al. Attitude Organization and Change* (New Haven: Yale University Press, 1960), p. 28.

in abilities (e.g., capacity for comprehending the meaning of what others say) or in motives (e.g., strong desire to avoid considering adverse consequences stressed by the communicator).

Kinds of response. Attitudes are commonly described as predispositions to respond in characteristic ways to particular objects. In analysing attitudinal responses different writers have stressed three areas: emotional or affective responses (evaluations), cognitive responses (beliefs), and overt behavioral responses. What are the interrelations between these different measures of attitude? This problem was investigated by manipulating experimentally one type of response so that it became inconsistent with other components and studying the type of reorganization produced.

A second factor considered in response patterns was duration of opinion change. There are a number of problems concerning the degree to which new opinions are retained. For example, powerful interference may arise from later exposure to competing communications which foster rejection of the opinions recommended in the first communication. Even with no subsequent counter-pressure, an individual may forget the incentive material learned from the communication, so that after a short period he fails to recall those ideas favoring continued acceptance. On the other hand, the individual may initially show great resistance during the communication but subsequently appear to accept it "spontaneously." Representative findings from research in this area will be discussed in this paper.

STUDIES OF THE ROLE OF THE COMMUNICATOR

The effectiveness of a communication is commonly assumed to depend to a considerable extent upon who delivers it. We shall deal primarily with situations in which the effects are attributable to a single, clear-cut source — an individual speaker who communicates directly to the audience and gives his own views on an issue. We shall refer to this kind of source as a "communicator."

The limited area chosen for investigation in our research program concerns factors related to credibility of the source. Analysis of this area will focus on three problems. How do differences in the credibility of the communicator affect: 1) the way in which the content and presentation are perceived, 2) the way its fairness is evaluated, and 3) the degree to which attitudes and beliefs are modified?

Perception of the communicator. In an experiment by Hovland, Harvey, and Sherif,[1] the credibility of the communicator and the content of his message were varied. The investigators were interested in among other things audience perception of the communication as it related to beliefs.

The topic discussed in this study was prohibition of alcohol. (The subjects came from a dry state where this was a lively issue.) From a series of nine statements ranging from extreme dry to extreme wet each subject indicated: the position most acceptable to him, other acceptable positions, the position most objectionable to him, and other objectionable positions. The most extreme dry statement was, "Since alcohol is the curse of mankind, the sale and use of alcohol, including light beer, should be completely abolished." A moderately wet statement was, "The sale of alcohol should be so regulated that it is available in limited quantities for special occasions." A more extreme wet stand was, "Since prohibition is a major cause of corruption in public life, lawlessness, immoral acts, and juvenile delinquency, the sale and use of alcohol should be legalized."

Several groups of subjects were selected whose stands on the issue were known such as WCTU members. These groups were compared with unselected groups of college students. In a subsequent session "wet" groups received a "dry" or "moderately wet" communication; "dry" groups received a "wet" or "moderately wet" communication; unselected groups received a "dry," or "moderately wet," or "wet" communication. After the communication, opinion measurements and reactions to the communications were obtained.

Subjects who received the "moderately wet" communication were asked to rate on a scale from extreme dry to extreme wet what they believed to be the position advocated by the communicator.

[1] C. I. Hovland, O. J. Harvey, and M. Sherif, "Assimilation and Contrast Effects in Reactions to Communication and Attitude Change," *Journal of Abnormal and Social Psychology,* 1957, *55,* pp. 244-252.

The results of this part of the experiment are shown in Figure 7-1.

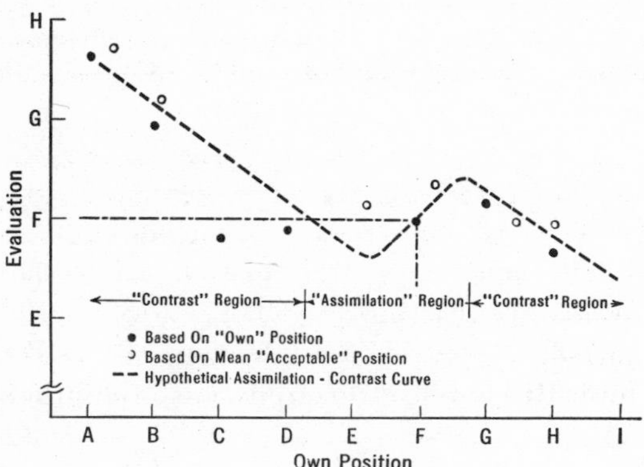

Figure 7-1. Average placements of position of moderately wet communication (F) by *Ss* holding various positions on the issue, plotted against hypothetical assimilation-contrast curve.

From a previous study we predicted that positions differing only slightly from one's own would be assimilated while larger differences between one's own position and that of the communication would be exaggerated, showing a contrast effect. Figure 7-1 bears out this prediction. Individuals who themselves held a position very close to that actually presented by the communicator were able to rate it accurately with respect to what was advocated. Those a little further away in either the pro or con direction tended to distort the communication to be saying something closer to what they themselves believed (assimilation effect). Those whose own position was at considerable variance with that of the communicator tended to view the content as more unlike their own position than it really was (contrast effect).

Evaluation of the fairness of the communication. The above study also provided data concerning how members of the audience with pro attitudes and con attitudes on the prohibition issue rated an identical speech on the subject. Figure 7-2 shows that those whose own position was similar to that of the communicator rated the statement as "fair and unbiased" to a significantly greater degree than those whose position was opposed to that of the communicator even though each group that was compared heard the same talk. Those with an opposed stand regarded the communication as propagandistic and unfair.

Effects upon opinion. It has been found that when a communication is presented by a highly respected source, it will be judged more fair and unbiased

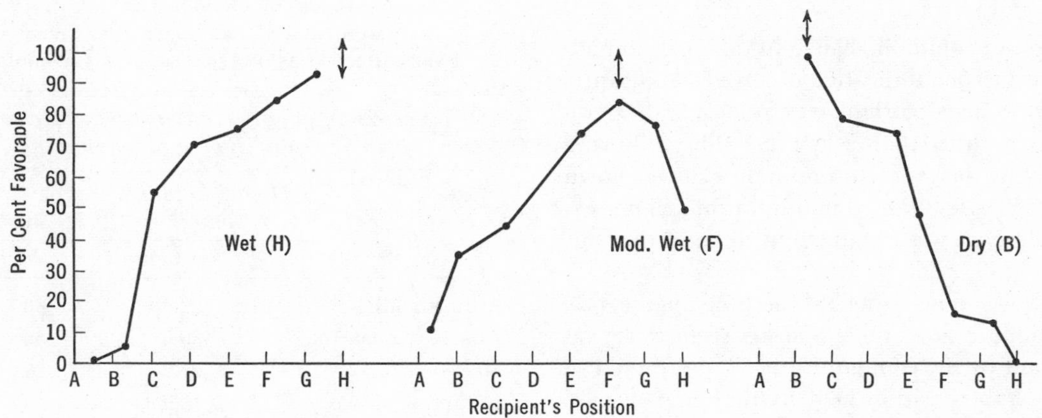

Figure 7-2. Percentage of favorable evaluations of wet (H), moderately wet (F), and dry (B) communications for *Ss* holding various positions on prohibition (based on mean acceptable statement).
(Positions of communications indicated by arrow)

than the identical communication presented by a communicator thought to be untrustworthy. In an experiment primarily set up to determine the duration of effects of communications, data were obtained by Hovland and Weiss[2] on the extent to which the perceived credibility of the communicator affects his influence. Four different topics were selected, each presented to some subjects by a source of high credibility and to other subjects by one of low credibility. Affirmative and negative versions of each topic were employed.

Each of the subjects received a booklet containing one article on each of four topics with the name of the source given at the end of each article. The four topics were the sale of antihistamine drugs, the feasibility of building an atomic submarine (the study was done in 1949), responsibility for the then-current steel shortage, and the future of movie theaters. A questionnaire administered before the communication obtained judgments from the subjects as to the trustworthiness of a long list of sources, including the specific ones used. Opinion questionnaires on the topics discussed were administered before, immediately after, and a month after the communication.

The results of the experiment showed that differences in initial attitudes towards the sources definitely affected audience evaluations of the article. Even though the communications being judged were identical except for attribution of the source, the presentation was considered to be less fair and the conclusions less justified when the source was of low rather than high credibility. These data are presented in Table 7-5.

Furthermore, opinion change in the direction advocated by the communication occurred significantly more often when it originated from a high credibility source rather than a low one. The following table presents the results on opinion change shown immediately after the communication. The expected difference was obtained on three of the four topics.

By way of summarizing this section on the role of the communicator, these findings seem clear: (a) What is said by the communicator is interpreted in the light of the position held by the recipient; (b) an identical message is differently evaluated in

[2] C. I. Hovland and W. Weiss, "The Influence of Source Credibility on Communication Effectiveness," *Public Opinion Quarterly*, 1951, *15*, pp. 635-650.

TABLE 7-5

EFFECTS OF HIGH AND LOW CREDIBILITY SOURCES ON EVALUATIONS OF FAIRNESS AND JUSTIFIABILITY OF IDENTICAL COMMUNICATIONS

A. Per cent considering author "fair" in his presentation

Topic	*High Credibility Source*		*Low Credibility Source*	
	*N**	*Per Cent*	*N*	*Per Cent*
Antihistamines	31	64.5	27	59.3
Atomic Submarines	25	96.0	36	69.4
Steel Shortage	37	24.3	26	19.2
Future of Movies	29	93.1	33	63.7
Mean		65.6		54.9

B. Per cent considering author's conclusion "justified" by the facts

Topic	*High Credibility Source*		*Low Credibility Source*	
	N	*Per Cent*	*N*	*Per Cent*
Antihistamines	31	67.7	27	51.8
Atomic Submarines	25	80.0	36	44.4
Steel Shortage	37	32.4	26	26.9
Future of Movies	29	58.6	33	42.4
Mean		58.2		41.8

* N = number of cases used.

TABLE 7-6

NET CHANGES OF OPINION IN DIRECTION OF COMMUNICATION FOR SOURCES CLASSIFIED BY EXPERIMENTERS AS OF HIGH OR LOW CREDIBILITY*

Net percentage of cases in which subjects changed opinion in direction of communication

Topic	*High Credibility Sources*			*Low Credibility Sources*	
	N	*Per Cent*		*N*	*Per Cent*
Antihistamines	31	22.6		30	13.3
Atomic Submarines	25	36.0		36	0.0
Steel Shortage	35	22.9		26	−3.8
Future of Movies	31	12.9		30	16.7
Mean		23.0			6.6
Difference			16.4		
p			<.01		

* Net changes = positive changes *minus* negative changes.

terms of fairness and impartiality by individuals whose own stands on the issue differ; (c) identical communications presented by communicators who are highly respected are judged more fair and unbiased than those by communicators thought to be less expert or less trustworthy; (d) the extent to which opinions are changed is affected by the degree of credibility of the communicator.

STUDIES OF THE CONTENT OF THE COMMUNICATION

The variables we shall now discuss have been lively issues in the history of rhetoric. These issues are: The effectiveness of emotional appeals in a communication; the relative advantage of having the first word (primacy effect) as opposed to having the last word (recency effect); and the advisability of presenting both the pro and con arguments in a communication.

Emotional appeals. The effects of using one kind of emotional appeal were studied in an experiment by Janis and Feshback.[3] Three different intensities of "fear appeal" were used in a standard communication on dental hygiene. A 15-minute illustrated lecture was prepared in three different forms, all of which contained the same essential information about causes of tooth decay and the same series of recommendations concerning oral hygiene. The three forms of the talk differed only with respect to the amount of personal threat presented. Form 1 contained a strong appeal, emphasizing the painful consequences of tooth decay, diseased gums, and other dangers. Form 2 presented a moderate appeal in which the dangers were described in a milder and more factual manner. Form 3 presented a minimal appeal which rarely alluded to the consequences of tooth neglect. The fear appeals were designed to stimulate emotional reactions in order to motivate the audience to conform to a set of recommendations. The strong appeal used personalized threat references (This can happen to you!) and vivid photographs of diseased mouths.

The entire freshman class of a large high school was randomly divided into four groups. Each group received one of the three dental communications and the fourth group, used as a control, received a communication on another topic. Immediately after exposure to the communication, the students were asked about their feelings while the talk was being given. The results indicated that the strong fear group felt more worried about the health of their teeth than the other two groups, and the moderate group felt more worried than the minimal group.

The main concern of this experiment was with the effectiveness of the different levels of fear in inducing the audience to accept the recommendations presented, and further, with exploring the potentially adverse effects of strong fear arousal. Five questions concerning dental hygiene practices were presented to all subjects one week before the communication and again one week later. These questions, which asked the students to describe the way they were currently brushing their teeth, covered practices about which all forms of the talk contained specific recommendations.

The results shown in the table below reveal that the greatest amount of conformity to the recommendations occurred in the *minimal* fear group,

TABLE 7-7

EFFECT OF THE ILLUSTRATED TALK ON CONFORMITY TO DENTAL HYGIENE RECOMMENDATIONS

Type of Change	*Group: Strong (N = 50)*	*Moderate (N = 50)*	*Minimal (N = 50)*	*Control (N = 50)*
Increased conformity	28%	44%	50%	22%
Decreased conformity	20	22	14	22
No change	52	34	36	56
Total	100	100	100	100
Net change in conformity	+8%	+22%	+36%	+0%

Reliability of Differences	*Critical Ratio*	*Probability Value*
Control vs. minimal	2.54	<.01
Control vs. moderate	1.50	.07
Control vs. strong	0.59	.28
Strong vs. moderate	0.95	.17
Strong vs. minimal	1.96	.03
Moderate vs. minimal	0.93	.18

[3] I. L. Janis and S. Feshback, "Effects of Fear-Arousing Communications," *Journal of Abnormal and Social Psychology*, 1953, *48*, pp. 78-92.

Form 3. The strong-fear group showed less change than the minimal-fear group and did not differ significantly from the controls. The data show a fairly consistent trend which suggests that as the amount of fear-arousing material is increased (above some undetermined minimal level) conformity to the communicator's recommendations tends to decrease. Similar results occurred with regard to other recommendations.

In addition to greater persuasiveness, the minimal-fear appeal also produced the greatest resistance to counter-propaganda. The importance of using the "proper" toothbrush and avoiding the "wrong" kind was a major theme of all the talks and was one of the main opinions on which changes were produced by the communication. In the questionnaire testing post-communication attitudes, all subjects read a brief statement which contradicted this particular theme of the original communication. The minimal-appeal group resisted more strongly changing their opinions to agree with the new, counter-propaganda appeal than did the other two groups. The results are shown in Table 7-8. The reason minimal fear was more effective, the authors suggest, is that the strong fear appeal aroused interfering motivations in the subjects, causing them to be inattentive to the communication, to ignore or minimize the threat, or to feel aggressive towards the communicator.

TABLE 7-8

EFFECT OF THE ILLUSTRATED TALK ON REACTIONS TO SUBSEQUENT COUNTERPROPAGANDA: NET PERCENTAGE OF EACH GROUP WHO CHANGED IN THE DIRECTION OF AGREEING WITH THE STATEMENT THAT "IT DOES NOT MATTER WHAT KIND OF TOOTHBRUSH A PERSON USES"

Type of Change	*Group: Strong (N = 50)*	*Moderate (N = 50)*	*Minimal (N = 50)*	*Control (N = 50)*
More agreement	30%	28%	14%	44%
Less agreement	38	42	54	24
No change	32	30	32	32
Total	100	100	100	100
Net change	−8%	−14%	−40%	+20%
Net effect (experimental minus control)	−28%	−34%	−60%	

Reliability of the Differences in Net Change	*Critical Ratio*	*Probability Value*
Control vs. minimal	3.66	<.001
Control vs. moderate	2.05	.02
Control vs. strong	1.71	.05
Strong vs. moderate	0.36	.36
Strong vs. minimal	2.03	.02
Moderate vs. minimal	1.66	.05

Organization of presentation. The second factor we shall consider is the organization of a communication. What effect does the order of presentation have upon an audience? A Law of Primacy in persuasion had been put forth by Lund stating that the side of an issue presented first will have greater effectiveness than the side presented subsequently. Other researchers, however, had found that greater change was produced by that side of the issue presented last. This finding suggests a recency effect rather than a primacy effect.

A number of studies have been carried out under our program in order to unravel some of these complexities.[4] A study of Luchins [5] was concerned with evaluating the effects of various sequences of information communicated about an individual on the impressions formed about that person's personality. Subjects were presented with a written description of an individual's behavior during the day. Part of the information was a paragraph reporting Jim (the stimulus person) acting in a very friendly, outgoing way (Extrovertive, or E, description):

> Jim left the house to get some stationery. He walked out into the sun-filled street with two of his friends, basking in the sun as he walked. Jim entered the stationery store which was full of people. Jim talked with an acquaintance while he waited for the clerk to catch his eye. On his way out, he stopped to chat with a school friend who was just coming into the store. Leaving the store, he walked toward school. On his way out he met the girl to whom he had been introduced the night before. They talked for a short while, and then Jim left for school.[6]

[4] C. I. Hovland *et al.* (Eds.), *Order of Presentation in Persuasion* (New Haven: Yale University Press, 1957).

[5] *Ibid.*, pp. 33-61.

[6] *Ibid.*, p. 34.

Another paragraph described Jim behaving in a more withdrawn way, in similar situations to those above. (Introvertive, or I, description.) Two other descriptions were obtained by combining the E and I descriptions, resulting in an EI sequence, or an IE sequence.

Thus, four experimental groups were set up, two of which received the combined or inconsistent information and two of which received either one description or the other. In all groups, subjects were asked to form impressions about Jim, and then to write a paragraph describing him. Rating scales on relevant traits, such as "forward," "friendly," etc., were presented and recall of the content of the communication was assessed by having the subjects fill in incomplete sentences. The descriptive paragraph written by each subject was compared through content analysis with the actual information contained in the E and I descriptions. When the responses were analyzed for primacy-recency effects, the results shown in Table 7-9 were obtained. (It should be noted that if an index of primacy-recency is positive, it points to primacy, whereas if it is negative, it points to recency.)

The table indicates that all of the differences are positive, thereby testifying to the predominant influence of the primary description. Thus, the material presented first was considerably more influential than that presented second in determining what were thought to be the principal personality characteristics of the individual described. It was remarkable also how many of the subjects received the incompatible information without realizing that there was any conflict of interpretation involved. Over a third of the subjects stated they had not been aware of any contradictions or inconsistencies.

Later experiments were carried out by the same author to see what procedures might weaken or eliminate the primacy effect. He reasoned that the primacy effect he had obtained had many similarities to the phenomenon of "set," or *Einstellung*, which he had found operative in problem-solving behavior, where subjects frequently persisted in attacking new problems the same way they had solved previous ones even though far simpler solutions were possible. In a replication of the primacy-recency experiment previously described, Group I was run under the original conditions as a control group. Group II was explicitly warned about possible "first impression" fallacies before any information was presented. Group III was warned between the first and second blocks of information, while Group IV had an arithmetic task injected between the two blocks of information. Results showed that there was a progressive decrease in primacy effect and increase in recency effect from Group I to Group IV. Thus, the primacy effect found in presenting contradictory information in the same communication was reduced by interpolat-

TABLE 7-9

Survey of Results in Experiment 2

(N: Group E, 40; Group EI, 135; Group IE, 135; Group I, 40)

	% E Responses				*% I Responses*				*Primary-Recency*		
	Group				*Group*				*Index*	*Index*	*Mean*
Item	*E*	*EI*	*IE*	*I*	*E*	*EI*	*IE*	*I*	*1*	*2*	*Mean*
Written impression	88	41	20	0	0	24	49	82	+21	+25	+23
Friendly-unfriendly	90	71	54	25	0	19	31	55	+17	+12	+15
Forward-shy	50	33	17	0	0	51	67	95	+16	+16	+16
Social-unsocial	85	60	46	5	0	30	41	85	+14	+11	+13
Aggressive-passive	55	26	18	5	45	55	62	75	+8	+7	+8
Sentence *re* store	93	58	30	12	0	19	41	62	+28	+22	+25
Sentence *re* students	88	63	34	8	0	23	44	77	+29	+21	+25
Sentence *re* girls	97	59	29	3	0	19	46	87	+30	+27	+28
Total questionnaire	80	51	31	7	6	30	48	77	+20	+18	+19

ing other activities between the blocks of information and by warning the subjects against the fallibility of first impressions.

Other experiments have shed light on still other factors which may determine whether or not the primacy effect will occur. Hovland and Mandell[7] attempted to replicate an earlier study by Lund[8] which had shown the effect. But the later study did not confirm the first. One difference between the original study and the replication was that, in the former, the regular teacher presented both sides of the issue to his students, whereas in the latter, somebody from outside the school came to present rival views. Thus, the students in the Lund experiment may have been motivated to learn the first side of the communication as part of their class work and probably were not expecting there would be a second side. This suggests that where the audience is aware that the issue is a controversial one and that there are two sides, they will not be so heavily influenced by the side that comes first.

A personality factor which interacts with order of presentation was investigated by Cohen.[9] Subjects who had a high desire for understanding were not differently influenced by different orderings of the same communication, but those subjects who had relatively weak desire for understanding were more influenced by order.

Commitment is another factor which may lead to a primacy effect. Hovland, Campbell, and Brock[10] presented one side of a controversial issue to one group of subjects, and asked them to write their opinion on the issue for publication in a magazine read by their peers. A control group wrote out anonymous opinions. When the other side of the issue was presented later, the authors found that the public expression of opinion tended to "freeze" the subject's views and make them resistant to influence by the other side of the issue.

The effects of presenting "one side" versus "both sides." Two patterns are usually available to the communicator; he can present only the points that support his position, or he can present his position and refute the opposing arguments. Which is more effective?

Experimental data on the problem are provided by Hovland, Lumsdaine, and Sheffield.[11] In this study, two experimental groups of 214 soldiers each and a control group of 197 received communications which argued that finishing the war in the Pacific would be difficult and take at least two years after VE day. Beliefs about the issue were tested before the communication and immediately after. One experimental group was given a fifteen-minute talk including only the arguments for thinking that the war against Japan would be a long one. The material contained much factual information stressing Japan's advantages and resources. The second experimental group was given a communication which contained the same arguments but also some consideration and refutation of arguments on the other side, e.g., concerning Japan's weaknesses. To evaluate the effectiveness of the two programs, subjects were asked to estimate the probable length of the war with Japan.

Both programs were found to be extremely effective, with marked changes in the same direction shown for both experimental groups. No advantage of one program over the other for the audience *as a whole* was revealed. When, however, certain critical factors were taken into account, advantages for opinion change of one pattern over another began to appear.

The initial stand of the listener was one such factor. Figure 7-3 shows that presenting both sides of the issue persuaded more of the men who were at first opposed to the communication, e.g., men who expected a short war, than did presenting only the one side.

On the other hand, the program giving the one-sided picture was more effective for the men who initially favored the stand taken, i.e., those who already agreed that the war would take at least two years. Another finding was that the program which presented both sides was more effective with better educated men, while that which presented one side was more effective with less educated men. The authors conclude that obtaining information about

[7] C. I. Hovland and W. Mandell, "Is There a 'Law of Primacy in Persuasion'?" in *ibid.*, Ch. 2.

[8] F. H. Lund, "The Psychology of Belief," *Journal of Abnormal and Social Psychology*, 1925, *20*, pp. 174-196.

[9] A. R. Cohen, "Need for Cognition and Order of Communication as Determinants of Opinion Change," in Hovland *et al.*, *Order of Presentation in Persuasion, op. cit.*, Ch. 6.

[10] C. I. Hovland, E. H. Campbell, and T. Brock, "The Effects of 'Commitment' on Opinion Change," in Hovland *et al.*, *Order of Presentation in Persuasion, op. cit.*, Ch. 3.

[11] C. I. Hovland, A. A. Lumsdaine, and F. D. Sheffield, *Experiments on Mass Communication* (Princeton, N. J.: Princeton University Press, 1949), Ch. 8.

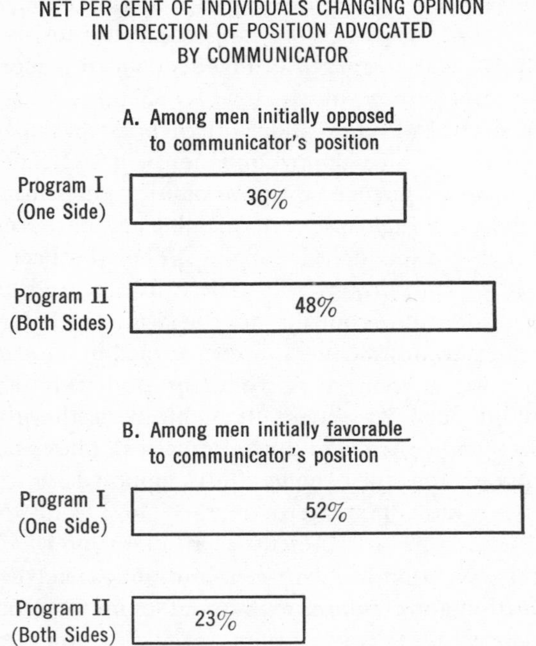

Figure 7-3. Effects of a One-sided vs. a Two-sided Presentation on Beliefs.

the educational level and initial position of an audience might be of considerable value in choosing the most effective type of presentation.

In the above experiment, effects of the communication were measured only in terms of immediate changes in opinion. It was not possible to compare the effects of one-sided versus two-sided communications in terms of resistance to subsequently presented "counter-propaganda." A more recent study by Lumsdaine and Janis[12] explored this question more fully. It was conducted several months before the announcement by President Truman that Russia had produced an atomic explosion. It compared the effects of two forms of a persuasive communication. Both forms consisted of a transcribed "radio program" in which the same communicator took the position that Russia would be unable to produce large numbers of atomic bombs for at least the next five years.

Program I, the one-sided presentation, contained only the arguments that supported this conclusion, such as: Russian scientists have not yet discovered all the crucial secrets; they cannot learn all of them through espionage; even after acquiring all the know-how Russia does not have sufficient industrial potential to produce the bombs in quantity. Program II, a two-sided presentation, contained the same arguments presented in identical fashion but also presented and discussed arguments for the other side of the picture. Examples were: Russia has many first-rate atomic scientists; Russian industries have made a phenomenal recovery since the war; Russia has uranium mines in Siberia. The total content of both programs was designed to lead to the conclusion that Russia would be unable to produce atomic bombs in quantity for at least five years. Except for the presence of the opposing arguments, the two communications were identical; Program II was recorded first, and Program I was constructed by simply deleting the opposing arguments from the tape recording.

One experimental group received the one-sided program (I) and another the two-sided program (II). A week later half of each group was exposed to a counter-communication and the other half was not. The counter-propaganda consisted of a second communication in which the same issue was discussed by a different commentator who argued that Russia had probably already developed the atomic bomb and within two years would be producing it in large quantities. All groups were given an initial questionnaire several weeks before the experiment to determine initial level of opinion and a final questionnaire at the end of the experiment. The main question designed to measure the effects of the communications was: "About how long from now do you think it will be before the Russians are really producing large numbers of atomic bombs?" This question was asked in both the initial and the final questionnaires.

As in the earlier experiment, there was little overall difference in the effectiveness of the two programs for those groups that were not exposed to counter-propaganda. The results for the groups that were exposed to counter-propaganda show that Program II was decidedly superior to Program I.

Generalizations which can be made from this section on content of the communication are: (a) A two-sided presentation is more effective in the long run than a one-sided presentation when, regardless of initial opinion, the audience is exposed to subse-

[12] A. A. Lumsdaine and I. L. Janis, "Resistance to 'Counter-propaganda' Produced by a One-sided versus a Two-sided 'Propaganda' Presentation," *Public Opinion Quarterly,* 1953, *17,* pp. 311-318.

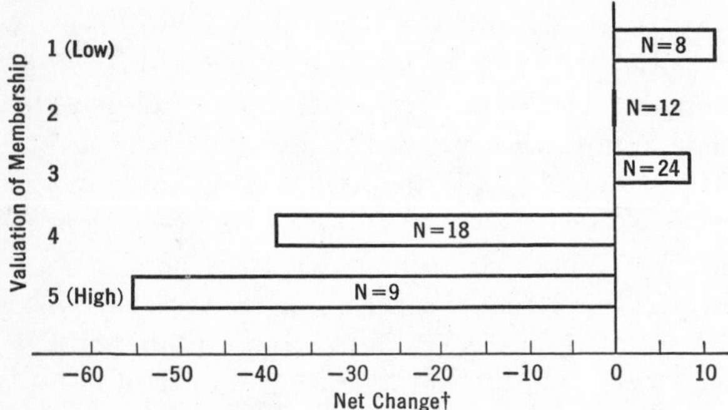

Figure 7-4. Opinion Change in Response to Counter-norm Communication for Scouts with Various Degrees of Valuation of Membership.* ("Private" Samples Only.)

*Combining categories 1, 2, and 3 and comparing them (in terms of net change) with 4 and 5 combined, $p < .02$ using one-tailed test.

†Net change equals the per cent changing in direction advocated by the communication minus the per cent changing in the opposite direction.

quent counter-propaganda, or when, regardless of subsequent exposure to counter-propaganda, the audience initially disagrees with the commentator's position; (b) a two-sided presentation is less effective than a one-sided presentation if the audience initially agrees with the commentator's position and is not exposed to later counter-propaganda; (c) as amount of fear-arousing material is increased, conformity to the communication tends to decrease; (d) an opinion or attitude arrived at under minimum fear is more resistant to counter-propaganda than an opinion or attitude developed under strong fear; (e) primacy effect seems to be superior to recency effect in communicating blocks of information which are incompatible; (f) personality factors and degree of commitment affect whether the primacy or the recency effect will occur.

STUDIES OF AUDIENCE PREDISPOSITIONS

Group membership. In addition to being affected by the factors discussed above, the effects of a communication are determined by the characteristics of the recipient. One important characteristic of a recipient is the strength of his tendency to conform to norms of groups of which he is a member.

A study by Kelley and Volkart[13] tested the hypothesis that members who value the group highly will be less influenced by a communication contrary to group norms than will members who place a lower value on their belonging. The members of 12 Boy Scout troops served as subjects, and the communication, contrary to the Scouts' emphasis on camping and woodcrafts, etc., argued that today's youth would profit more from learning about cities and city activities. One week before and immediately after the communication, a scale measuring attitudes towards woodcraft as opposed to city activites was administered.

The results are presented in Figure 7-4. The inverse relationship between how much the boys valued the group and amount of opinion change produced by a counter-norm communication was supported by the data. The boys who valued their membership less tended to change in the direction advocated by the communication (as shown by the positive net change) while the high valuation members actually changed in the opposite direction, suggesting that the communication had a boomerang effect in this group of subjects.

Individual personality predisposition. A number of our studies appear to indicate some individuals are consistently more influenced by communications than are others, regardless of source, topic, or medium. We shall refer to this characteristic as "persuasibility."

General persuasibility is demonstrated in the studies of Janis and Field.[14] The procedure devised by these experimenters to assess general persuasibility consisted of (1) an initial questionnaire on opinions, (2) Booklet I containing five persuasive communications on topics included in the initial questionnaire, and (3) Booklet II presenting a second series of five persuasive communications on exactly the same topics as the first series but taking

[13] H. H. Kelley and E. H. Volkart, "The Resistance to Change of Group-Anchored Attitudes," *American Sociological Review*, 1952, *17*, pp. 453-465.

[14] I. L. Janis and P. B. Field, "A Behavioral Assessment of Persuasibility: Consistency of Individual Differences," *Sociometry*, 1956, *19*, pp. 241-259.

diametrically opposite positions. After each communication, the subjects were asked the same opinion questions as in the initial questionnaire. A general persuasibility score was assigned to each subject on the basis of his opinion changes in response to both booklets. In order for an opinion change to be counted as such, the subject who had changed his initial opinion in one direction in response to the communication in Booklet I must change following the Booklet II communication all the way back to his original position or beyond on the provided scale.

The results of the Janis-Field investigations indicate consistent individual differences in persuasibility. Further corroboration came from a study by King[15] on adolescents.

Other evidence concerning persuasibility and factors which influence it comes from studies conducted by Abelson and Lesser[16] using first-grade children for subjects. These authors devised three tests of general persuasibility:

1. The Persuasibility Booklet, consisting of pairs of unfamiliar objects. The communicator showed each pair of pictures to the subjects, first indicating her own preference for one of the objects and then asking the subjects to state their preferences.

2. The Incomplete Stories test. Each story described a situation involving a mother (or father) and child, in which the parent figure stated a novel opinion, fact, or bit of advice. The subject was asked to tell what the child in the story would think or do in response.

3. The Recorded Opinions measure. Unusual questions were posed to the subjects and they were asked to give their opinions. Before giving their views, the subjects heard a tape recording on which either two adult voices (one male and one female) or voices of children expressed unanimity of opinion in favor of one choice. Subjects were then asked to state their own preferences.

Two additional measures were obtained. One was a parent rating of the subjects on persuasibility and the other a teacher rating of the same trait.

The results of these procedures yielded statistically significant intercorrelations among the various measures, showing that subjects who were influenced on one topic or one source tended toward persuasibility over the other topics and in relation to all the sources (parents, teachers, experimenters, peers).

Some studies have attempted to determine what other personality variables are concomitant with high and low responsiveness to verbal communications. Janis and Field[17] investigated the hypothesis that high persuasibility is related to low self-esteem. Using a self-rating personality inventory they found small but significant correlations between high persuasibility and measures of inadequacy feelings and social inhibitions.

The hypothesis is presented by Lesser and Abelson[18] that low self-esteem and high persuasibility stem from the same type of previous experience, namely, negative reinforcement of disagreement and discrepancy. Similarly these authors believe that aggressiveness and low persuasibility stem from the same antecedent factors, viz., parental rejection and/or lack of firmness in parental control. In any event, their prediction that persuasibility would be positively correlated with submissiveness and negatively correlated with aggressiveness was substantiated, at least for the boys among the school children they studied.

Disparity between male and female subjects in the personality correlates of persuasibility were found by Janis and Field,[19] King,[20] and Abelson and Lesser.[21] They interpret this as indicating the influence of culturally sex-typed roles which outweigh personality differences in relation to persuasibility. Personality differences may serve as indicators of level of persuasibility in boys, but the culture seems to demand of girls greater acquiescence to prestigeful sources of information and a pattern of frictionless social relationships, with the result that girls tend to be more susceptible to influence regardless of their personality traits.

This section on audience predispositions points to the following personal factors which determine persuasion by communications: (1) when communi-

[15] B. T. King, "Relationships between Susceptibility to Opinion Change and Child-Rearing Practices," in I. L. Janis, *et al.*, *Personality and Persuasibility* (New Haven: Yale University Press, 1959), Ch. 10.

[16] P. Abelson and G. S. Lesser, "The Measurement of Persuasibility in Children," in *ibid.*, Ch. 7.

[17] I. L. Janis and P. B. Field, "Sex Differences and Personality Factors Related to Persuasibility," in *ibid.*, Ch. 3.

[18] G. S. Lesser and R. P. Abelson, "Personality Correlates of Persuasibility in Children," in *ibid.*, Ch. 9.

[19] Janis and Field, *op. cit.*

[20] King, *op. cit.*

[21] Abelson and Lesser, *op. cit.*

cations are contrary to norms of groups to which persons belong, those who value the group highly are less influenced than are those who place a lower value on their membership; (2) those persons who hold themselves in low esteem are more persuasible in general than are those high in self-esteem; and (3) but with respect to this last factor, there seem to be important cultural differences between the sexes which serve to over-shadow personality predispositions among the females.

KINDS OF RESPONSE

Consistency between attitudinal responses. Attitudes are typically defined as "predispositions to respond in a particular way toward a specified class of objects." Being predispositions they are not directly observable or measureable. Instead they are inferred from the way a person reacts to particular stimuli. Saying that a man has an unfavorable attitude toward foreigners leads us to expect that he will perceive their actions with distrust, will have strong negative feelings toward them and will tend to avoid them socially. Thus when we study attitudes what we observe are the evoking stimuli, on the one hand, and the various types of observable responses, on the other. The types of observable responses that are commonly used as indices of attitudes fall in three major categories; cognitive, affective, and behavioral.

It is known from prior research and common experience that while frequently one index can be used to predict another, there are many situations where the different response measures yield different results; e.g., an individual behaves in a way not predictable from the way he feels about the issue. Several of our researches have been directed at the problem of determining the factors that influence the degree of consistency or disparity between the different attitudinal responses. Our general methodology has been to manipulate experimentally one type of response and then to determine the impact upon the other related measures.

Rosenberg[22] attacked this problem by inducing change in affect (or feeling) by hypnosis and then determining corresponding changes in beliefs. Post-hynotic suggestion was the means used to bring about the change in feeling without directly changing beliefs.

Subjects were given a questionnaire concerning their affective responses to seven social issues. A week later, the hynotic session took place. Before and again after the half-hour interval, during which the subject was hypnotized and given the suggestion to change his feelings about two of the issues, his beliefs regarding the issues were assessed. (The subjects were led to think that there was no connection between the testing and hypnotic sessions. They were later informed of the true purpose of the experiment.) During the hypnotic session, the subject was commanded to *feel* differently about the issues; e.g., "When you awake you will be very much in favor of the idea of Negroes moving into white neighborhoods. . . ." He was told he would have no memory for the suggestion being made until a signal was given. Upon awakening from the hypnotic trance, the subject again answered the affect questionnaire and the beliefs test. The latter required the subject to rate each of 31 values as to its importance for him, and also the extent to which the particular value was either furthered or blocked by the object of the attitude. For example, one of the values which the subject rated in importance for him was, "America having high prestige in foreign countries." The subject also indicated his estimate of the extent to which this value would be attained or blocked by "Negroes moving into white neighborhoods," "allowing members of the Communist Party to address the public," and so on through all seven issues.

The results of the experiment showed that the hypnotized subjects had affect change scores on the manipulated issues that differed at the .001 level from those of the control subjects in the predicted direction. As for the major prediction concerning *belief* changes, the results showed that the hypnotic subjects underwent more cognitive change than did the controls (Table 7-10).

The relationship between behavior and belief has been the subject of a number of studies in our program. The question asked is to what extent does conformity to a view which is not necessarily one's own lead to true attitude change in the direction of that view? The problem is important because differing interpretations of findings have led to a lively controversy in psychology and also because the situation involved is one that occurs often in real life.

[22] M. J. Rosenberg, "An Analysis of Affective-Cognitive Consistency," in M. J. Rosenberg, *et al., Attitude Organization and Change* (New Haven: Yale University Press, 1960), Ch. 2.

TABLE 7-10

COMPARISON OF EXPERIMENTAL AND CONTROL GROUPS

Index	*Difference Between Groups (Mann-Whitney x)*	*p*	*Direction of Difference*
Mean affect change score for five attitude objects on which the experimental subjects were not manipulated	.07	>.90	—
Affect change score for high-interest attitude object	3.30	<.001	Exp.> control
Cognition change score for high-interest attitude object	2.62	<.01	Exp.> control
Mean change in importance of values associated with the high-interest attitude object	3.15	<.002	Exp.> control
Mean change in instrumentality of high-interest attitude object	3.80	<.0002	Exp.> control

King and Janis [23] designed a study to investigate the effects of active participation on opinion change. They compared the opinion changes of two experimental groups: "active participants" who were induced to play a role which required them to deliver a persuasive communication to others, and "passive controls" who merely read and listened to the same communication. The subjects were male college students who met in small groups. They were told they were being given an oral speaking test which involved giving an informal talk and listening to two other talks. Opinion changes were measured by comparing each student's post-communication answers with those he had given in an opinion survey four weeks earlier.

In the experimental session the subjects were asked to give the informal talk based on a prepared outline. Each active participant was instructed to act the role of a sincere advocate of the position, while the others listened and read the prepared outline. Each subject in turn delivered one of the communications and was exposed to the other two.

Each of the communications took an extreme position on a controversial issue concerning future events. The events included a drastic decline in movie attendance and increased theater closings, a severe meat shortage in two years, a cure for the common cold in one year.

The results presented in Table 7-11 indicate that for two of the three communications, the active participants were more influenced than the passive controls. Although in the third communication the experimental and control subjects showed the same amount of opinion change in the direction of the communication, the active participants had more confidence in their post-communication opinions. Thus, the findings support the conclusion that a change in behavior may lead to a change in attitude.

Further work on the relationship between cognition and behavior has been carried out by Brehm [24] working within the Festinger "cognitive-dissonance" theory framework.[25] His experiments typically involve asking an individual to choose among several alternatives and observing changes in his evaluation of the alternatives after he has made his choice. He finds that cognitive and affective responses normally change to support the choice; selected alternatives are evaluated more favorably, for example, and rejected alternatives less favorably following the decision. Even when the person has no choice but is confronted by the necessity of having to undertake an undesirable activity, he tends to reevaluate its desirability. However, the subjective feeling of choice, Brehm concluded, is highly important in bringing about change in attitude toward activities.

[23] B. T. King and I. L. Janis, "Comparison of the Effectiveness of Improvised Versus Non-Improvised Role-Playing in Producing Opinion Changes," *Human Relations,* 1956, *9,* pp. 177-186.

[24] J. W. Brehm, "A Dissonance Analysis of Attitude-Discrepant Behavior," in Rosenberg, *et al., op. cit.,* Ch. 5.

[25] L. Festinger, *Theory of Cognitive Dissonance* (Evanston, Ill.: Harper & Row, Publishers, 1957).

TABLE 7-11

COMPARISON OF ACTIVE PARTICIPANTS WITH PASSIVE CONTROLS: CHANGES IN OPINION ESTIMATES FOLLOWING EXPOSURE TO PERSUASIVE COMMUNICATIONS

Experimental Groups	*Change in Opinion Estimates* * *Net Change (Slight or Sizable)*	*Net Change (Sizable)*	
Communication *A:* (Movie Theaters)			
Active participants (N = 31)	71%	45%	$p = .01$
Passive controls (N = 57)	58%	21%	
Communication *B:* (Meat Shortage)			
Active participants (N = 29)	62%	41½%	$p = .01$
Passive controls (N = 57)	52%	17%	
Communication *C:* (Cold Cure)			
Active participants (N = 30)	53%	40%	$p > .30$
Passive controls (N = 53)	51%	45%	

* The "net change (slight or sizable)" is defined as the percentage changing in the direction advocated by the communication minus the percentage changing in the opposite direction. The "net sizable change" in the case of Communication *A* was the difference between the percentage who lowered or raised their estimate by 5,000 or more. For Communication *B*, a sizable change was 25 or more; for Communication *C* it was 5 or more.

Duration of changes in attitude. Once a person's attitude has been changed by a communication, the next question becomes how long does this change persist? What factors determine whether the attitudes will quickly revert back to the pre-communication attitude or whether they will endure? Some studies showed a sizable carry-over effect over time, but others showed quick reversion to the original attitude, and still others revealed that the delayed effects of a communication may be greater than those immediately after presentation.

This latter finding has been referred to as the "sleeper effect." It was first reported in a study by Hovland, Lumsdaine, and Sheffield.[26] These experimenters chose for their communication "The Battle of Britain," a film produced by the Army to show the accomplishments of the British in withstanding German air attacks. The film was selected because it had previously been found to elicit large opinion changes. The experimental design involved four groups of soldiers, two experimental and two control. All were initially given an opinion questionnaire. Five days after the film presentation one pair of experimental and control groups were given the questionnaire again, and a second pair received the after-questionnaire nine weeks following the film showing. It will be noted that each group of men received the after-questionnaire only once.

Memory of the factual information in the film showed a characteristic decrease with time. Opinion changes, however, showed an average *increase* with the passage of time. This increase was not found in all items, but there was a reliable increase with time in the effects on a number of opinions. The investigators suggested a number of hypotheses to account for this "sleeper effect," as they termed it.

One hypothesis advanced was that the increase in agreement might have been due to the disappearance of initial skepticism. If it should happen that the source of the communication is regarded with skepticism or antipathy, there may be little agreement with his opinion. However, if the discounted source is forgotten more quickly than the content of the communication (or "dissociated" from the content), agreement with the recommended opinion should increase with time.

The first experiment to investigate further this hypothesis was one by Hovland and Weiss to which reference has already been made.[27] They used identical communications on four different topics. To half the subjects these were presented by sources considered trustworthy, and to half by sources considered untrustworthy. The topics were "The Future of Movie Theaters," "Atomic Submarines," "The Steel Shortage," and "Antihistamine Drugs." Opinion questionnaires were presented to the subjects before the communication, immediately after it, and four weeks later. Measures were taken on memory for factual material, memory for source, and opinion on the issues. The communications were presented

[26] Hovland, Lumsdaine, and Sheffield, *op. cit.*, Ch. 7.

[27] Hovland, Janis, and Kelley, *Communication and Persuasion*, pp. 17-31.

to college students who read them without knowing that tests of retention would be administered. Initially the communications presented by the untrustworthy sources were discounted by the audience and had less effect on opinion than those presented by trustworthy sources. With the passage of time, however, the initial differences attributable to source disappeared, so that when subjects were re-tested after a period of four weeks the amount of opinion change retained from the two sources was approximately equal. It was above the point initially obtained for the negative source and below that for the positive source. (See Figure 7-5.) Thus when the source of an opinion is lost the tendency to discount it may also be lost, with a net increase in the degree of acceptance of the communicator's conclusion.

The section discussing studies of the kinds of response patterns affected by persuasive communications may be summarized as follows: (1) Changes in affective responses or, more generally, in opinions may be brought about by changes in beliefs about the issue or by changes in overt behavior with respect to the issue; (2) the changes which occur in affective responses and opinions are such as to make them more consistent with beliefs and behaviors, especially when the person feels he has exercised some choice in getting himself into the situation of inconsistency; (3) with the elapse of time following a persuasive communication, opinions may change to conform more closely to the conclusions of a communicator who was initially deemed untrustworthy; (4) this delayed change ("sleeper effect") results from the tendency of persons to forget the source of communications—when they are reminded of its untrustworthiness, the delayed influence is negated.

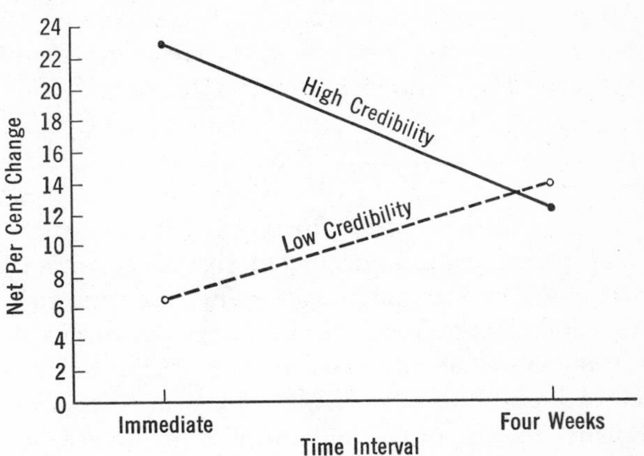

Figure 7-5. Retention of Opinion Change. Changes in extent of agreement with position advocated by high credibility and low credibility sources immediately after exposure to communication and four weeks later.

*ATTITUDE ORGANIZATION IN ELEMENTARY SCHOOL CLASSROOMS**

By Jules Henry

The word *organization* in this paper is used to stand for order and determinateness as distinguished from disorder and randomness. The emotions and attitudes of prepubertal children in our culture are not, on the whole, directed toward generalized social goals, but focused rather on the peer group and parents. From the point of view of an observer who has in mind the larger social goals, like the maintenance of stable economic relations, common front against the enemy, maintenance of positive attitudes toward popular national symbols, and so on, the emotions and attitudes of prepubertal children in our culture may be viewed as lacking order. The adult, on the other hand, is supposed to have so organized his tendencies to respond to the environment that his emotions, attitudes, and activities subserve over-all social goals. While it is true that attitudes and feelings are bent toward social goals even from earliest infancy,[1] many institutions combine to organize these attitudes and feelings so that ultimately a social steady state will be maintained. The elementary school classroom in our culture is one of the most powerful instruments in this effort, for it does not merely sustain attitudes that have been created in the home, but reinforces some, de-emphasizes others, and makes its own contribution. In this way it prepares the conditions for and contributes toward the ultimate organization of peer- and parent-directed attitudes into a dynamically interrelated attitudinal structure supportive of the culture.

This organizing process is comparable to, though not identical with, the reorganization of attitudes and resources that takes place as a society shifts from a peacetime to a wartime footing. During a period of peace in our society, adult hostility and competitiveness may be aimed at overcoming competition in business or social mobility, while love and cooperation are directed toward family and friends, and toward achieving specific social and economic ends *within* the society. With the coming of war the instruments of government seek to direct hostility and competitiveness toward the enemy, while love and cooperation are directed toward the armed forces, civilian instruments of war (price controls, rationing, civilian officials, etc.), and national symbols. From the point of view of an observer *within the war machine,* the civilian attitudes at first seem random and unorganized. He wants to change them so that from *his point of view* they will seem organized. The situation is similar, though not identical, with respect to the child: to an observer inside the head of even some psychotic children, attitudes and behavior may seem organized. But to the observer on the outside, whose focus is on social goals, the child seems *un-* or *dis*-organized. The prime effort of the adult world is *to make child attitudes look organized to adults.* The emphasis in this paper is on the description of the process of organizing child attitudes as it can be observed in some middle-class urban American classrooms.

THE WITCH-HUNT SYNDROME

One of the most striking characteristics of American culture since the settlement has been the phenomenon of intragroup aggression, which finds its pathological purity of expression in witch hunts.[2] It comes as a frightening surprise to democratic people to find themselves suddenly in terror of their neighbors; to discover that they are surrounded by persons who carry tales about others while confessing evil of themselves; to perceive a sheeplike docility settling over those whom they considered strong and autonomous. The *witch-hunt syndrome* therefore, as constituting one of the key tragedies of democracy, is selected for the elucidation of the organization of attitudes in our culture. In this

[1] J. Henry and J. W. Boggs, "Child Rearing, Culture, and the Natural World," *Psychiatry,* 1952, *15,* pp. 261-271.

[2] M. L. Starkey, *The Devil in Massachusetts* (New York: Alfred A. Knopf, Inc., 1949).

* From *American Journal of Orthopsychiatry,* 1957, *27,* pp. 117-133. Used by permission of the author and publisher. These materials are being expanded by the author in *Culture Against Man* to be published by Random House.

witch's brew *destructive criticism* of others is the toad's horns, *docility* the body of the worm; *feelings of vulnerability* the chicken heart; *fear of internal (intragroup) hostility* the snake's fang; *confession of evil deeds* the locust's leg; and *boredom and emptiness* the dead man's eye. The witch-hunt syndrome is thus stated to be a dynamically interrelated system of feelings and actions made up of destructive criticism of others, docility, feelings of vulnerability, fear of internal aggression, confession of evil deeds, and boredom.

The witch-hunt syndrome in full panoply was observed in but one of the dozen classrooms in four schools studied in the research which I discuss here. Thus it seems a relatively rare phenomenon. But the question I set myself to answer is, How could it occur at all? What are the attitudes, present in the children, that were organized by this teacher into the syndrome? How could she do it? With what materials did she work? She did not create out of nothing the attitudes she manipulated in her "Vigilance Club" in this fourth-grade classroom in a middle-class American community. She had to have something to start with. The argument of this paper will be that the feelings and tendencies to action which this teacher organized into the witch-hunt syndrome in her class are present in an *un*organized state in other classrooms. Given a certain type of teacher, he or she will be able to develop into a highly specialized, tightly integrated system in his classroom those attitudes which are present in differently organized state in the children in all classrooms. Let us now look at a meeting of the Vigilance Club.[3]

1. In the extreme back of the room is a desk called the "isolation ward." A child has been placed there for disciplinary reasons. The Vigilance Club of the class is holding a meeting. . . . Officers are elected by the group. The purpose of the club is to teach children to be better citizens. The order of procedure is as follows: the president . . . bangs her gavel on the desk and . . . says, "The meeting of the Vigilance Club will come to order." Each child then takes from his or her desk a booklet whose title is *All About Me* . . . and places it on top of his desk. The vice-president calls the name of a child, gets the child's booklet, and places it on the teacher's desk. The president then calls on the child and asks, "———, have you been a good citizen this week?" The president says, "Name some of the good things you have done," and the child tries to recall some, like opening doors for people, running errands, etc. Next the president asks the class if it remembers any good things the child has done. Each point is written in the child's booklet by the teacher. The president then . . . says to the child, "Name the bad things you have done. . . ." The child reports the wrongs he has committed during the week, and the class is asked to contribute information about his behavior. This too is written in the booklet by the teacher, who also reprimands the student, registers horror, scolds, etc. . . . When one child reports a misdemeanor of another the teacher asks for witnesses, and numerous children sometimes volunteer. . . . The child in the "isolation ward" reported some good deeds he had done; the children reported some more, and the isolated child was told he would soon be released. . . . [During this meeting some children showed obvious pleasure in confessing undesirable behavior. One child, by volunteering only good things of the students, seemed to be using the situation to overcome what seemed to the observer to be her unpopularity with the class.]

Before analyzing this protocol for the attitudes present in it, it will be well to look at some events that occurred in this classroom on another day.

2. During the game of "spelling baseball" a child raised her hand and reported that Alice and John had been talking to each other. This occurred when neither child was "at bat." The teacher asked Alice if this was so, and she replied that it was, but John denied having spoken to Alice. The teacher said that John must have listened to Alice, but he denied this too. Then the teacher asked whether there had been any witnesses, and many hands were raised. Some witnesses were seated on the far side of the room, and hence could not have seen Alice and John from their location in the room. All those testifying had "seen" Alice talking, but denied John's guilt. Alice was sent to the "bull pen," which meant that she had to sit on the floor behind the teacher's desk, and could no longer participate in the game. . . .

3. Mary raised her hand and said, "It hurts me to say this. I really wish I didn't have to do it, but I saw Linda talking." Linda was Mary's own teammate, had just spelled a word correctly, and had gone to first base. The teacher asked Linda if she had talked, and Linda said, "No, I just drew something in the air with my finger. . . ." She was sent to the "bull pen."

In these examples we see intragroup aggression; docility of the children in conforming, with no murmur of protest, to the teacher's wishes; and confession of "evil." In such a situation children develop feelings of vulnerability and fear of detection. Let us now look for these phenomena in classrooms presided over by teachers who seem to represent the more normal American type, in comfortable, middle-class, white communities: teachers who are consci-

[3] In order to prevent identification of teachers and children, the names of my student observers are not used.

entious and reasonably gentle, but creatures of their culture, and humanly weak. We begin not with internal aggression as expressed in spying and talebearing, but with the milder, though closely related phenomenon of carping, destructive criticism. While this occurs throughout the sample, I give here examples only from a fifth-grade classroom in the same school system.

4. Bill has given a report on tarantulas. As usual the teacher waits for volunteers to comment on the child's report.

Mike: The talk was well illustrated, well prepared. . . .

Bob: Bill had a piece of paper [for his notes], and teacher said he should have them on cards. . . .

Bill says he could not get any cards.

Teacher says that he should tear the paper next time if he has no cards.

Bob: He held the paper behind him. If he had had to look at it, it wouldn't have looked very nice.

5. Betty reports on Theodore Roosevelt.

A child comments that it was very good but she looked at her notes too much.

Teacher remarks that Betty had so *much* information.

Bob: She said "calvary" [instead of "cavalry"].

6. Charlie reads a story he made up himself: "The Unknown Guest." One dark, dreary night . . . on a hill a house stood. This house was forbidden territory for Bill and Joe, but they were going in anyway. The door creaked, squealed, slammed. A voice warned them to go home. Spider webs, dirty furniture . . . Bill wanted to go home. They went upstairs. A stair cracked. They entered a room. A voice said they might as well stay and find out now; and their father came out. He laughed and they laughed, but they never forgot their adventure together.

Teacher: Are there any words that give you the mood of the story? . . .

Lucy: He could have made the sentences a little better. . . .

Teacher: Let's come back to Lucy's comment. What about his sentences?

Gert: They were too short. . . .

Charlie and Jeanne are having a discussion about the position of the word "stood."

Teacher: Wait a minute, some people are forgetting their manners. . . .

Jeff: About the room: the boys went up the stairs and one "cracked"; then they were in the room. Did they fall through the stairs or what?

Teacher suggests Charlie make that a little clearer.

Lucy: If he fell through the step. . . .

Teacher: We still haven't decided about the short sentences. Perhaps they make the story more spooky and mysterious.

Gwynne: I wish he had read with more expression instead of all at one time.

Rachel: Not enough expression.

Teacher: Charlie, they want a little more expression from you. I guess we've given you enough suggestions for one time. (Charlie does not raise his head, which is bent over his desk as if studying a paper.) Charlie! I guess we've given you enough suggestions for one time, Charlie, haven't we? (Charlie half raises his head, seems to assent grudgingly.)

The striking thing about these examples is that the teacher supports the children in their carping criticism of their fellows. Her performance in this is not, however, consistent; but even where, as in Example 6, she seems at one point to try to set herself against the tide of destruction, by calling attention to the possible artistry in Charlie's short sentences, she ends up supporting the class against him, and Charlie becomes upset. Thus teacher, by rewarding the children's tendencies to carp, reinforces them. Teachers, however, are able to make their own contributions to this tendency. The single example given below will serve as illustration:

7. Joan reads us a poem she has written about Helen Keller . . . which concludes with the couplet:

> "Helen Keller as a woman was very great;
> She is really a credit to the United States."

Teacher (amusedly): Is "states" supposed to rhyme with "great"?

When Joan murmurs that it is, the teacher says, "We'll call it poetic license."

From time to time one can see a teacher vigorously oppose tendencies in the children to tear each other to pieces. The following example is from the sixth grade:

8. The Parent-Teachers Association is sponsoring a school frolic, and the children have been asked to write jingles for the publicity. For many of the children the experience of writing a jingle seems painful. They are restless, bite their pencils, squirm around in their seats, speak to their neighbors, and from time to time pop up with questions like, "Does it have to rhyme, Mr. Smith?" . . . At last Mr. Smith says, "All right, let's read some of the jingles now." Child after child says he "couldn't get one"; but some have succeeded. One girl has written a very long jingle, *obviously the best in the class.* However, instead of using Friday as the frolic day she used Tuesday, and several protests were heard from the children. Mr. Smith defended her. "Well, so she made a mistake. But you are too prone to criticize. If *you* could only do so well!"

It will be observed that all the examples are taken from circumstances in which the child's self-system is most intensely involved; where his own poetry or prose is in question, or where he has worked hard to synthesize material into a report. It is precisely at the points where the ego is most exposed that the attack is most telling. The numerous instances in the sample, where the teachers, by a word of praise or a pat on the head, play a supportive role, indicate their awareness of the vulnerability of the children. Meanwhile, as I have pointed out, the teachers often fall into the trap of triggering or supporting destructive impulses in the children.

The carping criticism of one's peers is a form of intragroup aggression, which can be quite threatening and destructive. Talebearing, however, countenanced by some teachers more than by others, can be an overwhelming threat to autonomy. While telling on others can be organized into the patrol-monitor complex (prestige through controlling and telling), useful perhaps in maintaining order in large school populations, its operation within the classroom may have serious consequences. Let us look at a couple of examples:

9. Second grade. As teacher asked the children to clear their desks one boy raised his hand, and when called on said, "Jimmy just walked by and socked me on the head."

Teacher: Is this true?

Jimmy: He hit me first.

Teacher: Why don't you both take seats up here (in front of the room). I'm not sure people like you belong in the second grade.

10. Sixth grade special class for bright students.

The children are working on their special nature study projects. Joseph passes where Ralph is working. Ralph (to teacher): Joseph is writing too much on his birds.

Teacher: Joseph, you should write only a few things.

In our sample, telling on other children in the classroom is infrequent outside the class in which the Vigilance Club was formed. Destructive criticism is the preferred mode of attack in most other classrooms. The ease with which tendencies to attack peers can be organized into telling on others, however, is illustrated by the monitor-patrol complex, and by the Vigilance Club (Example 3).

COMPETITION

Competition is an important element in the witch-hunt syndrome. Since witch hunts involve so often obtaining the attention and approval of some powerful central figure, the examples of competitiveness that I shall cite illustrate how approval and attention seeking occur as the child attempts to beat out his peers for the nod of the teacher. It would be easy to cite examples from the protocols of the merciless laughter of children at the failures or gaucheries of their classmates. I am interested, however, more in showing the all-pervading character of the phenomenon of competition, *even in its mildest forms.* The first example is from a fourth-grade music lesson:

11. The children are singing songs of Ireland and her neighbors from the book *Songs of Many Lands. . . .* Teacher plays on piano while children sing . . . . While children are singing some of them hunt in the index, find a song belonging to one of the four countries, and raise their hands before the previous song is finished in order that they may be called on to name the next song. . . .

Here singing is subordinated, in the child, to the competitive wish to have the song he has hunted up in the index chosen by the teacher. It is merely a question of who gets to the next song in the index first, gets his hand up fast, and is called on by the teacher.

The following examples also illustrate the fact that almost any situation set by the teacher can be the occasion for release of competitive impulses:

12. The observer enters the fifth-grade classroom.

Teacher: Which one of you nice polite boys would like to take [observer's] coat and hang it up? (Observer notes: From the waving hands it would seem that all would like to claim the title.)

Teacher chooses one child . . . who takes observer's coat. . . .

Teacher: Now children, who will tell [observer] what we have been doing?

Usual forest of hands . . . and a girl is chosen to tell. . . .

Teacher conducted the arithmetic lesson mostly by asking, "Who would like to tell . . . the answer to the next problem?"

This question was usually followed by the appearance of a large and *agitated* forest of hands; apparently *much competition to answer.*

Thus the teacher is a powerful agent in reinforcing competition.

It has already been pointed out that carping criticism helps to settle in the child a feeling of vulnerability and threat. In this connection it is significant that *the failure of one child is repeatedly the occasion for the success of another.* I give one illustration below from the same class as the one from which I have taken Example 12.

13. Boris had trouble reducing 12/16 to lowest terms, and could get only as far as 6/8. Much excitement. Teacher asked him quietly [note how basically decent this teacher is] if that was as far as he could reduce it. She suggested he "think." Much heaving up and down from the other children, all frantic to correct him. Boris pretty unhappy. Teacher, patient, quiet, ignoring others, and concentrating with look and voice on Boris. She says, "Is there a bigger number than 2 you can divide into the two parts of the fraction?" After a minute or two she becomes more urgent. No response from Boris. She then turns to the class and says, "Well, who can tell Boris what the number is?" Forest of hands. Teacher calls, Peggy. Peggy gives 4 to be divided into 12/16, numerator and denominator.

Where Boris has failed Peggy has been triumphant; *Boris's failure has made it possible for Peggy to succeed.*

This example and also Example 6 are ones in which the discomfort of the child was *visible,* and such instances may be multiplied. They illustrate how vulnerable the children feel in the presence of the attacks of the peer group in the classroom. But since these are children who face the world with serious anxiety to begin with, the classroom situation sustains it. Let us look at some stories created by these very children, and read by them to their classmates. We have already seen one, Example 6, Charlie's story of "The Unknown Guest." Here are *all* the stories read to their classmates by these children during an observation period.

14. (a) Charlotte's story: "Mistaken Identity." One day last year my family and I went to the hospital to visit somebody. When we were coming out and were walking along my father hit me. I came up behind him to hit him back, but just as I was about to do it I looked back and he was behind me! I was going to hit the wrong person!

(b) Tommy's story: "The Day Our House Was Robbed." [Observer has recorded this in the third person.] He was coming home from school one afternoon. He knew his Mom was away that afternoon. He started to go in the side door, but decided, he doesn't know why, to go round the back. He found the door open, went into the kitchen, looked into the front room where he saw a thief. Tommy "froze stiff" (chuckle of appreciation from the class), ran out, shouted "Stop thief" as the man ran out after him. He went to a neighbor, rang the bell, called his mother at the store. The cops came, asked qustions, but the man had gotten away with $99 and his mother's watch. If he had gone in the side door he would not have had a chance to see the man. Changing to the back door "may have saved my life." [Teacher's only remarks about this story were: 1) instead of having said "froze stiff," Tommy should have said "froze stiff as something": 2) he should have left out the word "then" in one place; 3) he could have made the story clearer; 4) he changed from the past to the present tense.]

(c) Polly's story: "Custard the Lion." Custard the Lion was the most timid animal in Animal Town. The doctors couldn't cure him. Then they found a new medicine. It had strange effects, but Custard wanted to try it. When he did he felt very queer. (Child gives details of queer feeling.) But he soon realized he wasn't afraid of anything. [Teacher's first remark: "You didn't let us hear the last sentence."]

(d) Dan's story: "The Boy Hero." Bill wanted to be a fireman, so he went to the firehouse. The Chief was telling him to go home when the bell clanged. While the Chief was getting into the engine, he didn't see that Bill was getting on too. (Class or teacher picks up flaw in sentence and it is reread correctly.) The Chief said O.K. as long as Bill was aboard, "But you're not to get into no mischief." (Class choruses, "Any. . . .") Everyone was out of the fire except a little girl and her doll. The firemen cannot figure out what to do, but Bill, seeing a tree near the house, climbs it over the protests of the firemen. He misses the girl on his first try, but gets her on the second. While sliding down the tree she slips and almost falls, but grabs Bill's pants, and they make it to safety. . . . [Children's remarks center on position of "clang, clang, clang" in the story. Teacher talks about how to use direct quotations, which, it seems, Dan had not used properly.]

(e) Bertha's story: Title not recorded. The story is about Jim who was walking home past the Smith's house one night and heard a scream. Penny Smith came out and said there was a robber in the house. When the cops came they found a parrot flying around in there, and Penny's parents told her to shut the parrot up before she read mystery stories again. [This story was followed by much carping criticism, which was terminated by the teacher's telling Bertha to change the story to suit the class.]

These stories contain elements of anxiety and even of terror. As each child finishes, the carping criticism of students and teacher then reminds him of his vulnerability. As the child sends out his cloud of fear, it returns with the leaden rain of hostility.

DOCILITY

It comes as a somewhat shocking surprise, perhaps, to middle-class parents, to find their children described as "docile." Yet we have already seen the perfection of docility in the Vigilance Club, and we shall presently see its manifold forms in more normal classrooms.

15. First grade. The children are to act out a story called "Pig Brother," which is about an untidy boy. The teacher is telling the story. One boy said he did not like the story, so the teacher said he could leave if he did not wish to hear it again, but the boy did not leave.

16. In gym the children began to tumble, but there was much restless activity in the lines, so the teacher had all the children run around the room until they were somewhat exhausted before she continued the tumbling.

17. Second grade.

The children have been shown movies of birds. The first film ended with a picture of a baby bluebird.

Teacher: Did the last bird ever look as if he would be blue?

The children did not seem to understand the "slant" of the question, and answered somewhat hesitantly, yes.

Teacher: I think he looked more like a robin, didn't he?

Children, in chorus: Yes.

Item 17 is one of a large number of instances, distributed throughout all grades, in which the children exhibit their docility largely through giving the teacher what he wants. Thus in the elementary schools of the middle class the children get an intensive eight-year-long training in hunting for the right signals and giving the teacher the response wanted. The rest of the examples of docility document this assertion.

18. Fourth grade.

(a) An art lesson.

Teacher holds up a picture.

Teacher: Isn't Bob getting a nice effect of moss and trees?

Ecstatic Ohs and Ahs from the children. . . .

The art lesson is over.

Teacher: How many enjoyed this?

Many hands go up.

Teacher: How many learned something?

Quite a number of hands come down.

Teacher: How many will do better next time?

Many hands go up.

(b) Children have just finished reading the story "The Sun Moon and Stars Clock."

Teacher: What was the highest point of interest—the climax?

The children tell what they think it is. Teacher is aiming to get from them what *she* considers the point of climax, but the children seem to give everything else but.

Bobby: When they capture the thieves.

Teacher: How many agree with Bobby?

Hands, hands.

10. Fifth grade.

This is a lesson on "healthy thoughts," for which the children have a special book depicting, with appropriate illustrations, specific conflictful incidents among children. The teacher is supposed to discuss each incident with the children in order to help them understand how to handle their emotions.

One of the pictures is as follows: A sibling *pair* is illustrated by *three* boys: 1) One has received a ball. 2) One is imagined to react with displeasure. 3) One is imagined to react benignly and philosophically, saying, "My brother couldn't help being given the football; we'll use it together."

Teacher: Do you believe it's easier to deal with your thoughts if you own up to them, Betty?

Betty: Yes it is, if you're not cross and angry.

Teacher: Have you any experience like this in the book, Alice?

Alice tells how her brother was given a watch and she envied him and wanted one too; but her mother said she wasn't to have one until she was fifteen, but now she has one anyway.

Teacher: How could you have helped—could you have changed your thinking? How could you have handled it? What could you do with mean feelings?

Alice seems stymied. Hems and haws.

Teacher: What did Susie (a character in the book) do?

Alice: She talked to her mother.

Teacher: If you talk to someone you often then feel that "it was foolish of me to feel that way. . . ."

Tommy: He had an experience like that, he says. His cousin was given a bike and he envied it. But he wasn't "ugly" about it. He asked if he might ride it, and his cousin let him, and then, "I got one myself; and I wasn't mean, or ugly or jealous."

Before continuing it will be well to note that since the teacher does not say Alice was wrong the children assume she was right and so copy her answer.

Two boys, the dialogue team, now come to the front of the class and dramatize the football incident.

Teacher (to the class): Which boy do you think handled the problem in a better way?

Rupert: Billy did, because he didn't get angry. . . . It was better to play together than to do nothing with the football.

Teacher: That's a good answer, Rupert. Has anything similar happened to you, Joan?

Joan can think of nothing.

Sylvester: I had an experience. My brother got a hat with his initials on it because he belongs to a fraternity, and I wanted one like it and couldn't have one; and his was too big for me to wear, and it ended up that I asked him if he could get me some letters with my initials, and he did.

Betty: My girl friend got a bike that was 26-inch, and mine was only 24; and I asked my sister what I should do. Then my girl friend came over and was real nice about it, and let me ride it.

Teacher approves of this, and says, Didn't it end up that they both had fun without unhappiness?

Here we note that the teacher herself has gone astray, for on the one hand her aim is to get instances from the children in which they have been yielding, and capable of resolving their own jealousy, etc.; yet, in the instance given by Betty, it was not Betty who yielded, but her friend. The child immediately following Betty imitated her since Betty had been praised by the teacher.

Matilde: My girl friend got a 26-inch bike and mine is only 24; but she only let me ride it once a month. But for my birthday my mother's getting me a new one, probably (proudly) a 28. (Many children rush in with the information that 28 doesn't exist.) Matilde replies that she'll probably have to raise the seat then, for she's too big for a 26.

As we go on with this lesson, we shall continue to see how the children's need for substitute gratification and their inability to accept frustration are the real issues, which even prevent them from getting the teacher's point. We shall see how, in spite of the teacher's driving insistence on her point, the children continue to inject their conflicts into the lesson, while at the same time they gropingly try to find a way to gratify the teacher. *They* cannot give the "right" answers because of their conflicts; teacher cannot handle their conflicts, even perceive them, because *her* underlying need is to be gratified by the children. The lesson goes on:

Teacher: I notice that some of you are only happy when you get your own way. You're not thinking this through, and I want you to. Think of an experience when you didn't get what you want. Think it through.

Charlie: His ma was going to the movies and he wanted to go with her, and she wouldn't let him; and she went off to the movies, and he was mad; but then he went outside and there were some kids playing baseball, so he played baseball.

Teacher: But suppose you hadn't gotten to play baseball? You would have felt hurt, because you didn't get what you wanted. We can't help feeling hurt when we are disappointed. What could you have done; how could you have handled it?

Charlie: So I can't go to the movies, so I can't play baseball, so I'll do something around the house.

Teacher: Now you're beginning to think! It takes courage to take disappointments. (Turning to the class) What did we learn? The helpful way . . .

Class: is the healthy way!

Before entering the final section of this paper, we need to ask: Why are these children, whose fantasies contain so many hostile elements, so docile in the classroom; and why do they struggle so hard to gratify the teacher and try in so many ways to bring themselves to her attention (the "forest of hands")? We might, of course, start with the idea of the teacher as a parent figure, and the children as siblings competing for the teacher's favor. We could refer to the unresolved dependency needs of children of this age, which make them seek support in the teacher, who manipulates this seeking and their sibling rivalry to pit the children against each other. Other important factors, however, that are inherent in the classroom situation itself, and particularly in middle-class classrooms, ought to be taken into consideration. We have observed the children's tendency to destructively criticize each other, and the teachers' often unwitting repeated reinforcement of this tendency. We have taken note of the anxiety in the children as illustrated by the stories they tell, and observed that these very stories are subjected to a carping criticism, whose ultimate consequence would be anything but alleviation of that anxiety. Hence the classroom is a place in which the child's underlying anxiety may be heightened. In an effort to alleviate this he seeks the approval of the teacher, by giving right answers and by doing what teacher wants him to do under most circumstances. Finally, we cannot omit the teacher's need to be gratified by the attention-hungry behavior of the children.

A word is necessary about these classrooms as middle class. The novel *Blackboard Jungle*[4] describes schoolroom behavior of lower-class children. There we see the children *against the teacher,* as representative of the middle class. But in the classes I have described we see the *children against each other,* with the teacher abetting the process. Thus, as the teacher in the middle-class schools directs the hostility of the children toward one another and away from himself, he reinforces the competitive dynamics within the middle class itself. The teacher in lower-class schools, on the other hand, appears to become the organizing stimulus for behavior that integrates the lower class, as the children unite in expressing their hostility to the teacher.

CONFESSION

The Vigilance Club would have been impossible without confession, and the children's pleasure in

[4] E. Hunter, *The Blackboard Jungle* (New York: Simon and Schuster, 1954).

confession. But, as with the other parts of the syndrome, confessing occurs in other classrooms also; it can be elicited when the proper conditions are present, and the children can be seen to enjoy it—to vie with one another in confessing. Let us follow the lesson on "healthy thoughts" a little further. We will see how confession occurs as the children seek to give teacher *precisely* what she wants.

20. Teacher asks if anyone else has had experience like that [of two children who have just recited], where they were mean and angry.

Dick: He has a friend he plays baseball with, and sometimes they fight; but they get together again in a few minutes and apologize.

In this first example we note one of the important aspects of the confession element in the syndrome: the culprit must have given up his evil ways, and now be free of impurities.

In response to Dick's story, teacher says: You handled it just right. Now let's hear about someone who had a similar experience and didn't handle it just right.

Tom: His little brother asked for the loan of his knife, but it was lost, and he got angry with his little brother for asking. [This knife story follows a sequence of several stories about knives told by other children. The exuberance of knife stories following immediately on the teacher's approval of the first one suggests that some of them are made to order and served up piping hot for teacher's gratification.]

Teacher: Now Tom, could you have worked it out any differently? (Observer notes that Tom seems to enjoy this confession; certainly he is not abashed or ashamed.)

Tom: Later he asked me if he could help me find it. He found it in a wastebasket, and then I let him borrow it.

Harry: Sometimes I get angry when my friends are waiting for me and . . . (observer missed some of this) and my little sister asked if she could borrow my auto-racing set, and I hit her once or twice. (Class laughs.)

Here we see another factor so important to the flourishing of the syndrome: the audience gets pleasure through the confessor's telling about deeds the audience wishes to commit: who among Harry's listeners would not like to have hit his sister, or anyone, "once or twice"?

The teacher then goes on: What would you do now—would you hit her?

Harry: Now I'd probably get mad at first, but let her have it later.

Thus Harry has mended his ways—in teacher-directed fantasy at least—and returned to the fold.

So far we have had confession of mean and angry thoughts and violence. We shall now see confession to unacceptable fear. In all cases the teacher says what type of confession she wishes to hear, and what the resolution should be of the unacceptable behavior; and the children vie with one another to tell commensurable tales, as they derive pleasure from the total situation—through approval of the teacher, expression of their own real or fantasied deviations, and the delight of their peers. In these situations the pleasure of the peer group is seen to derive not so much from the "happy ending" the children give their stories but rather from the content of the story itself. It is interesting that no carping criticism appears; rather the entire situation is a jolly one. It seems that within unspoken limits the children permit one another to boast of "evil" behavior because of the deep pleasure obtained from hearing it. Thus impulse expression becomes a device for role maintenance in the classroom.

The lesson proceeds:

Two children enact a little skit in which they have to go to the principal to ask him something. One of them is afraid of the principal, the other is not. The moral is that the principal is the children's friend, and that one should not be shy.

Gertrude: Well, anyway, the principal isn't a lion, he's your friend; he's not going to kill you.

Teacher: That's right, the principal is a friend, he says hello and good morning to you. . . . Have you ever felt shy?

Meriam: The first year I sold Girl Scout cookies I didn't know how to approach people; and the first house I went to I didn't know the lady; and I stuttered and stammered, and didn't sell any cookies. By the second house I had thought it all out before I rang the bell, and I sold two boxes. (Triumphantly.)

Teacher: It helps to have self-confidence.

Ben now tells a story, with a happy ending, of being afraid of a principal. Then Paul tells a story, amid gales of laughter, about his being scared on a roller coaster. By this time there is so much excitement among the children that the teacher says: Wait a minute—manners!

John: He was scared to go on the Whip-the-Whirl (scornful laughter from the class); but after he went he liked it so much that he went eight times in a row. (This is well received.)

Many hands go up. Teacher waits. . . .

Michael: He was at Pleasure Park on the ferris wheel (scornful Aw from the class) and a girl kept rocking it, and I started to get green (roar of laughter).

Teacher: Now we'll have to stop.

Certain phenomena not emphasized before appear in this section. Confession is used by the authoritative figure, the teacher, to strengthen attachment to significant but potentially terrifying figures like school principals, and to polish up cultural shibboleths like "self-confidence." For the child storytellers confession becomes an opportunity for bathing in the emotional currents of the peer group, as the child stimulates the group's approval through presentation of group standards, and awakens group pleasure as the peer group responds to its own anxiety about weakness, and experiences resolution of the anxiety through the happy ending. With a perfect instinct for what is right, each child provides catharsis for his peers. By presenting himself as weak, he enables his peers to identify with him; and then, as he overcomes his weakness, he enables his companions, too, to feel strong.

What this lesson on healthy thoughts may have accomplished by way of creating a permanent reservoir of "healthy thoughts" is difficult to say, but that it helped create solidarity among the students, and between them and the teacher is clear from the fact that when she suddenly shifted ground to say, "Do you think you are wide enough awake for a contest in subtraction of fractions?" the children responded with a unanimous roar of "Yes," as if she had asked them whether they were ready for cookies and ice cream!

Thus in this lesson, in which all have participated more with their *unconscious* than with their conscious emotions, solidarity has been achieved. Teacher thought she was teaching the children to have healthy thoughts, but she was showing them how to gratify her. The children sensed this and struggled to gratify her, while they sought acceptance by their peers also. The essential difference between this teacher and the one who perpetrated the Vigilance Club is that though the latter tended to demolish solidarity among the children while placing the teacher in supreme command, the lesson on healthy thoughts tended to a dubious solidarity among all. *Both teachers organize some of the same elements in the children, but into different configurations, of total feeling and behavior.*

BOREDOM

It seems unnecessary to document the fact that children become bored in class, for much of modern thinking and curriculum arrangement is aimed at eliminating it. The shifts at 15-minute intervals from one subject to the next in the elementary school classrooms is one example of this effort. Boredom, which means emotional and intellectual separation from the environment, is an insupportable agony, particularly if the emotional vacuum created by such separation is not filled by gratifying fantasies, or if it is filled by terrifying ones. To fill this vacuum people in our culture will throw themselves into a great variety of even relatively ungratifying activities. Since in this situation, bored children attack almost any novel classroom activity with initial vigor, the witch-hunt syndrome or any modification thereof helps to overcome boredom: better to hunt than be bored. In a full and satisfying life there is no place for witch hunts. The school system that can provide a rich program for children has no need of Vigilance Clubs, nor even of lessons on "healthy thoughts."

DISCUSSION AND CONCLUSIONS

In this paper I have used suggestions from communications theory in an effort to order the data obtained from direct observation of elementary school classrooms. Information, the central concept of communications theory, refers to measurable differences in states of organization. In human behavior, as seen in the classroom under discussion, we observe *qualitative shifts in state,* for *different teachers organize the same underlying emotional characteristics of the children to achieve different organizations of the emotions.* One teacher so organizes the children's emotions as to accomplish an intensification of the fear of intragroup aggression, while she turns the children's hostility toward one another. A different teacher may organize the emotions of the children so that a euphoria in which students and teacher are bathed in a wave of emotional gratification is achieved. The great skill in being a teacher would seem to be, therefore, a *learned*-capacity to keep shifting states of order intelligently as the work demands. This does not mean the traditional classroom order, where you can hear a pin drop, but rather the kind of order in which the *emotions of the children are caught up and organized toward the achievement of a specific goal.* It is not necessary, perhaps, that even the most prominent emotions of the children, like competitiveness, for example, form part of the organized whole. Yet, on the other hand, it is difficult to see how, in the present state of our culture, competitiveness can be overlooked. It would seem, perhaps, that the important outcome to avoid is that the competitiveness should become destructive of peers, while reinforcing dependence on the teacher.

The phenomenon I have labeled "docility" occurs because of the absolute dependence for survival of the children on the teacher. That is to say success in school depends absolutely on the teacher, and self-respect, as a function of the opinion of others, in the home or among peers, is in part a function of success or failure in school. In these circumstances the child's capacity to respond automatically to the signals he gets from the teacher is bound to acquire somewhat the appearance of instinctive behavior. Although it occurs at a much higher level of integration than instinct, the child hunts for the proper signals from the teacher, and the child's responses take on instinctual quality. They *must;* otherwise, like the nestling who does not open its mouth when the mother arrives with a worm, he will never eat the ambrosia of teacher's approval, so necessary to his survival. In this situation both children and teacher easily become the instruments of their own unconscious processes, as they, like Joseph and his brethren, fall on each other's necks in a shared ecstasy of exuberant dependence. Teacher and pupil will have gratified each other, but it remains an open question whether the children will have learned what the curriculum committee planned.

We see in the organization of the components of the witch-hunt syndrome an important phase in the formation of American national character, for tendencies to docility, competitiveness, confession, intragroup aggression, and feelings of vulnerability the children may bring with them to school, are reinforced in the classroom. This means that independence and courage to challenge are observably played *down* in these classrooms. It means, on the other hand, that tendencies to own up rather than to conceal are reinforced—a development which, in proper hands, might become a useful educational instrument. It means, further, that while many teachers do stress helping others they may inadvertently develop in the children the precise opposite, and thus undermine children's feelings of security. One could come from a very secure and accepting family and yet have one's feelings of security and acceptance threatened in these classrooms. On the other hand, what seems most in evidence from the stories they make up is that the children come to school with feelings of vulnerability which are intensified in the classroom.

Meanwhile we should try to understand that all the teachers in the sample were probably trying to be good teachers,[5] and all the children were trying to be good pupils. Their unconscious needs, however, naturally dominated their behavior. The teacher who organized the Vigilance Club probably thought she was teaching her children to be upright and honest, and to perform good deeds, but her unconscious tendencies caused these worthy inclinations to seek the wrong expression. All teachers need conformity in the classroom in order that the children shall absorb a respectable amount of academic knowledge. But the teacher's (often unconscious) need for acceptance by the children, and her fear (sometimes unconscious) of her inability to control free discussion, compel her to push the children into uncritical docility at times, while they seek her approval.

The creation of stories, and their discussion by the class, are accepted principles of progressive education. But the teacher's own (at times unconscious) need to carp and criticize gets in the way of her adequately developing the creative and supportive possibilities in her charges. Thus these are not "bad," "vicious," or "stupid" teachers, but human beings, who express in their classroom behavior the very weaknesses parents display in their dealings with their children. The solution to the problem of the contradiction between the requirements of a democratic education on the one hand, and the teachers' unconscious needs on the other, is not to carp at teachers, and thus repeat the schoolroom process, but to give them some insight into how they project their personal problems into the classroom situation.

[5] I am indebted to B. Bettelheim for this suggestion.

*REFERENCE GROUPS, MEMBERSHIP GROUPS, AND ATTITUDE CHANGE**

By Alberta Engvall Siegel and Sidney Siegel

In social psychological theory, it has long been recognized that an individual's *membership groups* have an important influence on the values and attitudes he holds. More recently, attention has also been given to the influence of his *reference groups,* the groups in which he aspires to attain or maintain membership. In a given area, membership groups and reference groups may or may not be identical. They are identical when the person aspires to *maintain* membership in the group of which he is a part; they are disparate when the group in which the individual aspires to *attain* membership is one in which he is not a member. It has been widely asserted that both membership and reference groups affect the attitudes held by the individual.[1]

The present study is an examination of the attitude changes which occur over time when reference groups and membership groups are identical and when they are disparate. The study takes advantage of a field experiment which occurred in the social context of the lives of the subjects, concerning events considered vital by them. The subjects were not aware that their membership and reference groups were of research interest; in fact, they did not know that the relevant information about these was available to the investigators.

The field experiment permitted a test of the general hypothesis that both the amount and the direction of a person's attitude change over time depends on the attitude norms of his membership group (whether or not that group is chosen by him) and on the attitude norms of his reference group.

This hypothesis is tested with subjects who shared a common reference group at the time of the initial assessment of attitudes. They were then randomly assigned to alternative membership groups, some being assigned to the chosen group and others to a nonchosen group. Attitudes were reassessed after a year of experience in these alternative membership groups with divergent attitude norms. During the course of the year, some subjects came to take the imposed (initially nonpreferred) membership group as their reference group. Attitude change after the year was examined in terms of the membership group and reference group identifications of the subjects at that time.

THE FIELD EXPERIMENT

The *S*s of this study were women students at a large private coeducational university. The study was initiated shortly before the end of their freshman year, when they all lived in the same large freshman dormitory to which they had been assigned upon entering the university. At this university, all women move to new housing for their sophomore year. Several types of housing are available to them: a large dormitory, a medium-sized dormitory, several very small houses which share common dining facilities, and a number of former sorority houses which have been operated by the university since sororities were banished from the campus. These latter are located among the fraternity houses on Fraternity Row, and are therefore known as "Row houses." Although the Row houses are lower in physical comfort than most of the other residences for women, students consider them higher in social status. This observation was confirmed by a poll of students,[2] in which over 90 per cent of the respondents stated that Row houses for women were higher in social status than non-Row houses, the remaining few disclaiming any information concerning status differences among women's residences.

[1] M. Sherif and C. Sherif, *Groups in Harmony and Tension* (New York: Harper & Row, Publishers, 1953).

[2] S. Siegel, "Certain Determinants and Correlates of Authoritarianism," *Genetic Psychology Monographs,* 1954, *49,* pp. 187-299.

* From the *Journal of Abnormal and Social Psychology,* 1957, *55,* pp. 360-364. Used by permission of the authors and publisher. This study was supported by grants from the Committee for the Study of American Values at Stanford University and from the Stanford Value Theory Project.

In the Spring of each year, a "drawing" is held for housing for the subsequent year. All freshmen must participate in this drawing, and any other student who wishes to change her residence may participate. It is conducted by the office of the Dean of Women, in cooperation with woman student leaders. Any participant's ballot is understood to be secret. The woman uses the ballot to rank the houses in the order of her preference. After submitting this ballot, she draws a number from the hopper. The rank of that number determines the likelihood that her preference will be satisfied.

In research reported earlier,[3] a random sample was drawn from the population of freshman women at this university, several tests were administered to the *S*s in that sample, and (unknown to the *S*s) their housing preferences for the forthcoming sophomore year were observed by the investigator. The *S*s were characterized as "high status oriented" if they listed a Row house as their first choice, and were characterized as "low status oriented" if they listed a non-Row house as their first choice. The hypothesis under test, drawn from reference group theory and from theoretical formulations concerning authoritarianism, was that high status orientation is a correlate of authoritarianism. The hypothesis was confirmed: freshman women who listed a Row house as their first choice for residence scored significantly higher on the average in authoritarianism, as measured by the E-F scale,[4] than did women who listed a non-Row house as their first choice. The present study is a continuation of the one described, and uses as its *S*s only those members of the original sample who were "high status oriented," i.e., preferred to live in a Row house for the sophomore year. In the initial study, of the 95 *S*s whose housing choices were listed, 39 were "high status oriented," i.e., demonstrated that the Row was their reference group by giving a Row house as their first choice in the drawing. Of this group, 28 were available to serve as *S*s for the follow-up or "change" study which is the topic of the present paper. These women form a homogeneous subsample in that at the conclusion of their freshman year they shared a common membership group (the freshman dormitory) and a common reference group (the Row). These *S*s, however, had divergent experiences during their sophomore year: nine were Row residents during that year (having drawn sufficiently small numbers in the housing drawing to enable them to be assigned to the group of their choice) and the other 19 lived in non-Row houses during that year (having drawn numbers too large to enable them to be assigned to the housing group of their choice).

E-F scores were obtained from each of the 28 *S*s in the course of a large-scale testing program administered to most of the women students at the university. Anonymity was guaranteed to the *S*s, but a coding procedure permitted the investigators to identify each respondent and thereby to isolate the *S*s and compare each *S*'s second E-F score with her first.

To prevent the *S*s from knowing that they were participating in a follow-up study, several procedures were utilized: *(a)* many persons who had not served in the earlier study were included in the second sample, *(b)* the testing was introduced as being part of a nation-wide study to establish norms, *(c)* the test administrators were different persons from those who had administered the initial tests, *(d)* *S*s who informed the test administrator that they had already taken the "Public Opinion Questionnaire" (E-F scale) were casually told that this did not disqualify them from participating in the current study.

The *S*s had no hint that the research was in any way related to their housing arrangements. Testing was conducted in classrooms as well as in residences, and all procedures and instructions were specifically designed to avoid any arousal of the salience of the housing groups in the frame of reference of the research.

The annual housing drawing was conducted three weeks after the sophomore-year testing, and, as usual, each woman's housing ballot was understood to be secret. In this drawing, each *S* had the opportunity to change her membership group, although a residence move is not required at the end of the sophomore year as it is at the end of the freshman year. If an *S* participated in this drawing, the house which she listed as her first choice on the ballot was identified by the investigators as her reference group. If she did not, it was evident that the house in which she was currently a member was the one in which she chose to continue to live, i.e., was her

[3] S. Siegel, *op. cit.*

[4] T. Adorno, *et al., The Authoritarian Personality* (New York: Harper & Row, Publishers, 1950); H. G. Gough, "Studies of Social Intolerance: I, Some Psychological and Sociological Correlates of Anti-Semitism," *Journal of Social Psychology*, 1951, *33*, pp. 237-246.

reference group. With the information on each *S*'s residence choice at the end of her freshman year, her assigned residence for her sophomore year, and her residence choice at the end of her sophomore year, it was possible to classify the subjects in three categories:

A. Women ($n = 9$) who had gained assignment to live on the Row during their sophomore year and who did not attempt to draw out of the Row at the end of that year;
B. Women ($n = 11$) who had not gained assignment to a Row house for the sophomore year and who drew for a Row house again after living in a non-Row house during the sophomore year; and
C. Women ($n = 8$) who had not gained assignment to a Row house for the sophomore year, and who chose to remain in a non-Row house after living in one during the sophomore year.

For all three groups of *S*s, as we have pointed out, membership group (freshman dormitory) and reference group (Row house) were common at the end of the freshman year. For Group A, membership and reference groups were disparate throughout the sophomore year. For Group B, membership and reference groups were disparate throughout the sophomore year. For Group C, membership and reference groups were initially disparate during the sophomore year but became identical because of a change in reference groups.

As will be demonstrated, the Row and the non-Row social groups differ in attitude norms, with Row residents being generally more authoritarian than non-Row residents. From social psychological theory concerning the influence of group norms on individuals' attitudes, it would be predicted that the different group identifications during the sophomore year of the three groups of *S*s would result in differential attitude change. Those who gained admittance to a Row house for the sophomore year (Group A) would be expected to show the least change in authoritarianism, for they spent that year in a social context which reinforced their initial attitudes. Group C *S*s would be expected to show the greatest change in authoritarianism, a change associated not only with their membership in a group (the non-Row group) which is typically low in authoritarianism, but also with their shift in reference groups, from Row to non-Row, i.e., from a group normatively higher in authoritarianism to a group normatively lower. The extent of attitude change in the *S*s in Group B would be expected to be intermediate, due to the conflicting influences of the imposed membership group (non-Row) and of the unchanged reference group (Row). The research hypothesis, then, is that between the time of the freshman-year testing and the sophomore-year testing, the extent of change in authoritarianism will be least in Group A, greater in Group B, and greatest in Group C. That is, in extent of attitude change, Group A < Group B < Group C.

RESULTS

Group norms. From the data collected in the large-scale testing program, it was possible to determine the group norms for authoritarian attitudes among the Row and the non-Row women at the university. The E-F scale was administered to all available Row residents ($n=303$) and to a random sample of residents of non-Row houses ($n=101$). These *S*s were sophomores, juniors, and seniors. The mean E-F score of the Row women was 90, while the mean E-F score of the non-Row was 81. The E-F scores of the two groups were demonstrated to differ at the $p<.001$ level ($\chi^2=11.1$) by the median test,[5] a nonparametric test, the data for which are shown in Table 7-12.

TABLE 7-12

FREQUENCIES OF E-F SCORES ABOVE AND BELOW COMMON MEDIAN FOR ROW AND NON-ROW RESIDENTS

	Residents of Non-Row Houses	*Residents of Row Houses*	*Total*
Above Median	36	166	202
Below Median	65	137	202
Total	101	303	404

Attitude change. The central hypothesis of this study is that attitude change will occur differentially in Groups A, B, and C, and that it will occur in the direction which would be predicted from knowledge of the group norms among Row and non-Row residents in general. The 28 *S*s of this study had a

[5] S. Siegel, *Nonparametric Statistics: For the Behavioral Sciences* (New York: McGraw-Hill Book Co., Inc., 1956).

mean E-F score of 102 at the end of their freshman year. The data reported above concerning authoritarianism norms for all women residing on campus would lead to the prediction that in general the *Ss* would show a reduction in authoritarianism during the sophomore year but that this reduction would be differential in the three groups; from the knowledge that Row residents generally are higher in authoritarianism than non-Row residents, the prediction based on social group theory would be that Group A would show the smallest reduction in authoritarianism scores, Group B would show a larger reduction, and Group C would show the largest reduction. The data which permit a test of this hypothesis are given in Table 7-13. The Jonckheere test,[6] a nonparametric *k*-sample test which tests the null hypothesis that the three groups are from the same population against the alternative hypothesis that they are from different populations which are ordered in a specified way, was used with these data. By that test, the hypothesis is confirmed at the $p<.025$ level.

TABLE 7-13

FRESHMAN-YEAR AND SOPHOMORE-YEAR E-F SCORES OF SUBJECTS

Group	*E-F Score* End of Freshman Year	*E-F Score* End of Sophomore Year	*Difference*
A	108	125	—17
	70	78	—8
	106	107	—1
	92	92	0
	80	78	2
	104	102	2
	143	138	5
	110	92	18
	114	80	34
B	76	117	—41
	105	107	—2
	88	82	6
	109	97	12
	98	83	15
	112	94	18
	101	82	19
	114	93	21
	104	81	23
	116	91	25
	101	74	27
C	121	126	—5
	87	79	8
	105	95	10
	97	81	16
	96	78	18
	108	73	35
	114	77	37
	88	49	39

DISCUSSION

Substantively, the present study provides experimental verification of certain assertions in social group theory, demonstrating that attitude change over time is related to the group identification of the person—both his membership group identification and his reference group identification. The hypothesis that extent of attitude change would be different in the three subgroups of *Ss*, depending on their respective membership group and reference group identifications, is confirmed at the $p<.025$ level; in extent of change in authoritarianism, Group A < Group B < Group C, as predicted.

Another way of looking at the data may serve to highlight the influence of membership groups and reference groups. At the end of the freshman year, the *Ss* in Groups A, B, and C shared the same membership group and the same reference group. During the sophomore year, the *Ss* in Group A shared one membership group while those in Groups B and C together shared another. From membership group theory, it would be predicted that the extent of attitude change would be greater among the latter *Ss*. This hypothesis is supported by the data (in Table 7-13); by the Mann-Whitney test,[7] the change scores of these two sets of *Ss* (Group A versus Groups B and C together) differ in the predicted direction at the $p<.025$ level. This finding illustrates the influence of *membership* groups on attitude change. On the other hand, at the conclusion of the sophomore year, the *Ss* in Groups A and B shared a common reference group while those in Group C had come to share another. From reference group theory, it would be predicted that attitude change would be more extensive among the

[6] A. R. Jonckheere, "A Distribution-Free, k-Sample Test Against Ordered Alternatives," *Biometrika*, 1954, *41*, pp. 133-145.

[7] S. Siegel, *Nonparametric Statistics, op. cit.*, pp. 116-127.

subjects who had changed reference groups (Group C) than among those who had not. This hypothesis is also supported by the data (in Table 7-13); by the Mann-Whitney test, the change scores of these two sets of *S*s (Groups A and B together versus Group C) differ in the predicted direction at the $p<.05$ level. This finding illustrates the influence of *reference* groups on attitude change. Any inference from this mode of analysis (as contrasted with the main analysis of the data, by the Jonckheere test) must be qualified because of the nonindependence of the data on which the two Mann-Whitney tests are made, but it is mentioned here to clarify the role which membership and reference groups play in influencing attitude change.

The findings may also contribute to our understanding of processes affecting attitude change. The imposition of a membership group does have some effect on an individual's attitudes, even when the imposed group is not accepted by the individual as his reference group. This relationship is shown in the case of Group B. If the person comes to accept the imposed group as his reference group, as was the case with the *S*s in Group C, then the change in his attitudes toward the level of the group norm is even more pronounced.

Methodologically, the study has certain features which may deserve brief mention. First, the study demonstrates that it is possible operationally to define the concept of reference group. The act of voting by secret ballot for the group in which one would like to live constitutes clear behavioral specification of one's reference group, and it is an act whose conceptual meaning can be so directly inferred that there is no problem of reliability of judgment in its categorization by the investigator. Second, the study demonstrates that a field study can be conducted which contains the critical feature of an experiment that is usually lacking in naturalistic situations: randomization. The determination of whether or not a woman student would be assigned to the living group of her choice was based on a random event: the size of the number she drew from the hopper. This fact satisfied the requirement that the treatment condition be randomized, and permitted sharper inferences than can usually be drawn from field studies. Third, the test behavior on which the conclusions of this study were based occurred in a context in which the salience of membership and reference groups was *not* aroused and in which no external sanctions from the relevant groups were operative. This feature of the design permitted the interpretation that the E-F scores represented the *S*s' internalized attitudes.[8] Finally, the use of a paper-and-pencil measure of attitude and thus of attitude change, rather than the use of some more behavioral measure, is a deficiency of the present study. Moreover, the measure which was used suffers from a well-known circularity, based on the occurrence of pseudo-low scores.[9]

SUMMARY

In the social context of the lives of the subjects, and in a natural social experiment which provided randomization of the relevant condition effects, the influence of both membership and reference groups on attitude change was assessed. All subjects shared a common reference group at the start of the period of the study. When divergent membership groups with disparate attitude norms were socially imposed on the basis of a random event, attitude change in the subjects over time was a function of the normative attitudes of both imposed membership groups and the individuals' reference groups. The greatest attitude change occurred in subjects who came to take the imposed, initially nonpreferred, membership group as their reference group.

[8] Sherif and Sherif, *op. cit.*, p. 218.

[9] Adorno, *op. cit.*, p. 771; S. Siegel, "Certain Determinants . . ." *op. cit.*, pp. 221-222.

The American Teacher

Adults in the School and Community

part THREE

Adults in The Educational Setting

VIII

THE AMERICAN TEACHER

*OCCUPATIONAL CHOICE AND THE TEACHING CAREER**

By Egon G. Guba, Philip W. Jackson, and Charles E. Bidwell

A career may be studied according to its internal and external aspects.[1] Internally the career reflects the individual's picture of his life, involving whatever commitment to goals he may have developed, his understanding of his relation to various social institutions, his values, his needs, and the like. Externally the same career embraces the succession of roles that the individual plays during his life. Since the roles occupied in the course of a career are always embedded within some institutional matrix, such as the family, the school, the factory, or the office, the career may be viewed as the means by which individual and collective lives are articulated.

From the individual's point of view, his career is to a very considerable extent a problem in choice. With some degree of clarity, he will have developed a commitment to one of the career lines found in his society, and this commitment provides a goal toward which he may strive. His problem is to choose jobs or other roles in such a way that movement toward this goal is maximized. From society's point of view, a career is very largely a matter of the progressive limitation of choice. An individual's initial personal and social situation imposes limits on those roles he may occupy, and, as Hall and others have shown,[2] each role which he does occupy further limits the range of new roles among which he may choose. In addition, if an individual in a particular role is unable to meet its demands, his continued occupancy within the role and his move-

[1] See the definitive article by E. C. Hughes, "Institutional Office and the Person," *American Journal of Sociology*, 1937, *43*, pp. 404-413.

[2] O. Hall, "Types of Medical Careers," *American Journal of Sociology*, 1949, *55*, pp. 243-253; and "The Stages of a Medical Career," *American Journal of Sociology*, 1948, *53*, pp. 327-336. See also H. S. Becker, "Role and Career Problems of the Chicago Public School Teacher," *American Journal of Sociology*, 1951, *57*, pp. 423-426; and W. A. Peterson, *Career Phases and Inter-Age Relationships: the Female High School Teacher in Kansas City*. Unpublished doctoral dissertation, University of Chicago, 1956.

* From *Educational Research Bulletin*, 1959, *38*, pp. 1-12, 27. Used by permission of the authors and publisher.

ment into succeeding roles in the career line are questionable.

The career thus appears to be especially fertile ground for studying the interaction between the pressures of personality and the demands of society in producing an individual's behavior. A number of questions concerning this interaction arise at once. One major question is whether the definition of the roles comprising a given career line so limits behavior that only specific types of personalities identify it as potentially rewarding and enter its preliminary stages. If personality types for a given career do exist, they may be identified and ways in which the nature of the career limits the recruitment of its personnel may be determined.

A related problem is the extent to which successive career demands, as they become more specific, exert continually stronger pressures upon the individual so that the personality type appropriate to the career tends to fall into a single pattern. A corollary to this problem is the extent to which demands arising from the career roles force out those individuals whose personalities are inconsistent with the dominant career type.

Such questions immediately suggest a third: the adequacy of the behavior of individuals whose personalities conform quite closely to the career type as contrasted with deviates from that type who, for some reason, have remained within the career. Such adequacy might be determined through the perceptions of colleagues and superiors and through self-examination. Closely related to this question is another: the manner in which both conforming and deviant individuals within a career assess the adequacy of that career and of its institutional framework. This assessment might well be made in terms of personal satisfaction or fulfillment, achievement potential, organizational efficiency, and like factors.

The present paper, based upon preliminary data on the American public-school teacher, represents a heuristic approach to the three major questions which have been raised. Data relevant to each of the questions give rise to certain hypotheses about the teaching career. Perhaps these hypotheses suggest a general approach to the study of career types and more specifically indicate promising means to illuminate the nature of the teaching career itself.

The hypotheses have their genesis in two different sets of data collected by the authors over the past two years. First, data which had been collected primarily for the purpose of describing a sample of 366 practicing teachers in a study of administrative behavior suggested the existence of differing personality patterns at various stages of teaching experience.[3] Second, personality data collected routinely from the participants in a special teacher-training program at the University of Chicago proved to be related to the staff's evaluations of success in the program and of future success in teaching. Both sets of data indicated the possibility of collecting material which would illuminate the nature of the career lines found in the teaching profession.

The major personality instrument utilized in these studies was the *Edwards Personal Preference Schedule,* a paired-comparison type of questionnaire which purports to measure a number of normal personality variables based upon the list of manifest needs proposed by H. A. Murray.[4] Briefly, these may be summarized as follows:

Achievement—to accomplish demanding tasks; to be able to do things better than others.

Deference—to yield to the leadership and judgment of others.

Order—to organize one's work and personal life systematically.

Exhibition—to talk cleverly for the sake of impressing others; to be the center of attention.

Autonomy—to act without regard to the opinions of others.

Affiliation—to form many strong friendships and to share experiences.

Intraception—to observe and analyze the behavior of one's self and of others.

Succorance—to gain encouragement and sympathy from others when one is depressed or hurt.

Dominance—to lead; to make decisions and to influence others.

Abasement—to feel timid and inferior to others and accept blame for things that go wrong.

Nurturance—to show sympathy and generosity toward those who are in trouble.

Change—to seek new experiences and new acquaintances.

Endurance—to work at a task until it is completed.

Heterosexuality—to be interested in members of the opposite sex and in the subject of sex.

Aggression—to show anger and criticize others openly.

---

[3] These data were collected under the auspices of the Midwest Administration Center, The University of Chicago. The study was supported in part by a grant from the University's Social Sciences Research Committee.

[4] A. L. Edwards (New York: Psychological Corporation, 1954).

In an attempt to obtain corroborative data for the findings suggested by the University of Chicago sampling, this test was administered to teacher-trainee groups at a Midwestern state university; a Southern Negro college; and a private, urban teachers' college. In each case the group was compared to a normative sample consisting of liberal-arts students of both sexes and widely differing ages. The data from both the original and the subsequent studies form the basis for the present hypotheses.

In the initial study, the Edwards test was administered to 366 public-school teachers drawn from 24 schools in a nine-county area surrounding Chicago.[5] Teachers of both sexes and at all levels from first grade through high school took part. Since this study provides a base line in terms of which trainee data may be interpreted, its results are summarized here. In examining them, one must keep in mind the higher average age of the sample (34.9 years) and the fact that liberal-arts students constituted the normative group.

The findings showed that the needs most characteristic of this group of teachers were high deference, order, and endurance and low heterosexuality, dominance, and exhibition. Marked variations, however, were found among subgroups divided by sex, teaching level, and years of experience. The six needs may probably be taken as representative of an emergent occupational pattern found most prominently among what will be termed the "veteran teachers," that is, teachers of ten or more years of experience. Conspicuous by their absence are such needs as achievement, intraception, and nurturance, which might have been expected for a teacher group. Interestingly, the characteristics seem to fit the cultural stereotype of the teacher as sexually impotent, obsequious, eternally patient, painstakingly demanding, and socially inept. Again, it should be emphasized that these needs showed great variability, especially in regard to sex groups and length of teaching experience, and that therefore such sweeping generalizations will obviously be in error in a great many individual cases.

Close analysis of the findings just reported, especially in terms of experience groupings, led the authors to administer the Edwards test to the groups of teacher trainees already described. The three hypotheses growing out of the studies are, of course, only suggested rather than proved by the data; the presentation thus has only heuristic validity.

The first hypothesis is based upon the preliminary steps taken by an individual who will occupy a future professional role. Two choices which occur at the early stages of his career line are of paramount importance in understanding the direction of his occupational movement and the particular pressures which will impinge upon him during the early years of his professional life. First, at some point the individual must explicitly decide that he desires membership in a specific occupational group. Second, he must select the particular training institution in which he wishes to prepare for this profession. One might logically expect the former choice to precede the latter, as indeed it must in the case of those students who choose to enter institutions whose primary function is to prepare members of only one profession. For many, however, the order of these choices is reversed. The decision to enter a specific profession is made only after the individual has spent one or two years in the institution in which he will ultimately receive his professional preparation. Such individuals would be "school oriented" rather than "profession oriented."

It seems probable then that for those students who choose to enter teachers' colleges, the choice of a training institution is secondary to the decision to become a teacher. Those who want the most "direct" route to the public-school classroom have the opportunity in a teachers' college of becoming acquainted early with professional problems and techniques; reduced tuition and lowered academic requirements may also be attractive. Since such persons seem to be more "profession oriented" than are those who enter multi-purpose institutions, there is a strong possibility that in many respects they closely resemble practicing professionals. Indeed, the resemblance between their personality structure and their perception of the teaching task may have been a major factor in their original decision to teach.

On the other hand, future teachers who choose to enter multi-purpose institutions should not resemble as closely the practicing professional. For these persons, presumably, the decision to enter a particular institution either preceded the decision to become a teacher or at least was of equal or greater

[5] See P. W. Jackson and E. G. Guba, "The Need Structure of In-service Teachers: An Occupational Analysis," *School Review,* 1957, *65,* pp. 176-192.

importance. Among these "school oriented" persons, one might expect to find the same kind of resemblance between their view of the demands of the institution and their personality structure that one might find between the demands of teaching and the personality structure of the students in a teachers' college.

This reasoning may be condensed in the following statement which we shall call Hypothesis One: *Trainees who choose to enter a multi-purpose institution display personality configurations responsive to the press of the institution rather than to the press of the profession. Conversely, trainees who choose to enter a professional school such as a teachers' college display personality configurations which resemble those of practicing professionals.*

Data relevant to this hypothesis are shown in Table 8-1 which gives the need structure of four female[6] teacher-trainee groups. Those needs for which the trainee groups are significantly higher than the normative group of liberal-arts students are shown by asterisks, while needs for which the trainee groups are significantly lower than the norms are shown by minus signs. Needs for which there is no significant difference between the trainee and normative groups are shown by zeros.

Consider first the University of Chicago–trainee group with an *N* of 28. It will be recalled that veteran teachers were significantly high in deference, order, and endurance and significantly low in exhibition, dominance, and heterosexuality. The Chicago group does not differ significantly from the normative group of liberal-arts students in any of these variables; instead the group is significantly high in achievement and intraception, traits quite typical of University of Chicago students and by no means confined to the teacher-trainee group. The rigorous academic demands of the Chicago curriculum require high need achievement from students; those who do not display this quality are

[6] Only data for women are considered in the present paper since the number of men available for study was too small to yield reliable findings.

TABLE 8-1

TRAINEE GROUPS COMPARED TO LIBERAL-ARTS NORMS ON THE PPS NEED VARIABLES

Need	*State University (124)*	*Private Teachers' College (35)*	*Southern Negro University (110)*	*University of Chicago (28)*
(1)	*(2)*	*(3)*	*(4)*	*(5)*
Achievement	0	0	*	*
†Deference	0	*	*	0
†Order	0	*	*	0
‡Exhibition	–	–	–	0
Autonomy	0	0	–	0
Affiliation	*	0	–	0
Intraception	0	0	*	*
Succorance	0	0	0	0
‡Dominance	0	–	–	0
Abasement	–	0	*	0
Nurturance	0	0	*	0
Change	0	0	–	0
†Endurance	0	*	*	0
‡Heterosexuality	0	–	–	0
Aggression	0	0	0	0

0 Not significant.
– Significantly low (P = .05 or less).
* Significantly high (P = .05 or less).
† Variables on which veteran teachers are significantly higher than the norms.
‡ Variables on which veteran teachers are significantly lower than the norms.

quickly eliminated. Before they enter this institution, most students know of the particular teaching methodology used at the undergraduate level. Here emphasis is placed upon the small discussion group where students are asked to analyze critically works of art, literature, and the like. The zest with which the students adopt this analytic orientation becomes understandable when considered in the light of their high intraceptive needs. Thus clear evidence indicates that the need pattern of these teacher trainees conforms to an institutional press rather than to a professional press even though the professional choice has already been made.

Also data for the state university with an N of 124 show very little relationship between the need pattern of the trainees and that of veteran teachers. Indeed, the two groups have in common only a significantly low need for exhibition. Unlike the veteran teachers, the state-university group is significantly high in affiliation and significantly low in abasement. Although the authors cannot claim as much familiarity with this student group as with the Chicago trainees, they believe that this pattern closely resembles the stereotype of the group-oriented, other-directed undergraduate. Whatever its particular causes, this profile is markedly different from either the veteran-teacher pattern or the Chicago pattern. If we may assume that the pattern of high affiliation and low exhibition and abasement is, as it were, the cultural norm for this institution, students apparently choose this school because of congruence between their personalities and the demands of their chosen profession.

Looking now at the data from a Southern Negro college with an N of 110, we see again a remarkable deviation from either of the other multi-purpose institutions and from the veteran-teacher pattern. Like the veteran teachers, these Negro teacher trainees do show high deference, order, and endurance and low exhibition, dominance, and heterosexuality; but they differ in seven other needs. The group shows also high achievement, intraception, abasement, and nurturance and low autonomy, affiliation, and change. Examination of the need structure indicates that the pattern is a cultural one for Southern Negro students rather than for teacher trainees. The peculiar social situation faced by the Southern Negro makes the interpretation of these data extremely difficult. Since institutional choice is probably severely limited for this group, one might not expect to find the same kind of "school oriented" patterns previously discussed. Nevertheless, the high scores displayed for such needs as achievement and intraception suggest a degree of congruence between personality structure and institutional demands which is not typical of students in teachers' colleges.

Finally we turn to the data collected from 35 students of a private teachers' college in the Chicago area. These students have chosen to be teachers and have selected the quickest, and probably what they regard as the best, training route into the profession—a well-managed "technical" school with none of the fads and frills of the usual college campus. The results are indeed startling. Without exception, the need pattern of this group is identical to that of veteran teachers. Although the average age of these students does not differ from that of the other groups and although all are full-time students, they have nevertheless already developed a need pattern typical of teachers with ten years service.

The importance of these data is enhanced when one considers that relatively few teachers are actually trained in teachers' colleges. A recent survey indicates that in 1954–55 the public and private teachers' colleges prepared only 20.4 per cent of the total number of persons completing training that year. During the same year, private liberal-arts colleges and universities prepared 31.6 per cent of the total, and public colleges and universities 48 per cent.[7]

In the light of these figures, the data are highly suggestive. Multi-purpose institutions apparently are able to develop a unique press to which students conform despite their choice of a profession which has a markedly different personality press. On the other hand, institutions designed particularly for the task of teacher training impose a personality press which conforms remarkably to the professional press. The problems of how personality requirements are developed in schools—the unique set in multi-purpose colleges and universities and the markedly consistent pattern in teacher-training institutions—of how students make their choices, and of why some students wish to submit to two personality patterns remain to be solved.

Interestingly, the length of time spent by the student in the training institution apparently has

[7] T. M. Stinnett, "The Teachers College Myth," *Journal of Teacher Education,* 1956, 7, p. 368.

little or no effect upon his personality structure. For each group of trainees discussed in this paper, Edwards PPS data were collected for both Freshmen and Seniors; no significant differences on any of the needs were found. These results accentuate the strength of the press imposed by the training institution and also the effectiveness, in terms of personality, of the formal and informal means by which prospective teachers select their training institutions and are selected by them. Here again is an interesting area for further work.

The previous considerations suggest that, since most persons who enter teaching come from multipurpose schools, the personality-need patterns of novice teachers differ markedly. What then is the effect of teaching experience upon this initial divergence? Do groups which differ initially because of the kinds of institution which produced them continue to differ as experience is accumulated? The data collected suggest Hypothesis Two: *Teaching experience operates to erase the particular need structure which was congruent with the press of the institution and produces a pattern that is present in all teaching groups regardless of their academic background.*

Table 8-2 gives relevant data which show the need structure of 209 female teachers divided into five groups on the basis of the type of institution from which they received their Bachelors' degrees: liberal-arts colleges, public and private teachers' colleges, and state and private universities. Although these teachers represent all levels of experience, the five groups display a remarkably consistent pattern of needs which resembles in most details the picture for the veteran-teacher group previously described. If only teachers of high experience were included, the two sets of data would probably coincide even more sharply.

The correspondence is perhaps most easily seen by inspecting the needs known to be significant for veteran teachers. Three of the six needs significant for them—deference, dominance, and endurance—are concurred in by *all five* subgroups; an additional need, order, by all except the state-university

TABLE 8-2

PRACTICING TEACHER GROUPS COMPARED TO LIBERAL-ARTS NORMS ON THE PPS NEED VARIABLES

Need	*Liberal Arts Colleges (67)*	*Public Teachers' Colleges (60)*	*Private Teachers' Colleges (16)*	*State Universities (33)*	*Private Universities (33)*
(1)	*(2)*	*(3)*	*(4)*	*(5)*	*(6)*
Achievement	0	0	0	0	0
†Deference	*	*	*	*	*
†Order	*	*	*	0	*
‡Exhibition	0	–	–	0	0
Autonomy	0	–	0	0	0
Affiliation	0	0	0	0	0
Intraception	0	0	0	0	0
Succorance	0	0	0	0	0
‡Dominance	–	–	–	–	–
Abasement	0	0	0	0	0
Nurturance	0	0	0	0	0
Change	0	0	0	–	0
†Endurance	*	*	*	*	*
‡Heterosexuality	–	0	–	0	–
Aggression	0	0	0	–	0

0 Not significant.
– Significantly low (P = .05 or less).
* Significantly high (P = .05 or less).
† Variables on which veteran teachers are significantly higher than the norms.
‡ Variables on which veteran teachers are significantly lower than the norms.

students. In addition, the tendency for low heterosexuality in the original group of veteran teachers is duplicated in three of the five groups; that for low exhibition in two groups of the total. Interestingly, many of the scores which do not show significant variations from the norm tend toward the direction established by the veteran teachers. For the variable heterosexuality, for example, the two groups that fail to show significant differences have mean scores that are lower than the norms. One group that fails to show a significant difference for exhibition actually has a lower mean score than the two groups that show significance, but its small number of available cases makes this value statistically unimportant.

Only three other need variables are significant, and these only in single cases. Autonomy is significantly low for public teachers' colleges, and change and aggression are significantly low for state universities. It is clear that these nonconforming significances are relatively weak. Possibly they are accidental or peculiar to the particular samples chosen.

That Hypothesis Two is tenable thus seems clear. Somehow, through educational experiences the initial personality differences of teachers coalesce into a common personality pattern. Whether or not this process occurs by genuine change in nonconformist personalities or by attrition as nonconformists drop out remains a moot question.

The leveling process introduced by teaching experience suggests a progression from some personality pattern or patterns unlike that of the veteran teacher to a pattern common to all experienced teachers. The question may well be raised, "Does the point along this line of progression at which a teacher happens to be affect the public school involved?" In other words, what is the relative professional effectiveness of conformant and deviant teachers? Also, how do they regard their professional status and behaviors? Preliminary study suggests Hypothesis Three: *For a given school, the more nearly the teachers approximate the typical teacher-personality pattern, the less likely are they to feel satisfied, effective, and confident in the ability of their administrative officials, but the more likely is the administration to regard them as effective.*

In the original study of 366 teachers discussed earlier in the paper, teachers rated themselves on effectiveness, satisfaction, and confidence in their principals' leadership; the principals rated the teachers on effectiveness. The four criteria were then examined in relation to a metric developed to permit direct comparison of individual teachers with the teacher-personality pattern. The metric, known as the Teacher Need Conformity or *TNC* score, was a standard score obtained by weighting original raw scores according to their conformity with or deviation from the veteran-teacher profile. A *TNC* score in excess of fifty indicated a subject who had in general a profile similar to that of the typical teacher but who possessed the important needs to a greater extent than average; a score of less than fifty indicated one whose profile deviated from that of the typical teacher.

After these scores had been developed, a mean *TNC* score was computed for each of the 24 schools in the study. Data for the five schools with the highest *TNC* means and the five with the lowest means were retained for further analysis. For each of these groups, consisting of 103 and 73 cases respectively, means were obtained for the four criteria, for which ratings on a six-point scale were available. The means of the criteria were then compared by the usual t test. Because of the nature of the rating scales, a smaller *TNC* mean indicated greater satisfaction, effectiveness, or confidence. The results are shown in Table 8-3. The five high-*TNC* schools

TABLE 8-3

SIGNIFICANCE OF THE DIFFERENCE IN MEAN CRITERION SCORES FOR THE FIVE HIGH- AND FIVE LOW-*TNC* SCORE SCHOOLS*

Criterion	*Means*†		t	p
	High-Mean Schools	*Low-Mean Schools*		
(1)	(2)	(3)	(4)	(5)
Confidence in principal	1.845	1.541	7.12	.001
Effectiveness (self-rating)	2.612	2.486	4.20	.001
Satisfaction (self-rating)	2.262	1.932	9.54	.001
Effectiveness (principal rating)	2.369	2.534	3.89	.001

* The degrees of freedom were approximately 175.

† A high mean indicates a lower value for the criterion; conversely, a low mean indicates a higher value.

have lower mean levels of confidence, effectiveness, and satisfaction as determined from teacher self-ratings than do the five low-*TNC* schools; however, effectiveness ratings given by principals are higher in the high-*TNC* schools. All findings are significant beyond the .001 level.

The significance of these data is undoubtedly very complex. Clearly, though, teachers who have personalities like that of the veteran teacher are valued by principals. Yet apparently the more one becomes like the typical teacher in terms of need structure, the less likely one will be satisfied, feel effective, or have confidence in the principal's leadership. It is difficult to advance reasons for this apparent anomaly. One might hypothesize that the deferent, orderly, enduring teacher is a boon to the administrator, an asset to someone who is concerned with the effective functioning of a social institution. Yet these very attributes might be linked with a rather negative self-image. One is reminded here of the stereotype of the office clerk whose services are highly valued yet who is so self-deprecating that he is afraid to ask his boss for a raise. It might also be conjectured that the data reflect a real change in satisfaction, effectiveness, and confidence as the teacher realizes more and more how far from ideal everyday teaching practices and school procedures really are. Unfortunately, the dynamics of the process involved in the changing need structure experienced by the teacher remain hidden for the present; much work is necessary before the questions posed by these findings are answered.

SEX ROLE AND THE CAREER ORIENTATIONS OF BEGINNING TEACHERS*

By Ward S. Mason, Robert J. Dressel, and Robert K. Bain

There has been considerable concern in recent years with the shortage of qualified public school teachers, particularly at the elementary level. This situation has been brought about by a number of complex and interrelated factors. These include: (a) the imbalance between the low birth rate of the 1930's and the high birth rate since 1945, resulting in fewer college-age students to be prepared as teachers just at the time there are more students to be taught; (b) trends toward earlier marriage and earlier motherhood; (c) military service requirements; (d) strong competition from other occupations for trained manpower; and (e) the relatively low pay and social status accorded to public school teachers.

There are at least two approaches for bringing the supply of qualified teachers into line with the demand. The first is to train a higher proportion of college graduates for teaching careers and to obtain their actual entry into teaching. There are rather obvious limits to this approach. In recent years both the number and proportion of college graduates meeting state certification requirements have increased so that today about one college graduate out of three is prepared to enter the classroom.[1] Similarly, three out of four of those prepared take teaching jobs the year after college graduation.[2] It would appear that little more can be expected by way of a larger proportion of our skilled manpower entering teaching without creating manpower shortages in other areas.

The second approach is to utilize more efficiently those who have already been trained and qualified as teachers. One of the factors indicative of the efficiency of manpower utilization is the rate of leaving the profession. A recent study by the U.S. Office of Education indicates an annual rate of loss

[1] National Education Association, *The Postwar Struggle to Provide Competent Teachers* (Washington, D.C.: National Education Association, 1957), p. 109.

[2] National Education Association, *Teacher Supply and Demand in Public Schools, 1959* (Washington, D.C.: National Education Association, 1959).

* From *The Harvard Educational Review,* 1959, *29,* pp. 370-383. Used by permission of the authors and publisher. This is a revision of a paper read at the annual meeting of the American Sociological Society in Seattle, Washington, August 28, 1958. The research on which the paper is based was conducted as part of the regular research program of the U.S. Office of Education.

among classroom teachers of 10.9 per cent.[3] In the study reported here, it was found that *half* of the teachers teaching for the first time in 1956-57 expected to leave teaching, either temporarily or permanently, within five years. Similarly, in a study of 1,000 University of Illinois graduates qualified to teach, Charters found that over a ten-year period, 40 per cent did not teach at all; of those who entered teaching, half had dropped out after two years; and that of the 2,400 man-years of teaching produced, 50 per cent was produced by 12 per cent of the graduates.[4] An important contribution could be made, then, by identifying some of the factors related to the career decisions of teachers and identifying the characteristics of those who would, over a lifetime, contribute the most years of teaching service.

Our purpose in this paper is to study the career orientations[5] of a special sub-group of teachers, namely teachers just beginning their careers. Role concepts provide a useful approach to the problem.[6] We are, of course, studying an occupational role. Our thesis is that an understanding of the career orientations of teachers must start with the relationship between sex role and occupational role. Of course many factors are ultimately related to career orientation, but the effect of these variables is generally mediated by the sex role. Certainly we would expect that maternity and childrearing responsibilities have massive effects in differentiating the career patterns of men and women, and such important differences in life-situation would have wide ramifications. For example, we would expect that the importance of salary in determining career plans is quite different for men and women. While men are generally breadwinners for a family, women most often are providing only for themselves or else their salary represents a supplementary family income. This is a complex area, and many relationships need to be studied. However, within the limits of this paper it will be possible to study only some first-order relationships between sex role and career orientation, together with the influence of sex role on the relationship between job satisfaction and career orientation.

THE SURVEY DESIGN

This paper will report some data from a survey of beginning public school classroom teachers conducted by mail in the Spring of 1957.[7] The sample design called for a 10 per cent systematic probability sample of the beginning teachers in the nation. The general procedure was to select a sample of school districts, stratified by pupil enrollment. The districts so chosen were asked to supply the names and addresses of their beginning teachers. The teachers on these lists were then sampled in turn; there was thus a two-stage sample. Sampling rates varied from stratum to stratum in each stage, but were always such that within a given stratum the product of the school district and beginning teacher sampling rates was equal to .10. In this way, each beginning teacher in the nation had an equal probability of selection.[8]

The population of school districts sampled in the first stage was defined as public school districts in the continental United States maintaining any grades from kindergarten through grade twelve, excepting schools operated by the federal government or directly by a state.[9] In the second stage, a beginning teacher was defined as "a regular full-time teacher who devotes half or more of his time to classroom teaching at any level from kindergarten through grade twelve who has not held a regular full-time paid position for a full term prior

---

[3] W. Mason and R. K. Bain, *Teacher Turnover in the Public Schools: 1957-58* (Washington: U.S. Government Printing Office, 1959).

[4] W. W. Charters, Jr., "Survival in the Teaching Profession: A Criterion for Selecting Teacher Trainees," *Journal of Teacher Education,* 1956, *7,* pp. 253-255.

[5] We use the term "career orientations" as a general term to denote specific career plans, occupational attitudes, and occupational values.

[6] See for example "A Language for Role Analysis," in N. Gross, W. S. Mason, and A. W. McEachern, *Explorations in Role Analysis: Studies of the School Superintendency Role* (New York: John Wiley & Sons, Inc., 1958), Ch. 4.

[7] Some preliminary findings of this survey are reported in W. S. Mason, *The Beginning Teacher: A Survey of New Teachers in the Public Schools, 1956-57,* U.S. Office of Education Circular No. 510 (Washington: U.S. Government Printing Office, 1958).

[8] In applying tests of statistical significance to this sample we are aware that we are using formulas designed for simple random sampling with a systematic, stratified, and clustered sample. The proper formulas are unknown, and it seemed useful to make the tests with the formulas available, noting that the results must be qualifid by this reservation. The .01 level of significance has been used throughout.

[9] Five public school districts which reported that they were staffed by members of a religious order were later eliminated from the sample.

to the current school year (1956-57) in any school system."[10]

Usable replies were received from 7,150 beginning teachers, or 89 per cent of those to whom questionnaires were sent. This number was estimated to comprise 84 per cent of the total number of teachers specified by the sample design.[11] Such a high rate of response minimizes the effect of non-response bias. To test for non-response bias, respondents were compared with non-respondents using information available for both groups. This information was on sex, teaching level, pupil enrollment of the teacher's school district, and marital status of women teachers. Differences between respondents and non-respondents on these characteristics were large enough to be statistically significant, using the chi square test, with the exception of the difference with respect to pupil enrollment of the teacher's school district. However, the proportion of non-respondents was so low that their somewhat atypical nature had little effect on the representativeness of the returns with respect to the characteristics mentioned. For example, although 37 per cent of the respondents were men while only 29 per cent of the non-respondents were men, the proportion of men in the entire sample of beginning teachers was 36 per cent, which is only one percentage point less than the proportion among the respondents. With respect to any characteristic, then, the amount of bias among the non-respondents would have to be large to bring into question the representativeness of the returns.

The questionnaire contained eight pages of items on such matters as social origins, qualifications for teaching, teaching assignment, economic status, job satisfaction, occupational values, and career plans.

CAREER ORIENTATION AND SEX ROLE

Teaching is an occupation in which large numbers of both men and women are to be found. Many occupations can be said to be either "men's occupations" or "women's occupations," and in studying them it is reasonable to start with an assumption that sex role is a constant factor. Although teaching is thought of popularly as a woman's occupation, actually at least one out of four public school teachers is a man, and among the beginning teachers reported on here, 36 per cent were men.

It is, of course, a commonplace that men and women have different degrees and kinds of involvement in the occupational system. Almost without exception, men engage in an occupation even though they might not have to from an economic standpoint, and most of them sooner or later have families to support. Although there is a minority of women both single and married who have strong commitments to their jobs, most women enter the occupational world only as a short adventure between school and marriage, or else they work as a means of supplementing the family income.

These considerations are fully applicable to the beginning teachers studied in the present survey. Table 8-4 shows that, when asked about their career plans, fully 70 per cent of all the women said they expected to leave teaching some time in order to become homemakers. These are divided between the 58 per cent who hoped to return to teaching later and the 12 per cent who did not plan to return. Only 16 per cent expected to teach continuously until retirement. If we combine this latter group with the 58 per cent who expected to return to teaching from homemaking, we have 74 per cent of the women with at least a partial or contingent commitment to teaching. Only 9 per cent of the women beginning teachers expected to move to non-teaching educational positions, and 6 per cent expected to leave for non-educational employment.

The men show a completely different pattern in their career plans. Of course, the homemaking alternatives do not apply, and their answers are completely within the occupational area. Only 29 per cent of the men expected to teach continuously until retirement. The most frequently expressed ambition of the men was to "continue in the field of education until retirement, but . . . move from classroom teaching into some other area of education eventually." In all, 51 per cent of the men made this choice. Another 19 per cent expected to leave education for another occupation. Thus, most men do not see teaching as a terminal occupation

[10] This definition appeared on the form sent to school districts, together with some more specific instructions concerning the inclusion or exclusion of certain borderline cases.

[11] This is an estimated response rate because the number of beginning teachers among non-respondent school districts was unknown and had to be estimated.

TABLE 8-4

PERCENTAGE DISTRIBUTIONS OF THE CAREER PLANS OF MEN AND WOMEN BEGINNING TEACHERS

Career Plan[a]	*Men* (N = 2,602)	*Women* (N = 4,548)
Committed to education	%	%
Expect to continue teaching *until retirement*	29	16
Expect to leave teaching in order to devote my time to *homemaking:* WOULD want to return to teaching later	—	58
Expect to continue in the field of education until retirement, but hope to move from classroom teaching into some *other area of education* eventually	51	9
Total	80	83
Non-educational plans		
Expect to leave teaching in order to devote my time to *homemaking:* WOULD NOT want to return to teaching later	—	12
Expect to leave education for *another occupation*[b]	19	6
Total	19	18

[a] Italics added for emphasis. They did not appear in the original questionnaire.

[b] Includes "other non-educational plans."

NOTE: Due to rounding the percentage totals do not add to 100.

or career, but as a stepping stone to some other position, either in or out of education. It is virtually impossible for all of the men who expressed the ambition to enter non-teaching educational positions (mostly administrative and supervisory positions) to achieve this goal. Those who do not succeed in making this move may remain as teachers, but others may leave for other occupations when they find their path of mobility blocked. The fact previously mentioned, that despite the heavy inroads which homemaking makes among the women teachers, the proportion of men among the total teaching population is much smaller than the proportion of men among the beginning teachers, may indicate a heavy exodus of men to either non-teaching or non-educational positions or both.[12]

CAREER PLANS AND PROFESSIONALIZATION

The most frequently expressed plans of men and women beginning teachers as indicated in the previous section have, in different ways, implications for the professionalization of teaching. Our purpose here is not to present a full analysis of teaching as a profession, but merely to make some inferences from the findings on career plans.

One of the hallmarks of the full professions (e.g., law or medicine), it may be suggested, is that the occupational role is institutionalized as the dominant role in the sense that, in conflicts between the role expectations of the occupation and those of some other social role, the occupational demands are given precedence. For example, a doctor would be expected to leave a family gathering to attend to an emergency case. Our findings regarding career plans indicate that, for most women, teaching is a contingent role rather than a dominant one: they will teach *if* they do not marry, *until* they have children, *when* the children are all of school age, *if* their husband's job takes them to a community that has an attractive teaching vacancy, etc. This situation makes it difficult to build up and maintain professional organization and standards. As Lieberman has commented,

> It should be obvious that the fact that so many women teachers drift in and out of teaching means that it is very difficult for teachers to achieve occupational solidarity. The woman teacher interested chiefly in marriage and a home is not likely to take a strong interest in raising professional standards and in improving the conditions of teaching. Indeed, such women are frequently opposed to raising professional standards; such action runs contrary to their personal long term interests. The difficulties of building a strong professional teachers' organization should be manifest. The turnover in membership is apt to be so high that teachers' organizations must spend a considerable portion of their resources just to maintain stable membership.[13]

[12] At least part of the difference is accounted for by the lower proportion of men recruited in previous years.

[13] M. Lieberman, *Education as a Profession* (Englewood Cliffs, N. J.: Prentice-Hall, Inc., 1956), p. 253.

None of this is intended to disparage the professional commitment of the many individual women teachers who are thoroughly devoted to their work. Nevertheless, a contingent commitment is a central tendency for women beginning teachers, as it probably is for women in most occupations, and this tendency very likely inhibits the development of the professionalization of the occupation.[14]

Another characteristic of the professions is that they are terminal occupations or careers. It is probable, for example, that few physicians aspire to become hospital administrators; being a physician is a career in itself. But the large number of men beginning teachers who expect to leave the classroom for administrative and supervisory positions, not to mention those who plan to leave education altogether, makes it appear that for many men the teaching phase of their job history is likely to be rather transitory. Of course it might be argued that if we spoke of "educators" rather than "teachers" the career orientations of men would appear in quite a different light. However, our interest in this paper is with teaching *per se* and the availability of qualified personnel *in the classroom*. That many men remain in education as administrators in no way results in maintaining staffs of classroom teachers. Furthermore the roles of teachers, principals, superintendents, supervisors, and the rest are too diverse to be assimilated to a single category except for the most general purposes.[15] Thus, in different ways, the most common career orientations found among men and women beginning teachers are impediments to the establishment of teaching as a full profession.

INTRINSIC AND EXTRINSIC FACTORS

If the occupational role is the dominant role for men but not for women, it should follow that the occupational plans of men would depend more on factors *intrinsic* to their work—for example, nature of supervision, opportunity for advancement, working conditions, and so on—while the occupational plans of women should depend more on factors *extrinsic* to their work—for example, marital plans, or the age of their children. Evidence is available regarding this hypothesis from a question which asked, "Regardless of the likelihood of your leaving teaching within the next five years, under what conditions would you leave voluntarily (or for what reasons do you expect to leave)?"[16] Data for this item are shown in Table 8-5. The two extrinsic categories used to code responses to this open-ended question were "family reasons" and "depends on another person." The predominantly female concern with these factors is apparent. The intrinsic categories are "pay," "social status," "working conditions," and "if teaching is no longer satisfying." Some of these reasons are mentioned by only a small proportion of either sex, but the strong male concern with pay and working conditions is striking, and the differences between the sexes are in the expected direction in all cases. The other categories cannot be readily classified as extrinsic or intrinsic.

A corollary of this hypothesis is that the relationship between the degree of job satisfaction and career plans should be higher for men than for women. Teachers were asked to rate 22 specific aspects of their teaching position on a four-point scale from "very satisfactory" to "very unsatisfactory." Fifteen of these items were used to form an H-technique Guttman scale with five contrived items.[17] The reproducibility of the scale is .93. Table 8-6 shows the relationship between these satisfaction scale scores and career plans for men and women separately. The fact that the women have two categories of career plans not available to the men creates a problem of analysis. The degree of relationship in each of the two parts of this table has been measured by use of Tschuprow's coefficient, or T, which is a contingency coefficient with a maximum value of 1.0 for tables with an equal number of rows and columns.[18] In the present case, T for the men is .53,

[14] For the impeding effects of contingent commitment on organized efforts to professionalize another occupation, see R. K. Bain, *The Process of Professionalization: Life Insurance Selling.* Unpublished doctoral dissertation, University of Chicago, 1959.

[15] For a discussion of education as a unitary profession, see Lieberman, *op. cit.*, pp. 152-156.

[16] This question followed one which asked, "What is the likelihood of your leaving classroom teaching within the next five years?"

[17] For a discussion of this scaling technique, see S. A. Stouffer *et al.*, "A Technique for Improving Cumulative Scales," *Public Opinion Quarterly*, 1952, *16*, pp. 273-291.

[18] A description of Tschuprow's coefficient may be found in G. U. Yule and M. G. Kendall, *An Introduction to the Theory of Statistics* (New York: Hafner Publishing Co., 1950), pp. 52-57.

and for the women it is .42, which indicates a higher relationship for the men, as expected. Unfortunately, the sampling distribution of T is unknown and therefore we cannot compute the significance of the difference between the two measures. However, in view of the large number of cases on which the findings are based, we shall tentatively accept the proposition that the career plans of men are more highly related to their job satisfaction than are those of women beginning teachers.

An interesting pattern is observable in Table 8-6. Although the job satisfaction of men beginning teachers is highly related to their intention either to teach until retirement or to leave education for another occupation, the relationship to going into a non-teaching job in education is much weaker. This latter relationship also shows a slight tendency to be curvilinear, with both the most and least satisfied men teachers being less likely to choose this alternative. Among the women, however, the more dissatisfied they are with teaching the more likely they are to seek an administrative post. This suggests that when dissatisfied with teaching, men have more alternative occupations from which to choose and are more likely to think of an occupation outside of education; on the other hand, the less satisfied women have a more restricted perspective and think in terms of a move into other educational positions as an escape from teaching.

At the outset it was mentioned that teaching is often thought of as a woman's occupation. It is clear from the data that women beginning teachers have higher job satisfaction than men. On every one of the 22 questionnaire items dealing with the teacher's job satisfaction, the percentage of women replying "very satisfied" was higher than for men, and the higher satisfaction of the women on the satisfaction scale is statistically significant. Because women are less concerned with factors intrinsic to their work, it may be that they make fewer demands on their jobs and thus are more easily satisfied. Other studies indicate that women are more satisfied than men in other occupations as well.[19]

[19] L. G. Thomas, *The Occupational Structure and Education* (Englewood Cliffs, N. J.: Prentice-Hall, Inc., 1956).

TABLE 8-5

PERCENTAGE DISTRIBUTIONS AND COMPARISONS OF THE REASONS AND POTENTIAL REASONS FOR LEAVING TEACHING GIVEN BY MEN AND WOMEN BEGINNING TEACHERS[a]

Reasons for leaving	*Men* ($N = 2,602$)	*Women* ($N = 4,548$)	*Difference*[b]
Extrinsic reasons	%	%	%
Family reasons	1.6	68.2	66.6*
Depends on another person	1.2	12.3	11.1*
Intrinsic reasons			
Pay, salary, standard of living, etc.	49.8	5.2	44.6*
Social status of teaching	2.2	0.5	1.7*
Working conditions	11.5	3.4	8.1*
Personal failure in teaching	2.2	1.2	1.0*
Lack of satisfaction from teaching	3.4	1.8	1.6*
Not classifiable as intrinsic or extrinsic			
Enter another occupation	40.5	11.5	29.0*
Return to school	4.8	4.0	0.8
Highly hypothetical condition not elsewhere classified (e.g., "If I were to inherit a great deal of money")	2.3	4.3	2.0
Other	9.1	3.9	5.2*

[a] The subjects were asked to respond to the following question: "Regardless of the likelihood of your leaving teaching within the next five years, under what conditions would you leave voluntarily (or for what reasons do you expect to leave)?"

[b] Differences marked with the asterisk are significant at the .01 level. A one-tailed t-test was used for the extrinsic and intrinsic reasons, for which an hypothesis was available. A two-tailed t-test was used for the remaining reasons, for which no hypothesis was available.

NOTE: Due to the fact that the subjects were allowed to give more than one reason the totals of the percentages do not equal 100.

TABLE 8-6

A. PERCENTAGE DISTRIBUTIONS AND TESTS OF SIGNIFICANCE OF CAREER PLANS OF MEN TEACHERS AS RELATED TO JOB SATISFACTION

(N = 2,602)

Job satisfaction scale score		*Teach until retirement*	*Stay in education but not teaching*	*Leave for new occupation*[a]	*Leave for Homemaking*	
					Would return	*Would not return*
(high)	5 (N = 265)	41	50	9	—	—
	4 (N = 269)	39	54	7	—	—
	3 (N = 372)	31	53	16	—	—
	2 (N = 579)	29	52	19	—	—
	1 (N = 636)	24	52	24	—	—
(low)	0 (N = 481)	21	48	30	—	—

X^2_{10} = 2230 P = .001 T = .53

B. PERCENTAGE DISTRIBUTIONS AND TESTS OF SIGNIFICANCE OF CAREER PLANS OF WOMEN TEACHERS AS RELATED TO JOB SATISFACTION

(N = 4,548)

Job satisfaction scale score		*Teach until retirement*	*Stay in education but not teaching*	*Leave for new occupation*[a]	*Leave for Homemaking*	
					Would return	*Would not return*
(high)	5 (N = 749)	18	7	3	58	13
	4 (N = 791)	19	8	4	60	9
	3 (N = 875)	17	8	5	60	10
	2 (N = 1,021)	15	8	5	58	13
	1 (N = 676)	10	10	7	57	16
(low)	0 (N = 436)	12	13	11	49	16

X^2_{20} = 3465 P = .001 T = .42

[a] Includes "other non-education plans."

NOTE: Due to rounding the total percentages do not necessarily equal 100.

OCCUPATIONAL VALUES AND SEX ROLE

We have emphasized the differences in satisfactions and career plans between men and women beginning teachers. It is especially interesting that these differences exist despite a considerable amount of selectivity[20] in the recruiting process.

One of the major clues to the process of occupational choice is the occupational values which people hold. What are the important things which people hope to find in an occupation? We are fortunate in having some comparative data available in this area. In a study of the occupational values of college students, Morris Rosenberg had a sample of 2,758 Cornell University students rate a set of ten values as high, medium, or low in importance

[20] By "selectivity" or "the selection process," we refer to the entire process by which persons qualify for and enter an occupation. This is, of course, both a matter of self-selection and institutional selection.

as criteria for "an ideal job or career." [21] Comparable data were obtained for the beginning teachers in our sample. The results, in terms of the percentage rating each value high, are shown in Table 8-7 for men and women separately in each sample.

First, let us note that Rosenberg had found that there were several sets of these values which were similar and could be grouped together. The items involving "people rather than things" and being "helpful" he called *people-oriented values;* the three dealing with "money," "status," and "security" he called *extrinsic reward values;* and the two reading "provide an opportunity to use my special abilities and aptitudes" and "permit me to be creative and original" he called *expressive values.*

The selection process is highlighted in several ways in Table 8-7. In the first place, the occupational values of the beginning teachers, who have already entered an occupation, are quite different from those of the college students, who were planning to enter many different occupations. For the men the difference between students and teachers is statistically significant for all ten items, and for

[21] M. Rosenberg, *Occupations and Values* (Glencoe, Ill.: The Free Press, 1957).

TABLE 8-7

PERCENTAGES AND COMPARISONS OF MEN AND WOMEN CORNELL UNIVERSITY STUDENTS AND BEGINNING TEACHERS RATING OCCUPATIONAL VALUES HIGH

Occupational value[a]	*Cornell Students*[b]			*Beginning Teachers*			*Difference between students & teachers*		*Difference in heterogeneity*[c]
(Numbers)	*Men (2,008)*	*Women (750)*	*Difference*	*Men (2,602)*	*Women (4,548)*	*Difference*	*Men*	*Women*	
People-oriented values									
Give me an opportunity to work with *people* rather than things	39	59	—20*	69	79	—10*	—30*	—20*	—10*
Give me an opportunity to be *helpful* to others	37	53	—16*	80	85	—05	—43*	—32*	—11*
Extrinsic rewards									
Provide a chance to earn a good deal of *money*	36	19	+17*	21	17	+04*	+15*	+02	—13
Give me a social *status* and prestige	25	15	+10*	31	30	+01	—06*	—15*	—09*
Enable me to look forward to a stable *secure* future	63	51	+12*	68	67	+01	—05*	—16*	—11*
Self-expression									
Provide an opportunity to use my *special abilities* and aptitudes	78	80	—02	81	81	——	—03*	—01	—02
Permit me to be *creative* and original	49	54	—05*	62	68	—06*	—13*	—14*	+01
Other values									
Leave me relatively *free of supervision* by others	46	40	+06*	29	27	+02	+17*	+13*	—04*
Give me a chance to exercise *leadership*	38	29	+09*	56	45	+11*	—18*	—16*	+02
Provide me with *adventure*	14	17	—03*	22	27	—05*	—08*	—10*	+02*

[a] Italics added here for emphasis; they did not appear in the original questionnaire.
[b] Rosenberg, *op. cit.*, p. 49.
[c] A negative sign indicates a smaller difference between men and women in the teacher sample than in the student sample.

NOTE: The asterisk is used to indicate those differences which are significant at the .01 level.

the women the difference is statistically significant for eight out of the ten items.

Teaching is clearly an occupation which attracts those with high people-oriented values; the beginning teachers chose both of these items in much higher percentages than did the college students. On the other hand, the percentage placing a high value on earning a great deal of money was lower among the teachers, especially among the men. Of the remaining values, the biggest differences involved the relatively high value placed by teachers on leadership and being creative and original.

The differences in occupational values of men and women are also of interest in this table. Some rather large differences in the values of men and women students can be seen, and all ten differences are statistically significant. The two people-oriented items, which are highly valued by teachers, are seen to be primarily feminine values (that is, held more often by women) in the general student population, while the extrinsic rewards items are primarily masculine values.

Of primary importance here are the disparities in these sex differences between the students and the teachers (see the last column of the table, labeled "difference in heterogeneity"). Our hypothesis was that, as a result of the selective process, the occupational values of men and women would be more similar among the teachers than among the students. We find that the differences are in the expected direction in seven of the ten items. For six of these seven, the differences are statistically significant, while none of the differences contrary to the hypothesis is significant.

Some of the patterns in these shifts are noteworthy. We have seen that the people-oriented values are feminine values and are values of importance to the teachers generally. Although both men and women teachers are much higher than the students on these values, the greater similarity between the two sexes is a result of the greater difference between men students and men teachers. On the other hand, the extrinsic-rewards items were more important to men than women in the college group. On the money item, the smaller difference between the sexes occurs through the selection of men as beginning teachers who place a relatively low value on earning a great deal of money. The pattern for the other two extrinsic-rewards items, status and security, is quite different. These, too, tend to be masculine values, but the smaller sex difference occurs through the selection of women beginning teachers who place a relatively *high* value on status and security.

SUMMARY AND CONCLUSIONS

In a questionnaire study of a national sample of beginning teachers, a number of differences were found in the career orientations of men and women which have implications for the general relationship between occupational role and sex role.

Relatively few new teachers intended to stay in teaching until retirement. A large proportion of women expected to leave teaching, at least temporarily, for homemaking responsibilities, indicating that for them their sex role was dominant over their occupational role. On the other hand, many men hoped to move from classroom teaching into administrative and supervisory positions. Both the contingent career commitment of the women and the limited commitment of the men were seen to be impediments to the professionalization of teaching.

If the sex role is dominant over the occupational role for women but not for men, it was hypothesized that the career plans of men would be more closely tied to factors intrinsic to their work and to their job satisfaction, while the career plans of women would depend more upon extrinsic factors and be more independent of job satisfaction. Support was found for both hypotheses. Also, women were found to be more satisfied with teaching than men.

Finally, it was found that although beginning teachers were more similar in their occupational values than a group of college students planning to enter many different occupations, there were still important differences in the occupational values of men and women beginning teachers.

It would appear that school administrators concerned with retaining their teaching staff must seek in part different solutions for their men and women teachers. For the men, they must find ways of making teaching a more attractive and rewarding occupation; for the women, they must search for social inventions which will reduce the conflict between occupational and family responsibilities, and make simultaneous performance in the two roles more feasible.

*TEACHER-PUPIL ATTITUDES AS RELATED TO NONPROMOTION OF SECONDARY SCHOOL PUPILS**

By Patrick D. Rocchio and Nolan C. Kearney

Within the past few years numerous studies have been made regarding nonpromotion of pupils. Most of these studies, such as the one by Sandrin,[1] have been concerned primarily with the effects of nonpromotion on the personality of the pupil rather than with the personality of the teacher who fails the pupils. A number of studies[2] have dealt with the incidence of failure by subject matter and with the number of boys and girls failed by teachers. There now appears to be a need for an investigation comparing the attitudes of teachers who fail many pupils with the attitudes of those who do not fail many pupils. The writers contend that greater attention should be given to teachers' attitudes, since they are among the important factors which can make secondary school experience both enjoyable and beneficial.

THE PROBLEM

The purpose of this study was to determine whether there was a relationship between the per cent of pupils failed by secondary teachers and the attitudes of these same teachers toward pupils. More specifically, the study was designed to answer the following question: Is there a relationship between the failure rate of the teacher (per cent of pupils given failing marks by the teacher) and his attitudes toward pupils as measured by the *Minnesota Teacher Attitude Inventory?* Since the age, sex, and subject matter taught by the teacher may be thought to affect his failure rate, the study attempts to provide answers to the following preliminary questions: (a) Is there a difference in failure rate between male and female teachers? (b) Are there differences in failure rates among the subjects of the curricula? (c) Is there a relationship between failure rate and age?

THE INSTRUMENT

The *Minnesota Teacher Attitude Inventory* was the instrument utilized to appraise the teacher's attitude toward pupils. Research over a period of years has shown that this instrument is capable of differentiating between teachers who get along well with pupils in interpersonal classroom relationships and those who do not. A validity coefficient of .60 was obtained between the *MTAI* and a combination of several teacher-rating criteria.[3] The results of these studies have shown that the *MTAI* can predict the aspects of teaching ability that depend upon teacher-pupil relationships as well as intelligence tests can predict college marks.

Inspection of the individual items of the *MTAI* shows that they were selected from the following

[1] A. A. Sandrin, *Social and Emotional Adjustment of Regularly Promoted and Regularly Nonpromoted Pupils* (New York: Bureau of Publications, Teachers College, Columbia University, 1944).

[2] B. Bristor, "Subject Failures," *National Association of Secondary School Principals Bulletin,* 1946, *30,* pp. 146-148; B. K. Farnsworth and J. B. Casper, "A Study of Pupil Failure in High School," *School Review,* 1941, *49,* pp. 380-383; R. A. Norsted, "To Mark or Not to Mark?" *Journal of Education,* 1938, *121,* pp. 81-84; M. C. Schinnerer, "Failure Ratio: 2 Boys to 1 Girl," *Clearing House,* 1944, *18,* pp. 264-270.

[3] For further information see: R. Callis, "Change in Teacher-Pupil Attitudes Related to Training and Experience," *Educational and Psychological Measurement,* 1950, *10,* pp. 718-727 and "The Efficiency of the Minnesota Teacher Attitude Inventory for Predicting Interpersonal Relations in the Classroom," *Journal of Applied Psychology,* 1953, *37,* pp. 82-85; W. W. Cook and C. J. Hoyt, "Procedure for Determining Number and Nature of Norm Groups for the Minnesota Teacher Attitude Inventory," *Educational and Psychological Measurement,* 1952, *12,* pp. 562-573; W. W. Cook and C. H. Leeds, "Measuring the Teacher Personality," *Educational and Psychological Measurement,* 1947, *7,* pp. 399-410; W. W. Cook *et al., The Minnesota Teacher Attitude Inventory, Manual* (New York: The Psychological Corporation, 1951); C. H. Leeds, "A Second Validity Study of the Minnesota Teacher Attitude Inventory," *Elementary School Journal,* 1952, *52,* pp. 398-405; and C. H. Leeds and W. W. Cook, "The Construction and Differential Value of a Scale for Determining Teacher-Pupil Attitudes," *Journal of Experimental Education,* 1947, *16,* pp. 149-159.

* From *Educational and Psychological Measurement,* 1956, *16,* pp. 244-252. Used by permission of the authors and publisher.

areas: (a) Teacher's attitudes toward the status of children, toward classroom situations involving discipline, and toward methods employed in dealing with such problems; (b) teacher's knowledge of child development and of child behavior related to ability, achievement, motivation, and personality development; (c) personal reactions of the teacher, such as his likes and dislikes; (d) teacher's knowledge of principles of education related to philosophy, curriculum, and administration. This knowledge and these attitudes are part fo the teacher's philosophy of education. The teacher's practices in the nonpromotion of pupils as they relate to the knowledge and attitudes measured by the *MTAI* are investigated in this study.

THE SUBJECTS

The subjects utilized in this investigation were secondary teachers of a public school system located in a mid-western city of approximately three hundred thousand population. More than 90 per cent of the secondary teachers are included in this study. In all, 395 teachers cooperated in the investigation.

Since a significant difference in mean *MTAI* scores has been found between teachers of academic and non-academic subjects,[4] these two groups were analyzed separately. Teachers of academic subjects are those who teach such subjects as English, social studies, science, foreign languages, and mathematics. Teachers of non-academic subjects are those who teach such subjects as art and crafts, music, business, homemaking, industrial arts, and physical education. Many teachers in certain fields of academic subject matter were not included in the study because their number in the specific field was too small to give stable statistics. For this reason teachers of speech, journalism, and foreign languages were excluded. The number of industrial arts and homemaking teachers taken separately was too small to give stable statistics; they were combined to make one group under the non-academic classification of subject matter. In cases where any one teacher taught two subjects, he was included under the subject in which most of his teaching was done. For example, if a teacher taught three hours

[4] P. Rocchio, *Teacher-Pupil Attitudes as Related to Teachers' Personal Characteristics and Pupil Adjustment.* Unpublished doctoral dissertation, University of Minnesota, 1954.

TABLE 8-8

THE MEAN MTAI SCORE AND MEAN FAILURE RATE CLASSIFIED BY SUBJECT MATTER AND SEX FOR SECONDARY TEACHERS OF ACADEMIC SUBJECTS

Subject Matter	*Sex*	*N*	*MTAI Score*	*Failure Rate*
English	M	13	43.54	1.15
	F	78	41.19	1.18
Sub-total		91	41.53	1.18
Mathematics	M	15	36.20	1.47
	F	17	24.47	1.53
Sub-total		32	29.97	1.50
Science	M	20	35.20	0.90
	F	10	37.50	1.40
Sub-total		30	35.97	1.07
Social Studies	M	42	36.74	1.43
	F	38	29.21	1.42
Sub-total		80	33.16	1.43
Total	M	90	37.29	1.28
	F	143	35.76	1.30
Grand Total		233	36.35	1.29

TABLE 8-9

THE MEAN MTAI SCORE AND MEAN FAILURE RATE CLASSIFIED BY SUBJECT MATTER AND SEX FOR SECONDARY TEACHERS OF NON-ACADEMIC SUBJECTS

Subject Matter	*Sex*	*N*	*MTAI Score*	*Failure Rate*
Art and Crafts	M	8	57.63	1.00
	F	10	44.70	0.50
Sub-total		18	50.44	0.72
Commercial	M	13	34.15	0.62
	F	23	18.91	1.83
Sub-total		36	24.42	1.39
Industrial Arts and	M	31	15.00	0.71
Homemaking	F	32	29.09	1.03
Sub-total		63	22.16	0.87
Music	M	9	7.11	0.33
	F	9	7.78	0.67
Sub-total		18	7.44	0.50
Physical Education	M	17	25.53	0.59
	F	10	23.90	0.00
Sub-total		27	24.93	0.37
Total	M	78	23.95	0.65
	F	84	25.26	1.02
Grand Total		162	24.63	0.85

of English and one hour of social studies, he was considered an English teacher for purposes of this study. None of the teachers in this study taught both an academic and a non-academic subject. Table 8-8 presents the mean *MTAI* score and mean failure rate for teachers teaching subject matter within the academic classification, and Table 8-9 presents this same information for teachers teaching subject matter within the non-academic classification.

SOLUTIONS OF PRELIMINARY PROBLEMS

To test whether there were significant differences in mean failure rate among teachers of various subjects and between the sexes within each subject matter classification, the analysis of variance was used.[5] These analyses are presented in Tables 8-10 and 8-11 for teachers of academic and non-academic subjects, respectively. The results of these analyses indicate that there were no significant differences in mean failure rates among the teachers within the academic classification, nor within the non-academic classification of subject matter. Nor was there a significant difference in mean failure rate between male and female teachers within each subject matter classification.

The correlation coefficients between failure rate and age are presented in Table 8-12. When the teachers were separated into academic and non-

[5] The assumptions of this analysis were tested and accepted at the 5 per cent level of significance.

TABLE 8-10

TEST OF THE SIGNIFICANCE OF DIFFERENCES IN MEAN FAILURE RATES AMONG SUBJECTS AND BETWEEN THE SEXES FOR SECONDARY TEACHERS OF ACADEMIC SUBJECTS*

Source of Variation	*df*	*Sum of Squares*	*Mean Square*	*F*	*P*	*Conclusion*
Subjects	3	.1919	.0640	1.	.05	Accept
Sex	1	.0420	.0420	1.	.05	Accept
Residual	228	45.0723	.1977			
Total	232	45.3062				

* The interactions of subject matter and sex were found to be non-significant and pooled with error.

TABLE 8-11

TEST OF THE SIGNIFICANCE OF DIFFERENCES IN MEAN FAILURE RATES AMONG SUBJECTS AND BETWEEN THE SEXES FOR SECONDARY TEACHERS OF NON-ACADEMIC SUBJECTS*

Source of Variation	*df*	*Sum of Squares*	*Mean Square*	*F*	*P*	*Conclusion*
Subjects	4	1.0143	.2536	1.149	.05	Accept
Sex	1	.0608	.0608	1.000	.05	Accept
Residual	156	34.4378	.2208			
Total	161	35.5129				

* The interactions of subject matter and sex were found to be non-significant and pooled with error.

TABLE 8-12

CORRELATION COEFFICIENTS BETWEEN FAILURE RATE AND AGE CLASSIFIED BY SEX AND SUBJECT MATTER FOR SECONDARY TEACHERS

Subject Matter	*Sex*	*r*
Teachers of Academic Subjects		
English	M	—.13
	F	.24*
Mathematics	M	—.30
	F	.38
Science	M	—.11
	F	.40
Social Studies	M	.41†
	F	—.02
Total		.16
Teachers of Non-academic Subjects		
Art and Crafts	M	.39
	F	.23
Commercial	M	—.21
	F	.12
Industrial Arts and Homemaking	M	.25
	F	.08
Music	M	—.31
	F	—.27
Physical Education	M	.08
	F	.00
Total		.15

* Significant at the five per cent level.
† Significant at the one per cent level.

academic categories,[6] and the relationship between failure rate and age again estimated, the correlation coefficients were found to be .16 for the academic group and .15 for the non-academic group. In both cases, these correlation coefficients were found to be non-significant.

SOLUTION OF MAJOR PROBLEM

The correlation coefficients between *MTAI* scores and failure rates by sex and subject matter are presented in Table 8-13. When the teachers were separated into academic and non-academic categories,[7] and the relationship between *MTAI* scores and failure rates again estimated, the correlation coefficients were found to be −.38 for the academic group, and −.23 for the non-academic group. In both cases, these correlation coefficients were found to be significant at the one per cent level. These results indicate that low scores on the *MTAI* tend to be accompanied by high failure rates.

An examination of Table 8-13 indicates that even though all of the correlations are not significant in the "statistical" sense, the general trend is in the same direction—there is a negative relationship between *MTAI* scores and failure rates of the teachers. Moreover, when these results are interpreted in the light of the school system's policy of "continuous" promotion, they become even more significant than the figures show. It is postulated here that teachers who scored low on the *MTAI* would have failed even more pupils if they were freed to do so.

CONCLUSIONS

Since a low and non-significant correlation was found between failure rates and ages for teachers of both academic and non-academic subjects, the failure rates of the teachers cannot be interpreted in terms of this factor. Nor can failure rate be interpreted in terms of the sex of the teacher or the subject which he teaches. Since a significant relationship was found between *MTAI* scores and failure rates, the differences in failure rates among the teachers may be interpreted in terms of their attitudes toward pupils. The high school teacher with undesirable teacher-pupil relations, who creates an atmosphere of fear and tension, and thinks in terms of the *subject matter to be covered* rather than in terms of what the pupils need, feel, know, and can do, is more likely to fail pupils than a teacher who is able to maintain harmonious relations with his pupils and who is interested in pupils as *pupils.*

TABLE 8-13

CORRELATION COEFFICIENTS BETWEEN MTAI SCORES AND FAILURE RATE CLASSIFIED BY SEX AND SUBJECT MATTER FOR SECONDARY TEACHER

Subject Matter	*Sex*	*r*
Teachers of Academic Subjects		
English	M	−.10
	F	−.21
Mathematics	M	−.38
	F	.03
Science	M	−.27
	F	−.65*
Social Studies	M	−.42†
	F	−.54†
Total		−.38†
Teachers of Non-academic Subjects		
Art and Crafts	M	−.28
	F	−.05
Commercial	M	−.26
	F	−.02
Industrial Arts and Homemaking	M	−.53†
	F	−.38†
Music	M	.13
	F	−.14
Physical Education	M	−.11
	F	.00
Total		−.23†

* Significant at the five per cent level.

† Significant at the one per cent level.

[6] Before the teachers were pooled into academic and non-academic groups, a test for homogeneity of regression coefficients of failure rate on age for each subclass within the academic and non-academic classification was tested and accepted at the 5 per cent level of significance.

[7] Before the teachers were pooled into academic and non-academic groups a test of homogeneity of regression coefficients of failure rate on MTAI scores for each subclass within the academic and non-academic classifications was tested and accepted at the 5 per cent level of significance.

SOCIAL SCIENTISTS AND RECENT THREATS TO ACADEMIC FREEDOM*

By Paul F. Lazarsfeld and Wagner Thielens, Jr.

INTRODUCTION

In the spring of 1955, 2,451 social scientists in 165 colleges were subjects for a rather lengthy interview. The purpose of the study was to learn their reaction to what, in the study, is called the "difficult years." By this term we mean the period of accusations and investigations concomitant to the security problems of the cold war and symbolized by the activities of the late Senator from Wisconsin.

The origin of the study was a debate which had been going on for a while among prominent educators. Some claimed that professors had become afraid to teach and that the effect of the difficult years on higher education in this country was formidable; others felt that it was a passing episode, not much different from what happened after the first world war. The Fund for the Republic sponsored a study to find out how much apprehension existed among teachers. After some discussion, it was decided to devote the available budget to a large number of interviews in a specific group of teachers, rather than to spread them thin over all disciplines and all levels. What was loosely called a social scientist includes sociologists, economists, historians, political scientists, social psychologists, geographers, and anthropologists. The sampling was done in two steps. First a stratified sample of all 900 accredited colleges was drawn, including teachers colleges but excluding business schools. Within each of the colleges a probability sample taken from the faculty lists was set up. The number of refusals on the college as well as on the individual level was very small.

The first tool developed was a so-called index of apprehension. The respondents were given a list of about twenty situations developed in an elaborate set of pretests. They were asked whether in recent years they were especially worried about community gossip and misrepresentation by students, whether they had toned down their writings or changed their reading lists in order to avoid political difficulties; whether they had become more cagey in their personal relations with colleagues and students, etc. The professors were classified according to the number of such symptoms of apprehension they reported. This kind of an index is subject to the usual limitations inherent in any attitude test. Our main report[1] discusses its foundation in great detail. In the present context only one specific aspect of the approach is relevant. The apprehension index was clarified by a large number of cross-tabulations against other information available from the interviews. The main finding is that the apprehension so measured really consists of three elements: (a) fear for one's job security, (b) general concern about the state of academic freedom, and (c) defiant resistance to the prevailing attacks. In future psychologically-oriented studies it will certainly be desirable to separate the three elements. For the purpose of the present study it seemed more realistic to treat this attitude syndrome as a single variable.

Once the basic classification had been achieved the next task was to find out the factors which determine variations in the extent of apprehension. As usual, a large number of correlations was available. After they had been carefully studied it became possible to organize the material around two pivotal variables, one pertaining to the professor himself, and one to the college in which he teaches. A pivotal variable, in general, has the following characteristics: it is relatively highly correlated with the main criterion, to-wit, apprehension; it is also well correlated with other items, which in turn are associated with the criterion; and, most of all, the substantive meaning of the pivotal characteristic is such that it makes a larger number of the findings understandable in the light of other sociological and psychological knowledge, as well as of common

[1] P. F. Lazarsfeld and W. Thielens, Jr., *The Academic Mind* (Glencoe, Ill.: Free Press, 1958).

* From *Social Problems,* 1958, *5,* pp. 244-266. Used by permission of the authors and publisher.

sense. The pivotal variable pertaining to the college is its quality; we shall return to it at the conclusion of this paper. The pivotal characterization of the professor will be called, hereafter, his permissiveness. The nature and role of permissiveness is the main topic of the following pages.

In an initial chapter of the main report [2] a large amount of general information on the social scientists is reported. In addition to the usual demographic characteristics, two findings stand out. For one, our respondents have what one might call a strong inferiority feeling. By a series of questions it was gauged how they think various community leaders would rate the professorial job as compared to occupations like, for instance, lawyer or bank manager. The large majority of our respondents feel that congressmen and businessmen would give the professor a very low prestige rating. The second finding pertains to the political vote of the social scientists: it is strongly on the side of the Democratic party, the traditional home of American minorities. In a somewhat exaggerated sense, one could say that our respondents think of themselves as a discriminated-against minority.

But all this background material didn't seem to fully account for the role these social scientists played and the reaction they had during the difficult years. Step by step the notion of permissiveness forced itself upon us, until it turned out that it has considerable relevance beyond the immediate purpose of the study. It seems worthwhile, therefore, to bring it to the attention of readers who have general interest in the sociology of the academic profession. This paper is essentially a chapter of the main report. But in a final section we will summarize some findings from other chapters which show the implications of the data we present here and explain why, in our opinion, they signal a rather crucial social problem for American higher education.

The problem of terminology and classification. It is notoriously difficult for the social scientist to find terminology which isn't prejudiced by everyday language. We therefore have to explain what the aim of the proposed classification is and why it is referred to under the polarity of permissive-conservative. We began by singling out the respondents who would go quite far in restricting the freedom of their students. They would not permit them to form a Socialist League, allow them to invite Owen Lattimore as a guest speaker on the campus, etc. About one professor out of five belongs in this group. We could have called them restrictive but didn't do so, for two reasons. For one, this is a pejorative term, while the term conservative is freely used when these men talk about themselves. Secondly, this group of non-permissive teachers have attitudes toward authority, education, and personal conduct which correspond closely to what one of their spokesmen, Russell Kirk, described as "a program for conservatives."[3] So much for one end of the index. But how about the other end? The men and women there might have been called liberals or progressives. But each of these terms has acquired so many meanings in recent years that the colorless term "permissive" seemed more desirable.

And yet this does not prevent possible misunderstandings. We needed some indicators which would single out those teachers who were willing to tolerate unorthodox activities even if they didn't agree with them. But heterodoxy differs from one period to the next. There was a time when acceptance of radical scientific thought would have been pertinent, as for instance an early espousal of Darwinism. Later an intense concern with women's suffrage or with the beginnings of social legislation doubtless made persons controversial. But these issues no longer provide us with appropriate indicators of permissiveness. There can be little doubt that at the time of this study the problem of tolerating Communists offered the only possible choice. The best way of singling out highly permissive professors in the spring of 1955 was to ask how they felt about other people who wished to discuss or express Communist ideas. It is important to understand that we are dealing with our respondents' permissiveness to other people's ideas and not their own views and beliefs.

Two questions in our questionnaire lend themselves readily to such a classification. Our respondents were asked whether students who wanted to join the Young Communist League ought to be allowed to do it. Of our total sample 38% said "yes," 53% said "no" and 9% could not make up their minds. They were also asked whether an admitted Communist teaching in a college should be

[2] *Ibid.*

[3] R. Kirk, *A Problem for Conservatives* (Chicago: Regnery, 1954).

allowed to remain on the campus. Thirty-five per cent would allow him to teach, 45% would not, and 20% could not make up their minds. Those answering both questions affirmatively are classified as "highly permissive," those giving only one such answer as "quite permissive."

By now it should be fairly clear how our classification worked. On the conservative end our respondents approved a number of restrictions which by the standards of the academic community (as established by our survey) were rather rare. According to whether a respondent advocated most or only some of these prohibitions, he was classified as "quite conservative" or "somewhat conservative." On the permissive end the two questions just mentioned were used as indicators. This left a middle group, which was defined in the following way: they did not advocate any of the unusual restrictions; at the same time, they were opposed to both of the two freedoms for Communists.[4] We could have called this group "neutral"; but in view of data to be reported presently, the thinking of this group is certainly not characteristic for the general population. Even if we were to compare them with other professionals, they would turn out as relatively more permissive. In order to bring this out we used an asymmetric terminology, presented in Table 8-14.

TABLE 8-14

CLASSIFICATION OF OUR SAMPLE BY A PERMISSIVENESS INDEX

Highly permissive	543	22%
Quite permissive	505	21%
Somewhat permissive	697	29%
Somewhat conservative	354	14%
Clearly conservative	352	14%
	2,451	100%

The first two groups (43%) we shall sometimes combine as "clearly permissive." If we were to follow a pattern which once prevailed in research we would say that permissiveness is what the permissiveness index measures. But this is not at all the practice which our study followed. It is true that we have to establish indices by general considerations like the ones presented in the preceding pages; but then we feel obliged to bring out the meaning of the index by relating it to other data available. Before using the classification of Table 8-14 to show the role of permissiveness during the troubles of the difficult years, we want to show that our classification has quite broad connotations. The permissive and the conservative teachers differ in many aspects of their general ideological outlook. This will be shown in the next two sections.

[4] Included in this middle group are a number of "contradictory" cases, who would, e.g., let a Communist teach, but would forbid Lattimore to be a guest speaker on the campus. Actually these cases can be explained through the analysis of qualitative comments provided, e.g., by a respondent who disagrees with Lattimore on a specific issue of Far Eastern policy. In the main report these cases are discussed in detail.

EDUCATIONAL PHILOSOPHY

When this study was designed, we wondered how a cross-section of social science teachers look at some of the educational problems characteristic of their profession, and incorporated a few short questions on the matter in the interview schedule. This information will now be used to establish an important point about permissiveness.

We hoped to find out whether teachers felt professionally obliged to instill into their students an enthusiasm for a better society. But we feared that in the threatening climate of the difficult years only a small proportion of social scientists would openly subscribe to such a philosophy if the question were put directly. Therefore, to make it easier for our respondents to reveal a reforming spirit, if they had one, we suggested to them a parallel with the less embattled and indeed almost universally accepted ideal of American society, the notion of technical progress. This was the rather elaborately worded question:

> In engineering school education, it is said to be important for students to understand the prevailing state of the mechanical arts. In addition, their education should prepare them to make their *own* original contribution and to accelerate new developments.
>
> Some say this is directly comparable to the *intellectual* training of students in the social sciences. It is agreed that these students should be prepared to make their own original contribution to help society better meet the needs of its people.
>
> How important do you see this element of creative preparation in the teaching of the social sciences to undergraduates?

Whether we underestimated the willingness of teachers to acknowledge their devotion to social reform, or whether the parallel with technical progress induced them to overstate such a belief, is hard to say. The results in any case showed more teachers attaching importance to the element of creative prepartaion than we had anticipated. The wording of the alternatives provided, and the distribution of answers, is reported in Table 8-15.

TABLE 8-15

Urgent part of undergraduate teaching	36%
Quite important part of undergraduate teaching	40%
Minor part of undergraduate teaching	11%
Not proper function of undergraduate teaching	2%
Honestly have never given it much thought	7%
Don't know	3%
No answer	1%
	100%

Three-quarters of the professors consider a better society an urgent or quite important goal of their teaching. In fact, the prevalence of such a view is further reinforced if we look at some of the comments volunteered by the apparently more hesitant teachers. Many of these, directing their answer to the term "own original contribution" in the wording of our question, explained that they didn't mean students should not be prepared to contribute to a betterment of society but only that they doubted whether the average student would ever have the ability to do so.

A second question of relevance here dealt with a familiar, even stereotyped, issue: should social scientists try to sensitize students to think and care about major social problems or focus more on providing them with factual information about how society works? Strictly speaking, these are of course meaningless alternatives. One cannot seriously attempt to solve problems without a detailed understanding of the facts, and social facts can only be understood as outward manifestations of underlying concepts developed as a result of intellectual social concerns. It is, however, a well established research experience that such a vaguely formulated stereotype can often tap a respondent's more basic beliefs. The distribution of answers is reported in Table 8-16.

TABLE 8-16

If you had to make a choice, in general which of these two approaches do you think ought to be emphasized more in teaching the social sciences to students in their first two years of undergraduate study?

1. To give students a basic grounding of facts in the subject	40%
or	
2. To get students thinking about the problem areas in the subject?	39%
Hard to decide	19%
No answer	2%

Although 76% of the respondents in Table 8-15 felt that creative preparation is at least quite important in undergraduate teaching, only 39% go on to place special stress on problem areas. Not all apparent problem areas, of course, are destined to develop into the wave of the future; it is quite possible that many of the controversies currently seen by social science teachers may eventually die away without leaving any significant impression on our society. Notwithstanding, comparison of the two results seems to suggest that a considerable body of teachers do not realize—or do not agree with what seems evident to us—that it would indeed be difficult to help students prepare themselves to make original contributions to society without getting those same students to think about the unresolved problem areas in society which social science can deal with.

The two items, in dealing with the goals of social science teaching, can help to clarify our index of permissiveness. For the more permissive respondents want most to instill in their students a searching and innovating attitude toward the problems with which a society is confronted. The evidence is reported in Table 8-17.

Both emphasis on creativeness and on problems decline as we move from the highly permissive to the clearly conservative respondents. One should notice that the second line in Table 8-17 shows a much sharper trend of this kind than the first. Perhaps the problem-fact alternative has something of the character of a projective question, whose answers express not so much a rational decision as a feeling for the kind of spirit which should permeate social science teaching. It is a general senti-

TABLE 8-17

THE RELATION OF EDUCATIONAL GOALS TO PERMISSIVENESS[5]

	Highly Permissive	*Quite Permissive*	*Somewhat Permissive*	*Somewhat Conservative*	*Clearly Conservative*
Percentages in each group who:					
Consider social creativeness an urgent matter	50	41	39	37	32
Consider problems more important than facts	68	59	47	36	28

ment in favor of a creative spirit which seems to be caught by our permissiveness index.

Educators not only differ in the objectives of their profession but also in the methods by which these goals can be reached. How should controversial issues in the classroom be handled? At this point the general problem of civil liberties and the specific features of the student-teacher relation merge. If one had to describe the classical civil liberties position, one would surely single out as a cardinal feature the belief in the ultimate value of controversy. Free competion in the marketplace of ideas, it is held, will in the end bring the greatest benefit to society at large. Do our respondents feel that this principle also applies to the college campus? To find out we asked the following question:

> Some claim there hardly exists an area in the social sciences which does not lend itself to value judgment—that is, subject to difference of opinion. Now, in general, for the courses you teach, which emphasis would you lean to?

Respondents were then handed a card on which three positions were suggested, and asked to choose one. The wording of the alternatives and the frequency with which they were chosen is reproduced in Table 8-18.

TABLE 8-18

1. Such controversial matters should be discussed frequently in undergraduate teaching because of the educational value of such discussion	68%
2. One should answer such questions honestly when they come up but not seek out such discussion	27%
3. In times like these, it is better to avoid the discussion of such controversial issues as much as possible	1%
Don't know, or no answer	4%

The results indicate a near unanimity among our respondents. Practically none say they avoid opportunities for the discussion of controversial matters. More than two-thirds of these social scientists, in fact, seek them out. But the matter needs more careful scrutiny. A teacher truly believing in the value of free discussion should probably himself become genuinely involved in this interchange of ideas. If he does not, there remains an uneasy suspicion that he looks upon the discussion of controversial matters rather as an educational device than as a serious effort towards intellectual enlightenment. This possibility is strongly suggested by a second question which, together with the distribution of answers, is given in Table 8-19.

TABLE 8-19

In teaching subjects which might require questioning of traditional values, which of these two approaches do you personally feel is a better educational policy for teachers to follow:

1. After proper discussion, to argue in a measured way for his own point of view	38%
or	
2. To give all sides of the question impartially without revealing his own views	44%
Hard to decide	17%
No answer	1%

[5] The percentage figures reported in this table are computed after the elimination of those who decline to choose an answer. The size of this undecided group can be seen in Tables 8-15 and 8-16 and presently in Tables 8-18 and 8-19. By and large, the proportions who cannot make up their minds are the same on all levels of permissiveness.

TABLE 8-20

THE RELATION OF TWO QUESTIONS ON EDUCATIONAL METHODS TO THE PERMISSIVENESS OF THE RESPONDENTS[6]

	Highly Permissive	*Quite Permissive*	*Somewhat Permissive*	*Somewhat Conservative*	*Clearly Conservative*
Percentages in each group who:					
Seek out controversy	82	80	72	61	54
Present own point of view	56	52	45	31	42

The consistent believers in free expression of opinion have been reduced almost in half. Can controversial issues genuinely be discussed if the teacher himself is not willing to present his own point of view? In comparing the two questions on educational methods, we thus find the same suggestions of uncertainty as when we compared the two items on educational goals. Experience has taught social researchers that pronounced differences in the distribution of answers to questions dealing with the same basic topic are often indicative of ambivalence among the respondents.[7]

Even so, the two items on classroom methods again contribute to an understanding of our permissiveness index, as can be seen from Table 8-20.

There is a clear tendency toward avoiding free discussion of controversial issues as we move from the permissive to the conservative teachers. The one exception can be found in the second line of Table 8-20. In the last column there is an increase in the readiness to argue one's own point of view. Special tabulations show that this rise is due to the teachers in denominational schools. At many of these colleges, the existence of a revealed truth is taken for granted; consequently, the exposition of this truth is considered a duty of the teacher.

Altogether, then, the meaning of permissiveness is fairly clear. The permissive professor is tolerant of both colleagues and students concerning the main heresy of the difficult years. And this attitude is likely to go hand in hand with the belief that exploring new ideas is an essential part of social science teaching and discussing controversial issues with students an important educational process. But on the latter point a reservation has to be made. The discussion of controversial issues in the college has become a major symbol for the defenders of civil liberties. It is often said that a retreat on this point is the principal damage American education suffered during the difficult years. If this is so, then it is disturbing to notice how much uncertainty and confusion appears to exist among social scientists themselves. How can a civil liberty be defended if it is poorly thought through? There is an obvious need for greater clarity among the teachers themselves. What is meant by a controversial issue in the classroom? What are the various ways in which a controversial issue can be handled in the classroom? What are the possible consequences for students of the different approaches a professor can take? As far as we know, there exists hardly any literature on this point, let alone systematic study. Inadvertently, then, our survey may have disclosed a weak point in the armor of the defenders of academic freedom.[8]

In spite of this reservation, there can be little doubt that the large majority of the social science

[6] See footnote 5.

[7] There are two attenuating circumstances which might make the gap between the statistical findings of Tables 8-18 and 8-19 somewhat less drastic. From qualitative remarks we know that the wording of the question reported in Table 8-19 created difficulties. We used the term "argue in a measured way." Quite a number of the respondents listened mainly to the word "argue" and refused an affirmative answer, stating that they would express their point of view but would not argue for it. With a different wording the discrepancy between Tables 8-18 and 8-19 might have been somewhat smaller. It is also interesting that in Table 8-19 we find 17 per cent undecided respondents, while in Table 8-18 the number of "Don't knows" is negligible. We are inclined to suggest that this is an indicator of the atmosphere created during the difficult years. It is still all right to let students have their say; but a teacher has to be careful, not only in what he does, but even in what he says proper educational policy should be.

[8] Most social science teachers will agree that it is difficult to discuss controversial matters like religion or sex in the classroom, even when they are free to proceed without any interference from the outside. One reason for this is the lack of any consistent educational theory or cumulative experience in the conduct of such discussions.

professoriate is permissive and, as will be shown below, considerably more permissive than the population at large. They feel that any society has shortcomings and can be improved. Many are willing to introduce this spirit into their teaching. Saying this, we face exactly the embarrassing situation which some of our respondents described: we feel obliged to stress that this does not imply in any way that the academic profession is a group of Communist sympathizers.

HERESY, YES—CONSPIRACY, NO

One of the most interesting findings in the Stouffer report[9] tells what aspect of Communism Americans distrust most. Participants in his study distinguish between the elements of conspiracy in the movement on the one hand, and its incompatibility with American ways of thinking, and especially with religious feelings, on the other hand. Stouffer offers strong evidence that the average American is hostile to Communism much more on the latter ground. It is experienced as a heresy, a threat to the traditional values of family and country.

Social science professors make the same distinction and make it even more explicitly. But many draw a different conclusion. They consider the conspiratorial aspect of Communism dangerous. On the other hand, they either do not take the heresy as seriously, or feel they have no right to fight it except by free discussion. At the time of the Stouffer survey (1953), as well as of our investigation (1955) most experts were in agreement that the danger of acute infiltration of conspiratorial Communists into defense work or government planning agencies had been reduced to a minimum. That the general public nevertheless believed Communism in America a much greater danger than it was considered to be by social scientists is largely due to a difference in attitudes toward unorthodox ideas. This can be seen in a variety of ways. The disagreement in general assessment is quite marked. Forty-three per cent of Stouffer's national sample considered Communism a great or a very great danger, compared to 15% of our respondents. But the social scientists make finer distinctions. Six per cent of the general population would not fire a Communist in a defense plant and 26% would allow one to continue as a clerk in a store, a difference of 20%. With professors the same difference is 65%: 82% would not fire a Communist from a store while only 17% would not eliminate him from a defense plant. In situations, then, where sabotage can actually occur, the professor and the average American are pretty much in agreement; but when suppression of undesirable opinions rather than security is involved, the professors are considerably more tolerant.

Frequently our respondents testify directly as to this distinction. We can single out those who, in check-list answers, consider Communism a very great danger but would not oppose a Communist student organization or the retaining of a Communist colleague. Quite a number volunteer remarks to explain this response pattern. One professor of economics at a Methodist college puts it this way:

> A Communist is a very great danger—a potential saboteur. But Communism is no danger to mass political thought.

In spite of his denominational affiliation, this teacher feels that the chances of an ideological influence on Americans are small. A professor of history at an Eastern private college says it in almost the same words:

> Communists are a very great danger as an espionage group, but their ability to influence public opinion is nil.

Some strongly anti-Communist professors feel that a temporary attraction to Communist ideas will not harm students in the long run. A professor of psychology at a Midwestern private university states that an admitted Communist is a dangerous person to have students exposed to, yet adds:

> But I would still be willing to have them exposed. Students handle rabbits with syphilis.

And a young historian at a private Southern university provides, so to say, the theory for his position when he explains why he would allow a Young Communist League in spite of the fact that he considers Communism a great danger:

> It's good for them to get it out of their system.

It is worthwhile to dwell a moment longer on this distinction between Communism as a conspiracy

[9] S. A. Stouffer, *Communism, Conformity and Civil Liberties* (Garden City, N.Y.: Doubleday, 1955).

TABLE 8-21

THE RELATION BETWEEN TWO PERMISSIVE RESPONSES, ONE PERTAINING TO TEACHERS AND THE OTHER TO STUDENTS

	Admitted Communist teacher should be—			
	Not fired	*Fired*	*Don't know, No answer*	*Total*
Young Communist League—				
Should be allowed	598	145	185	928
Should not be allowed	198	888	217	1303
Don't know and no answer	65	60	95	220
Total	861	1093	497	2451

and as an ideology. When the two items in our permissiveness index are cross-tabulated, we obtain Table 8-21.

About an equal number of respondents (somewhat more than a third) give an affirmative answer to each of the two questions.[10] And by and large the answers are quite consistent. If we look at the four figures in the upper left corner we find that most of the professors either are permissive on both counts or on neither of them. But interestingly enough, there are 145 teachers who would allow a Young Communist League though they would fire a Communist teacher; while 198 respondents take the opposite position. The divergence of opinion is by no means paradoxical; it can be explained in the light of our preceding analysis.

Both these groups are as a matter of course opposed to Communism as a conspiracy, and in most cases even as a political movement. Both belong to the sizable minority who are willing to respect heretic opinions even if they do not agree with them. But they differ, so to say, in their assessment of what one can expect from a student and a professor. In a somewhat exaggerated form we can put the matter as follows: Some respondents think that students' ideas need not be taken too seriously, whereas professors have a certain mysterious power making the transition from an idea to an act more of a clear and present danger. Others, in contrast, look at professors as abstract thinkers, but at young people as not having enough judgment to understand the line between heretic thought and conspiracy.

To show this, we will quote a number of the professors composing the two groups. Among the 145 respondents who would fire an admitted Communist teacher, comments of the following kind were volunteered:

> My objection to a Communist teacher is that he has already committed himself to rigid ideas and he is not a free intellectual agent.
>
> Membership in the Party would be incompatible with what I regard as a standard of academic integrity and responsibility.
>
> I am not objecting to nonconformists. It is the dogmatism of orthodoxy, whether Nazi or Communist, that I consider unfits him to be a teacher.
>
> If they were not under orders from the Communist Party, they could teach, but they are under discipline and therefore unfit to teach.

The idea of conspiracy appears here in two forms. One refers to party discipline, with the obvious implication that a Communist teacher might engage in dangerous action if an opportunity offered itself. The second aspect is somewhat more attenuated: even though it be only a matter of intellectual judgment, the Communist is not free and therefore is not to be trusted. These respondents at the same time would not forbid Communist student organiza-

[10] By an affirmative answer we mean one indicating Communists should be allowed to teach and a Young Communist League be allowed to form. We notice in passing that our respondents are much more undecided in regard to a colleague than in regard to students. Partly this is undoubtedly due to a greater empathy with fellow teachers. But the handling of Communist professors has also been more discussed in public; the ferreting out of all the divergent implications of the various alternatives probably contributes to a greater hesitancy in making a final judgment.

tions which they regard mainly as debating clubs. There are occasionally additional points of view which clarify this response pattern. A few teachers approve of Communist student organizations because through them it is easier to keep their activities under surveillance. Occasionally the public relations aspect comes in: a Communist teacher is more conspicuous than a Communist student.

It is easy to predict what comments we will find among teachers who take the opposite position, those who would forbid a Young Communist League but not fire a Communist teacher. Contrary to the previous group, they feel that a Communist student group would do harm to themselves and to the society.

By definition a Young Communist League wouldn't be a political party in the usual sense, but would be dedicated to the overthrow of the existing government.

They should study now, and they will have time later to take part in political activities. It will only instill prejudice.

We should protect students from the harm it will do them in the future if they have joined a Communist League.

Inversely, these respondents would not fire a Communist colleague because they do not take him too seriously.

As a matter of policy every college ought to have a resident Communist. More people would know why they are against it. But I don't mean an underground one, or all the benefits would be lost.

There could be a Communist who subscribes to the economic system and not the political; a person who subscribes to the overthrow of the government shouldn't be left in a position to do damage, but profession of social and economic beliefs should not be grounds for dismissal.

This remark is interesting because it implies a double standard. This respondent would respect the freedom of expression of a colleague but not of his students. He not only is unaware of this, but he even contradicts himself in an argumentation. He feels obliged to explain why he is against a Young Communist League: "The Party itself has been made extra-legal." He doesn't notice that this same, and incidentally mistaken, argument would also apply to professors. His attitude probably shades into the position which quite a number of teachers in this group take. Their concern with the preservation of tenure rights overrides other considerations.

In addition to the intrinsic interest of these comments, they indicate how unlikely it is that the professors who take a permissive position have Communistic sympathies themselves. They are permissive *in spite* of their disagreement with the Communist position. There are undoubtedly some Communists among social science professors, as among any other occupational group. Maybe a few could be found, for instance, among the 160 teachers who assert that the American Communist Party is no danger whatever. But the hard test of reality makes it quite convincing that the permissive teacher is far removed from any subversive activities. We know which of them have served as consultants to industry and other organizations. It develops that the probability of such employment is higher, the more permissive a respondent is. This, of course, is partly explained by the fact that, as we shall see soon, the more permissive professors are also the more expert professionally. But partly it is probably due to their greater flexibility. Men and women who have more understanding for other people's convictions may also be likely to bridge more successfully the gap between the academic and business world. And certainly no one will suspect that businessmen have a tendency to hire subversives as advisers.

This concludes our digression into a subject which under normal circumstances would not have deserved so much attention: while one aspect of permissiveness is a tendency not to interfere with other people's opinions, even when they are heretic opinions like Communism, it does *not* mean that the permissive teacher shares or approves of extreme positions himself. But this assertion should not becloud the positive element of dissent. For the permissive teacher is likely to align himself with the more unconventional and nonconservative causes.

PERMISSIVENESS AND DISSENT

We now return to an issue which we raised earlier and which is important if one wants to clearly understand the nature of a pivotal characteristic. The classification along the permissive-conservative axis was based on a few questions, mainly concerned with what should or should not be allowed on the campus. We set out to show that the index so formed was well related to the more general educational philosophy of our respondents. Now we shall see that it is also indicative of what one might call a general political outlook. What evidence do we have on this point? Firstly, the answers to a general question about teachers' political views are given in Table 8-22. The distribution of replies, incidentally, is interesting by itself. From the meaning of an average one would expect to find that an equal number of teachers consider themselves more liberal and more conservative; actually there seems to be a premium on thinking of oneself as more liberal—we will come back to this point later. In the present context what matters is the fact that of the highly permissive respondents 57% consider themselves politically more liberal, while among the clearly conservative ones, only 20% classify themselves this way. On the two extremes, then, our respondents deviate by about 20% up and down from the average; the middle group has about the same proportion of "more liberal" teachers as the whole sample. But we have much more detailed and stronger evidence on how closely our index is related to other indicators of the respondents' general ideological position.

TABLE 8-22

On political matters do you feel that you are more liberal or more conservative than the other members of your faculty?

More liberal	39%
Same	39%
More conservative	12%
Doesn't know	10%

As discussed earlier, a vote for the Democratic Party may have a symbolic meaning of protest. By and large, in the last few decades the Democratic Party was also considered the proponent of economic and social innovation. No wonder, then, that we find a sharp interrelation between permissiveness and Democratic vote, as shown in the top row of Table 8-23.

It could be countered that our respondents are mistaken and that the "New Republicanism" is more deserving of the support of intellectuals concerned with improvements in the government and social system. But what matters in the present context is whether permissiveness implies a concern with social criticism and social change. This can be seen again from the second line of Table 8-23. There we present data on magazine reading. For each group the proportion of teachers is given who read one of the three liberal magazines: *The Reporter, The New Republic,* and *The Nation.* Again the result is clear-cut: the more permissive a social scientist, the more likely he is to read at least one of the three magazines. Finally, we know how often our respondents discuss civil liberties cases with friends and read news items on such matters. The proportion of teachers giving affirmative answers to at least one of the two matters is reported in the third line of Table 8-23.

A last set of data will round out the picture. We asked our respondents two questions, which while related to college matters, imply general principles. One of these questions pertained to the teacher's

TABLE 8-23

INDICATIONS THAT DISSENT IS RELATED TO PERMISSIVENESS

	Highly Permissive	*Quite Permissive*	*Somewhat Permissive*	*Somewhat Conservative*	*Clearly Conservative*
Percentage of Democrats in 1952 two-party vote	91	78	62	53	31
Percentage reading at least one of three liberal magazines	62	57	44	29	13
Percentage showing high interest in civil liberties matters	70	64	51	46	42

TABLE 8-24

	Highly Permissive	*Quite Permissive*	*Somewhat Permissive*	*Somewhat Conservative*	*Clearly Conservative*
Percentages who:					
Welcome teacher's oath	3	7	14	27	52
Stress faculty rights	80	73	64	54	46
Are members of AAUP	58	55	54	40	34

oath. In some colleges an oath was required and there the professors were asked whether they welcomed signing it. In the other colleges the question was put on a hypothetical basis: If an oath were required, would they refuse, sign with reluctance, or welcome the opportunity. The first line of Table 8-24 shows how sharply our five classes of social scientists differ on this point. Only three per cent of the very permissive ones would welcome an oath, but 52% of the very conservative ones provide this response.

Our other pertinent questionnaire item has to do with the problem of public relations, which has often been commented upon by students of the American college scene. Robert Hutchins calls concern with public relations the main motive driving trustees toward conformity. We wanted to know how social scientists feel about the matter, and Table 8-25 shows how we worded the inquiry.

The second line of Table 8-24 shows that 80% of the highly permissive professors would give priority to faculty rights but only 46% of the clearly conservatives. The permissive teacher then is strongly opposed to the oath, and if he has to make a decision between the public relations problems of his college and the interest of his profession, he is inclined to hold out rather for the latter. He is relatively more oriented toward his professional group at large than toward the specific college at which he works. We could call him more union-minded and it wouldn't be only a metaphorical use of the term. There is a tendency for more permissive teachers to be more often members of the American Association of University Professors, which can be seen from the third line of Table 8-24. Thus while the permissiveness end of our index doesn't mean extreme radicalism it does indicate a strong element of dissent from things as they are and a feeling that solidarity with one's professional group is important.

TABLE 8-25

If you had to make a choice, in a case in which a member of the faculty is accused of being subversive or of engaging in un-American activities, which do you think it most important for the college administration to protect—the reputation of the college or the rights of the faculty members?

The reputation of the college	11%
Both	15%
The rights of the faculty members	65%
No answer	9%

We have now considerably clarified this pivotal concept, but especially the findings of Table 8-24 suggest that, before we turn to the role of permissiveness in the broader context of our study, we raise one more question: Is it a matter of purely personal taste or a relevant aspect of the whole professional life of a college teacher?

THE PROFESSIONAL RELEVANCE OF PERMISSIVENESS

Social scientists could be tolerant of other people's opinions; they could have a searching attitude regarding the current state of society and feel that their teaching should imbue their students with a similar spirit. Yet this might be a private state of mind—like, for instance the preference for a certain type of music or of food—without characterizing the profession as a whole. For an attitude to be relevant in this larger sense, we should expect to find that the leaders of the profession display it prominently, that prestige is attached to it, that it forms part of the cement of friendship groups, and that the average member would hesitate to deviate from the general norm. In a sense we have already assumed that much of this is true. In a chapter of our larger study we reported that many teachers find themselves under cross pressure between the more conservative mood of the larger community and the more permissive atmosphere on the campus. This suggests that permissiveness is a relevant characteristic of campus life.

Only a special study could give conclusive evidence on this point. Our data, however, make it quite plausible. First of all, we can demonstrate that the permissive teachers are more likely to achieve professional distinction. In the course of the study we developed a measure of professional achievement through an index of productivity; while this measure is mainly based on publications, we were able to show that it is broadly indicative of academic merit. Now, Table 8-26 demonstrates how the proportion of productive scholars goes up as we move from the very conservative to the very permissive respondents. It should be remembered that by its very nature our index of productivity goes up with age. Permissiveness, however, has the opposite tendency; younger people are much more likely to be permissive. It is therefore necessary to study the relation between permissiveness and productivity separately for different age groups. This is done in Table 8-26. For each age level (represented by a row), the proportion of productive social scientists is highest in the highly permissive group and goes down continuously to the clearly conservative.[11] It is not essential to unravel the causal nexus implied in Table 8-26. Partly, permissive social scientists are more integrated in their profession and can therefore devote themselves more successfully to their academic work. At the same time, expressing permissive viewpoints might facilitate getting well known, having, therefore, easier access to publishers, and so on. By a relevant characteristic we mean such an overall effect resulting from many interactions. A similar terminal outcome can be sensed in another finding.

One of our items asked how respondents felt about personal relations within the faculty. If permissiveness is a relevant characteristic on the campus, then we should find that where a group of colleagues have similar attitudes—either permissive or conservative—the cohesion between the members should be greater than in a faculty which is split on the matter. For an irrelevant characteristic this would not hold true: the good relations between social scientists are probably relatively unaffected

[11] The relation between permissiveness and age is as follows:

Age	*Highly Permissive*	*Quite Permissive*	*Somewhat Permissive*	*Somewhat Conservative*	*Clearly Conservative*
40 years or younger	328	258	299	127	126
41-50	125	132	188	86	101
51 years or older	98	115	201	140	121

Without further data, it is difficult to interpret this relationship satisfactorily. It could be that increasing age makes people more conservative. But the finding might also be due to some process of selection which voluntarily or unvoluntarily eliminates the most permissive people from the academic field. For the purpose on hand, it should be clear that the figures just given form the base for the per cent figures reported in Table 8-26.

TABLE 8-26

THE PROPORTION OF PRODUCTIVE PROFESSORS WITHIN GROUPS AT THE VARIOUS LEVELS OF PERMISSIVENESS

Age	*Highly Permissive*	*Quite Permissive*	*Somewhat Permissive*	*Somewhat Conservative*	*Clearly Conservative*
40 years or younger	34	32	26	24	18
41-50	65	63	59	51	41
51 years or older	73	73	66	56	52

by their feelings about baseball or food. To make an appropriate test, we restricted ourselves here to the 77 schools for which we have enough interviews for the computing of rates to make sense. At each of these schools at least 13 respondents were interviewed. This number (chosen a bit arbitrarily: 14 or 15, or perhaps 12, would have served) insures against too much weight being given the replies of any single respondent in forming an over-all school rate. By determining the proportion of permissive professors for each of these schools, we may classify the colleges themselves according to the spread of permissiveness on the faculty. In somewhat loose language, we can then speak of permissive institutions and conservative ones, as distinguished from those where the faculty is divided. Table 8-27 corroborates our expectation. In permissive as well as in conservative colleges the proportion of respondents who consider their relations with colleagues unusually good is higher than in the two middle groups which are more divided.

Several studies have shown that the sharing of beliefs *which are relevant to a group* facilitates friendships among the group and that, inversely, close personal contacts lead to a similarity of relevant attitudes. If this general finding is accepted, then Table 8-27 with its intimation that faculties divided on permissiveness are likely to be socially less satisfied as well, supports the relevance of conservatism and permissiveness for social scientists.

Now that we have somewhat clarified the meaning of permissiveness, its frequent occurrence among social scientists, and its relevance for their work, time may be taken out for speculations: What makes these teachers permissive?

THE PROFESSIONAL MIND

We can think of several reasons why there is a natural selection of permissive persons in the recruitment of professors. For a young man coming from a business background, an academic career involves a break in tradition. The business community has an understandable affinity with the conservative credo, with its belief in the value of tradition and authority, its corresponding distrust of people who critically scrutinize institutions like religion and the family, and its belief in the social advantages of private property and the disadvantages of too much state interference in economic affairs. Take, now, a son or daughter who for some reason—be it rebellion from parents or intellectual curiosity—has begun to question these values; he or she will look for new ones, and be more hospitable to unorthodox possibilities. In our terminology, such an individual will be permissive.

If the prospective teacher comes from a professional background he is likely to have grown up in an atmosphere of permissive ideas and—barring special circumstances—will carry them into his own academic work.

Once he is on the campus, socio-economic circumstances also militate against a conservative affirmation by the academic man. College professors are among the lowest paid of all professions requiring comparable training. This might not be decisive if the lack of economic advantages were counterbalanced by considerable prestige, as is true for certain ecclesiastic and judicial positions in America and for the university professor in Europe. But such is not the case with college teachers in this country.

TABLE 8-27

SATISFACTION WITH FACULTY RELATIONS IN COLLEGES CLASSIFIED BY DEGREE OF AGREEMENT ON PERMISSIVENESS

	Permissiveness of the Faculty			
	Mainly Permissive	*Divided, majority permissive*	*Divided, majority conservative*	*Mainly conservative*
Proportion of respondents who are highly satisfied with faculty relations	43	32	31	48
Number of professors	631	664	362	197
Number of colleges	21	27	18	11

We know that our respondents believe their occupation is not highly esteemed in the community; the higher the professional status of a professor, in fact, the more strongly he feels that his prestige is low in the outside world. The reasons are not difficult to trace. An important factor is the organization of education in America. The American college is a strange combination of an extended high school and the beginning of a truly academic training center. One hundred fifty thousand college professors staff these schools. Many of them may not deserve special prestige. But the elite among them, who properly compare themselves with the small number of university professors in other countries, find that they have in no way comparable prestige and influence because, for the general public, they are indistinguishable from the large mass of all other college teachers.[12] One might answer that the American professor could derive his self-respect from the prestige he has within his own profession and could forget about what the community thinks of him. Leaving aside the psychological unrealism of such an idea, the very size of the American professoriate makes it improbable. In a small professional group there can be a high degree of social acoustics. What a man says will be quickly appraised by the others and such appraisal could matter very much. But in a large profession it takes a long time before a single voice is heard, and the lack of an echo deprives the single individual of another means of psychological support. Small economic returns, little prestige on the outside, and scarce means of mutual prestige reinforcement—little wonder that the very position of the professor in the American social structure is not likely to make him feel that everything in it is unqestionably for the best.

What has been said so far is true in general for the academic world. The social scientist faces an additional situation deriving from the nature of his work, which is likely to strengthen a basically permissive attitude. A great discovery of anthropology was that there are social systems completely different from ours and yet viable. A major contribution of historians is the idea that in other periods the modes of thinking and the forms of social relations were different from ours and require reconstruction for contemporary understanding. The intellectual task involved in these and many similar endeavors of the social scientist is contingent on his ability to visualize a state of human affairs radically different from that of today. While it is true that the social scientist is subject to the same laws of evidence as are his colleagues in all other divisions of knowledge, for him ultimate scholarly accomplishment must depend upon a kind of imagination which has initially to be akin to criticism and therefore is not consonant with the intellectual mood of the conservative.

Occupational self-selection, then, certain features of the American social structure, and the very task of the social scientist make permissive tendencies probable to begin with. Once these conditions and functional consequences have come into play, an additional process sets in. Any group which inclines to a professional ethos, be it medical doctors or businessmen or civil servants, will tend to reinforce it by mutual interaction. It is naive to believe that there is a conspiracy by which faculties exclude from appointment candidates with a conservative mind. The mere balance of power, which in most colleges is on the side of the trustees and the administration, would preclude such a possibility in the long run. What actually is likely to happen is this. Many people drift into occupational pursuits without any clear ideological commitments. They could develop either the conservative or the permissive tendencies in their thinking and their personality. But two factors crystallize and reinforce the non-conservative component. For one, they see that professional success goes more often to permissive seniors. Furthermore, once permissive colleagues are in the majority, even a slight numerical differential may build up to a considerable effect on the uncommitted man. By mere chance he is likely to find friendships among the less conservative; the result will be a slow atrophy of conservative potentialities unless they were very strong to begin with. This is a process to which we have referred before: the development of norms by mutual interaction. And it applies to faculties as well as to any other group.[13]

Irrespective then of one's own predilection, one

[12] At least one other comparison with Europe is worth mentioning. Here the teacher in the grade school, the one with whom every American has contact, is usually a woman. Especially in small towns, she does not have nearly the prestige of her male counterparts in European villages and towns.

[13] The recurrent disagreements among the armed services provide an interesting parallel. Self-interest and selective perception would explain that the majority in the Army and Navy are often on different sides of a controversy. But the *extent* of in-group agreement on both sides can only be explained by a process of mutual reinforcement.

has to accept it as a "fact of nature" that among social scientists in 20th Century America permissiveness characterizes the prevailing climate of opinion. Our speculative digression has tried to explain this in terms of the experience of the typical academician. But we also probably face here a trend which considerably over-reaches individual experience. The historian Carl Becker is one of those who might see in our data corroboration of a much broader development:[14]

> Until recently the chief function of the sophisticated, the priests and scribes, has been to stabilize custom and validate social authority by perpetuating the tradition and interpreting it in a manner conformable to the understanding of common men. During the last three hundred years . . . there has emerged a new class of learned men, successors to the priests and scribes, whose function is to increase rather than to preserve knowledge, to undermine rather than to stabilize custom and social authority.

This is to say that a permissive professoriate, or an equivalent in some other part of the social fabric, is needed now to help society adjust to novel conditions while discarding outmoded patterns. It is thus the function of the social scientist to be sensitive to innovation in society, to be permissive in the full sense of our analysis.

As usual, when one meets such a situation one question has to be raised. Why doesn't the system veer into extremes? Why aren't all social scientists violent radicals? The general answer is obvious. Checks and balances in the form of trustees and administrators make such an outcome unlikely; and personality types inclined toward radical action would, in general, not be prone to choose classroom teaching as an occupation. A cross-sectional study like ours does not permit tracing out these kinds of ramifications. It happens, however, that we have a few data which shed some light on the restraining factors in the situation.

One of them returns to the distinction between generalized and local sources of gratification. We have already pointed out that the permissive teachers are more oriented toward the profession at large and the conservative social scientist more toward the local college institution.[15] It seems that an inverse relationship also holds true: the profession at large is more likely to reward the permissive professor than is the local institution, including its own faculty. We asked each professor whether he had been a member of a college committee which was entrusted with some administrative function and whether he was or had been a department head. It is not the most permissive group which has had these local honors. This is true in spite of the fact that, as we know, the most permissive social scientists furnish the largest proportion of highly productive scholars and the largest proportion of men and women called in as consultants by business firms. We are inclined to interpret this finding in the following way: When a faculty wants to see its interests represented on a committee, it is not inclined to pick the man with the greatest professional prestige, but the one who is likely to be most successful in negotiations with the constituted authority. The natural choice is a middle-of-the-roader, and it is indeed among them that we find the highest proportion of such representatives. In the case of a departmental chairman, this tendency would be even stronger, because very often they are not selected by the teachers but appointed by the administration. It is often claimed that academicians recoil from administrative assignments and committee positions. Still, these involve a certain amount of honor which is undoubtedly attractive to many persons. If the local honors are going to somewhat more conservative professors, then here we have one countervailing force which would set limits on the reward connected with permissiveness in the academic community.

A second such restricting factor is age. By and large in a more or less conservative community people tend to grow more conservative with age. We have already seen that this is also true for our social scientists: the proportion of permissiveness is largest in the youngest age group. There are several indications that this is not the result of temporary political circumstances. The depression generation has now reached well past the age of forty and they are more conservative than the most recent recruits to the profession. It also happens that our geographers who are much less permissive to begin with don't show a decline of permissiveness with age. What actually seems to happen is that age exer-

[14] C. Becker, *Progress and Power* (Stanford: Stanford University Press, 1936).

[15] In another part of the study it is shown that the attitude of conservative professors is more affected by academic freedom incidents in their own college, while the permissive professors know more about and are relatively more agitated by incidents which have aroused national attention. The parallel is clear to Merton's comparison between local or cosmopolitan community leaders.

cises a dampening effect on the innovating spirit with which younger people enter the social sciences. The equilibrium is maintained because each generation brings its own momentum into the system, replacing an older generation who have become less permissive.

We have another set of data which seems to indicate that the respondents of highest permissiveness are less favored by salary increases, but our information on this point is somewhat vague. The indications are strong enough to deserve further explorations wherever more precise data on salaries should be available.

In spite of all these qualifications our data leave no doubt that permissiveness is among the prevailing norms in the social science profession. As such, it has all the prerequisites of a pivotal characteristic. And we can now use it to summarize some of our major findings.

PERMISSIVENESS AND APPREHENSION

From all that has been said so far one result is almost a foregone conclusion: the more permissive a social scientist, the more apprehensive will he be. For a succinct picture, Table 8-28 gives a condensed cross-tabulation of the two indices.

TABLE 8-28

THE RELATION BETWEEN PERMISSIVENESS AND APPREHENSION*

	Apprehension Score			
Level of Permissiveness	*0*	*1 and 2*	*3 to 6*	*Total*
Clearly permissive	241	444	363	1048
Somewhat permissive	207	311	179	697
Conservative	294	299	113	706
	742	1054	655	2451

* For further details, see the footnote to Table 8-20.

In some respects this table corroborates previous findings. If apprehensive people are more permissive, this means that many teachers are not subdued by their apprehension. They are willing to go on record that unorthodox colleagues and students should not be interfered with. Also, the relationship reminds us of a common element in both attitudes: being permissive means looking at the contemporary scene with more critical eyes, and apprehension, it will be remembered, has a marked component of alertness to civil liberties. A third link between the two positions deserves more careful documentation.

Our data show that it was the permissive teacher who bore the brunt of the attacks on colleges during the difficult years. At three points in our questionnaire respondents had the opportunity to tell whether they themselves had come under fire. They were asked whether their own academic freedom had been threatened, whether they had ever been reported unfavorably to higher authorities, and whether they had felt pressures to conform to the prevailing climate of opinion. Table 8-29 shows that on each of the three matters permissive teachers much more frequently report unpleasant episodes.

This result cannot be taken lightly. We have seen that the permissive social scientist is most representative of his profession. He furnishes much of the academic leadership; his way of thinking is in harmony with the intellectual tasks entrusted to him; his educational philosophy is relatively more consistent. It is not surprising that being under attack makes him more apprehensive. But the attacks themselves now appear in a new light. They are not only directed against single individuals: they

TABLE 8-29

PROPORTION OF RESPONDENTS ON VARIOUS LEVELS OF PERMISSIVENESS WHO HAD UNPLEASANT EXPERIENCES

	Highly Permissive	*Quite Permissive*	*Somewhat Permissive*	*Somewhat Conservative*	*Clearly Conservative*
Percentages who:					
Reported own academic freedom threatened	32	24	19	14	7
Were reported to higher authorities	21	19	16	14	7
Felt pressure to conform politically	30	23	19	17	7

might endanger the very nature and quality of social science teaching. This point decidedly deserves our further attention. But first, one other aspect of the situation needs to be discussed: the role of party politics.

In Table 8-30 we report the relation between permissiveness and apprehension separately for Republicans and Democrats. If we compare the proportion of apprehensive respondents among the two groups of voters, we find that Democrats are considerably more apprehensive than Republicans on each level of permissiveness. It seems likely that professors in both political camps looked at the attacks during the difficult years as to some degree party inspired. Irrespective of their own attitudes and the extent to which they might therefore be subject to attacks, the Democrats felt considerably more endangered than the Republicans.[16]

If our interpretation of this finding is correct, it harks back to a problem serious for any popular government. One function of parties is to crystallize issues and thus to mediate between the interest of various sectors of the nation. But sometimes the process gets reversed. There are issues of national concern on which no genuine disagreement among the general population is possible. And still, such issues are sometimes seized upon by parties and thus become sources of division from which it is difficult to find a rational base for compromise. Foreign policy has most often provided pertinent examples in the United States as well as in other Western democracies. We seem to have here a similar case. Basically all Americans will agree on both the need for national security and for civil liberties. Nevertheless, even as sophisticated a group as the teachers in our study ends up by experiencing the problems involved as party issues. It might very well be that men of good will are not fully aware of this fact and that a finding like Table 8-30, if better known, could have a salutary effect.

We return to the major issue, the fact that attacks on permissive professors are at the same time directed against the more distinguished and representative sector of the professoriate. Many readers might feel that this is not serious. Even if a few good social scientists were endangered, there were undoubtedly many equally good ones who remained safe because they were less permissive. Besides, the argument might run, the conservative sector of the professoriate should be strengthened anyhow. Thus the whole problem would be reduced to a matter of individual human rights, serious enough in itself but not affecting American colleges at large. But the matter is not that simple. It is at this point that our second pivotal variable enters: the quality of the college.

THE ROLE OF THE COLLEGE

Offhand, it seems very difficult to classify colleges by their quality. And yet for the purpose of statistical comparison, the matter isn't as complicated as it seems. In the course of the study we developed an index of college quality based on a few available items of information: proportion of Ph.D.'s on the faculty, number of library books per student, proportion of graduates who were successful in post-graduate work, etc. The index so formed permitted the classification of colleges into four quality groups.

17 The third line of Table 8-30 gives for the total sample a more detailed account of how apprehension rises with permissiveness. The relation is considerably stronger than was visible in the condensed form of Table 8-28.

TABLE 8-30

PROPORTION OF APPREHENSIVE RESPONDENTS IN SUBGROUPS CLASSIFIED BY 1952 VOTE AND LEVEL OF PERMISSIVENESS*

	Highly Permissive	*Quite Permissive*	*Somewhat Permissive*	*Somewhat Conservative*	*Clearly Conservative*
Per cent apprehension among:					
Republicans	48	32	33	24	22
Democrats	62	54	50	49	32
Total Sample	61	50	44	37	25

* For purposes of this table a respondent is considered apprehensive who reveals 2 or more out of a possible 6 "symptoms" of apprehension.

In three ways it was possible to get reassurance on this classification. For 45 colleges we had additional information from the College Entrance Examination Board. For these schools we knew the ratio of applicants to admissions, the scholastic test level of the admitted students, and the distances from which they came. In other words, we had information on the demand for the college, and the correlation with our quality rating based on objective characteristics was very high indeed.

Furthermore, we had corroboration from the data in our own survey. In the high quality colleges 66% of our respondents had a high productivity score, while in the low quality group, only 26% of highly productive scholars were in our sample of social scientists. Finally, we submitted our classification of colleges to a number of experts in the field, and their impressions agreed most closely with our statistical ranking. Thus pending a detailed discussion in our main report, the reader of this paper can accept our classification with confidence. He will then appreciate the importance of Table 8-31.

The table shows that the high quality colleges have almost three times as many clearly permissive social scientists as the colleges in the low quality class. The reason for this is rather obvious from our previous discussion. In the profession at large, the more productive men and women are more permissive; an administration therefore which wants a good faculty has little choice but to accept a considerable proportion of permissive faculty members, irrespective of its own ideology. Actually, as we show in another part of the main report, the trustees and administrators of the high quality colleges are themselves more permissive in terms of academic freedom granted to their faculties.

TABLE 8-31

Distribution of Professors' Permissiveness in Schools of Various Quality Ratings

	Quality Rating of School			
Attitude of Professor	*High*	*Medium High*	*Medium Low*	*Low*
Clearly permissive	58%	44%	27%	22%
Somewhat permissive	30	33	24	19
Conservative	12	23	49	59
	100	100	100	100

The social implications of the findings are very great. A chapter of our main report, following the one reported in this paper, shows that high quality colleges were much more frequently attacked during the difficult years. This result in turn derives from their having a more permissive faculty. But the fact remains that the brunt of the accusations and attacks were directed against the top-level colleges. The difficult years were thus a danger to American higher education as an institution and not only to the civil rights of the individual professor.

This is shown in those parts of our main study which describe in detail the incidents which occurred in the various colleges and the consequences. In our 165 schools we were able to trace approximately 1,000 episodes, ranging from congressional investigations to attacks by a local newspaper. We did not find a breakdown of morale, because there was considerable solidarity among teachers which strengthened the element of defiance in each individual's apprehension. But what the study found was a beginning corrosion of morale. One out of five professors had probably become more cagey in his research and in his writings. Many more had experienced a deterioration in his relations with students and colleagues. Most frequent and affecting more than half of our respondents, was a withdrawal from the larger community. Teachers refused to give speeches to local organizations and avoided writing in general magazines on controversial issues. Many refrained from participation in conventional party meetings. This had a two-fold disadvantage. The local community lost valuable talents; in turn, the professors lost the opportunity to test his thinking on the realistic stage of public life.

The description and analyses of these incidents fill about one-third of our main report. However important it might be to show the impact of the difficult years, it isn't the main service which a social research study like ours can render. In the long run what contributes most is the development of basic variables which can serve to analyze a variety of historical situations. The three outstanding ones in our effort were the index of apprehension, the index of college quality and the index of a teacher's permissiveness. The present paper concentrated on the last of the three, but it is hoped that it gives a general idea of the procedures employed, the results obtained, and the social implications derived.

IX

ADULTS IN THE SCHOOL AND COMMUNITY

*CONFLICT AND ROLE BEHAVIOR IN THE EDUCATIONAL SETTING**

By Jacob W. Getzels

Not only are there more demands and constraints upon the educator than upon most other occupational groups but there are more *contradictory* demands and constraints. Although the teacher is expected to be a good citizen, he is barred from many of the roles which are the marks of good citizenship. Outspoken participation in a political party, for example, to say nothing of a socially controversial (even though legal) movement is prohibited. Partisanship in local politics can be a cause for dismissal.[1]

Although the teacher is expected to be a mature person—indeed a model of maturity for his students—his personal behavior is often circumscribed by rules and regulations prescribed for him by others, who, incidentally, need not, in fact do not, themselves abide by the same rules. As one teacher reports, "I don't lead a natural life. I wouldn't dare smoke or drink. When I go to public meetings where the parents and guests smoke, I have to say no. If the parents can smoke, why can't I?"[2]

Even in school matters, presumably the sphere of his own particular competence, the educator is liable to cross-pressures in opposition to his own best judgment. For example, the School Executive Studies found that twenty per cent of the superintendents reported facing incompatible demands from their religious and educational affiliations.[3] The members of their church wanted them to act one way, other people in the community in another way. One Catholic superintendent—and he speaks

[1] W. B. Brookover, *A Sociology of Education* (New York: American Book Company, 1955), pp. 230-262.

[2] *Ibid.*, p. 245.

[3] N. Gross, "Some Contributions of Sociology to the Field of Education," *Harvard Educational Review*, 1959, *29*, pp. 275-287.

* Prepared especially for this volume while the author was at the Center for Advanced Study in the Behavioral Sciences, Stanford, California.

for other denominations as well—said he faced these situations constantly:

> Sometimes, the situation gets pretty touchy. I want to keep my good relations with the Church. Don't forget—most of my school committee members and the local politicians belong to my church. Take this example: one of the Catholic groups wanted to let the kids out early from school. They were having some special meetings, and they wanted the kids to be there. I knew that wouldn't be right. It wasn't fair to the other kids. So what did I do? I refused to give an official O.K. to the request, but at the same time I simply winked at it [letting them out early]. I would have offended them if I'd stopped the kids from going, and I just couldn't afford to do that. It really left me bothered.[4]

In all the instances cited (and more could have been given) what was at issue was one form or another of *conflict*—conflict between one position the educator occupied and another, conflict between the educator's needs and the expectations held for him by his "patrons," conflict among the values of the patrons themselves, and so on. These conflicts are a matter of vital concern not only to the educator who must somehow cope with them but also to the community which may be quite unaware of what it is doing and of the effect the conflicts are having upon the education of its children.

In short, the problem of conflict in the educational setting is a crucial issue for conceptual clarification, empirical investigation, and practical solution. What, for example, are the various types of conflict, for clearly not all conflicts are of the same kind? What are the sources of the different kinds of conflict? What is the relationship among them? What are the consequences of conflict? Can a framework be formulated to handle the various issues of the problem within a single set of terms and relationships? Although numerous separate studies have been done on various aspects of the problem, they are quite sundry in point of view and language, and the findings cannot readily be related to each other without at least an attempt to integrate the diverse phenomena into a single conceptual scheme.

Accordingly, the purpose of the present paper is two-fold: 1) To describe a model of social behavior —for conflict is of course a social phenomenon— that attempts to integrate within a single framework many of the phenomena bearing on the problem of conflict; and 2) To generate from the model a classification of the kinds and sources of conflict, and to cite a number of research studies to illustrate these types of conflict.

[4] *Ibid.*, p. 284.

THE GENERAL MODEL

The framework we are proposing has already been elaborated elsewhere,[5] and only those dimensions of immediate relevance to the issue of conflict will be sketched here. The framework presumes interpersonal or social behavior as functioning inevitably within the context of a social system. It conceives of the social system (whether a single classroom, a whole school, or a community) as involving two classes of phenomena, the publicly mandatory and the privately necessary, which are viewed in this paper as conceptually independent and phenomenally interactive. There are on the one hand institutions with certain roles and expectations that will fulfill the goals of the system. There are on the other hand individuals with certain personalities and need-dispositions inhabiting the system, whose interactions comprise what is called social behavior. This behavior can be understood as a function of two major analytic elements, 1) institution, role, and expectation, which together refer to the *nomothetic* or normative dimension of activity in a social system and, 2) individual, personality, and need-disposition, which together refer to the *idiographic* or personal dimension of activity in a social system. We represent these dimensions and variables pictorially in the diagrams on the following page. To comprehend the nature of social activity and conflict, we must understand the nature and relationship of these elements.

[5] The same general set of concepts and categories have been applied to other areas of the educational setting, and portions of this paper are drawn from: J. W. Getzels, "A Psycho-sociological Framework for the Study of Educational Administration," *Harvard Educational Review*, 1952, *22*, pp. 234-246; J. W. Getzels and E. G. Guba, "Social Behavior and the Administrative Process," *School Review*, 1957, *55*, 423-441; J. W. Getzels, "Administration as a Social Process," in A. W. Halpin (Ed.), *Administrative Theory in Education* (Chicago: Midwest Administration Center, University of Chicago, 1958), pp. 150-165; J. W. Getzels and H. A. Thelen, "The Classroom as a Unique Social System," in N. B. Henry (Ed.), *The Dynamics of Instructional Groups* (Chicago: University of Chicago Press, 1960), pp. 53-82. Our debt to the work of Talcott Parsons will be evident.

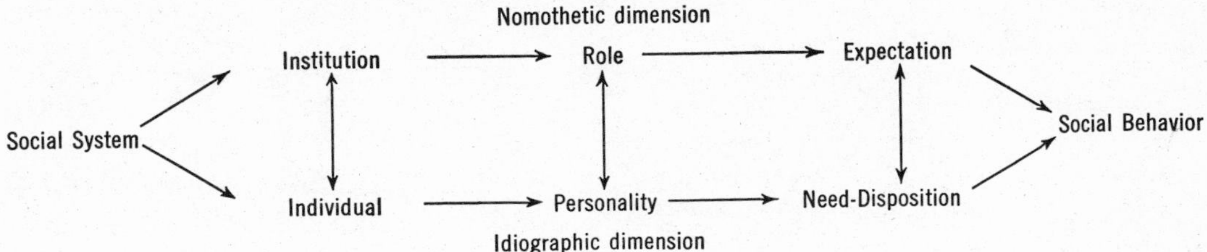

The term institution has received a variety of definitions. For our purposes it is sufficient to say only that all social systems have certain imperative functions that are to be carried out in certain routinized patterns. The agencies established to carry out these functions for the social system may be termed institutions. In this sense, we may think of education as an institution fulfilling certain requirements of the social system of which it is a part.

The most important analytic units of an institution are the roles, which, to use Linton's phrase, are the "dynamic aspects"[6] of positions and statuses, and may be defined by the expectations (the rights, privileges, and obligations) to which any incumbent of the role must adhere. A crucial characteristic of roles is that they are complementary. Each role derives its definition and meaning from other related roles. Thus, the role of teacher and the role of pupil cannot be understood or implemented except in relation to each other. In performing the role behavior expected of him, the teacher "teaches" the pupil; in performing the role behavior expected of him, the pupil "learns" from the teachers.

But roles are of course implemented by flesh and blood individuals, and no two individuals are alike. Each stamps a particular role with the unique style of his own personality. Social behavior is not only a function of public mandate but of private necessity, and of course public mandate and private necessity may not coincide. Not all teachers "teach," not all pupils "learn"—at least not in the same way. It is not enough to know only the nature of the roles and expectations within an institution—although, to be sure, institutional behavior cannot be understood apart from these—but we must know also the nature of the individuals inhabiting the roles, and how they perceive and react to the expectations. Just as we analyzed the institutional dimension into the component elements of role and expectation, so we may analyze the individual dimension into the component elements of personality and need-disposition.

The term personality like the term role has received a variety of definitions. For our purposes it is sufficient to conceive of it as the dynamic organization within the individual of those need-dispositions that govern his unique perceptions and reactions to the environment and to its expectations. The central analytic units of personality are the need-dispositions which we may define with Parsons and Shils as "individual tendencies to orient and act with respect to objects in certain manners and to expect certain consequences of these actions."[7] In order to understand the behavior of *specific* role-incumbents in *specific* institutions, we must know both the role-expectations and the need-dispositions involved.

Within this framework then, a given act is conceived as deriving from the interaction between the nomothetic and idiographic dimensions of our model. When the nomothetic axis is maximized—as in the case of rigid expectations for the military man—behavior still retains some personal aspects because no role is ever so closely defined as to eliminate all individual latitude. When the idiographic axis is maximized—as in the case of the less rigid expectations society has for the artist—social behavior still cannot be freed from some role prescription. Indeed, the individual who divorces himself entirely from such prescription is said to be autistic and his behavior a-social and paratactic.

[6] R. Linton, *The Study of Man* (New York: Appleton-Century-Crofts, Inc., 1936), p. 14.

[7] T. Parsons and E. A. Shils, *Toward a General Theory of Action* (Cambridge: Harvard University Press, 1951), p. 114.

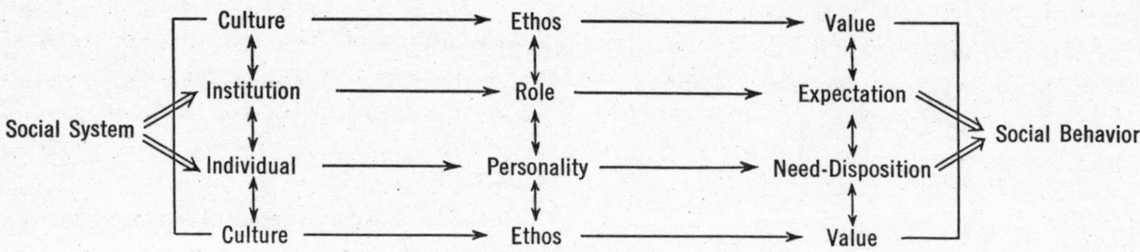

Like all theoretical formulations, the present framework is an abstraction from reality. Certain factors and relationships have been brought into the foreground, others relegated to the background.[8] By focusing on the sociological dimension with the central concept of role and the psychological dimension with the central concept of personality, we have omitted other dimensions and variables of social behavior. We should like to mention one other set of concepts, those deriving from the anthropological dimension.

Institutions and individuals are embedded in a culture with certain mores and values. The character of institutional roles and individual personalities is related to the particular ethos of culture, and the specific expectations and need-dispositions to its values. The educator, for example, cannot devote himself effectively to a classical education when that kind of education is no longer supported by the ethos. The pupil cannot ordinarily be expected nor will he want to learn for the sake of learning when learning is not a cultural value. In this sense, we must bear in mind that interacting with the sociological and psychological dimensions is the cultural dimension. By way of summary, we may present the dimensions and central concepts of the framework pictorially as in the diagram above.

In pointing to certain general fulcra of conflict in role behavior. this model, we believe, can help clarify and systematize the nature and sources of strain in the educational setting as a specific case.

FULCRA OF CONFLICT: SOME DERIVATIONS FROM THE MODEL

We shall identify for illustrative purposes five major types and sources of conflict, although these do not necessarily exhaust the list.

Conflicts between cultural values and institutional expectations. We may mention first an obvious and, in the educational setting, prominent type of conflict, the conflict between the expectations of the specific institution and the values of the general culture. Consider the following instance. It is expected by the school (or at least we assume it is expected or should be expected) that the child will work hard in order to achieve to the fullest extent of his intellectual potentiality and creativity. Accordingly, the child must be motivated to sacrifice immediate ease for ultimate attainment. Recent commentaries suggest, however, that our cultural values are coming to prize ease and sociability more than intellectual independence and achievement.[9] In this sense, the criteria of worth in the classroom and in society at large are incongruent, and to the extent of such incongruence, both teacher and pupil are subject to conflict.

Or consider the following data in relation to potential conflict for the so-called gifted or creative

[8] D. O. Hebb says, "To deal with behavior at present, one must oversimplify. The risk, on the one hand, is forgetting that one has oversimplified the problem; one may forget or even deny those inconvenient facts that one's theory does not subsume. On the other hand is the risk of accepting the weak-kneed discouragement of the vitalist, of being content to show that existing theories are imperfect without seeking to improve them. We can take for granted that any theory of behavior at present must be inadequate and incomplete. . . ." *The Organization of Behavior* (New York: John Wiley & Son, Inc., 1949), p. xiii.

[9] See, for example, D. Riesman, *et al.*, *The Lonely Crowd* (New Haven: Yale University Press, 1950); A. Wheelis, *The Quest for Identity* (New York: W. W. Norton & Co., 1958); W. H. Whyte, *The Organization Man* (New York: Simon and Schuster, Inc., 1956). The problem of conflict among the values of sub-cultures is of course important but will not be dealt with here.

child, and indeed for the gifted or creative teacher, if not for all pupils and all teachers. Spindler[10] analyzed the responses of some 328 graduate education students to such open-ended statements as "The individual is . . . ," "Intellectuals should . . . ," and to paragraphs they wrote describing their concepts of the "Ideal American Boy." From the open-ended sentences, results like this were obtained: "Artists are . . . ," "queer," "perverted," "nuts," "effeminate" (a negative-hostile category of 38%), "different," "people," "few," (a neutral category of 35%), "creative," "smart," "original," "interesting" (a positive category of 25%); "Intellectuals should . . . ," "be more sociable," "be more practical," "get down to earth" (a mildly derogative category of 36%), "keep it under cover," "drop dead," "shut up" (an openly hostile category of 20%), "apply their intellect," "study," "create," "think" (a neutral to positive category of 40%).

Spindler also asked the graduate students to describe the "Ideal American Boy." A content analysis of this technique revealed that the desirable features of character are ranked in the following order, from highest number of mentions to lowest number:

> He should be *sociable,* like people, and get along well with them; he must be *popular,* be liked by others; he is to be *well-rounded,* he can do many things quite well, but is not an expert in anything in particular; he should be athletic (but not a star), and healthy (no qualifications); he should be *ambitious* to succeed, and have clear goals, but these must be acceptable within limited norms; he must be *considerate of others,* ever-sensitive to their feelings about him and about events; he should be a *clean-cut Christian,* moral and respectful of God and parents; he sould be patriotic; and he should demonstrate *average academic ability* and *average intellectual capacity.*[11]

Leadership, independence, high intelligence, high academic ability, individuality, are mentioned relatively infrequently (in about 20% of the paragraphs). As Spindler points out, introspective behavior is devaluated (even intellectuals are held in suspicion by many). Deviancy is to be tolerated only within the narrow limits of sociability, of general outwardness, and of conformity ("Artists are perverts.").[12]

[10] G. D. Spindler, "Education in a Transforming American Culture," *Harvard Educational Review,* 1955, *25,* pp. 145-146.

[11] *Ibid.,* pp. 147-148.

[12] *Ibid.,* p. 148.

But it is exactly these culturally devalued characteristics—independence, high intelligence, high academic ability, creativity—that education is supposed to foster. In the strain between cultural values and institutional expectations is one type and source of role conflict in the educational setting.

Conflict between role-expectations and personality dispositions. Conflicts of this type occur as a function of discrepancies between patterns of expectations attaching to a given role and patterns of need-dispositions characteristic of the incumbents of the role. Typical of this kind of conflict are the army sergeant with high need for submission, the lighthouse keeper with high need for affiliation, the authoritarian teacher in a permissive school, the administrator with a high need for abasement, and so on. In all these cases there is a mutual interference between nomothetic expectations and idiographic dispositions, and the individual must choose whether he will fulfill individual needs or institutional requirements. If he chooses to fulfill requirements (it is not, of course, always a matter of conscious choice) he is in a sense short-changing himself, and is liable to unsatisfactory personal adjustment; he is frustrated and dissatisfied. If he chooses to fulfill his needs, he is shortchanging his role and is liable to unsatisfactory role performance; he is inefficient and ineffective.

Lipham[13] recently studied this problem in the educational setting. On the basis of the present model and preceding work in the area, he argued that the role of school administrator could be defined in terms of a number of crucial expectations. The administrator is expected, for example, to exert himself energetically, to strive for higher status, to relate himself successfully to other people, etc. He hypothesized that persons having a basic personality structure characterized by such needs and dispositions will suffer less strain in fulfilling the administrator role and will therefore be more effective than persons whose needs and dispositions are in conflict with the role expectations.

Accordingly, he assessed by interview and personality instruments (including the Adjective Check List and Sentence Completion techniques) the personality structure of two samples of 21 principals

[13] J. M. Lipham, *Personal Variables Related to Administrative Effectiveness,* Unpublished doctoral dissertation, University of Chicago, 1960.

each within a single school system, one sample having been rated highest in effectiveness by the superintendent and his staff, the other sample lowest. The results confirmed the hypothesis; the more effective principals tended to score significantly higher in activity drive, social ability, emotional control, mobility drive, and so on, than did the less effective principals. The less effective principals tended to score higher on such needs as abasement, which are in conflict with the expectations for the principal role.

Conflicts between roles and within roles. There is a range and variety of conflicts that occur when a role incumbent is required to conform simultaneously to a number of expectations which are mutually exclusive, contradictory, or inconsistent so that performance of one set of requirements makes performance of the other set of requirements impossible, or at least difficult. These role conflicts are evidence of dislocations in the nomothetic dimension of the social system and may arise in several ways.

DISAGREEMENT WITHIN THE REFERENCE GROUP DEFINING A GIVEN ROLE. There are numerous instances of this type of conflict in the school setting. The principal of the school may, for example, be expected by some teachers to visit them regularly to give constructive help, and by others to trust them as professional personnel not in need of such supervision. Or, the pupil may be expected by some teachers to emphasize the mechanics of writing, the substance being useful only for the practice of correct form. Other teachers might emphasize the content and substance, the form being merely a vehicle for the communication. Or, perhaps at a more fundamental level, the entire purpose of school and of education (and therefore of the various roles in the school) may be defined differently by different educators even within the same school system.

Prince,[14] for example, asked the question: Are there differences in the basic beliefs and values among educators of different age groups? To answer the question, he constructed a forced-choice questionnaire containing 64 pairs of items, one item in each pair representing a "traditional" value, and the other an "emergent" value, respondents being required to choose the more desirable alternative. Here are some sample pairs:

14A. Feel that "right and "wrong" are relative terms.
14B. Feel that I should have strong convictions about what is right or wrong.
30A. Feel that discipine in the modern school is not as strict as it should be.
30B. Feel that the change from strict discipline in the modern school is a good thing.
31A. Feel that the most important thing in school is to gain knowledge useful to me in the future.
31B. Feel that the most important thing in school is to learn to get along with people.
64A. Strive to be an expert in something.
64B. Do many things quite well but not be an expert in anything.

The instrument was administered to 98 teachers varying in age from the twenties to the sixties. It was found that the younger the teacher, the more frequent was the tendency to choose the emergent belief as desirable; the older the teacher, the more frequently he tended to choose the traditional belief as desirable. The same effect was found for principals. Prince compared the responses of ten principals under 47 years of age with the responses of ten principals over 47 years of age. There was a statistically significant difference (at the .01 level) in the responses of the two groups, the younger principals being consistently more emergent than the older principals.

DISAGREEMENT AMONG SEVERAL REFERENCE GROUPS, EACH DEFINING EXPECTATIONS FOR THE SAME ROLE. To illustrate with an example somewhat outside the immediate context of the public school, the university faculty member may be expected by his department head to emphasize teaching and service to students but by his academic dean to emphasize research and publication. Although these two sets of expectations for the same role are not necessarily opposed to each other, it is clear that the time given to implementing the one set can be seen as taking time from implementing the other set, and to this extent they conflict.

Or, consider the definition of the superintendent role as viewed by superintendents and their board members and of the school board member role as viewed by superintendents and school board members. Gross, Mason, and McEachern[15] studied the

[14] R. Prince, *A Study of the Relationships between Individual Values and Administrative Effectiveness in the School Situation,* Unpublished doctoral dissertation, University of Chicago, 1957.

[15] N. Gross, W. S. Mason, and A. W. McEachern, *Explorations in Role Analysis: Studies of the School Superintendent Role* (New York: John Wiley & Sons, Inc., 1958).

agreement and disagreement of these two groups of "role definers." The instrument used was a series of statements, e.g., "Read most of the professional journals," to which 105 superintendents and 508 school board members were required to choose one of the following responses: (A) Absolutely must; (B) Preferably should; (C) May or may not; (D) Preferably should not; (E) Absolutely must not. The investigators found that on 63 per cent of the items there were statistically significant differences (at least at the .05 level) between the distributions of responses given by the two groups.

Here, for example, are some sample results adapted from the more detailed and precise analysis of the original report. With respect to expectations for the superintendent role, the board members and superintendents differed on such expectations as: "Keep a watchful eye on the personal life of his subordinates" (66 per cent of the board members gave "Absolutely must" or "Preferably should" responses, 26 per cent of the superintendents gave such responses); "Defend his teachers from attack when they try to present the pros and cons of various controversial social and political issues" (70 per cent of the superintendents gave "Absolutely must" responses, 29 per cent of the board members gave such responses); "Help teachers to get higher salaries" (46 per cent of the superintendents gave "Absolutely must" responses, 8 per cent of the school board members gave such responses). With respect to expectations for the school board member role, the groups differed on such items as: "Appoint only teachers nominated by the superintendent" (50 per cent of the superintendents gave "Absolutely must" responses, 23 per cent of the school board members gave such responses); "Concern itself with administrative problems" (56 per cent of the board members gave "Absolutely must" or "Preferably should" responses, 27 per cent of the superintendents gave such responses); "Allow the superintendent to spend as much as a day a week away from his own school system engaging in professional activities not directly related to his job" (56 per cent of the superintendents gave "Absolutely must" or "Preferably should" responses, 24 per cent of the board members gave such responses).

Contradiction between the Expectations of Two or More Roles Which an Individual is Occupying at the Same Time. It is here that we have the problems arising from the fact that role incumbents in the educational institution are inevitably also role incumbents in other groups and institutions which may have opposing expectations. Conformity to one set of expectations may involve non-conformity to the other set of expectations.

Consider, for example, the adolescent attempting simultaneously to be an outstanding student and a popular member of the "gang." In a recent study Coleman[16] found that only 5.3 per cent of 3,830 high school students felt that their friends "would envy and look up to them" for being appointed an assistant in the biology laboratory because of their good work; 50 per cent felt that their friends "would kid them about it, but envy them." Coleman suggests:

> The ambivalent response illustrates the conflicting feelings of adolescents about scholastic success; privately wanting to succeed and be recognized themselves, but (in most adolescent groups) publicly making fun of the success of others, and disowning interest in scholastic success. Thus it is not only that scholastic success counts little in the adolescent culture; extra effort devoted to scholastic matters often counts negatively and is discouraged.[17]

He makes the following generalization:

> The result of these norms produces in students a conflict of motivation; put very simply, to be one of the fellows and not work too hard in school, or to work hard in school and ignore the group. Different teenagers resolve the conflict in different ways. Whichever way it is resolved, it sets an artificial dilemma. On the one hand are sociable average students (who could do better); on the other hand are a few academically-oriented, highly competitive isolates. A boy or girl can be oriented to academic achievement *or* to being popular, but it is hard to be both.[18]

Getzels and Guba[19] studied certain aspects of the teacher role. They posed the following questions: What are the expectations held for teachers as reported by the teachers themselves? How do these expectations accord with the expectations of other roles the teacher occupies? More specifically, in what

[16] J. S. Coleman, "Academic Achievement and the Structure of Competition," *Harvard Educational Review*, 1959, *29*, pp. 330-351. Also see pp. 87-94 of this volume.

[17] *Ibid.*, p. 340.

[18] *Ibid.*, p. 345.

[19] J. W. Getzels and E. G. Guba, "The Structure of Roles and Role Conflict in the Teaching Situation," *Journal of Educational Sociology*, 1955, *29*, pp. 30-40.

ways are the several sets of expectations inconsistent? How do these inconsistencies, i.e., role conflicts, vary from one teaching situation to another? What are the effects of such conflicts on the teacher?

Their initial attempt to answer these questions was based on extensive interviews with 41 teachers drawn from four school systems in two states. Three major areas of conflict were identified, each stemming from a central role a teacher occupied in addition to the teacher role.

(1) The socio-economic role. Teachers are usually assumed to be members of at least a quasi-professional group for whom middle class standards of living are expected. But in comparison with persons for whom similar standards are expected, the teacher receives a salary inadequate for implementing the expectations. Many of the strains felt by teachers arise not only because they are underpaid, but because they are expected to maintain standards of taste and living which are out of their financial reach.

(2) The citizen role. Most adults in a community are assumed to be responsible citizens whose judgment regarding their own conduct can be trusted. But the teacher is often not granted the same confidence. He may, for example, be required to participate with more vigor in church affairs than his neighbors, but with less vigor in political matters than his own beliefs dictate. Although the teacher resides in the community, his citizenship may be only second-class, since the expectations placed upon him in his role of teacher restrict the freedom of his role as citizen.

(3) The professional role. The teacher is expected to be a specially trained person with expertness in a particular field. Certification of this professional training and competence is required by the community, and persons without such professional certification would not be hired as teachers. In practice, however, the teacher's professional standing and prerogatives may be challenged by almost anyone who has succeeded only in becoming a parent or paying a tax bill. Not only may the school administrator encroach upon the teacher by prescribing more or less minutely what he may or may not do, but the community itself may dictate classroom content and procedures in direct opposition to the teacher's best professional judgment. Thus, conflict ensues. The teacher is expected to be a professional person with special competencies but, he is simultaneously expected to submit to others at crucial points in his own field of competence.

On the basis of the interview material, a group questionnaire was developed, and the responses of 166 teachers in six school systems analyzed. Among the results with respect to the distribution of role conflicts and the effects of role conflict on the teacher, the following findings may be noted.

(a) Some role conflicts seem to be *situationally independent*. They have equal impact in all teaching situations sampled, and appear to be independent of local conditions. For example, on a six point scale from "practically no teacher would agree" (scale score 0) to "very many teachers would agree" (scale score 6), the item, "Although the community expects a teacher to maintain the same standard of living as, say, a minor executive or a successful salesman, the salary typically paid a teacher is too small to make this possible," received a total mean scale score of 2.7 with a range of 2.0 for the low scoring school and 3.2 for the high scoring school.

(b) Some role conflicts seem to be *situationally variant*. They have some impact in all teaching situations but may be substantially aggravated or ameliorated by local conditions. For example, the item, "While the average person is usually free to experiment with places of amusement and entertainment, making his selection from among them in terms of his own choice, the teacher can go only to 'nice' places, *i.e.,* approved by the community at large," received a total mean score of 2.1 with a range of 1.4 for the low scoring school and 3.1 for the high scoring school.

(c) Some conflicts seem to be *situationally specific*. They are unrecognized in most teaching situations, but seem to have considerable impact in particular localities. For example, the item, "Even though dancing may be an accepted form of social recreation in the community, the teacher who dances is often thought of as somewhat immoral," received a negligible total mean score of 0.4, but it had a mean score of 2.6 in one school.

Regarding the effect of role conflict on the teacher, the data were analyzed as to what kinds of teachers were "more troubled" or "less troubled" by the conflicts. Among the groups who were "more troubled" (at least at the .05 level of significance) were:

Male teachers, as compared with female teachers; younger married teachers trying to set up appropriate standards of living, as compared with unmarried teachers or older teachers; teachers who come from communities they perceive as different from the community in which they teach, as compared with teachers from communities they perceive as similar to the one in which they teach; teachers who have fewer friends than they would like to have in the community in which they teach, as compared with a sufficient number of friends; teachers who feel that their relationship with the administration is not adequate and satisfying, as compared with those who feel that it is.

Conflicts deriving from personality disorder. If the preceding types of conflict derive from certain dislocations between cultural and institutional dimensions, between institutional and individual dimensions, and from within the institutional dimension itself, there is a type of conflict that occurs as a function of certain dislocations within the individual himself. The effect of such personal instability or maladjustment is to keep the individual at odds with the institution either because he cannot maintain a stable relationship to a given role or because he misperceives the expectations placed upon him. Existential objects and events have minimal representation in his private world, and there is little correspondence between his private world and the worlds of other role incumbents with whom he must interact. In a sense, no matter what the situation, the role is detached from its institutional setting and function and used by the individual to work out his personal needs and dispositions, however inappropriate these may be to the goals of the social system as a whole. It is exactly this type of conflict that selection procedures for potential role-incumbents attempt to circumvent when they screen out individuals characterized by one form or another of psychopathy.

Conflict in the perception of role expectations. Opposition among role incumbents as to their mutual rights and responsibilities is not solely a function of personality disorder, and the broader issue may be stated as follows: How is it that some teachers and some pupils, or some superintendents and some board members—or to generalize the case, some complementary role incumbents—seem to apprehend at once their reciprocal obligations and privileges, while others take a long time to reach such understanding, if they reach it at all?

The relevant concept we should like to apply here is "selective perception." We may conceive of any publicly prescribed role relationship as enacted simultaneously in two separate private situations. one embedded in the other. On the one hand is the prescribed relationship as perceived and organized by the one role incumbent in terms of his goals, experiences, and information. On the other hand is the same relationship as perceived and organized by the other role incumbent in terms of *his* goals, experiences and information. These private situations are related through those aspects of the existential objects, symbols, values and expectations that overlap in the perceptions of both individuals. When we say two complementary role incumbents understand each other, we mean that the area of this overlap in perception is maximal; when we say that the two complementary role incumbents misunderstand each other, we mean that the area of such overlap is minimal.

In a recent study of the perception of expectations for the superintendent role by superintendents and by various reference groups (teachers, parents, school board members, businessmen, etc.), three specific patterns of conflict relevant to the present general formulation were identified.[20] One tendency was for the superintendent to perceive the expectations of a reference group accurately but not to concur with their views. A second tendency was for the superintendent to believe there was no difference in his view of the expectations and the views of the reference group, when, in reality, significant differences did exist. A third tendency was for the superintendent to believe there was a difference in his view of the expectations and the views of the reference group, when, in reality, significant differences did not exist.

An item from the pilot study may serve as an illustration. The item was "I expect the superintendent to: Choose his friends from people who are important in social, civic, and business affairs." Three types of responses on a five point scale from "strongly agree" (scale score 1) to "strongly disagree" (scale score 5) were obtained. One response was the superintendent's expression of his own expectations; a second response was the superintendent's estimate of the expectations of the reference group; a third response was the actual expectation given by the reference group. Among the findings was that al-

[20] S. P. Hencley, *A Typology of Conflict between School Superintendents and Their Reference Groups,* Unpublished doctoral dissertation, University of Chicago, 1960.

though the superintendent scored 2.0 when he expressed his own expectations, and he estimated 3.0 for the school board reference group and 3.5 for the business reference group, the school board actually scored 3.5 (tendency one above) and the business group actually scored 2.4 (tendency three above).

Whatever the kind of conflict (and the specific effects of these different types of conflict need systematic examination), it seems clear from recent research that the proper functioning of certain role relationships in the educational setting depends on the degree of overlap in the perception of expectations by the several complementary role incumbents. Stated in extreme terms, the basic hypothesis underlying these investigations was that when the perception of expectations overlap, the participants in the relationship feel satisfied with the work achieved, no matter what the actual behavior or accomplishment; when the perception of the expectations does not overlap, the participants feel dissatisfied.

Ferneau[21] studied the interaction of consultants and administrators in a school setting. A problem-situation instrument was constructed in which varying expectations for the consultant role could be expressed. The instrument was given to 180 administrators who were known to have had the services of educational consultants and to 46 consultants who were known to have provided this service. Each administrator and each consultant was also asked to evaluate the outcome of the consultation. It was then possible to compare the expectations for the consultant role held by the consultant himself and by the consultee, and to analyze the effect of the congruence or discrepancy of these expectations on the evaluation of the actual interaction.

The results confirmed the hypothesis. When an administrator and a consultant agreed on the expectations, they tended to rate the actual consultation favorably; when they disagreed, unfavorably. And apparently the evaluation of success or failure was in measure independent either of the particular expectations or of the manifest behavior—provided that the participants' perception of the expectations, whatever their character, overlapped.

[21] E. Ferneau, *Role-Expectations in Consultations,* Unpublished doctoral dissertation, University of Chicago, 1954.

Moyer,[22] in a study along similar lines, investigated by a Q-sort technique the relationship between the expectations of teachers and of administrators for leadership in the educational setting and the effect of congruence or discrepancy in these perceptions upon teacher satisfaction. Again, the results were consistent with the hypothesis: the greater the agreement between teacher and principal on the expectations for leadership, the more favorable the attitudes toward the work situation.

SUMMARY AND CONCLUSION

Attention has often been called to the abundance of constraints and demands—and of *contradictory* constraints and demands—in the educational setting. The present paper attempted to systematize the relevant issues and phenomena within a single framework, and to illustrate a number of the pertinent role behaviors and types of conflict by reference to specific empirical studies. We should like to add several comments by way of conclusion. First, we should like to make clear that we have nowhere intended to imply that conflict is inevitably an evil. On the contrary, certain types of conflict, like certain types of necessity, give rise to productive transformations and inventions. And second, because of limitations of space, we have not been able to say anything about conflict resolution, although this is clearly a crucial issue. Certain modes of attenuating strain are implied in the theoretical framework and in the empirical studies, and further work in this area is indicated. Finally, we should like to point out that the present model of social behavior (and the classification of conflict and role behavior derived from it) is not the only possible formulation, or indeed that it is even in some ultimate sense the "right" one. We would suggest that it does seem useful at this time in clarifying various phenomena bearing on the subject, and we would hope that ensuing theoretical and empirical work would make the needed additions and revisions in the present effort.

[22] D. C. Moyer, *Teachers' Attitudes toward Leadership as They Relate to Teacher Satisfaction,* Unpublished doctoral dissertation, University of Chicago, 1954.

LEADERSHIP BEHAVIOR ASSOCIATED WITH THE ADMINISTRATIVE REPUTATION OF COLLEGE DEPARTMENTS*

By John K. Hemphill

INTRODUCTION

The effectiveness of administration within educational institutions is rarely assessed in a systematic or formal manner. Consequently, in research on problems of educational administration, the staff of the Ohio State Leadership Studies[1] has looked for methods for making reasonable estimates of the administrative effectiveness. This paper is concerned with characteristics of the "reputation for being well administered" as a criterion of the quality of administration in college departments.

Opinions of his peers, co-workers, or "buddies" about the quality of an individual's performance have been demonstrated to provide useful criterion data.[2] The question of whether analogous opinions can be found that will reflect the quality of educational administration is suggested immediately. Are departments of a college characterized by a reputation for their administrative excellence? If such reputations exist do they reflect valid differences in administrative practices? One part of a more comprehensive study of the departments within a single Liberal Arts college provides some evidence to support the proposition that the "reputation for being well administered" is useful criterion information.

PROCEDURE

The study. This report concerns only a portion of a larger study of the leadership and administration of 22 college departments in a moderately large midwestern university.[3] The larger study had as its general purpose, the testing of the applicability of research methods being developed by the Ohio State Leadership Studies to the university situation. These methods consisted of series of questionnaires and rating forms which had been used previously in military,[4] business,[5] and public school systems.[6]

Cooperation necessary for the study was first secured from the dean of the Liberal Arts college and the 22 department heads. Later all faculty members were informed of the nature and objectives of the study by means of (a) a letter of introduction signed by the dean, (b) personal meetings with each department's faculty, and (c) written instructions for completing a packet of questionnaires to be submitted anonymously. Although participation was voluntary, 234 of the 322 faculty members returned their questionnaires after two follow-up letters.

The questionnaires were distributed in four types of packets made up as follows:

Type A: (These questionnaires were distributed to the 22 department heads)

1. Background Information Questionnaire
2. Leader Behavior Description Questionnaire (self description directions)
3. Responsibility, Authority and Delegation scales[7]

[1] The Ohio State Leadership Studies, initiated in 1946 by Carroll L. Shartle, have been planned as a ten-year program of research on leadership and administration problems in military, business, industrial, educational, and civilian governmental organizations. The research reported here was supported by a grant received from the Rockefeller Foundation for the study of administration in education. Melvin Seeman and Andrew W. Halpin, as members of the staff of the Ohio State Leadership Studies, have conducted related studies of public school administration.

[2] R. J. Wherry and D. Fryer, "Buddy Ratings: Popularity Contest or Leadership Criteria?" *Sociometry*, 1949, *12*, pp. 179-190.

[3] Vernon Jon Bentz, Psychologist, Sears, Roebuck and Co., assisted in planning this study, and collected the data.

[4] A. W. Halpin, "The Leadership Behavior and Combat Performance of Airplane Commanders," *Journal of Abnormal and Social Psychology*, 1954, *49*, pp. 19-22.

[5] C. G. Browne, "A Study of Executive Leadership in Business: I. The R. A. and D. Scales," *Journal of Applied Psychology*, 1949, *33*, pp. 521-526.

[6] M. Seeman, "Role Conflict and Ambivalence in Leadership," *American Sociological Review*, 1953, *18*, pp. 373-380.

[7] R. M. Stogdill and C. L. Shartle, "Methods of Determining Patterns of Leadership Behavior in Relation to Organization Structure and Objectives," *Journal of Applied Psychology*, 1948, *32*, pp. 386-391.

* From *The Journal of Educational Psychology*, 1955, *46*, pp. 385-401. Used by permission of the author and publisher.

4. Reputational Ranking Form

Type B: (These questionnaires were distributed to a randomly selected third of the members of each department's faculty)

1. Background Information Questionnaire
2. Leader Behavior Description Questionnaire (*General* form with directions to describe the actual behavior of the faculty member's department chairman)
3. Group Dimensions Description Questionnaire
4. Reputational Ranking Form

Type C: (These questionnaires were distributed to a second randomly selected third of the members of each department)

1. Background Information Questionnaire
2. Leader Behavior Description Questionnaire (*General* form with directions to describe the behavior of an "ideal" leader of the faculty member's department)
3. Leader Behavior Description Questionnaire (*Specific* form, with directions to describe the actual behavior of the faculty member's department chairman)
4. Reputational Ranking Form

Type D: (These questionnaires were distributed to a third randomly selected third of the members of each department's faculty)

1. Background Information Questionnaire
2. Status Position Scales
3. Status Perception Scales[8]
4. Group Dimensions Questionnaire
5. Reputational Ranking Form

The four-way division of the work of completing the large battery of forms and questionnaires was necessary in order to reduce the formidability of the requests made of each faculty member.

Only the Background Information Questionnaire, the Group Dimensions, the Leader Behavior Description Questionnaire, (General Form) and the Reputational Ranking Form are of immediate interest in this paper. Each of these four questionnaires is described briefly in the following paragraphs.

BACKGROUND INFORMATION QUESTIONNAIRE. This form secured data concerning the respondent's department affiliation, age, sex, academic rank, degree held, length of time in his department, length of association as a member of an academic faculty, publications, affiliation with other professional organizations, and general job satisfaction.

THE LEADER BEHAVIOR DESCRIPTION QUESTIONNAIRE. This questionnaire is the product of the joint efforts of the staff of the Ohio State Leadership Studies. Its development is described by Halpin,[9] and Fleishman.[10] The form used in this study consisted of 150 items; however, only 30 of this number were actually scored. This decision was based upon an extensive factor analysis of all the items. Two scores are obtained: (a) Consideration and (b) Initiating Structure.

Consideration refers to leader behavior that is characterized by warm friendly relations with group members and concern with group member welfare. The following items are typical of this dimension:

He looks out for the personal welfare of individual members.

He treats all members as his equal.

He puts suggestions by the group into operation.

He gets group approval on important matters before going ahead.

Initiating Structure refers to leader activities that introduce organization, new ways of doing things, and new procedures for solving group problems, etc. The following are typical Initiating Structure items:

He lets members know what is expected of them.

He encourages the use of uniform procedures.

He asks that members follow organizational lines.

He tries out his new ideas in the group.

THE GROUP DIMENSION QUESTIONNAIRE. The development of this questionnaire is described in detail by Hemphill and Westie.[11] It yields scores on 13 dimensions or characteristics of groups:

1. *Autonomy* is the degree to which a group functions independently of other groups and occupies an independent position in society (13 items).
2. *Control* is the degree to which a group regulates the behavior of individuals while they are functioning as group members (12 items).
3. *Flexibility* is the degree to which a group's activities are marked by informal procedures rather than by adherence to established procedures (13 items).
4. *Hedonic Tone* is the degree to which group membership is accompanied by a general feeling of pleasantness or agreeableness (5 items).
5. *Homogeneity* is the degree to which members of a group are similar with respect to socially relevant characteristics (15 items).

[8] For a description of the use of Status Perception and Status Position scales see M. Seeman, "Some Status Correlates of Leadership," in A. G. Grace (Ed.), *Leadership in American Education* (Chicago: University of Chicago Press, 1950) and also footnote 6.

[9] A. W. Halpin, *op. cit.*

[10] E. A. Fleishman, "Leadership Climate, Human Relations Training and Supervisory Behavior," *Personnel Psychology,* 1953, *6,* pp. 205-222.

[11] J. K. Hemphill and C. M. Westie, "The Measurement of Group Dimensions," *Journal of Psychology,* 1950, *29,* pp. 325-342.

6. *Intimacy* is the degree to which members of a group are mutually acquainted with one another and are familiar with the more personal details of one another's lives (13 items).
7. *Participation* is the degree to which members of a group apply equal effort to group activities (10 items).
8. *Permeability* is the degree to which a group permits ready access to membership (13 items).
9. *Polarization* is the degree to which a group is oriented and works toward a single goal which is clear and specific to all members (12 items).
10. *Potency* is the degree to which a group has primary significance for its members (15 items).
11. *Stability* is the degree to which the group resists changes in its size and in turnover of its members (5 items).
12. *Stratification* is the degree to which a group orders its members into status hierarchies (12 items).
13. *Viscidity* is the degree to which members of the group function as a unit (15 items).

The respondents (faculty members) describe their departments by indicating how well the items assigned to each dimension characterize their respective departments as groups.

THE REPUTATIONAL RANKING FORM. This form is based on the methodology of the "nominating technique."[12] The form was prefaced with these directions:

It is desirable to ascertain an estimate of departmental reputation." *Not including your own department,* rank the five departments in the Liberal Arts College that have general reputations on the campus for being "Best Led" or "Best Administered" departments.

You are not asked to give your own personal evaluation, but asked to give the general reputation of the department, using as your point of reference what "most people in the College of Liberal Arts would agree" that a given department has as a given reputation. For example, you may personally think a certain department is poorly led but know that the reputation of that department on the campus is generally higher than your own personal opinion would rate it. In making the ranking use this general campus reputation.

Similar instructions also were given with a request for the five departments that were reputed to be "Least Well Led" or "Least Well Administered." With completion of the form the respondent had indicated his knowledge of the campus reputations of ten departments and by implication had placed the 12 remaining departments in a category not distinguished by reputations of being either well administered or poorly administered.

[12] J. G. Jenkins, "The Nominating Technique: Its Uses and Limitations," *American Journal of Psychology,* 1947, *2,* p. 43; C. L. Vaughn, "The Nominating Technique," in G. A. Kelly (Ed.), *New Methods in Applied Psychology* (College Park, Md.: University of Maryland Press, 1947).

ANALYSIS OF DATA

The analysis of data was planned in a manner to provide tentative answers to many questions that are raised when reputational information is suggested as a criterion of quality of administration. Among these questions are:

1. Is there any degree of consistency or agreement among the individuals who report knowledge of reputations of the different departments?
2. Are these reputational rankings made by individuals qualified to know existing campus opinions?
3. What characteristics of a department or of the behavior of its chairman are reflected in the department's campus reputation with respect to quality of administration?

Scoring of the reputational rankings. A relatively arbitrary scoring procedure was adopted for the purpose of summarizing the data secured by the reputational ranking forms. Each nomination received by a department was assigned the weight according to the following scheme:

Nomination	*Weight*
First Best Administered	5
Second Best Administered	4
Third Best Administered	3
Fourth Best Administered	2
Fifth Best Administered	1
First Less Well Administered	−5
Second Less Well Administered	−4
Third Less Well Administered	−3
Fourth Less Well Administered	−2
Fifth Less Well Administered	−1
Not nominated for either category	0

The score derived for each department was the sum of the weights assigned to the nominations that were received. Scores ranged from −271 to 305. The distribution of the scores for the 22 departments is given in the sixth column of Table 9-1.

TABLE 9-1

DEPARTMENTAL ADMINISTRATION "REPUTATION" SCORES DERIVED FROM TWO MATCHED SAMPLES OF RESPONDENTS AND FROM THE TOTAL NUMBER OF RESPONDENTS

Sample A (N = 33)		*Sample B (N = 33)*		*Total Sample (N = 133)*	
Dept.	*Scores*	*Dept.*	*Scores*	*Dept.*	*Scores*
A	9	A	2	A	16
B	−29	B	−30	B	−83
C	47	C	80	C	203
D	−46	D	−40	D	−112
E	49	E	73	E	223
F	−9	F	−18	F	−14
G	−53	G	−37	G	−138
H	16	H	9	H	31
I	45	I	19	I	100
J	−41	J	−54	J	−122
K	89	K	72	K	252
L	−8	L	−5	L	−24
M	0	M	0	M	4
N	101	N	68	N	305
O	−35	O	−26	O	−87
P	−74	P	−70	P	−271
Q	−1	Q	9	Q	13
R	−29	R	−12	R	−53
S	−27	S	−31	S	−80
T	19	T	−2	T	25
U	−17	U	−12	U	−56
V	3	V	1	V	3

RESULTS

The presentation of the results of the analysis of the data will be organized in respect to the three major questions that were asked about the characteristics of "reputation for being well administered" as a criterion of administrative effectiveness.

What is the degree of consistency or agreement among the reputations reported for the various departments? This question was answered by establishing two samples of respondents and determining the agreement between the two sets of reputation scores derived from the two samples. The two samples of respondents included only those who had made relatively complete nominations (8, 9 or 10, of the five best administered and the five less well administered) and was constituted so as to have an approximately equal number of respondents from the various departments in each sample. Table 9-1 shows the "reputation scores" of the department as derived from the two samples. The correlation between the two sets (Sample A vs. Sample B) of "reputations" scores is .94. If the Spearman–Brown prophecy formula is applied to this coefficient, we may estimate the reliability of these reputation scores as .97.

We, therefore, can have considerable confidence in the existence of a campus reputation with respect to the quality of departmental administration. Evidently, this reputation is known and can be reported with a high degree of agreement among members of the college faculty.

What are the characteristics of those faculty members who completed the Reputational Ranking Form? Not all of the faculty members who cooperated in the study by returning questionnaires completed the Reputational Ranking Form. Many faculty members indicated on the face of the form that they were unaware of campus opinion about the administrative reputation of departments. Others made only a portion of the ten nominations requested. It was possible to establish two groups of respondents on the basis of their responses to the Reputational Ranking Form. Group I consisted of 73 faculty members who provided at least eight of the ten nominations requested. Group II consisted of 101 faculty members who completed the other questionnaires in their packets but failed to make a single nomination on the Reputational Ranking

TABLE 9-2

AGE OF RESPONDENTS COMPOSING (*a*) A GROUP OF 73 WHO RETURNED THE REPUTATIONAL RANKING FORM COMPLETED AND (*b*) A GROUP OF 101 WHO RETURNED THE FORM BLANK

Age	*Returned Completed Forms (N = 73)*	*Returned Blank Forms (N = 101)*
Over 70	2	2
65-70	5	2
60-64	6	4
55-59	8	8
50-54	16	8
45-49	14	6
40-44	10	26
35-39	7	18
30-34	5	26
25-29	0	0
Under 25	0	1

Form. A comparison of data available on the characteristics of these two groups of respondents indicated that those faculty members who provided nominations differed from those who did not in that they were considerably older and, what is perhaps more important, had been members of the faculty for a longer time. (Tables 9-2 and 9-3).

TABLE 9-3

LENGTH OF TIME A MEMBER OF THE COLLEGE FACULTY OF RESPONDENTS COMPOSING (*a*) A GROUP OF 73 WHO RETURNED COMPLETED FORMS AND (*b*) A GROUP OF 101 WHO RETURNED BLANK FORMS

Length of Faculty Membership	*Returned Completed Forms (N = 73)*	*Returned Blank Forms (N = 101)*
Over 6 years	44	25
Four to 6 years	5	5
Two to 4 years	15	31
One to 2 years	7	21
Six months to 1 year	2	15
Less than 6 months	0	4

From Table 9-2 we note that 51% of the respondents who returned completed forms were over 50 years of age. This compares with 24% of the respondents who returned blank forms.[13]

Referring to Table 9-3, we see that 60% of the respondents who returned completed forms had been members of the faculty 6 years or more. This compares with 25% of the respondents who returned blank questionnaires.[14]

It is to be expected that campus reputations of college departments are known through long associations of faculty members. Individuals who are relatively "new" on the campus are likely to be unaware of events that were significant in establishing a department's reputation with respect to its administrative excellence. We interpret the tendency of more mature (older) and better qualified (a member of the faculty for a longer length of time) faculty members to complete this form to indicate a face validity of the information we obtained. We also must accept the fact that judging campus reputation of departments may be a meaningless and impossible task for a large portion of the younger faculty.

Is the reputation of departments for being well administered related to the style of the department chairman's leadership? The packets of questionnaires that were distributed to the members of each department included the Leader Behavior Description Questionnaire, General Form. One third of the members of each department completed this questionnaire to provide their descriptions of the leadership behavior of the chairman of their respective departments. A second third of the members of each department completed this same questionnaire but with instructions to indicate what an "ideal" chairman for their department should do. For 18 of the 22 departments descriptions were available of the "actual" and the "ideal" behavior of the chairmen from at least 2 and as many as 17 department members. For each of these 18 departments, an average Consideration score and an average Initiating Struc-

TABLE 9-4

AVERAGE SCORES ON CONSIDERATION AND INITIATING STRUCTURE OF DEPARTMENT CHAIRMEN AS DESCRIBED BY THE DEPARTMENT MEMBERS

Depart-ment	*Consideration*			*Initiating Structure*		
	Ideal	*Actual*	*Discrep-ancy*	*Ideal*	*Actual*	*Discrep-ancy*
A*	44.0	45.3	1.3	44.7	42.7	2.0
B	51.0	42.0	9.0	46.5	30.7	15.8
C*	49.3	48.1	1.2	45.5	43.5	2.0
D	43.0	24.3	18.7	34.3	33.0	1.3
E*	46.4	42.1	4.3	36.9	36.7	.2
F	45.5	38.3	7.2	44.8	44.5	.3
G*	53.0	35.0	18.0	50.0	26.5	13.5
I*	47.8	49.6	1.8	41.8	49.2	7.4
J	45.5	49.5	4.0	42.0	25.5	16.5
K*	47.3	41.1	6.2	38.4	38.9	.5
L	47.3	40.0	7.3	42.7	32.5	10.2
N*	49.0	44.8	4.2	39.6	37.8	1.8
O	49.3	43.7	5.6	47.0	44.3	2.7
Q*	48.0	47.0	1.0	36.3	39.0	2.7
R	50.3	38.3	12.0	40.8	34.0	6.8
S	50.0	34.0	16.0	40.5	25.0	15.5
T*	46.6	49.2	2.6	39.7	40.2	.5
U	51.0	43.2	7.8	38.8	35.8	3.0

* Above the median on "reputation."

[13] The difference between the means of the two groups (47.8 and 40.5) is significant at the .01 level ($t = 4.8$).

[14] The difference between the means of the two groups (4.30 and 2.72) is significant at the .01 level ($t = 4.7$. The first three categories of Table 9-3 were combined to make this test.

ture score were calculated. Table 9-4 presents the average scores for both "actual" and "ideal" leadership behavior and the "discrepancy" between these sets of scores.

Pearson product-moment correlation coefficients were computed to express the relationship between each of the two dimensions of actual leadership bebehavior and the "reputation" score of the departments. Correlations were also computed to express the relationship between the absolute discrepancy (either positive or negative) between "actual" and "ideal" leadership behavior on the two dimensions and the "reputation" score. These data are presented in Table 9-5.

By reference to Table 9-5 it can be seen that there is some relationship between the style of leadership of the department chairman as this is viewed by department members and the department reputation on the campus for being well or poorly administered. This is especially true if we view the departure of the actual behavior of the department from what is held by members of his department to be ideal behavior. Departments that achieve a reputation for good administration are those departments led by chairmen who attend to both of the facets of leadership measured in this study, i.e., they concern themselves with (1) organizing departmental activities and initiating new ways of solving departmental problems, and at the same time with (2) developing warm considerate relationship with members of the department.[15]

If we examine the leadership patterns of department chairmen closely we note a conjunctive relationship between Consideration and Initiating Structure suggesting that a minimal amount of both types of behavior are required for the acquisition of a good reputation and that an excess of one type of behavior does not compensate for the lack of the other. An excess of Consideration behavior cannot compensate for a deficiency in Initiating Structure and vice versa. If a cutting score of 41 on Consideration and 36 on Initiating Structure are applied simultaneously, the reputation of the department in terms of being above or below the median are successfully identified in 16 out of 18 cases. (These cutting scores were selected by inspection of the data and may have no specific significance.) The data for this comparison are given in Table 9-6.

The chi square value of the data of Table 9-6 is 8.00, significant beyond the .01 level of probability.

A further means of examining the conjunctive relation between these two facets of leadership behavior is available for the discrepancy score. The total of the two discrepancy scores of department chairmen correlates —.63 (.01 level of probability)

[15] This finding is congruent with the results of a similar study conducted within the Air Force and reported by A. W. Halpin, *op. cit.*

TABLE 9-5

CORRELATION COEFFICIENTS EXPRESSING THE RELATIONSHIP BETWEEN THE ADMINISTRATIVE "REPUTATION" SCORES OF 18 COLLEGE DEPARTMENTS AND FOUR LEADERSHIP SCORES OF THE DEPARTMENT CHAIRMEN AS DESCRIBED BY DEPARTMENT MEMBERS

Score	*Mean*	*S.D.*	*Correlation with Reputation Score*
Reputation	21.7	133.8	—
"Actual" Consideration	42.2	6.4	.36
Discrepancy between "Actual" and "Ideal" Consideration	6.9	5.6	—.52*
"Actual" Initiating Structure	36.8	6.7	.48*
Discrepancy between "Actual" and "Ideal" Initiating Structure	6.3	6.9	—.55*

* A correlation coefficient of .47 is significant at the .05 level.

TABLE 9-6

THE RELATIONSHIP BETWEEN THE REPUTATION ACHIEVED BY COLLEGE DEPABTMENTS AND THE CONSIDERATION AND INITIATING STRUCTURE SCORES OF DEPARTMENT CHAIRMEN TAKEN CONJUNCTIVELY (N = 18)

Chairman's Leadership	*Above Median Reputation*	*Below Median Reputation*
	Departments	
Score of 41 or larger on Consideration *and* a score of 36 or more on Initiating Structure	A, C, E, I, K, N, Q, T	O
Score of less than 41 on Consideration *or* a score of less than 36 on Initiating Structure	F	B, D, G, J, L, R, S, U

with the reputation scores. These last two reported results suggest strongly that if department chairmen meet the expectations of their facilities with respect to *both* Consideration and Initiating Structure the department is more likely to achieve a favorable reputation on the campus.

In the remainder of the presentation of results we shall examine characteristics of the departments for relationship with their administrative reputation.

Are the characteristics of their department as seen by department members related to the reputation of their department? The Group Dimensions Questionnaire was distributed to two thirds of each department's members. The questionnaire provides a score on each of 13 group characteristics (see pages 320-321). This score was calculated as the average of the descriptions supplied by those department members who completed this questionnaire. Average scores based on a minimum of two members' descriptions were available for 18 of the 22 departments. Pearson correlation coefficients were computed for each of the 13 dimensions and the reputation score. The correlations are presented in Table 9-7.

None of the correlations reported in Table 9-7 is statistically significant. There appears to be no relationship between the manner in which department members characterized their respective departments by use of the Group Description Questionnaire and the "reputation" of the departments for being well administered. This lack of relationship highlights the significance of the earlier reported relationship between the behavior of the department chairman and administrative reputation. It points to chairman behavior specifically, rather than general impressions about the department as the more likely determiner of reputation.

TABLE 9-7

CORRELATION BETWEEN EACH OF THIRTEEN GROUP DIMENSIONS (AVERAGE SCORES) AND DEPARTMENT'S "REPUTATION" FOR BEING WELL ADMINISTERED (N = 18)

Correlation: Reputation vs.	*Mean*	*S.D.*	*r**
Autonomy	34.4	4.0	.09
Control	28.7	3.4	—.07
Flexibility	37.6	5.8	.02
Hedonic Tone	18.8	2.1	.16
Homogeneity	33.1	3.7	—.05
Intimacy	48.4	4.4	—.02
Participation	46.4	4.5	.29
Permeability	22.5	4.3	—.04
Polarization	38.4	5.6	.05
Potency	51.1	4.6	.05
Stability	15.1	2.8	—.06
Stratification	40.7	5.1	.05
Viscidity	35.5	8.1	.04

* An r of .47 is required for significance at the .05 level.

Are there relationships between "demographic" characteristics of departments and their reputation? Examination was made of each of the following "demographic" characteristics of the 22 departments and their reputation scores:

1. Age of faculty members (Average)
2. Size of the department (Number of members)
3. Length of service to the department of its faculty members (Average number of years)
4. Length of academic experience of each department faculty (Average number of years)
5. Academic rank of members (Per cent Associate Professors or Professors)
6. Educational attainment of faculty of the departments (Per cent with Ph.D)
7. Publications record of department members (Index based on number and "quality" of publications)

Only one of these seven "demographic" variables showed a relationship with reputation. It was found that large departments tended to receive higher reputation scores (r between number of members and reputation = .58, significant at the .05 level). Two hypotheses were advanced in an effort to account for this relation. *First,* it was suggested that larger departments might require more Initiating Structure behavior on the part of their chairmen and since Initiating Structure had been shown to be related to "reputation" the relationship with department size could be a function of the same underlying variables.[16] The *second* explanation involved the suggestion that the significance of administration in larger as compared with smaller departments is well recognized by those responsible for the selection of department heads and that in the case of larger departments more care had been exercised. In other words, in very small departments, chairmen might be appointed on the basis of seniority without much regard for other qualifications, but in large departments demonstration of

[16] In previous research a relation between size of group and leader centered direction had been observed. In J. K. Hemphill, *op. cit.*

ability to assume administrative responsibility would be involved in a much larger measure in the selection of a chairman.

The first of the two hypotheses could be checked in part by determining the relation between the size of the department and the Initiating Structure behavior of their chairman. This correlation was computed and found to be .11, which is not significant. The available evidence rejects the first interpretation.

SUMMARY AND DISCUSSION

The campus reputations of 22 departments for being well administrated were secured from members of the faculty of a Liberal Arts college by use of a nominating form. As parts of the same research study data were also available concerning (a) the leadership behavior of department chairmen as viewed and as wanted by department members, (b) group characteristics of departments as viewed by department members, and (c) demographic characteristics of the departments. An examination was made of the relationship among these data in an effort to assess the usefulness of campus opinion as a criterion of quality of administration. The following conclusions resulted from the analysis:

1. Administrative reputation of the college department was reliably reported by faculty members. Agreement between two independent samples of respondents was very high ($r = .94$).

2. Older and more mature faculty members provided a larger proportion of the reputation information than "younger" or "new" members of the faculty. In fact, it appears many new members of the college faculty were not aware of the departments' reputations.

3. Reputation for being well administered is related to the leadership behavior of department chairmen as this behavior is described by department members. Those departments with best reputations for good administration have chairman who are described as above the average on *both* Consideration and Initiating Structure and who more nearly meet the behavior expected of an ideal chairman. It appears that optimal amounts of both of these types of behavior are required in order that a department earn a reputation for good administration.

4. With the exception of size, all group characteristics of the departments, both demographic characteristics, and those described by means of the Group Description Questionnaire are unrelated to reputation for good administration.

5. Larger departments tend to have better administrative reputations than smaller departments. This fact is independent of the Initiating Structure activity of the chairman and may indicate only that more care is exercised in selecting chairmen of large departments.

In conclusion, it appears that reputation may provide a criterion of excellence of administration. Many questions remain to be investigated concerning the limits within which such reputation may be useful. Certainly, qualified respondents must be found who have had the opportunity to become acquainted with events and opinions bearing on quality of administration. However, in many organizations a pool of qualified respondents may be available in the senior members of the groups. Our study involved only one college faculty. We know nothing about how differences between organizations may affect the availability and quality of opinion regarding administrative reputation. However, in view of the dearth of techniques available for assessing quality of administrative performance and importance of the problem, the suggestion of the usefulness of the reputation criterion reported here should be followed up.

*POLITICAL ALIENATION AS A FORCE IN POLITICAL ACTION**

By Wayne E. Thompson and John E. Horton

The outlines of community power structure and its close relationship to socio-economic status have become increasingly established in research.[1] Emerging from such research is a picture of power concentrated in the hands of a minority in key organizational roles—typically in business and industry—with the larger portion of the community playing a relatively small, essentially acquiescent part in community affairs. On a broader scale, social class, variously indexed, frequently has been used as an independent variable in studies of political participation, and such studies show a convergent trend.[2] In general, although a cleavage of interests and the development of active interest groupings is clear, a frequent response pattern found among the lower socio-economic strata is withdrawal from political activity. In other words, there typically is a relatively high incidence of nonvoting and expression of disinterest among the lower socio-economic status categories. Some writers have suggested that such apathy or indifference is in part a result of feeling politically inefficacious,[3] and this view is tentatively supported by findings such as those of the Michigan researches which show that a sense of political inefficacy is itself inversely related to socio-economic status.[4]

Yet apathy or indifference may not be the only correlate of political inefficacy. Haer finds that lower class position is associated with low intensity of feeling regarding sources of community power; but he also finds a higher incidence of unfavorable attitudes toward sources of community power within the lower SES category.[5] As Agger and Ostrom put it:

> The Non-Participants appear to be the most irrelevant of any category [in a typology of participation]. Yet their apparent apathy may be exaggerated or misinterpreted . . . although the analogy may not be particularly useful in terms of probable developments in the community, the apathetic, habitual non-voters in Germany came to life with a bang when Hitler opened up meaningful channels of political activity and convinced the apathetics that their lot could be dramatically improved by "politics." [6]

The suggestion is that political inefficacy may result in *political alienation* which involves not only apathy or indifference as a response to awareness of powerlessness, but also diffuse displeasure at being powerless and mistrust of those who do wield power. Given the opportunity for expression, political alienation would be expected to be translated into either an undirected vote of resentment or an organized vote of opposition.

For the most part, national elections do not provide such an opportunity, and it may well be that this explains the empirical findings which tie feelings of political inefficacy to apathy. Given the two

---

[1] Cf., among others, F. Hunter, *Community Power Structure* (Chapel Hill: The University of North Carolina Press, 1954); R. J. Pellegrin and C. H. Coates, "Absentee-Owned Corporations and Community Power Structure," *American Journal of Sociology*, 1956, *61*, pp. 413-419; D. W. Olmstead, "Organizational Leadership and Social Structure in a Small City," *American Sociological Review*, 1954, *19*, pp. 273-281; G. Belknap and R. Smuckler, "Political Power Relations in a Mid-West City," *Public Opinion Quarterly*, 1956, *31*, pp. 73-81; and R. E. Agger and V. Ostrom, "Political Participation in a Small Community," in Eulau, Eldersveld, and Janowitz (Eds.), *Political Behavior: A Reader in Theory and Research* (Glencoe, Ill.: The Free Press, 1956), pp. 138-149.

[2] Cf. B. R. Berelson, P. F. Lazarsfeld, and W. N. McPhee, *Voting* (Chicago: University of Chicago Press, 1954); P. F. Lazarsfeld, B. R. Berelson, and H. Gaudet, *The People's Choice* (New York: Columbia University Press, 1948); A. Campbell, G. Gurin, and W. E. Miller, *The Voter Decides* (Evanston, Ill.: Harper & Row, Publishers, 1954); R. Centers, *The Psychology of Social Classes* (Princeton, N. J.: Princeton University Press, 1949).

[3] D. Riesman, *The Lonely Crowd* (New Haven, Conn.: Yale University Press, 1950), pp. 187-190; and M. Rosenberg, "Some Determinants of Political Apathy," *Public Opinion Quarterly*, 1954, *18*, pp. 349-366.

[4] Campbell *et al.*, *op. cit.*, pp. 191 ff.

[5] J. Haer, "Social Stratification in Relation to Attitudes toward Sources of Power," *Social Forces*, 1956, *35*, pp. 137-142.

[6] Agger and Ostrom, *op. cit.*, p. 146.

* From *Social Forces*, 1960, *38*, pp. 190-195. Used by permission of the authors and publisher. An earlier version of this paper was presented at the annual meetings of The American Sociological Society, Seattle, August 1958.

party system, the compromising nature of national politics, and the limited chance to vote on specific issues, the "politically alienated" would be predicted in national elections more likely to be found among the nonvoters. But in local referenda it is possible for voters more clearly to perceive their action as participation in the decision-making process. Thus, on local referenda the politically alienated are provided the opportunity to express their alienation. It is widely recognized that such issues attract an exceptionally high number of voters predisposed to a negative vote; and very often the rallying cry of these voters is not so much concerned with the issue at hand as with preventing an ill-defined "them" from putting "this" over on "us."

As we see it, political alienation is a peculiarly sociological concept. Although probably related to the "quasi-paranoia" of misanthropy, it is not a personality variable in the usual sense. Neither is it directly an expression of cultural values or interests *per se,* although obviously it implies acceptance of the cultural prescription that every man shall have a voice in civic affairs. Rather, political alienation is most accurately understood as an emergent response to social structure in action, a reaction to perceived relative inability to influence or to control one's social destiny.

Conceptualized in this way, political alienation clearly would be expected to be associated with objectively-determined relative powerlessness in the community; and given the interrelationship between class, status, and power structures in American society, it follows that political alienation would be expected to be associated with lower socio-economic status however indexed. *In fact, it may be that political alienation is a mediating factor between SES and political participation which provides an alternative to "subcultural orientation" or self-interest explanations of political behavior of the lower SES categories.*

EMPIRICAL EVIDENCE REGARDING POLITICAL ALIENATION AND ITS EFFECTS

In March 1957, a school bond referendum provided the authors with the opportunity to do preliminary research on voting behavior in local referenda.[7] Unlike most research which has considered the effect of political inefficacy upon the *extent* of political participation, the research reported here focused upon the relationship between political alienation and *content or direction of attitude and vote.*

The index of political alienation is a score which combines the following item and measure:

1) *an item* on which the respondent indicates his perception of his role in the power structure of the community, viz., "People have different ideas of just how they fit into community affairs. Would you say that you are:

a person who contributes to community decisions
a person who is active, but not one of the decision-makers

just an ordinary person in the community
not really a part of the community at all"

(The first two answer categories define what we call the "actives" within the community structure; the last two define what we call the "passives.")

2) *a measure* of the belief that the exercise of political power is separated from the activities of the "ordinary citizen." This measure was devised through the use of the Guttman scaling technique and consists of the following items:

Agree-Disagree: It doesn't matter which party wins elections, the interests of the little man don't count.

Some people say you can usually trust local officials because they are your neighbors and friends, others say that elected officials become tools of special interests no matter who they are. What do you think?

Agree-Disagree: Local officials soon lose touch with the people who elected them.

Agree-Disagree: If people knew what was really going on in high places, it would blow the lid off things.

[7] The data presented here were gathered just after an upstate New York community had voted upon, and defeated, the school bond proposal. The interviews were conducted by the students in the senior author's course in political sociology as a class project. Although a successful attempt was made to obtain at least five interviews from each of several tracts of the community based roughly upon socio-economic differentials, no further systematic attempt was made to obtain a random sampling of the community and the respondents cannot be so considered. In all, 227 interviews were completed, of which 207 could be used in the analyses. The data should be considered suggestive, not definitive, of the effects of political alienation.

The extreme instance of political alienation so indexed is the person who is passive in community affairs and expresses a negative view on each of the above four items;[8] and the extreme instance of nonalienation is the person who is active in the community and expresses a positive view on each.

Objective position in the social structure of the community is indexed by interviewer ratings of socio-economic status, occupation of the head of the household, educational attainment of the interviewee, and the interviewee's age. Attitude on the bond issue was determined by asking the respondents to indicate whether they were very favorable, favorable, neutral, unfavorable or very unfavorable; vote, of course, is either "yes," "no," or "did not vote."

POLITICAL ALIENATION AS A FUNCTION OF SOCIAL POSITION

The data consistently show that the alienated are largely recruited from people of lower socio-economic status, whether indexed by interview ratings, occupation, or educational attainment. Thus the data suggest support for the proposition that people who hold lower objective positions in the social structure of the community are the more likely to be politically alienated. Over all, the picture is one of the way in which those who more probably lack control of economic power feel estranged from civic power. Obviously, this reflects an accurate perception of the facts of life as they are lived in contemporary American communities: for the most part, economic power does mean social power and civic power as well. But although economic power is perhaps the most important aspect of community structure, the fact that it is only one of many aspects should be emphasized. There are affluent citizens who nevertheless fall among the politically alienated. Moreover, although statistically scanty, some evidence that factors other than economic are important is suggested by the fact that every farmer in the study population is among the alienated. Hypothetically, this reflects concentration of power among the townspeople although it is exercised over surrounding areas as well.

Perhaps a more convincing illustration, those who are young—roughly 21 to 30 years of age—are as likely as those who are old to be politically alienated, with the least alienation occurring among the "mature adults."[9] This suggests further that

TABLE 9-8

POLITICAL ALIENATION AS RELATED TO POSITION IN THE COMMUNITY SOCIAL STRUCTURE

	*Political Alienation**		
	Percentage "Alienated"		*Percentage "Not Alienated"*
Interviewer Ratings of Socio-Economic Status:		*Per cent*	*Per cent*
Upper SES Categories	(50)	38	62
Middle SES Category	(81)	49	51
Lower SES Category	(76)	63	37
Occupation of Head of Household:			
Managers and Officials	(29)	33	67
Professionals	(55)	38	62
White Collar Workers	(47)	47	53
Laborers	(69)	68	32
Farmers	(7)	100	—
Educational Attainment of Interviewee:			
College Graduate	(86)	35	65
Some College Training	(52)	58	42
High School	(51)	62	38
Less than High School	(18)	83	17
Age of Interviewee:			
"Young"	(31)	66	34
"Mature"	(58)	38	62
"Middle-aged"	(72)	53	47
"Elderly"	(29)	57	43
"Old"	(17)	65	35

* The political alienation score is dichotomized, combining the most alienated and the least alienated categories. Numbers within parentheses are the percentage base in each case.

[8] Negative (alienated) responses are:

"It doesn't matter which party wins the elections, the interests of the little man don't count."

"Elected officials become tools of special interests, no matter what."

"Local officials lose touch with the people who elected them."

"If people knew what was really going on in high places, it would blow the lid off things."

Coefficient of Reproducibility of the measure = .94; Error Ratio = .57.

[9] Cf. Agger and Ostrom, *op. cit.*, p. 139, Table III.

political alienation is associated generally with lack of institutionalized power, in this instance whether among those who, on the whole, have not yet "arrived" or those who are largely "has beens."

POLITICAL ALIENATION AS A FACTOR IN POLITICAL ACTION

But the significance of political alienation lies in the area of the dynamics of community development: that is to say, political alienation would be one thing if the alienated accept their lack of institutionalized civic power and express their feeling of alienation in political disinterest and nonparticipation; it would be quite another thing if, imbued with norms which hold that all citizens have and should exercise civic rights and responsibilities, the alienated systematically express their alienation in political action, presumably as a negative attitude and a protest vote. The latter is what is hypothesized; and the data suggest that this is in fact the case. The politically alienated do not show appreciably less interest in the issue; and while they are less likely to have voted, fully three-quarters did manage to do so (Table 9-9). Beyond this, the alienated clearly tend to hold an unfavorable or a very unfavorable attitude toward the issue in question (Table 9-10); and this unfavorable attitude is translated into a negative vote by the alienated voter who goes to the polls.

However, it is possible that the relationship shown is spurious, for the indices of position in the community social structure—which are highly related to alienation—also are indices of special interests, particularly of economic interests. People in lower economic categories do tend to "vote their pocketbooks" as do the older people who depend upon a fixed income and the younger people who are just getting started financially. Moreover, quite apart from the fact that educational level in itself indexes financial wherewithal, one would expect that the more highly educated would generally place a higher value on improved educational facilities. Consequently, it may be that a negative attitude and vote directly expresses self-interest or cultural orientation even as alienation expresses relative powerlessness, with the same indices being used to measure each. It is important, therefore, to examine the relationship between alienation and attitude on the issue while holding constant the indices of position and interest.

TABLE 9-9

APATHY AS RELATED TO POLITICAL ALIENATION

	Political Alienation	
	"Alienated" (106)	*"Not Alienated" (101)*
	Per Cent	*Per Cent*
Interest in the Issue:		
Percentages Showing Much Interest: (Read own and opposition literature)	24	25
Percentages Showing Some Interest: (Read own literature only)	45	48
Percentages Showing Little Interest: (Did not read literature regarding the school bond issue)	31	26
Voting Behavior:		
Percentage Who Voted	74	84
Percentage Who Did Not Vote	26	16

TABLE 9-10

ATTITUDE TOWARD THE SCHOOL BOND ISSUE AS RELATED TO POLITICAL ALIENATION

	"Alienated"	*"Not Alienated"*
	Per Cent	*Per Cent*
Very Unfavorable or Unfavorable Attitude	60	33
Favorable or Very Favorable Attitude	40	67
	100	100

For the most part, it would seem that the variables so indexed are important in their own right; but more to the point here, *the relationship between political alienation and attitude persists independently of the indices of social position* (Table 9-11). In

TABLE 9-11

ATTITUDE TOWARD THE SCHOOL BOND ISSUE AS RELATED TO POLITICAL ALIENATION, HOLDING CONSTANT POSITION IN THE COMMUNITY SOCIAL STRUCTURE

	Percentages Who Were Unfavorable or Very Unfavorable Toward the Issue	
	Among the "Non-alienated"	*Among the "Alienated"*
	Per Cent	*Per Cent*
Interviewer Ratings of Socio-Economic Status:		
Upper SES Categories	19 (31)	63 (19)
Middle SES Categories	36 (42)	49 (39)
Lower SES Categories	46 (28)	69 (48)
Occupation of Head of Household:		
Managers and Officials	32 (19)	80 (10)
Professionals	15 (34)	43 (21)
White Collar Workers	40 (25)	41 (22)
Farmers and Laborers	55 (22)	72 (54)
Educational Attainment of Interviewee:		
College Graduates	25 (57)	41 (29)
Less than College	43 (44)	68 (77)
Age of Interviewee:		
"Young"	30 (10)	43 (21)
"Mature"	24 (37)	43 (21)
"Middle-aged"	35 (35)	67 (37)
"Elderly" and "Old"	47 (17)	78 (17)

every instance, the alienated are more likely than the "non-alienated" to hold an unfavorable attitude on the issue at hand. To be sure, certain of the differences are small, e.g., the middle SES category as compared with the upper and lower categories, the white collar workers as compared with other occupational groupings, and the younger people as compared with those who are older.[10] In general, however, the evidence for political alienation as a significant factor still stands.

POLITICAL ALIENATION AND SELF-RATING OF CLASS POSITION

Just as the effect of political alienation is independent of interest as indexed by objective social position, so it appears to be independent of social class interest indexed by self-ratings of class position (Table 9-12). Here, as before, the two factors are themselves interrelated, but in their relationship to attitude on the school bond issue each is important in its own right.

TABLE 9-12

ATTITUDE TOWARD THE SCHOOL BOND ISSUE AS RELATED TO POLITICAL ALIENATION, HOLDING CONSTANT SELF-PERCEIVED SOCIAL CLASS POSITION

	Percentages Who Were Unfavorable or Very Unfavorable Toward the Issue	
	"Upper Class, Middle Class"	*"Working Class, Lower Class"*
	Per Cent	*Per Cent*
"Non-alienated"	28 (79)	52 (21)
"Alienated"	57 (62)	66 (44)

In part, the significance of this relationship lies in the separation of self-perceived power position in the community from self-perceived social class position in a more general sense. One could argue that this may be an empirical illustration of dimensions of social stratification, subjectively perceived. But the central significance of the point in the present context again is the fact that the influence of political alienation seems to persist.

[10] The hypothesized influence of self-interest provides a systematic basis for interpreting these variations in the influence of political alienation: (1) the middle SES category and the white collar workers are the more probably upwardly mobile whose aspirations and expectations for their children largely negate the influence of political alienation, particularly when the issue has to do with educational facilities; (2) the interest in education among college graduates is manifested in such manner that political alienation is less significant among them than among the less well-educated; (3) the relatively small effect of political alienation among the "young" and the "mature adults" reflects the greater probability of having or expecting to have children of school age. For the younger citizens, a vote for improved school facilities quite literally is a vote for the future; (4) the relatively small effect of political alienation among the low SES categories, and in particular among laborers, is the result of economic interest and educational disinterest of people in this subcultural stratum.

ALIENATION AND "FAITH IN PEOPLE"

To this point we have built our case upon the proposition that a differential distribution of power in the community is reflected in an attitude of political alienation which, in turn, is translated into a vote of protest against the "powers that be." As far as community issues are concerned, the effect is a kind of desultory conservatism which nevertheless has impact upon the course of development of the community, in the form of a brake if nothing else. But negativism of this sort immediately suggests that a less clearly sociological interpretation might also be in order, namely, that personality factors here find expression in socially significant action.

To provide data to test the proposition that political alienation has an effect on political attitudes independently of more central personality variables, items were included from the "Faith in People Scale," first developed by Rosenberg and since used by several researchers at Cornell and elsewhere.[11]

There is no question that political alienation and "faith in people" are interrelated: among those of the highest faith in people scores only two-fifths were alienated, while among those of the lowest faith in people score, fully three-quarters were alienated. In other words, alienation which is specific to the arena of community politics would appear to reflect a kind of generalized alienation from mankind. But in their effect upon attitude toward the school bond issue, the two factors appear to be independently significant (Table 9-13). Only among those of least "faith in people" is political alienation unimportant, a matter perhaps of a generally disgruntled attitude expressing itself as negativism in spite of nonalienation with regard to political affairs. The interpretation would seem to be that personality factors are also of importance, but that excepting the extreme instances of misanthropy, political alienation continues to be important in its own right.

TABLE 9-13

ATTITUDE TOWARD THE SCHOOL BOND ISSUE AS RELATED TO POLITICAL ALIENATION, HOLDING CONSTANT "FAITH IN PEOPLE"

	Percentages Who Were Unfavorable or Very Unfavorable toward the Issue		
	High Faith in People Score	*Medium Faith in People Score*	*Low Faith in People Score*
	Per Cent	*Per Cent*	*Per Cent*
"Non-alienated"	27(70)	33(18)	67(13)
"Alienated"	52(46)	62(21)	69(39)

SUMMARY

In this paper, the concept of political alienation is developed as a factor relevant to political behavior, particularly to protest voting in local referenda. Political alienation is defined as a combination of perceived lack of power in community affairs and distrust to those who hold power positions; and as such it is hypothesized to be closely related to lower socio-economic status.

Empirical data are presented which provide tentative substantiation of both the hypothesis that political alienation is inversely related to socio-economic status and the hypothesis that political alienation leads to an attitude on a given issue which represents a protest against the existing power structure in the community. However indexed, a deprived position in the social structure appears to be a significant factor which contributes to political alienation: those whose status precludes maximal effective action in the community are the more likely to feel politically alienated. Further, those who are politically alienated are the more likely to hold a negative attitude and to vote "no" when they go to the polls. Moreover, the effects of

[11] Cf. especially M. Rosenberg, "Misanthropy and Political Ideology," *American Sociological Review*, 1956, *21*, pp. 690-695; and G. Nettler, "A Measure of Alienation," *American Sociological Review*, 1957, *22*, pp. 670-677. Our measure includes the following three items:

"Some people say that most people can be trusted. Others say you can't be too careful in your dealings with people. How do you feel about it?" [Positive response: Most can be trusted.]

Agree-Disagree: "If you don't watch out, people will take advantage of you." [Positive response: Disagree, Undecided.]

"Would you say that most people are more inclined to help others or more inclined to look out for themselves?" [Positive response: Help others.]

Coefficient of Reproducibility = .95; Error Ratio = .42.

political alienation appear to hold independently of the effects of self-interest, "subcultural orientation," and more general misanthropy.

It would be presumptuous, of course, to generalize from the data presented here to the extent of attributing to political alienation the defeat of the bond issue in question; and it would be impossible to offer these data as suggesting that political alienation is the key to the common experience of defeated school bond issues, airport bond proposals, fluoridation issues, and the like. But it does seem clear that feelings of political futility, political inefficacy, or political alienation must be given a second look, that the significance of such attitudes may not fully lie within the context of the question of political apathy. Putting it another way, in our attention to political behavior *and to the rationalizations people give for their actions,* we may have neglected the latent attitudes and potentially explosive position of the alienated voter.

GLOSSARY*

Ability grouping. subdividing a group of pupils into smaller groups of relatively equal ability, either in some one subject or in general ability.

Aggression. hostile action; action that causes fear or flight in another animal, or that — failing such effect — brings the aggressor into forceful contact with the other animal; or any psychological equivalent for such attack.

Alienation. loss or lack of relationship, esp. where or when relationship is to be expected.

Analysis of covariance. the extension of the methods used in the analysis of variance to include two or more related variables. Adjustments are made in the experimental variable on the basis of its known correlation with one or more other variables that might affect the experimental outcome.

Analysis of variance. a method for determining whether the differences (expressed as variance) found in a dependent variable, when it is exposed to the influence of one or more experimental variables, exceed what may be expected by chance. The F test is a measure of the probability of the beyond-chance difference.

Anxiety. a fusion of fear with the anticipation of future evil.

Assimilation. a process of perceiving or apperceiving in which the new content is so similar to a familiar content that the two seem almost identical.

Attention span. the number of distant objects that can be perceived in a single "momentary" presentation.

Attitude. an enduring, learning predisposition to behave in a consistent way toward a given class of objects; a persistent mental and/or neural state of readiness to react to a certain object or class of objects, not as they are but as they are conceived to be. It is by the consistency of response to a class of objects that an attitude is identified. The readiness state has a directive effect upon feeling and action related to the object.

Authoritarian character. one who craves unquestioning obedience and subordination. This is the defining quality, but various other qualities are believed to be generally associated with it, such as a servile acceptance of superior authority, scorn for weaknss, rigidity, rejection of out-groups, conventionality, desire to have everything clearly marked off and determined (intolerance of ambiguity), cynicism.

Authoritarian personality. the whole pattern of personality characteristics said to be common to those of authoritarian character (which see).

Autonomy. independence; self-regulation.

* All definitions are abstracted from Horace B. England and Ava Champney English, *A Comprehensive Dictionary of Psychological and Psychoanalytical Terms* (New York: David McKay Company, Inc. The student is encouraged to consult the original source for alternative meanings and more extensive treatment for each term.

Belief. an emotional acceptance of a proposition or doctrine upon what one implicity considers adequate grounds.

Catharsis. release of tension and anxiety by emotionally reliving the incidents of the past, especially those that have been repressed, and honestly facing the causes of difficulty.

Chi square or χ^2. a means of estimating whether a distribution differs from expected values to such a degree as to be evidence for the operation of nonchance factors. It is the sum of the quotients obtained by dividing the square of each difference between an actual and the expected frequency by the expected frequency.

Clique. a tightly organized group of persons, esp. one that tends to exclusiveness.

Conflict. the simultaneous functioning of opposing or mutually exclusive impulses, desires, or tendencies; or the state of a person when opposed impulses or response tendencies have been activated.

Conformity/social. behaviors or attitudes that are regulated by the norms, prescribed roles, standards, or consensus of a group in which a person is a member; or behaviors and attitudes that resemble the modal behaviors and attitudes of the other members of the group.

Contagion/social. the spontaneous imitation, by other persons in a group, of a behavior initiated by one member but without overtly shown intention to stimulate such imitation.

Contingency coefficient or *C*. a measure of the extent to which one set of data is found associated with another set more often than is to be expected by chance when each is expressed in several categories. As a measure of correlation, it does not assume that the successive categories are intervals on a continuous variable; they may be qualitative categories.

Contrast. heightened awareness of difference resulting from bringing together two items of any sort, either simultaneously or in close succession.

Correlation coefficient. a number that indicates the strength of the tendency by two or more variables to vary concomitantly. Perfect correspondence between the two is expressed by +1.00; perfect inverse correspondence is expressed by −1.00; complete lack of correspondence, i.e., independence of the two variables, is expressed by 0.00.

Culture. the pattern of all those arrangements, material or behavioral, whereby a particular society achieves for its members greater satisfactions than they can achieve in a state of nature. It includes social institutions and "knowledge, belief, art, morals, custom, and any other capabilities and habits acquired by man as a member of society." (*E. B. Tyler*)

Cumulative scale. a scale in which the items can be arranged in an order so that a testee who responds positively to any particular items also responds positively to all items of lower rank order.

Degrees of freedom. the number of observations (persons, test items, trials, scores — whatever a sample is composed of) minus the number of independent restrictions, i.e., of the number of prior calculations based on the sample, used in estimating a given statistic. Knowing the degree to which the sample is free or open to such variation permits a better estimate of what the prediction from another sample will be.

Dependency. a lack of self-reliance; the tendency to seek the help of others in making decisions or in carrying out difficult actions.

Discrimination. prejudicial treatment; any difference in action premised upon a prejudice, or upon the class or category by which an individual is typed, rather than upon his relevant characteristics: e.g., race discrimination, treating a person in a given way because of his race or ethnic group.

Domination. control of the behavior of others, esp. by coercion.

Ego. that aspect of the psyche which is conscious and most in touch with external reality.

Ethnocentrism. the tendency to exalt the superiority of the group (esp. the national or ethnic group) to which one belongs and to judge outsiders, often contemptuously, by the standards of one's own group.

Extrinsic reward. a reward that has, for the subject, no intrinsic or logical relation with the performance rewarded.

Feedback. a direct perceptual report of the result of one's behavior upon other persons: e.g., the perception of the return smile that greets one's own.

Frame of reference. a system of standards or values, usually merely implicit, underlying and to some extent controlling an action, or the expression of any attitude, belief, or idea.

Frustration. the blocking of, or interference with, an ongoing goal-directed activity.

Group acceptance. the responses of group members to a single member, or candidate for membership, that establish his role and status in the group structure.

Group decision. a judgment or conclusion arrived at by group discussion and representing either a consensus or a majority vote of the members.

Group goal. any goal proposed for or accepted by a group.

Group/social. two or more persons who interact and influence each other, and who are recognized in some special way because of the interaction.

Group structure. the relationships between the members of a social group (dominance, subordination, friendship, etc.) and its attributes as a group (size, group goals, cohesiveness, we-feeling, etc.) which define its relation to other groups or persons.

Guttman scale. *see* Cumulative scale.

Hostility. tendency to feel anger toward, and to seek to inflict harm upon, a person or group.

Identification. accepting as one's own the purposes and values of another person (or of a group); merging or submerging one's own purposes and values with the other.

Idiographic. pertaining to, or characterizing, an account of particular or individual cases or events.

Influence. an attribute of a person — whether due to status, role, or personality — whereby he produces an effect upon others.

Inhibition. a restraint upon behavior by group standards or by overt group action.

Intelligence. the ability to undertake activities that are characterized by difficulty, complexity, abstractness, economy, adaptiveness to a goal, social value, and the emergence of originals.

Interaction. mutual or reciprocal influence between two or more systems; esp. social interaction, that relation between animals in which the behavior of either one is stimulus to the behavior of the other.

Intrinsic reward. a reward so closely associated with the successful performance of a task that, for a given subject, it cannot be separated or distinguished from the end state.

Item analysis. the determination of the effectiveness of a test item for making the required discriminations between persons, i.e., of item validity.

Laissez-faire leadership. a kind of leadership in which the leader exercises a minimum of control, or even of guidance or assistance.

Leadership. the initiation, direction, or control of the actions or attitudes of another person or of a group, with the more or less willing acquiescence of the followers.

Level of aspiration. the standard by which a person judges his own performance as a success or a failure, or as being up to what he expects of himself.

Likert procedure. a method of constructing and scoring attitude scales: subjects are asked to indicate, on a three- or five-step scale, the degree of their agreement-disagreement with a statement.

Membership group. a group in which a person is an actual accepted member.

Morale. a prevailing temper or spirit, in the individuals forming a group, which is marked by confidence in the group, self-confidence with respect to one's role in the group, group loyalty, and readiness to strive for group goals.

Motive. a specific personal or organismic factor controlling behavior; any state or event within the organism that (under appropriate circumstances) initiates or regulates behavior in relation to a goal.

Nomothetic. characterizing procedures and methods designed to discover general laws.

Nonparametric statistics. the statistical operations that are available when it is not possible to assert that the frequency distribution is normal (as is the assumption of the statistics most commonly used).

Norms. a frame of reference or a standard by which behavior is judged in a given social group.

Open-ended question. a question that defines the general topic inquired about but leaves to the option of the person replying both the form and the substance of the reply. The answer may be a gesture, a single word, or an extended comment.

Opinion. a belief that one holds to be without emotional commitment or desire, and to be open to revaluation since the evidence is not affirmed to be convincing. It is capable of verbal expression under appropriate circumstances, at least to oneself.

Pecking order. a graded and accepted order of privilege, priority, and dominance, established in a small face-to-face group by aggression and intimidation. So called from the description of the behavior of barnyard fowl: A pecks B, B pecks C, C pecks D, and D runs from any of them.

Peer group. the group with whom a child associates on terms of approximate equality.

Perception. an event in the person or organism, primarily controlled by the excitation of sensory receptors, yet also influenced by other factors of a kind that can be shown to have originated in the life history of the organism.

Power/social. the ability or authority to control other persons, to obtain their obedience, to compel their actions.

Prejudice. a particular attitude or sentiment that inclines or predisposes the individual to act, think, perceive, and feel in ways that are congruent with a favorable or (more often) an unfavorable judgment about another person or object.

Press. stimuli or stimulus objects that (for a given person) more or less regularly constitute a unit because the separate parts mean the same thing or are aspects of the same thing, and are reacted to as a unified object.

Prestige. the attribute of being highly regarded by associates so that one's actions strongly influence others.

Primacy/law of. the hypothesized principle that the first acts in a series tend to be better learned and to show especial resistance to forgetting.

Projective technique. a procedure for discovering a person's characteristic modes of behavior (his attitudes, motivations, or dynamic traits) by observing his behavior in response to a situation that does not elicit or compel a particular response—i.e.,to a relatively unstructured, ambiguous, or vague situation.

Rank order correlation. a method of computing the relationship between two variables when scores on these variables are stated in ranks rather than in magnitudes.

Recency/law of. the principle or postulate that a given item is more likely to remind a person of some recent associate than of one more remote in time; that, other things being equal, what is learned is remembered in proportion to its recency.

Reference group. any group with which a person identifies and/or compares himself to such an extent that he tends to adopt its standards, attitudes, and behaviors as his own.

Repression. the exclusion of specific psychological activities or contents from conscious awareness by a process of which the individual is not directly aware. Exclusion includes preventing entry into, forcing out of, or continuously preventing return to, consciousness.

Rigidity. relative inability to change one's action or attitude when the objective conditions demand it; clinging to a no-longer-appropriate way of acting or feeling.

Role. the behavior that is characteristic and expected of the occupant of a defined position in the group.

Role conflict. the situation in which a person is expected to play two roles which, it seems to him, cannot be harmonized.

Role-playing. acting according to a role that is not one's own; imitating a role.

Sanctions. penalties for violation of legal and social imperatives (or rewards for conformity).

Self-concept. a person's view of himself; the fullest description of himself of which a person is capable at any given time.

Social class. a grouping or division of a society, made up of persons having certain common social characteristics which are taken to qualify them for participation on roughly equal terms with others of the group in important social relations, and to restrict (but not prohibit) many kinds of social interaction with those outside the group. There is usually a recognition by all of a hierarchy of upper, middle, and lower classes (sometimes with subdivisions), but this hierarchy is not necessarily one of worth or power.

Social climate. collectively, those folkways and mores of a community or larger unit that seem to the social scientist to be characteristic of the society.

Socialization. the processes whereby a person (esp. a child) acquires sensitivity to social stimuli (esp., the pressures and obligations of group life) and learns to get along with, and to behave like, others in his group or culture; the process of becoming a social being; or the result of those processes.

Social mobility. movement within a given culture from one class to another, esp., movement upward from a class of lower to one of higher status.

Sociometric test. a variety of rating in which the rater names those in his group who possess certain specified qualifications.

Standard score. any derived score using as its unit the standard deviation (or some fraction thereof) of the population that is regarded as the criterion group.

Standard deviation. a measure of the dispersion or variability of a whole distribution. It is computed by summing the squared differences of each measure from the mean, dividing by the number of measures, and extracting the square root.

Statistical significance. the degree of probability that, in an infinite series of measurements of the kind in question, the value or score actually obtained will not by chance alone occur with significant frequency, hence can be attributed to something other than chance.

Stereotype. a relatively rigid and oversimplified or biased perception or conception of an aspect of reality, esp. of persons or social groups.

Subculture. a division of a cultural group or population consisting of persons who share special cultural characteristics at the same time that they share the major characteristics of the whole culture.

Suppression. a conscious exclusion of disapproved desires.

***t*-test.** a test of statistical significance, appropriate when the number of cases is small.

***U* test.** a nonparametric test of the significance of the differences between means for unmatched groups.

Values. an abstract concept, often merely implicit, that defines for an individual or for a social unit what ends or means to an end are desirable.

Value system. the more or less coherent set of values that regulate a person's conduct, often without his awareness that they do so.

Variance. the square of the standard deviation.

INDEXES

INDEX OF NAMES IN INTRODUCTION

NOTE: Starred names (*) represent names not included in the principal index. All other names also appear in the Index of Names in Readings.

Adelson, J., xxi
Anderson, R. C., xxii
Arsan, K., xxii

*Blake, R. R., xx
*Brand, H. H., xx
Brookover, W. B., xix, xxi

Campbell, E. Q., xxi
Cartwright, D., xxii
Charters, W. W., Jr., xv-xxiv
Chatterjee, B. B., xxii
Coleman, J. S., xxii
Cook, S. W., xxi

Douvan, E., xxi
Festinger, L., xxiii
Flanders, N. A., xxii
Foshay, A. W., xxiii

Gage, N. L., xv-xxiv
Getzels, J. W., xix, xxiv
Goodrich, H. B., xxi
Gottlieb, D., xix, xxi
Gronlund, N. E., xxii
Guba, E. G., xxiv
Gump, P. V., xxiii

Hanfmann, E., xxii
Havumaki, S., xxii
Heider, F., xxiii
Heist, P., xxi
*Helson, H., xx
Hemphill, J. K., xxiv
Henry, J., xviii, xxiii
Hoehn, A. J., xxiii
Horton, J. E., xxiv
Horwitz, M., xix, xxiii
Hovland, C. I., xix, xxiii

Kahl, J. A., xxi
Kearney, N. C., xxiv
Knapp, R. H., xxi
*Koffka, K., xx
Kounin, J. S., xxiii

Lazarsfeld, P. F., xxiv
Lewin, K., xvi, xxi
Lippitt, R., xxii

McKeachie, W. J., xxiii
Mason, W. S., xxiv
Moreno, J. L., xxii

Newcomb, T. M., xxiii

Osgood, C. E., xxiii

Pace, C. R., xxi
Page, E. B., xviii, xxiii
Pettigrew, T. F., xxi
*Pitts, C. E., xvii
Pollie, D., xxiii

Rocchio, P. D., xxiv
Roe, A., xxi
Runkel, P. J., xxii
Ryan, J. J., III, xxiii

Selltiz, C., xxi
Sherif, M., xx, xxii
Siegel, A. E., xxiii
Siegel, S., xxiii
*Smith, M. B., xx, xxii
Speisman, J., xxiii

Tannenbaum, P. H., xxiii
Thielens, W., Jr., xxiv
Thistlethwaite, D. L., xxi
Thompson, W. E., xxiv
Torrance, E. P., xxii
Tumin, M. M., xxi

Van Egmond, E., xxii

*Waller, W., xxi
Wann, K. D., xxiii
Watson, G., v-vii, xvi
White, R. K., xxii

Zander, A., xxii

INDEX OF NAMES IN READINGS

Abelson, P., 249, 250
Ackerman, N. W., 22
Adams, R. G., 155, 160
Adelson, J., 21-35
Adorno, T. W., 22, 32, 265, 268
Agger, R. E., 327, 329
Alden, E., 194
Allport, G. W., 68, 156, 160
Anastasi, A., 18
Anderson, H. H., 155, 158, 160, 182, 183, 185, 189
Anderson, R. C., 153-162
Angelino, H., 19
Arrington, R. E., 184
Arsan, K., 133-140
Asch, M. J., 158, 160
Asch, S. E., 205
Atkinson, J., 219

Bacon, M., 122
Bailey, S. K., 58
Bailey, W. C., 4
Bain, R. K., 278-286
Barbe, W. B., 133
Barker, R. G., 192, 204, 208
Barry, H., 122
Barton, P., 61
Baruch, D., 204, 209
Becker, C., 305
Becker, H. S., 271
Belknap, G., 327
Bennett, E. B., 156, 160
Bentz, V. J., 319
Berelson, B. R., 327
Berkowitz, L., 155, 160
Best, S., 78
Bettelheim, B., 263
Bidwell, C. E., 271-278
Bills, R. E., 155, 157, 158, 160
Blackwood, P., 153, 161
Blizzard, S. A., 56
Bloom, B. S., 74
Boggs, J. W., 254
Bonney, M. E., 104
Bovard, E. W., 155, 156, 157, 160
Bower, R. T., 41
Brandwein, P., 153, 156, 157, 161
Brehm, J. W., 252
Bremer, N., 133
Brewer, J. E., 182, 183, 185, 189
Bristor, B., 287
Brock, T., 246
Bronfenbrenner, U., 21, 98, 101, 104
Brookover, W. B., 3-11, 13, 21, 157, 161, 309
Browne, C. G., 319
Burke, C. J., 207
Burke, H. R., 158, 161
Burnett, R. W., 153, 161
Buros, O. K., 20
Burrus, B., 61
Burton, W. H., 153, 155, 161

Callis, R., 287
Campbell, A., 327
Campbell, D. T., 177
Campbell, E. H., 246
Campbell, E. Q., 51-57
Carter, L. F., 159, 161
Cartwright, D., 107-114, 115, 161, 162, 203
Casper, J. B., 287
Centers, R., 327
Charters, W. W., Jr., 7, 11, 12-21, 279
Chatterjee, B. B., 173-181
Chein, I., 58
Child, I. L., 122
Christie, J. R., 35
Clark, B., 8
Clark, W., 185
Clifton, D. E., 181
Coates, C. H., 327
Coch, L., 110
Cohen, A. R., 115, 218, 246
Coleman, J. S., 8, 87-94, 315
Coleman, W., 19
Collins, M. E., 46
Collister, F. G., 99
Cook, S. W., 40-51, 44, 80-87
Cook, W. W., 287
Cooley, C. H., 108
Cope, A. H., 69
Cronbach, L. J., 153, 159, 161
Cuber, J. F., 3
Cutler, R., 58

Darley, J., 65, 66, 70
Davis, A., 4, 12-21, 181
Davis, J. A., 88
Deese, J., 218
Deignan, F. J., 155, 157, 161
Dembo, T., 204, 208
Deutsch, M., 46
Dispenzieri, A., 211
DiVesta, F. J., 158, 161
Dollard, J., 181, 196, 203
Doob, L. W., 196
Douvan, E., 21-35
Dressel, R. J., 278-286
Drews, E. M., 35-39, 133, 140

Eason, W., 58
Edwards, A. L., 233, 272
Eells, K., 12-17, 19, 20, 36, 181, 182, 185
Eglash, A., 157, 161
Eldersveld, S. J., 327
Eulau, H., 327

Farnsworth, B. K., 287
Farquhar, W. H., 157, 161
Farwell, E., 65
Faw, V. A., 155, 156, 161
Feldman, J., 88
Ferneau, E., 318
Feshback, S., 243
Festinger, L., 111, 156, 161, 174, 252
Fiedler, F. E., 133
Field, P. B., 249, 250
Flanders, N. A., 155, 156, 157, 161, 162-172
Fleishman, E. A., 320
Foa, U. G., 203
Form, W., 8
Foshay, A. W., 226-238
Fowler, W. L., 20
Freedman, M., 69
Freeman, F. N., 12
French, J. R. P., Jr., 110, 113, 115, 194
Freud, A., 35
Freud, S., 108
Friedman, M., 221
Fryer, D., 319

Gage, N. L., 173-181
Gardner, B. B., 4, 13
Gardner, M. R., 4, 13
Gaudet, H., 327

Gekoski, N., 159, 161
Getzels, J. W., 309-318
Gilbert, E., 41
Gnagey, W. J., 195
Goldman, 196, 204
Goodrich, H. B., 68, 71
Gordon, M. M., 3
Gottlieb, D., 3-11, 13, 21
Gough, H. G., 24, 39, 265
Grace, A. G., 320
Grambs, J. D., 153, 154, 161
Greenacre, P., 35
Greenbaum, J. J., 65, 66, 68, 71
Gronlund, N. E., 97-106
Gross, N., 7, 52, 279, 309, 310, 314
Guba, E. G., 271-278, 310, 315
Guetzkow, H., 155, 157, 158, 161
Guilford, J. P., 20, 134
Gump, P. V., 190-195
Gurin, G., 327

Haer, J., 327
Hagenah, T., 70
Haggard, E. A., 17
Haigh, G. V., 157, 158, 161
Hall, O., 271
Halpin, A. W., 310, 319, 320, 324
Hanfmann, E., 123-125
Harding, J., 42, 58
Hare, A. P., 155, 161
Hartley, E. L., 21, 141, 205
Harvey, O. J., 126, 240
Havighurst, R. J., 4, 5, 9, 12, 14, 21, 30, 181
Havumaki, S., 162-172
Hebb, D. O., 312
Heider, F., 174, 175, 196, 200, 202
Heintz, R. K., 111
Heist, P., 65-73
Hemphill, J. K., 155, 159, 161, 319-326
Hencley, S. P., 317
Henry, J., 254-263
Henry, N. B., 9, 310
Herrick, V. E., 12
Heyns, R. W., 155, 161
Hildreth, G., 185
Hoehn, A. J., 181-189
Hoffer, C., 8
Hoffman, M. L., 32
Hogrefe, R., 42
Holland, J., 9
Holland, J. L., 66, 71
Hollander, E. P., 69
Hollingshead, A., 5, 6, 181
Holzinger, K. J., 12
Hood, W. R., 126
Hopson, A. L., 80-87
Horowitz, E. L., 43
Horton, J. E., 327-333
Horwitz, M., 196-212
Houser, L., 9
Hovland, C. I., 239-253
Hoyt, C. J., 287
Hughes, E. C., 271
Hughes, M. N., 181
Hunter, E., 260
Hunter, F., 327
Huntington, R., 126
Hurwitz, J., 115
Husband, R. W., 158, 161
Hutchins, R. M., 301
Hutt, M. L., 218
Hyman, H. H., 51
Hymovitch, B., 115

Iverson, W. J., 153, 154, 161

Jahoda, M., 22
Jackson, P. W., 271-278
Janis, I. L., 239, 243, 247, 249, 250, 251, 253
Janowitz, M., 327
Jenkins, J. G., 321
Jersild, A. T., 203, 235
Johnson, D., 157, 162
Jonckheere, A. R., 267

Kahl, J. A., 3
Kearney, N. C., 287-290
Kelley, H. H., 239, 248, 253
Kelly, E. L., 157, 161
Kelly, G. A., 321
Kendall, M. G., 282
Kenkel, W. F., 3
King, B. T., 249, 250, 251
Kirk, R., 292
Klineberg, O., 12
Kluckhohn, C., 35
Knapp, R. H., 65, 66, 68, 71
Koch, S., 174
Kounin, J. S., 190-195
Krumboltz, J. D., 155, 158, 161
Kuhlen, R. G., 99
Kutner, B., 58

Lambert, W. E., 155, 161
Landsman, T., 155, 156, 157, 161, 162
LaPiere, R. T., 41
Lazarsfeld, P. F., 51, 291-308, 327
Lazarus, R. S., 218
Learned, W. S., 65
Lee, F. J., 196, 197
Leeds, C. H., 287
Lesser, G. S., 249, 250
Levin, H., 204, 206, 209
Lewin, K., 35, 108, 109, 110, 111, 155, 156, 158, 161, 204, 208
Lieberman, M., 281, 282
Lindquist, E. F., 222, 225
Lindzey, G., 58, 68
Linton, R., 311
Lipham, J. M., 313
Lippitt, R., 109, 110, 112, 115, 141-153, 155, 158, 162, 203
Liss, E., 35, 39
Loeb, M. B., 4, 5, 181
Lorge, I., 18, 19, 20, 21
Low, J. O., 4
Luchins, A. S., 244
Lumsdaine, A. A., 246, 247, 252
Lund, F. H., 246
Lunt, P. S., 4
Lynd, H. M., 4
Lynd, R. S., 4
Lynn, K. S., 21

McClelland, D. C., 11, 21, 22, 26, 36, 214, 217, 219
Maccoby, E. E., 21, 141, 204, 206, 209
McConnell, T. R., 65-73
McCurdy, H. G., 155, 161
McEachern, A., 52, 279, 314
McKeachie, W. J., 155, 157, 158, 161, 212-219
MacKinnon, D. W., 72
McNemar, Q., 221, 224
McPhee, W. N., 327
Maier, N. R. F., 213, 218
Mandell, W., 246
Mandler, G., 218
Marrow, A. J., 113
Mason, W. S., 52, 278-286, 279, 314
Matsler, F., 65-73
Mattson, L., 58
Meeker, M., 36, 181, 182, 185
Melzack, R., 35
Merton, R. K., 305
Meuwese, W., 133
Miller, N. E., 196
Miller, W. E., 327
Minard, R. D., 42, 43
Mitchell, B. C., 12
Monroe, J., 58
Moreno, J. L., 98, 101, 104, 105, 106
Morsh, J. E., 173
Mowrer, O. H., 196, 204
Moyer, D. C., 318
Murray, H. A., 35, 73, 272
Mursell, J., 154, 161
Myrdal, G., 58

Nettler, G., 332
Neugarten, B. L., 181
Neuman, S. E., 156, 157, 161
Newcomb, T. M., 8, 21, 113, 141, 174, 205
Newman, H. H., 12

Niyekawa, A., 80
Noll, V. H., 20
Norsted, R. A., 287

Oliver, P., 133
Olmstead, D. W., 327
Oonk, S., 133
Osgood, C. E., 174
Osler, S., 218
Ostlund, L. A., 157, 161
Ostrom, V., 327, 329

Pace, C. R., 8, 73-79, 74, 75
Page, E. B., 219-225
Parsons, T., 9, 310, 311
Pastore, N., 200
Patterson, F. K., 153, 154, 161
Pearson, G. H., 35, 39
Pellegrin, R. J., 327
Perkins, H. V., 155, 156, 157, 161
Peters, C. C., 156, 161
Peterson, W. A., 271
Pettigrew, T. F., 51-57
Polansky, N., 112, 115
Pollie, D., 212-219
Preston, M. G., 111
Prince, R., 314
Proshansky, H., 58

Rappaport, D., 33
Rasmussen, G. R., 155, 157, 161
Raven, B., 115
Redl, F., 112, 115
Reed, M. F., 182
Rehage, K. J., 157, 158, 162
Riecken, H. W., 200
Riesman, D., 50, 312, 327
Roach, M. E., 9
Rocchio, P. D., 287-290
Roe, A., 21
Rogoff, N., 77
Roseborough, M. E., 155, 158, 162
Rosen, B., 10
Rosen, S., 115
Rosenberg, M., 284, 285, 327, 332
Rosenberg, M. J., 239, 250
Rotberg, R., 61
Runkel, P. J., 173-181
Ryan, J. J., III, 190-195
Ryan, M. W., 42, 45

Saenger, G., 41
Sandrin, A. A., 287
Sanford, N., 69
Sarason, S. B., 218
Sarnoff, I., 32
Saupe, J. L., 20
Savage, M. L., 173
Schinnerer, M. C., 287
Schmidt, W., 157, 158, 161
Sears, R. R., 196, 204, 206, 209
Seeman, M., 319, 320
Seidman, J., 30
Selltiz, C., 80-87
Shartle, C. L., 319
Sheatsley, P. B., 51
Shedd, C. L., 19
Sheffield, F. D., 246, 252
Sheldon, W. D., 155, 156, 157, 162
Sherif, C. W., 126, 264, 268
Sherif, M., 126-132, 161, 240, 264, 268
Shils, E. A., 311
Shoben, E. J., Jr., 36
Siegel, A. E., 264-268
Siegel, S., 264-268
Simmel, G., 108
Simpson, G. E., 58
Sinha, A. K. P., 218
Slomowitz, M., 157, 162
Smith, H. C., 157, 162
Smith, M., 10
Smuckler, R., 327
Speisman, J., 212-219
Spindler, G. D., 313
Srole, L., 4
Starkey, M. L., 254
Stein, M. I., 74
Stern, G. G., 69, 70, 74, 79
Stinnett, T. M., 275
Stogdill, R. M., 319
Stone, C. P., 18
Stone, G., 8
Stotland, E., 115
Stouffer, S. A., 51, 52, 282, 297
Strevell, W. H., 133
Strodtbeck, F. L., 11
Sussman, M. B., 126
Swanson, G. E., 205

Tannenbaum, P. H., 174
Taylor, D. W., 18
Taylor, I., 46
Teahan, J. E., 35-39
Teevan, R., 216
Thelen, H. A., 155, 158, 162, 310
Thibaut, J. W., 200
Thielens, W., Jr., 291-308
Thistlethwaite D. L., 73, 77, 78
Thomas, L. G., 284
Thompson, O., 156, 162
Thompson, W. E., 327-333
Thompson, W. R., 35
Thurstone, L. L., 20, 151
Tiegs, E. W., 185
Titus, H. E., 69
Toby, J., 52
Tom, F., 156, 157, 162
Torrance, E. P., 21, 133-140
Trow, M., 8
Tryon, C. M., 101
Tumin, M. M., 51, 57-64
Tyler, R. W., 12

Van Egmond, E., 114-123
Vaughn, C. L., 321
Vener, A., 8
Vernon, P. E., 68
Volkart, E. H., 248

Walker, H., 41
Walkley, R. P., 44
Wann, K. D., 226-238
Ward, A. W., 19
Ward, J. N., 158, 162
Warner, W. L., 4, 5, 13, 21, 36, 181, 182, 185, 186
Warrington, W. G., 20
Waterhouse, T. S., 133
Waterman, A., 221
Watson, F., 153, 161
Watson, G., 35
Webster, H., 65, 69
Wechsler, D., 207
Weinberg, R., 80
Weiss, W., 242, 253
Weissman, M. P., 69, 70
Westie, C. M., 320
Wheelis, A., 312
Wherry, R. J., 319
Whipple, G. M., 12
White, B. J., 126
White, L. D., 208
White, R. K., 109, 141-153, 155, 158, 162
Whyte, W. H., 312
Wilder, E. W., 173
Wiley, D., 221
Williams, P., 65-73
Williams, R. M., Jr., 42, 45
Wilner, D. M., 44
Wilson, E., 8
Wilson, M., 161
Winterbottom, M. R., 36
Wischmeier, R. R., 155, 162
Wispe, L. G., 155, 157, 158, 162
Withall, J., 155, 158, 162
Wood, B. D., 65
Wright, H. F., 192

Yonge, G., 65
Yule, G. U., 282

Zajonc, R., 174
Zander, A., 114-123, 161, 162, 203
Zeleny, L. D., 155, 156, 162

SUBJECT INDEX

Ability grouping
and creative thinking tasks, xxii, 133-140
and disruptive group tension, 139-140
review of research, 133
Academic achievement, *see* Scholastic achievement
Academic freedom, xxiv, 291-308
Achievement, *see* Scholastic achievement
Achievement motive
and examination anxiety, 217-219
and parent-child relations, 35-36
and social mobility, 22-23, 26-27, 34
syndrome, 10-11, 27
see also Motivation
Acquaintance potential, in intergroup contact, 43
see also Interaction-potential
Activities Index, 74, 78-79
Administrative reputation of college departments, 319-326
Administrator
behavior, 319-326
expectations of, 318
role conflict, 309-310, 313-314
Adolescent
social mobility, xxi, 21-35
values, 8-9, 88-94
Aggression
and counter-aggression, 237-238
and leadership style, 147-148
and social climate, 109
student perceptions of, 230
teacher perceptions of, 230-231
verbal versus physical, 229-230
and witch-hunt syndrome, 254
see also Hostility
Aggressive autocracy, 146-149
Alienation
and social mobility, 23, 34
and voting, xxiv, 327-333
see also Political alienation
Allport-Vernon-Lindzey Study of Values, 68-70, 72-73
American Association of School Administrators, xvi
American Educational Research Association, xvi
American Sociological Association, xvi
Anderson-Brewer teacher contact index, 182-184
Anxiety
and classroom examinations, 212-219
and teacher criticism, 258, 260
see also Motivation
Apathetic autocracy, 146-149
Apathy, and voting, 327-333
see also Political alienation
Apprehensiveness, of social science professors, 291, 306-307
Aspiration, *see* level of aspiration
Assimilation-contrast effect, 241
Association for Supervision and Curriculum Development, xvi
Athletics in high school, 88-90, 92-94
Atmosphere, *see* Social climate
Attention span, 201-202, 207-208
Attitude
concept, 250
consistency between belief and feelings, 250-251
toward election issues, 327-333
toward minority groups, 9, 42-48
of mothers toward children, 36-39
organization of, in students, xxi, 254-263
of pupils toward misbehavior, 192-194
toward school desegregation
and age, 59-60, 63
and exposure to mass media, 62-63
measure, 59
of ministers, xxi, 53-54
and religion, 60, 63
and social class, 61, 63
and social mobility, 62-63
of Southern whites, xxi, 57-64
of social science professors, 291-308
of students toward clothing, 8-9
of teachers toward pupils, 287-290
toward out-group, 126-127, 131-132
see also Liberal attitude
Attitude change
and attributes of communicator, 239-243
and audience predispositions, 239, 248-250
and communication content, 239, 243-248
and discipline techniques, 191-195
and group contagion, 164-172
inner resistance to, 168-171
and intergroup contact, 41-47, 80-81
and leadership style, 111
and membership group, xxiii, 264-268
persistence through time, 252-253
principles of, 111-114
and reference group, xxiii, 264-268
and role playing, 251-252
and teaching style, 162-172
Attraction to group
and attitude change, 248-249
bases of, 233-236
and behavior change, 111-112
Attribution of causality, 200, 202
Audience-child, 190-195
Audience predispositions, and attitude change, 239, 248-250
Authoritarianism
in families of gifted children, 39
effects of membership group on, 264-268
effects of reference groups on, 264-268
in low-productivity colleges, 69, 72
measure, 69, 265
and social mobility, 22

Authoritarian leadership, *see* Leadership style
Autistic hostility, *see* Hostility
Autocratic leadership, *see* Leadership style
Autonomy, and social mobility, 23, 28-30, 34

Balanced state, 174
Behavior
of college department heads, 323-325
considerate, among students, xxiii, 226-238
influence of, on attitude, 251-252
observation categories, 116
and social power, 114-125
and student intelligence, 114-123
of teacher toward lower-class students, 181-189
of teacher and student hostility, 196-212, 254-263
see also Considerate-inconsiderate behavior
Behavior change
concept, 107-108
and discipline techniques, 191, 193
and group decision, 109-110, 156
principles of, 111-114
in teachers, 173-181
in workshops and training courses, 110-111
Belonging, *see* Group membership
Bond issue election, 327-333

California Test of Mental Maturity, 134
Camp, studies of group relations in, 126-132
Campus, *see* College
Career, *see* Job satisfaction, Occupational, Teaching career, Vocational interests
Catharsis
during examinations, 213-219
and reduction of hostility, 204-209, 211
see also Confession
Civil liberties, views of professors on, 300-301
Class, *see* Social class
Classroom management
effects on student attitudes, 254-263
techniques, xxiii, 190-195
see also Teaching style
Clergy, role of, in school desegregation, 51-59
Cognitive dissonance, xxiii, 174, 252
College
academic social system, 305-306
choice of, 273-276
interaction of foreign students and Americans, xxi, 80-87
leadership of department chairmen, xxiv, 319-326
production of scientists and scholars, 65-73
productivity index, 65, 308
social climate, 73-79
and threats to academic freedom, xxiv, 291-308
see also Professor
College Characteristics Index, 74-79
College press
clusters of characteristics, 75-76
differences across colleges, 75
and productivity of colleges, xxi, 73, 76-78
similarities among colleges, 74-75
and student personality needs, 78-79, 274-276
College productivity
and environmental press, xxi, 69, 71-73
explanations for differences in, 65-73
and liberalism of social science faculty, 308
and social climate, 79
and student-faculty relations, 78
and student personality, xxi, 69, 71-73
and student selectivity, 66-68
and values, 65-66, 68-70, 72-73, 76-78
and vocational interests, 69-73
see also Productivity
Commitment to teaching, 280-281
Communication
effects of, on attitude change, 239-253
between scientists and practitioners (pp. v, vi of Foreword), xix
and hostility, 113
and strain toward symmetry, 174-175
see also Feedback, Interaction
Communism, attitudes of professors toward, 292-308
Community social structure and voter attitudes, 329-330, 332-333
Competition
and ability of high school students, 90-92
and attitude organization, 257-258
boy-girl, and sociometric choice, 104
in creating group conflict, 130
Confession, as component of witch-hunt syndrome, 260-262
see also Catharsis
Conflict, *see* Culture, Group conflict, Role conflict
Conformity, *see* Norms
Conservative, *see* Liberal attitude
Considerate-inconsiderate behavior
agreement on, 227-228
as basis for popularity, 228-229
of college department heads, 323-325
and friendship-seeking, 231, 238
functions of, 237-238
instances of, 226-227
and status, 231-233
Consultant's role, 318
Contagion, *see* Group contagion
Controversial issues in college classroom, 295-296
Cooperation, *see* Intergroup cooperation
Cornell method, *see* Guttman scale
Counter-aggression, 237-238
Creativity
Counter-propaganda, resistance to, 247-248
Creativity
in classrooms, xxii
effects of ability grouping on, 133-140
tests, 134-135
see also Gifted student, Intelligence, Scholastic Achievement
Credibility of communicator, 240-243
Criteria for selecting readings, xviii-xix
Cross-cultural contact, *see* Intergroup contact
Cross-pressure, 51
Cross-sex friendship choices, 102-106
Cultural
bias in intelligence tests, xxi, 13-19
differences in problem-solving, 14-15
differences of social classes, 13, 20
Culture
of adolescent society, 87-94
and analysis of social systems, 312
values in conflict with educational goals, 312-313
Cumulative scale, *see* Guttman scale

Davis-Eells Games Test, 17-20
Decision-making process
 in children's groups, 114-123
 in school desegregation, 47
Democratic leadership, *see* Leadership style
Dependency on teacher, 163-172, 263
Desegregation of schools
 and change in social norms, 50
 attitude toward, 42-48, 57-64
 decision-making process, 47
 influence of group sanctions, 50
 influence of reference groups, 49-50
 opposition versus hostile action, 41
 and personality of leaders, 50-51
 resistance to, 57-64
 role of ministers in, xxi, 51-57
 role requirements of board members, 49
 social psychological analysis of, xxi, 40-51
Desist-technique, *see* Clasroom management
Deviation from norms and behavioral change, 112
Discipline, *see* Classroom management
Discrimination
 against Chinese, 41
 against lower-class students, 5-6, 14-16, 181-189
 against Negroes, 41
 see also Desegregation of schools, Group conflict
Divide and conquer techniques in teaching, 172
Docility in students, 254-255, 258-260
Dominance, among kindergarten children, 123-125
 see also Leadership, Power
Dominative behavior, *see* Leadership, Teaching style
Downward mobility, *see* Social mobility
Drop-out, 4, 6, 99

Educational philosophy, of professors, 293-297
Edwards Personal Preference Schedule, 272
Ego psychology and social mobility, 33-34
Election, school bond issue, 327-333
Elmtown, 5-6
Emotional appeals and attitude change, 243-244
Environmental press, *see* College press
Environment and heredity in intelligence, 12-13, 18
Equilibrium theory, xxiii, 173-181
Examinations
 effects of teacher comments, xxiii, 219-225
 and student anxiety, xxiii, 212-219
 see also Learning, Scholastic achievement, Test motivation
Expectations, of teacher's power, 197-212
 see also Role, Self-expectations
Extrinsic-reward value of occupation, 285-286
Extrinsic satisfaction in teaching, 282-284

Faculty-student relations in high productivity colleges, 78
Failing marks awarded to students
 age and sex of teacher, 289-290
 and teacher attitudes toward pupils, xxiv, 290
 teaching field, 288-289
Faith in People Scale, 332
Fallibility of the IQ, 20-21
 see also Intelligence tests
Fear of failure, *see* Achievement motive
Feedback from pupils to teacher, 173-181
 see also Communication, Interaction
Foreign student interaction with Americans, xxii, 80-87
Friendship
 and formation of camper groups, 128-129
 and reduction of group conflict, 131-132
 relations and liberalism of professors, 302-303
 see also Attraction to group, Group membership, Sociometric choice
Frustration, and student hostility, xxiii, 196-212
F scale, 69, 265
Future orientation, 23, 27-28

Gifted student
 attitude of mother toward, 35-39
 culture conflicts regarding, 312-313
 see also Creativity, Intelligence, Scholastic achievement
Grades, *see* Failing marks, Scholastic achievement
Group
 as agent of change, 111
 concept, 126
 as medium of change, 111-112
 social structure of, 128-129, 132
 as target of change, 111-114
 see also Interaction, Intergroup contact, Leadership, Status
Group acceptance, *see* Status
Group atmosphere, *see* Social climate
Group attraction, *see* Attraction to group
Group cohesiveness and teaching style, 162-172
Group conflict
 and competitive activities, 130
 experimental creation of, xxii, 130
 and within-group solidarity, 130, 132
 see also Intergroup contact
Group contagion and change in pupil opinion, 164-172
Group decision, 109-110, 156
Group Dimension Questionnaire, 320-321
Group dynamics
 application of theory, 107-114
 concept, 108
 and social technology, 114
Group formation, experimental inducement of, 128-130
Group goals, superordinate, 127, 131-132
Group membership
 effects on attitude, 264-268
 and mental health, 108-109
 and sense of belonging, 111
 and social mobility, 25-26
 see also Reference group, Sociometric choice
Group norms, *see* Norms
Group sanctions
 among camp boys, 129-130
 on ministers in school desegregation, 54-55
 in desegregation decisions, 50
Grouping, *see* Ability grouping
Guttman scale, 8, 59, 85, 328-329

Harmony of groups, *see* Intergroup cooperation
Heredity and environment in intelligence, 12-13, 18
Heterogeneous grouping, *see* Ability grouping
Higher education, *see* College
Homogeneous grouping, *see* Ability grouping

Hostility
autistic, and blocked communication, 113
effects on learning, 201-202, 207
and teacher behavior, xxiii, 196-212
see also Aggression, Classroom management

Identification, and social mobility, 30
Idiographic dimension of social system, 310-311
Influence
of children differing in social power, 114-123
of group on members, 111-112
of intelligent children, 114-123
through mass media, 109-110, 239-253
and status in group, 112
teacher, and opinion change in pupils, 162-172
of teacher on pupil misbehavior, 190-195
see also Domination, Leadership, Teaching style
Influentials among Little Rock ministers, 53
Information, regarding need for change, 113
Inhibition of hostility, 203-209
Initiation of structure, 323-325
Integrative behavior, *see* Leadership, Teaching style
Intelligence
environment and heredity, 12-13, 18
of high-achieving students, 90-92
and interpersonal behavior, xxii, 114-123
social class differences in, 12-13, 17-18
and social mobility, 32-33
and social power, 117
see also Creativity, Gifted student, Scholastic achievement
Intelligence tests
assessment of Davis-Eells Games, 19-20
cultural bias in, xxi, 13-17
and scholastic achievement, 10
and social class, xxi, 12-21
Interaction
among boys under differing leadership styles, 147
and considerate behavior of students, 231-233
foreign students and Americans, 19, 80-87
in homogeneous and heterogeneous groups, 139-140
and interaction-potential, 84-85
among kindergarten children, 123-125
and organization of student attitudes, 254-263
social psychology as the study of, xv
teacher-student, xxii, xxiii, 78, 162-212, 254-263
Interaction-potential, 82-85
see also Acquaintance potential
Intercultural relations, and leadership training, 110-111
see also Intergroup contact
Intergroup contact
acquaintance potential, 43
and attitude change, 80-81
attributes of participants, 45-46, 80-81
characteristics of situation, 43-45, 82
factors influencing foreign students and Americans, 86-87
involuntary, 43-45
interaction-potential, 82-83
norms, regarding, 43-44
and reduction of conflict, 130-132
status of participants, 43, 45-46
see also Group conflict, Interaction
Intergroup cooperation, xxii, 130-132
Intergroup hostility, *see* Group conflict
Intragroup, *see* Group
Intrinsic satisfaction in teaching, 282-284
Item analysis, of intelligence tests, 15

Job satisfaction
and agreement in role expectations, 318
and personality of teachers, 277-278
and sex of teachers, 282-284

Kindergarten children, social structure, xxii, 123-125
Kuhlmann-Finch Test, 19
Kuhlmann-Anderson Test, 116

Laissez-faire leadership, *see* Leadership style
Language forms, social class differences in, 15, 17
Leader Behavior Description Questionnaire, 320
Leadership
changes in, 132
of college department heads, xxiv, 319-326
effects on group life, xxii, 146-150
emergence among camp boys, 128
training, in workshops, 110-111
and types of dominance among children, 124-125
see also Dominance, Influence, Leadership style, Power
Leadership style
and aggressive behavior, 109, 147-148
autocratic, xxii, 141-162
of college department heads, xxiv, 323-325
democratic, xxii, 141-162
and effect on group members, 141-153
and group productivity, 148
laissez-faire, 141-153
and personality, 144-145
review of research on, 153-162
see also Leadership, Teaching style
Leading crowds in high school, 88-89, 92-93
Learner-centered teaching, *see* Teaching style
Learning
effects of hostility on, 201-202, 207
and examination anxiety, 212-219
and teacher comments on examinations, 219-225
and teaching style, 154-162, 201-202, 207-209
see also Failing marks, Scholastic achievement
Legitimate power, 197-212
Level of aspiration, influence of group on, 108-109
Liberal attitude
and apprehensiveness among professors, 306-307
index, 292-293
and professional productivity, 300
and the social science profession, 304-306
see also Attitude, Professor

Mass media
and attitude toward desegregation, 62-63
influence through, 109-110, 239-253
Mental health, and group relations, 108-109
Mental hygiene value of teacher-pupil contacts, 182-189

Methods of teaching, *see* Classroom Management, Teaching style
Metropolitan Achievement Test, 185
Middle-class standards of school, 5-6, 14, 16
Middletown, 4
Minister's role, in school desegregation, xxi, 51-59
Minnesota Multiphasic Personality Inventory, 71
Minnesota Teacher Attitude Inventory, xxiv, 287-288
Minority group, *see* Group conflict, Intergroup contact, Desegregation of schools
Misbehavior of students, methods of correcting, 190-195
Mobility, *see* Social mobility
Morale, and teaching style, 154-162
Mother, *see* Parent-child relations
Motivation, and teacher comments on examinations, 219-225
  see also Achievement motive, Anxiety, Personality, Test motivation

National Merit Scholarship winners, 66-73, 77
Needs, *see* Achievement motive, Personality
Negro
  discrimination against, 41
  personality needs, 274-275
  see also Desegregation of schools
Nomothetic dimension of social system, 310-311
Norms
  in definition of group, 126
  deviation from, and resistance to change, 112
  governing intergroup contact, 43-44
  and influence of communication, 248-249
  of high school culture, 8
  of liberalism among social scientists, 301-306
  toward school desegregation, 50
  see also Values

Observational method
  in boys' camp, 127
  in boys' club, 145
  categories, in observing children, 116
  of creative thinking, 135-136
  of dominative-integrative teacher behavior, 182-184, 186
  of social relations among kindergarten children, 123
Occupational
  aspirations, 10, 24, 32-33
  choice, 271-286, 303-306
  orientation of teachers, 278-282
  plans, of teachers, 281-284
  values, 284-286
  see also Job satisfaction, Teaching career, Vocational interests
Omnibus Personality Inventory, 69
Opinion, *see* Attitude, Attitude change
Organization of arguments, and attitude change, 244-248

Paired comparison method, in observations, 123
Parent-child relations
  and achievement motive, 35-36
  and gifted children, 35-39
  and social mobility, 31-32, 34
Parental Attitude Scale, 36-38
Pecking order in classrooms, 232-233
People-oriented value of occupation, 285-286
Perception
  accuracy of, 179-180, 317-318
  of actual teacher behavior, 176-179
  of ideal teacher behavior, 176, 178-179
  of liberalism in fellow professors, 300
  of need for change in group, 113
  of role expectations among superintendents, 317-318
  by teachers, of student behavior, 116, 119-120, 122-123, 173, 176-177, 227-228, 230-231
Permissiveness, index, 292-293
  see also Liberal attitude
Personality
  attributes and communication effectiveness, 246
  authoritarian, 22, 39, 69, 72, 264-268
  and career demands, 272
  in colleges differing in productivity, xxi, 69-70, 72-73
  and conflict with role expectations, 313-314
  disorders and role conflict, 317
  general persuasibility, 249-250
  of leaders in school desegregation, 50-51
  measure, 69, 74
  and need-dispositions in analysis of social system, 310-311
  needs and college press, xxi, 78-79
  needs of teachers, 260, 263, 273, 276-277
  and satisfaction with teaching job, 277-278
  and social mobility, xxi, 21-35
  of teacher trainees, 274-276
  and teaching effectiveness, 277-278
Persuasibility
  as a personality attribute, 249
  and self-esteem, 249-250
  sex differences in, 250
  see also Influence
Persuasion, modes of, through communication, 239-253
Pivotal variable, 291-292, 299-301, 306
Play, of kindergarten children, 123-125
Political activity, professor's tolerance of, 297-299
Political alienation
  and attitude toward school election issue, 330-333
  and faith in people, 332
  index, 328-329
  and interest in school election issue, 331
  and position in social structure, 329-330, 332-333
  and voting behavior in school election, 331
  see also Alienation
Political party of professors
  and liberal attitude, 300, 307
  and apprehensiveness, 307
Popularity
  and considerateness, 228-229
  and status in high school, 88-89, 92-93
  see also Friendship, Sociometric choice, Status
Power
  and interpersonal behavior of children, 114-123
  legitimate, 197-212
  and student intelligence, 117
  reduction by teacher, 196-212
  of teacher, and discipline techniques, 194-195
  of teacher as source of pupil anxiety, 217, 219
  see also Dominance, Influence, Leadership
Powerlessness, *see* Alienation, Political Alienation, Power
Prejudice, *see* Attitude
Press, *see* College press
Prestige, *see* Status
Primacy versus recency in presentation of arguments, 244-246

Principal
overlap in expectations with teachers, 318
role conflict of, 313-314
see also Administrator
Problem solving
and interpersonal behavior of children, xxii, 114-123
rigidity in, 201-202, 208
social class differences in, 14-15, 17
Productivity
index, for college, 65, 307-308
and leadership style, 148
of social science professors, 302
and teaching style, 154-162
see also College productivity, Learning
Professor
descriptions of leader behavior, 323-325
reports of department reputation, 322-323
threats to academic freedom, xxiv, 291-308
see also Liberal attitude, Teacher
Progressive Achievement Test, 185
Projective technique, 28
Promotion, *see* Failing marks
Pupil, *see* Student
Pupil ratings of teachers, 173-181
Pupil-teacher relations, *see* Teacher-student relations

Recency versus primacy in presentation of arguments, 244-246
Reference group
and attitude change, xxiii, 264-268
conflicting role expectations in, 314-319
and decision to desegregate schools, 49-50
of high school students, 6, 9
of ministers in school desegregation, 54-55
see also Group
Reform goal of social science professors, 293-294
Repression, 204-209
Reputation of college departments, 321-322
Rigidity, *see* Problem solving
Ripple effect in classroom discipline, 190-195
Role
analysis, xxiv, 51, 54, 309-318
of authoritarian leader, 143-145
of boys in camp groups, 128-129
and career lines, 271-272
of democratic leader, 143-145
and expectation in analysis of social system, 310-311
expectations for boys and girls, 115, 122
expectations, overlap in, 318
of laissez-faire leader, 143-145
of school board member, in desegregation, 49
sex, and occupational, 279
see also Role conflict
Role conflict
concept, 51-52
of ministers, in desegregation, xxi, 51-57
and modes of resolving, 56-57
and perceptions of expectations, 317-318
and personality of principals, 313-314
and reference group, 314-317
between superintendent and school board, 314-315
of teachers, 315-317
see also Culture, Role
Role playing and attitude change, 251-252

Sanctions, *see* Group sanctions
Satisfaction, *see* Job satisfaction
Scholars, production by colleges, 65-73, 307-308
Scholastic Aptitude Test, 67-69, 71-73, 77
Scholastic achievement
and attitudes of mother, 38-39
and examination procedures, 212-225
and intelligence, 90-92
and parent-child relations, xxi, 35-39
and social class, 10-11
and social climate of high school, 87-94
and status system in high school, 88-94
and teacher behavior toward students, 189
and values, 11
see also Creativity, Examinations, Failing marks, Gifted student, Learning
School board
and control of school, 7
decision to desegregate, 48-49
and superintendent, role conflict, 314-315
School-community relations, 312-313, 327-333
School policy
control of, 7
decision to desegregate, 47
and interscholastic athletics, 93-94
Scientists
communication with practitioners (pp. v, vii of Foreword), xix
production by colleges, 65-73, 307-308
see also Professor
Segregation, *see* Desegregation of schools
Selective perception, 317
Self-concept, and social mobility, 24, 30-31, 34
see also Self-evaluation, Self-expectations
Self-depreciation in homogeneous and heterogeneous groups, 138-140
Self-esteem, *see* Self-evaluation
Self-evaluation
and ability grouping, 138-140
among elementary pupils, 233-236
and persuasibility, 249-250
see also Self-concept, Self-expectations
Self-expectations
of ministers in school desegregation, 54
in model of role conflict, 51-52
and sense of guilt, 56
see also Role, Self-concept
Self-expression value of occupation, 285-286
Sleeper effect, 252-253
Snowball technique in interviewing, 53
Social class
and attitude toward school desegregation, 61, 63
and clique associations in high school, 6
differences among participants in intergroup contact, 45-46
and differences in teacher behavior, xxiii, 181-189
and educational attainment, 5, 9-10
and intelligence tests, xxi, 12-21
measure, 185
and political alienation, 327-333
and pupil education, xxi, 3-11
and pupil hostility, 260
role of teachers, 316-317
self-rating, 331
Social climate
and aggression in children, 109
of colleges, xxi, 73-79
of high schools, xxii, 87-94
in interracial contact situations, 44

and leadership style, 146-150
and productivity of colleges, 73
see also Culture, Norms, Values
Socialization, 9, 34
Social mobility
and attitude toward school desegregation, 62-63
and group membership, 25-26
and intelligence, 32-33
motivational factors in, xxi, 21-35
and parental relationships, 31-32, 34
and public schools, 4-5, 9-10
see also Social class
Social power, *see* Power
Social psychology
concept, xv
of education, xv-xxiv
and practical problems (pp. v-vii of Foreword), xv
of school desegregation, xxi, 40-51
see also Group dynamics
Social reform goal of social science professor, 293-294
Social scientists, *see* Scientists
Social stratification, *see* Social Class
Social structure
and considerate behavior, 232-233, 237-238
in definition of group, 126
in groups of campers, 128-129, 132
among kindergarten children, xxii, 123-125
position in, and political alienation, 329-330, 332-333
Social system
of college administration, 305-306
of high school, 8-9
theoretical model, 310-312
Society for the Psychological Study of Social Issues (p. vi in Foreword), xvi, xvii
Sociodynamic effect, 101, 106
Sociodynamic law, 98, 106
Socio-economic status *see* Social class
Sociometric choice
cross-sex, 102-106
criteria, 99-100, 102-103
distributions, 98-105
by grade level, 98-99, 102, 104-106
mutual, 104-106
and number of choices, 100-101
typical classroom patterns, 97-106
variations by schools, 103-104
see also Friendship, Group membership
Sociometric test, 9, 97-104
Sociometry, xxi, 97-104
Status
and academic achievement, 88-94
and athletics, 88-90, 92-94
among campers, 129
and considerate behavior, 231-233
of disciplined pupil, effects on audience, 195
and educational goals of school, 89
and group estimates of performance, 129
and influence in groups, 112
of leading crowd, 88-89, 92-93
of participants in intergroup contact, 43, 45-46
and popularity, 88-89, 92-93
of social science professors, 304-306
Strain toward symmetry, 174-175
Stratification, *see* Social class
Stress
and discipline techniques, 191
during examinations, 212-219
in heterogeneous groups, xxii, 139-140
see also Anxiety
Strong Vocational Interest Blank, 69
Student
anxiety, xxiii, 212-219, 258, 260
attitudes, xxiii, 8-9, 162-172, 191-195, 254-268
behavior in classroom, xxiii, 114-125, 133-140, 190-195, 226-238, 254-263
gifted, 35-39, 312-313
hostility, xxiii, 196-212, 254-263
perceptions, 176-179, 230
personality, 18, 69-70, 72-73, 78-79, 171-173, 272, 274-276
power, xxii, 114-125, 196-212
relations, xxii, 3-11, 80-106, 114-125, 133-140, 226-238, 254-268
status, 88-90, 92-94, 129, 195, 231-233
values, 65-66, 68-70, 72-73, 76-78, 88-94
vocational interests, 68-73
see also Adolescent, Creativity, Intelligence, Learning, Scholastic achievement, Teacher-student relations
Subculture, *see* Culture, Social Class
Suggestibility; *see* Persuasibility
Summer camp, studies of group relations in, 126-132
Superintendent
perceptions of role expectations, 317-318
role conflicts, 309-310, 314-315
Superordinate goals, *see* Group goals
Suppression, of hostility, 204-209

Teacher
administrator agreement in roles, 318
attitudes toward pupils, measure, 287-288
attributes and failing marks awarded pupils, 287-290
behavior, xxiii, 173-189
comments on examination papers, xxiii, 219-225
discipline techniques, 190-195
gratification by pupils, 260, 263
job satisfaction, 282, 284
middle-class values, 5-6, 16
occupational orientations, 278-286
perceptions, 116, 119-120, 122-123, 179-180, 227-228, 230-231
personality, 273, 276-278
power as source of student anxiety, 217, 219
role conflict, 309-318
see also Professor, Teacher-student relations
Teacher-centered teaching, *see* Teaching style
Teacher's oath and liberalism of social science professors, 301
Teacher-student relations
accuracy of perceptions, 179-180, 317-318
interaction, xxii, xxiii, 78, 162-212, 254-263
see also Professor, Student, Teacher, Teaching style
Teaching career
commitment to, 280-281
of public school teacher, xxiv, 271-278
and sex of beginning teacher, xxiv, 278-286
see also Job satisfaction, Occupational
Teaching style
autocratic-democratic, 153-162
and change in pupil opinion, 162-172
dominative-integrative pupil contacts, 182-189
and professors' liberalism, 295-296
and pupil hostility, xxiii, 196-201
review of research on, 153-162
Tension, *see* Anxiety, Stress
Test motivation, 16-17
see also Achievement motive, Examinations, Intelligence tests

Trustworthiness of communication, 241-242, 253

University, *see* College
Upward mobility, *see* Social mobility

Values
of adolescents, 8-9, 88-94
of American society, and conflicts in school, 312-314
in analysis of social system, 312
emergent versus traditional, 314
intellectual, in colleges, 65-66, 72 73, 76-78
occupational, 284-286
regarding education, 4-6, 8
and scholastic achievement, 91
teaching of, xxiii, 226-238
see also Norms
Vocational interests
and college productivity, 69-73
measure, 69
see also Job satisfaction, Occupational

Voting
of liberal professors, 300
on school bond issue, 327-333
see also Political activity, Political alienation, Political party

Witch-hunt syndrome, 254-263
Worker productivity, and participation in decisions, 110

Yankee City, 4-5